Trauma, Trials, and Transformation

Trauma, Trials, and Transformation

Guiding Sexual Assault Victims through the Legal System and Beyond

Judith Daylen, Wendy van Tongeren Harvey, and Dennis O'Toole

Trauma, Trials, and Transformation: Guiding Sexual Assault Victims through the Legal System and Beyond
© Irwin Law Inc., 2006

Published in 2006 by
Irwin Law
Suite 206, 14 Duncan Street
Toronto, Ontario
M5H 3G8
www.irwinlaw.com

ISBN-10: 1-55221-114-2   ISBN-13: 978-155221-114-4

Library and Archives Canada Cataloguing in Publication

Daylen, Judith Lynne, 1950–
    Trauma, trials, and transformation : guiding sexual assualt victims through the legal system and beyond / Judith Daylen, Wendy van Tongeren Harvey, and Dennis O'Toole.

Includes bibliographical references.
ISBN-13: 978-1-55221-114-4
ISBN-10: 1-55221-114-2

1. Rape victims—Legal status, laws, etc.—Canada. 2. Trials (Rape)—Canada. 3. Rape victims—Psychology. 4. Rape victims—Rehabilitation. 5. Sex crimes—Canada. I. O'Toole, Dennis Michael, 1953- II. Van Tongeren Harvey, Wendy III. Title.

KE8928.D39 2006   345.71'02532   C2006-905351-0
KF9325.D39 2006

The publisher acknowledges the financial support of the Government of Canada through the Book Publishing Industry Development Program (BPIDP) for its publishing activities.

We acknowledge the assistance of the OMDC Book Fund, an initiative of Ontario Media Development Corporation.

Printed and bound in Canada.

2 3 4 5   10 09 08

Summary Table of Contents

Detailed Table of Contents

[CHAPTER 2]

The Personal Impact of Sexual Crimes 35

[CHAPTER 4]
Law and the Human Factors   *101*

[CHAPTER 7]

Preparing for Court   *233*

[CHAPTER 9]
Sentencing *335*

[CHAPTER 10]
Seeking Compensation   377

[CHAPTER 11]

Personal Growth and Transformation 427

Foreword

Violence against women and children worldwide takes many forms, and sexual assault is one of them. Sexual assault and other gender-based crimes are committed in a number of ways. Without being exhaustive, the list includes: incest, pedophilia, rape, systemic rape as a form of warfare, trafficking in women and children, honour killings, genital mutilation, stoning, slavery, pimping, child pornography, aborting female fetuses and killing newborn females, domestic assault, and sexual assault on city streets. These crimes are so pervasive that the international community, in an attempt to impel countries to action, has adopted a number of declarations, conventions, and protocols. The *Convention on the Elimination of All Forms of Discrimination Against Women* and the *Convention on the Rights of the Child* are two measures that address violations of a most fundamental human right — the right to life. Sexual abuse, in particular, is a profound violation of the respect, consideration, and the dignity that every human being deserves. It is a crime against human rights. The consequences of these crimes, especially for women and for children, are incommensurable. The pain and suffering as well as the loss of happiness and enjoyment of life and health — in particular, mental health sometimes even leading to suicide on the part of victims — cannot be overstated.

In our own society, recent history has seen an increased awareness of sexual crimes and a better understanding of the people who perpetrate them, but these offences continue to present unique challenges to our mental health and legal systems. Sexual offences generally occur in private with no witnesses, are often committed by people who know the victim well, and frequently leave little or no physical evidence. Although sexual offending is prevalent in our communities, fear, social stigma, and lack of knowledge too often prevent victims from coming forward. Offences of this sort are significantly under-reported to authorities, and may be reported years after the offence has occurred. In those instances where a sexual crime is reported and prosecuted, the impact is felt not only by the victim, but also by a wide and concentric circle of people, from family members and friends, to law enforcement and legal professionals, to mental health workers and concerned community members. With increased awareness and concern about these crimes has come the challenge for us all to respond more effectively to the needs of victims, communities, and society as a whole.

Responding more effectively to the problem of sexual offending is a deceptively simple proposal. Deceptive because the goal of reducing sexual offending is straightforward, but the means to achieve that goal are complex and the subject of much debate and contention. The last twenty-five years have seen a significant evolution in the criminal justice system towards a better understanding of the victims' realities, and towards progress in meeting societal needs. The choice to report a sexual crime is a very personal and individual decision, but it is a decision best made with adequate knowledge of the consequent psychological and legal challenges. Those who choose to engage with the legal system will find a variety of views and agendas that might not be congruent with their own. The accused offenders, their supporters, the needs and goals of society, and possibly the demands of the media can all stand in opposition to a victim's wants and needs and to those of their supporters.

Ultimately, the law should promote justice and improve the social conditions for all — regardless of gender, race, religious beliefs, or sexual orientation — but it cannot do so without the participation of those citizens it serves. *Trauma, Trials, and Transformation* explores issues that are important to consider when making the frequently difficult choice of whether or not to report a sexual crime. This book also provides a comprehensive outline of ways to achieve the goal of holding the offender accountable. It is a source of information for communities who wish to build victim assistance programs, and it is a valuable resource for anyone seeking to use their experiences as a means to achieve personal growth. When a victim takes the courageous step of confronting the perpetrator in a public forum, she is not only pleading her own case, but may also be a catalyst for systemic change that promotes equality for others in similar circumstances. Those whose experiences motivate them towards a deeper commitment to the service of others will find inspiration in the stories of people who have used their traumatic experiences as a stepping-stone to help others.

This book is invaluable for lawyers as well as other professionals, victims as well as lay people. It is comprehensive as it looks at the issue of sexual assault from many angles, from the legal to the physical and psychological perspective. It is easy to read and it strikes me as an incredibly useful, practical, and effective tool for many actors in the judicial system, as well as for victims. It is an exciting addition to the literature on the subject and I am sure it will be very well received by the legal community and the community in general. I do not think that there is another book on the subject that draws on the law as well as on psychology and empathy for victims, while still being fair and balanced.

Honourable Claire L'Heureux-Dubé
Retired Justice, Supreme Court of Canada

Acknowledgments

THIS BOOK WAS PUT together with the help of many talented people. We thank Diane Sirkia who assisted us with research; Brian Sutherland who in the early stages took our rough data and turned them into a manuscript; Jane Cameron and Catherine MacArthur whose computer skills brought consistency to the work; and Keren Freed who helped with the initial editing. We thank Jane Howard Baker and Laurie Soper who helped reframe the book at the early stages. Keith Beale provided thoughtful drawings that illustrated the points made and, although we did not include them in the final manuscript, we appreciate his contributions.

We are also indebted to respected colleagues who provided invaluable feedback and comments: Randy Mackoff, Brenda Knight, John Yuille, Donna Diggens, Anne Sheane, Laura Woods, Diane Turner, Gisela Ruebsaat, Linda Light, Georgia Peters, and Nick Bala.

We would also like to thank the Honourable Claire L'Heureux-Dubé, who provided a foreword to this book and has inspired many with her passionate, creative, tempered, and principled legal works.

We particularly want to thank our spouses, John Yuille, Leo van Tongeren, and Donna Diggens, and our families for their support, patience, and generosity in allowing this exercise to unfold to completion.

Judith Daylen
Wendy van Tongeren Harvey
Dennis O'Toole

Introduction

A practical resource

WE HAVE WRITTEN THIS book as a guide for anyone who has been sexually assaulted and who wants to hold the offender accountable. It is also for those who are called upon to play a role in the resolution of a sexual crime, and for professionals who work in this area. If someone has sexually assaulted or abused you, it may feel like you face insurmountable obstacles on the road to recovery or in pursuing justice. Your emotional reactions to this crime, to the responses of others to you, and to the workings of legal process can be frustrating and complex. The goal of this book is to facilitate your emotional journey and to demystify some of the legal system complexities. We provide current information and references to multiple resources to assist those who want to expand their understanding and knowledge.

Sexual assault and childhood sexual abuse are crimes that put unique demands on everyone involved; not only the person who is assaulted, but a wide circle of community members. The crime has substantial impact on family, friends, mental health professionals, those who investigate the crime, and the many professionals who work in the justice system. It is our hope that the information provided here will help those affected by sexual crimes respond more effectively to the challenges we all face before, during, and after legal proceedings.

Based on our first-hand experience

TO WRITE THIS GUIDE, we have drawn on our first-hand experience in the courts, our direct professional experience with those who have been sexually assaulted or abused, and our review of the legal and psychological literature. The authors are a Crown prosecutor and two clinical psychologists. Collectively, our professional experience spans over sixty-five years. We have worked with hundreds of victims, and thousands of other people involved in the resolution of these crimes. The book is infused with the collective experience of all these people.

A blend of the legal and the psychological

WHAT SETS THIS BOOK apart from other, similar legal guides is a focus on both the legal and the psychological perspective. Effective navigation of the complex legal system terrain requires not only knowledge of that system, how it works, and who the main players are, but it also requires that you be emotionally and psychologically equipped for the journey. The legal and the psychological are not always easy companions; your emotional needs may, at times, be in conflict with the requirements of the court. We point out some of these tension points and make suggestions about avoiding or defusing them.

Writing this book was a mutual effort, with a lot of back and forth among the authors. However, Wendy van Tongeren Harvey, as the lawyer of our threesome, is responsible for most of the legal material, Judith Daylen took the lead with the psychological material, and Dennis O'Toole gave the book its voice and helped see the forest through the trees.

The "big picture"

ONE OF THE GOALS of this book is to present information from a wide range of perspectives so that you have a better idea of "the big picture" and your place in it. It is important to be aware of the diverse and competing interests that you will encounter. You will find a variety of perspectives within the legal system itself—the police, the judge, the prosecutor, the defence lawyer, your own lawyer in civil litigation, victim assistance personnel, and various support persons will all have views and agendas that might not match yours. The accused offenders, their supporters, the needs and goals of society, and possibly the demands of the media can all stand in opposition to your wants and needs, and those of your supporters. It is easy to feel like your needs are lost among the competing needs of many other individuals and agencies. However, we believe that you will be better equipped to handle these challenges if you have a greater understanding of the views and objectives of the various other players in this process, both within and outside the legal system.

Guiding principles, assumptions, and premises

WE BELIEVE IT IS important to articulate the principles, assumptions, and premises that have guided the development of this book. These flow from our philosophical values; we believe in the resilience of the human character and we maintain an optimistic outlook about the all too human, fallible, but viable and ultimately progressive legal system. You can read the following list and decide if this book is for you. These principles, assumptions, and premises are not recorded in any particular weighted or valued order.

- All sexual assaults are wrong — they are crimes.
- The criminal justice system in Canada, although not perfect, is a viable method for responding to breaches of the criminal law. The civil justice system in Canada, although similarly imperfect, is also a viable method for seeking compensation for harm you have suffered.
- The process of taking a criminal or civil case through the system is extremely complex and beyond the control of one person.
- The complainant is not in charge of the case.
- There are places in the legal system where the complainant has no choice or extremely limited choices. However, there are places where the complainant has choices available, and she should know about these.
- Participating in the court process is an inherently stressful process, and has the potential to trigger a crisis in the complainant's life.
- Knowledge can equip complainants to manage the stress of court more effectively.
- There is wide variability in the psychological impact of sexual crimes. Even when crimes appear objectively similar, the experience disables some victims, while others show few or no long-term effects, and many fall in between these extremes. Being a victim of sexual assaults does not have to carry a life sentence of being psychologically "damaged goods."
- There is no specific cluster of symptoms or psychological syndrome unique to sexual assaults. Although there are some similarities in victims' responses to sexual assaults, the differences outweigh the similarities.
- Your thoughts and beliefs affect the way you feel; challenging your internal dialogue or shifting your perspective can lead to dramatic changes in your emotional responses and your experiences.
- Resilience, or the ability to bounce back from crisis, can be learned.

- Learning resilience skills and other coping strategies can help victims feel less stressed, more in control, and can lead to more effective functioning as witnesses and advocates for their case.
- The requirements of the legal system can sometimes conflict with victims' therapeutic needs or path toward recovery. We believe that victims should make informed decisions about their own priorities.
- Participating in court, like managing any crisis, requires help and support from others.
- Participating in legal proceedings can lead to personal growth, empowerment or transformation.
- All victims of sexual crime who participate in the criminal or civil justice systems contribute to those systems and to our society. One person's participation can lead to changes in others' attitudes, understanding, or actions, or perhaps contribute to changes in the legal system.
- There is no single path through the adversities of dealing with sexual crimes or court proceedings. We provide some guidance and some suggestions, but each victim must chart his own path.

The book's language

WE HAVE ATTEMPTED TO write this book in everyday, accessible language, avoiding whenever possible legalese and psychological jargon. The downside of this is that when dealing with legal and mental health professionals, you may encounter language that you do not understand. To assist you in your communication and understanding of legal concepts, we have included a glossary of common terms used in this context.

In our work, we have encountered a number of terms used to refer to someone who has been sexually victimized. Most common of these terms are "victim," "complainant," and "survivor." We have had to choose carefully which of these terms we use because these words sometimes suggest political and social meanings that go far beyond the words themselves. To our minds, none of these words is wholly satisfactory. The term "survivor" is often used as an empowering expression in self-help books and in other literature about sexual assault victims, but it is not a legal term. We chose not to use this term because, as a euphemism for victimization, it does not adequately or accurately capture the range of human circumstances that we are attempting to address in this book. We have instead chosen to use the terms "victim" and "complainant." The *Criminal Code* defines a complainant as a "victim of an alleged offence."

We appreciate that the term victim may have negative connotations for some, suggesting powerlessness, or vulnerability. In the legal context, use of the term victim implies that a crime has been committed before it has been proven, so the term complainant is preferred. However, this term is limited because it applies only to victims of alleged sexual crimes who have reported the crime to police. Aware of these various limitations, we have chosen to refer to those sexually victimized as either victims or complainants. We use the term victim where appropriate because we believe that its meaning is universally understood and it covers all the situations discussed in our book. The term complainant is also used because it is legally neutral regarding whether or not the alleged crime has been committed.

You will also notice that we direct much of the book toward an anonymous "you." We prefer being able to speak directly to those for whom the book was primarily written — the victims of sexual crimes, the "you" to whom we are generally speaking. If you are a victim of a sexual crime, please do not over-personalize the "you" references in this book; some or many of the statements may not apply specifically to you. As we emphasize throughout, there are vast individual differences among people's reactions, needs, and responses to sexual crimes.

For those readers who have not been sexually victimized, we ask that you take into account our rationale for speaking directly to those victimized, without feeling alienated from the discussion yourself. We expect the topics discussed will be relevant to anyone who is trying to understand the legal process and psychological issues in sexual assault cases. We believe that the information in this book will better equip those wishing to provide support or services to victims of sexual crimes.

The book's structure

WE START THE BOOK with an overview of sexual crimes. These legal issues can be complex so this chapter is, by nature, somewhat dense. However, this information is foundational for much of the discussion that follows so we encourage readers to be patient here. The focus then shifts to the personal impact of sexual crimes, ways to cope, and issues of healing. After providing an overview of some important human factors involved in the legal process, including the matters of stress and memory, we offer some psychological strategies to meet these challenges and to build resilience. We then move to a detailed discussion of the criminal justice system and ways complainants can best prepare for their role in the prosecution of the offender. We dedicate one chapter to an examination of civil litigation and summarize some alternative methods of seeking redress following a sexual crime. The final chapter is devoted to the topics of systemic change and personal growth, illustrated with stories of inspirational people who transformed their lives and those around them in the aftermath of traumatic experiences.

You will see that we start each chapter with a vignette, which illustrates the relevant topics. We have drawn these stories from our professional experiences and we hope they will give some of the abstract topics a more human focus. At the end of the book, you will find Appendices containing supplementary information and additional references.

Using the book

WE DESIGNED THIS BOOK to follow a logical sequence from describing behaviours that are sexual crimes, to dealing with the impact, to reporting the crime, taking an offender to criminal or civil court, and using your experiences as opportunities for personal growth. Each chapter represents a link in the chain of events from trauma to potential transformation. Ideally, the book would be read from beginning to end, but we understand this will not always be the case, so we constructed the chapters so they can be individually used as a guide for a specific topic. We do caution people to read any particular chapter in its entirety, as information taken piecemeal or out of context can be misleading and potentially harmful.

Caveat

YOU ARE NOT TO interpret the contents of this book as legal advice specific to your case. Every case is unique. We highly recommend that you seek your own legal counsel to address questions pertinent to your particular situation. It also is important to emphasize that this book is not a "cure-all." We are not offering psychological advice or counselling to address your specific emotional needs. We recommend that you seek professional counselling or therapeutic support to assist you in dealing with any of your psychological concerns or needs that are significantly interfering with your life.

Sexual Crimes in Canada

Vignette One

A high school soccer coach knocks at the door of one of the student players on his team, a fifteen-year-old female who is home alone. She answers
the door, invites him into the foyer, and after a five-minute conversation
about the team's schedule the coach, without invitation, touches her
shoulders, moves his hands to her breasts, and then attempts to rub her
vaginal area. This behaviour upsets her greatly and after the initial surprise, she pulls herself free and pushes him away. When the coach leaves,
she locks all the doors. After recovering from her shock and confusion,
she telephones her parents to tell them what happened. The police are
called and charges are laid against the coach, who is now the accused.
The young girl then becomes the complainant. As her coach, the twenty-
four-year-old accused knows the complainant, and he happens to know
she keeps a diary because she has written in it during soccer trips. He also
often sees her going out socially with various boys who he assumes are
her boyfriends. During the investigation, he tells police the girl has been
sexually active and was giving him indications that she wanted to have sex
with him. The Crown prosecutor must now decide how best to proceed.

SOME SEXUAL BEHAVIOURS ARE clearly a violation of body and spirit;
others are not so readily characterized. In this chapter, you will find a discussion of sexual crimes as Canadian law now defines them. We discuss
the central issue of consent and its relevance to adults, youth, and children.
You will also find a review of current knowledge regarding perpetrators of
sexual crimes. If you have questions about whether someone's behaviour towards you constitutes a sexual offence, this chapter should help. Although

it may be dense and difficult to read, this chapter provides a necessary foundation for understanding sexual crimes.

The vignette above is one example of a sexual assault, and we will refer to it at the end of this chapter to demonstrate some of the principles discussed. Many victims of sexual crimes are left feeling powerless, alienated, and confused. Gaining a better understanding of the reality and nature of sexual crimes is a means to empower oneself. Increased knowledge will also aid in making key decisions about your personal options when an assault occurs. Some sexual behaviours are legal while others are not, so this chapter will help clarify when and how someone has contravened your legal rights.

A key principle of law is that nobody can physically touch or hit another individual without that individual's consent, although it is not always clear when someone has crossed this boundary. A person's sexual conduct towards another can be a violation of that person's integrity, or can be a violation of society's sense of decency, or both. Recognizing this fact, Canada's Parliament has sought to amend the *Criminal Code* in accordance with changing societal norms and knowledge.[1] This means that the law can change and what was once illegal may no longer be so and vice versa. A wide range of conduct now constitutes a sexual crime in Canada; below we provide a review of those behaviours currently regarded as sexual offences in this country.

As you read this chapter, bear in mind that it represents a brief summary of complex legal principles that have evolved over many years. We have simplified these principles and minimized legal language to help clarify complicated issues. Our discussion is organized to assist the reader in understanding current practices, rather than mirror changes in the law over time. Some basic facts should help you understand how a court determines which acts are sexual crimes in Canadian law.

WHAT IS A SEXUAL CRIME?

THE *CRIMINAL CODE*[2] OF Canada outlines which activities are illegal sexual behaviours. The *Criminal Code* defines sexual offences in Canada, and the Crown counsel, who represents the state, relies solely on it to prosecute. If you want the most current legal perspective on sexuality and the law, you should consult the *Criminal Code,* which is available at most libraries, through your local courthouse, or at the Canada Justice web page on the Internet.[3] Since Parliament amends the *Criminal Code* regularly, we recommend that you read the version of the law in effect at the time of the commission of any offence to know precisely what the Crown must prove in a given case. It is common for laypersons to use terms, such as "rape" or "assault" to describe their sexual victimization, but when it comes to proof in court these words may or may not be used. Legal language is precise and the Crown must prove the offence as the law technically defines it.

Each sexual crime is defined by its own unique features. Sexual assault has been a specific offence in the *Criminal Code* since January 1983, and is one of many sexually related offences. Incest is another offence with unique features or components. In any particular case, a single sexual act can result in one or more criminal charges. An adult who has intercourse with a thirteen-year-old girl is committing sexual assault, because she is under the age of consent. If the adult knows the girl is a blood relative (daughter, sister, grandchild), the adult is also committing incest and authorities could bring charges for both offences. In prosecuting the case, a Crown lawyer would have to establish all the features of the specific charge to get a conviction. To obtain a conviction on the incest charge, the Crown would have to show that the girl was a blood relative of the adult, that the adult knew this, and that the adult had sexually penetrated her. A charge of sexual assault in this case would require showing that the girl was under fourteen years of age and that the accused had knowledge of her age. For each charge, the Crown must not only prove that the wrongful act occurred but also that the accused intended to do what he did.

Some people are taken aback when they see that authorities have charged the accused with two or more offences (such as sexual assault and incest) for a single act against the victim. Having three charges brought for one act does not necessarily mean the accused will receive a sentence that is three times more severe, but it does give the Crown more leeway to conduct a successful prosecution. Even if the first or second of the charges are not proven beyond a reasonable doubt, the third charge may be.

Criminal Code changes

THE MOST OBVIOUS FORM of sexual violation is sexual aggression or sexual activity that clearly takes places without consent. The old terms used to describe forced sex are "rape" and "indecent assault." In response to the women's movement in Canada, Parliament formulated a new approach to these types of crimes. Sweeping changes were made to the *Criminal Code* on 4 January 1983 and a new approach to sexual crimes against children became law on 1 January 1988.[4] These dates are not the only times the *Criminal Code* was changed, as its evolution is ongoing, but they are the dates of major changes.

Since 1983, sexual assault is the charge applied when one forces sexual activity on another against the person's wishes, or has sexual contact with someone under the age of fourteen. Part VIII of the current *Criminal Code* deals specifically with these offences against a person's sexual integrity. Changes were made because the old terms were gender specific, which is discriminatory. Under the old definitions, the law could convict a man of indecently assaulting a woman, yet a woman who indecently assaulted a man was not charged with an offence. As well, the definition of rape had an "all or nothing" character. It recognized vaginal penetration to be the most serious feature of the offence, giving less importance to the violent aspects of the behaviour. The new language of the *Criminal Code* acknowledges more clearly the violent nature of "sexual assault" along with the sexual violation caused by it.

Further, the current *Criminal Code* comprehensively defines situations where consent is irrelevant because a victim submitted due to the abuse of power or authority, did not have the capacity to consent, or consented but then withdrew consent.[5] The former *Criminal Code* permitted a husband to force himself on his wife with no legal consequence, as the law did not consider this rape. In 1983, when the word "rape" was dropped as a legal term, Parliament amended the *Criminal Code* so a husband could be charged with sexual assault of his wife. For a history of *Criminal Code* changes and terminology, please refer to Appendix 1.

The *Criminal Code* defines offences at the time of commission

ALONG WITH OUR UNDERSTANDING of law and psychology, the *Criminal Code* is continually evolving. When reading this section it is important to remember that police officers charge a person with an offence based on the *Criminal Code*'s wording and definition of sexual crimes at the time the activity took place. For example, if a husband forced sexual intercourse on his wife today, that would be sexual assault as defined by law. However, if a woman reported today that her husband forced intercourse on her in

December of 1982 before the law changed, authorities could not lay charges of rape (the wording used in 1982) because the legal definition of rape at that time did not include forced intercourse in marriage. In contrast, if a man forced intercourse on a woman who was not his wife in December 1982 and then again in February 1983, he would be charged with rape for the first offence and sexual assault for the second offence because the law relevant on those two dates had changed.

SEXUAL ASSAULTS AS CURRENTLY DEFINED BY THE *CRIMINAL CODE*

AS ACKNOWLEDGED BY THE Supreme Court of Canada, "Having control over who touches one's body, and how, lies at the core of human dignity and autonomy."[6] Violation of a person's integrity in a sexual manner is the basis of the crime of sexual assault and can result in criminal charges. How authorities decide if a sexual crime has been committed will become clearer as you read this chapter, but we will begin with a discussion of the components that make up a sexual assault. To prove that a sexual assault has occurred, the prosecutor must show that (1) there was touching, (2) the touching was of a sexual nature, (3) there was an absence of consent, and (4) the accused knowingly and intentionally perpetrated the sexual acts.

The *Criminal Code* now defines three levels of sexual assault, meant to distinguish increasingly dangerous situations and the degree of harm to the victim. The maximum penalty for those convicted of these crimes increases with the added seriousness.[7]

The three levels of sexual assault are:

- Sexual assault with no weapon and no bodily harm (level I)
- Sexual assault with a weapon, or with bodily harm (level II)
- Aggravated sexual assault with wounding or maiming, which causes permanent bodily harm (level III)

Depending on the seriousness of a level I sexual assault, authorities can charge the assailant with an indictable offence (the most serious sort of crime, subject to a maximum sentence in a federal penitentiary) or a summary offence (a less serious crime, subject to a maximum of eighteen months). If the decision is made to proceed by indictment, with the potential for maximum penalties, the court process can be more rigorous. The accused has a choice of which court the trial will be held in; if the Supreme Court is chosen, the proceedings will include a hearing, called a "preliminary hearing" or "inquiry," which is similar to a trial before the actual trial. A summary offence is always tried in Provincial Court without a preliminary hearing. The *Criminal Code* specifically defines sexual assault level I as a hybrid offence that can proceed either by indictment or by summary conviction, and sexual assault levels II and III as straight indictable offences.

Sexual assault with no weapon or bodily harm (level I)

SECTION 271 OF THE *Criminal Code* covers offences where the assailant applies force without consent, but no weapon is used, no bodily harm is caused, and no threat is made against a third party. This section may cover situations ranging from an unwanted kiss, to the placing of a hand on a woman's breast without her approval, to sexual penetration without consent. Depending on circumstances, this offence can lead to a charge laid by indictment (maximum ten years in prison) or by summary conviction (maximum eighteen months in prison).

Sexual assault with a weapon or bodily harm (level II)

SECTION 272 OF THE *Criminal Code* deals with the more serious charge of sexual assault involving threats or actual use of a weapon, threats to a third party, or some form of bodily harm to the victim. When the assailant intends to harm the victim beyond the injury of sexual assault, the crime is of a more serious order. This is an indictable offence, for which the maximum penalty is fourteen years in prison. The assailant need not use the weapon — it may simply be carried or its use threatened. This law applies to imitation weapons as well. If the weapon used is a firearm, as defined by the *Criminal Code*,[8] the court must impose a minimum sentence of four years. The *Criminal Code* does not designate a minimum sentence for any other weapons.

The reference to "bodily harm" in this section means cuts, bruises, and minor wounds that result in some impairment, but also includes psychological harm. Psychological harm may be difficult to demonstrate, but convictions can occur. In some cases, an expert witness can reasonably testify to its presence. However, neither science nor the court presumes that psychological harm necessarily results from every instance of sexual assault or abuse.

Section 272 also deals with threats to a third party. This covers cases where an assailant persuades one to engage in an unwanted sexual act by threatening harm to a third party whom the victim wants to protect, usually a child. The court considers that this coercion increases the seriousness of the assault to the same extent as the use of a weapon.

Aggravated sexual assault (level III)

SECTION 273 OF THE *Criminal Code* outlines the most serious level of sexual assault. Termed "aggravated sexual assault," it refers to cases where the victim is wounded, maimed, disfigured, or the victim's life is endangered. This charge proceeds by indictment with a maximum sentence of life in prison, and a minimum of four years imposed when a firearm is used. These crimes may leave the victim with permanent physical and/or psychological damage. These crimes occur less frequently than other levels of sexual assault reported in Canada. Figures from 1997 suggest that of the sexual crimes reported to the police, approximately 88 percent were level I sexual assaults, while 2 percent were level II and level III. "Other" sexual offences, primarily offences against children, accounted for the remaining 10 percent of reported crimes.[9] These figures suggest the majority of sexual offences do not involve weapons or bodily harm.

CONSENT — A KEY ISSUE

WHEN DECIDING IF A sexual activity constitutes a sexual assault in law, the Crown must prove that the complainant did not consent. The issue of consent is a key issue when dealing with two equally functioning adults. Violent, forced sex is obvious evidence of a sexual assault, but there are instances when the absence of consent is not as obvious. Legislators and the courts have done a great deal in recent years to distinguish between sexual assault when there is no consent (an essential ingredient of the offence) versus when a defence of honest and mistaken belief of consent exists (because the accused got the facts wrong and does not have a guilty mind).

Lawmakers have also had to address situations in which the two parties are not equal in capability or personal power. This situation arises with sexual activity between an adult and a child, between an adolescent and a person who has authority over him, such as a high school sports coach, or if one person has a mental disability and does not appreciate the nature or consequences of the sexual contact. In trials where the issue of consent between two capable adults is disputed, the legal determination is rarely clear. There are rarely other witnesses and each person has a different version of what happened. We will frequently return to the question of consent because it is such a complex issue that must be addressed in every sexual assault complaint. The issue of what is sexually acceptable behaviour and who can consent to sexual contact reflects some of our society's most deeply held values and beliefs. In this book, we focus on illegal sexual behaviour while appreciating that the legal issues reflect complex and changing societal standards.

What constitutes consent?

CONSENT REQUIRES VOLUNTARY AGREEMENT to engage in sexual activity. What constitutes consent is not to be confused with what the accused thought the complainant did or did not consent to. The courts will look to what was in the complainant's mind at the time of the sexual contact to determine if consent was present or not. If the complainant says there was no consent and this is accepted by the court, then that component of sexual assault is established, making the accused's interpretation of the complainant's actions irrelevant to that component of the offence.

There is no such thing as "implied" consent in Canadian law. The complainant either voluntarily consented or did not. If the complainant says "no" and the accused interprets this as "yes," there is no defence in the eyes of the law. Section 265(3) of the *Criminal Code* also says that no consent is given if the complainant submits or does not resist due to fraud, the exercise of authority, the use of force, or the threat of force to the complainant (or to someone else, such as the complainant's child). In addition, the *Criminal Code* (section 273.1) says that no consent exists if

+ The consent was given by someone other than the victim (for example, the victim's spouse or father).
+ The victim was incapable of consenting because of an inability, temporary or permanent, to exercise proper judgment or consent (for example, the victim was asleep, intoxicated, or had a severe cognitive impairment).
+ The accused, such as a teacher, physician, or coach, induced the victim by abusing a position of trust, power, or authority (for example, "I will get you to the nationals if ...").
+ The victim expresses, by word or conduct, a lack of agreement to engage in the activity.
+ The victim later revoked an initial consent by words or conduct.

What constitutes honest mistaken belief in consent?

IF BELIEF IN CONSENT is to result in exoneration, a person must have taken reasonable steps to ascertain that consent was given. Defendants in sexual assault cases often claim they believed the victims gave consent, but the *Criminal Code* explicitly states that professing belief is not a defence when there is not sufficient evidence to support that claim. The *Criminal Code* specifically addresses some rationales about consent that, on their own, cannot be used by the defendant as proof of consent. An accused cannot interpret silence, passivity, or ambiguous conduct by the victim as consent and expect to rely on mistaken belief as a defence. Similarly, there is no defence if the defendant's belief arose due to a state of self-induced intoxication, recklessness, wilful blindness, or failure to take all reasonable steps to determine if the victim freely gave consent.[10]

The expression of belief in consent must also have an "air of reality," if it is to be an acceptable defence. The leading case regarding communication of consent is that of *R. v. Ewanchuk*, where Major J. of the Supreme Court of Canada stated:

> In order to cloak the accused's actions in moral innocence, the evidence must show that he believed that the complainant communicated consent to engage in the sexual activity in question. A belief by the accused that the complainant, in her own mind, wanted him to touch her, but did not express that desire, is not a defence. The accused's speculation as to what was going on in the complainant's mind provides no defence.[11]

The accused will be convicted if the Crown can prove that the accused had a guilty mind. This means that the accused engaged in sexual behaviour knowing that there was no consent. In the *Ewanchuk* case, the accused heard "no" but assumed "yes," which is not an acceptable defence, so he was convicted.

We must also make a distinction between what the accused believed about the complainant's consent, and what was believed to be the law. Ignorance of the law is not an acceptable excuse and is not grounds for exoneration. If the accused admitted knowing that the complainant was thirteen years old but believed it was legal to have sex with anyone over the age of twelve (the legal age at the time being fourteen years of age), the accused does not have a legitimate defence. Whether the accused honestly believed this is irrelevant. On the other hand, if there is evidence that suggests: the accused was honestly mistaken regarding the consent and believed that the victim agreed to sexual contact, or the accused genuinely attempted to find out the consenting partner's age (going beyond merely asking the victim's age) and honestly believed that the person was over fourteen years of age, then this is an acceptable defence.

THE WIDE RANGE OF SEXUAL OFFENCES

SOME SEXUAL MISCONDUCT IS readily recognizable as a criminal offence. When a man breaks into a home, or grabs a woman on a dark street, and engages in vaginal penetration through force or threats, there can be no argument that a crime has occurred. Other behaviours may not be easily recognized as criminal offences. Some of these behaviours might not be specifically named in the *Criminal Code,* but can be components of other criminal offences. These other, sometimes hidden, sexual crimes include

- Spreading diseases
- Indecent, intrusive, and sexually exploitive acts
- Sexual assault by a spouse
- Date rape
- Use of drugs or alcohol to obtain sex
- Sex and power imbalance

Spreading diseases

WHEN A COMPLAINANT CONTRACTS a communicable disease following consensual sex, without being informed that the accused had the disease, authorities can lay charges. The issue is the risk to the complainant where consent was given under false pretenses, and authorities can charge the accused with criminal negligence causing bodily harm or aggravated assault. The Crown must be able to demonstrate that the accused knew of the disease at the time and that the complainant was not infected before the sex act took place. Even if the latter condition cannot be proven, the accused could still be charged with attempted aggravated assault.

If sexual activity takes place, and the accused knowingly withholds the existence of a serious sexually transmitted disease, such as the HIV virus, and the partner is not infected, the law is less clear. There is controversy as to whether this is enough to invalidate consent and allow the court to find the infected person guilty of assault even without infecting the partner. The prosecution must demonstrate that the failure to disclose an infection created a significant risk of serious bodily harm to the partner, so that these guidelines, for example, would not apply to a failure to disclose the common cold. To prosecute successfully, the Crown must also prove that the complainant would not have consented to the sexual activity if the accused's health status had been disclosed. Prosecuting such cases is complex and requires expert evidence to answer such questions as whether the disease state created a significant risk, how one is infected, and what the incubation periods are.

In the event that the accused knows of the existence of a communicable disease and has sex with someone else for the sole purpose of infecting that person, the resulting charge would be attempted aggravated assault. If the sexual contact causes an infection, this is an aggravating factor so the charge would be aggravated assault or assault causing bodily harm. This degree of responsibility is difficult to prove in these cases. If the victim of such an assault were to die, in order to bring murder charges the Crown would need to prove that the accused intended to kill or at least intended to inflict bodily harm knowing it could lead to death, or was reckless in the face of this fact.[12] Causation would also be an important issue as it often is difficult to prove the accused is the one responsible for the infection.

Indecent, intrusive, and sexually exploitive acts

THE LAW CONSIDERS CERTAIN behaviours illegal if they are wilful, indecent acts performed in public, or any other place, when the objective is to insult or offend others, or where children are sexually exploited. This includes exposing one's genitals to a child under fourteen years old for a sexual purpose, transmitting indecent material by mail, or making indecent phone calls. It is also an offence to use electronic devices to surreptitiously observe or record a person who expects privacy in a place like a washroom, while showering, or while having consensual sex. A person who films children in illicit poses for a sexual purpose can also face charges.

Sexual assault by a spouse

AS NOTED EARLIER, PRIOR to 1983, there were no legal sanctions against a husband sexually penetrating his wife without her consent, perhaps reflecting the lingering belief that a man should have property rights over his wife. *Criminal Code* changes made in 1983 addressed this legal inequity. Today a husband or wife has no legal right to force any form of non-consensual sex on a partner; any forced sexual activity with a spouse is a crime. Surveys indicate that sexual coercion in marriage occurs relatively often (10 to 25 percent of women surveyed reported it)[13] but few spouses report this crime to police.

Date rape

DATE RAPE IS ANOTHER example of a widely used everyday term for unwanted sexual advances that is not consistent with legal language. As with other intimate relationships, dating or friendship does not override legal restrictions. Familiarity can cause the line between appropriate and inappropriate sexual behaviour to become blurred. In a relatively common date rape situation, a couple begins by engaging in mutually consensual hugging, kissing, petting, or foreplay. They become progressively more intimate and, at some point, one partner (usually the woman in a heterosexual relationship) either protests verbally or submits when there is conduct on the part of her partner that makes her feel afraid to resist openly. Her partner may continue escalating the sexual activity using both verbal insistence and physical persuasion until vaginal penetration takes place despite a lack of consent. As stated previously, this is not referred to as a "rape" if it occurred after 1 January 1983. The proper technical legal term was changed to "sexual assault."

If the woman is not yelling for help or resisting physically, the man may claim to interpret her verbal protests as part of the seduction game. Given that each partner is interpreting the event from different perspectives, and given that victims do not typically report these scenarios as sexual assault, the assailant may repeat his behaviour and his partner may continue to feel victimized, sometimes without the awareness of her partner. In some cases, the woman may never see him again and he may never learn the reality and impact of his behaviour; he may remain oblivious or in denial. However, the message is becoming clearer from society and the legal community that "no" means "no." Unwanted sexual advances constitute sexual assault under the law and this includes advances that the victim resists solely by saying "no" or using equivalent body language.

Coercive sex is not okay — it is a crime. Nevertheless, a high proportion of young people continue to think it is okay to coerce a woman to have sex. In a Toronto study, a group of men and women were asked, "If a girl engages in necking or petting and she lets things get out of hand, is it her own fault if her partner forces sex on her?" The survey showed 31 percent of males and 22 percent of females said "yes." In another study, 60 percent of Canadian college-aged males admitted they would commit sexual assault if they were sure they would not be caught. [14] Given these attitudes, it is not surprising that date rape seems to be a relatively common occurrence. Research has indicated that 20 to 68 percent of adolescents have experienced date rape. It has been estimated that as many as 99 percent of these sexual assaults are not reported to the police. At minimum, these figures suggest serious miscommunication in relationships, a subject worthy of further examination.

Use of drugs or alcohol to obtain sex

THE *CRIMINAL CODE* SPECIFIES that if drugs or alcohol have incapacitated a person (the victim), consent is absent. As well, those accused cannot rely on their impaired state (and therefore lack of control or memory lapse) to absolve themselves from the crime of sexual assault.[15] Further, merely intending to use substances to obtain sex from a partner is illegal. Section 212(i) states it is an offence to give or cause a person to take drugs or alcohol if the intent is to stupefy or overpower the person in order to have sexual intercourse.

An evidentiary issue can arise in cases where the victim claims to have been drunk when unwanted sex occurred and therefore does not remember the incident. The defence may fill in the blanks for those parts of the narrative during which the victim claims to have been unconscious. Details the defence supplies are likely to be a demonstration that the victim gave consent for sex. The issue then becomes a matter of credibility and whether there is reasonable doubt that consent was given.

Sex and power imbalance

SECTION 265(3) OF THE *Criminal Code* stipulates that there is no consent, regardless of the victim's age, if the perpetrator obtained agreement for sex by the exercise of authority. This section applies no matter what the ages of the parties, such as the circumstance where an employee feels the need to engage in sex with an employer in order to keep a job. Although this section calls for the "exercise" of authority, it may be enough that the employer only pursued sex in the "context" of a power position. As Boyle stated in her book on the topic, "conservative legal advice would be to refrain from sexual contact with anyone in one's power."[16]

SEXUAL OFFENCES AGAINST CHILDREN AND YOUTH

OFFENCES RELATED TO ILLEGAL sexual activity against children and youth are not in Part VIII of the *Criminal Code* where sexual assault is found (namely Offences against Persons and Reputation). They are in Part V, called Sexual Offences, Public Morals and Disorderly Conduct. In this part of the *Criminal Code*, one will find the sexual offences that Parliament has decided, for public policy reasons, should be illegal. Sex with children is one of those activities that Canadians, through their elected representatives, believe should be outlawed.

Currently in Canada, the age at which a person can legally consent to sexual activity with an older person (more than two years older) is fourteen years of age, but there are some stipulations. In these situations, even when the complainant is over the age of fourteen but under the age of eighteen, the judge will look at the relationship between the parties to determine if it is a sexually exploitive one. If so, consent is not a defence. Even if the adolescent appears to go along with the sexual activity, the consent is not valid by law. Section 153 of the *Criminal Code* stipulates some of the relevant circumstances that apply, including a position of trust, authority, or dependency in the relationship. Other characteristics of the relationship also considered are the age of the young person, the age difference between the suspect and the young person, the evolution of the relationship, and the degree of control or influence over the young person. From this information, the judge may infer the relationship is a sexually exploitive one. If the accused is in a real or perceived position of power to solicit sex from the victim, whether through maturity or social position, this is a crime.

Parliament recognizes certain conditions are necessary if agreement to sexual contact is to be truly voluntary. One of these conditions is that the person is old enough to appreciate the consequences of having sex. In Canadian law, this age has been set at fourteen years of age. No one in Canada under the age of fourteen can legally consent to sex with someone two or more years older. As noted above, in some situations legal consent requires the person to be aged eighteen or older (see discussion below). There is an ongoing controversy about the age of consent in Canada with some advocating for the age to be raised to sixteen years of age, the standard in most of North America. In 2005, although lawmakers did not go so far as to raise the age of consent, they did recognize that a fourteen-year-old could be sexually exploited in ways that Canadian law does not prohibit. Parliament addressed this concern in legislation proclaimed on 1 November 2005 in Bill C-2, expanding the definition of sexual exploitation for victims between the ages of fourteen and seventeen years. At this writing, federal legislation has been tabled to raise the age of consent from fourteen to sixteen, although this remains a contentious issue.

When "yes" is not consent

ALL FORCIBLE SEXUAL ASSAULT offences that apply when an adult is victimized apply equally to children (from birth to fourteen years of age) and youth (over fourteen but under eighteen years of age). Beyond this, Part V of the *Criminal Code*, sections 150.1 through 153, addresses some specific issues regarding children and youth. As with Part VIII of the *Criminal Code*, the key issue in Part V is consent. The law presumes that persons under fourteen years of age need special protection due to their immaturity, lack of knowledge, lack of personal power, and restricted freedoms in our society. Even though the child or young person might willingly comply with, or agree to engage in sexual activity, section 150.1 of the *Criminal Code* says that no consent exists due to the young age. Any sexual activity with a person under fourteen years of age by an adult (or a youth more than two years older) is an offence no matter what the child said or did. This is the crime previously referred to as statutory rape. The following summarizes sexual behaviours with children that are currently crimes in Canada:

- Sexually touching anyone under the age of fourteen
- Invitation to a child under the age of fourteen to sexually touch someone else
- Sexual exploitation of a youth, over the age of fourteen but under the age of eighteen, by someone in a position of trust or authority, or by someone upon whom the youth is dependent or where the court infers there is an exploitive relationship
- Luring a child through the Internet
- Engaging a prostitute under the age of eighteen
- Anal intercourse with a person, other than a spouse, under the age of eighteen
- Bestiality in the presence of a child under the age of fourteen

Sexually touching anyone under the age of fourteen
Section 151 defines "sexual interference" as sexually touching someone under the age of fourteen. If found guilty of an indictable offence, the offender can

face up to ten years in prison, with the minimum penalty set at forty-five days. Alternatively, if the offender is convicted of a summary offence, the maximum penalty is eighteen months with a minimum penalty of fourteen days. In such a situation, the accused may plead that the accused thought that the victim was of legal age to consent. The law requires that one take reasonable steps to ascertain the age of a person before engaging in sexual activity if there is any reason to believe that person is underage. In one Toronto case, the suspect claimed his victim, a girl aged thirteen, told him she was seventeen years old and he believed her. In court, the girl denied that she had said any such thing. In addition, the man lived in her housing complex, knew the girl, knew her mother, and frequently saw the girl playing with her friends. The jury found him guilty of sexual assault for engaging with a person under the age of fourteen. Although we do not learn the reasons why a jury makes its decision, one can infer that the accused did not raise a reasonable doubt about the issue of mistaken age. The jury was likely not convinced that he could think she was aged seventeen, and concluded that he did not take reasonable measures to verify that she was as old as she allegedly claimed.

Inviting a child to sexual touching

Section 152 of the *Criminal Code* makes it illegal for an older person to invite children under the age of fourteen years to touch themselves, to touch the older person, or to touch someone else for a sexual purpose. An offence is committed if a child actually does the touching but it is not necessary to go that far to establish that an offence has been committed. Charges for the full offence can be brought if the accused merely gestures or verbally invites the child to do some touching, even if the touching does not subsequently occur. This offence is subject to the same minimum and maximum penalties as sexual interference discussed above.

Sexual exploitation by someone in a position of trust

Youth between the ages of fourteen and eighteen years do not require the same broad protection as children, but the law does provide protection from sexual exploitation in certain relationships. Sexual activity with a person between the ages of fourteen and eighteen years old, by a person in an exploitive relationship, in a position of trust or authority, or upon whom the youth is dependent, is an offence whether or not the young person willingly participated. In these cases, the offender need not have used a position of power to coerce the sexual activity; it is enough that the relationship exists. These cases hinge on demonstrating that a relationship of trust, authority, or dependency existed, as between youth and coaches, teachers, religious leaders, or foster parents. We have yet to see if the court will consider that sexual exploitation exists in the circumstance where a significantly older person, without a meaningful emotional connection, provides a youth with drugs, alcohol, parties, or gifts in exchange for sexual favours. With a summary conviction, the charge of sexual exploitation is punishable by a minimum fourteen days and a maximum eighteen months in jail. If convicted of an indictable offence, the minimum penalty is forty-five days up to a maximum of ten years in jail.

Luring a child through the Internet

Technological advances in communication and information processing have led to new and innovative ways of victimizing others including children. To address this problem, section 172.1 of the *Criminal Code* makes it an offence to use the Internet for sexual exploitation. It is now an offence to lure a person under the age of eighteen via the Internet, for the purpose of engaging in a sexual offence, such as sexual assault, sexual exploitation, or making pornography. Luring a person under the age of sixteen for the purpose of abduction is now an offence, as is luring a person under the age of fourteen for any sexual purpose. A summary conviction carries a maximum penalty of six months in prison and/or a two-thousand-dollar fine. If the charge proceeds by indictment, the maximum penalty is five years in prison.

Child prostitution

The *Criminal Code* specifies that sex with a person under eighteen for consideration is illegal; in other words it is illegal to engage in sex with a prostitute. The minimum penalty for this indictable offence is six months and a maximum penalty of five years incarceration. As well, the law considers it a serious offence to live off the avails of a prostitute under the age of eighteen; therefore, this crime is punishable by a minimum term of two years imprisonment with an allowable maximum of fourteen years.

Anal intercourse with a child or youth

The *Criminal Code* makes it illegal for any person to engage in anal intercourse unless it is in private, between a husband and wife, or between two consenting adults both of whom are aged eighteen or older. This means it is an offence for an older person to engage in anal intercourse with a person under the age of eighteen. In this instance, the behaviour at issue is the anal intercourse, not the question of consent. Unlike sexual exploitation, the relationship of trust or authority is not an essential part of the offence. Some have argued this section of the *Criminal Code* is discriminatory against gay sex, and certain judges have ruled it unconstitutional under the *Charter of Rights and Freedoms*.[17] In these situations, anal intercourse is considered in the same manner as other sexual acts. The Crown will look at the facts of each case reported and determine if the act of sexual penetration was without consent. If the intercourse was without consent, the charge may be sexual assault or sexual exploitation, rather than anal intercourse. If convicted of anal intercourse by indictment, the maximum penalty is ten years in jail.

Bestiality in the presence of a child

Bestiality, which is sexual contact between a human and an animal, is a criminal offence. In the same section that prohibits bestiality is the offence of committing bestiality in the presence of a child under the age of fourteen, or inciting a child to do the same. The Crown can choose to prosecute this offence either by indictment or by summary conviction (a dual or hybrid offence). In this case, the maximum penalty is ten years in jail when convicted by indictment.

SEXUAL OFFENCES AGAINST PERSONS WITH DISABILITIES

SECTION 153.1 OF THE *Criminal Code* extends further protection against sexual assault for persons of any age with a physical or mental disability. Due to their relative dependency, consent is again the main issue. The law recognizes the right of adults with a disability to engage freely in sexual activity, but it also establishes special conditions when the sexual relationship is with a person in a position of trust or authority, or the person with a disability is dependent on the sexual partner. There is no consent if the person, due to a mental illness or intellectual delay, cannot understand the nature or consequences of his actions, or in other words is incapable of giving consent. Consent cannot come from someone other than the person with a disability, nor can anyone counsel that person to engage in sexual activity by abusing a position of trust or authority.

OTHER SEXUAL OFFENCES

SECTIONS 155, 159, 160, and 170 to 172 in Part V of the *Criminal Code* deal with the following offences:

+ Incest — sex between known blood relatives (brother, sister, parent, or grandparent)
+ Corruption of a minor or coercion of a dependent under the age of eighteen by parents, guardians, or house owners to engage in sexual activity

Incest

A CRIME OF INCEST is committed if the parties, knowing they are blood relatives, as parent and offspring, grandparent and grandchildren, or siblings, engage in sexual penetration. The Crown does not need to prove a lack of consent, or even consider the ages of the parties involved. There are recorded cases where both the daughter and the father have been convicted of incest for their sexual relationship. The *Criminal Code* does stipulate that if one party is under restraint, duress, or fear from the other, that party is not guilty of incest. The most common scenario is father/daughter incest where authorities charge the father not only with incest, but for other acts as well. If the activity took place after 4 January 1983, the additional charge would be sexual assault. The essential elements to be proven for these two offences are very different, so caution must be taken when laying charges. If the Crown brought only a charge of sexual assault and a lack of consent was not proven, the court could not then be called upon to convict for incest if that offence had not already been charged. The maximum penalty for this straight indictable offence is fourteen years in prison.

Corruption of a minor

PARENTS AND GUARDIANS HAVE a legal duty to protect their children from living in a home that would corrupt them by exposing them to adultery, sexual immorality, and habitual drunkenness (*Criminal Code* section 172). Parents are also criminally liable if they procure their children for the purpose of having them engage in illegal sexual activity (*Criminal Code* section 170). Equally, an owner, occupier, or manager of premises will be found criminally liable if she knowingly permits illegal sexual activity with a person under the age of eighteen to take place there (section 171). Convictions for these two latter charges bring minimum penalties and, if the person is under the age of fourteen, the sentences are harsher than if the corrupted person is aged fourteen to seventeen years.

When indecent is not illegal

THE GENERAL POPULATION MAY regard some less frequently practised sexual behaviours as indecent or bizarre, but the law attempts to be objective when making decisions about the legality of sexual acts between consenting adults; consent once again being the key legal issue in separating acceptable from unacceptable behaviours. The dictum made famous by Prime Minister Pierre Trudeau, "There's no place for the state in the bedrooms of the nation," is a guiding principle. The government of Canada considers sexual acts between mutually consenting adults to be a private matter. Sexual behaviour crosses a legal line when consent is absent, which includes many of the circumstances and offences described in this chapter.

The other line of demarcation is fantasy. Studies show that many law-abiding Canadians have unusual sexual fantasies, some involving activities that, if carried out, would be criminal. The *Criminal Code* law applies only to actions taken, not to what a person keeps uniquely in one's mind. Nonetheless, there is an exception to this rule. When a known sexual offender, who has repeatedly committed offences, continues to fantasize about illicit sexual activity, the offender may be at risk to offend again. Where there is evidence that the offender is at a precarious stage of the crime cycle, such as fantasizing about sex with children, the authorities may seek a court order restricting the offender's freedom to prevent a sex crime from taking place. This is different from charging the offender with a criminal offence — it is a preventative measure. Freedom can be restricted under a court order but authorities cannot bring new charges for the simple act of fantasizing.

PREVALENCE OF SEXUAL OFFENDING IN CANADA

SEXUAL CRIMES ARE PREVALENT in Canadian society. There were 39, 829 reported sexual assaults in Canada in the year 2002.[18] That is about 8 percent of all violent crimes. The vast majority of sexual assaults (some 96 percent) were of the non-weapon, non-aggravated variety. These numbers represent the reported crimes and do not necessarily reflect the actual rates of sexual crime or crimes of a sexual nature that do not fall within the definition of sexual assault. Nevertheless, there is no question that sexual crimes are a significant problem in Canada, a problem that not only damages individual lives, but also consumes vast amounts of the health and justice system resources. When victims do make a complaint, the pursuit of justice requires enormous expenditures of money by the courts, law enforcement agencies, and mental health systems. In short, sexual offending is a serious problem that directly or indirectly affects us all.

Sexual offences are the least reported violent crimes

WE KNOW THAT CANADIANS do not report to the police every time a crime is committed. Reasons for not reporting are diverse and include fear of the consequences, feelings of shame, distrust of authority, or cynicism that something helpful will actually come from the effort. Of all violent crimes that take place in our communities, sex-related crimes are the most under-reported. Researchers estimate that between 50 and 95 percent of all sexual offences remain unreported. Data from the 2004 Statistics Canada General Social Survey on Victimization suggest that the vast majority of sexual offences (88 percent) go unreported. It is possible that even these high numbers underestimate the rate of unreported sexual offending in this country. Studies indicate that certain features of a sexual offence, such as the pattern of offending, the relationship between the parties, and circumstances of the victim, are meaningful predictors of whether a report to the authorities is likely. Where a victim knows the assailant, such as in a marital or date rape, 99 percent of the cases may go unreported. Similarly, a male is not likely to report a sexual assault by a female, or if he does, he may not be taken seriously.

WHO ARE THE VICTIMS?

It can happen to anyone

THERE ARE CERTAIN GROUPS in our society who are more vulnerable to victimization than others are, but sexual assault can happen to anyone, regardless of gender, economic, social, or cultural status. Even a 240-pound kick-boxer, who understandably feels safe from attack by most people, was once a vulnerable child and may once again be vulnerable during his elderly years. Moreover, if you deem yourself less vulnerable than others are, you no doubt have family, friends or children who may be subjected to victimization. Sexual crimes are human crimes that affect us all in one way or another, and it is only as a society that we can hope to reduce their impact and occurrence. Unless we wrap our family and ourselves in some sort of metaphorical cocoon against life, which is neither possible nor advisable, we must be realistic about the possibility of victimization. We do not mean this caution to sound alarmist or to be a scare tactic, but we want to make an objective analysis of the reality of sexual crimes. As we talk about the statistics of sexual offending, we should not lose sight of the fact that the numbers represent real people who each bring to the courts and health system a uniquely personal history.

Female victims

ALTHOUGH ANYONE CAN BE sexually assaulted, females are the primary victims. Current numbers estimate that 80 percent of sexual assault victims are females. Of the 20 percent who are male victims, most were assaulted during childhood and their assailant was typically another male. Sexual assault appears to be a gender-biased crime, with females typically the victims and males most often the offenders.

Social scientists and feminists have offered analyses to explain the female vulnerability to rape as being deeply rooted in a patriarchal social structure. Society has generally accorded males supremacy and ultimate authority in both the home and state affairs. Legal and social systems have historically supported male dominance, which may reflect a deep-rooted sense that this is the "natural law." From this frame of reference, women and children are by definition subordinate and in need of both protection and guidance by the male members of society. Further, although there may be some cross-cultural differences in the expression of sexual violence, there do not appear to be many, if any, "rape-free" societies. Sexual violation appears to be widespread wherever there are relational power differences, such as those between men and women, adults and children, or between the powerful and powerless. In her 1975 groundbreaking book, *Against Our Will: Men, Women and Rape,* Susan Brownmiller made the point, now widely accepted by experts, that sexual assault is a crime primarily motivated by violence and power rather than by sexual desire. Therefore, sexual assault against women may be primarily the use of sexuality by males to establish dominance and control over women. This is most clearly seen in circumstances where social controls break down (for example, war zones) and rape becomes epidemic.

Male victims

IT WAS NOT SO long ago that most people thought the percentage of male victims was much lower than the 20 percent cited above. Males have proven even more reluctant than females to report sexual crimes due to the associated stigma and the limited recognition by authorities that males can be victimized, not only by other males, but by females as well. When an older male forces himself sexually on a young female, she is a victim, but when an older female takes sexual advantage of a young male, others may view him as "lucky." Although as many as one in five males may experience some sort of sexual violation in their lifetime, typically when they are young, it is only recently that attention has turned to this topic. With an increasing number of high profile male athletes, celebrities, and First Nations residential school victims coming forward to talk about their abuse, awareness regarding male victims is growing.

Age of victims

RECORDS SHOW THAT SEXUAL assault victims range in age from new-born to the elderly. When the assault is forceful and involves vaginal or anal penetration, infants and young children can sustain particularly horrific physical damage. In pre-verbal children, there is often only physical damage to indicate a sexual assault has occurred. Unfortunately, children and youth make up the majority of sexual assault victims. While this group makes up only about 20 percent of the population, they are victims in 60 percent of all reported sexual assaults. Records indicate that 60 percent of female victims and 80 percent of male victims are under the age of eighteen. Over 90 percent of all reported sexual assaults are against people under the age of thirty-five.

Low-income, underprivileged, and isolated communities

IN SOME COMMUNITIES, SEXUAL assault rates are higher than average. Factors such as poverty, drug and alcohol abuse, and social disorganization can increase the risk to vulnerable groups. Statistics from some First Nations groups indicate particularly high rates of childhood sexual abuse, as much as three times the national average. One Northwest Territories study found that 80 percent of First Nations girls and 50 percent of the boys under eight years of age had been sexually abused.

Other vulnerable groups

SOME OFFENDERS TARGET THE particularly vulnerable, such as those who reside in institutions and are reliant on others for their care, in the hope they will avoid detection. In recent history, we have the example of First Nations children attending residential schools away from their homes and families, as well as children in schools for the deaf or blind, who were subjected to repeated sexual abuse by caregivers placed in charge of their well-being. There are also documented cases of caregivers, or relatives of caregivers, committing sexual assaults against persons who have profound intellectual or physical disabilities.

Sex-trade workers are another group who are particularly vulnerable to both physical and sexual assaults by their johns, pimps, and others on the street. Research with female sex-trade workers indicates that approximately 75 percent have been vaginally penetrated by force while working as a prostitute. The fact that many prostitutes were sexually abused as children and carry the emotional burden of that abuse does little to temper the attitude that "they deserve what they get" for working the streets. Recent high profile cases of serial homicides in the sex-trade community have underscored the larger societal attitude toward groups held in low esteem. Not only did the male offenders feel at liberty to abuse and murder the prostitutes, those outside their community gave little notice to their disappearance. Moreover, those cases that did come to the attention of authorities tended to be investigated with less than the usual vigour until advocates drew public attention to the case.

WHO ARE THE OFFENDERS?

THERE IS NO SIMPLE or straightforward answer to this question. Just as there is a wide range of sexual offences, there is a wide variety of offender characteristics. While some sexual offending is the consequence of a long-standing and entrenched perversion on the part of the perpetrator, other offences can be committed due to ignorance of appropriate behaviours and their consequences. Ignorance, however, is no excuse before the law so we all have an obligation to be aware of what constitutes unacceptable sexual behaviour. Those who are prone to unusual or powerful sexual urges must learn appropriate boundaries and adequate impulse control, while others can empower themselves by learning about their rights, and when and how those might be violated.

Sexual offences can range from the unobtrusive rubbing of the offender's body against a victim on a crowded bus, to taking nude pictures of a child, to violent penetration and maiming. This wide diversity of sexual behaviours reflects a wide range of human personalities, experiences, arousal patterns, and opportunities. Offenders can be young or old, male or female, hence it is difficult to outline any specific qualities or personal histories that will reliably predict, on an individual basis, those who will commit a sexual offence. An offender can be someone with a long history of antisocial and criminal behaviours or an otherwise upstanding, respected member of the community. To some extent, we can speak in generalities: males are more likely than females to be offenders and those who offend once are at higher risk to offend again. However, trying to identify specific predictive characteristics that identify potential sexual offenders is fraught with difficulties. There are no infallible methods of identifying potential sex offenders.

Some common myths associated with sex offending suggest that offenders are people who have uncontrollable impulses or sexual urges, are all mentally ill, or are seduced by their victims. As a group, those convicted of sex offences do not appear to have uncontrollable sexual impulses nor do they display a higher incidence of mental illness than others. The idea that the victim somehow encourages the assailant by wearing provocative clothing or subconsciously provoking an assault is equally unsupported. Further, society has tended to view females as victims and males as offenders, but there is accumulating evidence in the literature that female offenders are neither non-existent nor rare. Although males commit the majority of sex offences, research suggests females, acting alone, may account for approximately 6 percent of sexual abuse against females and 14 percent of sexual abuse against males.[19]

The causes of sexual offending are not simple or straightforward. Accumulating knowledge suggests that such behaviour is the result of interacting factors, such as early experiences (both good and bad), beliefs, conditioning, and biological characteristics. Considering all these biological, psychological, and social factors (the bio/psycho/social model), often gives a better understanding of individual sex offenders and allows clinicians some ability to form treatment plans and to predict continued risk.

Although there are currently several well-researched instruments used by clinical psychologists to estimate the risk of re-offence by sex offenders, these instruments must be used with caution and with full understanding of their limitations. Perhaps the more relevant questions are how do we deal with sexual offenders once they have been identified by their behaviours, and what steps can we take to lower the rate of sexual offending generally?

To begin, we know we cannot rely on the word of the offender alone to predict risk. As with other compulsive behaviours, such as substance abuse, you cannot count on offenders to give an accurate account of their thoughts, feelings, or behaviours. Researchers have developed risk assessment tools that use information generated by the offender but also include other sources of information and objective criteria (such as compliance with supervision, historical facts, and access to victims). Forensic psychiatrists and psychologists have developed standards for assessment designed to assist the courts in tackling these difficult issues. Functional assessments that take into account the unique biological, psychological, and social factors that were important in each offender's crime cycle are now the norm. Gone are the days when the offender's physician could appear in court and legitimately defend the offender by saying "he was a nice man and would not re-offend."

Provincial and federal corrections agencies have also had to come to terms with the growing numbers of sex offenders moving through the system. Lowering the risk of re-offence by an identified sex offender calls for a coordination of services — a multifaceted approach.

Most victims know their assailant

AS FOR THE CIRCUMSTANCES in which sexual assault and abuse occur, we are now aware that these crimes are predominantly inflicted on people who know their assailants. Assaults by strangers in the dark on deserted roads do occur—and it is a fear that most of us carry with us. However, in reality, 60 percent of reported sexual assaults occur in private homes, about 40 percent occur in the victim's home, and half occur in daylight hours. Furthermore, most studies agree that persons known to the victims commit more than 80 percent of these crimes. The assailants include family members, friends, neighbours, and business colleagues. Complex psychological dynamics arise when those most trusted, such as parents, spouses, close friends, priests, teachers, or coaches perpetrate sexual assaults. Increasing knowledge has brought this crime much closer to home and changed the way that we view our own vulnerability and others around us. An example of changing attitudes is the earlier discussion about how we have increasingly had to come to terms with the reality of sexual assault within marriage.

YOUNG OFFENDERS

YOUNG OFFENDERS, BETWEEN THE ages of twelve and eighteen, commit many sexual crimes in Canada. Inappropriate sexual acts by teens are still often dismissed or minimized as being just experimentation or harmless curiosity, but this is not the case. A youth who commits a sexual offence against a younger child, or is sexually aggressive with a peer-aged victim, typically knows the behaviour is wrong. The perpetrator generally bribes, manipulates, or threatens the victim not to tell anyone about the sexual acts. The reasons why an adolescent offends sexually derive from the interaction of biological, social, and emotional factors, and the most effective way of reducing the risk of re-offence in most offenders is through programs that address these factors.

At one time, the court treated youth who committed crimes in the same manner as adult offenders, but that thinking has changed. Punishment alone is not seen as a sufficient deterrent to criminal behaviour and more severe forms of punishment do not result in an equivalent drop in the crime rate. Current reasoning holds that the best way to provide long-term protection for society is through early intervention and rehabilitation. While young offenders are considered to be in a state of immaturity and dependency compared to adults, they are nevertheless held responsible for their crimes beginning at the age of twelve; however, they are typically not held accountable to the same degree as adults are. The primary goals of the *Youth Criminal Justice Act* (*YCJA*) are to create a system that takes into account a victim's interests, fosters responsibility in young people, ensures accountability through meaningful consequences, provides effective rehabilitation and reintegration into the community, and reduces over-reliance on incarceration for non-violent offenders. The Act discourages charging young people if other options will suffice, and reserves jail sentences for those who commit violent crimes.

The *Criminal Code* defines criminal conduct that applies equally to youth and adults, but when accused of a crime the law prosecutes a young person differently than an adult. A youth is dealt with, and if charged is prosecuted, under the *YCJA*, and the case is heard in youth justice court rather than in the criminal court where adult cases are tried. Legal principles and procedures are similar between the two courts but there are some important differences. The *YCJA* articulates principles that encourage the court to keep young people out of jail and out of the criminal justice system whenever possible.

Extrajudicial measures

WHERE THE POLICE OR the Crown feel that a young person's behaviour can be properly managed without court attendance, the case can be dealt with using extrajudicial measures. These measures include, taking no further action, a warning, a caution, a referral to a community program, or a referral to the extrajudicial sanctions program. The first step is to determine if a youth can be appropriately dealt with by these means. In making a decision, the court will consider the seriousness of the offence, the nature and number of previous offences committed, or other aggravating circumstances. When appropriate, the Crown may refer the matter to the extrajudicial sanctions program. In that case, the youth would meet with a youth justice committee whose purpose is to work out the differences between the youth, the victim, and community members. There must be sufficient evidence to proceed with the prosecution of the offence when referring for extrajudicial sanctions. A victim is informed if a matter is dealt with by this extrajudicial route rather than by prosecution.

Sentencing of young offenders

WHEN THE COURT FINDS a youth guilty of a crime, the sentencing judge faces the same difficult choices that apply when sentencing an adult. Sentencing is not meant to be retribution, but a means for positive action. A sentence should be a statement that the person's criminal actions are unacceptable, and an acknowledgment of harm done by that person. A sentence should also help to prevent further criminality through rehabilitation. The sentencing judge's task is to find a sentence that will serve all these purposes.

Custodial sentences in both the adult and the youth systems are reserved for the most serious crimes and for repeat offenders. When sentenced to jail, a young offender goes to a youth facility and attends rehabilitative programs designed for that age range. Under the *YCJA*, judges have the option to impose an adult sentence on a youth. This can occur if the youth is at least fourteen years of age, is charged with an indictable offence punishable by more than two years in custody, and a youth sentence is an inadequate response for that youth. In some cases (for example, murder or aggravated sexual assault), it is presumed that the youth will be sentenced as an adult unless the youth shows reason to not be so sentenced. Whether or not the court sentences a youth as an adult depends on the nature of the crime and consideration of individual characteristics, such as the risk to re-offend, emotional development, and physical maturity. If sentenced to an adult term, the young person could go to an adult facility or stay in youth jail until mature enough to enter the adult system.

When a youth is sentenced to an adult sentence, the case remains in the youth justice court. Under the youth system, the maximum penalty for serious crimes other than murder (such as aggravated sexual assault) is three years in custody. When the Crown proceeds summarily, the maximum sentence in youth court is eighteen months, just as it is for an adult.

Rights of young persons

IN GENERAL, A YOUNG offender has the same rights as everyone does, with some exceptions. To begin, a young offender is not convicted of a crime but instead is "found guilty." This may seem like a trivial matter of semantics but it allows the young person to answer "no" truthfully when asked if he has been convicted of a criminal offence. In addition, the *YCJA* protects the identities of young offenders along with young victims and witnesses. A young offender can be identified if given an adult sentence, and after he turns eighteen years old, information can be published that would identify the young offender. If a young person stays out of trouble for a period of three years after completing a sentence, authorities destroy the youth record. The period of good behaviour is five years for the more serious indictable offences, after which time a youth record can be destroyed. If the young person becomes an adult and commits further criminal offences during this period, the youth record becomes part of the adult criminal file and remains a public record for the rest of the offender's life. The record of a young person transferred to adult court is treated in the same manner as an adult record. In terms of sexual offences, the names of young offenders are not added to the national sex offender registry unless they receive an adult sentence and the court orders them to register.

VIGNETTE ONE: EXAMPLE OF A SEXUAL CRIME

VIGNETTE ONE, LEADING INTO this chapter, illustrates many of the principles outlined above. As is the case with many victims, the fifteen-year-old girl knew her assailant, and his actions left her feeling confused, shocked, and unsafe. Fortunately, she had a support system that allowed her to feel safe to tell her parents and to report the incident, which is not always the case. After investigating her assault, the police would prepare a report for the government's lawyer, the Crown counsel. In this case, the Crown would likely proceed with a summary charge (less serious than an indictable offence) unless the accused had a serious history of sexual offences on his record. That the accused touched her without her consent could itself result in a charge of sexual assault; but since the complainant is under the age of eighteen and the offender is in a position of trust and authority, consent is irrelevant. The Crown also would likely lay a charge of sexual exploitation. If the Crown does not prove the lack of consent beyond a reasonable doubt, the accused could be convicted of sexual exploitation.

After charges are laid, the accused must consider if he will plead guilty or not guilty. There may be plea discussions whereby the Crown would offer to accept a plea to one of the charges and outline to the defence what its position on sentencing would be. The Crown lawyer may want to hear what the defence considers the sentence should be before deciding to take a plea. The defence counsel would want some agreement about what sentence the Crown will ask of the judge. If the offence took place after 1 November 2005, the minimum penalty for sexual exploitation would be fourteen days. There is no minimum sentence for a sexual assault conviction.

The court appearances, whether they be remands, a guilty plea, or a trial, will all take place in the courthouse nearest to the alleged crime scene. Before the actual trial begins (or during the trial if issues arise that make this relevant), the defence lawyer might make an evidentiary application for copies of all, or parts of, the complainant's diary (section 278.2 provides a process to require a witness to bring material evidence to court). The defence might also ask the judge for permission to question the girl or others about other times she has had sex with the accused or with other persons (section 276 states that the judge may deem such information admissible if it is relevant to the issue at trial). The defence would have to show that the diary contents and/or questions about previous sexual behaviour with either the accused or someone else are relevant to enable the accused to provide a full defence.

As the legal arguments develop in the trial, the lawyers might cite relevant sections of the *Criminal Code* and case law. The defence might argue that the client's actions were not sexual and the girl misinterpreted his intentions. The prosecutor could cite *R. v. Chase*[20] to argue that what the coach did was not merely physical aggression but was a sexual assault, a behaviour that violates the sexual dignity of the complainant. Therefore, even if the accused only grabbed the girl's shoulders and made lewd or violent sexual remarks, if the sexual integrity of the girl was violated he could be charged with a sexual offence under the law (sections 265 and 271), equivalent to grabbing her vagina or breast.

Alternately, the accused may argue that the girl was leading him on, and that she consented to the activity. He might also say he interpreted her actions as an indication that she wanted to have sex with him and he is therefore entitled to an acquittal because the Crown did not prove the necessary intent. Another issue would be the allegation that the accused, as the complainant's coach, was in a position of trust and authority over her, making his actions an offence even if she agreed to his advances. In fact, even if the girl had wanted sex and had invited his advances, sexual activity with her would be illegal because she was between the ages of fourteen and seventeen years.

If the court found the accused guilty as charged, the lawyers would use the *Criminal Code* sentencing principles (sections 718.1–718.2) and relevant case law to make their arguments for an appropriate sentence. Typically, the defence would argue that the accused should receive a sentence near the lower end of the sentencing spectrum, while the prosecutor would likely submit that a harsher penalty is required as a means of deterrence.

ENDNOTES

1   Parliament amended the *Criminal Code*, below note 2, in 1983 when Bill C-127 repealed the offences of rape and indecent assault and created the offences of sexual assault level I, II, and III. Subsequent amendments in 1992 (Bill C-49 was passed as S.C. 1992, c. 38) enacted s. 273.1, which reiterated that consent meant a voluntary agreement to engage in the sexual activity, and provided further guidance on circumstances in which consent was not obtained.

2   *Criminal Code*, R.S.C. 1985, c. C-46 [*Criminal Code*].

3   Online: www.canada.justice.gc.ca/en/dept/pub; www.canlii.org.

4   Sexual intercourse with a female under fourteen years of age and gross indecency, to name two, became sexual interference, sexual invitation to touch, and sexual exploitation. See Robin F. Badgley, *Sexual Offences Against Children* (Ottawa: Library of Parliament, Research Branch, 1984) [Badgley Report]. *Criminal Code*, ss. 150.1, 273.1, and 265(3).

5   *Criminal Code*, ss. 150.1, 273.1, and 265(3).

6   *R. v. Ewanchuk* (1999), 131 C.C.C. (3d) 481 at para. 28 (S.C.C.) [*Ewanchuk*].

7   In addition, if a victim dies while an offender is perpetrating a sexual assault, the charge is first degree murder and the penalty is life without consideration of parole until twenty-five years. *Code*, s. 230.

8   For an offender to receive the minimum four years for use of a firearm to intimidate, the police need to have seized it, done forensic testing, and ensured it fits the *Code* definition. It is not enough that the victim says the weapon looked like a gun. If there is not definite proof of it being a firearm, the charges will still be sexual assault with a weapon and its use will be an aggravating factor in sentencing.

9   Canadian Centre for Justice Statistics, Statistics Canada, *Uniform Crime Reporting Survey*. Online: www.statcan.ca.

10 *Criminal Code*, s. 273.2.

11 *Ewanchuk*, above note 6 at 499.

12 See, for example, online: www.cbc.ca/story/canada/national/2005/11/14/HIV-trial_051114.html.

13 David Finkelhor & Kersti Yllo, *License to Rape: Sexual Abuse of Wives* (New York: Holt, Rinehart & Winston, 1985). See also online: www.vaw.umn.edu/documents/vawnet/mrape/mrape.html#bergen1996.

14 Helen Lenskyj, *An Analysis of Violence Against Women: A Manual for Educators and Administrators* (Toronto: Ontario Institute for Studies in Education, 1992).

15 *R. v. Daviault* (1994), 93 C.C.C. (3d) 21 (S.C.C.), which allowed the defence of intoxication for an accused whose ingestion of alcohol put him in a state of automatism, was overturned by Parliament with s. 33.1 of the *Code*. Since its enactment, it has been challenged successfully in Ontario and the N.W.T.

16 Christine Boyle, *Sexual Assault* (Scarborough: Carswell, 1984) at 71.

17 *Canadian Charter of Rights and Freedoms*, Part I of the *Constitution Act, 1982*, being Schedule B to the *Canada Act 1982* (U.K.), 1982, c. 11 [*Charter*].

18 Julian V. Roberts, *Criminal Justice Processing of Sexual Assault Cases* (Ottawa: Statistics Canada, Canadian Centre for Justice Statistics, 1994).

19 David Finkelhor & Diana Russell, "Women as Perpetrators: Review of the Evidence" in David Finkelhor, *Child Sexual Abuse: New Theory and Research* (New York: Free Press, 1984) at 171–87.

20 [1987] 2 S.C.R. 293.

2

The Personal Impact of Sexual Crimes

Vignette Two

A sixty-five-year-old man, Tony, exposes his penis to a fifty-four-year-old woman, Liz, while she is working in a retail store. Following this event, Liz develops anxiety and depression, conditions serious enough to interfere with her ability to work. She no longer feels safe, although she had previously been very comfortable and secure in the store. She is preoccupied with thoughts of the offender and feels that he specifically targeted her. These emotions and thoughts do not subside and they keep her from returning to her job. Her co-workers, some of whom also saw Tony's penis, are puzzled at what they see as Liz's extreme reaction to a relatively minor event and some suspect she is exaggerating her symptoms to get time off work. People make remarks to the effect that she should "just get over it." Liz believes this herself; she feels inadequate and weak because she cannot put the experience behind her. These negative thoughts and feelings increase her depression and anxiety to the point where she feels in need of professional help.

THIS CHAPTER PROVIDES INFORMATION about the ways that sexual crimes can affect you. This discussion is not an exhaustive examination of psychological dynamics but a conceptual framework on which you can build an understanding of your experiences and their social/emotional impact. You will learn that there is no "normal" response to sexual assault, as each of us brings a unique history and perspective to such ordeals. A broader understanding of your experiences can help reduce anxiety about what is normal or abnormal, can improve your coping ability, and can help you deal more effectively with stress caused by legal system.

During the last three decades, knowledge about how sexual assault and childhood sexual abuse affects victims and their families has greatly expanded. The pioneering work of Ann Burgess and her colleagues in the mid 1970s raised awareness of the tremendous impact that sexual assault can have.[1] By the 1980s, knowledge about the prevalence and the impact of childhood sexual abuse had grown. Over the last few decades, new information has continued to accumulate, increasing our understanding of the nature and impact of sexual crimes. Below we have summarized relevant research data and clinical experience in an attempt to reduce the misconceptions and confusion that can occur around such an emotionally charged subject. Misunderstandings can occur if information in this chapter is taken out of context or read piecemeal, so we advise you to read the complete chapter before making any personal decisions or judgments.

SHARED AND UNIQUE REACTIONS

AS YOU READ THIS and the upcoming chapters, and think about the way a sexual crime has affected you, you should be alert to some important issues. There is no single, telling response or set of responses to a sexual assault. People may share reactions that are similar to those of others and have some reactions that are uniquely their own. Consequently, as is true with most important life experiences, you will find that the road to understanding and resolution is partly a road travelled by others and partly a journey uniquely your own. What follows is not an exhaustive exploration of the impact of sexual crimes; it is an overview to help people understand the breadth and complexity of potential psychological, physical, and social consequences. Below are four central principles you should take into consideration when trying to understand your experiences and reactions to sexual abuse:

- There are wide ranging emotional consequences.
- Psychological problems can have many causes.
- Emotional effects tend to shift and change over time.
- It is important to ask, "Does this symptom truly apply to me?"

A wide range of consequences

SEXUAL CRIMES CAN AFFECT a person in a variety of ways, and we list some of the possible consequences below. The presence or absence of distressing symptoms depends on many factors, such as the severity of the assault, relationship of victim to the assailant, passage of time, and personality characteristics and history of the victim. There is no specific "syndrome" caused by sexual crimes. Instead, there is wide variability in personal responses. Bear this in mind as you read this chapter, and avoid stereotyping yourself or others as having to conform to a predetermined notion of a "sexual assault victim." You may identify with a few, many, or none of the potential problems in the following list:

- Physical injuries
- Chronic pain
- Wide-ranging fears, including phobias
- Post-Traumatic Stress Disorder symptoms
- Panic attacks
- Mood swings and depression
- Suicidal thoughts
- Low self-esteem or altered self-concept
- Guilt
- Shame
- Anger, hostility, and/or aggression
- Eating disorders
- Substance abuse
- Doubts about sexual orientation
- Sexual dysfunction or promiscuity
- Problems in intimate relationships
- Distrust of others
- Changes in perception of the world

Some individuals will be extremely damaged and debilitated by their sexual victimization. For some, reading and discussing these difficult topics will not be an option at this point in their life. They may not be able to concentrate or sufficiently process the necessary information. For others, their emotional turmoil may overwhelm their ability to cope. It is a sad reality that those who have been most psychologically damaged are often the least able to seek redress in either criminal or civil court. It is also the case that severe psychological difficulties can sometimes be used against sexual assault victims to discredit their evidence. However, there are steps you can take to lessen this possibility, and we will address these.

When we consider the potentially damaging effects of sexual crimes, we also acknowledge that long-standing or severe psychological difficulties are not an inevitable outcome of an assault. Those who exhibit few or none of the symptoms or problems often associated with sexual assaults can experience self-doubt and feel alienated from other victims. If you find yourself in the paradoxical situation of asking, "What's wrong with me?" because you do not match the descriptions you have read of victims of sexual assault, it is important to understand that this does *not* mean that there is anything wrong with you. Different people respond to the same experience in different ways.

Further, the absence of psychological symptoms or reactions following an assault does not mean that the assault did not occur. The notion that sexual assault victims are inevitably or irreversibly damaged by their experiences can lead to misconceptions in court. The credibility of an adult or childhood victim might be questioned if they do not conform to the stereotype of a sexual assault victim and are functioning "too well." In some cases, it may be necessary to educate court officials and help them understand the reality of the complainant. This would entail looking to the individual to see how the victim has been specifically affected by the crime, rather than relying on a stereotype.

Psychological problems can have many causes

SINCE THERE IS NO "syndrome" specific to being sexually assaulted, we cannot confirm or disconfirm that someone has been the victim of a sexual crime based solely on one's behaviour or psychological problems. A wide range of other types of stressors, medical problems, or mental health conditions can also cause the types of difficulties that are associated with sexual victimization. As you read about the psychological difficulties that might arise from sexual crimes, you may recognize negative emotions or psychological symptoms that you have experienced at other times in your life, or may be experiencing now, that are unrelated to any victimization.

For example, you may have been depressed following the death of a loved one, or some other significant loss. You may experience frequent anxiety in response to an array of factors: living with an angry spouse, worrying about your finances, raising your children, dealing with an aging parent, experiencing pressures at work, facing a dreaded medical procedure, to name a few possibilities. Just the day-to-day hassles of life can be very stressful.

You may also experience psychological symptoms and distress related to a medical condition or other psychiatric condition that you have. People diagnosed with schizophrenia, for example, are particularly vulnerable to stressful events.

It is evident, given these complexities, that not all symptoms you identified in the preceding list may be directly or solely due to your experience of sexual assault. The precise cause of your psychological difficulties will become an important issue if you pursue civil litigation. Your lawyer may retain an expert, typically a psychologist or psychiatrist, to sort out these complexities for the court. However, at this stage the precise cause of your psychological difficulties is less important than identifying the psychological concerns you currently have. Identifying your psychological issues can help you make decisions about engaging in legal proceedings. Identifying and understanding your feelings, thoughts, and reactions is also an important step towards your individual road to recovery or personal growth.

Effects tend to shift and change over time

LIFE IS A PROCESS; birth, growth, and aging are its ever-changing characteristics. In a constantly shifting world, change is one thing that we can count on. None of us remains the same over time. As we evolve, as our life circumstances change, our thoughts and feelings about our experiences also shift. Victims of a sexual crime can expect their emotional reactions and perceptions of their experiences to change with time.

Fear may dominate in the period following the assault, but then the fear may subside and be replaced by sadness or anger. These new predominant feelings will then be subject to change in their turn. Expect this process to occur frequently on your path to healing. For some victims, the impact of sexual crime will be strongest in the days, weeks, or months following the assault, with few or no lingering effects. For others, distress may fade quickly after the sexual assault only to re-emerge later (sometimes many years later), perhaps to a degree more debilitating than the initial reactions. Some individuals work through the impact of the sexual assault and its meaning subtly but steadily over time, so they eventually feel psychologically stronger than before. There can also be a period of shock following a sexual assault, during which you may be numb to many of your emotions. Be careful that you are not masking your symptoms with drugs, alcohol, or other methods of distraction. Emotional effects generally lessen with time but unexpected or suppressed emotional reactions can emerge at any time, sometimes triggered by some other external event.

Particular dates or times of year may trigger thoughts or memories of emotional events in our lives. For some victims, anniversary dates of the assault can trigger upsetting thoughts or feelings. Major life events — even positive ones like getting married or having a child — can trigger intense, distressing memories and emotional reactions related to the sexual assault. Among those sexually assaulted in childhood, a resurgence of strong emotions and upsetting thoughts may emerge when their own child or other children in their life reach the same age they were when the assaults took place.

For those who choose to pursue a legal course of action against their assailant, be aware that there will likely be times during this process (from reporting to police through various pretrial procedures to the trial itself, or during civil litigation) when strong emotional responses are apt to occur or recur. Although talking about past hurtful experiences with someone you trust can be helpful, talking in-depth about these distressing issues with strangers or in front of the offender (as may happen in court) can be upsetting or painful. We discuss methods of coping with these potential situations in subsequent chapters.

Does this truly apply to me?

THERE IS A NATURAL tendency in all of us to imagine we have the symptoms we are reading about. This tendency usually does most of us little harm beyond needless anxiety, like some doctors-in-training who worry that they suffer from each new ailment and disease they encounter. However, if you have been sexually assaulted or abused, there is potential danger in believing that certain symptoms apply to you when they do not.

This type of mistaken belief could negatively influence your recovery and generate needless anxiety. It could also negatively affect the legal outcome of your case. Therefore, when reading this book and thinking about these issues, we caution you to be careful in deciding whether you believe that a particular symptom or problem applies to you. Challenge it before you accept it. Ask yourself, "Does this truly apply to me?" or "Is this particular problem due to something else?" Is the symptom in question frequent and obvious, or is it something minor that you experience occasionally? Remember that no single set of symptoms applies to all victims. Bear in mind that you are a unique individual with unique experiences, and when reading about the range of psychological symptoms outlined, make a particular effort to decide which truly apply to you.

THE PERCEPTIONS AND EXPERIENCES OF OTHERS

EVEN IF MANY OF the reactions or perceptions discussed in this and subsequent chapters are not ones that you have experienced, it will be helpful for you to understand the sorts of psychological issues that others, for example, family, friends, the police, and mental health and legal professionals may assume that victims are experiencing. To assist you in overcoming their misperceptions, and having the reality of your own experience understood, it might be helpful to know how others may perceive you. Reading this chapter may also help you better understand the experiences of others who have been sexually assaulted and who may have reacted differently than you have. Taking into account the experiences and perspectives of others can be useful as you interact with a wide range of individuals in the legal system. Being able to entertain a variety of perspectives can also be a very important part of your own recovery process.

EVERYDAY STRESS

A DISCUSSION OF THE extraordinary stress that you may face following a sexual assault or during legal proceedings must begin with an examination of the daily hassles we all face. Stress is an inevitable part of life, and a distressing or traumatic event only adds to daily tensions. At any point in our lives, we will be experiencing more or less pressure from stressors, such as poor health, finances, relationships, family responsibilities, school, work, or mental health challenges. Sometimes we do not realize that positive events (for example, a promotion or marriage) are also causing stress. Virtually anything that changes our lives or challenges our personal resources is stressful. However, a manageable amount of stress in our lives is actually a good thing. Manageable doses of pressure are stimulating, motivating us to be productive and to move our lives in positive directions. Stress becomes a negative force when it overwhelms our capacity to cope and interferes with our daily functioning. Ongoing high stress can lead to medical problems ranging from aches and pains to chronic illness, or to mental health problems like overwhelming anxiety and depression.

As we discuss psychological reactions to sexual assault or to the court process, it is important to bear in mind this backdrop of everyday stressors. The pressures in your everyday life are not suspended during times of crisis. Stress you feel in one part of your life interacts with stressful feelings from other aspects of your life. As we discuss feelings of fear, anxiety, depression, anger, and distrust that may result from an assault, remember that these overlay your everyday problems of living. As you read on, keep in mind the four principles outlined above that apply to emotional reactions. As well, try to look beyond the damages that you have suffered, pace yourself according to your current emotional needs, and be mindful of the subtleties of your reactions. Consideration of these issues will be particularly important as you move through challenging periods of your life.

In the following section, we discuss in detail some of the emotional reactions that may follow a sexual assault. Rather than attempting to discuss all potential reactions, we have chosen to highlight the types of psychological responses that can, in our experience, emerge during the court process and interfere with your ability to be an effective spokesperson for your case. Some of these understandable reactions to sexual crimes are as follows:

- Anxiety — short and long-term physiological changes
- Depression — physical and emotional flatness
- Anger — hostile, aggressive urges
- Mistrust — loss of faith in others

ANXIETY: "FIGHT OR FLIGHT"

OUR HUMAN BODIES HAVE an automatic reaction to danger, frequently referred to as the "fight or flight" response. When we perceive a threat to our safety, our body instinctively shifts into survival mode. Our nervous system releases neurochemicals that trigger immediate biological reactions to help us either confront or escape the danger. Our heart rate and respiration increase, blood pressure goes up, and energy, in the form of stored sugars, is released to increase muscle tone. As well, our attention narrows, focusing primarily on the danger of the moment and ignoring other information that is not crucial to our survival. Victims of frightening assaults can have the intense sensory experiences of blood pounding in their veins, rapid breathing, nausea, dry mouth, sweating, or trembling. These physiological responses are the body mobilizing for survival.

In a study of selected rape victims, almost all reported feeling numerous physical and emotional reactions at the time of the assault, but within just a few hours some of their feelings changed. Not all changed in the same way, some increased while others diminished. For example, although physical responses, such as a racing heart and rapid breathing decreased significantly within two or three hours, other responses, such as shaking and tightened muscles were still evident. Other stress symptoms, such as headache had significantly increased. For some victims, feelings of confusion decreased, but social withdrawal and depressed mood were more pronounced.[2]

Those sexually assaulted in extremely frightening circumstances may find themselves still trembling hours after the event, even though the danger has passed. Some may feel emotionally numb for a lengthy period, while others may experience a flooding of images or emotions associated with the assault. In some cases, the initial biological response unexpectedly comes back, an "echo" of the original response, complete with sensations of trembling, pounding heart, or feelings of fear, triggered by some event that brings back the memory of the original experience.

These bodily reactions are adaptable and understandable responses to a very frightening or traumatic experience. How long it takes for the physical effects of anxiety or the fear response to lessen varies individually. For most individuals, physical reactions have quieted significantly within hours or days, and then gradually decrease with time. For others, the physical reactions may continue long-term, causing considerable distress.

For some victims of traumatic experiences, including those who were repeatedly and severely sexually abused as children, these fear-based anxiety reactions may become chronic, sometimes being evident in their day-to-day functioning. On the other hand, anxiety responses may diminish only to happen again suddenly and unexpectedly many years later. Typically, this recurrence is triggered by some significant event, and the court process can sometimes provide such a trigger. When these physical reactions are intense, long-lasting, and interfere with a person's functioning, they can make up a constellation of symptoms known to mental health professionals as Post-Traumatic Stress Disorder (PTSD).

PTSD symptoms

PTSD IS AN ANXIETY disorder that some people develop after being exposed to life-threatening or terrifying experiences, such as being in combat, in a serious car accident, in a natural disaster, in a robbery at gunpoint, or being a victim of a physical or sexual assault. People often respond to these types of experiences with extreme fear, horror, or helplessness and they may subsequently develop PTSD symptoms.

Experiencing some PTSD symptoms after a traumatic event is not unusual, but the majority of trauma victims do not develop full-blown, diagnosable PTSD, a disorder that causes significant distress and disruption in a person's life. Furthermore, for those diagnosed with PTSD, the frequency and intensity of the symptoms typically decreases within three months, to the point that the diagnosis no longer applies to them.[3] On the other hand, some individuals continue to have distressing PTSD symptoms many years after their traumatic experiences.

Diagnosis of PTSD requires assessment by a qualified mental health professional who evaluates the severity and extent of the symptoms experienced. Taken individually, symptoms of PTSD are relatively common, normal reactions to highly stressful experiences, but when they cluster together, and occur over time, they can become a significant problem requiring professional intervention to relieve. Below are the major symptoms associated with PTSD. We do not suggest that you use this information to make a diagnosis for yourself or someone else, but use it to gauge if a professional opinion is needed. The *Diagnostic and Statistical Manual of Mental Disorders* (DSM-IV-TR), a manual used by mental health professionals for diagnosis,[4] outlines three clusters of PTSD symptoms:

- Recurring, intrusive memories, thoughts, images, or dreams of the traumatic experience
- Persistent attempts to avoid reminders of the trauma or to numb certain feelings
- Persistent symptoms of nervous arousal that were not previously present (hyper-arousal)

Intrusive memories

INTRUSIVE RE-EXPERIENCING OF A traumatic event is one of the signature symptoms of post-traumatic stress. This may include having distressing memories, thoughts, or images of the sexual assault popping into your mind or repeatedly occurring in dreams or nightmares. These thoughts or images are unwanted and distressing. You may feel as though you cannot turn off your memory, as though you remember too much. This condition is sometimes referred to as "hypernesia" and is the opposite of amnesia, where you cannot remember what has happened. Dreams or nightmares can be particularly disruptive because they interrupt your sleep and, in turn, affect your daytime functioning. Those with a severe history of disturbing nightmares may fear going to sleep, leading to insomnia and a reliance on medication, drugs, or alcohol to induce dreamless sleep.

Less frequently, some individuals experience a dramatic type of response in which they literally feel as if the sexual assault is happening again in the present. This kind of momentary vivid re-living of a past event in the present is sometimes referred to as a "flashback." Those who experience such episodes testify to their frightening reality and hallucinatory character: "It felt as if I was right back there." Flashbacks often include the physiological responses that were experienced at the time of the actual sexual assault, such as sweating or trembling.

Unfortunately, the term "flashback" is frequently misused. Its colloquial use refers to a vivid memory or image of a past trauma that suddenly pops into your head, but this is not necessarily a flashback. In a clinically defined flashback, the person suddenly, unexpectedly, and momentarily loses touch with reality. In other words, the person is not psychologically present and actually "relives" some aspect of the past trauma. This is understandably a terrifying experience. It is important for you to try to distinguish flashbacks from other types of intrusive experiences, such as those described above. Mislabelling your experiences is something you want to avoid in court. Always try to be accurate with the language that you use in court, and avoid using technical terms you are unsure of because this can lead to misunderstandings and poor communication.

The trigger of an intrusive memory, image, or thought is sometimes easy to anticipate, for example, being in the place where the assault took place or a similar place, seeing the person responsible for the assault, or seeing someone who looks like the assailant. Normal sexual activity can also trigger intrusive thoughts, feelings, or flashbacks, even when you are having sex with someone who has never hurt you or someone you love deeply. Other triggers may be things you cannot predict or cannot prepare for, such as a colour, a scent, a word, a tone of voice, or something uniquely linked with the assault. When these unpredictable triggers occur, the haunting thoughts and images may seem to come out of nowhere.

In most discussions of intrusive experiences, it is generally assumed that intrusive memories, images, dreams, nightmares, and flashbacks accurately reflect what happened. Many people think of these experiences as images frozen in time that are exact copies or precise memories of what actually happened to them. Although this can be the case, things are not always this simple or straightforward. Just because an image is very vivid and feels real does not necessarily mean that it accurately reflects an actual experience. For example, most of us have had the experience of waking from a preposterous, physically impossible dream that is so vivid it takes us a few minutes to convince ourselves that it was not real. It is important to recognize that images, dreams, and flashbacks of traumatic events may not be completely accurate reflections of your actual experiences. This need not mean that the traumatic events did not occur, but it may be that not all details in your images of the event are accurate. Again, this understanding could be important when testifying in court.

It is also possible to experience false or pseudo-memories, sometimes referred to as "created memories." These can seem like actual memories even though they are not. As unsettling as this idea may be, we cannot always conclude that something happened in a particular manner just because we have certain mental images, thoughts, or feelings about it. Given these types of concerns, the court tends to be skeptical about information whose source comes solely from re-experiencing phenomena, such as dreams or flashbacks. Since the issue of memory is so fundamental and important to the court process, we dedicate an entire section to this discussion in Chapter 4.

Avoiding or numbing your feelings

WHEN EXPERIENCING REPETITIVE, UNWANTED thoughts or memories, it is understandable that we would try to find ways to escape the distress. Some victims attempt to avoid experiences, activities, places, conversations, or people that remind them of the sexual assault. This may include avoidance of activities that previously provided pleasure in their lives. One victim dearly loved horses from an early age until someone sexually assaulted her in a horse stable. She subsequently avoided horses, finding the thought of riding to be sickening. In attempting to avoid reminders of the sexual assault, she was denying herself a previously pleasurable and healthy activity.

Avoidance strategies may also include attempts to shut out close friendships and/or intimate sexual relationships. It is understandable why some victims might want to pull back from others, needing space and time to deal with the impact of their experiences. Yet by adopting this strategy long-term, you can deprive yourself of the kind of support that is important to your recovery. This avoidance strategy can lead to social isolation and increased feelings of alienation from others.

In some cases, attempts to avoid distressing thoughts and feelings can lead to withdrawal from the world to a degree that the person becomes numb, losing interest in what was formerly engaging, reducing expectations, and shutting down. In an attempt to mute or shut down overwhelming feelings, some victims turn to alcohol, drugs, or medications to numb themselves. While these strategies may initially appear to be helpful, you are replacing one set of problems with another if you become dependent on intoxicants, narcotics, or other numbing substances. By numbing your feelings, you also lose the chance to better understand and manage distressing feelings.

In certain cases, victims may numb their feelings at the time of the assault using a strategy called "dissociation." Victims who feel extremely frightened, distressed, or confused during a sexual assault may distance themselves from the experience as it is happening. Some victims mentally remove themselves from the situation so that, on some level, they can convince themselves that "this is not happening to me." Some people do this by mentally going to another place or time so they feel removed from what is actually happening to them. Others describe a feeling of melting into the wall or floating above their bodies so they feel physically removed from their own body as they watch the assault from above as if it is happening to someone else. Individuals who mentally remove themselves from a situation may remember few or no details about the event from which they dissociate. Their memory may be a blank, there may be a beginning and end but no middle to the experience, or there may be fragmentary details. In some cases, the person remembers the dissociated place well (for example, all the grooves and colours of the ceiling), but has little memory of the traumatic episode itself. We discuss this rare but important phenomenon further in the memory section of Chapter 4.

Hyper-arousal

PTSD IS ALSO CHARACTERIZED by high levels of anxiety, fear, and arousal — jitteriness, restlessness, and being easily startled or spooked. Some victims of trauma are easily startled by seemingly harmless things, such as a touch on the shoulder or by sounds that others can readily ignore. Some victims also may become constantly alert to possible threats in their environment — scanning crowds, looking over their shoulder when walking on the street, or checking out every noise inside or outside their home.

This kind of hyper-arousal can lead victims to use excessive amounts of energy worrying about safety, checking their surroundings, or restricting their activities and movements. Victims of trauma can become overly protective of others, such as their own children or other family members. Some adult victims of childhood sexual assault restrict their children's lives to a degree that limits their opportunities and personal growth.

Being worried, nervous, and jumpy much of the time can also affect a person's sleeping pattern. Being unable to sleep well at night or relax during the day can quickly drain your physical resources. You may end up feeling constantly tired, with little energy to do the things that you need to do to feel productive and worthwhile. Fatigue can also contribute to depressed mood or irritability.

Hyper-arousal can also negatively affect a person's ability to concentrate and maintain focus on specific tasks. You may readily become distracted and easily lose your train of thought, making any sustained activity, such as work or school, very challenging. The ability to concentrate will also decrease when you are under added stress like legal proceedings. Stress-related symptoms, such as having difficulty remembering, not responding fully to questions, or perhaps not comprehending questions, may compromise your ability to be an effective witness in court. Reducing your stress, or managing it more effectively, is your best strategy for improving your concentration.

Other anxiety responses

THERE ARE OTHER ANXIETY responses besides PTSD symptoms that victims of sexual crimes may experience. It is common to have fears about dating or going out to bars or dances, especially if the assault occurred in these contexts. Some sexual assault victims have specific fears of being in the dark, losing control, or being in enclosed spaces. Some victims sleep with their light on or keep their bedroom door open because they are afraid of being alone in the dark or in a closed room. These fears can generalize to include a greater range and number of feared items. If you are frightened of a particular enclosed space, you may begin to avoid similar places — you may choose to walk up the stairs instead of taking the elevator. People often learn how to work around these types of fears, but not without the personal cost of limiting and restricting their lives.

Mental health professionals refer to intense fears that are out of proportion to any threat, or that occur in the absence of danger, as phobias. Some victims of assault develop specific fears or phobias that seem excessive or unreasonable to those around them. Some develop a pervasive phobic response known as agoraphobia. People who suffer from this tend to feel extremely apprehensive when they are in places or situations from which they might have difficulty escaping (for example, a train, a bus, or a restaurant). One of the most common effects of agoraphobia is the fear of being outside one's own home alone. Agoraphobia may also include fears of being in crowds, standing in lines, or travelling on public transportation. Whatever the specific features of agoraphobia, the fear of leaving home or being in public can be very limiting.

Panic attacks may also be associated with agoraphobia, or may occur on their own. A panic attack occurs in the absence of any real danger when the person suddenly feels overwhelmed with intense fear or discomfort that usually lasts for ten minutes or less. Panic attacks bring on the intense physiological sensations associated with danger: sweating, trembling, difficulty breathing, pounding heart, nausea, chest pain, heart palpitations, and dizziness. These feelings often cause people to think that they are having a heart attack, losing control of themselves, or "going crazy."[5] After having had a panic attack in public, a person may limit activities outside the home for fear of losing control or becoming embarrassed.

Self-diagnosis

YOU MAY HAVE EXPERIENCED some of the symptoms discussed above. However, we want to caution you not to fall into the trap (and sometimes self-fulfilling prophecy) of self-diagnosis. This is particularly the case during periods of significant stress, which may affect your ability to make good judgments. If you do experience any of these anxiety symptoms frequently, and they are significantly interfering with your life, then we recommend that you consult a qualified mental health professional. There are effective treatments available that can greatly assist you. In Chapter 5, we provide stress-reduction, distraction, and grounding strategies that can help reduce PTSD and other anxiety symptoms in the short run, but connecting with a mental health professional is the best strategy for the long-term resolution of distressing symptoms.

DEPRESSION: DARK DAYS AND MOOD SWINGS

LIKE OTHER EMOTIONAL STATES discussed above, periodic depressed moods are a normal aspect of life — things happen to all of us that leave us feeling sad and gloomy, generally for a limited time. However, a depressed mood can be a significant problem when it is severe or continues for extended periods. In the aftermath of sexual victimization, you may not feel as emotionally stable as you once did; your day-to-day mood may seem less steady and predictable. You may experience more frequent mood swings, fluctuating between periods of sadness, irritability and/or hostility, and perhaps with periods of calmness or even exuberance. Some victims experience long-lasting depressed moods. Depression can occur because you are feeling shame, self-blame, guilt, or humiliation. The sexual assault may have been degrading, or the offender may have made the victim feel the assault was the victim's fault. These feelings can have an enormously negative impact on a person's self-esteem and self-concept.

Negative thoughts about yourself and others contribute to the development of a depressed mood. Then, when enveloped in this melancholy, you tend to view the world through a pessimistic, negative lens. Most of your thoughts and feelings reflect doom, gloom, and defeatism. In fact, a state of depression can even affect the type of memories you tend to recall — depressed people more often recall negative, painful, or unhappy memories. When depressed, you may recall few happy memories, or memories of personal satisfaction. Depressed mood, like anxiety, can also interfere with your ability to concentrate.

Rumination significantly intensifies depression. Ruminators repeatedly dwell on particular thoughts or feelings (often negative or catastrophic), hoping to understand and manage their moods more effectively. However, rumination tends to have the opposite effect; the depressed mood worsens. Ruminating is similar to a cow chewing its cud; the same pieces of information are repeatedly rehashed. This is not an effective problem-solving strategy because nothing gets resolved. The issue just keeps going around and around in your head. You do not get any closer to a resolution than a hamster does by running in circles in a revolving exercise wheel.

We are not suggesting that you ignore your thoughts and feelings — self-awareness and self-reflection are important aspects of your healing journey. Furthermore, rumination about important experiences is virtually inevitable at times. It only becomes a problem when you are preoccupied with your thoughts to the exclusion of other things in your life and your thinking process becomes an unproductive exercise. In Chapter 5, you will find a discussion of distraction strategies that can help you shift your mind away from unhelpful rumination or excessive worrying.

Feelings of profound unhappiness or sadness are characteristic of depression, resulting in recurrent bouts of crying, irritability, numbness, or withdrawal from others. For some people the negative feelings may reach the point of self-hatred and be expressed in acts of self-harm. When pervasive feelings of worthlessness and hopelessness enter the mix, individuals can suffer recurrent thoughts of dying or thoughts of killing themselves.

Loss of appetite and perhaps loss of weight may accompany a depressed mood, while for others, soothing their emotional distress with rich foods leads to weight gain. Sleep disruption is another commonly experienced symptom of depression. Some experience insomnia and disrupted sleep, while others sleep much more than they once did.

Loss of interest or pleasure in activities and other people are also possible consequences of a depressed mood. When depressed, you may find yourself withdrawing from others and shutting yourself off from interactions that you may have previously enjoyed. Your experience of fatigue, unhappiness, or irritability may also have a negative effect on your interactions with others, further increasing your depression.

Periodic or a low-level depressed mood is something you may effectively be able to address on your own (see strategies in Chapter 5). However, severe depression can be a serious mental health problem. If you have felt severely depressed for the majority of the day for as much as two weeks or if you have had thoughts about hurting or killing yourself, or hurting or killing someone else, seek immediate help from your family physician or a mental health professional. You may be suffering from a major depressive episode, which can have particularly dire consequences if not appropriately addressed.

Effective treatment or management of depressive symptoms is also important if you are participating in legal proceedings. If you are depressed, it will be difficult for you to feel sufficiently motivated to do what needs to be done in a court case and to persevere over the long haul of the legal process. Ruminative, negative thinking can eat away at your self-esteem and self-confidence and make it particularly hard for you to muster the strength needed to be effective. Depression also erodes the stamina that you will need to deal with the stress of legal proceedings. Poor concentration and a skewed recall of life events can affect your ability to speak clearly about what has happened to you. Depression is treatable; seek out a qualified professional to help you if you are struggling with this problem.

ANGER: THE GOOD, THE BAD, AND THE UGLY

BECAUSE IT CAN LEAD to violent behaviour and potentially severe consequences, society typically considers anger a negative emotion that one should try to eradicate from one's repertoire. Nonetheless, anger is an important emotion that acts as a signal to indicate threats to your well-being. Anger can help you protect yourself, and can be a strong incentive to make personal changes, or motivate you to act for an important cause. The anger caused by a sexual assault can also be a powerful motivation to report the crime to the police and to pursue legal redress.

Conversely, anger, which occurs on a continuum ranging from irritability or annoyance to fury and rage, can act against you. If your anger is very intense and out of proportion to its cause, or developmentally inappropriate (for example, having a temper tantrum as an adult) it can become a negative force in your life. As well, chronic anger can cause physical symptoms, including high blood pressure, headaches, body aches, or pain.[6]

Although victims of sexual crimes may experience powerful feelings of anger or rage following the assault, anger is not an inevitable result. Following a crisis or trauma, some individuals conduct themselves with considerable calm, but for others anger can simmer beneath the surface and be a tremendously difficult emotion to acknowledge or express. Some of these individuals may take a long time to "get in touch" with their anger while others never will. For certain individuals, anger can overwhelm almost all other feelings and drive most of their actions. Some express anger through cynical and sarcastic remarks, criticism, negativism, and/or insults. Anger can also be expressed in general irritability or grumpiness — always being "in a bad mood," or it may be vented verbally in screaming fits or loud tirades against others. The most damaging and frightening expression of anger is physical aggression against other people or objects.

The targets of anger may shift over time. Some victims understandably report feeling great anger toward their assailant, but if your assailant is someone you thought loved you and should have protected you, your feelings may not be so clear-cut. Along with, or instead of anger, you may feel deeply hurt and betrayed. In the same way, anger may be felt toward those you believe may not have done enough to prevent the assault. As an example, those abused by a father or stepfather may feel a lot of animosity toward their mother (or other caregiver) from whom they expected protection.

Following an assault, some victims may turn their anger toward those they perceive as not providing adequate emotional support, or those who do not appear to understand what they are going through. If the sexual assault occurred while you were in the care of a government agency, institution, or religious organization, you may feel angry toward these groups who did not act in your best interests and failed to keep you safe. Complainants also may direct anger toward the court system, which can at times be frustrating, unresponsive, or seem uncaring and unjust.

Sometimes the victim does not directly express anger toward the victimizer. Doing so may be too dangerous, or the victim may not have access to this person, or may have conflicted feelings about the person. Some victims take their anger out on "safer" targets like children, pets, or other people nearby, including friends and loved ones. Some victims find themselves becoming explosively angry at inconsequential events. They may vent their feelings by yelling, slamming doors, or throwing things, directed at no one in particular.

On the other hand, some victims end up directing anger recklessly against highly unsafe targets, such as people who are physically powerful and likely to respond aggressively. Clearly, this is an ill-advised, dangerous, and possibly self-destructive strategy. Another self-destructive behaviour is the heavy use of drugs or alcohol to stifle these feelings. Some individuals vent their anger directly on themselves. They may feel overwhelmed by anger for which they see no viable target, apart from themselves. They may feel anger toward themselves because they do not think that they are coping as they should, or they feel angry about limitations or difficulties that were caused by the sexual crimes. They may respond by punching or kicking walls or by purposefully hurting themselves (for example, hitting, pinching, cutting, or burning themselves).

While these types of coping strategies can provide some temporary relief from anger, they are obviously not healthy solutions. It is important to find effective ways of coping, of shifting the focus away from emotional turmoil and pain. We discuss some workable anger management strategies in Chapter 5, but those who are deeply entrenched in self-destructive behaviours may need professional help to see them through their distress.

It is important to keep in mind that anger outbursts are generally a poor strategy, but they can be especially counter-productive during court proceedings. When angry, you are more prone to misinterpreting and overreacting to what others say or do. Intense anger also can cloud your thinking. In the throes of anger, you may say things that you do not actually mean, leading to misunderstandings and alienation from others. Sometimes officials may ask questions that intentionally or unintentionally push your buttons. You may give the impression of being hot-headed, aggressive, vindictive, or worse. Being able to remain cool under pressure can be a valuable asset that you may want to cultivate — not just for court appearances, but also for your day-to-day life.

MISTRUST: A LOSS OF FAITH

SEXUAL ASSAULT CAN CAUSE you to see the world in general through a lens of distrust. The violation of trust perpetrated by the offender can generalize widely to other people. For some, being able to trust again may turn into a long-term struggle. Trust issues may be most evident as you contemplate legal proceedings, given that such proceedings require some degree of trust in numerous individuals, including people in positions of authority. The legal process will require you to disclose intimate, personal information to people that you do not know, something that is difficult to do even under ideal circumstances.

The extent to which you feel betrayed by your assailant depends largely on the trust and dependence you had on that person prior to the assault. The greater the dependency or trust, the greater your feelings of betrayal are likely to be. The more you feel betrayed, the more likely it is that you will have issues trusting others. If a family member, spouse, close friend, teacher, coach, clergyman, or peace officer has sexually assaulted you, the effect on your subsequent ability to trust others can be enormous.

The extent to which sexual crimes undermine a person's trust also depends to a large degree on the victim's general ability to trust. Growing up with a loving and emotionally supportive caregiver during your earliest childhood can provide a foundation on which you can rebuild a disrupted capacity to trust. Developing the ability to trust can be particularly difficult for individuals who have never had the benefit of loving or supportive caregivers. It can present a significant emotional challenge for these individuals when an offender violates their already fragile sense of trust.

For some victims, betrayal by the offender can lead them to lose confidence in their own perceptions and judgments about others. These individuals may ask themselves: "How can I trust anyone?" or "How can I even trust myself to know who can be trusted?" Feeling unable to trust your own judgments can severely affect your autonomy and decision-making. This can lead to feelings of helplessness and perhaps over-dependence on someone else to make decisions. For some, it can lead to generalized fear or anger and withdrawal from interactions with others.

Victimization can contribute to distrust of certain groups or categories of people. Those victimized by a male may have particular difficulty trusting other males. Those victimized by an authority figure may have particular difficulties in trusting people in positions of authority. Those sexually abused by a clergyman or priest may come to not only distrust the clergy, but may also develop distrust for religion in general. Those victimized in government-run facilities or institutions may distrust the government, and anyone who works for the government. This can be a barrier to effective participation in legal proceedings, particularly given the central role of the government in our justice system.

Going to court will require you to put your trust in at least a few people, beginning with the Crown lawyer or other legal counsel. Trust does not mean you unreservedly give personal control over to someone else, or blindly have faith in everyone you meet. It is a balance between having confidence in your own judgment and making the best use of advice from those close to you. Information contained in this book will hopefully broaden your understanding of yourself and the system, and help you to develop trust in your own judgments while relying on others when appropriate.

The challenge of relationships

MISTRUST CAN AFFECT YOUR relationships with friends and family in many indirect ways. Some victims experience strongly-mixed feelings about being with others. They may long for emotional support and human contact while also feeling a strong desire to pull away and isolate themselves. Shortly after being sexually assaulted or following disclosures of the assault to others, victims may withdraw to give themselves enough time and space to regroup. Understandably, they may feel safer, at least for a while, away from others.

Victims may also withdraw from others in an attempt to hide feelings of embarrassment or shame, or to cover up their feelings of self-doubt and confusion. Some victims withdraw from the touch of others or sexual intimacy, because it triggers memories of the assault. Although this helps them avoid some anxiety, it also deprives them of the comfort found in close, loving contact. Viewing yourself as being different, or somehow tainted or bad, can also be an alienating experience. Sexually abused children report that they sometimes feel as though others know of their abuse, or can somehow see they are "different," leading them to withdraw. Feelings of depression or anxiety can also make being in the company of others difficult and exhausting.

At the same time that victims of sexual crimes are withdrawing from others, they may feel a very strong need to be supported. They may desperately want the feelings of protection and reassurance that others can provide, but be unable to achieve this goal. Some victims may go out of their way to elicit care or attention from others only to withdraw when someone gets too close. Having mixed feelings about others — wanting support and needing some personal space — can be confusing both for the victims and for those close to them.

The behaviour of others affects you, and your behaviour affects them. If your moods seem volatile, erratic, or unpredictable, others may become frustrated or impatient with you, and may distance themselves from you. Being irritable, angry, or distracted can result in others reacting with annoyance or anger and pulling away from you. When you are feeling sad, unhappy, or depressed, others may find your negative mood distressing and therefore may avoid you. Withdrawing from the company of friends and family can lead them to feel abandoned or rejected by you. This can increase your isolation, leaving you with less support for healing or for the court process, and less likely to have the input of others to inform and broaden your own perspective.

Throughout this book we encourage you to reach out and make healthy connections with others. We consider this vital to your sense of well-being and important to enhance your participation in legal proceedings. We discuss strategies to strengthen interpersonal relationships in Chapters 4 and 5.

DISTRESS IS COMMON

IN THE PRECEDING SECTIONS, we have pointed out some of the reasons why it is important to understand and effectively manage your emotional and social responses to a sexual assault. We advise this approach not just for your own sense of well-being, but also to help you deal more effectively with the court process. That is not to say you should stifle any emotional distress during legal proceedings. The absence of emotional expressiveness is not expected, or advisable, and is certainly *not* a pre-requisite for participating in court. Those who work with offenders and victims understand that emotional distress is frequently associated with sexual crimes. The court will make considerable allowance for your feelings. However, the more you are able to tell your story in a coherent, honest manner and interact with authority figures in a non-confrontational, non-abrasive way, the more likely you are to get a sympathetic hearing.

YOUR UNIQUE JOURNEY

YOU ARE A UNIQUE individual with distinctive abilities, experiences, vulnerabilities, and strengths. At any particular juncture of your life, you will have distinctive stressors and supports. These qualities and experiences all influence your emotional responses, which are likely to be as unique as your life circumstances. It is not possible to spell out each of the diverse and wide-ranging factors that might influence one's emotional response to a sexual assault, however, some well-studied issues are worth noting. Your age, gender, ethnic or cultural background, beliefs and attitudes, experiences, and personal characteristics may broadly determine the way you react to a sexual crime. The circumstances and characteristics of the sexual crime itself are also important factors. These circumstantial and personal features will interact in unique ways to affect a person's reactions. The complexity of these interactions defy simple explanation, nevertheless, in the following section, we consider how these various factors, viewed individually, can influence one's particular responses and reactions.

Childhood

THERE IS NO SIMPLE formula to determine the impact of sexual crimes based on the age of the victim at the time the assault occurs. However, given the many developmental processes underway throughout childhood, children's reactions to sexual assaults frequently differ in many respects from the reactions of adults. In some cases, sexual assaults can significantly interfere with a child's cognitive, psychological, social, and/or sexual development. On the other hand, children also can be remarkably resilient, exhibiting few, if any, long-term effects.

To date we have no consistent evidence as to whether the negative effect of sexual abuse tends to be greater on a younger or an older child. In some circumstances, very young children may be protected by their lack of sexual understanding and limited ability to remember such incidents. Alternatively, sexual abuse at a very young age and critical stage of development, especially when the abuse is repetitive and causes fear or pain, can permanently alter a child's emotional development, disrupting the ability to bond with others, to trust, or to feel safe. Therefore, the limited cognitive development and understanding of a young child can lessen the long-term effects of abuse, but in other circumstances, the impact of the abuse may critically disrupt development.

In some cases of ongoing sexual abuse during childhood, thoughts, feelings, and behaviours related to the sexual abuse may become incorporated into the victim's developing personality and self-concept. A sexually assaulted child may grow up to be a different person had the abuse not occurred . Children who are abused by a primary caregiver, such as a parent, may experience considerable confusion. They may have ambivalent feelings about authority figures, which they have difficulty resolving. They may have difficulty trusting others, believing that all or most people are potentially dangerous and should not be trusted. Children sexually abused within their own homes can also be affected by the losses and disruptions caused if they are removed from their family and placed in foster care for protection. If the abusing family member is removed from the home, other family members may resent or blame the victim for changes in the family's circumstances.

In other cases of childhood sexual abuse, the impact on the victim's self-concept may not occur until years later. For example, young children who are abused under the guise of affection or of playing a game may be neither fearful at the time nor aware that they were being abused. The child may perceive the abuse as "normal" within the context of their lives at the time. However, if the sexually abusive incidents are later revealed and understood as being exploitive, wrong, or criminal, the impact on the victim's belief system, including a sense of self, can be intensely disorienting. In these circumstances, victims may feel as though they have lived a lie, that people were not what they seemed to be, and that they, themselves, may not be who they thought they were.

Childhood abuse can have various effects on school performance. Some children may become so distressed that they have difficulty concentrating in school. Some may become restless, irritable, and act out against other children in ways that interfere with school attendance and performance. On the other hand, for some abused children, school can become a haven, a refuge from the chaos of sexual abuse at home. Some of these children use school activities as an effective coping strategy, allowing them to be distracted from thoughts and feelings about the abuse and bolstering their self-esteem. These children may perform particularly well at school. Other sexually abused children may show no notable changes in their school performance or behaviour.

Childhood sexual abuse can also cause later disruption in the development of healthy sexuality and satisfying sexual relationships. Depending on the circumstances of their abuse, some childhood victims find it difficult to separate affection and friendship from sexual interest. They may behave in an indiscriminate manner, responding sexually to anyone who shows interest in them. Some victims of ongoing childhood sexual abuse may come to believe that their self-worth is based largely on their sexual availability. Instead of believing they have talent, intelligence, or character, they may come to believe that they have but one thing to offer, namely, sex. Sexuality can become the central aspect of a childhood victim's personal identity. Not surprisingly, a disproportionate number of prostitutes were sexually abused as children.

Sexual abuse during childhood can also lead to premature sexualization or sexual precociousness. Some victims have difficulty controlling their sexual urges or may view indiscriminate sexual contact as normal. As young children, these individuals may inappropriately touch other children. In some cases, sexually victimized children become adult sex offenders, with the resulting burden of legal sanctions and ostracism. It is important to emphasize that, while researchers continue to study this issue, evidence linking sexual victimization with subsequent sexual offending is limited. Although many sexual offenders claim they were sexually abused, it is clear that the vast majority of victims of sexual abuse do not go on to become offenders themselves. Childhood sexual abuse is merely one variable that can influence later sexual offending. Many childhood sexual abuse victims go out of their way to protect children from the abuse that they experienced.

Being male or female

WHILE HAVING A NUMBER of shared responses to sexual assault, the reactions of males and females can differ in some respects. Because the majority of victims of sexual crimes are females, most of the research literature has understandably focused on the female experience. The list of problems associated with sexual assaults given earlier in this chapter is based on research done with female victims. As more male victims (primarily those who are victims of childhood and adolescent sexual abuse) have come forward, and research data have accumulated, we have come to understand some effects of sexual crimes that may be specific to males. We present a few examples here to illustrate some potential gender influences.

Since our culture typically socializes males to believe that they should control situations and defend themselves whenever necessary, being a victim of sexual assault can pose challenges to a male's sense of manliness, self-worth, self-confidence, and self-esteem. Heterosexual males, sexually assaulted by another male, may express concern or confusion about their sexual identity. Because male victims may experience physiological arousal during the assault, some interpret their response as indicating an underlying homosexual orientation, even though they previously considered themselves heterosexual. Males sexually abused during childhood by adult males may experience confusion about their sexual preference during puberty, but there is no clear evidence that sexual assault causes a change in the victim's sexual orientation or long-term sexual preference.

Some male victims report no specific concerns about their masculinity, but they worry that others will view them as less manly if their victimization becomes known. Males can therefore be very reluctant to disclose their abuse. Although most male victims do not themselves become sexual offenders, they sometimes worry that their abuse may cause them to offend against children, or that others will believe that they are potential sex offenders. Sometimes these fears lead to avoiding having children and/or declining to participate in early childcare activities (for example, changing diapers or bathing children) and avoiding normal parental displays of affection.

Cultural issues

THE MULTI-CULTURAL NATURE OF Canada has heightened our awareness of how cultural issues can affect sexual assault victims. In recent years, we have become aware of the extensive sexual abuse of First Nations people in residential schools. Loss of their language, their culture, and access to family support not only made First Nations children more vulnerable to sexual abuse, but also exacerbated the impact of abuse. Family and community supports are important factors in healing and personal growth, so the loss of these supports is particularly damaging. The widespread institutional abuse suffered by First Nations people will likely affect their communities for generations to come.

In cultures that highly value female virginity, a female victim may suffer significantly not only in response to a sexual assault, but also when others learn of her experience. These victims can feel completely devalued within their culture. Their families may disown them and their community may consider them unfit for marriage. Recent immigrants to Canada who are victims of sexual assault may feel particularly isolated if their primary language is not common locally or their cultural beliefs differ significantly from those of others. Their isolation and lack of resources in their own language serves to increase the negative effects of sexual crimes.

Being deaf or blind

THOSE WHO ARE DEAF or blind can feel particularly isolated following a sexual assault. Although the majority of deaf people can communicate effectively in American Sign Language (ASL), regional access to interpreter services is often very limited or costly. Even communication within families may be very basic thus restricting the deaf person's ability to make a disclosure and to get family support. The same barriers can also limit access to community services and counselling for people who have been sexually victimized and are deaf. Additionally, some deaf individuals may be cautiously reluctant to communicate information about their experiences to another deaf person due to fears that the tightly knit deaf community will learn of their sexual assault experiences and will label the victims in some negative manner. The offender may also be a member of the same deaf community and avoiding contact with that person can be very difficult if the victim is to continue to participate in community functions.

Most sexual assault victims find it distressing to discuss the details of their assault, and this can be particularly distressing for deaf persons. The graphic nature of the American Sign Language gestures for sexual acts can trigger intense emotional and physiological reactions for the victim. Deaf children may be more vulnerable to perceived or real threats by a non-deaf offender since the ability to hear tends to confer more personal power on the assailant. As a result, the pressure to maintain secrecy can be heightened for the deaf. As well, deaf individuals abused within residential schools suffer the added consequences of alienation, abandonment, and loneliness associated with this unique environment.

Individuals who are blind or visually impaired face unique challenges as well. Blind persons may be more hesitant to report a sexual assault for fear that no one will believe that they can identify the offenders. It also can be more difficult to identify precisely what happened to the victim because those who are blind are unable to provide specifics about visually mediated details. Victims who are blind may also experience extreme anxiety following their assault because they are unable to be visually vigilant for self-protection. Heightened feelings of vulnerability for individuals who already feel particularly vulnerable can be paralyzing.

Being mentally challenged or physically disabled

INDIVIDUALS WHO ARE MENTALLY challenged and/or severely physically disabled are particularly vulnerable to sexual assault. Because many of these individuals are highly dependent on multiple or sequential caregivers for home or institutional care, they are at greater risk for abuse than are the general population. They may have few, if any, options to escape the abuse and little or limited ability to communicate effectively with others about the abuse. Furthermore, society too often thinks of individuals with intellectual challenges and/or physical disabilities as not being sexual. These individuals typically receive little or no sexual education or access to sexual abuse prevention programs that are suited to their level of communication. Not only does this lack of knowledge increase their vulnerability to a sexual crime, but it can also lead to increased confusion and distress in response to a sexual crime. For example, one individual believed that each time the offender forced her to have intercourse, his semen remained active in her body and she could, at any time in the future, get pregnant. These kinds of misunderstandings based on lack of information or conceptual ability can be chronically distressing and hard to assess and treat.

Further personal characteristics and vulnerabilities

PEOPLE'S BELIEFS AND ATTITUDES can play an important role in how a sexual crime affects them. If you believe that "bad things only happen to bad people," being victimized yourself could be devastating to your self-esteem, suggesting that you are not living your life the way you should, and that you are not the "good" person you believed yourself to be.

Strong religious beliefs can strongly mediate the impact of sexual assaults. Your faith can provide solace and meaning that helps alleviate the negative impact of a sexual assault. On the other hand, if you feel that a sexual assault represents a punishment by God, or is an indication of a sinful life, your reaction could be intense shame and guilt. Victimization can also present a strong challenge to religious faith, particularly when the offender is a trusted religious figure. There are examples of Canadian communities where individuals abandoned their religious affiliation after learning that a local religious figure was a sex offender. This illustrates how sexual assault can have a powerful effect on those not directly victimized.

Loss of a fundamental belief, whether religiously based or not, and the support that it provides, can have far-reaching consequences, both positive and negative. A well-developed belief system acts as a practical and moral compass to guide us through adversity and the multitude of decisions we must make each day. Most of us have drawn comfort and support from well-tested beliefs, but we also experience times when a strongly held, but erroneous, belief is a liability to us. We often do not examine our values closely until loss or trauma shakes long-held beliefs and routines, forcing us to find new meaning in our lives. While this experience can be terribly frightening and disorienting, it can also be liberating. In your efforts to understand and cope with a sexual assault, it may be helpful to examine the way you think about the world, affirming those beliefs that give you comfort and strength while challenging those that increase your anxiety or vulnerability.

Crime characteristics

CIRCUMSTANCES OF THE SEXUAL crime are also important in determining its impact. As outlined in Chapter 1, sexual crimes vary enormously in terms of severity, circumstances, frequency, motivation, and use of physical threats or violence. A sexual assault in your bedroom can cause anxiety about being alone in your own home, which may have previously been a source of comfort and sanctuary. Sexual assault by a stranger at a bus stop can have the opposite effect, causing anxiety when away from home and out in the world. As noted above, sexual assaults perpetrated within residential facilities, or in any similar situation where the victim has limited communication and no access to emotional support, can be particularly harmful.

Generally, someone who experiences an objectively minor sexual crime (for example, an offender purposely exposing his penis) will react quite differently than someone who experiences a more intrusive sexual crime (such as forced vaginal or anal penetration). More severe sexual assaults (for example, those including physical injuries or forced penetration) tend to result in more significant negative consequences than less severe assaults. It is important to emphasize, however, that the impact of a sexual crime for any one person may relate more to the victim's perception of the event and to personal characteristics, than to an outsider's view of the event. There is no simple, direct relationship between the severity of a sexual assault as it "objectively" appears to others and the effect it has on the victim. An event that may appear relatively minor to others may cause considerable distress for some individuals. An event that totally devastates one person may have seemingly little effect on another.

EXAMPLES OF VICTIM RESPONSES

THE FOLLOWING EXAMPLES ILLUSTRATE the wide-ranging responses to sexual crimes:

> As a child and young adolescent, a First Nations man was the victim of sexual assaults on multiple occasions at a residential school. A female, church-affiliated staff member at the school performed oral sex on him and forced him to perform oral sex on her. He described himself as being repulsed and sickened by having to put his mouth on this woman's genitals; he frequently vomited afterwards. He also was very distressed and confused by his body's reaction to the fellatio (he had erections). He felt betrayed by his sexual arousal, which evolved into strong feelings of anger and hatred when he had erections. This man subsequently abused his own genitals to the point of injury. He also had very conflicted and often violent relationships with women. He reported no enjoyment in sexual contact, noting that seeing female genitalia made him feel nauseous. His adult life was primarily characterized by severe alcohol abuse and multiple incarcerations for aggression. When he disclosed the sexual abuse in a therapy group in prison, several members of the group laughed and

told him he had "lucked out" to have sexual contact with a woman. This response heightened his confusion, anger, and self-loathing, causing him to further question his masculinity and sexual identity.

A young woman reported a history of emotional and psychological abuse by her father, an alcoholic drug user, who had continually criticized her during her childhood and adolescence. As a young girl, she came to believe that she was as worthless as he said she was. At the age of thirteen, her father sexually assaulted her (attempted sexual intercourse). The woman described the assault as being a very distressing experience in her life, however, over time the incident, paradoxically, had a liberating effect. She subsequently saw her father's sexual attack as so abnormal that she was able, for the first time, to view him as a very "messed-up" man whose opinions were of little value. After the sexual assault, she was able to take her father's critical comments less and less to heart. She saw him as the defective one, the unworthy one, rather than herself, and his negative impact on her life lessened from that point onward.

LOOKING BEYOND THE DAMAGES YOU HAVE SUFFERED

OUR DISCUSSION ABOUT THE impact of sexual assaults has necessarily focused on emotional pain and psychological reactions, but it is also important to keep this negativity in perspective. Even when sexual assaults have greatly affected you, their effects are not the only factors that determine who you are as a person. While you may be feeling a bewildering array of emotions, there are ways to restore balance in your life, and we discuss these in later chapters (see Chapters 3, 5, and 11).

The court process will focus almost exclusively on the sexual assault and the related harm and distress it has caused. We cannot emphasize enough the value of avoiding tunnel vision that frames your life only in terms of damage. It is important to take note of the other aspects of your life and self-concept that extend beyond the sexual crimes. This may include focusing on positive thoughts and memories of other times in your life, your areas of competence, and the important roles you play. Do not lose sight of positive, fulfilling experiences that you have had or hope to have. Purposefully place emphasis on your strengths and your accomplishments. If you are having difficulty seeing beyond the damages that you have suffered, meet with a friend or counsellor to brainstorm about your personal strengths. You could also make a list of the positive, quirky, unique things about you that go into making you who you are. Do not let a sexual assault exclusively define who you are, or what you will become. Remember, your humanity, your potential, your self, encompasses much more than the experiences of sexual assault. The court process, which is apt to focus on the negative, can cause us to lose sight of this fact.

REMEMBER — TAKE CARE OF YOURSELF

LEARNING HOW TO MANAGE stress and anxiety is a very important ability for you to acquire, and we will continue to discuss this issue as we move through subsequent chapters. You may have little experience giving yourself and your well-being top priority, but your ability to work, maintain relationships, participate fully in your life, and to consider participation in legal proceedings depends a great deal on your psychological and emotional well-being. This may seem like common sense advice but assault victims often neglect their self-care. If this kind of self-focus is not typical for you, now is a good time to consider developing and practising a new skill. We will be reminding you to pay attention to your needs and we will emphasize the importance of self-care throughout this book. We also recommend that you consult with a mental health professional if you are feeling emotionally overwhelmed, highly distressed, or if you feel in danger of hurting yourself or someone else. A mental health professional can help provide a balanced perspective on your life, a perspective that is often lost in times of crisis, and this could be invaluable to your healing journey. We provide information about finding appropriate mental health support in Chapter 3.

VIGNETTE TWO: A UNIQUE REACTION

THE WOMAN DESCRIBED AT the beginning of this chapter in Vignette Two had unique reactions to what objectively appears to be a minor sexual assault — a man exposing his penis. Many people might have dismissed the incident as the juvenile actions of an emotionally disturbed man. The man's behaviour, however, deeply affected the victim to the extent that she was unable to return to work and sought out psychological counselling. In counselling, the woman began talking about the sexual abuse she had endured as a child.

An adolescent boy who lived in her neighbourhood had befriended Liz. In her childlike way, she looked up to and admired this older boy, enjoying the attention she received from him. He eventually induced her to perform fellatio on him by introducing it as a game and giving her small gifts. Eager to please and not understanding the nature of her actions, Liz went along with his requests. When she matured, she realized how the youth had manipulated and used her. She felt embarrassed, tainted, and guilty because she had willingly complied with his requests.

For these reasons, Liz did not talk about her experiences to anyone but successfully put the memories "out of her mind." Throughout her adult life, she had worked hard and strived to demonstrate that she was a capable person, perhaps, in part, as compensation for her feelings of inadequacy and guilt. When Tony exposed his penis to her in the store, thoughts and feelings about her childhood abuse came back in full force. Her belief that she had successfully left her abuse experiences behind, that she was a capable woman in control of her life, and that she was secure as an adult were shattered. The loss of her central beliefs led to significant depression and anxiety. The counsellor focused on her adult strengths, helped put her experiences in perspective, and assisted in restoring belief in herself. As a result, Liz's depression lifted, her anxiety diminished, and she was able to return to work, albeit in a different store.

ENDNOTES

1 Ann W. Burgess & L.L. Holstrom, "Rape-Trauma Syndrome" (1974) 131 American Journal of Psychiatry 981–86.

2 Patricia Resick, *Stress and Trauma* (Philadelphia, PA: Psychology Press, 2001).

3 R.C. Kessler, A. Sonnega, E. Bromet, M. Hughes, & C.B. Nelson, "Post-Traumatic Stress Disorder in the National Comorbidity Survey" (1995) 52 Archives of General Psychiatry 1048.

4 American Psychiatric Association, *Diagnostic and Statistical Manual of Mental Disorders: DSM-IV-TR*, 4th ed., text revision (Washington, DC: American Psychiatric Association, 2000) [DSM-IV-TR].

5 DSM-IV-TR, above note 3 at 430.

6 Mary Beth Williams & Soili Puijola, *The PTSD Workbook: Simple, Effective Techniques for Overcoming Traumatic Stress Symptoms* (Oakland, CA: New Harbinger, 2002).

Starting Along the Healing Path

Vignette Three

Theresa, aged sixteen, goes on a date to see a movie with Christopher, a seventeen-year-old she knows from high school. On the walk back to Theresa's home, the couple stops in a park to swing on the swings and talk. Later that evening Theresa's older sister Helen finds her distraught and crying in her bedroom at home. Theresa says Christopher forced her to have sexual intercourse in the park. Although Theresa is hesitant, Helen convinces her to report the incident to police. When interviewed by the police, Christopher does not deny that he had sex with Theresa but he says it was consensual; nevertheless, authorities eventually charge Christopher with sexual assault and arrest him. In the weeks that follow, Theresa sleeps and eats poorly, loses weight, and does not go out much. Although she is quite athletic, she loses interest in exercise and her usual sporting activities. The preliminary hearing for her case is due to begin in six months, but Theresa grows emotionally distressed and overwhelmed. Her life feels dark and dismal, and she fears she will be emotionally incapable of carrying through with her case against the accused and thinks that going to the police might have been a mistake.

IN THE AFTERMATH OF a traumatic experience, we struggle to cope, but then we must move on. This chapter deals with the subject of healing and personal growth. Moving yourself in a positive, healing direction following a sexual assault not only helps you regain control of your life, but also puts you in a better position to pursue justice. This chapter discusses the goals of healing, a variety of healing approaches, and ways to choose a therapist.

So far, we have focused on the psychological difficulties and damages that may occur as a result of sexual assault. Frequently, understanding what has happened and weathering the initial emotional impact is the first priority for victims of such trauma. Having discussed some of those issues, we will now shift from a focus on damages to a consideration of the issues of recovery. One way you can shift your perspective is to look at your injuries as offering an invitation for personal growth. You will have to move on with your life one way or another, so why not decide to move in a healthy, positive direction. While anger and bitterness can be satisfying emotions in the short run, they are heavy burdens to carry for very long. Alcohol and drug abuse may help you numb the pain or briefly escape disturbing memories, but in the end these substances cause more problems than they resolve. Beginning the process of healing will not only help you to regain control of your life, but it will also put you in a better position to pursue justice.

Psychologist Sam Keen suggests the following about psychological injuries:

> In time, we may transform our liabilities into gifts. The faults that pock-mark the psyche may become the source of a man or a woman's beauty. The injuries we have suffered invite us to assume the most human of all vocations — to heal ourselves and others.[1]

The most important thing is that you pace yourself while you strive for emotional awareness and recovery from emotional pain. As you begin the healing process, we remind you to heed the advice given in the previous chapter about self-examination, particularly the following three issues:

- Ask yourself, "Does this symptom truly apply to me?"
- Look beyond the damages you have suffered.
- Take care of yourself.

WHAT IS HEALING?

WHEN WE THINK OF healing or recovery, many of us think of a return to "normal functioning," or living the way we did before the sexual assault happened. This is a reasonable and obtainable goal for some people; however, for many victims recovery may not entail a straightforward return to previous functioning. For example, recovery for those sexually assaulted during childhood or over long periods of time would not be a return to their pre-assault level of functioning. A forty-five-year-old assaulted at age six would not recover from the assault by obtaining the level of functioning of a six-year-old. Other victims of sexual crimes may not want to return to their previous ways of being that they now view as self-defeating or dysfunctional. In still other cases, a sexual crime may have changed a victim to the extent that recovery necessarily entails creating a new sense of self and a different way of relating to the world.

Recovery often means feeling "better," but what exactly does better look like? If you have experienced specific psychological symptoms or problems, such as Post-Traumatic Stress Disorder (PTSD), feeling better may mean that you no longer have flashbacks, or that they occur less frequently. Alternatively, it may mean that you can manage the associated distress and are not preoccupied with negative emotional responses. Recovery can also mean that you feel relatively good about yourself; you no longer experience debilitating shame or self blame related to your sexual assault, or perhaps your depressed mood lifts.

Recovery for some may mean no longer viewing the sexual crime as the defining experience of their life. From this perspective, a past trauma does not define who you are now or who you will be in the future. Instead, the sexual crime can take its place as one important event in a lifetime of experiences. You no longer think of yourself primarily as a victim or a survivor of sexual assault; you view yourself from a broader perspective. You are a human being who, like many others, has had your share of the good and bad that life can offer.

The most realistic goal for your recovery may not be to eliminate all your negative emotions or memories but, instead, to have a more balanced life that includes being emotionally, physically, interpersonally, and spiritually healthy. This holistic approach to healing is consistent with many First Nations traditions that focus on healing all aspects of the person and creating balance in a person's connection to both the physical and spiritual worlds.

For some people, an important part of their healing involves restoring the balance between themselves and their community. Through use of the Medicine Wheel and the Healing Circle, many First Nations people approach healing as a process that encompasses the entire community. The goal is to restore positive connections between the victim, the offender, the affected families, and the community at large. As described in the healing model from the community of Hollow Water,[2]

The process holds offenders accountable to their communities and fosters healing for all — those victimized, their victimizers, and the community .... Healing is a letting go — physically, mentally, emotionally and spiritually — of our hurt — the hurt that has been inflicted upon each of us, the hurt that we have inflicted on others .... Healing is a search for who we are, who we have been, and who we can become. Healing is coming to feel good about ourselves as individuals, as families, as communities and as a Nation .... Healing is coming to believe in ourselves, our families, our community, our Nation.

Often a major goal of healing is to find or restore meaning in your life. The sexual assault may have shattered some basic assumptions that you now need to rebuild. You may be struggling to come to terms with "why" questions, such as why the assault happened. To feel truly, deeply healed, you may need to find some meaning in what has happened to you that helps incorporate this experience into your lifetime of experiences and allows you to move on. This is often the final stage of healing but bears some thought and consideration from the outset. We address this issue to some extent in Chapter 11 where we explore the ways in which some victims of adversity or horrible tragedies have moved on to growth and transformation.

No matter how you might define recovery, it will not mean that you achieve a life in which you feel good all the time. To be alive is to experience negative emotions, such as sadness, anger, and fear at least some of the time. Recovery will involve your being able to manage your emotions, rather than having your emotions manage you. Being emotionally healthy means being able to experience the full range of human feelings, the painful ones as well as the positive ones, without becoming trapped in one limiting, negative state.

IS FORGIVENESS NECESSARY FOR HEALING?

SOME RELIGIOUS AND SPIRITUAL traditions suggest that forgiveness of the offender is necessary for the victim's healing. Others suggest that committing a sexual crime is unforgivable. If you are struggling with this issue, it may help you to think about what forgiveness means. Williams and Poijula provide a very helpful discussion about this issue in their PTSD workbook. They suggest that forgiveness is "a willful act that is for your benefit alone."[3] Forgiveness can lead to a letting go of anger and hatred that serves to free victims, at least to some degree, from the power the offender may have held over them.

It may also be helpful to think about what forgiveness is *not*. According to Williams and Poijula, forgiveness is not any of the following:[4]

- Dependent upon the offender's apology or remorse
- Condoning or excusing what happened to you
- Forgetting what happened to you
- Denying that any negative effects occurred
- Restoring your condition or your relationship with the offender to what it was prior to the assaults

Although forgiveness of the offender is not necessary for healing, forgiving yourself may be. This notion is expressed well in *The Courage to Heal*, a self-help book written for women who were abused as children.[5] As you read the following, think about how you might expand the message to include all victims of sexual crimes and personalize the words to meet your particular circumstances:

> The only forgiveness that is essential is for yourself. You must forgive yourself for having needed, for having been small. You must forgive yourself for coping the best you could. As one woman said, "I've had to forgive my genitals for responding. I've had to forgive myself for not being able to second-guess my father and avoid the abuse."
>
> You must forgive yourself for the limitations you've lived with as an adult. You must forgive yourself for repeating your victimization, for not knowing how to protect your own children, or for abusing others. You must forgive yourself for needing time to heal now, and you must give yourself, as generously as you can, all your compassion and understanding, so you can direct your attention and energy toward your own healing. This forgiveness is what's essential.

While finding some compassion for an offender can be a hugely difficult task for most people, it can also be an effective step toward healing. If you can manage to understand the motives, feelings, and thinking of the offender, this may help you achieve some degree of resolution and freedom from the negative effects of the assault. Compassion may help you to better understand the offender's behaviour during the legal process — the denials, the delays, the contradictions. You may come to see this person as a human being forced to confront some very unpleasant personal truths.

When an offender has admitted responsibility and truly accepted the consequences of the abusive actions, the question then becomes, "How can something positive be achieved from this point on?" Being respectful and compassionate does not mean being naïve and putting others at risk. That an offender says, "I will never do it again," is merely a statement for the present and not a predictor of the future. The offender may truly feel remorse, not want to hurt others, intend to go into treatment, and want to help the victim recover. These are positive feelings that may lead an offender to the door of a treatment program. Nonetheless, meaningfully changing the conduct of a sex offender is a challenging and often fruitless task. The propensity to offend may be deeply entrenched and, in the end, may only be something that is managed, not eliminated. Victims, lawmakers, and the community must balance compassion with a keen regard for the risks involved.

THE RECOVERY PROCESS

TO MAKE THE POINT once again, there is no list of recommended recovery goals and there is no single or simple roadmap for achieving any particular goal. You should decide what is important to you and take the time to formulate your own specific goals. Try to be as concrete and as detailed as possible. The following questions are a sample of what a therapist might ask you about the direction you want to take. Consider how you would answer these questions, and help clarify for yourself the path you want to take.[6]

- What do you need right now in order for you to feel better?
- How will you know when these needs are being met?
- How would you like your life to be different; what has to change?
- How will you know when the changes you seek are happening?
- What is your belief about your role in the healing process?
- What is your belief about the therapist's role in the healing process?

Regardless of the direction you choose, there are some generally accepted guidelines to getting started. Sexual assault leaves many people feeling unsafe and destabilized, so the first step is to find places (physical and emotional ones) where you feel safe. Create space where you are able to breathe freely and relax. You cannot confidently address other issues unless you have some degree of stability in your life. If you are at risk of self-harm or harm from others or towards others, these issues must take first priority. We discuss ways to address your safety concerns in Chapter 5. Your therapist needs to ensure that you have some basic coping skills that help you to function day-to-day. Until these basic safety conditions are established, a therapist should not be delving into potentially destabilizing issues, such as in-depth exploration of any abuse history. Some may choose to take their healing no further than the first stage of finding some stability and developing coping strategies; that is your choice to make.

In this chapter, we describe a number of different therapeutic methods that can help you along your recovery path. Whichever path or paths you may choose, bear in mind that no single therapeutic method or approach to healing is successful for all people or for all problems, but research indicates that certain treatments are generally more successful than others. We recommend that you give these research-supported treatments consideration when seeking treatment from a mental health professional.

Timing and pacing

THE TIMING AND PACING of your recovery is important. Moving too quickly can be destabilizing and can set you back. Moving too slowly can cause you to get discouraged or to give up prematurely. You will need to find the right balance for yourself by paying attention to your feelings, needs, and reactions along the way. It is also important to understand that, while you may address some problems more easily than others, some people may recover more quickly than you. The pace and timing of your recovery will be specific to you, your psychological needs, your past history, the types of sexual crimes you experienced, and the resources available to you.

Twists and turns along the way

THE ROAD TO RECOVERY typically includes backtracking, side-trips, and even breaks in the journey. In other words, you may not always travel from A to B in a straightforward manner. Gains can be followed at times by a step back or to the side, before you move forward again. You are likely to revert to old patterns or your "fall-back" position frequently. With time and practice, this will occur less and less as you develop new ways of thinking, feeling, and behaving.

Even when you are some distance along the path to recovery, you may face periods of a temporary relapse. Anxieties and fears can return, triggered by some crisis or stressor in your life, and participating in legal proceedings can be one such stressor. This is an understandable reaction. If this happens, apply the skills and understanding that you are acquiring, use the personal resources that you have developed, and remind yourself that temporary relapses are part of the process. Portia Nelson delightfully captures the twists and turns of the healing journey in the following poem:[7]

Autobiography in Five Short Chapters

1.

I walk down the street.
There is a deep hole in the sidewalk.
I fall in.
I am lost … I am helpless.
It isn't my fault.
It takes forever to find a way out.

2.

I walk down the same street.
There is a deep hole in the sidewalk.
I pretend I don't see it.
I fall in again.
I can't believe I am in the same place.
But it isn't my fault.
It still takes a long time to get out.

3.

I walk down the same street.
There is a deep hole in the sidewalk.
I see it is there.
I still fall in … it's a habit.
My eyes are open.
I know where I am.
It is my fault.
I get out immediately.

4.

I walk down the same street.
There is a deep hole in the sidewalk.
I walk around it.

5.

I walk down another street.

Be patient and thoughtful

EACH STEP IN THE process toward psychological health and well-being may be small and sometimes the progress may seem slow. You will likely try some things along the way that do not serve you well and you will likely have some setbacks. It is important for you to be both patient and compassionate toward yourself. This can be difficult for many of us. It may help if you try showing the same level of compassion towards yourself that you would show towards a friend. It can also be helpful to ask the same of your friends and family. Having supportive and understanding people in your life can provide valuable feedback and encourage you when progress seems slow. As with many endeavours, success relies on perseverance. Participation in therapy or engaging in any healing strategy requires time, effort, and ongoing practice before you learn what works for you. Balance this attitude with the recognition that not all approaches will work for you so if, after an honest effort, a therapist or technique is not giving you what you need, do not hesitate to move on and explore alternatives.

Going it alone

SOME OF YOU MAY have chosen to take your healing journey largely on your own. You may be relying on your religion, spiritual beliefs, or strength of character to guide you through. Books, articles, workshops, and seminars can help. Though going it alone is a difficult path, it can also be very rewarding. We urge you, however, to remain open to seeking some help along the way. At the very least, it helps to have someone who can be a sounding board for you and who can give you an outside perspective. It is often important to have a witness to your individual healing journey, someone who can observe your progress, support you, and give you some reference points along your journey. Later, you may appreciate having someone to reminisce with who knows what you have experienced. Be aware that this is not an easy task for friends and family, many of whom may not be able to shoulder that kind of responsibility. Professionals not only offer expertise in counselling, but they also relieve intimates of the burden of supporting a loved one who is in emotional pain.

SEEKING PROFESSIONAL HELP

SEEKING HELP WHEN NEEDED from a mental health professional does not have to mean that you are crazy, weak, or sick. All of us experience challenges that overwhelm us from time to time. High levels of stress, questioning the meaning of life, having difficulties with relationships, feeling trapped, or wanting to understand yourself better are neither illnesses nor weaknesses; they are human issues that confront all of us. With the help of a skilled mental health professional, you can find ways to effectively deal with these issues. Seeking help when needed suggests that you are attending to your psychological needs in a constructive manner, you have the courage to reach out, and that you are willing to change. These are qualities of personal strength, not weakness.

If you are struggling with mental health issues that significantly interfere with your ability to work, to relate well socially, or to deal effectively with the tasks of daily living, we encourage you to seek out a professional counsellor. The following issues are particularly important and indicate a need for professional input:

- High levels of anxiety day after day
- Not getting restful sleep, or having sleep disruption
- Disturbing PTSD symptoms
- Being preoccupied with thoughts of the assault
- Social isolation or withdrawal
- Thoughts or plans of self-harm, or harming others
- Chronic low mood and low energy

It is beyond the scope of this book to give a comprehensive or exhaustive overview of the numerous types of treatment available. Instead, we provide you with information about the major types of therapy offered by mainstream mental health professionals that can be effective in dealing with problems resulting from sexual assault. We focus on treatments that meet current acceptable standards of care and that are most likely to be considered acceptable by the legal system. We also give some criteria for you to consider when choosing your own therapist and we discuss ways that you might go about finding the right therapist for you. Although we do not discuss non-mainstream therapies, we provide information about some of the most popular and effective additions and alternative approaches to traditional individual therapy, including a description of a First Nations approach to healing.

Cognitive-behavioural therapy

THERE IS CONSIDERABLE RESEARCH indicating that cognitive-behavioural therapy (CBT) is an effective treatment for depression and anxiety, including PTSD symptoms.[8] CBT for depression focuses on identifying the negative thoughts and dysfunctional beliefs that underlie depression and examining feelings, such as helplessness and worthlessness. The therapist will challenge these negative ideas with more functional, realistic, and rational beliefs. Gaining a different, more functional perspective can be very effective in shifting a person's emotional state in a positive direction.

CBT techniques for addressing anxiety disorders often include some form of exposure to, or confrontation with, feared situations, events, people, or memories. This can be accomplished using imagery, rather than the actual situations. Repeated exposure to feared stimuli in a therapeutic environment, usually paired with some form of relaxation response (such as deep breathing) typically alleviates anxiety. CBT therapists also explore and confront unhelpful, inaccurate beliefs and thoughts related to the feared experience (for example, the sexual assault). They examine how the assault may have adversely affected beliefs about oneself and the world, and they challenge erroneous beliefs to help the client develop a more balanced perspective that can relieve distressing emotions. For example, successfully challenging a common belief that the victim somehow should have prevented the assault can alleviate associated feelings of guilt or shame. In Chapter 5, we describe several CBT techniques in some detail.

CBT is a structured form of therapy that is usually short-term (eight to twenty-four sessions). It takes a problem-solving approach that requires considerable collaboration between the therapist and the client. There are usually "homework" assignments for the client to complete between sessions, which include collecting information about the client's day-to-day functioning and practising those skills learned in therapy sessions.

Psychodynamic psychotherapy

PSYCHODYNAMIC PSYCHOTHERAPY INCORPORATES A range of techniques that can also include the cognitive behavioural methods discussed above, but the approach centres on the idea that psychological problems, or internal conflicts, arise from unconscious defence mechanisms developed early in life. The goal of the therapy is to help the client deal with any immediate psychological distress, then move on to change or replace the dysfunctional defence mechanisms with healthier functions. In the case of sexual abuse, the therapist would help the client integrate the traumatic experience into the client's life in a way that avoids unhealthy defence mechanisms.

There are many approaches to psychodynamic therapy, but all of them place considerable emphasis on the therapeutic value of the relationship between the therapist and the client. Although there are short-term forms of psychodynamic therapy, it is more often long-term, typically extending over several years of weekly sessions, especially in cases of complex trauma or long-term abuse during childhood. This therapeutic approach involves a great deal of introspection and reflection on the part of the client, and it can result in strong emotional reactions when past issues are raised.

There are case studies and anecdotal evidence suggesting that psychodynamic therapy can be effective in treating problems associated with trauma, including those caused by a history of childhood sexual abuse. However, because of its relatively unstructured nature and the length of this therapy, it is difficult to conduct research to determine its effectiveness. Currently, there is little definitive research available to indicate the efficacy of psychodynamic therapy for victims of trauma, however, this may be due more to the limitations of the research, rather than to the limitations of this form of treatment.

Eye movement desensitization and reprocessing (EMDR)

EMDR IS A RELATIVELY recent, somewhat controversial therapeutic technique that has been widely used to reduce anxiety, especially related to PTSD symptoms. The therapist induces eye movements by having the client follow an index finger while visualizing an upsetting image from her traumatic experience (for instance, some aspect of the sexual assault). This technique helps the patient integrate the emotions and sensations that occurred during a traumatic event. This is a short-term therapy that is usually effective in six to twelve sessions, although more sessions may be needed for more complex, multiple traumas. There is research indicating that EMDR can be effective in reducing PTSD symptoms. However, some researchers question whether the eye movements are essential, noting that the other components of the treatment are virtually the same as CBT. Some professionals have voiced concerns about the extent to which this procedure may change the client's memories of the traumatic experience, potentially causing problems in legal proceedings.

Other labels for psychotherapy

THERE IS A WIDE range of labels and descriptors mental health professionals may use to describe their particular approach to psychotherapy. Some of these labels reflect the values of the therapist (for example, Christian counsellor or feminist therapist), while some labels reflect the techniques used or the therapist's general approach to therapy (for example, Gestalt therapist, existential-humanist therapist, or Ericksonian, solution-focused therapist). Some mental health professionals may claim no specific label and describe themselves as being "eclectic" in their approach, meaning that they combine several approaches and techniques.

You may also encounter therapists whose primary focus is to be emotionally supportive. They may describe their approach as being "Rogerian" in reference to the client-centred methods developed by Carl Rogers. This type of therapy tends to be non-directive and unstructured, offering comfort and unconditional support, but research has generally found that this approach alone is not particularly effective in addressing problems associated with trauma.

Pharmacological (drug) treatment

RESEARCH HAS INDICATED THAT there are effective drug treatments for some forms of depression and anxiety, including some of the symptoms of PTSD. For example, medications can effectively address problems with insomnia. Psychiatrists are generally the ones to prescribe medication for mental health problems, although family physicians sometimes do so as well. Medication can be particularly effective to help overwhelming symptoms become more manageable, in turn making them easier to address in therapy.

Although drug treatment can be highly effective for some individuals, medications do not work for everyone. Furthermore, you may have to try several different types of medications (such as anti-depressants) before finding the one that works for you. Some clients find the side effects of the more powerful drugs to be intolerable, while some medications can be addictive and can interact negatively with other medications or foods. All medications require ongoing monitoring by a physician.

Those who have medication prescribed by a physician have the right to know why certain drugs are recommended and what effects to expect from the medications. Appendix 2 provides a list of questions that you can ask about some of the issues arising from drug treatments. You can read this list and determine which issues might be most relevant for you.

CHOOSING A MENTAL HEALTH PROFESSIONAL

IT IS EASY TO feel bewildered by the various labels that mental health professionals use to describe their particular approach to psychotherapy. Often these labels are not very helpful in illuminating how effective a particular therapist may be for you. However, there are ways and means to find the therapist who can best meet your needs, and we provide the following information in an effort to shortcut the "trial and error" approach that can be time consuming and expensive.

In choosing a professionally trained mental health practitioner, you are choosing to work with someone who has specialty training and is a member of a government-recognized regulatory body upholding standards for its members. Mental health professionals are required to meet certain minimum training qualifications and to maintain a professional code of conduct. They are accountable to a regulatory body that investigates complaints and that can withdraw the privilege of practising under its name. Below are some of the recognized groups of practitioners.

Psychiatrists

PSYCHIATRISTS ARE MEDICAL DOCTORS who go on to take specialized training in psychiatry. The College of Physicians and Surgeons gives them a licence to practise and holds them accountable to uphold professional standards and an ethical code of conduct. Psychiatrists can prescribe medication and their fees are paid by provincial health plans. They require a referral from a family physician and may have a waiting list. Although some psychiatrists provide psychotherapy, most focus primarily on managing symptoms or psychiatric illness with medications. If you choose to see a psychiatrist, the section above on drug therapies will be particularly helpful.

Psychologists

PSYCHOLOGISTS DO NOT HAVE degrees in medicine, rather, they have a university degree followed by specific, post-graduate training that leads to an advanced degree, including either a Master's (M.A., M.Ed.) or a doctoral degree (Ph.D., Psy.D.). The post-graduate degree will be in a specific branch of psychology, such as clinical, educational, or counselling psychology. To be granted registration in a province, a psychologist must meet the standards of that province's regulatory body for psychologists. While these standards may differ somewhat among provinces, the psychologist must meet specific educational requirements, complete a series of exams, and demonstrate clinical competence to qualify. Members are required to continue updating their training and must practise within their specific area of expertise according to regulations and a code of ethics set by their regulatory body. Provincial mental health programs typically cover only fees for a small range of psychological services. However, some private and employee health plans are more comprehensive.

Social workers

SOCIAL WORKERS IN PRIVATE practice are typically licensed by their own provincial regulatory body under an umbrella organization called the Canadian Association of Social Workers. Licensed or registered social workers hold undergraduate or graduate degrees in social work. In general, registration to provide counselling requires a Master's degree. Registered social workers must abide by a standard of practice including a code of ethics. As is the case with psychologists, provincial health care plans do not cover fees, but some private and employee health plans may.

Other counsellors and therapists

THERE IS NO REGULATION governing use of the titles counsellor or therapist. Anyone can call oneself a "counsellor" or "therapist," regardless of previous training or qualifications, or lack thereof. In British Columbia, some clinical counsellors are members of an Association of Registered Clinical Counsellors that sets some requirements for registration. However, this association is not a legislated regulatory body, therefore it has no authority to penalize misconduct by its members. By contrast, the regulatory bodies noted above have protocols for therapist referrals, for registering complaints against their members, and for bringing disciplinary action when necessary.

The value and limitations of professional credentials

YOU ARE MOST LIKELY to receive appropriate and effective treatment from mental health practitioners who have professional qualifications and the court is likely to give their opinions more regard. However, it is important to note that professional credentials do not guarantee either competence or effectiveness. Some fully qualified professionals fail to provide their clients with appropriate and effective treatment, and some even make things noticeably worse. Similarly, some non-professional counsellors and therapists provide excellent and effective services, while some are ineffective or even damaging. Training and experience both matter, but they are not always sufficient to make for a good counsellor or a good fit for your specific needs. Working with a mental health professional registered by a legally sanctioned body does give you the advantage of being able to lodge a complaint through the registration body if you are not satisfied.

What to look for when choosing a therapist

IF YOU FEEL YOU are ready to engage in psychotherapy, you will have the widest choice of options in the metropolitan areas of Canada. In smaller communities, your options will be more limited. Whatever your circumstances, finding the right therapist for you is an important step. We offer the following guidelines to help you make the right choice, a choice that will hopefully assist, rather than hamper, in your recovery and participation in legal proceedings. When possible, we recommend that you choose a mental health professional with the following qualities:

- Professional credentials (a member in good standing of a regulatory body with the power to sanction those who are incompetent or unethical in their practices)
- Specific training in and experience dealing with victims of sexual crimes
- Knowledge about the role of mental health providers within our legal system and experience working with clients who are involved in litigation
- Clear professional, emotional, and physical boundaries that allow you to feel safe in a therapeutic relationship

- The ability to clearly explain the potential benefits and limitations of the procedures used
- A willingness to explain and obtain your informed consent to engage in therapy
- The ability to explain confidentiality and its limitations in court cases
- The ability to work with you to outline realistic therapy goals and ways to meet those goals and know when the goals are met
- The ability to make you feel relatively at ease and safe and assist in developing a trusting relationship
- The ability to interact with you in a non-judgmental way
- The ability to actively listen to you, show respect towards you, and have your best interests in mind
- The ability to challenge your maladaptive beliefs in a respectful way and offer other perspectives

Apart from professional qualifications, the gender of your therapist may be important to you. A female assaulted or abused by a male may not wish to deal with a male therapist at any stage in her recovery process. Conversely, some women benefit from a male therapist because dealing with a man with clear boundaries who offers help, support, and empathy can help some women re-establish their trust in men. Men who seek therapy to deal with their victimization may find it more difficult to discuss what happened to them with another man, thus preferring to work with a female therapist. Men sexually assaulted by other men can also benefit from working in a positive therapeutic relationship with another male, as this can serve to restore trust and challenge underlying assumptions about male attitudes toward sexual victimization. It is up to you as the client to decide whether you feel more comfortable working with a female or male therapist. If choices are limited, or if you have concerns related to your therapist's gender, we encourage you to discuss these issues with your therapist in the early stages of your therapy.

For some victims seeking counselling, cultural similarity or common values with the therapist may be important. For example, as a First Nations person, you may prefer a First Nations counsellor. As a feminist or a person of strong religious faith, you may prefer a feminist counsellor or a religiously affiliated counsellor. It is understandable that people from a particular cultural background may want a therapist of that same background on the assumption that they will have commonalities and easy rapport, but this is not always the case. People from small communities often prefer to work with someone outside their community (and their culture) because of issues of trust and concerns about confidentiality.

What to be wary of

AS WE NOTED ABOVE, therapy can go awry. Certain therapists or therapeutic approaches may harm, rather than help. In some instances, therapeutic activities can compromise your legal case (see Chapter 4). You should question the approach of therapists who depart significantly from the guidelines outlined above. Bear in mind that communication is a two-way street, so you should take the liberty to discuss your concerns and note how the therapist responds. Open, non-defensive discussions are another hallmark feature of good therapy.

We encourage you to be particularly wary of therapists who do not appear to have appropriate personal boundaries. As a victim of sexual assault, you especially need to feel physically safe. You need to have a clear understanding about the boundaries of touch. For example, some people are "huggers," while some are not. You might feel comforted by a hug; on the other hand, you might feel violated by a hug. Clarify this with your therapist. It is reasonable for you to request not to be touched, if this is how you feel. Any form of sexual touching or harassment in therapy is totally unacceptable and just plain wrong. You should report any therapist who violates sexual boundaries to a regulatory body and to the police.

Appropriate emotional boundaries are more difficult to define than physical ones. It is essential to experience a sense of caring and support from your therapist, however, the relationship lines should always remain clearly drawn. This is a uniquely intimate relationship because you divulge your most personal thoughts and feelings; consequently, feeling close to your therapist is a typical response. While therapy is occurring, it is generally a mistake for a therapist to become friends with or get over-involved with a client. This behaviour can blur the lines between the professional and the social relationship and, ultimately, interfere with your progress in therapy.

Also, be wary of a therapist who falls into the trap of trying to "rescue" you. Yes, at times, you need assistance and support, but the primary goal of effective therapy is to help you acquire the coping skills that you need to function on your own, not to have someone else make decisions for you. A therapist does you no favour, in the end, if you become so dependent on the therapist's aid that you cannot make decisions for yourself.

We also encourage you to be wary of a therapist who wholeheartedly, without reservation, validates all your memories or dream images or flashbacks as accurately representing actual experiences. Nobody, except someone who was physically present at the time, can validate the accuracy of your memories. Your therapist *cannot* bear witness to your experiences. Your therapist can validate your feelings but cannot confirm the accuracy or source of your memories. A therapist who is well-acquainted with memory issues will help you to understand and deal with the strong feelings, doubt, indecision, and ambiguity that arise when dealing with memory retrieval, memory fragments, visual images, or physical sensations ("body memories"). We discuss these issues further in the memory section of Chapter 4.

If you are participating in legal proceedings, you should be particularly wary of therapeutic techniques, such as hypnosis, that could seriously undermine your legal case. Refer to the points raised in subsequent chapters regarding these concerns. Be an informed consumer — therapy is an important investment of your time, energy, emotional-self, and financial resources.

We are all liable to make bad decisions at times but, by becoming an informed consumer, you are in the best position to judge what is working or not working for you. Take into account that most therapy journeys have twists and turns. Everything may not always run smoothly or live up to your expectations. At times, you may be particularly sensitive to someone's challenges or you may feel disrespected, even when this was not intended. It is legitimate for you to talk with your therapist about any concerns that emerge. Ultimately, if the therapeutic process is not meeting your needs, you can take this experience and move on to another therapist who may be a better fit for you.

How to get appropriate referrals

IT IS WISE TO seek a lot of advice when you are going about the process of choosing a therapist. You can get referrals from friends, colleagues, and others who have faced similar problems. Regulatory bodies for mental health professionals often have referral lists that you can access. Check the listings of regulatory bodies in your province. Rape crisis centres or victim services usually have referral resources and your family doctor may be able to refer you to a specialist in the field. You also can ask your legal counsel or other lawyers with experience in sexual assault cases for names of mental health professionals who are familiar with court proceedings. If you have access to a computer, you may want to look for potential therapists on the Internet.

Not every referral will lead to the right place. Choosing a therapist is, in at least one important respect, the same as choosing a financial advisor, legal advisor, auto mechanic, hairdresser, or any other type of service provider. The main thing is to be an informed consumer and not to be afraid to ask a prospective therapist questions about the therapist's credentials and therapeutic approach. Only settle for what works for you. Not only can the right therapist help your recovery proceed more smoothly and effectively, the wrong therapist can make things worse both psychologically and legally.

The initial contact: you are not signing a lease

YOU CAN SEEK OUT more than one mental health referral, then telephone these professionals and ask to arrange a short telephone interview. Therapists differ in their billing practices, but an initial consult is often at no charge; clarify this with the therapist. You can then ask questions about the issues that are most important to you. You will find sample questions in Appendix 3. Asking some of these questions can help you judge the competency and appropriateness of a prospective therapist. You should also provide some information about yourself, such as the possibility of upcoming legal proceedings. Some therapists may be reluctant to provide therapy in these cases. When you find someone who seems to meet your needs, make an appointment to meet in person. You are under no obligation to continue beyond this preliminary meeting. If you do choose a particular therapist and find later that it is not working, you can always stop and switch to someone else. You also have the right to interrupt your therapy at any time to take a break, and then resume later when you feel better able to proceed. Your therapist should be amenable to timing therapy to meet your needs.

The purpose of the suggested questions in Appendix 3 is to help you determine how experienced and knowledgeable the therapist is, and if the therapist understands the interface between therapy and the courts. These issues will become clearer when we discuss specific legal matters later in the book. At this point, it is important for you to know that the court could require your therapist to write a report or testify. For example, if you pursue civil litigation, your lawyer could request that your therapist provide an expert opinion on how the sexual assault damaged you psychologically. This is not always the case and may not be advisable since your therapist is assumed to have your best interests at heart and therefore may not be likely to offer an unbiased opinion. It is also possible that either a lawyer or the court could request your therapy records. Both you and your therapist should bear this is mind and perhaps discuss how your sessions will be recorded. Accurate and suitable documentation of therapy is required of all mental health professionals and you have a right to read these records. You could arrange to review documentation and notes with your therapist to ensure that they are accurate. This gives you an opportunity to clarify any misconceptions and ensures that the record contents do not later upset or surprise you. You might also ask to add your own comments (clearly identified as yours) to the records in order to clarify a point made by the therapist.

Paying for therapy

AS NOTED ABOVE, PROVINCIAL medical plans cover only psychiatric fees. Sometimes, employee assistance plans or private insurance plans cover the costs of therapy with other mental health professionals, such as psychologists and social workers. If you were sexually assaulted at work, Workers' Compensation programs may fund counselling. Some provinces also have victim assistance programs that provide funding for counselling for victims of crime. As well, some specialized provincial programs provide funding for treatment. Funding for First Nations people sexually abused in residential schools may also be available. You can discuss funding possibilities with your therapist or seek information from provincial and national government websites. Funding to programs often changes, so it is worth your while to explore the current situation in your area.

Discuss fees and billing practices with your therapist. The costs of therapy vary widely. Some therapists also charge on a sliding scale based on the client's ability to pay. If you are proceeding with civil litigation, costs of therapy may be included in the compensation that you are seeking. The court may award funds to reimburse your therapy costs and may pay for future therapy. You cannot count on this, but it is important to keep records of any therapy costs so that you can later seek these costs if the court awards compensation. You also may need receipts for income tax purposes; therapy provided by a registered health care provider may be tax-deductible.

ADJUNCTS AND ALTERNATIVES TO INDIVIDUAL TREATMENT

Group treatment

THE THERAPEUTIC ISSUES DISCUSSED above largely apply to individual treatments, but there are also group therapies to consider. These include groups specifically designed for victims of sexual assault or adult victims of childhood sexual abuse. These groups may be quite structured and usually include considerable emphasis on psycho-education (learning about the dynamics and impact of sexual assault). There are also problem-focused groups that may target particular issues like PTSD symptoms. Victim organizations sometimes organize support or self-help groups without the participation of mental health professionals. Therapists can deliver cognitive-behavioural therapy (CBT) or other individual approaches in a group format, so there may be a wide variety of groups from which to choose. Treatment is usually delivered in a group format at residential substance abuse treatment programs.

Participation in therapeutic or support groups can be very beneficial but, as always, you should be aware of possible drawbacks. Groups are not suitable for everyone. Leaders of therapeutic groups frequently screen participants to determine if they are an appropriate fit. Participants may be required to demonstrate suitable social skills and a level of emotional stability. Someone who has suicidal thoughts may be at risk in some groups. Participants also should be able to establish some level of trust with others and be capable of maintaining confidentiality about issues discussed in the group. Some therapeutic groups require that participants also have an individual therapist.

Below are some potential benefits and problems that you should be aware of when considering group therapy:

- *Potential benefits of group treatment*
  - ▷ Acceptance and social support of other victims
  - ▷ Validation of your victimization experience, and awareness of commonalities with other victims
  - ▷ Reduction of feeling stigmatized and alienated
  - ▷ Increased knowledge about sexual crimes, their impact, and ways of recovery

- ▷ Ability to learn healthy ways in which others cope
- ▷ Provision of an expanded social network, which can reduce isolation and withdrawal from others and provide an opportunity for positive, healthy bonding
- ▷ Access to a wider range of perspectives
- ▷ Opportunity to disclose in a safe environment
- ▷ Lower costs than individual therapy

- ◆ *Potential problems of group treatment*
  - ▷ Groups can become chaotic or overwhelming without an effective leader
  - ▷ Inappropriate group members may sabotage the group or divert the focus away from group needs
  - ▷ Some members may not display appropriate personal boundaries
  - ▷ Some members may breach confidentiality or undermine the trust of others
  - ▷ Concern can arise in court that group participation may have contaminated your evidence. For example, if others discussed their sexual assaults, it may be suggested that you unconsciously incorporated details of their abuse into your own narrative

Culturally based treatment — a First Nations approach

TWENTY YEARS AGO, IT was found that First Nations individuals tended not to use the counselling services in proportion to their needs, and of those who did, half dropped out of counselling after the first session.[9] Researchers concluded that the main problem was one of cultural differences between the counsellors and the potential clients.

Professor Rod McCormick at the University of British Columbia published a study in 1995 that looked closely at the healing experiences of fifty First Nations volunteers.[10] Dr. McCormick concluded that these individuals, and by extension individuals from cultures whose traditions are different than those in mainstream North America, have a different world view that must be understood before effective counselling can take place. First Nations' world view is more spiritual and holistic than the prevailing Western perspective, emphasizing harmony and balance within an individual and between the person and the community. From the First Nations' perspective, the focus is not on ego development, but on transcending the ego, so that the self, as part of the community, becomes most important.

Some First Nations victims of abuse may turn for assistance to others in their community, such as Elders, but it may be foreign for them to share information or talk about their problems with strangers. To facilitate healing, the First Nations people studied by Dr. McCormick used a broad spectrum of approaches that extend far beyond "talk therapy," and included the following:

- Participation in community ceremonies
- Expression of emotion to others
- Learning from a role model
- Establishing a connection with nature
- Physical exercise
- Involvement in challenging activities
- Establishing a meaningful social connection
- Gaining an understanding of the problem
- Establishing spiritual connections to self and one's surroundings
- Obtaining help or support from others
- Self-care
- Setting goals
- Anchoring oneself in tradition
- Helping others

In Chapter 5, you will read about the types of coping strategies and techniques that are associated with resilience or the ability to cope effectively with stress. You will notice that there is considerable overlap between some healing resources used by the First Nations people and the resilience strategies that social scientists have identified as important for us all.

Resource and rape crisis centres

ASSISTANCE MAY BE AVAILABLE to you through the valuable work done by women's resource and rape crisis centres. These organizations are usually very accessible to female victims. Their mandate generally is to dispense information and deal with crises. Often staffed by caring volunteers with years of experience helping victims of sexual assault on the front lines, these centres typically provide invaluable support and caring, and sometimes provide safe places for you to volunteer your own time as your recovery progresses. These resources may be able to help you with daily needs, such as shopping for groceries, getting to appointments, speaking with your employer about time off, finding a therapist, or helping you to identify friends and family who can help. If they cannot provide these services directly, they may know who can.

Although less commonly available, there are some resource centres available for male victims of sexual crimes that offer support groups. Local rape crisis centres may be able to refer you to these. Cultural centres can also provide support services for some groups. Local Friendship Centres often provide First Nations people with valuable support and can help to find healing programs.

Self-help books

THERE IS CURRENTLY AN astonishing array of self-help books available on virtually every topic. By one estimate, approximately 2,000 new self-help books appear on the shelf each year.[11] It is virtually impossible to keep abreast of all these books, which vary greatly in their quality and usefulness. In our resource guide found in Appendix 4, we have listed a sample of self-help books. Some of these are truly outstanding resources that we recommend without qualification, while others we offer with some words of caution. Research indicates that self-help books, including those that target specific problems like depression and anxiety, can be as effective as therapeutic intervention for some people.[12] The difficulty lies in choosing a book that will meet your particular requirements. When choosing a self-help book, you must consider both the quality and usefulness of the material as well as the potential legal ramifications.

To illustrate the potential difficulties with some self-help books in legal proceedings, consider the following. In the early 1990s, considerable controversy arose about the possibility of complainants coming forward with "false memories" of childhood sexual abuse (see Chapter 4 for a discussion of these issues). In particular, concerns arose about various therapeutic procedures and techniques that might be overly suggestive or that might "contaminate" a person's memory of past abuse. The very popular self-help book for women who had been sexually abused as children, *The Courage to Heal* by Bass & Davis,[13] was criticized for being overly suggestive about the possibility of abuse in the absence of definitive memories of abuse. Although one can argue about whether or not the criticisms of *The Courage to Heal* were justified, complainants who read this book became vulnerable to attacks on their credibility in court.

The Courage to Heal has since been updated (a third edition was published in 1994) to address some of these concerns. In many respects, the current edition is an excellent self-help resource for women who have clear memories of their past sexual abuse. This edition was the top-rated book on sexual abuse as judged by a group of psychologists surveyed for the *Authoritative Guide to Self-Help Resources in Mental Health*.[14] There are other excellent, less controversial books listed in our resource guide. If you choose to read *The Courage to Heal*, we recommend that you read the current edition, rather than an older copy. Nevertheless, we caution the use of this text by victims who are planning to pursue legal action and whose memory of their assault is limited or vague.

Other publications and online resources

READING BOOKS WRITTEN BY or about people who have successfully coped with extremely difficult experiences, such as the death of loved ones, surviving cancer, or a sexual assault, can be inspiring. Such books can give you hope and motivate you to change your own life in positive and profound ways. With this in mind, we provide references for some of these inspiring books in our Appendix 4 resource guide. We also give brief summaries of several remarkable lives in Chapter 11 that illustrate how some people have transformed their lives following tragic experiences.

Online resources can also provide helpful information to assist you with your healing journey. With a few clicks, you can have access to enormous quantities of information on the web. This can be a very helpful source of information and ideas. The quality of information available varies dramatically, so you can find as much misinformation as accurate information, and often it is difficult to distinguish between the two. Not all sources are what they claim to be, so approach the Internet with caution. Those of you who do not have ready access to a computer can check with your local library. Larger urban areas also have Internet "cafés" where you can access the web for nominal fees. We have provided some reliable online resources in our resource guide.

Are you going too fast?

IN THIS CHAPTER, WE have provided a lot of information about various paths toward healing or recovery, which may seem overwhelming or bewildering. In their book, *Life after Trauma*,[15] Drs. Rosenbloom and Williams offer practical advice about how to pace yourself as you consider your options and begin making personal changes. Below is their checklist of warning signs that may mean you need to slow down a bit or put down this book. When you experience one or more of the following, it may be time to take a step back, take a break, and perhaps indulge in some self-care or soothing strategies.

- You begin to feel (or you feel more often) that you do not feel present in your body or surroundings, or you lose time (also known as dissociation).
- You begin to have flashbacks (or your flashbacks increase) of the trauma that intrude into your mind.
- You have feelings that seem unmanageable or that flood you.
- You experience irritability, strong anger, depression, fear, anxiety, sadness, or other feelings, particularly if they feel out of control or if you do not understand their source.
- You begin to injure yourself (or you injure yourself more frequently) in ways including cutting, scratching, burning, and substance abuse.
- You are behaving more compulsively in areas, such as eating, working, or sexual activity.
- You are completely numb or unable to feel any emotion.
- You have a desire to isolate yourself and avoid others.
- You experience a dramatic change in sleeping or eating patterns.

TENSIONS BETWEEN THE LEGAL SYSTEM AND HEALING

YOU NEED TO BE aware of tensions and incompatibilities between the legal system and your psychological needs. Our legal system attempts to protect the rights of both the accused person and the complainant in the pursuit of justice. Most of us would agree that this is a very important and appropriate principle of justice. To protect the rights of the accused in criminal proceedings, the court requires a stringent standard of proof—"beyond a reasonable doubt." The standard of proof is less stringent in civil litigation (based on the "balance of probabilities"), but evidence of wrongdoing is nonetheless required there as well. This means that in both criminal and civil court, your reports of sexual crimes and their impact on you will be treated as allegations that must be proven according to required standards. For many victims, having their story believed and validated by others is an important part of their healing process, especially for those victims whose claims of sexual abuse or assaults have previously been denied or dismissed. Validation may not happen in court, and not necessarily because people do not believe that the assaults occurred, but simply because the evidence presented does not meet the court's standard of proof. This evidentiary requirement of the law may create tensions between the needs of the court and your therapeutic needs. Outside the court system, you are free to pursue healing without providing evidence, but inside the courtroom, explanations and evidence will be the primary concern.

From the perspective of your legal counsel, an overarching goal is to collect sufficient evidence of the type and quality needed to satisfy the court's standard of proof. In some cases, your lawyer may have concerns that your evidence (your account of what happened to you) could be compromised or tainted by your engaging in therapy, and may ask you to avoid particular therapeutic techniques or certain types of therapy. The following are some examples of types of therapies or treatments that may compromise your legal case:

- Therapy whose goal is to retrieve memories of abuse. These memories are likely to be viewed by the court as unreliable or contaminated.
- Hypnosis for memory-retrieval or clarification of details. This does not include other uses of hypnosis aimed at changing problematic behaviours (for example, to stop smoking or lose weight).
- Participation in group therapy or group meetings where other victims are disclosing or discussing their experiences of sexual assault. The court may view this as a potential source of contamination of your memory.
- "New Age," non-mainstream forms of treatment, such as past life regressions. Some of these practices may be viewed negatively by the court and could reflect unfavourably on your credibility.

Because of these concerns, legal counsel might request that you postpone receiving treatment altogether until after the court proceedings. In addition to concerns that therapy could negatively affect your narrative about the assaults, some lawyers prefer that complainants avoid therapy prior to their court testimony so that they will not appear too "healthy" during the court proceedings. There may be a concern that juries and judges will give more credence to someone who fits the stereotype of a badly damaged or poorly functioning victim. In civil litigation cases, lawyers may be concerned about reducing your psychological damages before the parties have reached a settlement. If a complainant has notably recovered or healed, the case for compensation may be weakened.

If these concerns should arise, you will have to balance your own needs against requests from your legal counsel, but as we emphasize throughout this book, we encourage you to give your well-being sufficient priority. This does not mean that the concerns of the court have no merit. You may be able to reach a compromise that adequately satisfies the competing needs of the legal system and your psychological health. We cannot advise you how to resolve these types of dilemmas, but we suggest that you consider them and discuss your concerns with your legal counsel and therapist if you have one. If you are engaged in treatment with a qualified mental health professional experienced in dealing with court proceedings and litigation issues, you are less likely to encounter major problems. In our experience, having the help and support of a competent, experienced therapist during court proceedings can be a great advantage.

VIGNETTE THREE: FIRST STEPS TO HEALING

IN THE WEEKS FOLLOWING the sexual assault by her friend Christopher, sixteen-year-old Theresa, described in Vignette Three, experienced many of the symptoms of a depressive disorder including sleep disturbance, poor appetite, low mood, and feelings of helplessness and hopelessness. Being emotionally vulnerable, she isolated herself at home and did not want people to know what had happened to her. The only person she was able to talk to was her sister Helen, with whom she had a trusting and comfortable relationship. Helen seemed to understand what Theresa had been through: she supported Theresa and eventually encouraged her to seek help for her emotional distress. Theresa went first to her family doctor who prescribed a course of antidepressant medication for her. The medication relieved some of her symptoms, but she continued to feel overwhelmed, particularly when the Crown counsel office notified her of the date for a preliminary hearing in her case.

While the antidepressant medication did not solve her problems, it did elevate Theresa's mood to the point that she could think more clearly and she realized she would have to do more if she was to regain her emotional balance. She asked Helen to help her find a therapist. Helen contacted the referral service of their provincial psychological association and described her sister's situation. She received the names of several psychologists with appropriate expertise in the area of sexual assault. From this list, Helen picked a female therapist because she thought Theresa would be less comfortable talking to a male. Interestingly, Theresa did not warm to the chosen therapist whom she described as "too touchy-feely" in her approach. Theresa was disappointed and after two sessions decided not to go back because "therapy just isn't going to work." Helen suggested Theresa try once more with another therapist on the list, a male.

Theresa was quickly at ease with the new therapist who framed her difficulties in athletic terms. He suggested that Theresa think of the preliminary hearing as a marathon that she had to train for, language she immediately grasped. He reminded her of some helpful strategies that she had previously used as an athlete (such as staying focused on a goal, setting up a training schedule) and taught her some techniques that she could use to regain her emotional control (for example, progressive relaxation and visualization). Together, Theresa and her therapist developed a plan to help Theresa improve her diet, start exercising, socializing, and reconnecting with her friends. Theresa's view of herself as a broken and vulnerable person began to change. She began to think of herself as an athlete-in-training. The therapist encouraged her in each small step she took; her confidence increased and she began rebuilding her life. Although she was still emotionally fragile, Theresa began feeling healthier and emotionally stronger. She was able to recognize improvement in many of the small steps she took toward her goal of being able enough to testify at the upcoming trial.

ENDNOTES

1   Bill O'Hanlon, *Thriving Through Crisis: Turn Tragedy and Trauma into Growth and Change* (New York: The Berkley Publishing Group, 2004) at 75.

2   *The Four Circles of Hollow Water,* APC 15 CA (Ottawa: Solicitor General Canada, 1997) at 118–19.

3   Mary Beth Williams & Soili Poijula, *The PTSD Workbook: Simple, Effective Techniques for Overcoming Traumatic Stress Symptoms* (Oakland, CA: New Harbinger, 2002) at 174; based on Robert D. Enright & Richard P. Fitzgibbons, *Helping Clients Forgive: An Empirical Guide for Resolving Anger and Restoring Hope* (Washington, DC: American Psychological Association, 2000).

4   *Ibid.*

5   Ellen Bass & Laura Davis, *The Courage to Heal: A Guide for Women Survivors of Child Sexual Abuse*, 3d ed. rev. (New York: Harper & Row, 1994) at 165.

6   Directly quoted from Cheryl Bell-Gadsby & Anne Siegenberg, *Reclaiming Her Story: Ericksonian Solution-Focused Therapy for Sexual Abuse* (New York: Brunner/Mazel, 1996) at 19.

7   Bass & Davis, *The Courage to Heal*, above note 5 at 193.

8   Barbara O. Rothbaum & Edna B. Foa, *Treating the Trauma of Rape: Cognitive-Behavioural Therapy for PTSD* (New York: Guilford Press, 1998).

9   Rod McCormick, "The Facilitation of Healing for the First Nations People of British Columbia" (1995) 21(2) Canadian Journal of Native Education 251–322.

10   *Ibid.*

11   John C. Norcross *et al., Authoritative Guide to Self-Help Resources in Mental Health,* rev. ed. (New York: Guilford Press, 2003).

12   *Ibid.* at 4.

13   Above note 5.

14   Above note 11.

15   Dena Rosenbloom & Mary Beth Williams, *Life after Trauma: A Workbook for Healing* (New York: Guilford Press, 1999) at 13.

Law and the Human Factors

Vignette Four

A young woman, Carol, attends a private party at a rented banquet hall. When Carol leaves, a man from the party follows her into the parking lot, forces her into the bushes, and has anal sex with her. Bystanders hear her cries, run up to the scene and hold the assailant until the police arrive. Carol is taken by ambulance to the hospital where she is examined by a doctor. While at the hospital, she gives a full account of the assault to police. The Crown lays charges against the assailant. Three months later, when Crown counsel contacts Carol, the key witness in the trial, to go over her testimony, Carol remembers being in the parking lot prior to the assault and being in the ambulance after the assault, but she no longer has any memory for the assault itself. Crown counsel asks Carol to see a psychologist, an expert in memory issues, for an assessment and tells her the case will have to be adjourned until the assessment is completed. The Crown feels Carol's inability to give details of the assault in court will seriously weaken the case. Because of the adjournment delay, the court releases the accused on bail. Carol is very upset. She fears the assailant may attempt to harm her again, she thinks the Crown lawyer blames her for the adjournment, and she worries that her memory problems indicate that she has some serious mental disorder.

THE LEGAL SYSTEM HAS a long, venerable history, but it can be an intimidating experience with its arcane language and complex rules. Despite the focus on procedure and ritual, it is ultimately a system for people conducted by people and consequently imbued with human elements. In this chapter, we review some of the human factors that are important to consider when participating in this venue. We discuss memory issues, relationship dynamics, legal system stressors, and emotional buoyancy. The chapter ends with some thoughts about the personal benefits of participating in the court process.

Some crime victims can be dismayed and confused by their first experience with our adversarial court system. This reaction applies equally to those involved in civil litigation or criminal prosecution. In an adversarial system, each side presents a case before a court (judge alone or with a jury), whose function is to balance the rights of the defendant with those of the complainant to ensure that each side follows the legal rules when presenting its case. This adversarial, accusatorial method, which pits one side against the other, dominates most of what happens in a courtroom. It has ancient origins and a long history, but only recently have there been any noteworthy modifications recognizing the human factors important to the process.

To the non-professional, a court case conducted in this system can be a complicated, complex process. Court officials frequently use esoteric language that you may not understand and they will engage in rituals unfamiliar to you. In contrast, the justice personnel who make their living in this environment are comfortable with it. You may feel that the unfamiliar language and arcane courtroom rules hinder, rather than help, you tell your story. Some participants may wonder why their concerns appear to take a back seat to seemingly trivial details and obscure legal wrangling.

Although you might feel like an outsider, your role in the legal process is an important one. While you are not the one who steers or controls the case, as the complainant, you are the central witness. You provide valuable information and testimony when required, but you do not act as an investigator or prosecutor; you should turn these functions over to those "in the know," those with the necessary skills and competence to do the job well. To some, not being in complete control can be disconcerting, but the experience can also be liberating if you learn to trust those around you to prosecute the offender fully or to conduct your civil suit fairly.

When it comes to legal proceedings, we have to consider not only the adversarial context but also the influence of historical myths related to women and children, and the causes of sexual offences. In the past, authorities expected that the victim of a sexual crime (most often women and children) would report the crime immediately and failure to do so raised suspicions about the complaint. The law also considered children to be unreliable witnesses, and a woman's sexual reputation was used to undermine her credibility. For example, if a woman consented to sex on previous occasions, it was taken as evidence that she likely consented to sexual activity with the accused during the alleged offence. Further, to determine the victim's credibility at trial, the court, until recently, accepted her personal records willy-nilly, without consideration of privacy issues. Accumulating knowledge demonstrates that some of these myths and outmoded procedures are detrimental to fair legal practices.

After lengthy legal struggles, legislation now prohibits courts from using some of these spurious assumptions in the legal analysis of a case. Nevertheless, in the adversarial context, and in spite of prohibitions, lawyers do occasionally stray into arguments and positions based on this outdated thinking. Enlightenment is coming slowly in some quarters, but there are indications that Canadian law is evolving away from some of the narrow biases that have marked it in the past. This evolution is particularly evident in cases involving harm directly inflicted by one person on another, as in sexual crimes. There is a shift toward increased victim participation, particularly in the prosecution of young offenders and at the sentencing stage of adult offenders, where victim impact statements are now common practice. Increasingly, human factors that affect the legal process are being recognized and accommodations are being found that do not diminish the legal system's integrity.

In this chapter, we discuss some of the human elements that will be important when you take part in the legal system. We begin with an examination of memory processes; this includes a review of our current scientific understanding and its relation to court expectations that a victim provide an accurate and detailed account of past experiences. This section does not offer any easy solutions to the legal stressors encountered by a victim, but it does address the complexity of memory and reviews some long-standing misconceptions about human recall.

MEMORY

THE ABILITY TO RECALL events accurately typically plays a central role in legal proceedings related to sexual crimes. There may be limited physical evidence in a case, particularly with respect to crimes, such as childhood sexual abuse that occurred years before the prosecution begins. In this type of case, the primary evidence is generally the complainant's description of what the complainant remembers of the sexual assaults. The defendant is likely to contest these memories and offer a different version of what happened. The defendant's narrative, as well as that of the complainant, is highly dependent on memory, so the legal proceedings can hinge, to a considerable extent, on the examination of these memories. The judge and/or jurors have the task of trying to determine whose memory is more accurate. However, the relationship between people's experiences and the representation of those experiences in their memory is complex.

Complainants come into the legal arena with memories of varying quality. Some may have generally clear, vivid memories of the sexual assault, but some details may be missing, unclear, or forgotten. Others remember relatively few details, especially if the assault happened years ago. Some complainants, like Carol in Vignette Four, describe "blanks" or "holes" in their memories that may extend to part or most of their experience. Some are distressed by the vivid clarity of their memories, while others may be upset because they do not clearly remember much of what happened. How much or how little you recall will depend on many factors, and you will better understand those variables after reading this section.

First, a note of caution: whatever the extent and quality of your memories, recalling a traumatic sexual assault can sometimes evoke disturbing thoughts and feelings that emotionally overwhelm you. Regardless of issues relating to accuracy and quality of memory, the emotions aroused by these images can make it difficult for you to participate fully and effectively in legal proceedings. If you are feeling highly distressed or overwhelmed by your memories and they are having a significant impact on your day-to-day life, we recommend that you seek assistance from a qualified mental health professional. In the next chapter, we suggest some healthy strategies that you might try to change or diminish the effect of disturbing memories. These strategies can be particularly helpful during court proceedings, when memories of the assaults are likely to be triggered. By learning ways to manage the emotional impact of your memories effectively, you reduce their power, and you will feel better equipped to handle the challenges of participating in legal proceedings.

Different kinds of memory

THE STUDY OF HOW we remember is a complex and evolving field of research but, during the last few decades, science has gained valuable knowledge about human memory processes. Unfortunately, there are no quick and easy answers to how our memory works; many questions currently remain unanswered. It is beyond the scope of this book to provide a complete outline of the existing state of knowledge in this field; instead we focus on some basic information that can help you better understand the role that memory will play in both your legal experiences and your recovery.

Memory is a word that we use to label many different processes. Scientists have identified a variety of different types of memory, mediated by different parts of the brain, which serve different functions. Some types of memory are of little relevance to the topics in this book. "Procedural" memory, for example, is a kind of memory that permits the retention of sensory motor coordination — remembering how to walk, tie a shoelace, ride a bike, drive, and so on. Although this type of memory is extremely important, it plays little role in the context of sexual assault.

Another type of memory, known as "semantic" memory, is the source of our general knowledge. This type of memory permits us to remember words, their meanings, and general information we have acquired, such as knowing that Ottawa is the capital of Canada or knowing that January is the first month of the year. This type of memory pertains to knowledge not associated with a particular time or place so it is typically not of central concern in sexual assault cases. However, sometimes people may use their general knowledge to try to remember or reconstruct how something might have happened.

The most important aspect of memory in sexual assault cases is "autobiographical" memory, also known as "narrative" or "episodic" memory. When you remember a particular, personally experienced incident in your life, it is your autobiographical memory that enables you to do so. You rely on this type of memory to remember a sexual assault. Autobiographical memory develops some time between eighteen and thirty-six months of age. The absence of this type of memory in young infants is one of the reasons that we all suffer from infantile amnesia, an inability to remember personally experienced events before roughly two years of age.

Yet another kind of memory, called "script" memory, comes into play when a person experiences a similar event repeatedly. When several separate episodes of a similar nature occur, we tend to blend the separate episodes together to form a more general memory or script. In a script memory, you tend to forget the minor variations between individual events in the series, while remembering the common pattern. For example, if a babysitter makes a child perform oral sex in the family bathroom on a number of different occasions, the specific episodes will often blend into a common pattern retained in script memory. When asked to recall the assaults, the child's memory will largely consist of what generally happened, rather than specifics of each incident. Although a script memory forms the main part of memory for repeated sexual abuse, a victim also may remember some details from specific episodes, especially when something odd or different from the usual pattern occurred, for example, that it was the only time that the victim was wearing jogging shorts. This illustrates another feature of human memory discussed in more detail below — we tend to remember details or events that are unusual, that somehow stand out, provoke strong emotions, or that have particular meaning for us in our individual lives. We sometimes even describe these special experiences as being "memorable."

Memory is reconstructed

HUMAN MEMORY DOES NOT operate like a computer file or a video recorder. That is, we do not store away an unchanging copy of an event or a script. Instead, we reconstruct or recreate past events when trying to recall them. Rather than playing back a memory of a specific episode as we would a videotape, we piece the event back together. Thus, recall is synonymous with reconstruction — words we will use interchangeably in this text. The reconstructive nature of human memory has both advantages and disadvantages. One of the advantages is the increased number of incidents or number of scripts that we can retain over time. One of the disadvantages of memory's reconstructive nature is we may, at times, make mistakes when reconstructing an event or script.

Sometimes we have many "pieces" or details of an event to work with in our memory reconstruction. Other times, there may be very few specific, remembered details to work with. The amount and quality of details remembered depends on many factors, including how much attention was paid to details at the time, how long ago the event occurred, and one's emotional state at the time. When we put together our memory fragments to reconstruct an event, we tend to fill in the gaps based on our general knowledge, beliefs, and expectations. In this way, we can make mistakes when reconstructing a memory. Memory researcher Ulrich Neisser reported a vivid recollection of hearing about the invasion of Pearl Harbor on 7 December 1941.[1] He remembers hearing the news from a radio newscaster who interrupted a baseball game to make the announcement. Neisser considered this to be an accurate memory for several decades until he realized that there are no baseball games in December. Fifty years after the original event, Neisser suggests that he was likely listening to a football game at the time of the invasion announcement. He had apparently forgotten this detail and filled in the gap with the incorrect detail of a baseball game, perhaps because he was an avid baseball fan and this memory distortion was consistent with his personal interests and habit of listening to baseball on the radio.

Reconstructing an episode or a memory script is largely dependent on having appropriate cues. A cue is a reminder or hint about the nature of a particular event that helps in the reconstruction process. Cues can be smells, emotions, thoughts, pictures, diaries, or any other stimuli that assist in reconstructing an event. We know that we quickly forget most events and that the capacity to reconstruct an event can deteriorate rapidly with the passage of time. The primary reason we forget is that there are no cues to distinguish one event from another. That is, most events are routine, run of the mill, and there simply are not sufficient cues to permit the reconstruction of such blasé happenings. For example, remembering what you had for breakfast on a particular day four months ago is not possible when there is no cue to distinguish that breakfast from thousands other breakfasts. Of course, some people might claim to remember what they had for breakfast because they eat the same thing every day. However, such a person is operating from a script memory, not recalling a specific event.

Although we forget most events, we retain some for months, years, or even a lifetime. Memorable events are typically unique or they generate strong emotions. We may well remember a long past breakfast if that particular meal was somehow very different or emotionally charged. For example, you might never forget a breakfast in which you ate fried ants or a breakfast during which your lover proposed marriage. The uniqueness and importance of such an event provide cues that permit the reconstruction of the memory for that event over a long period. Frequently, thinking about or talking about an event can increase the ease with which a particular event is recalled.

Research indicates that memories of traumatic experiences, including memories of violence, tend to remain more vivid and consistent over time than memories of emotionally positive experiences, which progressively deteriorate. In describing this phenomenon, researchers from Dalhousie University referred to the "scars of memory" left by traumatic experiences.[2]

Although imperfect (memories are not "things"), this metaphor captures a quality of traumatic memories that victims of terrifying experiences may identity with — the indelible "scar" that these types of experiences can leave in the person's memory. Although scars can fade or become less distinct over time, they usually remain as reminders of a past trauma. Interestingly, scars also represent the healing process — moving from a painful, open wound to a healed scar.

Depending on the nature of the sexual assault, like a scar, it may stand out dramatically in a person's life and many of the details may be all too unforgettable, no matter how much the person may wish to forget about it. On the other hand, the details of some sex crimes, such as sexual touching and fondling during childhood, may become woven into the fabric of everyday life in ways that make the assaults seem commonplace at the time and less easily recalled.

Although we more readily remember vivid or unique experiences, vividness or uniqueness does not guarantee that you will reliably recall that event. Other factors figure into accurate reconstruction. Intense emotional reactions or altered states of consciousness (such as those caused by alcohol or drug intoxication) can affect recall to the point that little or no accurate memory of an event, including sexual assaults, is retained or accessible.

Emotional states and memory

YOUR EMOTIONAL STATE AT the time of an occurrence can affect the way in which the memory for that event is processed. We process emotionally stressful experiences differently than emotionally neutral events. Most people tend to remember stressful or upsetting experiences more readily than neutral events. Our emotional states can also serve as a memory cue. For example, when you are feeling particularly happy, you are more likely to remember past happy experiences. When depressed, you are more likely to recall negative, depressing experiences. This means that your current emotional state can affect the types of memories that you recall. For some of you, becoming upset or frightened, regardless of the cause, may cue a memory of the frightening sexual assault you experienced. You can see how people's lives can quickly become narrow if they attempt to avoid any sort of upsetting situation that could potentially cue distressing memories.

Extreme distress or fear appears to have unique effects on memory, some of which researchers still do not understand well. As we discussed in the context of PTSD, when a person goes through a life-threatening or extremely upsetting experience, which can include sexual assault, the body engages different mechanisms that alter the nature of perception as well as memory. Experiencing trauma causes a narrowing of the focus of attention during the traumatic event. When this occurs, the victim tends to focus on limited aspects of what is happening to the exclusion of other aspects of the experience. A victim may focus on external aspects of the threat, perhaps concentrating on the attacker or on a possible means of escape. During a traumatic assault, some victims focus primarily on their feelings, such as their fear, pain, or panic at the time. Some victims mentally escape or dissociate from what is happening by imagining they are in another place or time; for example, they may imagine themselves floating in space. The point of focus during a traumatic event has profound effects for later recall of the experience. Because we can explicitly remember only those things to which we have directed our attention, the victim's memory will be restricted to whatever was paid attention to during the sexual assault.

The intense emotions experienced during a traumatic event also can have an impact on memory after the event. As noted previously, some victims may experience "hypernesia," better than usual memory that may include a vivid reliving of the sexual assaults. When this occurs, memories of the assault feel outside of the victim's control, occurring without any conscious effort to recall them. In fact, the victim usually expends considerable effort trying to avoid the memories or any reminders of the past trauma. On the other hand, some victims may experience a loss of memory, or "amnesia," for some aspects of the traumatic event. Hypernesia for some details of the event and amnesia for other details can also co-occur. A very small proportion of victims experience a complete loss of memory for central aspects of the event or for the event having ever happened. This type of memory loss, which is too extensive to be explained by normal forgetfulness, is called "dissociative amnesia." Experts know little about why some people experience dissociative amnesia after a traumatic event. We do know that some people recover from dissociative amnesia; they later recall what happened to them, but precisely how this happens is not well-understood. We discuss these issues further in the following section pertaining to recovered memories.

Not only may the intense emotions felt during an event affect consolidation (storage) of memories at the time of the actual event, but your emotional state at the time of later recall can also affect reconstruction of the memory. When a person is recalling a traumatic event, the person may experience strong emotions associated with the event. On the one hand, these emotions may serve as cues for additional memories, but on the other hand, the intensity of these emotions can interfere with the person's ability to reconstruct the event fully. This can be important during a trial when you are required to testify about your experiences. If you are anxious and fearful on the stand, when asked questions about a traumatic event, your emotional arousal might cause some memory lapses or inaccurate recall. Part of the overall recovery process for some victims of sexual assault is developing the ability to recall the traumatic event without experiencing the overwhelmingly intense emotions that had usually been associated with it. Recall of the sexual assault may always be distressing, but you can lessen the degree of distress. As you will learn in upcoming chapters, preparation for court and the use of effective coping strategies can help you manage potential memory difficulties.

Physical condition and memory

OUR PHYSICAL CONDITION CAN affect the ability to recall events. A head injury, certain medical conditions, drugs, or alcohol can negatively affect our ability to remember. A person who receives a head injury during a sexual assault may have memory loss for all or part of the attack. A blow to the head that results in unconsciousness will obviously result in no memory for the period of unconsciousness, but it can also disrupt memory for events just prior to the head injury (retrograde amnesia) and for events following a return of consciousness (anterograde amnesia). Memories for events affected by amnesia are not necessarily lost permanently; victims may recover them in the weeks or years following the head injury. The extent of amnesia and ability to recall will depend on the severity of the head injury. The person's memory for the lost time period prior to the injury may come back over time in bits and pieces, although some permanent loss is possible. The greatest degree of memory impairment tends to occur right after the injury, with at least some improvement usually occurring over the next two to three years. In severe cases, impairment of learning and recall of new information may be permanent.

Other physical conditions can also negatively affect the memory process. It is common knowledge that a cerebral infarction (a stroke) or diseases, such as Alzheimer's, or other forms of dementia, can severely affect memory and the ability to learn new material. However, more benign, everyday conditions can also influence your recall ability. Any condition that negatively affects concentration or perceptual abilities, such as extreme fatigue or sleep deprivation, will diminish your capacity to remember, and age exacerbates these conditions. Fortunately, these sorts of memory impairments can be addressed by reducing stress and making improvements in diet, exercise, and sleep habits. Throughout this book, we make recommendations and outline strategies to improve your physical and emotional well-being; an additional benefit of this approach is to improve your ability to focus and concentrate. This will improve your capacity to learn and recall information, in turn, making you a more capable participant in your legal proceedings.

Another well-known cause of memory impairment is the use of substances, such as alcohol, street drugs, or certain medications. The extent of memory disturbance depends upon the type of substance, the amount consumed, interaction with other substances, and a person's biochemistry. Commonly, extreme alcohol intoxication results in severe memory impairment for events occurring during the period of intoxication or blackout. A victim who happens to be intoxicated during a sexual assault may not encode the experience well in memory. If this is your situation, you will have poor, or no memory for what happened while you were intoxicated. Unfortunately, your recall for this experience will not improve over time no matter what recall techniques you might try. Drinking moderate amounts of alcohol may or may not affect your memory. This will depend on how much you drank, over what period, what other substances you consumed, and how you are generally affected by alcohol consumption.

Some prescribed medications, such as sedatives, especially when taken in high doses or in combination with other drugs, also can negatively affect your encoding ability or your ability to provide coherent memories later on. The impact of recreational drug use on memory is unclear, but any drug use that alters perception or concentration can negatively affect the memory process and result in distorted or unclear recall. There are several substances known as "date rape" drugs that can also impair memory. Rohypnol (flunitrazepam), GHB (gamma hydroxybutyric acid), and Ketamine (ketamine hydrochloride) all cause significant perceptual disturbances and can cause blackouts, leaving the victim with no memory for that period of time. Again, effects of the drugs are variable, with victims possibly having no recall of an assault or only vague, incoherent memories.

Memory cues

AS NOTED ABOVE, RECONSTRUCTING or recalling an experience is largely dependent on having appropriate cues. These cues can be virtually anything you see, hear, smell, touch, taste, experience, or think about that somehow reminds you of a past event. Bodily sensations can serve as powerful cues to memories of a sexual assault. For example, a sexual assault victim who was anally penetrated may have vivid memories of the assault when touched on the rectum or the buttocks or when having a bowel movement, although the strength of repetitive cues, such as a bowel movement, tends to lessen or disappear over time.

Sometimes memory cues seem to come out of nowhere; a particular smell may suddenly trigger a forgotten detail about an assault, or a certain sound will produce a vivid image of your ordeal. On the other hand, you can purposefully expose yourself to potential memory cues and assist your recall. Returning to a childhood home or a school where someone sexually assaulted you might cue a flood of memories about what happened to you. In general, you are likely to find that the more frequently you think about, talk about, or write about a sexual assault, the more details you will remember. This is a natural aspect of recall; as you think about an event, you are likely to remember more details, and these details, in turn, can act as cues for further recall.

A similar recall process can occur during therapy, when discussion of the assaults and your personal history generates more cues, which, in turn, leads to further recall or reconstruction of details. These can be accurately reconstructed memories; however, inaccurate recall can also occur, especially if you feel pressured to recall past abuse or when highly suggestive or problematic therapeutic techniques are used. You should be wary of a therapist who suggests someone has sexually assaulted you when you have no specific memories of an assault having occurred. Similarly, be cautious of anyone who suggests that your healing depends upon recalling past abuse incidents that you do not now remember.

As discussed below, some therapeutic techniques may contaminate your memory, leading you to believe that things happened when they did not. It is also important to understand that your therapist cannot tell which memories are accurate and which are not. You should be wary of a therapist who reassures you that everything that you remember must be accurate; on the other hand, an overly skeptical therapist is not likely to be very helpful to you either. A well-informed mental health professional should take a more neutral position and inform clients that memories recovered in therapy may accurately reflect reality or may be partly true and partly inaccurate, or may be mistaken beliefs about events that never occurred ("pseudo" memories, as discussed below). Determining the objective truth of your memories to any degree of certainty may require some type of external validation, such as physical evidence or a witness. You may have to accept a degree of ambiguity and uncertainty about what has happened to you. Psychologically, your "felt truth" may be what is most important to you, even though this may never be objectively demonstrated or proven.

Enhancing recall

IT IS NATURAL THAT, with the passage of time, memories about specific experiences tend to fade. Although you may always remember that you were the victim of a sexual assault, you likely will forget some or many of the specific details, especially peripheral details, such as the colour of clothing, names, or dates.

A number of interview techniques or "aide memoirs" can improve recall and have a low risk of contaminating memories or prompting the recall of inaccurate details. These techniques consist of supplying particular kinds of cues, for example, drawing a floor plan of the place in which an assault took place can help cue accurate memories. Another technique has the victim remember the event in question as if watching it from the outside. When participating in legal proceedings, you may encounter a police officer or other interviewer who uses these or similar techniques to assist you in reconstructing your story.

Numerous other techniques, offered as ways to improve your memory, can actually result in contamination of your recall. Use of these types of techniques can be particularly problematic in legal proceedings, because they raise questions or doubts about the accuracy of your recollections. One such familiar technique is hypnosis. Practitioners conduct hypnosis in a variety of ways, and for many different purposes including behaviour change, such as smoking cessation. In a hypnotic trance, you become very relaxed and more open to suggestion by the hypnotist. Although research does not support the efficacy of hypnosis to recover traumatic memories or to improve the accuracy of recall, some continue to use it for these purposes. Because of the suggestive context in which hypnosis takes place, the hypnotized subject is vulnerable to various distortions in memory. The risk of memory distortion appears to outweigh the chances of obtaining useful information, making this a particularly perilous venture for anyone involved, or contemplating becoming involved, in the court process. In light of these risks, defence counsel will likely question the validity and reliability of any hypnotically induced details of a sexual assault. Due to the potential problems associated with hypnosis, we recommend that it be avoided as a memory enhancement technique by anyone participating in the legal process.

Guided imagery is a technique similar to hypnosis that can be very useful as a relaxation technique or as an aid to self-exploration. Although guided imagery may be helpful in therapy, it can also contaminate memory retrieval if it is overly suggestive. Relaxing and imagining yourself in the room where the offender assaulted you can help you remember details of what happened in that place — the image of the room could serve as an important memory reconstruction cue. However, if the image is "guided" by someone else, this can be problematic. It is not appropriate for someone to make specific suggestions about what may be in the room, what may have happened in the room, or how you may feel. You may incorporate these types of suggestions into your memory, whether or not they represent what actually happened.

Dream interpretation and the symbolic interpretation of drawings can also be useful techniques for self-exploration and self-understanding. However, the court will not consider these therapeutic techniques a reliable source of memory in court for the same reasons discussed above; the risk of memory contamination is unacceptably high.

From a therapeutic point of view, participating in group-counselling sessions or group discussions with other victims of sexual assault can be a very helpful process. Relating to others who have had similar experiences can be empowering and provide a context in which your story can be sympathetically heard. However, anyone who has memory loss related to past sexual assault experiences should be cautious about participating in a group before legal proceedings are completed. The group context where you hear many stories that may be similar to yours can be very suggestive to someone with few memories of one's own. In this instance, the potential exists for creating a false or unreliable memory. Those who have clear memories of their experiences or those who have completed the court process would not have the same type of concerns.

Regardless of which memory retrieval strategies you might use, there are circumstances in which the reconstruction of an event will be limited or impossible. As noted above, if a sexual assault occurred when you were extremely intoxicated or under the influence of a sedative or hypnotic drug, a memory may not have developed in the first place, so subsequent recall will not be possible. A similar situation arises when a victim "dissociates" during the course of the assault. Dissociation is a significant alteration in the way in which you perceive your environment and may occur at times of extreme trauma or stress. The degree of dissociation may vary from a person being aware of their circumstances and details of the assault but feeling it was somehow not real, to cases where the victim mentally leaves the event so that no attention was focused on the assault at all. In the latter case, the lack of attention focused on the assault will result in no memory being established, and a subsequent inability to recall the assault itself. You will only be able to recall those things that were the focus of your attention.

For some of you, the challenge may be to accept the reality of your assault while understanding that you may never know the details of what happened. Without sufficient memories, pursuing your case in criminal court may not be a viable option. Legal action will depend upon the specifics of your case and the availability of evidence other than your testimony. Talk to a lawyer about your circumstances to determine if you have a sufficient legal case. Since the standard of proof is significantly lower in civil court, you may be able to proceed civilly even if you cannot take your case to criminal court. If you are unable to remember the specifics of your experience, do not blame or criticize yourself; instead work on managing the emotions associated with the assault and on moving your life forward.

The recovered memory controversy

AS NOTED ABOVE, VICTIMS of traumatic experiences, including some types of sexual assaults, can develop amnesia for all or part of the traumatizing event. Some individuals have reported, even after many decades of being unable to recall the details of a sexual assault, that they have "recovered" their lost memory of what happened to them. These accounts began occurring with increased frequency during the early 1990s, primarily among adults who indicated that they had recovered memories of sexual abuse during childhood or adolescence, even though they had not previously remembered these experiences. These recovered memories were not of experiences merely forgotten, or of incidents put in the "back of the mind." The initial lack of recall extended beyond normal forgetting. These were experiences that, if previously asked about, the person would have honestly denied that the events had happened. In fact, many of these recovered memories were very distressing for the person who remembered them — memories one wanted to disbelieve or forget.

The phenomenon of recovered memories became very controversial during the 1990s. Some scientists and mental health professionals did not believe this type of memory recovery could occur. These professionals proposed that such memories were not authentic, but were "pseudo-memories" or "created" memories of childhood sexual assault that the complainants believed to be true even though the event or events had not happened. The position of these skeptical professionals was widely disseminated by a group, the False Memory Syndrome Foundation (FMSF), which advocated for those who stood accused of crimes based on recovered memories. FMSF outlined criteria that it said identified a syndrome associated with the creation of "false memories." However, it is important to note that mainstream psychiatry and psychology has not recognized this as a legitimate syndrome, so to date it is not a designated mental disorder and there is no validated diagnostic tool to provide evidence of false memory.

An acrimonious debate arose in reaction to the position put forward by FMSF, and created camps of experts on both sides of the issue. The notion of "false" or "created" memories, which we refer to as pseudo-memories, was hotly contested with some mental health professionals claiming that pseudo-memories of sexual abuse or sexual assaults do not occur. This is clearly not the case as studies have demonstrated that memory is susceptible to suggestion. We know what people remember seeing is influenced by what they are told they saw, what they hope they saw, and what they expected to have seen. A person can create a pseudo-memory of an event that did not happen and come to believe that the event actually did occur. Furthermore, a pseudo-memory can be extremely vivid and can evoke physical sensations and emotional reactions that seem to correspond to an actual event even when there was no actual historical event. A created memory or pseudo-memory can feel as real as an actual memory and, consequently, can be virtually indistinguishable from an actual memory.

On the other hand, there is also evidence that a person can have no recollection of a traumatic event, and then later recover an accurate, legitimate memory of the event. The therapeutic literature abounds with case histories of people who have recovered memories that appear to be legitimate. Unfortunately, most of these cases do not lend themselves to objective verification, leaving the question of legitimacy unanswered. However, there are some cases in which the historical accuracy of a recovered memory of sexual assault has been verified.[3] To date experts understand the mechanisms of recovered memory poorly, and much scientific work remains to be done before we will reliably be able to distinguish a pseudo-memory from an authentic recovered memory.

Since the early 1990s, the courts in Canada have had to confront these issues head on and have drawn some preliminary lines in the sand. Although the court has recognized the possibility of legitimately recovered memories, there has also been caution about the risk of pseudo-memories that do not reflect historical reality. Because it is very difficult, and sometimes impossible, to distinguish a pseudo-memory from an actual true recovery from amnesia, these cases remain very controversial. Hence, when a complainant makes an allegation of sexual abuse after a period of having no memory of the event, the court tries to determine if it is a case of traumatic amnesia or some other sort of forgetting. The situation where a person always remembered being abused but had not thought about the abuse in many years and then had occasion to remember it is different from a situation in which the person suddenly remembers abuse but previously had no prior knowledge or memory of ever having been abused. It may also be important to consider whether all or only part of the abuse experience was forgotten, or whether only the most traumatic parts were forgotten.

Even though a Crown prosecutor may believe that the complaint represents a legitimate case of memory recovered after amnesia, the prosecutor may decide not to proceed with criminal charges due to the controversy surrounding this type of evidence. The Crown may believe that the challenges presented by the defence counsel to this kind of recall evidence will diminish the likelihood of a successful prosecution and might expose the complainant to an emotionally difficult cross-examination. Some jurisdictions have developed policies that caution against proceeding with criminal prosecution in these cases unless there is corroborating evidence. Because the burden of proof is less stringent in civil litigation, a recovered memory case has a greater likelihood of proceeding in that court. Nevertheless, these cases will likely continue to provoke controversy and raise difficult legal questions.

Memory in the courtroom

THE VAGARIES OF HUMAN memory are not always compatible with the long established procedural needs and legal rules of the court. The mind is not a reliable recording device that we can count on for accuracy and clarity. There are changes in memory over time; we forget some details and remember new information, and this is to be expected. However, if your account of what happened is different in your various statements or testimony, the defence is likely to emphasize these inconsistencies and use them to call your credibility into question. In a courtroom, authorities will question your memory with a rigour that you typically do not experience in your everyday life. It is important to be prepared to address any inconsistencies in your testimony. Some discrepancies in your recall are likely to occur, so try not to be rattled or to take personally any questions about incongruities. Answer in an honest and straightforward manner, as most minor inconsistencies can be explained. On the other hand, if the magnitude of discrepancy is great, there may be some serious problems with the evidence, and this could greatly affect your case.

We address the issues of testifying and how best to tell your story in a later chapter but, to begin, you can use some practical strategies to organize and consolidate your recollections. Because memory tends to fade over time, if you are able to write out or record a detailed description of what happened soon after the sexual assault occurred, this will serve as an excellent memory aid for your future recall. Keeping a log of various memories as you recall them can also be helpful. You may be questioned specifically about the source of your memories, so keep track of when and how you recalled a particular memory. Record where you were and what was happening at the time of the recall, and make note of anything specific that cued the memory. The source or origin of your memories may be important in evaluating their reliability or credibility. Sometimes memories seem to come out of nowhere, with no identifiable cue. In these cases, record the circumstances of your recall. It is important to understand, however, that recordings of this type become evidence in your case and therefore must not be altered or destroyed. Later chapters will expand on the issues of evidence, disclosure, and record keeping.

RELATIONSHIP DYNAMICS

YOUR HISTORY MAY MAKE it hard to believe that anyone in a position of authority will be genuinely helpful to you. However, try to maintain an open mind and allow yourself to accept assistance when it is offered. Hopefully, you will receive helpful information and emotionally supportive responses from at least some of the people you encounter in the legal system and from your family and friends. On the other hand, it is also likely that some of the responses that you receive from others will seem more of an impediment than a help to you. The bottom line is that interpersonal stress or conflict is likely to occur during legal proceedings.

If criminal or civil proceedings move to the trial stage, you will encounter a number of different courtroom professionals. You may get to know some of them better than others. You will feel a personal connection with some people, but not others, and vice versa. It is worth remembering that they are all there in a professional capacity, each with a specific role and duties. Their job is not to befriend you but to make the process proceed fairly and smoothly. Depending on the person's role, establishing more than a professional relationship with a complainant could be inappropriate or unethical.

Apart from the complainant (or plaintiff in civil proceedings) and the accused (or defendant in civil cases), some or all of the following people are likely to be involved in courtroom proceedings. We will examine the function of these courtroom personnel in more depth as we move through relevant legal procedures in subsequent chapters. To see more in-depth descriptions of their roles you can refer to Appendix 5.

- Crown counsel — the lawyer who represents the state in prosecuting offenders.
- Defence counsel — the lawyer who represents the accused and makes sure they get a fair trial.
- Your lawyer — the lawyer who represents you in civil litigation. You do not typically have your own lawyer in a criminal case, but can retain one to advise you on specific issues.
- Judge — the person who ensures that the rules are followed, that the rights of the accused are protected, and that the interests of justice are served.
- Jury — twelve ordinary citizens who sit through the trial, listen to the facts presented and then make a decision about guilt or acquittal. Not all trials have a jury.
- Court clerk — manages the practical issues in a courtroom, for example, arranges for water, microphones, and electronic equipment, hands exhibits to witnesses, keeps records of the process, and prepares court participants for the entry of the judge.

- Court reporter — records and transcribes everything that is said while court is in session.
- Sheriff — physically protects the participants and the public from attack or intimidation. Can summon others into the courtroom in the event of a crisis.

Intentionally or not, some of these people and/or friends and family may be insensitive and hurtful when interacting with sexual assault victims. This happens often enough that the psychological literature has labelled it as "secondary victimization." Although we consider this to be a very important concept, we have chosen to refer to this as a source of interpersonal stress, rather than repeatedly using the term secondary victimization. We want to avoid equating or confusing the impact of insensitive or hurtful comments from others with the impact of sexual victimization. These are very different types of experiences with different effects. We also caution you not to fall into the "victim trap" of viewing virtually every negative or upsetting event in your life as examples of further victimization. This can lead to a distorted view of the daily tribulations that are a normal part of everyone's life. Viewing yourself as a victim to whom bad things "just happen" is an act of giving power and control over your life to others. Living your life in a healthy manner involves taking control where you can, being responsible for your own actions, and not being preoccupied by things out of your control.

Of course, during legal proceedings you will continue to interact with people outside the court system — your family, friends, co-workers, physicians, and perhaps mental health professionals. Throughout this book, we emphasize the importance of reaching out to others in your life and creating a network to support you through the legal process. Along with the support that relationships can afford you, they can also be the source of stress and tension. In Chapter 2, we alluded to the challenges posed by mistrust and misunderstandings following a sexual assault, particularly as these issues apply to the intimate relationships of family and friends. Participating in legal proceedings is likely to pose additional relationship stresses and can strain the relationships with those closest to you.

Ways you may experience interpersonal stress

VICTIMS OF SEXUAL CRIMES often encounter those who either deny or disbelieve their accounts of what happened. It is virtually inevitable that your participation in the criminal or civil justice system will raise questions that subtly or directly suggest that you are mistaken, lying, or exaggerating your experiences and how they affected you. As discussed below, legal language dictates that the court will refer to the "alleged" sexual crimes. Being the complainant, your motivations and actions will come under scrutiny. This is not a personal attack on you; it reflects an attempt to remain fair and impartial toward both the victim and the accused offender until the court gives its decision. Nonetheless, this type of language and scrutiny can leave you feeling disbelieved by others and unsure of yourself.

Some of the people close to you or people you encounter in the legal system may minimize or discount what happened to you and its impact on your life. Some may suggest that your experience was "no big deal" or that you should "get over it" and move on with your life. Friends and family members may also say or imply that you "should be over it by now." You may feel stigmatized or misunderstood when others appear to judge your reactions negatively. Some may criticize or ridicule you for being unable to concentrate, for being tearful, or for expressing your distress. In the course of civil litigation, people could suggest that your psychological symptoms reflect a "desire for financial gain, attention, or unwarranted sympathy."[4] These types of dismissive responses minimize the victim's emotional experience and can contribute to feelings of self-blame, inadequacy, anger, or withdrawal.

Directly or indirectly, people may attempt to shift the blame for the sexual crime onto the victim, rather than the offender, sometimes reflecting societal and cultural myths regarding sexual crimes. Even when people do not intend to blame the victim, being asked certain "why" questions about a sexual assault could trigger feelings of self-blame. You might feel blamed if someone asks why you went home with someone you met in a bar, or why you wore a short skirt. Similarly, being asked why you did not report childhood sexual abuse to an authority figure at the time can be guilt-inducing.

Interpersonal stress can also occur if authorities deny you assistance, services, or the compensation that you expect. One of the most difficult aspects of participating in lengthy legal proceedings is uncertainty about the outcome. Sometimes, the result may not be what you hoped for or expected. A legal technicality or unforeseen circumstance can lead to a judgment that seems neither just nor fair. Complainants sometimes feel "victimized all over again" when they go through a long, drawn-out, and extremely stressful legal proceeding with an unsatisfying decision or judgment.

Because communication between people is always a two-way street, others' interactions with you can go off course because of misperceptions, misunderstandings, or miscommunication by either party. You cannot control the behaviour of others, but you can change your own behaviours in a way that will decrease the likelihood of negative responses from others. Understanding the perspective of others and your own emotional landscape can begin a shift in perspective that also changes the impact others have on you. Below, we discuss the sources of stress that you may experience either in your close social or family relationships or with those that you encounter during the legal process, and we suggest some strategies that may help in these situations.

REASONS FOR NEGATIVITY

IT IS HARD NOT to take personally a negative response from someone else. Most of us want to be perceived in a positive light and are hurt when another person insults, ignores, or demeans us in some manner. When dealing with people whom we are meeting for the first time, or who only know us superficially, it is worth remembering that their behaviour toward us is based on limited information because they hardly know us; this is generally true of the professionals whom you will encounter. You will see that their responses often have more to do with their own circumstances than with your personal qualities; this also generally holds true for family and friends who care about us and know us much better. Below we address a few of the reasons why someone in the justice system, and others, might treat you poorly, and none of them in any way reflect your personal qualities.

Ignorance

AT LEAST SOME INSENSITIVE responses reflect "sheer ignorance" or lack of experience in dealing with traumatic events.[5] Some people who have no knowledge or experience related to victimization simply do not understand the effects of sexual assault. Due to their lack of understanding, people may unintentionally make hurtful, ill-informed comments, or they may exhibit little patience with your emotional struggles. People in your support system, from whom you may most need assistance, may inadvertently say hurtful, unsupportive things because they lack understanding about the kind of trauma you have experienced. Although insensitive comments by friends and family can sometimes be intentional, it is important to realize that their comments often may simply reflect their lack of knowledge.

Ignorance and insensitivity are not limited to non-professionals. Police officers, and legal and mental health professionals sometimes show surprising ignorance and insensitivity to the needs of sexual assault victims. This situation has improved significantly during the past twenty years as institutions provide courses and training to educate professionals about the dynamics of sexual assault and the needs of victims. Nonetheless, you may encounter some legal personnel or professionals who display obvious ignorance or insensitivity toward you.

Professional burnout

BURNOUT AMONG HELPING PROFESSIONALS is one factor that can lead them to treat you in an inappropriate or insensitive manner. Front-line workers, such as social workers, nurses, police officers, and government employees are often underpaid, overworked, and undervalued. Some of these professionals, who often work in extremely stressful circumstances, may be emotionally depleted and therefore unable to respond with sensitivity to your psychological and physical needs as a victim of a sexual crime. Some understanding of their circumstances can go a long way in establishing sympathy and rapport with them. As noted below, close friends and family members can also "burn out" when providing support over long stretches of time.

Limited psychological resources

SOME PEOPLE SIMPLY DO not have the psychological or physical resources needed to provide emotional support to a victim. Family and friends who have their own emotional or physical challenges may be so overwhelmed by their own issues that they do not have sufficient resources or patience to assist you. Given their own stress and limited resources, their responses to you may be, at times, non-supportive or hurtful.

Some individuals deal with stress by attempting to deny or discount the difficult aspects of life. If your friends or family depend on this type of coping strategy, they may attempt to ignore what you have experienced or minimize the extent of its negative consequences. Given these dynamics, they may be more apt to tell you to "just get over it" and "get on with your life."

Cultural beliefs and myths

HURTFUL AND INSENSITIVE COMMENTS from others often reflect wider cultural beliefs and myths. For example, some people hold to a "just-world philosophy."[6] This belief suggests that people "get what they deserve and deserve what they get." This philosophy is one way to make sense of the inexplicable, and serves to quell the fear that anyone can be a victim. There are also numerous rape myths including beliefs that "no means yes" or that wearing provocative clothes encourages attack. Related to pervasive homophobia in our culture, there also is a belief that males who are sexually assaulted by other males are somehow unmanly or "latent homosexuals." Some cultures continue to place extreme emphasis and value on a female's virginity. Identifying a daughter's worth solely based on her virginity has led families to disown her when she disclosed sexual abuse within the family. You may encounter people, either among your friends and family or among those from whom you may seek assistance, who continue to hold cultural beliefs and myths that lead to criticism or blaming of victims of sexual crimes.

EMOTIONAL BUOYANCY

IT IS IMPORTANT TO learn healthy ways of responding to inappropriate or negative comments, and to counter your feelings of being hurt, misunderstood, or denigrated. Failure to do this can lead to increasing feelings of victimization and self-blame. It can also impede your ability to tell your story and advocate for yourself in court. Instead of being weighed down by the negativity you encounter, you can strive to be emotionally buoyant or resilient. This advice applies equally to circumstances where people's comments are not mean-spirited but are perceived by you as hurtful. Sometimes statements are so subtle or guileless that we are not immediately aware why we are upset. Recognizing when people are making inaccurate, hurtful, or insensitive comments is the first step to helping yourself. Below are several strategies you can use when you encounter insensitive remarks. You will find similar strategies reiterated and discussed in more detail in Chapter 5. Many of the strategies outlined in the context of the challenges of the legal process will apply equally well in other circumstances as you go forward with your life.

De-personalize comments

IT CAN BE HELPFUL for you to distance yourself both emotionally and mentally from negative comments. You can do this by first considering the source of the comments. Do they reflect the other person's ignorance of sexual crimes, limited psychological resources, professional burnout, or inappropriate cultural beliefs or myths? Note when insensitive comments are a reflection of the other person's issues or the legal process, rather than a reflection of you. Being able to adopt this perspective, rather than automatically assuming such statements reflect your reality, can help you deal more effectively with these situations. This does not mean that you will be untroubled by insensitive remarks by others, but the goal is to bounce back and not to be devastated by them.

Analyze your own reactions

VICTIMS OF SEXUAL CRIMES can be understandably distrustful of others, and this, in turn, can make it hard to believe that anyone will be genuinely helpful to you. The experiences of some victims make them particularly angry and distrustful of authority figures or government officials, the very people they will be dealing with in legal proceedings. Your past negative experiences can lead you to perceive rejection or insensitivity in others even when unintended, or you may be overly defensive and particularly sensitive to people's remarks. On the other hand, you may have a tendency to become overly dependent on others, which may frighten you and lead you to push them away at crucial times. Whatever your personal dynamics, your way of interacting with others will affect the way others interact with you, and the way you interpret their responses to you. This is true for all of us. It is important to keep this in mind; we all need to take responsibility for our role in communicating with others.

When you react emotionally to comments by others, examine your responses. Ask yourself what pushed your buttons, what led you to feel upset, angry, depressed, guilty, or embarrassed. Recognize where you have some responsibility for a negative exchange, and where the responsibility lies chiefly with the other person. Eleanor Roosevelt once said, "No one can make you feel guilty without your consent." You can apply this general notion to virtually every emotional response you may have. Other people do not "make" us feel a certain way; we participate in creating our reactions. When you feel someone is pushing your buttons, look more closely at yourself. If you feel guilty in response to something said to you, examine your underlying thoughts associated with self-blame. If you feel ashamed for crying, look at what crying in the presence of others means to you. You may discover thoughts and beliefs that you have internalized or taken as your own based on your experiences or based on cultural beliefs, such as that crying in public reflects weakness. You may struggle with self-blame because the person who sexually assaulted you repeatedly shifted the blame to you, as offenders often do — "She was asking for it." As a result, you may be quick to blame yourself or to perceive blame when none is intended. Uncovering and challenging these underlying beliefs can help you gain a healthier perception of yourself and the things that people say to you. Turn negative encounters into experiences that help you grow.

Internally challenge and counteract negative messages

WHENEVER YOU ENCOUNTER INAPPROPRIATE negative messages from others, or negative beliefs of your own, it helps to counter with realistic, positive, or compassionate thoughts. One strategy is to contradict, in your own self-talk, the negative message that you received or the negative thought that you had. For example, when you perceive that you are being told either directly or indirectly that the sexual assault was your fault, you might repeat to yourself (and to the other person, if appropriate), "I am not responsible for the assault I experienced; the offender is." If someone says that you should "get over it now," you might say to yourself, "This person does not understand my situation. I am in the process of recovery. I need to deal with this in my own way." Anytime you find yourself feeling self-blame or guilt in response to the comments of others, you can repeat to yourself, "No one can make me feel guilty without my consent." Refuse to agree with inappropriate guilt-inducing thoughts. Countering negativity with positive statements and compassion builds strength as opposed to falling into an energy-sapping state of constant anger or self-denigration.

Avoid retaliation

WHEN SOMEONE UPSETS YOU with a comment, you may react by feeling angry and want to strike back either verbally or physically. However, it is not likely that either of these responses will be helpful to your recovery or to the legal proceedings. Although angry retaliation might feel good in the heat of the moment, these types of responses will ultimately undermine your recovery and your legal case. As Dr. Matsakis, author of an excellent handbook for victims of trauma, notes, "even when your desire to retaliate is entirely justified, an aggressive response only confirms the other person's belief that you are 'a nut case' or otherwise undeserving of assistance — which can lead to that person withholding what you in fact deserve and need."[7] It is to your benefit to avoid retaliation, and the strategies discussed above can help defuse situations that might otherwise lead to angry outbursts.

Challenge inappropriate comments

AVOIDING RETALIATION DOES NOT mean that you should passively absorb the ill-treatment by others. It is entirely appropriate and empowering to question or challenge inappropriate comments or remarks from others. If you are not sure about the meaning or intention of a particular comment, you can ask the person to explain. In a discussion about feeling shamed, Psychologist Charlotte Kasl offers some excellent suggestions of responses you might consider.[8] For example, if you are feeling inappropriately criticized or shamed, you could say: "It's not all right to talk to me like that," or "Please ask me what you want without all the innuendoes about how I did it wrong." You could also ask for clarification of intent by saying, "Could you tell me what you meant by that?" or even "That feels like a shaming remark — was that your intention?" Finally, if you do not like how you are feeling in response to someone's comments let the person know that you are feeling uncomfortable and then stop the conversation or change topics.

Learn to recognize constructive criticism

AS IS TRUE ABOUT most aspects of our lives and most topics in this book, the issues addressed in the preceding discussion are more complex than they may first appear. We have presented this information to alert you to the kinds of insensitive comments that you may encounter from others who have little compassion for, or understanding of, sexual victimization. It is important for you to counter them in ways that help you expose the underlying ignorance or insensitivity that provoked them, or to recognize your own negative self-perceptions.

Nevertheless, you should not automatically dismiss every negative comment made to you as representing the other person's ignorance or lack of understanding. Any of us can get stuck in emotionally unhealthy places, and we all occasionally rely on unhealthy coping tactics. It can be helpful if these tactics are revealed and challenged. If you automatically dismiss helpful comments and challenges to your assumptions as representing insensitivity or ignorance, you are in danger of remaining stuck in the same place, rather than moving forward in your healing journey. Learning to evaluate comments made by others and fairly deciding which ones to dismiss and which ones to consider further, can be a benefit. Feedback from a trusted friend, family member, or counsellor may assist you in finding the right balance between acceptance and rejection of others' comments. This is neither a simple nor a straightforward task, but you can accept it as a challenge. As you get better at separating constructive from hurtful criticism, you will grow as a person and be better able to cope more effectively.

UNIQUE STRESSORS

YOU ARE LIKELY TO encounter some strains and stresses in the court system that you are unaccustomed to in other parts of your life. These may ebb and flow during the process, but they typically begin when you first seriously consider participating in either criminal or civil proceedings. Stress is likely to intensify at predictable stages of the process, such as the initial police interviews, examinations for discovery in civil litigation, participation in court hearings, and appearing at the trial. In most cases, this stress will dissipate after the legal process ends. Some clinicians suggest that the stress associated with legal proceedings greatly diminishes within six months of the end of the criminal case or the civil claim settlement. Recovery depends upon the degree of stress experienced, the complainant's resilience, the available emotional support, and the outcome of the legal case.

It is important to appreciate that participating in the criminal justice system or in civil litigation is inherently a stressful process. We repeat this point often, not to frighten you away from participation, but to help you make decisions with your eyes wide open and to help you prepare yourself for the challenges presented by a lengthy court case. There are both similarities and differences in the types of stressors you will encounter in criminal proceedings as compared to those in civil litigation. We point out important differences as they arise. To help clarify these issues, in the following discussions we use the term complainant to describe the role of the victim in court proceedings generally (both criminal and civil), and we use the term plaintiff when specifically referring to civil proceedings.

Mental health professionals who work with victims involved in legal proceedings have called attention to the high level of stress frequently experienced. Some have suggested that the mental health profession should designate a specific diagnosis to recognize the stress caused by participation in the legal process.[9] To capture the anxiety and potential harm the civil litigation process can cause, professionals coined the term "critogenesis," to emphasize "intrinsic and often inescapable harms caused by the litigation process itself."[10] Although these professionals were referring primarily to plaintiffs in civil litigation, most of their comments also apply to complainants in criminal cases. The take-home message is that no one should take lightly participation in the legal process, criminal or civil. It is a highly stressful experience, a time of significant challenges and for some victims a time of crisis.

The adversarial proceedings

THE ADVERSARIAL NATURE OF the legal system can cause considerable anxiety and stress. Those involved do not automatically consider your version of events as being either accurate or true. From the outset, the court will refer to the crime you have reported as the "alleged" sexual assault. This designation is not meant to be either challenging or insulting to you; it merely reflects a basic tenet of our legal system: the court considers all accused persons innocent until proven guilty.

It can be difficult to have your version of events and your perceptions closely scrutinized. Questioning by an opposing lawyer can be intimidating. The wording of questions, as well as repeated questions, can be confusing. Given the dynamics of the adversarial process, you may feel verbally attacked and disbelieved during the court process. Sometimes you may feel as though you, the victim, are the one on trial. What may feel like a direct personal attack on you, can also be seen as the opposing counsel doing what is needed to best defend a client; in other words, one is doing the job one was hired to do. To the extent that you can keep this in mind and avoid personalizing the questioning, you can reduce the distress you are likely to feel.

Loss of privacy

TALKING ABOUT ONE'S SEXUAL experiences is difficult in the best of circumstances, but when the discussion of these private experiences is before strangers in a courtroom or the alleged offender, this can be extraordinarily stressful and painful. In subsequent chapters we discuss in considerable detail both the limitations and protection of your privacy in criminal and civil cases. Your identity can be protected from disclosure outside the courtroom, and a publication ban can be used to limit specific information from becoming public. Criminal court has protections that limit access to your private records and aspects of your past including sexual history. In civil court the rules are different and your life becomes more of an "open book." Being aware of these privacy issues can help you understand your rights and perhaps prepare you for a level of personal exposure you may not have encountered before.

Length of the process

LEGAL PROCEEDINGS CAN OFTEN be a lengthy process. Procedures, examinations, tactics, and delays sometimes stretch legal proceedings over several years. Some civil litigation cases have gone on for over a decade. Criminal proceedings tend to average one to two years, but can extend over longer periods. The numerous delays inherent in the legal process can result in rising and falling expectations that may seem like an emotional roller coaster.[11] You may mentally and emotionally prepare yourself, and arrange your life to meet a scheduled court date, such as the beginning of the trial, only to have the date postponed as it nears. This can sap your energy and be demoralizing. It will be important for you to face the likelihood of delays from the beginning. You should develop alternative actions and plans in the event of cancellations and postponements to help mitigate your disappointment. Putting positive, healthy coping strategies into place beforehand can help reduce stress and minimize the risk of turning to unhealthy ways of coping, such as using drugs or alcohol to manage emotional turmoil.

Some complainants remain largely focused on thoughts and feelings related to the sexual crimes throughout much of the legal process, which can significantly increase their stress. The stress of prolonged proceedings may also serve to exacerbate or further entrench symptoms of PTSD, depression, or other difficulties related to the sexual assault. We recommend that you work out a schedule for yourself when you embark on legal proceedings, and outline how you are going to fit this process into your life. It will be very important to your well-being that you not try to do more than you reasonably can do during this time of your life. It will also be important for you to schedule regular healthy, productive, fun, and distracting activities so you do not focus only on painful, difficult issues. Healthy ways of containing or compartmentalizing your thoughts and feelings are invaluable short-term coping strategies.

Over-focus on damages

ONE POTENTIALLY DETRIMENTAL ASPECT of the legal process is its primary focus on the injuries incurred by the complainant or plaintiff. Although there is some focus in criminal court on the physical and psychological injuries suffered by the victim of a sexual assault, this is particularly a concern in civil proceedings. The central issue in civil litigation is the harm or damage suffered by the plaintiff as a result of the sexual assault. The litigation process highlights psychological difficulties and problems in daily functioning. This can cause a notable shift in perspective for the victim. Some individuals, who have begun their recovery before attending court, have their optimism and confidence undermined by the persistent message that they are emotionally damaged. Hearing consistently negative messages from respected professionals can quickly demoralize a person and make it easy to adopt a "sick role." Hearing discussions of a poor prognosis (predictions about your future functioning) can increase one's feelings of hopelessness and powerlessness. This negative focus then becomes a self-fulfilling prophecy; the more an individual hears about being damaged, the more likely one is to doubt oneself and the less likely one is to take the steps necessary for recovery.

Once again, knowledge can be a powerful aid. Understanding the focus on damages in civil litigation can help you prepare to balance the ledger. Keep in mind that the focus of litigation is skewed; it represents only one perspective on you and your life. Adopt a wider perspective. You are more than the legal process will portray. Prepare a list of positive, valuable aspects of yourself and keep it posted where you will see it frequently. Repeat positive affirmations to yourself that you can really believe in. Seek out friends and companions who help reflect your worthy qualities and believe in yourself. Do not despair; the court process will end and your life will go on.

Negative impact on family, friends, and support system

AS NOTED ABOVE, YOU may feel misunderstood or inappropriately criticized by those close to you. As you relate to your family, friends, and others, it is important to keep in mind that participating in the legal process affects not only the complainants, but also those who function as their primary support system. The court process and its related stress can strain or disrupt relationships with your family and friends. Some people close to you may "burn out" in their attempts to help you deal with the challenges. Disruptions can also occur in your intimate sexual relationships. Focusing on your experiences of past sexual victimization can raise thoughts and feelings that interfere with your current sexual relationships. To reduce interpersonal tensions in these situations, keep lines of communication open with your intimate partner, friends, and family. It is also important to have a broad-based support system, so that you do not over-rely on any one person. Make space in your life to interact with family and friends in ways that do not focus your negative experiences or your emotional distress — take time to relax and play together. Be aware that people in your support network, including your closest family members, will need breaks of their own to recharge their energy. When you are feeling emotionally needy, it can be hard to see the needs of others. You may resent it when those close to you attend to their own needs, or you may feel abandoned. Try to balance your needs with the needs of those close to you.

You will also benefit from being clear about your own boundaries and your own limitations. Those close to you may have strong reactions to your victimization. It is not your role or responsibility to take care of or "fix" these emotional responses. Instead, you may need to suggest resources that they can draw from to help them cope more effectively. In our resource guide in Appendix 4, we provide a list of self-help references that offer this type of assistance. Individual, couple, or family counselling sessions can be very helpful to provide emotional support and information about victimization to partners or family members.

UNIQUE BENEFITS

IN LIGHT OF THE possible challenges outlined above, one might ask, "Why bother with legal proceedings?" Beyond punishment of the offender, and potential financial compensation through civil litigation, the legal process can "provide an opportunity for an individual to stand up for her or himself and to hold accountable those who have wronged and/or damaged him or her."[12] The legal process provides an opportunity for a victim to feel empowered by taking an active role against the offender. Making an informed decision to report your assault to the police or to launch a civil suit may represent, or actually help create, a shift in your self-perception from that of a passive, silent victim to that of a person who is asserting one's right to make a statement and to seek redress. Having your voice heard by the justice system can be very empowering.[13] Your actions may also serve a greater good of preventing future assaults by the offender, or changing social policies for the better. Individuals who enter the legal process by choice, with realistic expectations and goals, and who obtain what they consider an equitable outcome can feel vindicated and empowered by the process. These complainants are likely to experience a restored sense of personal integrity through enhanced self-esteem, feelings of restitution, and increased social acceptability.[14]

Lenhart and Shrier have identified the following characteristics in plaintiffs who have fared well emotionally in the civil litigation process.[15] We believe these personal strategies will also apply to complainants in the criminal justice system:

- Setting realistic goals
- Being able to attain and maintain some sense of control in the litigation process
- Having adequate social support
- Focusing on addressing psychological concerns and restoring equilibrium in your life independent of the litigation process
- Acknowledging and adequately coping with the inevitable losses, even when litigation has a favourable outcome

As much as possible, participation in legal proceedings should be an informed decision that takes into account your overall well-being: physical, emotional, interpersonal, financial, and spiritual. Because the legal process entails considerable stress and inevitable costs or losses, along with potential benefits, participation, either criminal or civil, should begin with a cost/benefit analysis in which you assess your personal and interpersonal resources. As you read more about the process in the following chapters, you will be in a better position to make these judgments.

VIGNETTE FOUR: MEMORY ISSUES

THE VIGNETTE DESCRIBED AT the beginning of this chapter provides an example of memory loss that mental health professionals call dissociative amnesia. Carol, the woman sexually assaulted as she left a party, had a clear memory of the sexual assault in the parking lot immediately following the assault and for several weeks thereafter. Three months later she continued to remember what happened before and after the assault — being at the party, being followed out by a man who had been pestering her to dance, being grabbed by him in the parking lot and pushed into the bushes, and then being in the ambulance and going to the hospital. However, Carol had no memory of the highly traumatic anal penetration that she had experienced after he pushed her onto the ground.

In his report, the psychological expert who assessed Carol explained his reasons for diagnosing Carol with dissociative amnesia, starting with the fact that "her loss of memory is too extensive to be explained by normal forgetfulness."[16] He further explained that although Carol had two glasses of wine at the party, her alcohol consumption was not sufficient to cause her memory loss — she remembered the incident well at the time and was able to describe it fully to police. Most likely, Carol was unable to recall the central aspects of the assault because this experience was so terrifying; she feared for her life as she was being assaulted. By dissociating or removing this traumatic experience from her conscious awareness, Carol was able to protect herself from the extreme distress of remembering or psychologically reliving the assault. Even though Carol said that she wanted to remember what happened to her so that she could testify, she was unable to remember these details. The psychologist recommended against the use of hypnosis in this case. He questioned the general usefulness of hypnosis for recovering a memory, and he noted that the suggestive nature of hypnosis would call into question the accuracy of any memories that Carol might recall as a result. Instead of using hypnosis, the psychologist employed other, non-suggestive techniques with Carol, but without success. The psychologist concluded in his report, "Over time, Carol may gradually begin to recall her dissociated memories; however, it is possible that she will never remember all of the details of her traumatic anal rape."

Due to Carol's memory issues, the court process was unavoidably extended, which upset Carol. She was told to expect rigorous questioning on the stand about her memory. In addition, it became clear to her that many people, including court personnel, do not understand memory issues well. As a result, Carol encountered insensitive comments and skepticism from others about her lack of memory. A family member even accused her of faking memory loss to get out of testifying. Carol felt disbelieved and thought about giving up. She asked the Crown to go ahead with the case without her testimony. However, the Crown explained that the rules of evidence require that, with few exceptions, as the complainant, she must come to court on the date of the trial to give her best recall of the events that are the subject of the charges. This is necessary because the complainant must be properly cross-examined by the defence on her version of events. The Crown thus encouraged Carol to testify, explaining that she needed only to tell what she could remember with as much detail as possible. Carol said that she really wanted the offender to be held accountable for what he had done, so she agreed to do her best to tell the court what she could remember about the assault. The case proceeded to trial.

At trial, with the help of the psychologist's expert testimony, the Crown lawyer was able to demonstrate that Carol's memory loss was likely due to the trauma of the sexual crime, and was understandable in that situation. Carol remained unable to recall the assault details at the time of the trial, but she was able to testify about the events before and after the assault, including her memory of giving her statement to police and her affirmation that she told the truth at that time. That testimony, plus the testimony of other witnesses and the medical examination, was enough evidence to convict the offender. Testimony given in court and the successful conviction of the accused resulted in Carol feeling vindicated. The expert's testimony helped Carol understand that her memory loss did not mean that she was "going crazy." Testimony during the trial also helped several of her family members gain a better understanding of her ordeal. Although some resentment lingered toward the family member who had accused her of faking her memory loss, Carol was able to attribute his remarks to his ignorance, rather than to any personal failings of her own. Carol's experiences in court helped restore some of her self-confidence. Although it had been a very stressful ordeal, she felt it had been worthwhile. She felt good about having been able to testify in intimidating circumstances and knowing that her testimony had contributed to the conviction of a dangerous sexual predator.

ENDNOTES

1   Ulric Neisser, *Memory Observed: Remembering in Natural Contexts* (San Francisco: W.H. Freeman, 1982).

2   S. Porter & K. Peace, *The Scars of Memory: A Prospective, Longitudinal Investigation of the Consistency of Traumatic and Positive Emotional Memories in Adulthood* (2006) [unpublished, archived at Dalhousie University, Department of Psychology, Halifax, NS].

3   Daniel P. Brown, Alan W. Scheflin, & D. Corydon Hammond, *Memory, Trauma Treatment, and the Law* (New York: W.W. Norton & Company, 1998); J.W. Schooler, "Cutting Towards the Core: The Issues and Evidence Surrounding Recovered Accounts of Sexual Trauma" (1994) 3 Consciousness and Cognition 452–69.

4   Aphrodite Matsakis, *I Can't Get Over It: A Handbook for Trauma Survivors* (Oakland, CA: New Harbinger, 1992) at 81.

5   *Ibid.* at 84.

6   *Ibid.* at 84–85.

7   *Ibid.* at 86.

8   The following examples are quoted directly from Charlotte Kasl, *If the Buddha Got Stuck: A Handbook for Change on a Spiritual Path* (New York: Penguin Compass, 2005) at 135.

9   "Forensic Stress Disorder," which is proposed as being similar to Post-Traumatic Stress Disorder (PTSD), has been suggested by Larry J. Cohen & Joyce H. Vesper, "Forensic Stress Disorder" (2001) 25 Law & Psychology Review 2–27.

10   T. Gutheil, H. Bursztajn, A. Brodsky, & H. Strasburger, "Preventing 'Critogenic' Harms: Minimizing Emotional Injury from Civil Litigation" (2000) Journal of Psychiatry and Law 5–18.

11   *Ibid.*

12   Larry H. Strasburger, "The Litigant-Patient: Mental Health Consequences of Civil Litigation" (1999) Journal of the American Academy of Psychiatry and the Law 203 at 206.

13   Mary Russell, *Measures of Empowerment for Women Who are Victims of Violence and Who Use the Justice System* (Vancouver: Ministry of Public Safety and Solictor General, 2002).

14   Above note 12.

15   Sharyn A. Lenhart & Diane K. Shrier, "Potential Costs and Benefits of Sexual Harassment Litigation" (1996) 26:3 Psychiatric Annals 132 at 133.

16   American Psychiatric Association, *Diagnostic and Statistical Manual of Mental Disorders: DSM-IV-TR*, 4th ed., text revision (Washington, DC: American Psychiatric Association, 2000) at 520.

5

A Psychological Tool Box

Vignette Five

Alma, aged thirty, is bathing her six-year-old daughter. When the girl gets out of the tub to be dried, the sight of her naked body suddenly and unexpectedly triggers a powerful reaction in Alma. She thinks, "This is the age I was when George first started touching me. How could he do that to such a vulnerable little girl?" Alma's mother married George (not Alma's biological father), when Alma was two years old. Beginning at the age of six and continuing until the age of nine, George frequently touched and caressed Alma's genitals, sometimes putting his mouth on her vagina. At the time George had told Alma that "This is the way daddies show their daughters how much they love them." Alma had put the abuse in the back of her mind and avoided thinking about it, but now that her daughter is six years old, Alma's perspective suddenly shifts. Her mother is still married to George and Alma fears that her daughter could be in danger from "grandpa." Fear for her daughter's safety galvanizes her resolve and Alma confronts George privately. George minimizes the abuse, saying he did nothing wrong and suggesting that Alma is being "hysterical." This encounter only escalates Alma's fears that George is a danger and she decides, for the first time, to take someone else into her confidence. With great apprehension, she talks to her husband, discloses her own abuse, and explains her concerns about their daughter.

IN THIS CHAPTER, WE focus on short-term coping techniques and specific stress-reduction strategies that will help you address the symptoms (fear, anxiety, depression, anger, and interpersonal distrust or social isolation) that we discussed in Chapter 2. We also discuss the issue of resilience, and long-term strategies for dealing with adversity and for promoting personal growth. Most of the coping strategies presented in this chapter are straight-forward and transferable; you can use them in a wide variety of situations, such as dealing with everyday issues in living, as well as when preparing for and attending court.

In Chapter 2 we discussed many psychological symptoms that could arise in response to a sexual assault, some of which can significantly inter-fere with a person's daily functioning. The first order of business for people suffering from psychological distress is to develop coping skills that will meet their immediate and basic needs. In this chapter, you will read about a variety of coping techniques that can help you reduce emotional distress and regain some control over your life. It is likely that some of these meth-ods will not appeal to you nor be successful for you, but you should find at least some that will be beneficial. As is true with many endeavours in life, the value of coping strategies is in the regular application of them. What might first impress you as a simplistic, ineffectual exercise can prove to be a valuable tool when put into consistent practice. Decide which approaches discussed in this chapter resonate best with you, and give them a try. Some techniques will be more useful or necessary than others are; consider them all and see which best meet your needs. Later in the chapter, we will broaden our perspective and focus on strategies that go beyond coping with acute problems to address long-term personal change. None of these strategies should be seen as advice for specific problems but as general mental health tools. Specific problems need to be treated on an individual basis, and we recommend that you see a mental health professional.

For ease of presentation, we have organized the various strategies into categories, as shown below, even though individual strategies may result in benefits in more than one category.

- Basic health-care, including strategies to help you sleep
- Fear reduction and safety enhancement strategies
- Stress reduction strategies
- Containment strategies that help you contain or moderate the ex-pression of an upsetting feeling or reaction, such as anger or some Post-Traumatic Stress Disorder (PTSD) symptoms
- Distraction techniques to help you focus your attention away from upsetting thoughts and images

+ Grounding techniques to help you stay in the present, focus, and minimize unwanted distraction
+ Mood altering strategies, including ways to counter periodic thoughts of self-harm or suicide
+ Strategies for the development of supportive relationships
+ Strategies for building resilience

BASIC HEALTH-CARE

YOU HAVE PROBABLY HEARD many of the oft-repeated recommendations for good health, but since these principles become particularly important during periods of extreme stress, we will outline them once more.

+ Eat regular meals that are nutritionally balanced and healthy.
+ Get adequate rest and sleep.
+ Exercise on a regular basis or engage in some type of healthy physical exertion, such as housework, yard work, or playing with children or pets.
+ Get regular medical check-ups.
+ Be particularly careful to follow prescribed medical regimes and/or take medications for diagnosed medical problems.
+ Drink an adequate amount of water throughout the day.

When you find yourself emotionally drained or stressed, you are more likely to neglect your basic needs. During court proceedings, or other periods of emotional intensity, you may need to schedule routine physical self-care into your daily routine. For example, you may need to schedule regular meals to ensure that you eat adequately. When attending court, it is a good idea to take along some healthy snacks so that you do not inadvertently go too long without eating. You also may need to schedule regular exercise breaks, such as a brisk walk. Even twenty minutes of moderate physical exertion per day can have tremendous physical and psychological benefits.

In our busy day-to-day lives, the essentials for good health often fall by the wayside, and we neglect, or ignore, our physical needs. On the other hand, anxiety and stress can make us extremely sensitive to some bodily functions and needs. In an attempt to ignore or suppress emotional responses, some people experience heightened physical reactions, and become focused on such things as physical pain. Owing to the close relationship between our emotional and physical well-being, observing the principles of stress reduction will also be a benefit in reducing bodily symptoms, such as pain. Of course, if you have physical concerns, the best place to start is with a thorough physical exam by a medical doctor.

The benefits of sleep

ALONG WITH ADEQUATE NUTRITION and exercise, sleep is essential to good health. Sleep deprivation can dull our senses, diminish our productivity, and make us less able to cope with adversity. Many of us are chronically sleep-deprived, which not only exacerbates our stress response, but it also leaves us with reduced energy, poor concentration, and increased susceptibility to disease. Anxiety and depression can significantly disrupt your sleeping patterns and negatively affect your ability to heal, so addressing your sleep needs is an important part of the healing process. Begin by sleeping in a location where you feel safe and secure. While a bedroom is the optimal sleeping environment, it is not always possible to rest there, especially if it is a place where violence has occurred. The following list of general techniques was developed to improve sleep patterns.[1]

- Physically exercise during the day, but not within three hours of bed-time.
- Do not nap during the day.
- Go to bed when you are sleepy or tired, not just because you think you should go to bed.
- Try not to drink anything within two hours of going to bed, to reduce the probability of having to get up during the night to go to the bathroom.
- Do not drink alcohol, coffee, or other caffeinated beverages and do not smoke cigarettes within two to three hours before bed.
- Do not read or watch TV in bed; these are stimulating and waking activities.
- Do not count sheep while lying in bed; this is a stimulating activity.
- Use your bed only for sleeping; get up after thirty minutes of being unable to sleep.
- Before going to bed engage in a boring, non-stimulating task. In particular do not get involved in anxiety-provoking activities or thoughts ninety minutes before going to bed.
- Write about your hopes and dreams every night before you go to bed to focus on positive things and free up your mind.

- If you tend to worry when you fall asleep, schedule a "worry time" during the day to deal with these issues. Be sure this is completed at least two hours before going to bed.
- Check with your doctor to see if any medications you are taking interfere with sleep.
- Wear earplugs or use a white noise machine (if it is safe not to hear in your environment).
- Take a warm bath about four hours before bedtime; give your body time to cool down after your bath to assist you in falling asleep.
- Keep your bedroom cool rather than warm.
- Do five or more repetitions of deep breathing exercises before you go to bed.
- Try progressive muscle relaxation beginning with your toes and ending with your head (see description below).
- Listen to calming music or a relaxation tape.

ENHANCING SAFETY AND COMFORT

FOLLOWING A SEXUAL ASSAULT, restoring a sense of physical safety and emotional security is paramount. Some victims may not even realize the extent to which they remain at risk of further harm. Below we offer a brief outline to illustrate the ways you can enhance your safety. We also encourage you to take the extra step of discussing your safety with those who can best assist you, such as local police or a victim services worker.

Apart from a need to protect yourself, to optimally deal with various stressors in your life you need places where you can feel relatively safe and secure. In the immediate aftermath of a sexual assault, you may not have felt safe anywhere. You may continue to fear for your general safety, but you should have at least some places where you feel secure. If you are going to participate in legal proceedings related to your sexual assault, it is especially important that you have a safe haven where you can retreat and recuperate.

Ideally, you should have several safe places where your fear subsides and you can relax. Your safe place may not be where you have typically felt safe. If you were a victim of assault in your home or at work, these places may no longer feel safe to you. For some, a public place, possibly a favourite restaurant or a spot in a park, may seem safer than an isolated private residence.

Your safe place might be a particular room in your home — perhaps your own bed or maybe anywhere in your home but your own bed. Regardless of where it might be, it is important for you to have somewhere you feel safe. If you have not yet found such a place, this should be a priority. If it means moving from where you are to another building or community, give it serious consideration. If this is a difficult issue for you, talk with a friend, family member, or counsellor to help assess your feelings and the advisability of making significant changes to your living arrangements.

Creating a safety plan

WITH THE HELP OF police, your friends, family, or your employer, you can design ways to protect yourself. Research and the work of experts have produced a body of knowledge designed to teach justice personnel about risk assessment and the development of safety plans for the victim. Police typically do not have the resources to stake out your home or place of employment, and it may seem to you that they do not offer much in the way of direct protection. If you feel a need to protect yourself, you may find it necessary to move or hide so that the offender cannot find you. Clearly, this situation will further disrupt your life and aggravate your emotional turmoil, but it is not an unusual scenario for complainants, particularly when awaiting the arrest of a serious offender, or dealing with an offender who is out on bail.

When thinking about your safety and considering a safety plan, you can divide the risks and needs into three domains: those related to yourself, those related to the offender, and those within the community. In each of these categories, you can find elements that contribute to your risk of danger or enhance your safety. As you devise a safety plan, think about how you can enhance your security or reduce your risk in each of these categories. Your plan might be quite different depending upon whether your abuser has or had a close relationship with you or is a stranger. The list below provides some examples of strategies in three domains that people have used to address their specific situation.

- *Yourself* — change door locks, go to a safe house, arrange for another place where you or your children can go, decide on different pathways out of your house, arrange to carry a cell phone, develop a code word that lets a support person know you are in danger, keep a journal of important events or threats

- *Offender* — request a restraining order, keep a copy of the order with you at all times, ask your work supervisor not to allow the offender in the building
- *Community* — get help from a local women's advocacy group or shelter, share your concerns or plans with a trusted friend or family member, arrange for someone to pick you up at a safe location when necessary

Enhance security with pets

RESEARCH HAS DEMONSTRATED THE important contribution that a pet can make to your sense of well-being and safety. The companionship and affection a pet gives you and the affection that you can safely express to your pet can be invaluable. Some animals can also provide a sense of personal security. A well-trained dog can be both a friend and a protector in times of danger, but training a dog for such purposes requires considerable time and energy. If you have a pet, you are likely already aware of the benefits. If not, you may want to consider getting one that suits your lifestyle in terms of care requirements and expense. It is important to recognize that pets require considerable time and attention, which can potentially represent an additional stressor in your life. You will need to balance the pros and cons of adding a pet as another member of your family. If you already feel overwhelmed with your current responsibilities, it may not be a good time for you to consider pet ownership. It may be more advisable to postpone getting a pet until you feel ready and able to take on further responsibilities, perhaps at the end of court proceedings.

Enhance emotional security with objects

ANOTHER TECHNIQUE TO HELP increase feelings of safety and security can come from objects that you associate with happiness and safety. These objects can be anything portable and safe that gives you positive feelings. Often small gifts from family or friends can serve this function, as can things you find on a relaxing, enjoyable holiday — a stone or a seashell from a beach. People have found comfort in all sorts of small objects — a piece of inexpensive jewelry found in a second-hand store, a bird's feather, a soft toy, or a religious relic. Having the object held or "blessed" by someone important to you, like an Elder, a spiritual leader, or a loved one, can enhance the meaningfulness of the object. The object should easily fit in your pocket so that you can touch it at any time without calling undue attention to yourself. Because such objects can be associated with positive feelings, strength, or the support of others, the object can be a powerful talisman to touch or hold when you are facing challenging moments, as you will in court.

STRESS-REDUCTION STRATEGIES

STRESS CAN EXERT POWERFUL effects on your mind and body. It can induce agitation, anger, tension, or depression. One of the most useful ways to counteract stress is to learn responses that are incompatible with the particular effects stress exerts on you. Relaxation is one of those contrary responses; you cannot be both relaxed and agitated at the same time. Learning how to relax properly can help you control or diminish the effects of stress. You should not confuse the term relaxation, as we use it here, with the act of lying on the couch and watching your favourite TV program. We are referring to a deeper, more therapeutic form of relaxation.

The process of deep relaxation begins with the development of some self-awareness; a greater understanding of your physical body and its reactions. Start noticing the ways in which your body responds to stress; how you tense in some situations and relax in others, and notice the associated bodily sensations. You may develop tension in your shoulders, neck, or back, or a tightness in your stomach, you may clench your jaw, or your breathing may change. Take note of where your tension accumulates when you are under pressure and use this knowledge to focus your efforts when relaxing.

Once you are able to sense when tension is building, you can take some steps to counteract it. The following techniques are some of the most commonly used relaxation strategies. Two of the techniques can help increase your self-awareness of your breathing and other physical signs of tension in your body, while the third technique, visualization exercises, can enhance your awareness of how your thoughts and mental images affect your emotional state. Focusing on relaxing images helps both your mind and your body relax. In our resource guide in Appendix 4, we indicate sources you can go to where these techniques are outlined in detail.

The key to using the following techniques effectively is to practise, practise, practise. These techniques become most effective when you learn them well and can quickly apply them when needed. Practise is best done during times of low stress; if you only attempt to learn or use the techniques when you are feeling extremely stressed, they are unlikely to be effective because you will be too distracted and your physical responses will be too intense. As you become more aware of your body's stress responses, you can learn to apply relaxation techniques at an early stage of tension, when they can be most effective and before your stress responses escalate in intensity.

Progressive Muscle Relaxation

LEARNING HOW TO RELAX the various muscle groups of your body is a powerful stress-reducing strategy. Stress usually results in muscles tightening, causing feelings of stiffness and pain, particularly in your back, shoulders, or neck. Progressive muscle relaxation is a way of systematically relaxing muscles in the body, usually beginning with the feet and moving throughout the body up to the head. You should practise this technique in a relaxed position by either sitting comfortably or lying on your back. You begin by focusing on a small muscle group, such as the muscles in your toes and feet, which you tightly tense for a few seconds followed by a complete release of the tension. This contrasts the feeling of tension with the feeling of relaxation. If practised regularly, you can become adept at releasing tension in your body and relaxing muscle groups throughout your body whenever necessary. You can enhance muscle relaxation by deep, slow breathing and by soothing self-talk. Telling yourself to "relax" or "let go of all the tension," helps calm your mind along with your body. Listening to one of the commercially available relaxation tapes will guide you through the process and will give you soothing messages you can later recall.

Breathing

YOU MAY HAVE NOTICED that whenever you feel stressed or anxious, your breathing changes; it may become rapid and shallow, or halting. Some people "forget to breathe" when they are anxious. In *The Resilience Factor,* psychologists Karen Reivich and Andrew Shatté explain the vicious cycle of increased anxiety that results from shallow breathing: "Because you are bringing in less oxygen to your lungs, less oxygen is being circulated through your bloodstream. The change in oxygen level sends off a warning alarm in your brain, causing more adrenaline to be released, which leads to even more anxiety, further shallow breathing, further oxygen depletion — a vicious cycle."[2]

To break this cycle, you need to shift your breathing from your upper chest to your diaphragm, which lies just above your abdomen, and underneath your lungs. When practising, it may help you to lie with your back on the floor with your hand on your abdomen so that you can feel the rise and fall as you breathe from your diaphragm. The higher your abdomen rises with each breath, the deeper and fuller your inhalations will be. With each deep breath, you will feel tension ebbing away as you exhale and your abdomen falls. Becoming aware of shallow breathing and then shifting to deeper and slower abdominal breathing will have a noticeable calming effect.

Visualization

VISUAL IMAGERY IS A powerful technique that you can use in many different ways. As you will see, it provides the underpinning for many other coping strategies in this chapter. One of the simplest and easiest types of imagery is to picture a calming and relaxing place or scene. You might imagine a favourite holiday place, a happy place from childhood, or a purely fanciful place where you imagine yourself to be safe and comfortable. You can make the image particularly vivid by imagining with all five senses. Think of sounds, smells, and tactile sensations, as you feel the sun on your skin or a breeze blowing through your hair. You might visualize a comfortable scene, imagine yourself engaged in some relaxing activity, or think of a piece of art that evokes positive, soothing feelings for you. The power of visualization lies in practising until you have conditioned your body to relax whenever you think of that particular image. By regularly practising visualization, you can mentally go to a place that quells your fear and helps you relax and feel safe.

Visualization techniques are particularly helpful when you are alone and needing to relax, for example, before going to bed at night. You may also find these techniques helpful when applied just prior to participating in stressful activities, such as police interviews, examinations, hearings, or appearances in court. Conversely, this type of strategy is not always appropriate. When you are engaged in activities that require mental sharpness and focus, some visualization techniques may be helpful just prior to your engaging in these tasks, but they may interfere with your ability to focus if used at the wrong time. Relaxing until you find yourself daydreaming or distracted is clearly inappropriate if you are working or driving a car. If this is an issue for you, you may want to try some grounding strategies, discussed below, rather than visualization strategies that could increase your distractibility.

CONTAINMENT STRATEGIES

BELOW ARE SOME CONTAINMENT strategies that can help you reduce the impact of distressing thoughts, images, or emotional responses. Self-help books and self-administered strategies may not be adequate for your long-term needs if you are suffering from chronic symptoms of PTSD. However, in the interim, while you seek professional help, or for those with only sporadic symptoms, we offer some strategies for symptom relief. Learning to contain upsetting memories and associated thoughts does not mean that you are indefinitely avoiding or denying these experiences. Instead, deliberate containment gives you the ability to put these upsetting memories aside when necessary or until you are ready to deal with them more fully. This can increase your sense of self-control and reduce your anxiety.

Dealing with upsetting memories, images, or flashbacks

THE FOLLOWING TECHNIQUES, FROM Williams and Poijula's workbook, *The PTSD Workbook,* can be used to contain upsetting memories, images, or flashbacks by temporarily putting them out of your mind.[3] Experiment with these approaches to see which will work best for you.

- Get the flashback or memory outside of your head by writing about it, talking about it, drawing, or making a collage of it.
- Put the flashback or memory into some sort of container — either actually write the memory on paper and put it in a container or symbolically place the memory in some sort of vault or container that can remain closed until you choose to open it.
- Imagine yourself spraying the memory or flashback with an imaginary cleaner that causes it to disappear.
- Draw or write about the flashback on a piece of paper and then get rid of the paper by shredding it, burning it, or burying it.

The following strategies offer a different approach: ways to confront painful memories or images in a gradual and healthy manner, without resorting to numbing, detrimental forms of avoidance, or dissociation.[4]

- Learn to tolerate painful emotions, such as fear, by learning to identify what triggers a painful emotion and then finding ways to reduce the power that triggers have over you (see discussion above).
- Find ways to look at your fears indirectly, including using writing, art projects, dancing, or creative movement, or music.
- Increase your contact with others, perhaps by joining an organization.
- Learn to appraise the threat of situations by using your head rather than your emotions. Think about how, or if, your safety is actually threatened. Devise a safety plan, as suggested earlier in this chapter.
- Keep physically safe and learn to stay in the "here and now."
- Use grounding techniques to separate your past trauma from your present reality.
- Pace yourself in how you deal with your trauma; for example, set up a certain time during the day or week that you focus on your trauma or work on related issues.

Identifying what specifically triggers your intrusive memories is an important step toward managing your emotional reactions. Start by making a detailed list of the things that are likely to provoke intrusive memories, images, or distressing feelings. It may help to organize these triggers into categories: visual cues, sounds, smells, tastes, physical sensations, places, and people. Once you have identified as many triggers as you can, you are in a better position to take steps that will allow you to control your reactions.

The relaxation and breathing techniques discussed above can be helpful in containing your responses to triggers. Having contact with supportive people in your life and avoiding unnecessary stress also can help reduce responses to triggers. You may be able to structure your life in such a way that you can avoid some important triggers (such as the place you were assaulted), but attempting to avoid all triggers would be onerous and restrictive, if not impossible. It is unrealistic to expect no negative feelings or reactions when encountering triggers. A more reasonable goal, at least initially, is learning how to manage upsetting reactions to triggers, although this will take some time and perseverance. Dealing with your responses to particularly strong triggers, such as seeing the perpetrator's face, could take years.

Considering these various factors, a viable long-term goal is to learn how to control or manage your emotional responses when you encounter a trigger, rather than expecting to have no reaction or trying to avoid every trigger. If you are having difficulty dealing with triggers or intrusive memories on your own, a cognitive-behavioural therapist could greatly aid you. In some cases, a course of appropriate medication also might be helpful.

Dealing with anger

TO REITERATE A PREVIOUSLY made point, anger is a natural, normal emotion. No matter how unpleasant anger may sometimes feel, you will no doubt have angry moments throughout your life. This is a typical human experience. Anger can give us a temporary sense of control and relief from feeling vulnerable. The real question, however, is how to express anger appropriately when it occurs. Although it may not always feel like it, you do have choices. The following ideas may help you learn ways of managing or containing angry reactions and avoiding destructive behaviours.

In her book for trauma survivors, Dr. Aphrodite Matsakis[3] suggests you begin to take control of anger by telling yourself the following:

> I'm okay. All that's happening to me is that I'm feeling angry. All I have to do with anger today is feel it. I can figure out later what to do about it.

> All I have to do now is ride with it. If I can just feel the anger without hurting myself or someone else, I am a success.

The following strategies can help you identify and learn to manage problematic anger:

- Even though anger may appear to come "out of the blue," it is generally preceded by bodily sensations such as jaw clenching, tingling sensations, heavy breathing, sweating, or muscle tension. Try to identify these sensations, which can then serve as warning signals to you.
- Anger usually builds from low to high intensity. It is much easier to deal with angry feelings before they spiral to the danger point or result in a violent outburst. When you feel yourself getting angry, take a break and let others know you need some time by yourself.
- When taking time out to deal with angry tension, do something that allows you to release the tension, for example, run, lift weights, or do some vigorous exercise.
- If you are not the sort to do strenuous exercise, try something else, for example, dance, bang a drum, or be creative in the way you blow off steam.

Here are some additional anger management strategies suggested by Williams and Poijula:[6]

- Put your anger into words or pictures that describe the feelings behind the anger. When writing about your anger, describe the triggers and bodily sensations that occur.
- Put your anger outside of yourself. Do not turn your anger against yourself or use it to criticize yourself. Try to let those who hurt you know why you are angry without criticizing or attacking them.
- When you become angry find alternative expressions for your anger, such as the following:
  - ▷ Going to the gym and working out
  - ▷ Taking a long walk
  - ▷ Ripping apart an old telephone book
  - ▷ Pounding a pillow
  - ▷ Playing racquet ball or a similar type of vigorous physical game
- Engage in a relaxation response that is incompatible with anger. For example, you can try breathing exercises, relaxation techniques, or meditation.
- Become aware of the anger-inducing messages that you say to yourself and then work on changing these messages. Realize that it is not other people who cause the angry feelings you feel. While others do things that upset you, it is your decision about how you will react to a person that leads to your expression of anger.
- Be aware of your self-talk and create a useful dialogue. Tell yourself you can control your anger; you do not need to fear it. When you hear yourself making defensive excuses, tell yourself to listen, ask questions, and make sure you understand the situation. There may be some room for agreement or compromise.

DISTRACTION TECHNIQUES

WHENEVER YOU BECOME PREOCCUPIED with upsetting thoughts, images, memories, or feelings, you may need to take a mental break and find a healthy distraction. You might distract yourself from unwanted thoughts by engaging in another mental activity, such as counting to yourself or using your watch or your pulse as a way to count.[7] Alternatively, you can distract yourself by getting involved in a vigorous activity that requires some mental focus, such as household chores or exercising.

Bill O'Hanlon suggests several types of mental games that can help shift your attention away from upsetting, non-productive thoughts.[8] He suggests quick games (under two minutes) that are engaging but not so difficult that they frustrate you further. The games should have an aspect of fun so your mood shifts from anxiety, anger, or sadness to a more pleasant emotion.

Examples of mental games suggested by Mr. O'Hanlon include the following:[9]

- Alphabet Game: Work your way through the alphabet, naming a person for each pair of initials (for example, AB — Annette Bening, BC — Bob Costas, CD — Charles Darwin, etc.).
- Categories: Choose a category and name as many items in the category as possible within two minutes. Examples of categories are vegetables, ski resorts, bones in the body, books written by Charles Dickens, Oscar-winning movies. Make the game more challenging by naming items within a category in alphabetical order (vegetables: asparagus, bok choy, carrots, etc.).
- Rhyming: Select a word and see how many rhymes you can come up with in two minutes.
- Mathematics: Count backwards from 2,000 by seven or rehearse the multiplication tables.
- Song Lyrics: This is a great way to shift your mood. Recite the lyrics from your favourite songs (stay away from depressing or overly sexualized lyrics).
- Poetry: Memorize an uplifting poem and then recite it when you need to refocus.

GROUNDING TECHNIQUES

IF YOU FEEL DISTRACTED when you should be focused, if you have moments of unreality where you do not feel present in your body, or if you experience flashbacks, you can use grounding techniques to bring you back to the "here and now." You can begin by reminding yourself: "I've made it through the worst part by surviving the sexual assault, and now I am here in the present; the sexual assaults happened in the past." You can also ground yourself by focusing on sights, sounds, and sensations in your immediate environment. More specifically, you might try one or more of the following grounding techniques:[10]

- Be aware of your physical body and how you look.
- Be aware of your movements in space as you walk.
- Exercise while being aware of what you are doing.
- Make a plan for the day and share your plan with someone else.
- Challenge yourself to a contest to increase the length of time you remain in the present.
- Watch television or a movie and tell yourself or others what you saw.
- Do routine activities in a different way, such as cleaning the house in a different order.
- Ask others to help you stay connected to them.
- Talk to yourself about the present.
- Hold a favourite or interesting object and focus your attention on that object in a way that allows you to stay in touch with reality.
- Feel your body's contact with furniture or the floor to remind you of your current location in space. You can intensify this feeling by stomping your feet on the floor or pushing your body against a chair.
- Shift awareness to current sensations or sounds by clapping your hands, washing your face with cold water, touching your tongue to the roof of your mouth, or repeatedly blinking your eyes vigorously.

MOOD-ALTERING STRATEGIES

SELF-SOOTHING TECHNIQUES CAN HELP you take the edge off upsetting emotions, lift your mood if you are depressed, or help you feel calmer when you are anxious. They can also reduce stress so that you are able to think more clearly. Although there is overlap here with the stress reduction strategies discussed above, in this section we focus more on strategies that can lift your mood when you are feeling depressed or down-in-the-dumps. We also include some ways to challenge periodic suicidal thoughts.

When you feel particularly depressed or anxious it is hard to think of anything that is soothing or relaxing. Hence, it is important to make a list of your self-soothing, restorative activities during a period of relative calm so you can refer to them when you need them most. The list should include activities that lift your spirits in a healthy way and do not undermine your general well-being. Having a drink of alcohol may make you feel better in the short run, but it can diminish, rather than support, your overall well-being particularly if alcoholism has been a problem in the past. Here, the focus is only on healthy coping strategies.

Making a list of mood-lifting activities is a very personal exercise — what works for you may not work for someone else. A general guideline for composing your list might be "less of what drains you and more of what feeds your life."[11] Activities on such a list may not give you the immediate relief of a stiff drink, but they are ultimately more far-reaching and helpful in lifting your mood. Once you make the list, keep it handy and use it when you need a mood-lifter or when your emotions tend to overwhelm you. Such reminders can keep you on track. Here are some ideas:

- Exercise vigorously or play sports
- Meditate
- Go for a walk
- Practise yoga
- Complete a home project you have been putting off (for example, reorganize a closet, or make a photo album)
- Practise relaxation techniques, such as imagery (discussed below)
- Watch a movie, especially a light comedy
- Take a refreshing shower or soothing bath
- Work in the garden or arrange flowers
- Listen to soothing music
- Dance
- Visit with trusted friends
- Spend time outdoors, enjoying nature
- Read an absorbing or light-hearted and fun book
- Play games
- Write in a journal
- Volunteer for local organizations
- Get a massage to help relieve muscular tension or pain
- Share a relaxed meal with a friend
- Have some quiet time
- Spend ten minutes thinking about things you are grateful for

Countering negative thoughts

ONE OF THE MOST effective ways to deal with a depressed mood is to address the underlying thoughts and beliefs that contribute to feeling worthless, helpless, hopeless, or sad. Dealing with chronic or serious depression may require the help of a professional, particularly if you are in danger of harming yourself or others, but there are steps you can take to improve your mood and functioning when the situation is less critical. Some excellent self-help books are available that deal specifically with the problem of mood disturbance and we list a number of these in our resource guide in Appendix 4, including *Feeling Good: A New Mood Therapy* by David Burns. While you decide which resources are appropriate for you, try some of the following strategies to help you get started in a healthy direction.

Your thoughts greatly influence your emotions, so cultivating self-awareness is an important first step in altering your mood. Notice your thoughts and the statements you make, and then notice how this affects your emotions. If you are depressed or tend to be a negative thinker, your mind will be filled with grey mutterings, such as "I'm no good at anything," "I'm no good, period," "I always screw up, no wonder no one likes me," or "I'm such a useless human being, I don't deserve anything good to happen; it's all hopeless, so I might as well give up now." These kinds of thoughts can become so habitual that you accept or barely notice them. Finding ways to turn off or turn down the volume and frequency of negative thoughts can greatly lift your mood. It can also work wonders for your self-confidence and feelings of self-worth.

Once you begin to identify these negative thoughts, you can employ some thought-stopping techniques and temporarily halt them. When negative thoughts come to mind, you can visualize an image, such as a stop sign or traffic light, which tells you to stop on that negative road, and dismiss those thoughts. Play with this technique and see if you can come up with phrases or images that diminish your negative thinking. A simple stop sign may not be powerful enough for you; perhaps you need a more compelling image, such as a train-crossing signal, complete with flashing lights, ringing bells, and descending barriers. With practice, you will find a suitable image that meets your needs.

In her delightfully readable and helpful book, *If the Buddha Got Stuck: A Handbook for Change on a Spiritual Path,* psychologist Charlotte Kasl illustrates another way to stop negative thoughts and to then take the next step of countering depressive thinking patterns with more positive, proactive thoughts:[12]

> Notice whenever your mind goes to negative or helpless thinking, and say, "negative," or "oops." Then have a pithy direct phrase to shift your perspective. "Okay, now what can I do?" "There's got to be a way." "People have changed their situation, so can I." "What's one step I can take today?" Shifting to proactive thinking is like jump-starting your system.

Countering feelings of shame

THOUGHTS AND FEELINGS OF shame can be particularly toxic to your well-being. Shame leaves you with chronic feelings that you are being bad or wrong, or that others are judging you to be an unworthy person. Shame can be paralyzing, devastating your self-esteem and inhibiting you from doing things for fear of judgment, all of which can lead you to withdraw from others. You can counter shame-inducing thoughts or feelings using strategies similar to those discussed above. Charlotte Kasl suggests using some of the following strategies to counter shame, which can also be adapted to address other types of distressing thoughts or feelings.[13]

- *Name it. Observe it.* Recognize when you are feeling shamed and ask yourself what happened or what thoughts you had before feeling shame.
- *Realize you are not your shame.* Say the following to yourself: "This shame is not my essential self. It is an intruder, like toxic chemicals or pollutants. It was put there when I was abused, left, hurt, shamed, seduced, teased, neglected, scolded, or not allowed to voice my thoughts or feelings."
- *Think of what you do not do for yourself because of your shame, and then give yourself the assignment of doing it anyhow.* This might include any of the following or more: "standing up for yourself, expressing feelings, initiating a conversation, asking for what you need, inviting someone to get together with you." Doing something proactive now can help you counteract the impact of the past.
- *Imagine having a new response to a shameful situation.* You can begin by imagining yourself "being centred, confident, and at peace with yourself in a situation that has previously triggered shame." You could stand up for yourself by using phrases and comments that ask

for clarification of the other person's intent or indicate that "it's not all right to talk to me like that." We gave examples in the previous chapter when we discussed how you can stand up to hurtful comments by others.

+ *If you get triggered into shame, call someone who is understanding and has a sense of humour.* Have a list available of people you can contact who lift your spirits. A list helps because when you are feeling shamed, you may even forget that you have friends.

+ *Go into big mind.* This means that you step back and view shame from a broader perspective. For example, you can say to yourself the following: "I am feeling the shame of being used or hurt. I am feeling the shame of exploiting others or hurting them. I am having the human experience of feeling shame. I am not alone. There are many people feeling shame right this moment. It's just a feeling, it will all pass."

Boosting self-esteem

IN ADDITION TO COUNTERACTING negative thoughts and feelings, it is healthy to generate self-affirming thoughts. Although it seems simplistic and perhaps silly, repeating these positive thoughts to yourself can go a long way to counteracting years of criticism and negative self-perceptions. Thoughts affect attitudes and feelings; consequently, consciously changing your thinking is a first step to changing perceptions about yourself. Shifting long-held perceptions does not occur quickly, but taking small, regular steps will reward you in the end. Williams and Poijula[14] suggest the statements below as examples of affirming thoughts that help shift feelings in a positive direction. Try repeating several of these affirmations daily. Not all will feel right, so use those that fit you, and feel free to develop your own. Be sure they are positive statements that have a ring of truth for you.

+ I have worth.
+ I am worthy of respect from myself.
+ I can do good work at my job.
+ I make a difference in my own life (or in the lives of others).
+ I am capable of changing and growing.
+ I am no longer a helpless child.
+ I am willing to accept love.

Another way to boost your self-esteem is to engage in activities that make you feel good about yourself or that promote self-confidence. Try turning your attention outwards in a constructive manner. For example, you might take a course to develop some new skill you have wanted to learn. You could become involved in an enjoyable hobby or activity you can do well. Being helpful and doing something for others can also help you feel good about yourself.

Dealing with suicidal thoughts and feelings

IF YOUR DEPRESSED MOOD is persistent and includes recurring, serious thoughts of self-harm or suicide, you should seek help from your family physician or a qualified mental health professional. If you are alone or without support, contacting a crisis line or going to your local emergency room is obviously advisable before such negative thinking leads to self-harm. Thoughts of self-harm are likely to subside as your mood improves, but this period can still be hazardous. As they feel better, some may find energy to carry out self-injurious plans that had previously seemed too difficult. Some have found it helpful to reflect on reasons they have to go on living, rather than dwell on reasons to hurt themselves. It may be important to live to see your children grow or to support certain loved ones. The reasons below are from a list developed in an online newsletter, Survivorship.[15] Use these as examples to create your own list of reasons to live.

- Because you deserve to live
- Because your life has value, whether or not you can see it
- Because life itself is precious
- Because you will feel better, eventually
- Because each time you confront despair, you get stronger
- Because if you die today you will never again feel love for another human being or see sunlight pouring through the leaves of a tree
- Because the will to live is not a cruel punishment, even if it feels like that at times; it is a priceless gift
- Because no one knows better than you the meaning of suffering, and agony deepens the heart
- Because you deserve the peace that will come after this battle is won, and it *will be* won, but only minute-by-minute
- Because it is critical that you survive

Supportive relationships

WE ARE SOCIAL CREATURES, and being able to rely on others can greatly assist with coping and rebuilding personal resources, but reaching out to others is not always easy, especially for victims of sexual assault who feel betrayed. Building or rebuilding trust takes time, energy, and courage. However, being able to turn to a trusted friend, family member, or mental health professional can help restore some calm to your life and provide you with an emotional safe haven when you are feeling overwhelmed. Since the issue of relationships is so important, we will spend some time on the topic of personal interactions.

In the preceding chapters we talked about strategies to deal with people in your life who may have different agendas and perspectives than you, and who may be hurtful in their interactions. We also have to consider those who love you and want to offer their support but who, for various reasons, may not know how to help you. All of us experience disruptions in our relationships, especially when we are dealing with difficult personal issues of our own. Issues of distrust, anger, anxiety, and depression can disrupt our relationships and support network, alienating us from previously meaningful contacts. The following strategies may help you reconsider the relationships in your life and perhaps expand your support network.

Make your own choices

ALLOW YOURSELF TO CHOOSE, as much as possible, the people in your life with whom you want to spend time. You may choose to avoid some relationships, either temporarily or permanently, because they have more negative than positive aspects. Those who truly care for you will understand your need to regroup; those who do not were not likely good friends to begin with.

Pace yourself

BE DELIBERATE IN MAKING contact with others. Closing yourself off from everyone will delay any real progress towards building healthy relationships again. Yet, if you quickly throw yourself into intense or demanding social encounters, it may prove too much and can overwhelm even the most resilient individual. You may need to move slowly, beginning with a few scheduled get-togethers and building up gradually.

Develop casual friendships

CULTIVATE CASUAL FRIENDSHIPS AND relationships. Not everyone needs to be, or can be a close friend. It is usually easier to relate to people on a more casual basis — for example, people with whom you work, play sports, or walk your dog. Have people in your life that you can socialize with, but with whom you may not share a lot of personal information. It can be a relief to be with people who are not likely to talk about your traumatic experiences. Charlotte Kasl offers some innovative ways to interact casually with others:[16]

+ If it feels safe to you, talk casually with someone at a checkout stand.
+ Call, go visit, or send a card to someone who is lonely or ill and wish them the best.
+ Pick out a bright or strong paint colour and get a friend to help you paint an accent wall in your living space.
+ Go shopping with a friend and try on clothes you thought you would never wear.
+ Call a friend from the past who has recently come to mind (he may only be a Google away) to say hello.
+ Call a friend and offer to do an exchange so you can get some help with a task that has got you stuck, for example, clearing out old clothes, cleaning up the garage, or painting a room.

Participate in group activities

ANOTHER WAY TO INTERACT with people on a casual basis is to join group activities. Seek out those that feel non-threatening or perhaps even healing. For example, take a course at a local community centre, join a meditation group, play a team sport, volunteer with a charity organization, participate in activities and rituals that celebrate your cultural heritage, join a book-reading club or a hiking group, make a quilt or build something with others, or join a group in your church. Group activities generally focus on the task at hand (such as bowling, bird watching, or hiking) and typically do not require the sort of closeness demanded in a one-to-one interaction.

Be selective about disclosure

DECIDE WHOM YOU WANT to tell about your experiences of sexual assault. Who and how you choose to tell can make a difference in your relationships. Not everyone needs to know all your experiences, thoughts, and feelings. For example, "Jane Doe," one of Canada's most well-known survivors of a home invasion sexual assault, chose not to disclose the assault to her parents. She carefully chose those in her life with whom she would share her story. She shared her story with some of her siblings, but not all of them. Some of her friends and colleagues knew her struggle and others did not. Jane Doe had the wisdom to know who around her could protect her, who had the strength and knowledge to help guide her, who had the strength to endure over the long term, and whom she needed to protect with her silence. More about Jane Doe can be found in Chapter 11 and in her book, *The Story of Jane Doe: A Book about Rape,* which chronicles her experiences with the criminal justice system.

Learn active listening

IMPROVE YOUR COMMUNICATION SKILLS by learning to listen well. This means not interrupting the other person, not taking the conversation back to yourself, and not thinking about or preparing your own response while the other person is talking. When you listen well and deeply, you focus on the other person and pay attention to what is being said without becoming restless or distracted. If the conversation exceeds your attention span or ability, let the other person know and take a break instead of faking it — your inattention is usually obvious.

Work on developing trust

DEVELOP SOME TRUSTING RELATIONSHIPS — people you can talk to and go to for emotional support. There is no easy way to do this. Start slowly and set clear boundaries for yourself. You will need to be discriminating — not all people are trustworthy. Trusting others always involves some risk. You will need to confront fears you have about trusting others and explore the thoughts and feelings that emerge for you. It will be important to learn to recognize and challenge old patterns, thoughts, and feelings that you bring from your experiences and other relationships (for example, memories of people who have betrayed you). The following comments from Charlotte Kasl offers some sage advice about developing trustworthy friendships:[17]

> Go toward people who are reliable, responsive, interested in knowing you, and supportive of your best self. Do not repeatedly put your energy into

people who are indifferent, unreliable and unresponsive to you. Remember to switch it around and consider that if you want solid friendships you also need to be reliable and responsive to those you would like to spend time with.

Diversify social contacts

REALIZE THAT NO ONE person can satisfy all your interpersonal needs or be your sole comfort and guide. There are many types of acquaintances, contacts, and relationships into which people enter. You may not have considered, or have forgotten about, or have yet to explore some types of relationships. Appendix 6 contains a support team checklist with which you can begin. Use this list to generate new possibilities for yourself and develop your own support team. We recommend that you fill out contact information for people on your list, so that you can readily connect with them when necessary. You may find only some of the examples listed here to be appropriate for you, but add others as you see fit. Post the list somewhere handy to remind yourself of important people available to you in your life and how you can contact them.

THE ROAD TO RESILIENCE

TO THIS POINT, WE have talked a lot about coping skills that are available for short-term relief of distress. We now want to expand our scope to include the types of coping skills associated with resilience, and being able to bounce back from adversity, including participation in legal proceedings. Building resilience is something that you can begin today, but will likely take you some time and effort to accomplish. Although the skills associated with resilience can help you recover from your assault, they are not specific to sexual assault; building resilience can aid you in all areas of your life.

The tragic terrorist attacks in the United States on 11 September 2001 changed the way many Americans viewed their lives and expanded awareness about the importance of resilience. Along with feelings of shock and loss, many Americans felt pronounced feelings of uncertainty. Psychologist, Russ Newman observed: "Now more than ever people seem open to reexamining their lives and finding new ways to cope."[18] In response to this perceived need, psychologists within the American Psychological Association (APA) gathered current research findings to help Americans learn ways of more effectively responding to and managing the fears and stresses of a post-9/11 world. To share this information with the public, the APA teamed with the Discovery Health Channel to launch an education initiative entitled "The Road to Resilience."

We have based much of this section on research and information provided by the APA, which you can also access on its website.[19] We present additional information drawn from other sources including two excellent books we highly recommend: *The Resilience Factor* by psychologists Karen Reivich and Andrew Shatté, and *Thriving through Crisis* by Bill O'Hanlon. Building resilience can help each of us cope more effectively with difficult, stressful experiences in our life. Learning these skills will reduce your stress and enhance your well-being, making you more effective in dealing with general life stressors and the specific stressors of participating in legal proceedings.

So what is resilience?

RESILIENCE IS THE ABILITY to adapt well and "bounce back" when faced with adversity, trauma, tragedy, or very difficult, stressful life experiences. As described by Karen Reivich and Andrew Shatté: "Resilience transforms. It transforms hardship into challenge, failure into success, helplessness into power. Resilience turns victims into survivors and allows survivors to thrive."[20]

Most of us do not feel psychologically prepared to handle extreme stress or adversity well, nevertheless, most of us know someone or know about someone who inspires us with her resilience and her ability to overcome terrible circumstances with apparent grace and integrity. Although resilient people may seem quite extraordinary, resilience is actually an ordinary quality. Most of us show resilience in some way or in some aspect of our life. No matter where you fall on the continuum of resilience, you can increase your ability to "bounce back" from life's challenges with spirit and grace. Of course, being resilient does not mean that you will avoid experiencing emotional pain, difficulties, or distress. Experiencing hardships is an inevitable part of life, but building resilience can help you significantly change how you deal with life's hardships and setbacks when they occur. Resilience can help you feel more in control, experience less stress, and like yourself better in the process of dealing with adversity.

The good news is that everyone can develop resilience. It is not something that certain people are born with; it is not a fixed feature or trait, like having black hair or blue eyes. Resilience is something you can learn, and something you can teach yourself. The not-so-good news is that there is no quick fix. Learning the skills to build resilience takes time but is ultimately worth the effort.

Ten ways to build resilience

YOU CAN USE MANY different strategies to build resilience, but as is generally the case, what works for one person may not work for another. You will need to try different approaches to see what works for you. Research studies have identified several specific resilience-building strategies. Below, we list the ten research-based strategies suggested by the American Psychological Association. Although we have changed the order of the ten items and added comments, the wording that is in quotation marks is directly from the APA's website.[21] The website briefly describes each of the ten strategies to keep the list user-friendly. We will be referring to items from this valuable list throughout the book so you may want to copy the list or mark its place for easy access.

As you read this list, you will notice it contains some of the strategies referred to earlier, including those used by complainants who tend to fare emotionally well during the legal process. You will also likely see strategies that you already use. This can help you identify strengths that you may take for granted or have not previously recognized. You may see items that you consider inappropriate or that may seem impossible for you, and some strategies listed may seem like common sense. There is no magic here; these strategies have been used by ordinary people to effectively deal with stress and trauma in their lives. Try to keep an open mind (an important resilience skill) as you read the following list.

American Psychological Association Top Ten List

1. *Make connections.* "Good relationships with close family members, friends, or others are important. Accepting help and support from those who care about you and will listen to you strengthens resilience. Some people find that being active in civic groups, faith-based organizations, or other local groups provides social support and can help with reclaiming hope. Assisting others in their time of need also can bene-

fit the helper." Making connections with others is an often-repeated theme in this book. Connecting with others is not only essential to successfully maneuvering your way through the legal system, but it is critical to your overall well-being. Sometimes, making connections requires being open to those who genuinely reach out to you. Other times making personal connections depends on your being able to reach out and include those who may have shut you out. With love and courage, you can open doors for both yourself and others.

2. *Take care of yourself.* Once again, we bring this to your attention. "Pay attention to your own needs and feelings. Engage in activities that you enjoy and find relaxing. Exercise regularly. Taking care of yourself helps to keep your mind and body primed to deal with situations that require resilience."

3. *Avoid seeing crises as insurmountable problems.* "You can't change the fact that highly stressful events happen, but you can change how you interpret and respond to these events. Try looking beyond the present to how future circumstances may be a little better. Note any subtle ways in which you might already feel somewhat better as you deal with difficult situations." This is a particularly important strategy for you to consider when dealing with court proceedings. It is easy to feel overwhelmed by the legal process, especially when so much of it lies outside of your control. However, it will help if you frame legal proceedings as a challenge, rather than a threat to you and learn to deal with the overall process one step at a time.

4. *Keep things in perspective.* "Even when facing very painful events, try to consider the stressful situation in a broader context and keep a long-term perspective. Avoid blowing the event out of proportion." Gail Cantor of Contegrity Designs[22] invites us to find strength in the magnificent expanse of time and our relationship to it. Ms. Cantor suggests the following exercise. Draw a series of five lines on a page with each one representing an expanse of time, illustrated below:

From the beginning of time until the end of time

From the beginning of life as we know it, until the end of life

Three millennia from 0–1000, 1001–2000, 2001–3000

From the birth of your oldest grandparent to the death of your youngest grandchild

From your birth until your death

Now, think about the choices you have to make today or during the court process and see where they fit on any of these time-lines. What appears so frightening or overwhelming today will merely be a dot on most of these time-lines. On others it will not even appear. The take-home message is that no matter what, your current feeling will pass and another will replace it. The feeling may come back, but that too will pass. Shifting your perspective in this way can diminish overwhelming feelings and may help you move from any "stuckedness" back into constructive action.

5. *Accept that change is a part of living.* "Certain goals may no longer be attainable as a result of adverse situations. Accepting circumstances that cannot be changed can help you focus on circumstances that you can alter."

6. *Move toward your goals.* "Develop some realistic goals. Do something regularly — even if it seems like a small accomplishment — that enables you to move toward your goals. Instead of focusing on tasks that seem unachievable, ask yourself, 'What's one thing I know I can accomplish today that helps me move in the direction I want to go?'"

7. *Take decisive actions.* "Act on adverse situations as much as you can. Take decisive actions, rather than detaching completely from problems and stresses and wishing they would just go away."

8. *Nurture a positive view of yourself.* "Developing confidence in your ability to solve problems and trusting your instincts helps build resilience."

9. *Maintain a hopeful outlook.* "An optimistic outlook enables you to expect that good things will happen in your life. Try visualizing what you want, rather than worrying about what you fear." Optimists, by definition, are happier, more hopeful people. However, "Pollyanna-like" optimism can be glib and empty, with no basis in reality and not the kind of optimism that builds resilience. Resilience is based in realistic optimism. Drs. Reivich and Shatté provide an excellent description of this type of optimism:[23]

Realistic optimism is the ability to maintain a positive outlook without denying reality, actively appreciating the positive aspects of a situation without ignoring the negative aspects. It means aspiring and hoping for positive outcomes, and working toward those outcomes, without assuming that those outcomes are a foregone conclusion. Realistic optimism does not assume that good things will happen automatically. It is the belief that good things may happen and are worth pursuing but that effort, problem solving, and planning are necessary to bring them about.

10. *Look for opportunities for self-discovery.* "People often learn something about themselves and may find that they have grown in some respect as a result of their struggle with loss. Many people who have experienced tragedies and hardship have reported better relationships, greater sense of strength even while feeling vulnerable, increased sense of self-worth, a more developed spirituality, and heightened appreciation for life." We discuss the possibility of growth and transformation later in the book (see Chapter 11).

ADDITIONAL WAYS TO BUILD RESILIENCE

RESEARCH HAS FOUND OTHER strategies that help some people deal more effectively with adversity and stressful experiences. See which of the following appeal to you. The key is to identify ways that fit with your personal style and abilities, and that can be part of your long-term strategy for fostering resilience.

Write about feelings and thoughts

RESEARCH HAS FOUND IMPROVED mental, emotional, and physical functioning associated with writing about upsetting experiences. Suggested guidelines for therapeutic writing are simple — write honestly and openly about your thoughts and feelings. You can do this more easily if you feel confident nobody else will be reading your notes. Some therapists suggest you accomplish this by writing about your feelings then immediately destroying what you have written.

Although this process can be therapeutic, it may have significant legal consequences if you are participating in civil or criminal court. Be aware that writing about your thoughts and feelings regarding a sexual assault can be considered evidence in a court of law. What is a therapeutic tool in one context can be considered evidence in the legal context. This means your personal writings, such as diaries or journal entries, can be subpoenaed by the court, read by a judge, and ultimately given to the defence. Further, destroying relevant personal writing may be equivalent to destroying evidence. Given the potential consequences, think carefully about engaging in this type of writing if you are involved in or contemplating legal action. We discuss these issues more thoroughly in Chapter 7.

Spiritual practices

THERE ARE MANY DIFFERENT religious and spiritual traditions from which you can draw strength. These are very personal choices based on your own values and beliefs. If you feel an emotional void in your life, you might benefit from exploring and perhaps charting your own spiritual path. You could talk to religious and spiritual leaders in your community, or explore these issues in books, films, and the worldwide web (see our resource guide in Appendix 4 for some examples).

There are also myriad ways to have spiritual experiences that do not require affiliation with any particular religious or spiritual tradition. Consider, for example, the following description of spirituality:[24]

> It's a passion for life, a feeling of connection, of being a part of the life around you. Many people experience this in nature, watching the ocean roll in, looking out over a vast prairie, walking in the desert. When you are truly intimate with another human being, when you are uplifted through singing, when you look at a child and feel wonder, you are in touch with something bigger than yourself. There is a life force that makes things grow, that makes thunderstorms and mountain ranges and perfect avocados.

Cultivating mindfulness

IGNORING, AVOIDING, OR DISTRACTING yourself from emotional distress, as discussed above, are all ways that we can manage our emotions in the short-run and this may be necessary in some situations, including testifying in court. However, these strategies also reduce self-awareness; they are actions that diminish our focus on the healing process and are therefore not good long-term strategies. When we shut down self-awareness, our growth and transformation stops and we may end up living the same painful cycles over and over again. Although we may appear to be rushing around with great zeal and energy (avoiding, distracting, or ignoring), it is often merely motion, not healing action.

To cultivate mindfulness, which is an antidote to distraction, try developing a different attitude toward time. Make an effort to slow down and take time, rather than attempting to leave time behind. We can compress or dilate time. The minutes are interminable while sitting in a dentist's chair having a tooth drilled, but they are fleeting when we are absorbed and entertained. We can distract ourselves and "kill time" in any number of ways, for example, numbing substances, gambling, television, or video games. We often do not appreciate the moment we are in; we are bored, feel emotional pain, or are fearful; we want to leave that moment behind in any fashion we can. If people escape from or repel these moments, they are typically prolonging their pain; they are making themselves less aware of their emotional needs and delaying the healing process.

Make an effort to accept emotional distress as your own; do not recoil from it but find motivation in it. By acknowledging and accepting your emotional pain, you begin to weaken its influence on you and begin to reclaim your personal power. Time can be an ally, rather than an enemy, as you become more fully aware of each moment and what it can bring. One way to accomplish this shift in awareness is through a process called mindfulness meditation.

In recent years, North Americans have shown great interest in various forms of meditation, a practice that developed out of Eastern spiritualism. One of the basic aspects of meditation is a focus on developing "mindfulness," which means learning to be aware of the present moment of your life in a non-judgmental, non-evaluative way. If you are mindful when eating a dessert, you are aware of the textures and various flavours you taste. You are aware of the experience of eating that dessert, rather than looking around the restaurant to see who you know or wondering whether the dessert is good for you or not. When you are mindful, you learn to be aware of your thoughts without getting lost in them; you learn how to recognize or acknowledge your thoughts and then "let go" of them. The goal is to quiet the constant chatter in your mind so that you are able to more fully experience each moment in your life.

Most forms of meditation involve quietly sitting and focusing your attention on your breath or on a particular word or object as you practise letting go of the thoughts and the "busyness" in your mind. Mindfulness can also be cultivated in your day-to-day life by paying moment-to-moment attention to your experiences, rather than your thoughts. When you wash dishes, notice the movement of your hands, the temperature of the water, and the sensation of soap on your skin. In this way, you can truly experience washing dishes, rather than getting lost in thoughts and other distractions. This is an experience of mindful meditation.

Research has shown meditation to have numerous health and psychological benefits, including stress reduction. Meditation has also been effective in helping people manage chronic pain and reduce depression. Jon Kabat-Zinn has developed a treatment program called mindfulness-based stress reduction (MBSR).[25] If this approach sounds interesting, you can read more about it or contact your local hospital or mental health association to see if a program is available in your area. There has been an explosion of books, magazines, websites, tapes, and CDs about meditation, and our resource guide in Appendix 4 lists a sample of these. You may also be able to find more information from meditation practitioners in your area and you could join a meditation group.

Embracing humour

LAUGHTER CAN HAVE A particularly potent, positive effect on mood. Physiologically, laughter increases blood circulation and heart rate, and lowers blood pressure and stress hormones, while enhancing the body's immune system. In addition to the ideas offered below to increase laughter in your life, you might consider building up your repertoire of lawyer jokes, to help bring some lightness into the heaviness of court proceedings (although we are not suggesting that you share your humour with the court, which does require a certain level of decorum).

Williams and Poijula suggest the following to create more laughter in your life and to enhance your sense of humour:[26]

- Know what makes you laugh.
- Know people who can make you laugh.
- Use jokes and collect them in a humour log.
- Laugh at life. Look for the ironic, the ridiculous, or the absurd in situations, reminding yourself of the saying, "one day we will laugh about this."
- Never miss an opportunity to play. Be spontaneous.
- Schedule fun time. Make scheduling fun time as important as scheduling work time.
- Celebrate successes big and small.
- Treat yourself. Indulge yourself in ways that reflect care and compassion.
- Do not wait to be happy, do it now.
- Smile, smile, smile. Physically smiling can actually lead to positive, happy feelings in yourself and others.

Expressing strong feelings and impulses

ONE QUALITY OF RESILIENCE is being able to regulate or manage your emotions so you can respond in a way appropriate to challenging situations. This means being able to manage how we express strong emotions and generally being able to remain calm under pressure. It does not mean you will never feel discouraged, angry, or upset, or that you will never be in a bad mood. As noted by Drs. Reivich and Shatté, "The expression of emotions, negative and positive, is healthy and constructive; indeed, proper emotional expression is a part of being resilient. But just as life's luster is dulled if we keep our emotions under total wraps, so does being a slave to your emotions interfere with your resilience and drain it from those around you."[27]

We each differ in the way we express our emotions and the ease in which we manage our behaviour. Some people appear to express negative emotions, such as anger, more strongly and perhaps more frequently than others do. They may have more difficulty controlling their impulses and regaining their composure after becoming upset. If this is true for you, you may often feel stuck in negative emotions, such as anger, fear, or sadness. Being stuck in strong feelings makes you less effective in stressful situations, less able to think clearly, and more likely to accept and act on your first impulsive belief about the situation. With this approach, you are not likely to solve your problems effectively; rather, things are likely to escalate and end without resolution.

Earlier, we outlined many effective techniques to reduce anxiety, calm yourself, or lift your depressed mood. However, to break the bonds of destructive emotional reactions, one of the most effective strategies is learning how to recognize the thoughts and beliefs that are the source of those emotions. You can then do a reality check and challenge those thoughts or beliefs that do not accurately reflect your situation. This method is fundamental to the cognitive-behavioural therapeutic (CBT) approach discussed in chapters 3 and 5. The goal is to "have your emotions and behaviours be productive, appropriate responses to the facts of the situation, not knee-jerk reactions to your ticker-tape beliefs (those thoughts that form a running commentary just below the surface)."[28] Some of the strategies outlined earlier to address feelings of shame are examples of this approach. While you can certainly learn these skills from self-help books, a skilled therapist trained in these techniques will facilitate the task considerably.

You may choose to regulate your emotional responses by practising a form of meditation that helps you "let go" of inappropriate emotions and their accompanying thoughts and beliefs. You might decide to practise the Buddhist tradition of "big mind" (as opposed to our usual, restrictive "small mind"), which we referred to earlier. With a big mind you can see the commonality of your own experience with that of others. When you are feeling an emotional reaction, such as anxiety, you can think in terms of having the human experience of anxiety. You then realize that you are not alone, as many other human beings are feeling that same emotion at that very moment. From this perspective you also realize, "it is just a feeling, it will pass." In this manner, you see your feelings as being normal, rather than their being a source of anguish, shame, or taking on the features of a personal defect. Letting go of your feelings becomes easier with practice.

Whatever strategy you choose, being able to regulate your emotional responses effectively is a critical skill for becoming resilient in stressful situations. You will find this skill particularly important during legal proceedings, which will inevitably trigger strong emotional reactions in you. It is almost certain that things said or occurring during this process will upset you. Nonetheless, you can learn how to manage your responses so they will be appropriate in the situation, allowing you to "bounce back" from the experience, rather than feeling devastated or being consumed by chronic negative feelings or anger.

Learn to think "outside the box"

TO DEAL WELL WITH difficult, upsetting situations, we need to have effective problem-solving strategies. We could approach the situation as a scientist would; collect information in a fair and objective way, analyze all the data in a logical manner, propose alternative explanations for the data, and then draw a conclusion that most accurately reflects the data. Regrettably, problem solving in the real world does not work this way. As noted by Drs. Reivich and Shatté, "When it comes to appraising ourselves, others, and situations, we are downright shoddy scientists. We collect incomplete data, we use shortcuts to process it that lead to biased appraisals and we make errors in interpretation that often support our favoured hypothesis."[29] In this way, we tend come up with only slight variations of the same old solutions we have found in the past. We get stuck, entrenched in our old ways of seeing, thinking, feeling, and doing. When this happens, we need to learn "to think outside of the box."[30]

Thinking outside the box is more easily said than done. Our human brains are wired to perceive the world in a particular way, unique to our species. For example, we visualize and sense the world very differently than a bumblebee or a bat does. Even within our own species, we each are born with unique abilities and limitations; some of us see the world in full colour, some in black and white, and some do not see it at all. Each of us has built our own perceptual "box" over many years. Millions of interactions with family, friends, and strangers within a society of deeply rooted influences contributed to the structure of this box. This is natural, it is our framework for viewing and navigating the world, but in the process of building our box, we have "fallen into thinking traps and developed radar to scan the environment for violations of rights, for loss and for future threat."[31] We have also learned how to screen out contradictory information and let in information that is consistent with our own particular views and biases. When these thinking traps begin to interfere significantly with our functioning, we need to break out of the box. We need to become more flexible and creative, more aware of our automatic thought processes, paying more attention to the issues that we have been ignoring. We can do this by examining our biases, questioning the first thoughts that pop into our head, and generating alternative explanations or solutions for the recurring problems we face. This returns us to a theme already repeated several times: developing self-awareness.

Breaking out of your box and developing effective problem-solving strategies requires that you first become aware of the erroneous ways you perceive and make sense of your experiences. These errors are what cognitive-behavioural psychologists refer to as "thinking traps." We all use a variety of thinking strategies at different times and in different circumstances, however, these strategies become "traps" when they are our default position, an automatic or systematic response that interferes with effective problem solving. Consider the following examples of thinking traps drawn from *The Resilient Factor* to see if you over-rely on any of these strategies.[32]

- *Using Tunnel Vision*: None of us can pay attention to or process everything in our environment. We have to select some things to pay attention to and ignore others. We "sample" from our environment, with some things getting more attention than others. With tunnel vision, you selectively sample from your environment along one dimension.

For example, you may focus only on negative aspects of yourself and others.

- *Magnifying and Minimizing*: This approach differs from tunnel vision in that you register more of what occurs during a situation, but you tend to either magnify the value or weight of some things or minimize that of others. Those who magnify the negative in situations tend to expect the worst; this is sometimes referred to as "catastrophizing."

- *Personalizing*: Those who personalize problems tend to see themselves as the cause of problems. This can sometimes be an accurate perception, and can be empowering because you can take steps to solve the problem by changing your own behaviour. However, if you automatically and systematically default to personalizing, you are ignoring other causes and you will not be able to take the appropriate steps to address the problem.

- *Externalizing*: Externalizing is the opposite of personalizing. Externalizers blame others or something outside of themselves whenever something goes wrong.

- *Over-generalizing*: Over-generalizing means that you over-extend a particular belief or view more globally in ways it does not apply. For example, "personalizers" who over-generalize will attribute virtually all problems to themselves, thereby wrongfully maligning their own character.

- *Mind Reading*: Mind readers believe that they know what others are thinking and they behave accordingly. Sometimes this also extends to expecting others to know what you are thinking and then becoming upset when others do not behave in keeping with your expectations. Mind readers tend to jump to conclusions. The best remedy for this tendency is to check in with the other person and clarify what is actually going on rather than assuming that you know.

Becoming aware of your tendencies to misinterpret or misread situations can help you evaluate situations more appropriately. Not only will this improve your problem-solving ability, but it will also improve your communication skills because you are more likely to ask appropriate questions and to have authentic conversations, rather than operating on false assumptions. Avoiding thinking traps will also enhance your ability to communicate effectively in court.

Be flexible and seek a balance in life

AS YOU WORK ON building resilience, remain flexible. You will likely need to modify your personal strategies as you and your circumstances change. Being flexible can help you achieve or maintain some degree of balance in your life. You may need to develop a number of problem-solving strategies for different situations. The APA offers the following examples to illustrate ways in which being flexible in your use of resilience strategies can help you balance competing needs.[33] You will see some parallels with the coping strategies discussed earlier.

- Do not be afraid to let yourself experience strong emotions, but also be aware of situations when it is best to avoid experiencing them in order to continue functioning.
- Step forward and take action to deal with your problems and meet the demands of daily living, then step back to rest and re-energize yourself.
- Spend time with loved ones to gain support and encouragement, and also nurture yourself.
- Rely on others, but learn to rely on yourself as well.

Patience

WHEN EMBARKING ON MAJOR life changes, such as those associated with building resilience, it is important to remember that the process takes time and effort. It took many years to become the person you are; you will not change years of ingrained habits overnight. Individuals begin the journey at different places and proceed at different paces. There are generally times when progress slows or you encounter setbacks, so go easy on yourself. Try not to resort to "shoulds" or "oughts," such as "I should be less anxious by now," or "I ought to be further ahead." Instead, acknowledge each small step forward that you take. Use the strategies discussed above to help make and sustain the changes. Be persistent but patient with yourself.

Get help when you need it

SEEK APPROPRIATE ASSISTANCE TO help you build resilience. Besides friends and family, you may want the assistance of a support group or a mental health professional. We have referenced several excellent self-help books in this chapter, but you can also find online resources, such as the APA's website, that will provide valuable information. Check the resource guide in Appendix 4 for these and other references. In the last chapter of this book, we tell the stories of some resilient people who have overcome tremendous obstacles to lead full and productive lives. These stories not only inspire us, but they also can motivate us in our individual journeys.

SOME FUNDAMENTALS OF PERSONAL CHANGE

AS YOU FINISH READING this chapter and consider the various ways and means you can use along the path of effective coping and self-development, you might want to reflect on some fundamental questions about personal change. Ask yourself, "What are my beliefs about personal change?" If you feel that significant life change is possible, you will be open to new experiences and to developing new skills. If you agree with the saying, "You can't teach an old dog new tricks," you are not likely to devote much effort to changing old behaviour patterns or learning new ways of coping with adversity. If you buy into the old-dog belief, you are likely to give up prematurely when the going gets tough, and the going is likely to be tough at times. This belief can become an excuse for inaction, or can operate as a self-fulfilling prophecy. To increase your chances of successfully developing new skills, we recommend that you vigorously challenge the old-dog belief. Think of ways that you actually have changed and new things you have learned in the last five years. Start noticing little changes that you make that might otherwise go unnoticed, and try the approaches suggested below to stack the deck in favour of changing your life for the better.

Small changes

START WITH SMALL CHANGES. Small changes are usually more manageable and over time can add up and lead to bigger or sustained changes. Begin the journey of a thousand steps by taking one small step in the right direction. In *Thriving through Crisis*, Bill O'Hanlon suggests that you begin by making small, random changes in your everyday habits, "which might highlight where you need to introduce something new in the areas you hadn't even noticed." Mr. O'Hanlon suggests the following small, random changes as good places to start:[34]

- *Change body behaviour:* Use your left hand rather than your right; get out of bed on the other side of the bed; wash your feet first instead of your hair in the shower; walk backwards into the house when you come home at night; gesture only with one hand during an animated discussion.
- *Change locations:* Sit at another place at the table; eat in the basement rather than the living room; take a different route to work; sit with your back to your partner when having a discussion; do what you usually do at home at the coffee shop (if appropriate) or at the park.
- *Change modalities:* Walk or ride the bus instead of driving; write out your arguments without saying a word; record the delivery of consequences you would have given your in-after-curfew child and leave the tape recorder near the door for your child to find when arriving home; talk to your spouse on the phone when you are feeling unheard even when both of you are at home.
- *Change the timing:* Stretch out what you usually do in five minutes to take a half hour; likewise, shorten the time involved; do what you usually do at a specific time at another, unexpected or unfamiliar time or day; start early, leave early; start late, leave late.

Once you commit to change and begin making steps toward changing your life, sustain your momentum by trying the following:[35]

- Remind yourself of the price you pay or will pay for not changing or not keeping the change going.
- Enlist friends or supporters to help you change, remind you, and keep you on track.
- Link change to positive consequences and activities (for example, "I keep myself exercising regularly by listening to favourite audio programs while I walk").
- Do not attend to the feelings and preferences of the moment but rather focus on the commitment to change or the new action or habit.
- Take the long-term rather than short-term view.
- Take risks — remember the old saying: "If you fall on your face, at least you are heading in the right direction: forward."

VIGNETTE FIVE: COPING AND RESILIENCE

ALMA, THE SUBJECT OF Vignette Five, has a powerful insight, triggered by the sight of her nude daughter. She realizes what a vulnerable and help-less child she was at the age of six, and her daughter inadvertently acts as a trigger for memories of sexual abuse by her stepfather that she had avoided thinking about for years. Faced with the realization that her stepfather could be a danger to her daughter, Alma must confront some issues she had long avoided. Alma's emotional response to the situation is complex. She is fearful for her daughter's safety, she is angry with her stepfather, and she is confused by his behaviour. She begins to doubt the reality of what she had previously considered to be a loving and caring childhood home. She wonders how her stepfather could have done such a thing to her if he truly loved her. She also questions her mother's love, because her mother did not protect her from the man that she had brought into their home.

Alma ruminates about these thoughts to the point that she loses sleep, cannot think clearly during the day, and she feels uncharacteristically sad and irritable. She has always thought of herself as an independent person and does not readily seek help from others, but her emotional turmoil is in-terfering with her ability to function normally. When her husband brings up the subject of her uncharacteristic moods and behaviour, she makes a decision to disclose her past abuse to him. Telling her story to her husband is very difficult and Alma realizes that she feels a lot of shame about what her stepfather did. Her husband responds by being very angry with George and he wants to contact the authorities immediately, but Alma dissuades him. She does not want to upset her mother or have the fact of her abuse be-come public knowledge; her immediate concern is for her daughter's safety. Her husband agrees not to do anything until his anger subsides and the two of them have a chance to carefully consider their options.

After telling her husband about the abuse, Alma's anxiety begins to decrease. She feels relieved to have an ally, and she is particularly reassured by seeing that her husband is supportive and not rejecting of her. She feared that the news of the sexual abuse might change his opinion of her or his feelings toward her, but that does not happen. Instead, he offers to help her deal with the situation in whatever way she thinks best. Together, the two of them tackle Alma's most pressing concern — the safety of their daugh-ter. They devise a safety plan in which their daughter will never be left unsupervised in Alma's parents' care. They go to the Internet and search for self-help literature on childhood sexual abuse. Once her daughter's safety has been addressed, Alma's anxiety lessens and she is better able to concentrate. She reads several helpful books and learns that there are practical steps she can take to improve her emotional health. She takes long vigorous walks to relieve her tension, which has the added benefit of clearing her mind and helping her sort things out. She learns relaxation techniques and starts sleeping better. She still feels shame about the abuse, thinking there must have been something wrong with her, but she learns to counter these thoughts with reminders that she is a good mother, an accomplished musician, and that as a young child she was not responsible for what her stepfather did to her.

Although her emotional health improves greatly, Alma is still angry with her stepfather and her feelings of shame stand as an impediment to her moving on with life. After considerable thought and discussion with her husband, she decides that she will no longer be silent. She decides that in order to recover fully from the sexual abuse, she needs to act decisively in a way she could not have done at six years of age. She wants to hold her stepfather accountable for his behaviour and protect other children from going through what she did. She decides to report her stepfather's conduct to the authorities and contacts a lawyer about the possibility of launching a civil lawsuit.

ENDNOTES

1   Adapted from list provided in Mary Beth Williams & Soili Poijula, *The PTSD Workbook: Simple, Effective Techniques for Overcoming Traumatic Stress Symptoms* (Oakland, CA: New Harbinger, 2002) at 80–81.

2   Karen Reivich & Dr. Andrew Shatté, *The Resilience Factor* (New York: Broadway Books, 2003).

3   Williams & Poijula, *The PTSD Workbook*, above note 1.

4   *Ibid.*

5   Aphrodite Matsakis, *I Can't Get Over It: A Handbook for Trauma Survivors* (Oakland, CA: New Harbinger, 1996).

6   Williams & Poijula, *The PTSD Workbook*, above note 1.

7   *Ibid.*

8   Bill O'Hanlon, *Thriving through Crisis: Turn Tragedy and Trauma into Growth and Change* (New York: The Berkley Publishing Group, 2004) at 204.

9   *Ibid.* at 204–5.

10 Williams & Poijula, *The PTSD Workbook*, above note 1.

11 Charlotte Kasl, *If the Buddha Got Stuck: A Handbook for Change on a Spiritual Path* (New York: Penguin Compass, 2005) at 41.

12 *Ibid.* at 17.

13 Quoted directly from Charlotte Kasl, *ibid.* at 134–35.

14 Williams & Poijula, *The PTSD Workbook*, above note 1 at 163.

15 Mari Collings, *Reasons Not to Kill Yourself*, online: www.stardrift.net/survivor/ bwreasons.html, as referenced in Williams & Poijula, *The PTSD Workbook*, above note 1 at 143.

16 Kasl, *If the Buddha Got Stuck*, above note 11 at 49.

17 *Ibid.* at 127–28.

18 Materials available on APA website online: www.apahelpcenter.org.

19 *Ibid.*

20 Reivich & Shatté, *The Resilience Factor*, above note 2 at 4.

21 Above note 18.

22 Online: www.contegrity.com.

23 Reivich & Shatté, *The Resilience Factor*, above note 2 at 56.

24 Ellen Bass & Laura Davis, *The Courage to Heal: A Guide for Women Survivors of Child Sexual Abuse*, 3d ed. (New York: Harper & Row, 1994) at 167.

25 Jon Kabat-Zinn, *Full Catastrophe Living: Using the Wisdom of your Body and Mind to Face Stress, Pain, and Illness* (New York: Dell (Bantam Doubleday Dell), 1990).

26 Williams & Poijula, *The PTSD Workbook*, above note 1 at 193–94.

27 Reivich & Shatté, *The Resilience Factor*, above note 2 at 37.

28 *Ibid.* at 74.

29 *Ibid.* at 54–55.

30 *Ibid.* at 160.

31 *Ibid.*

32 *Ibid.* at 95–113.

33 Above note 18.

34 Bill O'Hanlon, *Thriving through Crisis*, above note 8 at 104–5.

35 *Ibid.* at 118.

6

Going to the Police

Vignette Six

After many years of keeping her sexual abuse a secret, Halima, a twenty-one-year-old Muslim woman, decides to go to the authorities. A very good friend of her father, a man held in such great esteem by the family that the children called him "uncle," had sexually abused her from the age of eight to the age of eleven. The abuse began with caressing her genitals, having her touch him, and eventually led to intercourse. At a family gathering, Halima, so incensed at the high regard the family paid this man, confronts him about the abuse. The man becomes very defensive, denies the abuse, and when Halima persists, he threatens her life. Many of her family members rally to the man's defence and call Halima a liar. A day later, she receives a message on the answering machine at her apartment. Her abuser says she is filthy, a troublemaker, and is hurting her family by making these accusations. He also says if she tells authorities no man will ever marry her because she is not a virgin. Due to her fear of the man's threat and with the support of her female roommate, Halima goes to the police. At the police station, an officer takes her complaint and asks her to write out everything she can remember about the abuse and tells her to come back when she is finished. The officer later puts this narrative, her answering machine tape, and a statement directed by the police officer into her file. Based on this evidence, the Crown lawyer decides to charge the accused with sexual assault, sexual interference, and invitation to sexual touching.

WHEN YOU REPORT TO the police that a sexual crime has taken place, you are taking the first step in assigning criminal responsibility to the person who assaulted you. Although each reporting experience, and the police response that follows, is unique, there are common elements to the investigation of sexual crimes. In this chapter, we systematically walk you through the typical reporting procedures: police interviews, investigation, arrest of the accused, and decisions about laying charges. The goal of this chapter is to point out what you can expect when you report a sexual assault, and how the police will investigate your allegations.

There are a number of steps necessary before your case actually gets to criminal court. The first step is reporting the crime to the police who record the complaint. If, based on your account, the police determine the offender has likely engaged in criminal behaviour, they will investigate. When the investigation is completed and the suspect has had the opportunity to make a statement, the police (or sometimes the Crown lawyer) decide if they will lay charges and they determine what those charges will be. Once authorities have laid charges, the prosecuting lawyer then establishes the process for the accused to answer the charges in a court of law. Depending on circumstances, your case may go all the way to a trial and sentencing or it may be resolved at any of the steps along the way. See Appendix 7 for an overview of how a case would proceed through the complete criminal process. In later chapters, we discuss these steps in more detail.

Deciding whether to report your sexual assault is clearly a big decision, with emotional and legal consequences for you and those close to you. In the previous chapter, we touched on some of the potential emotional costs and benefits of pursuing your case in criminal court. The court process begins with your report to the police, so what you read in the last chapter should assist you to make a decision about reporting the crime. Given the many stresses encountered within the justice system, it is not surprising that most victims of sex crimes see significant obstacles to reporting.[1] Research suggests that 88 percent or more of all sexual assault crimes go unreported. These low reporting rates indicate a very unfortunate and disturbing reality: sexual crimes are the most under-reported of all types of crime.

There are many reasons why victims of sexual assaults never report their experiences to the police. Some victims do not realize that a criminal offence has occurred. These victims may feel violated but do not appreciate that they have legal recourse to hold the offender accountable. This can occur with child victims, victims sexually assaulted by husbands, victims who were too drunk to consent to sex, victims who were too afraid to say no to sex, or victims who blame themselves for what happened. Other victims do not report the crime due to threats or actual violence by the offender.

They are fearful of the harm that could befall them or their loved ones should they report. Individuals disenfranchised from mainstream culture, isolated within their community, or from divergent cultural backgrounds may experience additional obstacles to reporting sexual assaults.

Vulnerable people, such as sex-trade workers, the homeless, or new immigrants, may have little faith in the police or trust in the justice system. First Nations people may particularly distrust government or other mainstream authority figures due to a history of abuse in government-run residential schools or due to personal experiences of racism. Within some ethnic groups, a woman tainted by a sex crime falls to a rung lower on the community social ladder than the man who sexually assaulted her. She is the one ostracized and punished while the community protects the offender. Male victims have no fewer barriers to reporting. They may fear a stigma will attach to them if another male has sexually assaulted them. If the offender is a woman, the shame of the failure to defend himself or the perception that others do not view this as an assault may contribute to the male victim's silence and failure to report.

There may be one overriding reason or a combination of reasons deterring any particular individual from reporting a sexual crime. We note some of the most commonly given explanations for not reporting below:

- Fear of or threats by the offender
- Social stigma of being a sexual assault victim
- Embarrassment, shame, or blame for being sexually assaulted
- History of negative experiences or mistrust of police or other authorities
- Concern about the negative reactions, criticism, shame, or judgment of family, friends, or community
- Fear of being disbelieved, especially if the abuser is in a perceived position of power or esteem in the community
- Fear that private aspects of one's life will be exposed and judged by family, friends, or others
- Feeling that the assault was not serious enough

INCENTIVES FOR REPORTING A SEXUAL CRIME

DESPITE THE OBSTACLES TO reporting a sexual assault to the police, there are those who do come forward. It is from these people that we learn how to overcome some of the impediments to reporting. Below are some of the reasons that victims have given for coming forward. You may recognize some thoughts and feelings that have affected your own decision-making. Among other motivations, victims report sexual crimes to the police for one or a combination of these reasons:

- To protect themselves or others (for example, a younger sibling) from future harm
- To remove an abusive family member from the home
- To expose the offenders for who they really are
- To have their voices heard and the truth revealed
- To promote personal healing
- To make the offender finally accept responsibility and apologize
- To force the offender to get some help
- To provide others with an explanation for why the victim is a certain way
- To have what was done to the victim taken seriously
- To obtain justice — having the offender punished and publicly held accountable
- To qualify for criminal injury compensation programs
- To pursue civil action (the civil lawyers have told victims to report as a prerequisite to civil redress)
- To model for the victim's children the civic duty to report
- To make the abuse stop

Consider your motives

ALTHOUGH THE ABOVE ARE legitimate reasons to pursue a legal course of action, not all sentiments will serve you well. You could be setting yourself up for disappointment if your main motivation is to have the offender apologize or express regret. This common desire is understandable, but seldom achieved through the courts. As noted in Chapter 4, you will fare better throughout the legal process if you set realistic goals from the outset. This means appreciating that you have little control over the outcome of your case. The court's ultimate form of "justice" may seem neither just nor fair to you, so try not to over-invest in a particular outcome. A disappointing or distressing outcome does not have to derail your personal healing. Coming forward and speaking out, no matter what the court ultimately decides, can be an important step in your healing journey.

In terms of outcome for the offender, there are various sentiments that may motivate victims, such as a desire for revenge or a desire to have the offender incarcerated for the sake of community safety and rehabilitation. Interestingly, a large number of victims are motivated to bring charges in an effort to feel safe and to stop the abuse, rather than a desire to see the offender punished. Many victims say they just want the offenders to get help, which they will not seek on their own. Revenge, even when achieved, does not typically help with the healing process. A psychologically healthier perspective is to work toward public acknowledgment of the crime, immediate safety for you and other potential victims, accountability for the actions of those involved, and prevention of future assaults by the offender.

MAKING A DECISION TO REPORT

WHEN AND WHERE YOU decide to make a report should depend as much upon your current life circumstances as it does on your sentiments or motivations. Reporting a sexual crime is a major decision and you should consider the full landscape of your life before you do it. Be sure you will have the time, energy, and stamina to go the distance once you report. This means taking into account diverse issues including your physical health, emotional conditions, work situation, finances, social matters, and spiritual well-being. Some pressures in our life, such as chronic illness, are unavoidable and persistent, but rarely do situations arise in which we cannot exert at least some control to improve matters. If there are some temporary stresses you are dealing with, like a child's acute illness, new job pressures, pregnancy, or a residential move, you might want to take some time to deal with these issues before beginning legal proceedings.

A survey of these areas of your life can quickly point out where your strengths are or where you may need to make some changes before burdening yourself with more challenges. You will find a life stressors guide for this purpose in Appendix 8. This guide will help make some of these abstract issues more tangible and will help you think more concretely about personal preparations you can make. Photocopy and use it to assess which areas of your life may need some attention or change before proceeding with the decision to report or making other important decisions. You may want to fill out the life stress scale with a support person who is capable of understanding your situation and giving some guidance. The legal process can be arduous, and you do not want to add pressures to an already overburdened life. In the case of historical abuse, consider making your report at a time when you will be best able to meet the increased challenges you are likely to face.

ACTING ON THE DECISION TO REPORT

ONCE YOU HAVE MADE the decision to report the crime against you it is important to understand the full implications of your decision. When you report a crime to the police, your case begins. Reporting the crime is not an isolated feature of your case, as the police will record your words and actions starting from this point. If the suspect is charged, everything you tell police and the way you report it becomes evidence. Anything you say, even to people outside the reporting process, can also become evidence. For example, a complainant says to a friend of the accused, "He's a good guy; I can't believe that he meant to do this — maybe it was because he was drunk." The defence could later use this statement in court to indicate that the complainant did not believe the accused intended to assault her, and that he was mistaken on the issue of consent. Of course you are not going to stop talking to those around you, but be prudent, because what you say could show up at trial.

Be mindful that any aspect of your initial contact with the police can eventually come under scrutiny. For example, there have been cases in which the defence suggested that, because a certain person accompanied the complainant for the initial report, this was evidence of a conspiracy against the accused. The 9-1-1 recording of the victim reporting a crime can be recovered as evidence. It can be used to demonstrate that the complainant was intoxicated at the time of the crime or it might be used to suggest the complainant was not distressed at the time. Sometimes a defence lawyer will use the notes of the first responding officer to cross-examine both that officer and the complainant in an effort to expose inconsistencies in their account of the crime.

Where there is a problem with the authenticity of a complaint, it will frequently show up at the reporting stage. Based on this premise, complainants should expect the police to test their words and behaviour at this preliminary stage. Such testing is part of the process that will establish the validity of your claim; it is not intended to be a judgment of your character. Nonetheless, for the reasons outlined above, taking your complaints to the police can be a very distressing and anxiety-provoking experience, particularly if the offender is someone well known to you. You can ease the tension by preparing yourself mentally, emotionally, and physically in advance. We assist you in this process by outlining the steps to take in going to the police and what to expect when you do. Once you have read this section you can refer to Appendix 9 for a checklist of tips to make reporting go more smoothly.

Initial contact

IN THE IMMEDIATE AFTERMATH of a sexual assault, you can call 9-1-1 or whatever emergency response phone number is available in your area for assistance. Although the response time can vary depending on the circumstances, an emergency call generally results in a rapid response from the police, perhaps within minutes. If you are in danger at the time due to injuries sustained or due to the assailant being in your immediate vicinity, the 9-1-1 dispatcher can summon police and the appropriate medical help as well.

Regardless of your circumstances, we recommend that you initially contact the police by telephone, rather than showing up unannounced at your local police station. When the assault has occurred in the past, and you are not in imminent danger, you should report the crime by phone to the non-emergency police number listed in the front of your local telephone directory. When you call the non-emergency police number, the communications centre will transfer the call to a police officer, who will either ask you to come to the police station or will send someone to you.

Calling ahead gives you the opportunity to schedule an appointment at a mutually agreed upon date and time. This will prevent you from showing up when the station is closed, no one is available to take your report, or the staff is too busy to deal with you effectively. Although you can certainly go to the police without a prior appointment, calling ahead can reduce tension and confusion.

If the assault has occurred recently in your home, be sure to make this known because there may be evidence present that the police can collect. Similarly, if the assault happened recently and you have not seen a doctor for a medical examination, tell the responding officer this as well. The idea that a police car will come to their home upsets some complainants. Some fear this will make an already difficult situation worse by encouraging gossip among the neighbours. If this is the case for you, tell the operator about your concerns and discuss other options. An officer could possibly attend your residence in an unmarked car or it may be more appropriate for you to go to the police station.

When you telephone the police, have a pen and paper handy to jot down information that you will need. If you feel too overwhelmed to do this, you could arrange for a friend or family member to be with you when you phone and to take notes for you as you repeat information aloud. If there is no urgency and you prefer to make your report in person, arrange an appointment by telephone to meet an officer at the police station. In these cases, when you phone you can ask about general services or those specific to you that can make the reporting process go more smoothly. Asking specific questions ahead of time can help you feel better prepared when you actually meet with the police officer. You also can avoid wasting time and emotional energy on practical matters at the time when you actually want to make your report. For example, you might want to ask about the following:

- Directions to the nearest police station (including bus routes or parking facilities)
- Hours they are open to take non- emergency complaints
- If you can request a male or female interviewer
- How long you will be there
- If you can bring a support person
- If a victim services person will be available
- Availability of interpreting services, if necessary
- Wheelchair access, if necessary

The police officer who initially attends to a complainant or crime scene is called the "first responder" and is the person who decides what the police need to do next. First responders do not necessarily have training or experience in dealing with sex crimes; their job is to handle the initial stages of a criminal investigation. If the crime has just occurred, this may mean getting medical help, calling for an all-points bulletin, preserving crime scene evidence, or finding a suspect. The first responder will take short written statements from the complainant and any witnesses, or may have them write out their own statements. After asking some initial questions, the case may then be transferred to an experienced officer or detective trained to investigate that particular type of crime. Procedures can vary depending on the jurisdiction, with larger jurisdictions having more and specialized staff.

Preparing mentally

PREPARATION CAN MAKE THE reporting process go more smoothly, so in non-emergency circumstances take time to gather your thoughts before you actually meet with the police to file your report. Try to take care of practical issues in advance, such as the following:

- Setting aside an entire day for your report so you will not be worrying about time
- Arranging for childcare or other kinds of assistance you might need that day
- Setting up an enjoyable, distracting schedule or relaxing, healthy activity preceding the interview (a game, vigorous exercise, or watching an engaging movie)
- Taking along some light reading, a crossword puzzle, easy-to-carry craft work, or an electronic game to occupy your time if you have to wait at the police station
- Arranging to meet and talk afterwards with a trusted friend, family member, or therapist. This sort of debriefing is supportive and may help you remember any omissions

You can avoid having your case get off on the wrong foot by being prepared to provide the police with specific details about the assault. You should be able to provide the correct date of the offence and location of the crime scene. If your complaint is historic (the crime was not reported immediately), take the time to figure out as specifically and accurately as possible when and where it happened. You might draw a time chart on which you plot the years and relevant demographic information (see Figure 1). This clearly links together dates, ages, and activities. If you make such a chart for yourself, have it with you when you speak to the authorities. If you need to look at school records, rental agreements, or other reference documents to get the right dates, do so. Keep copies of these, as they could be valuable reference material as the case progresses. Be mindful that you could be asked to show the documents that back up your report.

Jotting quick notes in a day timer, diary, or even on scrap pieces of paper will help you keep facts straight, or at least remind you what you have said. Without written notes, you are unlikely to remember precisely what you said, especially over long periods; this is why the police keep notebooks. Jot down the facts as you remember them, in clear language and in legible writing, rather than your opinions or feelings. Remember that the defendant is entitled to ask to see any notes that you have relied upon that are related to the crime. Only very private notes of a personal nature that have minimal relevance to the case can be kept from the defence in a sex crime trial. If you make notes do not destroy them and be truthful about having them. The appearance of trying to hide something can damage your credibility. Later in the legal process, you will be allowed to go over the transcripts of statements you previously made, but you will not have access to the notes any officers made about you.

Figure 1   Time Chart

Year	Age	Grade, Employment	Significant events
1976	0		Born in Montreal
1977	1		
1978	2		
1979	3		Moved to Vancouver
1980	4		
1981	5	K	
1982	6	K–1	Parents divorced
1983	7	1–2	
1984	8	2–3	Moved to Victoria
1985	9	3–4	
1986	10	4–5	Father died
Etc.			

Preparing emotionally

AS ALWAYS, YOU CAN best deal with emotionally charged situations by using effective stress coping techniques, such as those reiterated throughout this book (see especially Chapter 5). In the case of filing a police report, it also helps to understand that your account becomes part of the investigative process. The questions asked of you are part of the information and evidence-gathering protocol used by police. These are questions typically asked of sexual assault complainants, so try not to personalize them.

After you have worked up the courage to report the crime to the police, especially if it is after a lengthy period of deliberation, you may feel annoyed, diminished, saddened, or even humiliated by the apparent emotional detachment of the police. Their seeming indifference to your plight may discourage you. Bear in mind that receiving sexual assault claims is part of police officers' jobs; they are trained to gather information in a neutral and calm manner. Their straightforward style of questioning can actually help you disclose evidence relevant to the crime. Stay calm, remember this moment will not last forever, and answer all questions as deliberately and thoughtfully as you can. If you omit details, refuse to answer some questions, or lie to or mistreat the police officer, your credibility may suffer and the strength of your complaint may be affected. A victim services worker from the police agency can help you emotionally with this part of the process. Ask for a referral at the earliest opportunity.

Prepare yourself physically

AS WE HAVE ALREADY noted, taking care of your physical health goes a long way to ensuring your mental and psychological well-being. Do your best to get adequate rest, exercise, and nutrition. This will be particularly important in the days just prior to your scheduled police report. This is often much easier said than done. Periods of increased stress often interfere with your sleeping and eating patterns, so do not add additional tension by berating yourself about these difficulties, just do your best to care for your body during this stressful time. Preparing for interviews and appointments in the ways discussed here are not only beneficial to your case but can also serve as a way to minimize unproductive anxiety. Instead of excessively ruminating and worrying about what lies ahead, use some of that nervous energy for constructive activities. You can walk off tension or prepare meals ahead of time. Because you may spend considerable time waiting at the police station, it is also a good idea to take drinks and snacks with you. If you take medication, make sure these are on hand and ready to take with you if need be. Although these sorts of preparations may seem excessive, taking care of such small, but important details as you go along can add up to a big advantage in the long run.

Evidence preservation

IN THE END, YOUR courage, certainty, and emotional preparation will not be sufficient on their own to hold your assailant responsible. The court must rely on evidence to decide innocence or guilt. When you decide to report the crime, make every effort to preserve physical evidence. In the immediate aftermath of assault, things should be left as they are until the police can come and gather evidence at the scene. Some people are aware that a bath or shower can wash away human body fluids and hair that would constitute evidence identifying sexual activity and could even implicate an offender, but people often do not consider other important items. Weapons used, marks and rips on clothing, things written by the suspect about the event (letters, notes), important recorded phone messages, personal items left, and fingerprints on common items can all be important to your case. If you choose to report weeks, months, or years after the event, much of the evidence may be lost, but consider what items may still be available. In the well-publicized case of Monica Lewinsky and former President Clinton, she had kept a dress stained with DNA evidence that corroborated her account of their sexual contact. Such DNA evidence can help resolve cases even years after the crime was committed.

Keep in mind that emergency centres record 9-1-1 calls on a master tape, and preserve them for a short period in case they are needed as evidence in subsequent court proceedings. The tapes are eventually destroyed if no specific request is made to preserve them. If you called 9-1-1 in great distress, you will remember little of what you actually said on the phone. Possibly, due to the confusion and shock of what has happened, or from embarrassment, you might say things based more on self-preservation or anger than on fact. Later on, authorities may play the tape and question you about it. We alert you to this because sometimes in making statements to police or testifying in court, complainants might report things differently. Forgetting what you said at the time of a 9-1-1 call or making erroneous statements due to emotional turmoil will appear to others as discrepancies in your account of the crime. If you say something in court that is different from what you said during the 9-1-1 call, the defence may use this to support the argument that your account is unreliable. The earlier in the process you can correct any inconsistencies, the better.

REPORTING OF SEXUAL CRIMES

IF SOMEONE STEALS YOUR car, you would most likely go to the authorities immediately or shortly after the offence was committed, and you would relate all the details of the theft as best you could. Victims of sexual crimes do not always report in this manner for a number of reasons, including confusion, uncertainty, shame, fear, embarrassment, or misunderstanding. Those assaulted when they were children may not completely understand what has happened to them until years later, or they may feel it necessary to protect the offender. When sexual assault victims do finally go to the authorities, they may find it traumatic or extremely embarrassing to recount their experience. For these reasons, sexual crimes are reported to the authorities in a number of ways that differ from the reporting of other crimes.

Third-party reports

THE REPORT OF A crime by a person other than the victim is called a "third-party report." Anyone can act as a third party in making such reports — a friend, family member, or anyone else who is concerned. Where the strength of the case rests significantly on the victim's version of events, the police will not proceed with charges based solely on the report of a third person; the victim must make a statement. Whether you are the victim or a third party aware of a sexual crime but hesitant to report it, one option is to consult a lawyer for advice on how to make a complaint while maintaining anonymity. A lawyer can communicate the complaint to the police to ensure that they get the relevant information without implicating the lawyer's client. If a child is at risk, the lawyer will inform you that you have an obligation to report and not to do so may constitute a contravention of the law.

Sex crimes involving children

YOUNGER CHILDREN RARELY REPORT sexual crimes directly to the police; instead, cases of sexual assault involving children frequently originate from a concerned adult. In fact, if you know that someone is sexually abusing a child, you have a legal obligation, according to provincial legislation, to report the crime to the local child protection agency or the police. Governments enacted this legislation to protect children who are vulnerable and not mature enough to make a report themselves. In most circumstances, reporting to the local child protection agency fulfills this legal obligation. If the sexual abuse is ongoing and it is important to intervene quickly, the most prudent course is to contact the police directly.

Reports to authorities often come from professionals who have close contact with children, such as doctors, school counsellors, teachers, or daycare workers. In the course of a medical or dental examination, doctors may see physical injuries to a child that could be the result of sexual abuse.

Ethically and legally, these professionals are obligated to report their findings to the proper authorities so they can investigate the matter and protect the child from further abuse. In contrast, the same doctor is not obligated to report evidence of sexual assault of an adult patient. In fact, privacy laws prohibit the doctor from reporting abuse of a patient without the adult patient's consent.

Reports may also originate from someone the child tells about the crime — the non-offending parent, a family member, a friend, or a teacher. This kind of reporting often raises questions about the validity of the complaint. If a child has told an adult about the abuse first, the courts have to consider whether the account is solely from the child, or partly from the recipient. This is why it is so important that an adult listen carefully to a child and make notes afterwards. The recipient of the child's disclosure must let the child speak, and not presume to "fill in the blanks" when the child is hesitant or unsure. Carefully worded, non-leading questions can encourage conversation in a manner that provides good information for caregivers and the authorities later.

A good strategy is to refrain from trying to question the child excessively before the police or social services interview the child. However, even experienced social workers and police sometimes fall into the trap of asking questions that may inappropriately direct the child's responses. Often people ask leading questions without even knowing they are doing so. The legal system is more likely to consider the report valid when the adult can reiterate the exact words a child said before the child was questioned. The ideal situation is to have experts interview the child as soon as possible following a disclosure.

Delayed reporting of sex crimes

DELAYED REPORTS, MONTHS OR even years after the assaults, present a unique challenge to the police and the prosecutor. The police want to solve crimes and they know their chances of success are better when untouched evidence is available.

When reporting is delayed, evidence is generally contaminated or lost, diminishing the chances of a successful prosecution. Delayed reporting may also raise questions about why the complainant is coming forward now, rather than before: "If this really happened, why did you not take the opportunity to report it before?" Until 1983, judges instructed the jury to consider the complaint suspect if the victim of a sex crime did not report the crime right away. That rule has now disappeared from court procedure, and nobody can assume the complaint is dubious due to a delay in reporting. Nevertheless, it is still an important issue and may cause people to speculate about the complainant's motives. The Supreme Court of Canada said this about the reporting issue in the landmark case of *R. v. D.D*:[2]

> A trial judge should recognize and so instruct a jury that there is no inviolable rule on how people who are the victims of trauma like a sexual assault will behave. Some will make an immediate complaint, some will delay in disclosing the abuse, while some will never disclose the abuse. Reasons for delay are many and at least include embarrassment, fear, guilt, or a lack of understanding and knowledge. In assessing the credibility of a complainant, the timing of the complaint is simply one circumstance to consider in the factual mosaic of a particular case. A delay in disclosure, standing alone, will never give rise to an adverse inference against the credibility of the complainant.

Be prepared to answer the question "Why now?" Although your first reaction may be to feel insulted or disbelieved, try to view this from an investigative perspective. The police and the defence lawyers need to understand why a complainant did not come forward immediately. Be prepared to explain truthfully and clearly any delay in reporting to the police. Take time to examine what your thoughts and feelings were at the time of the offence, and what circumstances led you to postpone your disclosure. Reflect on the timing issue until you are confident and clear about your reasons, and then make sure your explanation of the delay in reporting is accurate.

Reporting an assault you had previously denied

COURT OFFICERS WILL VIEW a delayed report differently from the situation in which you denied the abuse when initially asked. Suppose a hockey coach assaulted Joe, a twelve-year-old child on his team. Perhaps Joe's friends and family became suspicious of the coach's behaviour and someone asked Joe if any abuse was occurring. Joe was not ready to tell anyone about his experiences and denied any wrongdoing. Ten years later, he feels ready to disclose, and goes to the police. During the course of the ensuing investigation, the police interview people who tell them that Joe had previously denied any abuse. Joe's earlier denial then becomes part of the record, and it is consequently open to examination throughout the legal process. The defence lawyer will likely challenge Joe about the disparity between his two claims. Joe will have to admit that he was not honest when initially questioned. He should be given an opportunity to explain the inconsistency and, if the explanation for his initial dishonesty is not believed, his credibility with the police, the court, or the jury will be damaged. If a denial of sexual abuse is made under oath in court or in an affidavit, it will have an even more serious, deleterious effect on the complainant's credibility that could prove insurmountable in securing a conviction. Without strong confirming evidence or an admission by the accused, the prosecutor will have an extremely difficult task overcoming the doubt cast upon a case by an earlier denial under oath.

Reporting without pressing charges

WHEN SOMEONE REPORTS A crime to the police, the general expectation is that authorities will conduct an investigation and determine if the evidence is sufficient to press charges and proceed to court. Some complainants, however, want to report a sexual assault to the police without having charges brought. In these cases, the complainant just wants the assault to be on the record with the police. The complainant may be curious to see if the assailant has a record of sexual assaults, may want to warn others of the assailant's behaviour, or may want documentation in case the behaviour escalates. Some police agencies cooperate with complainants who want to do this; they simply keep a record of the incident. However, there are no guarantees. The police may discover the assailant is a suspect in another case or has a lengthy record and believe charges must be pursued. Alternatively, the police may know of an ongoing prosecution and inform the Crown of this new complaint. The Crown may decide that this new evidence should go to the jury as "similar fact" evidence to show the behaviour pattern of the accused thereby strengthening its case. There have been cases in Canada where hesitant witnesses have been compelled to give evidence against their will. If you have concerns about this, check with a lawyer before making a report.

Another challenge occurs when a complainant reports an assault, requests no charges, and then later reverses this decision and requests to have charges pursued. If the case does then go to trial, the initial record may be weak because the police would not have taken a full statement or conducted a full investigation. The police may have briefly noted the reasons given for not wanting to press charges initially or there may be no record at all. This gives the defence an opportunity to question the motives of the complainant and contest the sketchy details of the initial report. The chances of being able to reconstruct the facts of the assault may be slim, particularly after a lengthy lapse of time. If the defence disputes a complainant's motivation for pursuing charges in the first place, the reversal of a decision to press charges can be particularly problematic.

To guard against any misunderstandings about your intentions, if you want to report without charging, consider obtaining a copy of the police record to ensure that it accurately reflects what happened and records your intentions. If the police ask you to provide a statement, obtain a copy for your records and keep it in a safe place should you need it in the future. The police will not necessarily keep the kinds of records you would need to be successful in pursuing subsequent charges.

False reporting

ALTHOUGH THE VAST MAJORITY of reports are valid, people do make false reports for a variety of reasons, and this is a serious matter for you, for the falsely accused, and for the system. It is a criminal offence to make a false report to police. The report remains on police records, and can potentially become evidence used against you later in unrelated matters. A false report is like "crying wolf"; not only will authorities lose respect for the claims of the person who makes a false report, it can shade their opinions of others who make similar, but legitimate complaints. If for whatever reason you have made a false complaint you should seek legal advice immediately to understand your rights but also to prevent any further prejudice to the wrongfully accused.

THE POLICE INVESTIGATION

AFTER THE FIRST RESPONDER has taken a handwritten statement, any investigation will start with formal and controlled interviews by police officers assigned to the case. In the most serious cases, and in jurisdictions with a large population, the first responder will likely have submitted a report to officers who have specialized training in sexual assault investigations. Typically, these officers will be different from those who took the initial complaint. Their objective is to discover and collect evidence that either supports or refutes the complainant's allegation that a crime has taken place.

We encourage you to tell the truth as the best means of navigating the justice system but, in telling your truth, you may inadvertently use words in ways that complicate or confuse matters. Some complainants tell their story in a manner that suggests the listener knows at least some of the facts and can fill in the blanks. Do not make this assumption; imagine instead, that each person you talk to has never heard the story before, knows nothing about what happened, and is not assuming you were assaulted. You have the full responsibility to find the words that convey exactly what happened. You have to paint on a clean canvas with explanatory colours that demonstrate what really happened. Do not exaggerate. Do not minimize. Tell the truth as precisely as possible and with whatever details you can remember.

Warnings to tell the truth

SOME POLICE FORCES THINK it is a good idea to give a warning that if you do not tell the truth they will charge you with public mischief. Some of the statement forms have this written on them for the witness to read and sign. You might want to read the form carefully, think seriously before you sign it, and even get a copy of what you signed for your own file.

In come cases, the investigators may have concerns that complainants will change their minds, change their testimony, or not show up in court. This is most likely to occur when the complainant is in an intimate relationship with the alleged assailant. In such an instance, the police may opt for an interview process called a KGB statement, developed because of the *R. v. K.G.B.* case.[3] If, during your police interview, the officer takes a KGB statement you will be aware of this. It is a much more formal procedure than the regular statement-taking process.

When taking a KGB statement, an officer will come in and read a list of warnings to you related to the legal obligation to tell the truth to the police. He will ask if you prefer to swear to tell the truth or affirm to do so. The entire process is voluntary. In addition, he will tell you, and you will see, that both the oath or affirmation taking and the interview process are being videotaped. Having provided a KGB statement, if the complainant then testifies and denies the contents, the Crown may seek to have the taped interview put in as evidence that the crime happened as the complainant earlier stated. This is one way the Crown and police ensure that your original statement is reliable. If authorities decide to pursue charges, they will have confidence to proceed where historically they have seen a witness recant or fail to show up in court. If you have provided a KGB statement and later decide to deny the accusations, you may find that you are still a witness due to your original testimony. Because it is a sworn statement, the KGB has significant weight in court and ensures that the story will not go away.

Face inconsistencies early and directly

INCONSISTENCIES IN A COMPLAINANT'S account over the course of the reporting process, the investigation, and trial are common, and frequently become a crucial factor in the outcome of legal proceedings. You may have deliberately not told the truth for a number of reasons. You may have lied to your assailant as part of a survival strategy. Some victims lie and tell their assailant that someone is coming home, that they like him, or that they have a communicable disease, all in the hope of affecting the offender's behaviour and gaining escape. If you have used this type of strategy, it will likely be in your narrative to police and can be explained when necessary. Inconsistencies may also arise if you forget, or fail to mention, something in an earlier interview that you recall in a later interview or statement. For your own reasons you may deliberately tell authorities falsehoods that will be difficult to defend later. Whatever the discrepancy, the best approach is to address it directly and truthfully as soon as it becomes apparent.

Here is a hypothetical situation to illustrate the point. A boyfriend had sexually assaulted Margaret when she was twenty years old. She quickly called 9-1-1, but the police did not arrive for three hours. When another man assaulted her at age thirty-one, Margaret, remembering her first experience, was determined to make sure the police arrived more quickly so she told the 9-1-1 operator that her assailant had a knife and she was seriously injured, neither of which was true. When the investigating officer took her statement, she admitted lying to the operator. In court, the defence asked Margaret if she had lied to the operator in order to make the assault sound worse than it was. The lawyer then asked about the previous sexual assault when she was twenty years old. Had she lied about that too? What a mess! The judge has to decide whether her lying to the operator should affect her credibility. If she admitted lying about some details, could the court believe other aspects of her story?

In this hypothetical case, the Crown would deal with the situation by first requesting that the previous assault not be admitted as evidence except to the extent that it helps explain Margaret's later exaggeration. The Crown will suggest that her exaggeration was reasonable under the circumstances and that departure from the truth in that instance should not take away from her credibility in other aspects of the case. The defence may try to include the details of the previous sexual assault but there is case law that suggests it would have trouble convincing the court that these details are relevant. The defence will argue that the 9-1-1 call is but another example of a witness exaggerating her claims and therefore she should not be believed as a whole. To see a more detailed exploration of issues associated with factual inconsistencies, please refer to Appendix 10.

Sexual assault accusations are serious business. The accused and the defence lawyer are very concerned about the potential loss of liberty and the subsequent criminal record if the complainant's case is successful. Even if you are very sincere and scrupulous in your account, suggestions will likely be made that you are not. We encourage you to be honest and conscientious when dealing with authorities, and to document your story so those testing the complaint will see that you have been so.

INTERVIEWING THE COMPLAINANT

THE POLICE OFFICER RESPONSIBLE for an investigation will want to arrange an interview of the complainant. This is a very important part of the investigation and a part you should take very seriously even if you feel you have expended a lot of emotional energy making your initial report. The documents generated in the investigation phase will be used throughout the trial, and beyond in some cases. We recommend that you listen to the officer and read any instructions carefully. If you do not understand something, have it clarified and get independent advice if you feel the need. Know with whom you are dealing. Get the business cards or phone numbers of the people working on your case, and start to develop a congenial relationship with them; you may need to come back to them with more details, questions, and updates.

The police officer responsible for an investigation will want to have some background information before interviewing the complainant. You can expect that person to have read the reports of the first responding officer and to have checked your name and the suspect's name against the police databases. A good investigator will know if the complainant has made a report before, whether it is against the same suspect, and whether the complainant or the suspect (if identified) has a criminal record.

A criminal record or a previous false allegation by the complainant should not stop the investigation from taking place, but it may affect the decision to lay charges. If the defence counsel asks, the Crown will provide a copy of the complainant's criminal record after checking to make sure it is accurate. The Crown will also decide if previous convictions are relevant to the case; an impaired driving charge may not be, whereas a perjury charge might be. Witnesses are likely to be asked about their criminal records on the witness stand. Having a criminal record or denying that a record exists will both reflect negatively on the complainant's credibility.

Another issue of credibility arises if the complainant has a history of making allegations the police believe are false. Prior false allegations will certainly raise concern that the current complaint may also be false. In this situation, the investigators may not lay charges unless they have other evidence to corroborate the complainant's statement. Making previous false allegations is different from the situation where the complainant has made previous charges that could not be substantiated. In this case, the allegations may be valid, but there is not enough evidence to proceed. The fact of previous unsubstantiated complaints will likely be kept out of any subsequent trial. Neither the police nor the Crown should use these unsubstantiated complaints as a reason to discontinue the investigation as long as the new complaint is complete and reliable. The court recognizes that some people are in situations that make them particularly vulnerable to repeated sexual assaults. People in these vulnerable situations can help themselves by learning more about the legal process and by developing a safety plan and self-care skills. Victim assistance programs, women's shelters, and women's health centres can often help in this regard.

THE INTERVIEW FORMAT

THE POLICE MAY CONDUCT their interview with you in a number of different ways. The way they choose to record your behaviour and what you say can affect the credibility of your report and the course of the subsequent legal proceedings. Although you are a witness and not the investigator, with some cautions you can take appropriate initiatives to ensure the police are getting the necessary information from you and properly recording what you say. Be forewarned that giving a statement is an important process and most complainants are not aware what the important elements of a statement are. If you prepare a written statement on your own, you may inadvertently cause problems for your case. The statement you give to the police is not recorded as "just rough notes;" it will be used later in legal proceedings. If you have doubts about what is important or relevant, ask. You can simply say, "I don't know how to do it," "I need your help," or "I would prefer to do this with you; I'm not sure what's important." Do not sidetrack the case by giving irrelevant and potentially complicating information. Here are some guidelines to consider:

- If you do not feel comfortable with the officer who is conducting the interview, calmly explain your reasons why and work out an alternate plan. As an example, it may be that you prefer an officer of your own gender, for example.

- Do the interview face-to-face with the officer. Do not merely write out your own statement and hand it in. You need the assistance of a trained person who can guide you through the relevant narrative and questions so you do not leave out important information or file a complaint with superfluous, irrelevant material.

- It is best if you do the interview alone with the officer. Others present may influence you in subtle or not so subtle ways. (See further discussion below.)

- The interviewer should audiotape or videotape your responses. If you are under the age of eighteen, or have a disability that affects your communication, videotape is preferable. You need to speak clearly and at a pace that allows others to understand you. Try not to speak with your head down or your mouth covered.

- Stick to one complaint about one person at a time. Naturally, if you had two assailants at the same time, you will talk about what they did in the same interview. Otherwise, focus on one incident at a time and make sure you give all the relevant facts before moving on.

- Start by narrating details of the important events with minimal sidetracking. Once you have completed the "who, when, where, and what" of the complaint, go back and fill in details where called for. The officer can then ask you more directive questions about pertinent topics.

- Try to relate the events in chronological order. You may have only fragments of memory about some events, but try to order them as clearly and precisely as possible. Tell the officer when events are not clear for you or when events are out of chronological order.

- If you later realize that there are details you left out or that you were mistaken about something and want to correct this, go back to the officer and give another statement.
- Check with the investigator when the transcript is completed (weeks later) and explain that you would like to come back, listen to the tape, and make sure the transcription is complete.

If you are an adult reporting sexual abuse that occurred during your childhood or teenage years, the interview poses special challenges for both you and the police. The case depends on your ability to recall historical information. As discussed in Chapter 4, when the events happened years ago, particularly if the events were traumatic or chaotic, complex patterns of recall can occur.

In these historical cases, there may be a lot of ground to cover and, because there may be confusion in the recall process, interviews can go on for a long time. In some cases, you may have to go with the officer to actual physical locations to determine if landmarks still exist. To get details right, you may need to go through old photo albums, retrieve school records, find old clothing, or sort out names of friends and relatives from the past for interviewing purposes. Being very well prepared, with written material as a guide, when you attend the interview will help you cover all the necessary material.

Taking a support person

SOME POLICE OFFICERS WILL not allow a person to attend the interview with you. This will certainly be the case if the support person has evidence to offer, but may also become an issue if the support person interrupts or otherwise is seen to interfere with the process. Officers have good reason to be concerned because judges have expressed concern with interview evidence when another person in the room interrupts or tries to help or correct the witness. Such interruptions might make the tape inadmissible and seriously damage the Crown's case; so having a support person with you during the interview can make you feel better in the short term but may have unfavourable long-term consequences for your case. If a support person either has, or appears to have, some interest in the outcome of the case, the defence could later try to use this issue to weaken the complainant's case by suggesting this was not a real complaint but the result of a conspiracy to harm the accused.

Additionally, you may want to have that person as a support during the trial when the defence might raise objections that this person is too close to the facts. These issues are particularly relevant if the support person knows the accused. For example, coming to the police station with the offender's ex-wife or brother-in-law, may be seen as an attempt by that person not only to influence you, but also perhaps to put words in your mouth.

A more appropriate choice of support person is a counsellor, women's centre worker, victim assistance person, or a responsible adult who understands what the role of a supporter is and is seen to be neutral in the process. Such a person is not likely to be a witness in the trial so there would be no perceived conflicts. If you have any concerns about the police interview, you may consider seeking the assistance of a lawyer. Lawyers can give you ideas about how best to participate in an interview without jeopardizing the outcome.

Therapy is not a police officer's job

WHEN THE POLICE INTERVIEW you about your complaint, they conduct an "investigative" interview. This is different from a "therapeutic" interview designed to give you support and enhance personal growth. An investigative interview can feel very cold when what you prefer is a safe, warm haven from your pain or fear, but the police do not have training as therapists and meeting your emotional needs is not their role. The more they can encourage you to focus on the facts and provide the necessary information, the stronger the case will be against the offender. The officer should withhold judgment and take a neutral stance toward the complainant. The complainant's report of a crime is just one piece of evidence; it is not enough to prove that the crime occurred, but it is enough to begin an investigation. To do their job well, the officers have to examine the evidence with alternative hypotheses in mind, while respecting the person reporting the alleged crime. Once the details of the investigation are compiled, the court weighs relevant evidence to determine if a crime has occurred and whether the accused is criminally responsible.

The mandate of police agencies and the courts is to administer justice, not to meet your psychological needs. If you understand this distinction and are confident you can find the emotional support you need with other laypeople or professionals, you will have a much better chance of coming through this stage of legal proceedings without further insult or injury. Recognizing the importance of emotional issues, many police agencies now have victim support workers who may be present for the first police encounter. Although they are not therapists either, it is the job of these individuals to help you with your emotional needs by providing support, accompaniment, information, and referrals.

Managing documents and records

IF YOU EITHER GATHERED or prepared written, detailed accounts of your sexual assault, police should request that you produce these documents. With few exceptions, the police will give copies of these documents to the prosecutor. These documents can be of various sorts; you may have kept a journal or other personal writings that you consider private, or a calendar on the wall marked with relevant appointments and occurrences, or you may have obtained documents from third parties, such as a doctor or a counsellor. Where there is a privacy concern with any document, even if the prosecutor has a copy, the defence can only gain access if you waive your privacy rights or the court issues an order to release it.

You can expect some information will be released, such as information that helps prove who committed the assault, where and when it took place, and how it occurred. Other documents may well be protected. You must tell the police about any information you want kept private so they can keep it sealed and separate from other, less private documents. Not all of the record needs to be released, only those parts relevant to the case. If you want privacy for parts of the record, make the request and it will likely happen.

Hypothetically, let us assume that a female victim went to a sexual assault crisis centre at the time of the assault but did not report the crime to authorities for years. Before making a report to the police, she goes back to the centre and obtains a copy of the file detailing her initial visits there. If she relies on these records for her recall of events, she can expect defence to ask for and to receive, by court order, at least relevant parts of these documents. Later in the proceedings, she can expect people to question her about her visit to the crisis centre.

The law considers diaries to be private records, but all or parts of them may be released to the defence if the witness waives privacy rights or if the court so orders. The court would order the whole diary or parts of it released if it considers the information relevant in determining the guilt or innocence of the accused. The right of privacy gives way to the right of full answer and defence of the accused.

The police will likely take any private records from you for safekeeping. Later, the Crown will inform the defence about the existence, but not the content, of these records, and then seal them in anticipation of the defence making an application to see them. Later still, the court, after hearing from the complainant, will decide, in a hearing independent of the trial, if fairness to the accused demands that the records be released. Some provinces will provide a lawyer to assist the complainant whose records are the subject of such an application.

If the police do not ask for or do not take the private records, it is important that you keep them safe and ready for any later request to produce them. Do not destroy them, as this could result in an abrupt end to the prosecution. If you have any doubts about documents or records you have, talk to a lawyer about the best procedure to follow.

Telling the story in your own words

THE POLICE WILL LIKELY follow a predetermined structure to their interview. Most will begin by building some rapport with you to reduce your tension. They want to create a comfortable atmosphere that encourages you to reveal as much information as possible. Typically, they begin by encouraging a "free narrative," or "pure version" wherein you tell your story in your own words with few directives. They will ask open-ended questions, such as "Can you just tell me what happened, in your own words, beginning anywhere you like." The police must allow the complainant to tell the whole story first; this is the complainant's account and understanding of events, even though it may not be consistent with the facts. Only later will the police ask specific questions, such as "How long have you known this person?" or "What kind of car was it?"

If the assaults happened frequently over weeks or months, many details may be lost and the description may take on a particular narrative quality. For example, the complainant might say, "He would do this and he would do that." Consistent with the nature of script memory, as described in Chapter 4, a complainant may inadvertently merge one event with another. If, for instance, someone has been assaulted repeatedly, several incidents may be merged in his memory. What is described as one incident may be a combination of several incidents. The challenge for the police is to help the complainant separate one incident from another and clear up any confusion or inconsistency.

On the other hand, some in a series of incidents may stand out on their own. A specific episode may be retained in clear detail, perhaps because something unusual or unexpected happened, for example, a person may have walked in and interrupted the assault. The interviewing officer should provide the complainant every chance to talk about each episode as fully as possible. The complainant can name or label the various episodes in some meaningful way for easy reference and for ease of sequencing. If a particular program was on television during an assault, or Aunt Mabel interrupted on one occasion, these two episodes could be called the "Teen Idol time" or the "Aunt Mabel incident." This strategy helps organize your account and can prevent miscommunication.

Examining the details

INVESTIGATING OFFICERS WILL EXPLORE each separate assault in as much detail as possible, and they will want you to be specific about these details. They will want to know dates, times, and specific indicators. Be as precise and specific as possible without guessing. It would more helpful if you were able to indicate, "It was winter, after Valentine's Day, probably late February," instead of "Sometime last year;" or "It was late, at least two hours after midnight," instead of "It was night." The officers will ask you about the city, the street, the building, and the room in which the assault took place. If the assault took place in a vehicle, they will ask you to describe that vehicle and to indicate exactly where in the vehicle the assault occurred. Having someone quiz you on every detail can be very difficult, since it may feel like a challenge to your credibility and it may tax your recall. Do your best to provide the officer with sufficient details; but always avoid guessing or filling in details you cannot actually remember. If you do not remember something, do not be afraid to say so.

Even more challenging may the degree of intimate and private details the police want from you. They will want to know what led up to the incident. They may ask you what you and the alleged offender said and did before the assault. They may ask how you felt at the time and how you expressed those feelings. Although they may be difficult to discuss with a stranger, details of sexual activity are important. The following are some of the detail questions you can expect from the investigating officer:

- Who is the alleged offender? What is your relationship to the offender?
- Where did the assault(s) take place?
- When did the assault(s) take place? What date was it? What time of day was it? Was it during a holiday or some other event?

- What happened? How did it come about?
- What exactly was said? Use the exact words if you can.
- What behaviour did you consider to be an assault and why?
- What parts of the body were touched or contacted by you or the assailant?
- What were you wearing? Where are those clothes?
- Were there any injuries to you or the assailant?
- Were there any weapons used by you or the assailant? What happened to the weapons and where are they now?
- Describe the assailant's appearance and personal characteristics. Describe other aspects of the assailant: a car, an apartment, clothes, jewellery, and associates.
- Were intoxicants used and by whom? Provide details of type, amounts, and effects.
- Can you name any witnesses?
- Who have you told about the assault(s)?

Talking about sexual activity

TALKING ABOUT THE SPECIFICS of sexual contact can be difficult, but precision is very important because some words can mean different things to different people. To say, "We had sex," could mean oral contact, vaginal penetration, anal penetration, or something entirely different, depending on who is making the statement. Research conducted by Hilary Randall and Professor Sandra Byers at the University of New Brunswick in Fredericton[4] clearly demonstrates this reality. They interviewed 164 heterosexual Canadian university students, asking what activities they would classify as "having sex" and what behaviours constituted "unfaithfulness." The researchers discovered tremendous divergence in opinions. While 23 percent of the students believed that oral stimulation of another's genitals to orgasm constituted having sex, 77 percent did not consider this to mean having sex. Of the female students surveyed, 17 percent said anal intercourse with orgasm was not having sex, while only 10 percent of males were of this opinion. See Appendix 11 for the full survey of sexual behaviours.

To avoid any confusion or misunderstanding, the police and lawyers will want to know what part of the offender's body touched what part of the victim's body and who did precisely what. This may require that you use words that embarrass you, like ejaculation, oral sex, or anus. Comfort yourself in knowing that the person you are speaking to is generally at ease with this language and has heard it all before. Knowing these details will allow linkages to be made to other evidence, such as forensic findings, injuries, and statements from others. It will also make clear otherwise fuzzy statements, such as "We had sex."

No words are taboo

SOME COMPLAINANTS AND WITNESSES feel they should edit what they say because it is rude or vulgar to talk about explicit sexual details. This is particularly true for complainants who are unaccustomed to vulgar language in their daily life. They may feel the police will think less of them if they use sexual language. However, in this context, you must appreciate that it is a mistake to hold back needed information for fear of offending the police, lawyers, or the judge. You have permission when talking about what happened to tell it as it is. Use the most precise word you know to describe body parts or the sex act, and if during the incident the offender used foul or vulgar language, do not edit your report for your listener's ears. Professionals working in this area are accustomed to frank language, and you can give a full account only by quoting actual words. If this is difficult for you, share your discomfort with the person interviewing you and likely you will be put at ease. If you still feel unable to say the actual words, ask to write them out if that is more comfortable for you.

Children can have particular difficulty saying certain words to the police or other authority figures. Society typically forbids such language, so they think they will get in trouble even if they are quoting their offender. If you are supporting a child, a simple word of permission normally gets the child over this trepidation. Help the child understand that such language can be used in this context, but be careful not to influence the child in what to say.

Questions about other sexual encounters

THERE IS SOME CONTROVERSY over what questions the investigating police should ask about sexual acts between offender and complainant at times other than the assault. They may want a thorough exploration of the relationship, or the degree of previous intimacy between you and the offender. They may also want to know about your sexual history with other people, either previously or during the period of the assault. This may be important if there is medical evidence that suggests some sexual activity took place.

Once the matter goes to trial, the defence must apply for permission from the court to seek evidence including asking the complainant about sexual activity outside of the subject matter of the charges. The court may permit such questions if they are relevant to the case. If the questions are asked to show that the complainant consented before and therefore must have consented during the alleged assault, or that the complainant frequently has sex with a variety of people, suggesting that the complainant is immoral and should not be believed, the court will prohibit the questions. A problem occurs when the police ask questions during their investigation that the court would prohibit. Since these questions are in the recorded statement, they are relevant at trial as credibility issues.

A complainant does not determine which questions are asked or not asked in either the investigation or the trial. Investigators will ask questions about other sexual activity if they think it is important. In the event that questions are asked that you believe are not relevant, very personal, or both, you have some options. You can say that these are very personal and ask the officer to explain their relevance. If this approach does not clarify the issue, you can seek legal advice about the necessity to give answers to those particular questions.

The matter of which questions are relevant and necessary is not a simple one. This is a serious issue that has provoked ongoing debate. There has been tremendous effort expended to strike a balance between what is fair for the accused and invasive for the complainant. The courts continue to work on a case-by-case basis when deciding where the line should be drawn between providing full evidence and protecting the privacy of the complainant.

Talking about historic abuse

IF YOU ARE RECOUNTING incidents that happened repeatedly some time in your past, try starting with a solid foundation of well-known facts: who was the offender and within what time range did the events happen? Use an age chart, as outlined above, and make sure all dates are accurate. Refer to past documents, for example, school or medical records to help your accuracy. Once you have accurately described the general context, provide the narrative of what happened: "He was my teacher and he would touch me every time he got a chance during recess. This happened when I was in grade four, which was in 1960 and 1961 and I would have been nine to ten years old at the time." Once you have told the narrative, details that are more specific may be triggered: "He told me not to tell" or "He gave me a book as a gift." The police will investigate each of the specific incidents that you recall as a separate crime, so the more detail that you can provide the better. It is understandable if some of the details are just not there; do not try to fill in the blanks if there is no memory, as you may be creating detail, rather than recounting it.

When the interview is complete

THE POLICE WILL RECORD all the information collected during the initial report and the investigative interview. If the case proceeds, they will file written notes and will transcribe any audio or video recordings into a written record. The recordings are important to the later trial as this information will either support or challenge your credibility. All this information is available to both the prosecutor and the defence lawyer. If you do not want the defence to know your address or that of another person because there is a safety concern, you do not have to say the address and phone number on the tape. You can write it down and ask the police to keep it private. The Crown will erase addresses from the transcripts but may not always be able to erase addresses and other personal information from audio and videotapes.

Through human error, some things occasionally are omitted from the recordings. Later in court, you may claim that you gave the police some information at the time of the interview that they did not hear, record, or transcribe. It could also be that you intended to say something, and believe that you did, but you actually did not say it. Usually the officer reviews and checks the accuracy of the transcription once it has been prepared. There will be a note at the bottom of the transcript stating that someone has proofread it. The complainant or witness does not usually get an opportunity to do the comparison, because transcription is typically done weeks after the interview. Months or even years later, when the complainant reviews the statement with the Crown counsel for trial preparation, the complainant will have an opportunity to listen to the tape while reading the transcript.

If you are concerned about the recording procedures, you could consider asking the police for a copy of the taped statements and the transcript. You can then make the comparisons yourself and you will have an extra copy in case the original tape goes missing (this can happen). The down side to having this information is that the defence could accuse you of spreading the details of the assault to others, which is an accusation difficult to dispel.

Certainly, if the police give you a transcript of your statement, do not share it with anybody. Keep it sealed and tucked away so that no one can find it and improperly distribute it. Filing it in your personal office, your home safe, or a lawyer's office are examples of good security.

INTERVIEWING CHILDREN

THIS SECTION WILL BE largely for those who are supporting a child through the whole process of reporting a sexual crime to the police. You can best guide the child if you know some of the perspectives and dynamics considered by justice personnel when children are involved in a case.

The vast majority of sexual abuse allegations made by children are found to be true. False allegations, although infrequent, stand out in the public mind because they are shocking and they tend to be sensational stories the media want to cover. Detailed studies, including those by Jones and McGraw, 1987[5] and Thoennes and Tjaden, 1990,[6] have found that over 90 percent of children's allegations prove to be true. False allegations are most often complaints gone awry due to the influence of or misinterpretation by an adult. Children can recount central details of an assault as accurately as adults do when investigators use optimal interviewing practices.

Legal experts understand well that a poorly conducted child interview can be detrimental and could make or break a case. Over the last twenty-five years, there has been increasing pressure to improve the conduct and practices in child sexual assault cases. Today, professionals are generally aware that younger children are more suggestible to influence than are older children, that a free narrative is difficult to elicit from a young child, and that accuracy suffers if a trusted adult has told the child falsehoods. The child's report of the facts will be negatively affected if the interviewer

- Has biased views
- Is intimidating
- Asks questions that are beyond the ability of the child to understand at a certain developmental level
- Uses legalese, jargon, or other complex language
- Asks misleading questions
- Conducts the interview after a long delay in procedures
- Asks questions not central to the experience of the child, such as details peripheral to what took place

- Asks questions about events in which the child did not participate

In response to this evolving knowledge, police agencies have developed training programs, specialized services, and better techniques to use when conducting a child interview. In some jurisdictions, forensic psychologists conduct all the interviews for the police. Investigators should ideally video-tape the interview of a child, or an adolescent, instead of merely recording and transcribing it. A videotape of a well-conducted interview, done within a reasonable time following the event, is acceptable in court if the witness testifies that the contents are the witness' own genuine effort to tell the truth. This goes a long way in preventing a child from having to repeat details after months or years have passed before a trial begins.

Police have learned that they should guard against steering the interview based on what they know and believe about the reported incident or about other sexual assault cases. They should avoid naming a suspect or talking about the assault before the child raises those details on her own; and they should explain the reasons for the interview in simple language. They should not suggest to the child to "tell a story" or "pretend." They may use simple drawings to promote understanding but should generally avoid using anatomically correct dolls as props. There is controversy whether these props can lead to misinterpretation of the child's account so they are used judiciously to clarify information and usually only at the end of the interview.

Experience suggests that personal qualities of the interviewer are as important as knowledge. The best people to interview a child may be individuals who know little about the case and have no strong views about sexual offenders. To be maximally effective such interviewers should

- Ask non-leading questions
- Not be attached to a single hypothesis about the crime
- Avoid repeating close-ended "yes/no" or multiple choice questions
- Be patient, non-judgmental, and not demanding

Interviewing the child without the parent present

MOST POLICE OFFICERS PREFER that even responsible parents or care-givers not be present in the room when they conduct the interview. A parent's impulse to intervene in the investigation and in the interview itself is normal and expected. As parents, we see it as our job to protect and advocate on behalf of our children. This is our experience when we deal with their teachers, doctors, or sports coaches. Parents, supporting a child in a police interview, typically feel that they must remind the child about forgotten things, correct the child when they think that the child is mistaken, or challenge the police when they do not conduct the interview according to parental expectations.

Parents who are angry about their child's victimization, and are determined to see justice done, can be a negative influence on the investigation. They may not be aware of the guidelines that investigators must follow, or they feel that the guidelines are not helpful and not applicable in their case. A parent may even have serious misconceptions about how the police should do their job. Some parents feel that the best way to proceed is by interrogating the hesitant child until the truth comes out; the method that they use at home to discover which child shaved the family dog, ate the cookies, or instigated a fight among the siblings. It can be very frustrating for parents who have obtained a report of abuse while questioning their child at home, to find that the child reveals no such complaint during the subsequent interview when the police interviewer uses open-ended questions. The police know that an authoritarian interrogation will not produce the kind of evidence necessary for a successful prosecution, and that aggressive questioning could actually jeopardize the case.

Another real issue for the police is the multiplicity of unknown factors at the initial stages of an investigation. Until the police are able to establish rapport with the child, and feel confident that they have heard the child's complete story, they cannot be sure whom to implicate. The person who brought the child to the interview could potentially be complicit in some way. This is a further reason to interview the child alone.

Parents must show restraint when it comes to child victims and witnesses. They should resist the temptation to question or direct their child if a police investigation or litigation is ongoing. Interference can do more harm than good. Parents can inadvertently alter their child's story by seeking information, explaining things, or filling in the blanks. By doing so, they either change the child's evidence or create an aura of contamination that will result in others not trusting the stated facts.

Other issues for a child

FREQUENTLY, A CASE REQUIRES that a variety of people talk to the child, possibly requiring five to ten interviews. Authorities make every effort to minimize the child's stress by restricting the number of interviews, using non-uniformed, experienced interviewers, and using a "soft" interview room with appropriate props and tools for communication. As the case develops, however, more issues may arise, leading to more questions. It is normal for a child to get frustrated and state: "Why are you asking me this again?" "Don't you believe me?" "I don't want to talk about this anymore."

A parent or caregiver can play a key role in reassuring the child that this is a part of the police officer's job, that the police are doing their best to stop the abuse from happening again, that it is important for the child to answer the questions, and that all of this unpleasantness will pass. Parents can help normalize a child's life, reduce the strain, and demonstrate that better times are coming by continuing with the child's normal routines as much as possible.

We recommend that parents and caregivers inform themselves about recommended strategies to encourage resilience for children and youth. A helpful website for this purpose is www.apahelpcenter.org. As noted in Chapter 5, this website was established in part to encourage a public campaign for building resilience after the 11 September 2001 attacks on the World Trade Center in New York.

AFTER THE INTERVIEW

AFTER INTERVIEWING THE COMPLAINANT, the police may begin expanding the investigation by identifying and interviewing the accused, interviewing possible witnesses, and collecting any physical evidence.

Identifying the accused

IN CASES WHERE THE accused is a stranger to the complainant, the police are very cautious about identification procedures. In their initial contact with the complainant in a developing case where the assailant is at large, the police will ask for a physical description and will broadcast this to other officers. When the police officer testifies at trial, this initial description will likely be introduced as evidence. It is well known that people are not very good at identifying others, and serious mistakes have been documented; innocent people have been wrongfully convicted based on erroneous identification by witnesses. The main concern of the police is that nothing be done to influence the complainant's identification of the assailant.

After the complainant has given a physical description, and after following investigative channels, the police may determine a suspect. This may or may not be the actual offender. The next step is to show the complainant a series of photos and see if someone is picked out. When the police have identified a previously unknown suspect, they will follow very strict guidelines when presenting that information to the complainant. It is not proper procedure for the police to show just a lineup of photos. They will ask the complainant to look at a number of photos, one picture at a time, and will instruct the complainant not to identify anyone until all the photos have been examined. The complainant does not necessarily need to pick someone out, as the actual offender's photo may or may not be included; the police may have the wrong suspect. The police will record this process, at least in writing, but preferably on videotape, to show that they followed proper procedures. They will also record any other communication from the complainant about the suspect. If the complainant identifies a suspect and that choice coincides with other evidence that the police have collected, they will present that information to the court. No matter whom the complainant identifies during the early stages of investigation, the police will not reveal whether or not the choice is correct. The only advice the police or the Crown will give the complainant is "Look carefully and choose the person you think is the suspect." There should be no more clues than that.

Courts are very cautious about relying on an identification of the accused done solely in the courtroom. In fact, if the only evidence is the pointing out of the accused on the day of trial, the case will likely be too weak to gain a conviction.

The Crown strengthens its case if the complainant is able to identify the accused from a series of random photos shortly after the assault. The Crown further strengthens its case if it can present additional evidence placing the accused at the scene, such as DNA, other physical evidence, or other eyewitness testimony.

INTERVIEWING THE SUSPECT AND OTHERS

ONCE THE POLICE IDENTIFY a suspect, they will usually give the suspect an opportunity to provide a statement. Even when an accused fully admits to the crime by admitting to exactly what the complainant said was true, the case has not ended. An admission of guilt merely becomes more evidence against the accused that the judge will weigh in deciding the trial outcome. In order for the results of that suspect's interview to be admissible in court, there are two major issues to address.

To begin, the accused has rights before the law that the police must uphold. When they detain or arrest a suspect, they must inform the suspect of the charges and of the fact that there is no legal obligation to talk to the police until a lawyer has been contacted. The police are required to make every effort to ensure that the accused has legal counsel before they conduct an interview about an alleged crime.

Second, the suspect must make any statement voluntarily without oppression or trickery. The court equates this voluntary act with reliability. Forcing someone to make a statement increases the likelihood that the statement is false or inaccurate. Although the appeal courts have recognized the duty and essential need of the police to conduct suspect interviews, there is a line of acceptable conduct that when crossed makes the statement inadmissible. The court examines the conduct of the police to determine if they have induced the accused to make a particular statement. Although the police do use some ruses to elicit statements, there is a threshold of acceptability. Making offers that have some prosecutorial benefit, or were made deceptively or in an oppressive atmosphere, or by using tactics designed to break down the suspect emotionally will all contribute to making a statement inadmissible. It falls to the Crown to demonstrate that the statement is valid and admissible.

The suspect's statement is not shared

YOU WILL NOT KNOW if your assailant has confessed. The police and the Crown do not share such information in case they jeopardize the case by telling you too much and influencing your testimony. They may ask you questions related to what the accused said in the accused's statement but will not discuss the reason for the question. Do not second-guess these procedures or ask the Crown counsel what his strategy is. If you were to get an answer, it could damage your credibility and be used against you later on. Even if you are scrupulous about your conduct, the defence could still accuse you of collusion. It is best to stick to what you know, trust in the Crown to look out for the best interests of the case, and be able to respond truthfully that you did not collude or interfere with the police or Crown in any way.

Interviewing other people

DURING THE COURSE OF the investigation, the police will interview others who may have relevant information or knowledge, such as people living or working near the crime scene, the first person you spoke to about the assault, or the medical personnel who examined you. The complainant often provides these names directly to the police, but some complainants contact potential witnesses first and then invite them to talk to police. If you speak to a witness, it is very important that you have no discussion whatsoever about what you have told the police or what you expect the witness to say. Not only could this affect the witness' version of the facts, it may also be interpreted as collusion and sink the entire case in the minds of the lawyers. Friends and family members who are witnesses may have a period of distancing themselves from you during legal proceedings to ensure that there is not even the appearance of discussion between them and you, the complainant.

Some people really dislike being part of the legal proceedings and blame the complainant for their involvement. There have been instances of witnesses pressuring the complainant to have the Crown take friends and neighbours off the witness list. Interestingly, the defence may have subpoenaed some of these witnesses and the Crown often knows nothing of it. Whatever the case may be, if a complainant is getting pressure from people who do not want to testify, the complainant should tell those people that this is the legal professionals' decision. Give them the phone number of the Crown counsel or the police. If this pressure becomes more than a mere nuisance, tell the investigating officer what is going on and get some help to remind the witnesses that this is a police matter and they should not be harassing the complainant. In extreme cases, the court can issue protection orders to stop those who seriously harass the complainant.

COLLECTING OTHER EVIDENCE

APART FROM WITNESS STATEMENTS, the police will search for physical evidence of the crime. The first source of such evidence is the complainant's body, including physical signs of violence or sexual activity, samples of body fluids, and any other material that authorities can link to the offender. Much of this evidence may already have been collected if a medical examination followed the assault. Photos of your body showing evidence of assault may be important, particularly if authorities document them as being taken near the time of the assault. Torn clothing and other signs of violence can also serve as evidence, so do not be surprised if the police seize some of your clothing. You will not get these articles back until after the appeal period has passed following the trial. You might want to include this loss as part of any compensation claim.

The crime scene itself is the other primary source of physical evidence, especially if it has been relatively undisturbed after the assault. The police will visit the scene, take photos, and will collect objects or physical specimens (hair, fibers, blood, or semen) that they believe demonstrate that a crime took place, or link the accused to the scene. If the incident took place in your home, this process might require taking a chunk out of your mattress or a piece of the bedding. You may find yourself troubled not only about damages done by the offender, but by the investigators as well.

As the investigation progresses, the police may call upon forensic techniques and tests that are special analytical tools used to uncover evidence of the crime. This could include DNA testing, voice stress analysis, and electronic surveillance. They will not keep you apprised of the work that is going on in the background unless your direct assistance is required.

The medical examination

IF YOU HAVE NOT already had one, the police may ask you to have a medical examination. There have been some very sad stories over the years related to the medical examination. There are reports of women lying exposed, with their feet in stirrups for hours while physicians try to figure out how to do the examination or go off to see other patients who, in their minds, have needs that are more critical. Many doctors do not want to do these forensic examinations and give them a low priority. In part, doctors do not want the inconvenience and potential aggravation of attending court and being cross-examined. Efforts are being made to correct these problems. Practitioners can now use a sexual assault kit, designed to encourage the medical team to conduct a proper forensic examination. Now many hospitals have rosters of physicians (usually women) who are committed and trained to do this work. In another innovative step to improve the service provided to the complainant, nurses trained in forensic examinations have begun conducting the examinations.

With an eye to quality control, the sexual assault kit itself undergoes regular scrutiny. While the kit directs a rigorous examination involving the plucking and combing of hair (including pubic hair) and the sampling of bodily fluids from the vagina, anal cavity, and mouth, in practice these samples may or may not be necessary to prove the case in court. Prosecutors and police will tell you it is better to endure the pain and humiliation of the medical exam, rather than take the risk that some evidence may be lost, but the research literature does not fully support the usefulness of this approach.

That is not to say use of the kit or similar standardized procedures is fruitless, but ongoing research and observation will be necessary to ensure techniques developed are necessary and valid. Although the kit calls for a blood sample to check for drugs and alcohol, with the rising use of stupefying drugs a urine sample is needed as well. The urine has been stored in the bladder and may show traces of substances already cleared from the bloodstream. What elements are found in the urine will depend on how long it has been since the complainant voided. Urinalysis will not show relative amounts of drugs or help with timelines, but it could assist in explaining unusual behaviour, such as incoherence, memory problems, or unconsciousness in the complainant.

The police will take, record, and store any samples obtained during a medical examination, along with relevant articles of clothing. This material is important evidence and the investigation team will process it carefully since the Crown will have to demonstrate in court that these items came from the complainant and were uncontaminated by anybody else's biological substances when submitted to laboratory analysis. Without this formal approach to the collection of biological evidence, any benefits to matches or other findings by the lab are lost. This is why prosecutors prefer that the complainant cooperate by attending the medical exam with the police, rather than going to a medical examiner inexperienced in forensic work.

Not all complainants report to the police in the immediate aftermath of the crime, so medical evidence is often unavailable to the court. The lack of medical evidence should not dissuade victims from reporting the crime, as research indicates the absence of this evidence does not significantly alter the outcome of legal proceedings. Even if such evidence is available, how the forensic team collects, records, and tests it will determine its usefulness to the case.

The presence of police at the time of the medical exam will usually strengthen the case because they will record events and make sure procedures dovetail with legal requirements. A medical team trained in forensic practices can meet the same legal requirements by following proper procedures and maintaining security of the exhibits until the police take possession of them. Improper practices can lead to lost evidence or the inability to demonstrate the authenticity of samples. In one case, the Crown counsel was required to track down and call five additional people to prove the urine sample tested at the hospital lab was that of the complainant. This took up days of trial time simply because a hospital lab, rather than the RCMP forensic lab, tested the complainant's urine sample. The sample was important evidence in a case where the complainant alleged the offender had drugged and sexually assaulted her. The urine sample, but not the blood sample, showed traces of a stupefying drug. If, due to sloppy processing, the Crown could not use the results of the urine test, there would have been no physical evidence to substantiate the allegations.

Medical examination of the accused

AUTHORITIES CANNOT FORCE THOSE accused of a crime to undergo a medical examination to gather evidence. However, if a medical condition or history is important to the investigation and evidence can be obtained from the medical file, the police can obtain a warrant to search for medical records of the accused. This might be the case if the complainant is infected with the HIV virus and the accused is believed to be HIV positive. Further, if a body fluid sample is left at the crime scene, or on the complainant's body, there is provision in the *Criminal Code* that allows the police to investigate a linkage to the accused. This is typically done by obtaining samples from the accused (in the form of blood, mouth swabs, or hair samples) to determine if they match the crime scene evidence.

The accused cannot be forced to reveal a positive HIV status, but the information can be gained in a circuitous way. If the defence counsel is informed of the HIV status by the accused, the lawyer can pass the information on, without prejudice, to the complainant's lawyer or the Crown counsel. If there is confidence in the information, it may be used by the complainant to make health-related decisions.

CHARGE ASSESSMENT

WHEN POLICE FEEL THEY have collected all the available evidence, they will review the case and determine whether to lay criminal charges. In most provinces, the decision of whether or not to lay criminal charges is in the hands of the police. In British Columbia, Quebec, and New Brunswick, the Crown pre-screens the files before charges are laid. In other provinces, police review and lay charges. The Crown can stay charges later if it determines there is not sufficient evidence to prosecute. The case review takes place in the jurisdiction where the crime allegedly occurred, thus, if you go to the Dauphin, Manitoba police to report a crime that took place in Winnipeg, the file would go to the Winnipeg Crown.

The police and the Crown prosecutors will first look to the police report, which outlines the results of the investigation, and the documents attached to it. There must be sufficient evidence related to each element of the crime in order to charge the suspect. To lay a sexual assault charge there must be evidence showing that the accused engaged in sexual behaviour, applied force (touching is enough), acted intentionally, and did not have the complainant's consent. Each sexual offence will have its own essential parameters that determine if authorities can lay charges. Corroboration of the suspect's behaviour, by either physical evidence or third-party observation, will strengthen the case but this is not necessary. The law no longer has a requirement of corroboration for a conviction for a sexual offence. Authorities will look for any of the following factors when making their decision about laying charges:

- A credible complaint that is internally and externally consistent
- Physical evidence of sexual activity, alleged force, or the suspect's presence at the scene
- Confirming evidence from a third party (especially a neutral third party)

Factors that may result in the Crown or the police wanting evidence that confirms the complainant's version before laying a charge:

- A complainant who has a history of perjury or false complaints
- A complaint based on recovered memory
- A complaint where there is corroboration of the suspect's denial
- A complainant who may be motivated by anticipated benefits or goals other than criminal justice (such as a custody dispute)

Factors that may influence a decision not to charge the suspect:

- The complainant gives a story that suggests there should be obvious physical evidence, and has no explanation when none is found.

- The complainant significantly changes the story over time.
- The investigation reveals evidence of collusion and motive to make a false complaint.
- The accused provides a statement of denial that is accepted as reliable.

The charge assessment process is a judgment call fraught with difficulties. Opinions will vary depending on the knowledge, experience, and even the worldview of the person evaluating the facts. Two police officers, or Crown lawyers, in different parts of the country or even within the same office will view the claimant's credibility differently. The Crown and the police agencies deal with the subjective nature of decision-making by drafting policies, writing practice manuals, training personnel, and seeking second or third opinions in the more difficult cases. In some circumstances, these policy manuals are also accessible to the public. The Federal Department of Justice, Ontario Ministry of the Attorney General, and British Columbia's Criminal Justice Branch are examples of jurisdictions where the public can read the policies that the Crown lawyers rely upon. The public can access these policies via Internet links.[7]

The process is often delayed while the police follow up on matters requested by the prosecutor. This will mean that the police might come back to you, or interview more people, to answer questions on matters that the prosecutor feels are important to prove the case. Those involved understand that the investigation must be as complete as possible before laying charges. Authorities will proceed with charges only if the evidence gathered suggests that there is a substantial likelihood of conviction. In other words, the police will not lay charges at an early stage hoping to find new evidence later.

Sexual offences without violence or physical injury are offences that prosecutors can deal with either by indictment or by summary conviction. There is a general effort to keep cases considered less serious (for example, those without violence, weapons, or physical injury) at the summary conviction level if possible, to keep the case in provincial court, rather than relying on the supreme or superior courts. This procedural strategy actually benefits the complainant because it avoids having to testify twice — once at the preliminary hearing and once at the trial. The advantage to the accused is that the maximum penalty for sex crimes prosecuted by summary conviction is eighteen months.

Even if the Crown or investigating officers feel confident that there is enough evidence to lay the charges, and that there is a good likelihood that the accused will be convicted, they also have to be satisfied that it is not contrary to the public interest to do so. There are written polices to guide the police and the Crown in making decisions in the public interest. Usually there are factors that support the decision to charge, such as injury to the complainant or previous convictions of the offender, while other factors, such as an admission by the accused or criminal behaviour of a less egregious sort may favour discretion in bringing charges or opting for diversion.

Diversion is a procedure that gives the defendant a chance to make restitution or obtain treatment, rather than face charges. The conditions for diversion are set out in the *Criminal Code* section 717. The Crown will review the file and refer it to the office designed to administer the diversions program, usually the probation office, to consider the accused for the program. The probation office will inform the Crown of its decision, then the Crown makes the final decision. The accused admitting the offence, being willing to go the diversion route, and the complainant agreeing with this plan are important variables to be considered. If the offender continues to admit responsibility, cooperates with the probation office, and fulfills the conditions of the diversion agreement (which often includes an apology), then charges can eventually be stayed.

When authorities make the decision not to charge or to divert the defendant, they will contact the complainant in order to hear the complainant's opinion about the outcome of the legal process before making a final decision. There is controversy with this procedure because the complainants often feel under pressure and may not give a strictly voluntary agreement to diversion due to that pressure. This is particularly true in situations where the demands to divert come not through a positive support process, but negatively as intimidation from community members who want to protect the offender. Another area of controversy is the efficacy of diversion. While many consider diversion a progressive and positive alternative to charges and jail, there is no evidence that it works to prevent re-offending. There is, however, clear research evidence indicating that treatment programs for offenders in jail reduce re-offending. Some suggest that, since we do not know if diversion works, we should not take the risk of diverting sex offenders.

When police lay charges against your wishes

BOTH THE POLICE AND the Crown have a professional responsibility to act in society's best interest, rather than in the best interest of individuals. This means that they can lay charges contrary to the complainant's wishes. They may believe there is sufficient evidence to obtain a conviction, which would serve the public good. When this happens, you may ask that they drop the charges. You cannot do this yourself, but the Crown has the authority to do so. Although not required to heed your request, many police and Crown prosecutors will do so if you firmly believe that more harm than good will come from proceeding to trial. Alternatively, if authorities consider the offender dangerous and protection of society is a priority, the charges will remain and they will subpoena you as a witness.

IF CRIMINAL CHARGES ARE NOT APPROVED

WHEN POLICE LAY A charge, they swear a document called an "Information" before a justice of the peace. When they decide not to charge, and you believe charges should go forward, you still have some options. You can speak to a senior police officer or Crown prosecutor and ask for a review of the decision, or you can speak to a lawyer about laying a private Information through a justice of the peace. Be aware that the Crown can still stay this charge at a later stage if it feels there is not sufficient evidence to proceed further.

Unfortunately, in some cases, the accused has gone on to commit more offences and complainants feel powerless because officials rejected earlier charges. Some complainants are repeatedly victimized for years while falsely believing that to tell would be useless and would bring no protection. They feel that, because there was not enough evidence to proceed with the first complaint, the same circumstance will apply to subsequent complaints. This is an erroneous belief. Clearly, if the suspect re-offends, the victim is free to make a new report. Police will investigate the new accusation and it may be that for these offences the evidence will be sufficient to approve charges. Two very similar cases may result in different decisions. Variables, such as the particular experience of the investigator or the Crown, or type of evidence found, can be very important in determining the final decision. Having been through the process once, the complainant may also be in a much better position to articulate the complaint in a subsequent investigation.

Keep in mind that the criminal justice system can only do so much to resolve crimes of sexual assault. Charges and the ensuing legal proceedings rarely reflect the whole story, and criminal justice is not always the main issue for complainants. Many people are interested in seeing the offender's behaviour recognized as assault, and want the offenders to admit they were wrong and give some sort of public acknowledgment of the damages done. These issues can be particularly important if the offender was an authority figure or family member. You can refer to relevant sections in this book to explore how you might achieve your goals through non-criminal options for dealing with sexual offences, including a civil lawsuit.

THE ARREST

BY "ARREST" WE MEAN when the police take a person into custody by authority of the *Criminal Code* or a warrant of arrest. The *Criminal Code* specifies the grounds of arrest and the police cannot deviate from them. Although all sex crimes are indictable offences, the police do not always arrest the alleged offender. Once they lay charges, so long as the reported offence is not serious (such as a grabbing of the buttocks in a shopping mall), authorities may serve the suspect with a document called a "promise to appear," or "undertaking to appear," or may even request that the court registry simply mail the offender a summons to appear on a particular date.

The police do not take their authority to arrest lightly. Canadian criminal law requires that they have reason to believe the person committed a crime, and that they first obtain a warrant from a justice of the peace to take that person into custody. In some special circumstances, such as an emergent, on-the-scene, crime-in-progress situation, the police do not have to seek a warrant. When a warrant is issued, it spells out specific *Criminal Code* charges in very formal language. Police still have legal limitations in how they carry out the arrest. They cannot go into someone's house and make an arrest without another specific warrant. That means two warrants are required to arrest a person at home unless there is a crime in progress and people are at risk. Once apprehended, the police must inform accused persons of their rights and take them to a place where they have access to legal advice.

The police will arrest an offender when a complaint suggests reasonable and probable grounds that a serious offence has occurred, or after a warrant has been issued following charge approval. The police will arrest without either a warrant or charge approval, if they have reasonable grounds to believe a suspect has committed or is about to commit an indictable offence and the arrest is necessary to identify the accused, preserve evidence, prevent recurrence of the offence or another offence, and if there is reason to believe the accused will not attend court. When this occurs, the police must release the accused within twenty-four hours or they must lay charges and take the accused before a justice of the peace or judge. If no charges are laid, the officer in charge or the arresting officer can release the accused with or without conditions. In the case where charges are approved while the suspect is at large, the police or Crown counsel can ask for a warrant to arrest as part of the charge approval process. If officers make an arrest for a relatively minor sexual offence, they will normally release the accused without a hearing following initial processing.

Cases involving dramatic arrests, detention, or bail followed by severe restrictions on the suspect's freedom are in the minority. If someone unknown to the complainant commits a serious assault, and the risk for future offences seems high, authorities will detain the suspect. If the offender has a previous record of similar crimes, the police would most likely make an arrest, and the Crown would request that the court detain or put that person under strict community conditions (such as a curfew, no contact with children, or no alcohol). The same holds true if the sexual offence is a violent one. Under all of these circumstances, the police will arrest the accused in order to ensure the accused appears in court, to protect the complainant, and to lower the community risk while legal matters are resolved.

In most instances, victims know the offender and getting the case before the court is a legal process that proceeds routinely without arrest, bail hearings, or special conditions. In these circumstances, authorities allow offenders to go about their lives quite unrestricted until they appear before the court to answer the charges. Even when charges go forward, most offenders tend to cooperate with the police and the court, particularly if they have engaged legal counsel. They respond to requests by the police to provide information, and they appear as required before the court. Those innocent of the charges are eager to exonerate themselves and will do what the court asks in order to expedite the process. Those responsible for the crime are often just as eager to present themselves as law-abiding and cooperative citizens in order to convince the police, the court, and those who know them that they are not the kind of people who would commit such offences. Offenders are not likely to commit new offences at this stage because the risk of going to jail is quite real and their behaviour is being scrutinized. The exception occurs when the complainant and the offender are in a relationship. The offender will often try to communicate or interact with the complainant before the trial in spite of court orders that prohibit such actions.

The suspect's rights when arrested

OUR LEGAL SYSTEM PRESUMES innocence until a finding of guilt. At the time of an arrest, the court has not yet made a finding of guilt so the police must treat the suspect accordingly. The police recognize and acknowledge the seriousness of an arrest from the suspect's point of view. They should arrest in a respectful manner even when evidence against the suspect is strong. This means taking care, when reasonable, not to arrest at the suspect's place of work, at home, or in front of children. If you have any particular concerns about how a suspect will be arrested, talk to the police and they will often heed your requests to avoid unnecessary embarrassment to your family or the family of the alleged offender. This may be a particular issue if the suspect is an intimate of or is well-known to the complainant.

Under Canadian law, which includes "*Charter* rights" as set out in the *Canadian Charter of Rights and Freedoms*, at the time of an arrest, officers must inform a suspect of the right to the following:

- Be informed fully and promptly of the reasons for the arrest
- Be told of the right to have, and be permitted to retain and instruct, a lawyer
- Not talk to the police about the offence or the investigation
- Be taken before a justice of the peace or judge promptly to ensure the detention is legally justified

Waiting for police to make the arrest

THE DELAY THAT NORMALLY occurs between the report of an assault and the arrest can present special challenges for you. It can be a time of great fear, tension, and uncertainty. If you do not know the offender's identity, the police will likely ask you to provide a detailed physical description, from which they may construct a composite portrait. If the police have a suspect in mind, they may ask you to review a series of photographs one by one.

Through this process, you may be haunted by the fear that the offender will do you further harm. You may feel the offender has the advantage of knowing more about you than you know about the offender. If this is the case, you may benefit from constructing a safety plan as was discussed in Chapter 5.

On the other hand, most complainants know, have a close relationship with, or may even be living together with the offender at the time of the offence. If this describes your situation, the period between the report and the arrest can be as stressful as it is for those who do not know their offender, but for different reasons. Since you know the offender well, you may feel the desire to intervene directly to protect yourself or to prevent the offender from fleeing. Some complainants may utilize a friend or hire someone to monitor the offender's movements. This approach can do you more harm than good, both legally and psychologically. The offender may resent these intrusions and could report you for harassment. Your credibility with the authorities may suffer and in the worst-case scenario, the offender might report you for assault, voyeurism, or criminal harassment.

If you want the help of someone other than the police, it is best to get advice from a professional who understands the issue well. You can start by talking to a lawyer about your needs. Phone the law society in your province and ask about the lawyer referral service. Ask for assistance to find one near to you who understands criminal law. In most provinces, there is a service that allows you to get a half-hour consultation with a lawyer for a minimal fee. Alternatively, speak to a victim assistance organization or rape crisis centre; awareness of ways to develop safety plans to protect complainants pending arrest and trial is on the increase. If you have the funds to do so, you could consider hiring a specialist in either detective work or security to help ensure your safety.

The bail hearing

ONCE THE POLICE MAKE an arrest, the matters of safety and security may not be over. Any suspect arrested without a warrant must go before a justice of the peace within twenty-four hours or be released. In cases where the police have concerns about the accused fleeing or committing other offences, they will take the accused before a provincial court judge for a bail hearing conducted with the Crown and a defence lawyer. If the accused has not yet retained a lawyer, a legal aid duty counsel will assist until defence counsel is retained. The Crown has the burden of convincing the court to either release the accused with conditions or detain in custody. This can be a difficult task, especially when the alleged crime happened a long time ago, the accused has no criminal record, or the accused has no recent history of misconduct. The Crown will often ask for a no-contact order, restricting the suspect's unsupervised associations. Where children are the victims, a no-contact order may extend to all children under fourteen years of age in order to protect the known victims as well as the general community. The courts, however, are loathe to do this when the children are not the offender's victims and will often leave the issue of offender contact with the offender's own children up to governmental child protection agencies.

Some Crown lawyers will tell you that it is not appropriate for you to sit in on the bail hearing because it might reflect negatively on your evidence later. You may hear that it is better that you not know what the suspect says. If the assailant is a stranger to you, you definitely should not attend the bail hearing, because you must make your identification of the assailant from your memories of the event, and not from assumptions you may have drawn subsequently. In other words, if you see a person charged with the crime in the courtroom, this could potentially confuse you. When you make the identification later in the trial, you may be relying on your recollections of the bail hearing and not those of the crime. This sort of confusion can diminish the integrity of your evidence, and might even contribute to the conviction of an innocent person or the acquittal of a guilty one.

VIGNETTE SIX: UNEXPECTED CONSEQUENCES

WHEN HALIMA, THE YOUNG woman described in Vignette Six, went home from the police station to write an account of her sexual abuse, she started with her first memories and filled six pages with her thoughts, an analysis of her family, and an explanation of why her abuser was able to escape detection for so many years. She returned to the police station with this narrative and, with the investigating officer's direction, she gave a recorded statement. Halima's two statements about the abuse were quite different; the first was impressionistic and included her thoughts, feelings, and emotions. She talked about her disgust with the offender, her anger about the deference paid to him by others, her disappointment and sadness that family members took his side and did not believe her, and the alienation she felt from her family and community. The second, directed statement was more relevant to legal issues of who, what, where, and when. Both statements were information collected by the investigating officer, so both were considered evidence and made up part of her allegations. The first statement would prove to be problematic for Halima and the defence lawyer would use it to discredit her at the trial.

During the trial, the defence was able to attack Halima's credibility based on statements made in her first, unguided narrative. In that statement she had talked about the dynamics of her family, how family members had not protected her from the abuser and her fear that she would be punished if she revealed her abuse. None of this was particularly helpful in proving that the man had sexually abused her, but it did give a dark portrait of her family's ignorance and lack of support. If she had been given some guidance in preparing her statement, Halima would have understood that her impressionistic analysis was not what is required as an investigative statement and that its contents would take the trial places that were inflammatory and not relevant to the guilt or innocence of the accused. Members of her family who testified denied the negative portrait Halima painted of them and accused her of being vindictive. They accused her of lying and exaggerating out of bitterness and hatefulness toward the family friend. They also suggested that if her accusations were true she would have reported them much sooner, rather than waiting until her young adulthood. Working with the Crown lawyer, Halima was able to give a cogent and well thought out explanation for her delay in reporting, citing her shame and fear of family backlash. The Crown submitted that the family's reaction to her statement, rather than impugning her credibility, demonstrated the very dynamics she feared as a child and a young adult. The trouble caused by the first statement could have been avoided if more care had been taken, and more guidance given, during the initial reporting stage.

ENDNOTES

1　First study cited in Rosemary Gertner & Anthony N. Doob, "Trends in Criminal Victimization: 1988–1993," (1994) Vol. 14 No. 13 Juristat, cited in Tina Hattem, *Survey of Sexual Assault Survivors* (Ottawa: Canada Justice, Research and Statistics Division, 2000). Online: www.canada.justice.gc.ca/en/ps/rs/rep/2000/rr00-4a.pdf. Second study cited in Statistics Canada, *The Daily* (18 November 1993) at 7.

2　2000 SCC 43 at para. 65.

3　*R. v. K.G.B.*, [1993] 1 S.C.R. 740, 19 C.R. (4th) 1, 79 C.C.C. (3d) 257.

4　Hilary E. Randall & Sandra E. Byers, "What Is Sex? Students' Definitions of Having Sex, Sexual Partner, and Unfaithful Sexual Behaviour" (2003) 12:2 Canadian Journal of Human Sexuality 91.

5　David Jones & J. Melbourne McGraw, "Reliable and Fictitious Accounts of Sexual Abuse to Children" (1987) 2 Journal of Interpersonal Violence 27.

6　Nancy Thoennes & Patricia Tjaden, "The Extent, Nature and Validity of Sexual Abuse Allegation in Custody/Visitation Disputes" (1990) 14 Child Abuse and Neglect 151–63.

7　Online: www.attorneygeneral.jus.gov.on.ca/english/crim/cpm/defalt.asp.

Preparing for Court

Vignette Seven

Roy is thirty-two years old when his marriage breaks up due to his heavy drinking and anger problems. His divorce makes him realize he has some serious personal problems to resolve and he seeks out counselling. In therapy, he reveals that he was sexually abused from the age of eleven to fifteen by a foster father. While he can recount the basic facts of his abuse, he has difficulty discussing his emotional experiences. The therapist suggests he write about his feelings in a journal that he shows to nobody else, so he can be uninhibited and free to express his honest emotions, whatever they might be. The journalling works well as a therapeutic technique and Roy makes good progress in dealing with his emotional difficulties. When he is the age of forty, the police contact Roy and explain that they are investigating allegations of sexual abuse disclosed by other children in the foster father's care. When questioned, Roy admits the foster father also abused him and he gives police some of the details. The Crown counsel approves charges against the foster father and contacts Roy to plan for his testimony in court. In discussing the details of his abuse, Roy shows the Crown lawyer his journal and says this is the best source of information if the lawyer really wants to understand how the abuse happened. The Crown warns Roy that since she is aware of the journal, the fact of its existence but not its contents must be revealed to the defence. The defence will be entitled to apply for all or part of the journal if it is likely to be relevant to the case. In addition, she indicates that if she uses evidence from the journal, the defence will likely have to receive a copy, and Roy should be prepared for this possibility. She suggests Roy get advice from independent legal counsel on this issue. Roy insists that his journal is the best source of information, and that both he and the Crown should rely on it. He signs a waiver allowing the Crown to release a copy of the journal to defence.

THE PERIOD BETWEEN YOUR first report of a sexual assault and the actual trial can be lengthy, challenging, and frustrating. During this phase, you will have your first encounters with the justice system and will meet many of the important participants. While the waiting can be difficult, this time can also provide an opportunity to prepare yourself emotionally, to learn about the legal system, and to define your role in it. In this chapter, we discuss rules of disclosure, privacy issues, plea negotiations, your role in the preliminary hearings, and child testimony. We also outline strategies that can empower you and make you a more effective participant.

The pretrial period is sure to test even the most self-assured and competent individuals. Fear and frustration can be disorienting and can make even simple tasks challenging. Many complainants have made an effort to get on with life and to put the abuse behind them, but preparing for court often entails bringing many disturbing issues back to the forefront. There are appointments to schedule, meetings with new people, new relationships to build, and a disruption of routines. Not surprisingly, some complainants feel frustrated at not understanding the legal process or the complicated information people seem to expect them to absorb. During the pretrial stage, you will likely see and hear things you do not like, and you may be disillusioned if your image of the justice system is not reflected in reality. You will experience the enormity of the justice system and its unyielding nature, which can leave little opportunity to accommodate your needs. In light of this state of affairs, should you run for the hills and forget about any chance of justice? No, we believe not. Instead, we encourage you to gather information and prepare for the upcoming challenges.

Taking the initiative in your personal preparation for court is the strategy that can most effectively shift you from feeling stuck or overwhelmed to feeling capable and competent to manage the stress. How you perceive the court process and how you interact with others are two areas over which you can exert control. You have reported the crime, provided your statement to the investigators, and waited for the authorities to charge and arrest the accused. All of this may have taken weeks or months. Between the first court appearance and the preliminary hearing or trial, you will probably wait at least another six months. The whole process will take from one to three years — more if the defence appeals a conviction. This gives you ample time to prepare yourself. You can learn about the rules of disclosure, get to know the Crown prosecutor, and prepare yourself for the time you are going to testify. Because court preparation is especially important for the very young, we have dedicated a segment specifically to child testimony.

PREPARATION CAN MAKE A DIFFERENCE

IN AN IDEAL WORLD, your local victim assistance program would contact you to schedule a court orientation, provide you with emotional support, and arrange a meeting with the Crown prosecutor. The Crown, who would have received your file months before the court date, would be very familiar with your case before even meeting you for the first time. Regrettably, the world is not an ideal place, and even though justice personnel know this sequence of events is the best model to follow, very few jurisdictions have the resources available to assist in this way. Most often, the Crown lawyer is the only person available to prepare and support you. Although lawyers will do their best, heavy workloads may mean the Crown might not receive your file until a few days before you are scheduled to appear in court.

To ameliorate these system weaknesses, take the initiative with your preparation. Start by looking beyond the immediate legal necessities and look upon this as a potential growth experience. Keep yourself physically and emotionally healthy, examine your attitudes, and look at the competencies you would like to develop that would also be useful in other domains of your life. Set a goal that can have a positive outcome independent of the offender or the justice system verdict. You might decide to become more self-aware of how you react in a crisis or around people in authority. You may want to develop a better understanding of criminal law, to become a better public speaker, or to develop your self-confidence. Use the court process as a path along which you can move to achieve some of these personal goals. In a worst-case scenario in which you do not achieve any of your legal objectives, you can still achieve personal growth, which may be the greatest reward.

Below we outline some of the strategies you can employ to prepare yourself to participate effectively in the legal process. We also provide a preparation checklist in Appendix 12 that you can use as an organizational guide in preparing for court.

Recruiting a team to help you

PREPARATION TO TESTIFY AS a witness usually entails justice personnel acquainting you with the legal terrain and your place in it. You should learn what actions are permissible and advisable, what your testimony will entail, and what questions you will likely have to answer in court. Only the Crown lawyer should help with the evidence review, but others can help with the additional tasks of preparation. Make connections with people who can help you develop some of the strategies discussed in earlier chapters, such as building resilience, forming supportive relationships, finding a therapist if necessary, maintaining good health, and enhancing your personal safety and security.

There is a lot that you can do on your own to get ready. You can read books, search web pages designed to inform lay people on legal issues, see a therapist to strengthen yourself emotionally, or visit a courtroom to watch an unrelated trial. Visiting a courtroom is similar to a woman going to the maternity ward before she goes into labour to make the experience less disorienting. Hence, when it is time to have the baby she can concentrate on that important task instead of worrying about peripheral details that are unfamiliar to her. We suggest that if you do attend another trial as part of your preparation, choose a trial that is not a sexual assault case. This way you avoid being unduly influenced by unique procedural matters in that particular case, and there will be no question of having your memory tainted by testimony that you heard about another sexual assault.

A word of caution here; these preparations are not about taking charge of your legal case, they are about strengthening your ability to stand up to the task of being a complainant and a key witness to the criminal behaviour of the person who assaulted you. You should appreciate the difference between these two things. If, during your preparations, you find that you want to change what you said to police or add something you may have missed, make sure to first talk to the Crown lawyer for advice on how to handle these matters.

Who is the Crown prosecutor for your case?

TO FIND THE NAME of the Crown prosecutor assigned to your case, call the victim assistance agency in your community or the police officer investigating the case. You can also check the phone book for the court offices in the region where the crime took place. If you phone the Crown office, tell them who you are and that you want to start preparing for the upcoming trial in which you are a witness. The office personnel will then give you the name you are looking for. I have several times available during which you could attend a meeting. Crown offices are generally open between 9 a.m. and 5 p.m. Monday to Friday. If it is impossible for you to meet during the day, the Crown may be able to accommodate you after hours. This would be on the Crown's own time, without extra pay, but you might be accommodated to ensure that the trial goes well.

When the Crown prosecutor does call you in for a meeting, go. Try your best to keep any appointments and inform the Crown in advance if you cannot attend. Appreciate that the Crown benefits from meeting with you and going over your statements. Lawyers need this preparation too, and when they ask to see you, this is generally the time they are best able to accommodate you. Even though you may be tempted to procrastinate, it is not helpful if you miss appointments or wait until the last minute to meet with the lawyer. If several months have passed since the police laid charges, or the trial date is looming and you have not received a call, do not hesitate to call the Crown office and get matters started.

Some Crown prosecutors assigned to your trial may believe that minimal contact with you is best because they do not want to give the defence any basis to suggest that your testimony has been tainted. The chance of having the Crown lawyer take this approach varies from province to province. The prosecutor who operates in this way is likely to contact you just before the trial, and will simply want to know if you have read your statement, and then may ask you a few questions. If you feel the need for more preparation than this, we encourage you to call the Crown lawyer well in advance of the trial and devise a mutually workable plan.

It is useful to know what approach the Crown will take in your case. Chances are you will have a prosecutor who wants you to be well-prepared, ensuring that you understand the expectations of you, and that you are familiar with basic court procedures. The Crown will typically want to refresh your memory about the details of your statements to police, and will likely arrange a time to read it with you well before the court date. This will include going over those parts of the narrative that you will tell in court, organizing the information, and making certain that you get appropriate emotional support if necessary.

Crown prosecutors are lawyers, not counsellors. Although the nature of their work frequently places them in this position, some fit the role better than others do. If going through court is emotionally hard for you, you are better off to seek counselling help elsewhere. Although it is tempting to expect such support from the Crown, be aware of the Crown's limited resources and lack of training as a counsellor. The prosecutor has a tremendous amount to do in preparing all the witnesses, generating the legal strategy, dealing with the defence lawyers, and managing other eventualities that are bound to arise. Beyond the preparation of your evidence, if you are asking for more, you may receive the requested time and attention from the Crown, but keep in mind that time spent dealing with your emotional issues is time not spent preparing other aspects of the case that are important to a successful prosecution. The challenge is for the Crown to prepare you for the court process, to organize the evidence, and to assist with emotional difficulties where needed while not improperly affecting the answers that you will give in evidence. It is your story and your truth to tell, not the prosecutor's.

The Crown counsel initially assigned to your case may not be the lawyer who completes the case. Unfortunately, you cannot be guaranteed continuity in this respect. Due to the lengthy nature of the criminal process, Crown lawyers can be reassigned to other cases, seconded, transferred to another office, or be unavailable for a host of other reasons, before your case is completed. You may have to work with two or more Crown prosecutors in the course of your case. These transitions can be frustrating but are often unavoidable so some flexibility on your part may be necessary. There is an avenue of complaint through the supervising or administrative Crown counsel in your area whom you might want to talk with to see if the change of the lawyers is absolutely necessary.

YOUR FIRST MEETING WITH THE CROWN PROSECUTOR

A KEY STEP IN the preparation process is your first meeting with the Crown. The Crown needs to get ready for court, and generally wants to include you, as much as is appropriate, in the prosecution. Most victims of sex crimes who have made their complaint to the police feel some anxiety about the legal proceedings, but do want to proceed. The first meeting is your opportunity to discuss any concerns you have, how comfortable you are about telling your story in court, how you can effectively and comfortably present your evidence, and what you anticipate your reaction will be to cross-examination by the defence. The Crown cannot tell you what to say but can give you some idea of what to expect in court, and general guidance on how you can properly respond to various eventualities. This advice can be invaluable because once you take the stand you have only your own resources to rely on.

Organizing and recording

THE PRETRIAL PERIOD IS an opportunity to make sure you have correctly noted and organized important kinds of information. If you do not already have a system for organizing such things, this is the time to develop one. It can be as simple as buying a notebook and writing all the names and phone numbers in the back, or stapling in business cards. We suggest you make brief notes of all the phone calls and conversations related to your case. When you testify, the judge or defence lawyer may ask about your meetings with the Crown, or with support people or therapists, or about other related matters. If you have relevant dates noted down, it will help you to answer these questions accurately. You can use the notebook to refresh your memory before you testify. Be mindful that if you rely on your notebook during testimony, the defence may ask to see it while you are on the stand and could ask you questions about it.

Make a list of things to talk about

BEFORE THE FIRST INTERVIEW, write a list of questions you have about what is going on and what the Crown's expectations about your testimony are. The following is a list of inquiries you might want to make:

- What day am I required? Will I need to schedule time off work?
- Is this a preliminary hearing or a trial? (If it is a preliminary hearing, you will testify twice.)
- Does the accused have a lawyer? (If he does not, you may want to apply to prevent him from cross-examining you himself.)
- Is there a private place for me to wait away from the accused? (Not all courthouses have this and you need to be prepared if the accused is waiting in the same hall as you before you enter the courtroom.)
- Is there food at the courthouse? (Not all courthouses have food nearby and the waits can be lengthy.)

- What do I call the judge in this court? (A lower court judge is "Your Honour" and a higher court judge is "My Lord" or "My Lady.")
- Can I make a claim for mileage or meals? (Reimbursement may be provided by the court registry with assistance from the Crown office.)
- Can a support person sit near me in court? (There is provision for this in the law. Although you can apply for this on your own, the Crown usually asks for this on your behalf.)
- Can I have a copy of my statement? (You may be able to have a copy, but talk to the Crown lawyer, as there might be complications.)
- How will the examination-in-chief (questions the Crown will ask) be organized? Are there any legal issues around my testimony, such as the defence wanting access to my private records? Are there preparations I can make for this?

When meeting with the Crown you can also take the opportunity to discuss other issues that may be important to you. In some cases, the accused makes harassing or threatening attempts to contact the complainant. In cases where the complainants fear reprisal by the accused, they may want their address withheld in court. If the fear is great, some complainants may not feel that they can give their testimony on the stand in front of a public audience. It may be possible to arrange a publication ban or testimony by videoconferencing, so that the complainant does not have to come into the courtroom. Some witnesses do not want to swear on a Bible, in which case they can "affirm" to tell the truth without using the Bible. You should discuss these, or any other issues of concern, with the Crown in advance of your first court appearance.

Reviewing your report of the crime

AS PREVIOUSLY NOTED, THE police usually tape their interview with a complainant, and then have it transcribed. When transcription is completed, the investigator should read the transcript over while listening to the tape to make any corrections. However, this does not always happen, nor is it always done perfectly. Be aware that your statement can have inadvertent transcription errors that could cause unnecessary challenges to your credibility. Ideally, you will have met with the investigating officer after transcription was completed, listened to the tape, and ensured that the transcript accurately reflects what the two of you said during the initial interview. If you have not done this before the trial, ask the Crown to do the review with you. The Crown should have copies of the interview tape.

If you have already received and reviewed your statement with police, inform the Crown of this when you meet. If there are inaccuracies or changes necessary, this is the time to discuss them. The sooner the Crown knows about this the better. The Crown must provide every new piece of information to the defence, but there is a point in the trial where the prosecution cannot introduce new material unless it is favourable to the accused. If the defence receives the material too close to the trial date, it will seek an adjournment because it may need, or say it needs, time to deal with the new information. This possibility illustrates the importance of conducting a comprehensive investigation and solid preparation before the trial.

At the time of your first meeting, if you have not already received a copy of your statement, the Crown may get you a copy. This statement will be a key part of the evidence in the case, and the defence will study it in detail, so there are good reasons for you to review it well. You may find you cannot muster up the courage or the interest to read this on your own. If your spirit is flagging, we suggest that you not read the statement alone or in silence. Read it in the company of others who support you, or with music playing. Read it slowly several times, until you become very familiar with the contents and ideally somewhat emotionally detached from them. If you have no one to help with this task, ask the Crown prosecutor to read it with you. Some lawyers would prefer to review the statement with you in their office, rather than have you take it home. This is most likely preferable in cases where witnesses in the trial are close to each other and releasing copies may create an impression of collusion.

Although you should be very familiar with your initial police statement, do not memorize it. Your statement is there to refresh your memory but it is not a script. Although it may be challenging, in court you should be able to talk spontaneously about your memory of events. If you restate the document monotonously word-for-word, the defence may question your apparent inability to recall facts on your own. On the other hand, if you deviate from what you stated initially, the credibility of your claims may be challenged. You might want to analyze your statement as you would an essay in English class. Become familiar with the structure you followed, the points you made about certain events, and why you said things the way you did. You should be able to describe what the interview process was like for you, be familiar with what you said, and still be able to give your account with freshness on the stand.

Withholding information about the case from you

THE COMPLAINANT'S POSITION IS very different from that of the accused. The complainant is not a party to all the proceedings; it is not for the
complainant to make tactical decisions. The Crown counsel is the person
who has conduct of the case. Your major role, as complainant, is to be a witness, and it is crucial to the success of the prosecution that some important
facts are kept from you. Although you will review your own statement, the
less you know about the evidence that the Crown intends to call, the more
likely the court will find you credible. In some cases, such as when other
victims of the same accused are appearing as witnesses, your evidence will
have more weight if you are unfamiliar with what they have to say. It is best
if you do not even know their identity and have never spoken to them. This
may seem unfair, but you can see that if witnesses know what others are
going to say in a trial, they consciously or unconsciously may change their
evidence to best fit with the other facts. This must not happen. No one
benefits when extraneous facts unduly influence a witness' recall of criminal events.

AVOIDING TESTIMONY

MANY VICTIMS WANT NOTHING to do with testifying in a trial. The
reasons for this are varied and uniquely personal. In many cases, the true
reasons for avoiding testimony may not be obvious at first glance. It may
be that the complainants with valid complaints do not want to testify because, since first reporting the crime to police, their experiences have convinced them that it is not good for them or others that they care about to
continue with legal action. Some people may initially make false or exag-
gerated claims and later regret that they did so. If you have made a false
complaint about a sexual assault, and now want out, your wisest choice is
to seek legal advice. Remember, the Crown lawyer you have dealt with is
not your personal lawyer; this lawyer represents the state in prosecuting
criminal offences. Lying to the police, in an affidavit or while on the stand,
is a criminal offence; these are charges a Crown counsel would prosecute,
not defend. You will need to engage a defence lawyer to give advice on how
to admit your mistake.

   If, for whatever reason, you as the complainant do not testify, the consequences for a successful prosecution vary. If you are not available due to

health or other serious issues, and there is another witness willing to testify, or a confession by the accused, there might still be enough evidence
to proceed. In some cases, the court may admit as evidence what you have
said to others if you are not available to testify because of some unavoidable
reason that goes beyond mere reluctance. If the success of the case rests
solely on your evidence, and you cannot testify, then the court will dismiss
the charges.

If your sexual assault claim is a valid one but for some reason you do
not want to testify, you might again need to seek the assistance of your
own lawyer. In some cases, complainants attend the Crown interview and
explain their choice not to go on, but in other cases they do not even go to
the interview. The problem with the latter approach is that the Crown and
the police do not know the reasons for the lack of cooperation and will not
just let this slide. They will be wary of the reason for this non-cooperation
and may assume the accused or the accused's associates are threatening, or
at least improperly influencing, the complainant. If you do choose to meet
with the Crown and state that you do not want to go forward, the Crown
will likely try to find out why. At the very least, make sure the information
about your choice is accurate. In some cases, if people have chosen not to
participate based on erroneous information, discussion with the Crown
may diminish this impediment.

There will be cases where a complainant's testimony is essential evidence
against the offender. If the accused is known to the police or considered a
high risk to re-offend, the Crown may decide that the case must proceed
despite your wishes to drop out. In this situation, the Crown will tell you
that you do not have a choice other than to appear and answer the questions asked of you. You could receive a subpoena (a court order) requiring
your attendance. If you do not obey the subpoena, there will be a warrant
for your arrest, the police will apprehend you, and then release you with a
condition to appear in court and testify. If you fail to honour this condition and do not appear as directed, authorities will keep you in custody
until your testimony is complete. Although this is a very rare occurrence,
it does happen.

Sometimes, victims of a genuine sexual assault will create false stories or
deny that the sexual assault occurred. Again, the unique facts of each case
will determine what the consequences of the complainant's actions will be.
In some instances, the Crown can prosecute the matter without the complainant, while in others, the Crown will insist that the complainant tes-

tify, using a previously given statement to show the court the discrepancy in the original story. Other times the case will have to be dropped. Lying to the authorities can have long-lasting consequences not anticipated at an emotional time when deception looks like the only choice. Many complainants have lied about what happened to them and damaged their credibility, only to be sorry later when they want to be believed about a new incident of victimization. If you find yourself in the position of regretting that you reported an incident of abuse, try your best to find a solution that does not involve lying to the authorities.

Talking to the defence lawyer

A LEGAL APHORISM SAYS "there is no property in a witness." This means that the Crown cannot prevent you or the defence lawyer from talking to each other. The accused may request that the defence lawyer talk to you, thinking the lawyer can convince you to drop the charges. If the defence lawyer contacts you, it is your choice whether or not to speak with this lawyer. If you do, be aware that nothing you say is private or off the record, and it may come up in trial later. If you do not want to talk to the defence, politely decline. You can talk to the Crown about any attempts the defence makes to contact you.

Several years ago, a defence lawyer actively sought out the complainant and her father during a sexual assault case in British Columbia. The lawyer intimated that if the charges went ahead, the complainant's reputation in the community would be ruined. The Law Society judged the lawyer's actions to be unacceptable conduct and disciplined him.

There have been cases in which the complainant has sworn an affidavit with the defence lawyer recanting the original charges. Of course, when this happens, the Crown does not know whether the defence has improperly influenced the complainant or if the complainant was not telling the truth in the first place. Some women have come to the authorities and told stories years later of being intimidated into recanting a truthful story. Under these circumstances, the complainant's credibility is compromised to the point that little can be done to address the original charges.

When you, the complainant, are dealing directly with the lawyer for the accused, that lawyer is not acting with a concern for your best interests; rather, the lawyer is getting evidence from you to help the accused. If the defence takes a sworn statement from you indicating that you lied to the police, this could subject you to charges for public mischief or perjury and seriously taint your credibility as a witness. This statement will go on file and will be available to the police and the Crown if you are hurt or make a complaint again. Since the defence lawyer is representing the accused, and not looking after your interests, you might consider obtaining independent legal advice (not from the Crown lawyer) before acquiescing to any of this lawyer's requests.

RULES OF DISCLOSURE

DISCLOSURE REFERS TO THE stage of litigation where each party is required to reveal any documents that it has that are relevant to the case. Mutual disclosure and inspection is intended to make sure both parties "put their cards on the table" at an early stage. Nevertheless, you will see that the disclosure exercise is not a level playing field. Disclosure must be treated seriously because it can heavily influence the outcome of court proceedings. Failure to make proper disclosure by overlooking or destroying documents will damage that party's credibility at trial. A court can impose severe sanctions for noncompliance with the obligations of disclosure. The rules of disclosure will affect your role as a witness, so it is important that you are familiar with them.

The defence has a right to the fruits of the investigation

THE LAW STATES THAT the Crown must provide the defence with all relevant evidence, whether or not it forms part of the Crown's case or suggests that the accused is innocent. If either side withholds relevant details, the court will order it to make that disclosure.

Under disclosure rules in Canadian law, the Crown must provide the accused with the following information:

- Statements made to the police and the Crown prosecutor
- Statements made by other witnesses
- Police notes and continuation reports
- Police report that summarizes the investigation
- Lists of exhibits — items of evidence — that may be introduced in court
- Photographs taken by the police for their investigation

- Results of any forensic medical examinations
- Results of any forensic lab investigations related to the charge (for example, blood tests for drugs or alcohol levels)
- The accused's criminal record and the record of witnesses, if this is relevant to the case

Crown witnesses will not have access to any of the above information with the exception of their own statements. However, Crown prosecutors in sexual offence cases tend to disclose to the court all evidence in their possession except information that is irrelevant to the case, and information that will reveal personal details about you, such as your address. In the case of some personal records like diaries and journals, the Crown will tell the defence that they exist and the latter can then apply for access if they can demonstrate that those records are relevant to the defence's case. In cases of inadvertent withholding of information by the prosecution, the judge may adjourn the trial to allow the accused to integrate the new evidence into the defence case. In circumstances where there is purposeful, bad-faith withholding of information by the prosecution, the court will enter a judicial stay of the charges. This means that the case has ended.

THE RATIONALE FOR DISCLOSURE RULES

SOME PEOPLE QUESTION WHETHER these rules are fair; why should the accused person get to know everything while apparently not giving up any information? Although it appears that the accused does not have to disclose anything, this is not quite true. The reality is that the police do have powers to obtain and admit evidence from the accused, but they must follow the strict parameters of the law. Police can search and seize items with a warrant, obtain blood samples with a DNA warrant, or intercept and record conversations with the proper authorization, to name a few avenues available. Officers can use these procedures during the investigation and, for obvious reasons, there is no requirement that the accused be informed of the procedures at the time. The police must later provide all of this evidence to the accused or the defence lawyer to allow them to prepare for the defence at trial.

The reason for implementing rules of disclosure is well-established in Canadian law, and in many other countries that share our legal traditions. It is essential to a fundamental principle of our legal system that every effort be made to guarantee the right of the accused to a fair trial. Rules of disclosure have been entrenched in legal procedure to prevent oppression of the individual by the state. If there were no sanctions against withholding information, a falsely accused person could be wrongly convicted. Withholding information would deny accused persons a fair opportunity to defend themselves. Only if the accused know the full case against them can a defence be properly prepared.

The accused and the accuser do not have equal rights

AS THE FOREGOING INDICATES, the complainant and the accused in our justice system do not share the same rights. Without proper authorization, accused persons have no obligation to provide evidence to the state, just as they need not incriminate themselves by providing a statement to the police. The accused does not even have an obligation to testify in criminal court. The onus is fully on the Crown to prove the case against anyone charged with a crime. The law also recognizes that there is some advantage for the accused in that the Crown could be caught off guard by any eventual defence provided. Judges dislike having the defence reveal its strategies pre or mid-trial, as this would compromise the defendant's right to a fair trial. There are minor exceptions where the defence must give the Crown notice, for example, if it is calling an expert witness or is relying on an alibi as a defence.

On the other side of the ledger, the complainant's role is more circumscribed and any legal rights are more limited than those of the accused. A complainant is not involved in the prosecution process, apart from being an important witness. The complainant does have some rights, but judges are careful that any consideration given to complainants, or efforts made to encourage them to give evidence, in no way deprive the accused of a fair trial. There is an ongoing tension in our system to balance the rights of both parties.

To understand what might initially seem like an inequity of rights in favour of the defendant, imagine yourself falsely accused of a crime. Suppose someone accuses you of stealing a piece of valuable jewellery. The consequences of a guilty verdict are different for you than for your accuser. Unless the accusation is false, your accuser risks little, while you could end up with a criminal record and perhaps spend time in prison. In this hypothetical case, assume the main witness is a man named Vincent, who tells police you stole the jewellery. However, you know that you bought the jewellery from Vincent who, without your knowledge, had stolen the jewellery himself. If, through the rules of disclosure, the prosecution informs you that the only witness is Vincent, you can prepare your defence by investigating Vincent's criminal record, or trying to establish the original source of the jewellery. If the courts do not tell you ahead of time what evidence the prosecution will present, you will have no time before the trial to do this kind of investigation.

To continue this example, let us suppose that several other witnesses appear at the trial, unannounced, and back up Vincent's testimony. This pits your single testimony against the multiple testimonies of these other witnesses. If you had known about their identity before the trial, you and your lawyer would have had time to discover that they were all Vincent's associates and were perhaps involved in criminal activity themselves. This would assist you in discrediting their false accusation and exposing the truth. It is for these reasons that the court requires the prosecution to disclose all evidence, accusations, and identities of witnesses to the defence before the trial.

DISCLOSURE OF PRIVATE RECORDS BEFORE THE TRIAL

PERHAPS THE MOST DIFFICULT aspect of the disclosure rules relates to the very private information accumulated over the years either in your diaries, journals, employment records, or in the files of professionals from whom you have sought assistance. There is a special provision in criminal law designed to protect the privacy of this information when it is not relevant to the trial, although records created during the investigation are not subject to these same privacy rules. The provision starts with a *Criminal Code* (section 278.1) definition of the term "record"

> Any form of record that contains personal information where there is a reasonable expectation of privacy and includes ... medical, psychiatric, therapeutic, counselling, education, employment, child welfare, adoption and social services records, personal journals and diaries.[1]

How the defence gains access to private records

UNLIKE MANY OTHER ITEMS of evidence, the defence does not have automatic access to your personal records. It must apply to see these using a rather complex process outlined within the *Criminal Code*. This application cannot be made until a trial judge is appointed, consequently it will not happen until after the preliminary hearing and usually within a month or so of the trial.

In 1991, the Supreme Court of Canada laid the foundation for the conduct of the Crown in relation to disclosing the fruits of the investigation in a case called *R. v. Stinchcombe*.[2] The Court ruled that the Crown file was not to be treated as the property of the Crown, and that the contents were to be provided to the defence whether they supported the Crown's case or not. The *Stinchcombe* case pertained to a property crime and the Supreme Court did not address the unique nature of sexual crimes in that judgment. Until 1997, there was no process in place to protect the complainant's privacy in the prosecution of sex crimes, and it was easy for the accused to gain access to personal records. This represented a tragic flaw in our justice system that was not addressed until another case proved to be a wake-up call for stricter guidelines. In 1991 a Roman Catholic Bishop from British Columbia, Hubert O'Connor, was ordered to stand trial for sexual offences against four Aboriginal women.[3] In the course of this historic trial and subsequent appeals, the Supreme Court of Canada acknowledged the need to create a process for the release of third-party records in sexual offence cases that respected the privacy rights of the complainant (see Appendix 13 for a detailed account of this trial).

The Parliament of Canada responded to this case and others by passing Bill C-46 in May of 1997. It clarifies much of the uncertainty around the issue of disclosure and stipulates stricter guidelines for accessing personal records. Now the defence can apply for these types of records only after the preliminary hearing and once a trial judge is appointed. The defence must submit an application to the trial judge and must describe the requested record in detail, indicate who has it, and give reasons for needing the document.

The defence must give seven days' written notice that it is applying for these records to the three principals: the Crown, the person(s) about whom the record is written, and the person who has the record.

Be prepared to retain your own lawyer

IF YOU RECEIVE NOTICE of an application for the production of records, we recommend that you hire a lawyer to represent you. This issue is complex and potentially can be damaging to your privacy. Since the Crown is not your legal advocate, you cannot rely on the Crown to state your case and protect your privacy. If you cannot afford a lawyer, all Canadian provinces have legal aid available for such circumstances. There are policies in place that encourage the Crown to assist you to find a lawyer through legal aid. Information about procuring this sort of legal representation is available through the Crown prosecutor and through the victim assistance programs in each province.

To obtain private records, the defence would first notify you of its request. If you did not already have your own lawyer, you would contact the Crown assigned to your case and make an appointment. The Crown will ask you if you want to waive your right to privacy, which is protected under sections 278.1 to 278.91 of the *Criminal Code*. If you consider the content of the record sensitive and you do not want it revealed, you would so advise the Crown and be referred to another lawyer. Once retained, your lawyer would go into court and tell the judge why the content of these records should not be disclosed. The court would then read the records and make a decision. This hearing is confidential and none of what goes on there can be disseminated in any way.

Waiving your *Criminal Code* rights

YOU MAY DECIDE THAT it is acceptable for the defence to have the records it seeks. Having made that decision, you will sign a waiver to that effect and the court will release the records. The Crown will assist you with this as well but will likely prefer that you sign a waiver in the presence of your own lawyer so you can have privacy and make the decision based on independent legal advice. This waiver is more than a mere consent to release form. You should be aware of the rights that you are waiving in relation to these documents and the potential consequences at trial. Since these issues arise due to your role as a witness for the Crown, the Crown lawyer will assist you in dealing with them, and the costs of hiring another lawyer for this purpose should be covered by the Crown office.

How a judge decides to disclose a personal record

IF YOU DO NOT waive your rights to privacy, the trial judge deals with the defence's application in a closed courtroom, and ideally this process takes place before the trial begins. Bill C-2 prohibits any dissemination of information filed or discussed during the defence application for such third-party records. Nobody can publish or transmit this information in any way; to do so is a criminal offence. These strict guidelines are outlined in the *Criminal Code*.

The trial judge considers the defence's reasons for wanting the record, but also considers the impact of disclosure on you. The guiding question is "Will the documents likely be relevant to an issue in the trial and is producing them necessary in the interests of justice?" A mere assertion that the record is relevant is not enough. Section 278.3 of the *Criminal Code* lists eleven specific assertions that are not sufficient on their own to establish that a record is likely relevant. It is not sufficient merely to say the record is related to the complainant's treatment or counselling, that it may be relevant to the complainant's credibility, or that it contains information about the subject matter of the charge. The purpose of requiring the defence to give specific, detailed reasons is to prevent speculative requests for records based on stereotypical assumptions.[4]

Judges in sexual offence trials will not easily grant the request for the release of private records. The following reasons have been ruled insufficient grounds for the request: the complainant received medical, psychiatric, or psychological therapy or other counselling; the complainant has accused someone else of sexual assault; the complainant had sexual relations with the accused on occasions other than the one in question.

If the judge rules in favour of producing a record, there may still be conditions placed on its release. The judge will likely only release selected pages or notes, may stipulate that the record be edited to block irrelevant information, may prohibit making copies, could require that the record be viewed only in the court, and may order that the record be returned at the end of the appeal period. Even where something private about you is made available to the defence it does not necessarily mean that it will come up in trial. The Crown should object if, at any time, there is some indication that the defence is misusing the information in court, and the judge should make a ruling about that objection.

Preliminary hearing questions about private records

THE COURT ALLOWS A defence lawyer to ask the complainant questions at the preliminary hearing in preparation for a possible application to release personal records. The defence can ask you whether a record exists, its source, and its location. You can be asked if you kept a personal journal and if relevant subject matter is contained in it. The defence may want to know if the information in your records is related to the subject matter of the charge or other case issues, but cannot ask you about actual details of the information. Similarly, the defence can ask general questions about any therapy you underwent, for example, whether it was group, memory-based, or regression therapy? The defence can also ask if the counselling was focused on memory retrieval or if it helped you recall any memories. Most complainants are not likely to have their own lawyer at this stage, but the Crown lawyer and the judge should ensure that the defence lawyer only asks you proper questions about these matters.

Possible consequences of a record request

THERE WAS A TIME when all of this private material would automatically be handed to the defence without any consideration of the complainant's concerns. If you find yourself facing the unpleasant task of dealing with a record request, remember the courageous Canadian women who confronted this unfairness and contributed to changing the law so that respect for your privacy is now a matter of law. Although the process can be arduous, it is done in the interest of protecting your privacy. Below is a brief outline of what to expect of a record request and your role in the procedure:

- You may be preparing for trial and hear you have to go to court earlier than expected to answer a request for your private records. You will receive a notice with supporting papers in which the accused sets out why the material is being requested.
- You may have to help gather the records, particularly if a personal diary or journals are requested.
- You will have to decide if you consider the release a violation of your privacy. This may be obvious or you may not appreciate the consequences of the release and want some advice about this. The Crown can give you limited advice but, ideally, you should speak to a lawyer who is familiar with this specific type of application.
- At the hearing, your lawyer (not the Crown) will speak on your behalf. There may be other lawyers there too, representing those who hold your records, such as your doctor, psychologist, or a government agency (for example, Welfare, or Child Protection).
- If the records are released you may be asked questions during the trial about their content.

Publication bans and closed courtrooms

REGARDING ANOTHER PRIVACY ISSUE, judges have an obligation to inform you of your right to a ban on publication of your identity at the beginning of the proceedings. The Crown usually asks for this very early on. The accused also has the right to apply for a ban on the publication or broadcast of evidence taken at the preliminary hearing. Besides excluding witnesses so they do not hear each other's evidence, judges may also decide, upon application by the Crown, to close the courtroom and exclude the public from part or all of the preliminary hearings. The *Criminal Code* states this is justifiable only if such restrictions are in the interest of public morals, the maintenance of order, and the proper administration of justice. The Crown will normally ask for this type of exclusion when a young victim is testifying, but some courts do not want to close proceedings even under these sensitive circumstances. Whether a ban is granted depends on the judge and the particular circumstances of the case.

THE ARRAIGNMENT

ONE OF OUR "DUE process" constitutional rights is the right of an accused person to be told exactly what the accusations are when the police lay criminal charges. This happens during a procedure called the arraignment. At this time, the judge reads the charges that have been filed and asks if the accused understands the accusations. If the accused does not have a defence lawyer, this is the opportunity to get one. If the accused cannot afford a lawyer, the judge will appoint one for free, which is another constitutional right.

Once the judge is satisfied that the accused understands the charges and has had an opportunity to get a lawyer if one is wanted, the judge will ask how the accused pleads to the charges. If the accused pleads "guilty," then the court proceeds to the sentencing stage of proceedings. If the accused pleads "not guilty," the case goes to trial and the prosecution will have to prove beyond a reasonable doubt that the accused committed the crime.

THE PRELIMINARY HEARING

ONLY THE ACCUSED AND the Crown have a say in whether there will be a preliminary hearing; it is largely out of the hands of the complainant. If the accused claims not to have committed the crime, the accused must then make some choices. The accused may choose to have a preliminary hearing first and a trial later or may decide to have a trial only, which may not happen for many months. If a preliminary hearing is chosen, it will occur before the trial and will allow the judge to hear submissions of evidence from the prosecutor.

The preliminary hearing will be the first time you have a chance to tell your story in this forum in this way. Witnesses have said it was beneficial to go through a preliminary hearing because they received first-hand experience in giving testimony. Indeed, it is a unique setting and there is not another place in life where communication takes place quite like this. You will have to sit in one place until the hearing ends, tell a narrative of the event, and then face a series of questions based on information from both you and other sources until the questioners are satisfied.

Once the principal witnesses have told their stories, and other evidence has been presented at the preliminary hearing, the presiding provincial court judge then decides if there are sufficient grounds to warrant a higher court putting the accused on trial. Your testimony will help the judge make this decision. The question the judge must answer is "Could a properly instructed jury, having heard the evidence, reasonably convict the accused?" Most preliminary hearings for sex crimes result in a committal for trial. An example of when this would not be the case is where a complainant failed to identify the accused.

Following the decision to go to trial, the Crown will then define the crime as either an indictable or a summary offence (see Chapter 1). The Crown decides what charges are appropriate in light of the facts, and will consider whether the penalty for the crime should be more than the eighteen months maximum mandated by a summary conviction. A serious sexual assault with violence usually calls for a penitentiary term (over two years) so the Crown would proceed to deal with it as an indictable offence. Since the sentences are more severe for an indictable offence, the law subsequently grants the accused so charged certain rights. For one, the accused has the right to choose in which court the trial takes place. The accused can elect to have the trial in the lower provincial court with a judge only, in the higher superior court with a judge only, or in the higher superior court with a judge and jury.

The preliminary hearing is a critical event in the legal proceedings that follow any serious crime, but it is particularly critical to the defence team in sexual offence cases because this is its first access to the complainant. This is the defence's opportunity to learn what the Crown's case will be. The defence will hear what the complainant's evidence is and then will begin preparation for the trial. Depending on what the Crown's case looks like, the defence may or may not advise the accused to choose a superior court trial. After the preliminary hearing, if the accused is committed for trial and chooses a superior court venue, there is still the option of re-electing to choose the provincial court again with the Crown's consent.

Direct indictment — a rare occurrence

ALTHOUGH EXTREMELY RARE, THE preliminary inquiry may be skipped in one other situation. In certain cases, the Crown can apply for a direct indictment, meaning the offence is indictable, but the Crown asks that the court deny the offender the right to a preliminary hearing. This is a serious decision that departs from normal procedure, and requires the consent of the Attorney General. A direct indictment will occur when the investigation is complete, the Crown has strong evidence in a very serious, high profile case, and it would not be in the public interest to delay the process. Full disclosure of the Crown's case is the key to ensuring this procedure is fair to the accused. The cases of Paul Bernardo in Ontario, and the Martinsville child sexual abuse in Saskatchewan, proceeded under direct indictment. In the latter case, this prevented the children from having to testify more than once against each accused.

WHAT HAPPENS AT A PRELIMINARY HEARING

A PRELIMINARY HEARING IS a presentation of evidence against the accused. It may look like a trial in many ways. However, it is not a vehicle for proving guilt or innocence; it only establishes whether there is enough evidence to warrant a trial in superior court. For this reason, there are rules meant to streamline the preliminary hearing to deal with just those issues identified by the lawyers. If the evidentiary issue is specific, such as consent (the sex happened but the accused says the complainant wanted it), or identity (the accused claims not to be the offender), the defence may be prepared to admit certain facts in writing and then wait to hear what the complainant has to say on issues critical to the defence. If the issues are not so specific, there may be more questioning and more witnesses may need to testify at the preliminary stage.

In court, participants strive to reveal the truth through questions. The Crown will ask open questions so the complainants can speak of the important events through their own narrative. The defence will ask leading questions in a very different style from that of the Crown, and may want more specific or concrete responses from you. In a preliminary hearing, you can gain immense insight into the language you and others use. You learn how to listen carefully to questions and you may discover that using vague language is not a good approach. You become aware of how your body and mind react to certain questions, how you feel in the court setting, and what emotions are provoked by the presence of the accused. This valuable experience can help you prepare for the trial itself.

Although the hearing may seem like a trial, you might need to remind yourself that it is not. It might help to interpret questions as fact-finding tools instead of attacks, regardless of what the lawyer's intentions might actually be. A simple question, such as "Why did you do that?" may be asked in a tone that makes it sound more like "Why did you do such a stupid thing?" Suggesting that "You did really like this man" may imply that "You really did want to have sex with him." A statement like "You have told lies before" may sound like we will not believe a thing you say. You should be prepared to answer such questions with calm resolve and try to minimize the influence of any emotional turmoil and pain that you might feel.

Try to identify your emotional insecurities and distinguish them from other people's intentions, although this can be tough to do in a courtroom or a preliminary hearing. In one case, a defence lawyer stood to ask a question and the teenaged witness said, "Could you get away from me and stop towering over me like that?" She made this statement despite the fact that the lawyer was more than fifteen feet away from her at the time.

The Crown's goal at a preliminary hearing

THE CROWN HAS SEVERAL objectives during the preliminary hearing. These include presenting the evidence at hand efficiently, showing that it is sufficient for the case to go to trial, and perhaps giving the complainant an opportunity to testify in order to test the complainant's capability to testify at trial. If you can tell your story effectively at the preliminary hearing, and hold up under the pressure of questioning from a defence lawyer, you have a good chance of doing well at trial. If you falter at this stage, you will know you have a challenge ahead at the trial and can begin making appropriate preparations. After the experience of a preliminary hearing, some complainants or the Crown may decide that the case should not go any further, even in instances where the accused has been committed for trial.

The preliminary hearing is also a way of expanding your understanding of the judicial process and your place in it. Although nobody may speak of it in these terms, participating in the preliminary hearing can be a learning experience that contributes to your own personal growth and may represent a step toward resolution of the crime. A Crown prosecutor understands that the preliminary hearing is your first opportunity to tell your story publicly and to go on record with your complaint. The Crown understands that apart from the legal consequences, there are personal consequences for the complainant and others involved in the case. For those who can take on this challenge, there is the potential for a positive outcome beyond the judge's verdict.

The prosecution strategy

WHERE BOTH LAWYERS DECIDE to opt for a full preliminary hearing, the Crown may apply one of two strategies: short and simple, or full-scale. In the first approach, the Crown is likely to put you on the stand, and merely have you tell your story. Following cross-examination, the Crown would end the hearing. If the accused is committed for trial on this basis, the exhibits and other witnesses are retained for the trial itself. At the other strategic extreme is a full presentation of all evidence including photos, medical evidence, results of the police investigation, forensic lab results, and the testimonies by all of the witnesses. In this scenario, the presentation of evidence in the preliminary hearing is every bit as comprehensive as at the trial.

There are advantages to each approach. The first is obviously efficient in terms of court time usage. It will move the case along quickly and it saves all other witnesses the anxiety and inconvenience of testifying twice. The second approach entails a great deal of effort on behalf of the Crown, who has to go over all the exhibits and interview all witnesses. Full presentation has the advantage of ensuring that the Crown prosecutor at trial (who may not be the same Crown prosecutor at the hearing) will have a clear and complete map of the case from the start of proceedings. This is important because without a detailed plan, unforeseen matters are more likely to arise and the case may go off course. The preliminary hearing can act as a dry run ensuring exhibits are in order, appropriate forensic tests are completed, and witnesses are not contradicting each other.

Most preliminary hearings in sexual offence cases are conducted in a manner that falls between the extremes described above. Witnesses, other than the victim, are often necessary, particularly the investigating officers and the physician who examined the complainant after the incident. Frequently, the Crown will present this supportive evidence by way of admissions. The accused will admit certain facts for the purposes of the preliminary hearing so that the doctor, police officer who seized items, lab technician, or others do not have to testify at this stage. It is an expense and inconvenience for expert witnesses to testify twice, but the inconvenience may be offset by the experience gained. After being questioned at the preliminary hearing, the witnesses will better understand what is expected of them at trial.

Ideally, the Crown should get a full understanding of the case evidence by interviewing as many witnesses as possible before the preliminary hearing. Most Crown prosecutors will prepare for the preliminary hearing as thoroughly as for a trial. They will want to ensure that all material relevant to getting a committal for trial is available to the defence.

One final point about strategic planning for the preliminary hearing is worth considering. You may be extremely anxious about seeing the accused in court, and you may expect to feel frustrated, intimidated, or fearful in the accused's presence. If you anticipate that these feelings may significantly affect your ability to testify, you can apply for extraordinary supports, such as a screen that blocks your view of the accused. If you testify without such a screen at the preliminary hearing, the court may not grant the request for the trial, reasoning that since you did not apply for one initially, you must not really need it.

The defence strategy

THE DEFENCE LAWYERS, OF course, have very different objectives from the Crown in regard to the preliminary hearing, and consequently they employ different strategies. The optimal outcome for the defence at a preliminary hearing is clear and simple — to have the case against the accused end at this stage, with a discharge, no trial, and no criminal record. The defence pursues this goal as thoroughly and strongly as possible. If a discharge is not achievable at this stage, the next objective will be to create a transcript to use at the trial to demonstrate weaknesses in the evidence, which includes your testimony. To achieve these goals, the defence first needs to learn completely about the evidence against the accused. The defence lawyer will then look for ways to challenge the credibility of your evidence and that of any other witnesses. Questioning can therefore be relentless and at times aggressive during the preliminary hearing.

The defence lawyers may also try to create the groundwork for a subsequent application under the *Charter of Rights* for disclosure of private documents. They may question you about the existence of diaries, journals, or other third-party notes and records. The court should not allow the defence to ask you what any diary says or what you talked about in therapy, but they are entitled to ask questions that could establish the existence of a certain record and its potential relevance to the case. The sort of questions the defence asks, and the submissions made, will give the Crown a sense of what the defence strategy might be. This is an adversarial process and the defence has no obligation to inform the Crown in advance of what its position is. If the defence lawyers show their hand too early, they might put themselves at a disadvantage. They walk a thin line — advancing enough to accomplish their objectives in the hearing without revealing too much about any defence strategy they may have at this point.

If the evidence proves to be strong against the accused, and you are a strong, steady, and credible witness, experienced defence lawyers will change their objective. In this case, following the hearing, they may explain to their client the full extent of the case against the client, and discuss whether a guilty plea might be the best option.

Witness testimony

THE CROWN MAY CALL a variety of witnesses. Some might present physical evidence, such as exhibits seized by the police during their investigation, others may be asked to give an expert opinion. The defence has the right to cross-examine witnesses as the Crown calls them. Although the accused also has the right to present evidence at the preliminary hearing, this is rarely done. At the end of the evidence presentation, both the Crown and the defence counsel try to convince the court that their respective positions are valid, and that the accused should be either committed to trial or discharged. In some cases, the hearing may reveal evidence of charges not named on the

Information and the judge then has the jurisdiction to commit the accused on those offences as well. Since it is open to the Crown to add counts on the indictment based on evidence disclosed at the preliminary hearing, some judges prefer the Crown to bring any additional charges at this time.

The key evidence at the preliminary hearing is generally the complainant's testimony, so you can expect to face an aggressive challenge to your credibility by the defence. As in a trial, the court excludes the complainant and other witnesses from the courtroom, except when they are delivering their testimony. Excluding witnesses from hearing each other is fundamental in Canadian law. It protects the testimony of each witness from the influence or contamination of other evidence in the case. Witnesses should state only what they know of the facts and not what they may have concluded from outside information. Current research on memory tells us that people can unwittingly incorporate facts they have heard from others into their own recall and think that this memory reflects their actual experience, rather than the blend of perspectives it is.

After you have completed your testimony at the preliminary hearing, you have to leave the courtroom and cannot listen to the other evidence or submissions of counsel. There have been exceptions made to this rule. In the *Jane Doe* case the complainant hired her own lawyer who argued on her behalf that she be permitted to sit in on and listen to the evidence of others at the preliminary hearing. The court heard her testimony, gave her lawyer status to make the application to let her remain in the courtroom, and allowed the application with conditions. One of the conditions was that she not hear the testimony of the other women that her assailant had sexually assaulted.[5] Jane Doe has indicated in her book that she felt it would have been better to hire a lawyer earlier than she did in the proceedings, and would advise other sexual assault complainants to do the same.[6] She seemed to believe that things might have gone differently if she had counsel advocating on her behalf from the beginning.

Everything is recorded

THE LAW REQUIRES THAT a transcript be made of all the proceedings of a preliminary hearing, so every detail is recorded. This will likely afford you the first opportunity to see your story clearly outlined in writing. Both the Crown prosecutor and the defence want to ensure that important evidence is on record for later use; they rely on the preliminary hearing transcript to do this. Defence lawyers always refer to this record at the trial to strengthen their view or discredit a witness on certain points of evidence. The defence assumes that witnesses will reliably reproduce their preliminary testimony at trial because they made their statements under oath or affirmation.

It is a criminal offence for a witness to give intentionally false information; therefore, lawyers rely on the transcript to predict the trial's evidence. They build their trial strategies based on what witnesses say at the preliminary hearing. Most lawyers, particularly in cross-examination, ask questions designed to show what the witnesses recall, to commit them to a particular version of their story, and to create a transcript of that version for later use. Knowing this does not mean that you should try to create a particular transcript, rather you should answer the questions in a truthful and complete manner, alert to the importance of what you are saying at this stage of the proceedings. Be mindful that lawyers will use this transcript later in the trial. The only part of the transcript that you will be allowed to read is your own testimony. This applies to every witness. The accused, however, sees the entire transcript, which includes everyone's testimony.

How the hearing transcript will be used at the trial

SKILLED DEFENCE LAWYERS SEEK to use the preliminary hearing to illuminate factors helpful to their case. They are conscious of creating a transcript beneficial to their client. Later at the trial, jury members do not read the whole transcript but the defence can bring parts of it to their attention through witnesses. For example, here is part of the transcript from a fictitious preliminary hearing to illustrate this strategy:

DEFENCE LAWYER: You have known the accused for quite a while.

WITNESS: Yes.

DL: In fact, until this event happened, you were friends.

W: He thought so, but frankly he kind of weirded me out.

DL: But you are not afraid of the accused, are you?

W: Only when he drinks.

Later, here is what could happen during the trial:

DL: Why didn't you just leave if you didn't want sex?

W: I didn't leave because I was afraid.

DL: And I want to clarify one more time; my client had not been drinking, had he?

w: No, he had not been that time.

DL: And yet you say that you didn't leave because you were afraid?

w: Yes.

DL: What were you afraid of?

w: Of him.

DL: I suggest to you that you were not afraid of him.

w: Yes I was.

DL: Do you recall telling us at the preliminary hearing that you were not afraid of him?

w: No, I do not recall saying that.

DL: Show the witness the transcript. And you recall when you testified at the preliminary hearing that you were under oath to tell the truth?

w: Yes.

DL: Look to page 45 line 23. Question: But you are not afraid of the accused are you? Answer: Only when he drinks. Do you recall being asked that question and giving that answer?

w: Yes, I do.

DL: And was it true?

w: Yes it was.

DL: So you say you were too afraid to leave the room, even though he wasn't drinking.

w: Yes.

DL: And this is in a context where you had been on friendly terms with this man in the past?

w: Yes.

DL: The door was not locked was it?

w: It was open.

DL: But you chose to stay.

w: Yes.

Some lawyers even go so far as to read the transcript to the witness at the trial to ensure there is no deviation from what was said at the preliminary hearing. At the end of reading the passage, they ask the witness to adopt it as the truth. This is arguably not the correct use of the transcript but the judge may not always stop the defence lawyer. If the section in question is out of context or requires some explanation, you may say something about this at the time. The Crown should monitor the defence's use of the transcript and can clarify any misunderstanding or confusion in the cross-examination or later in re-examination. A witness can make being on the stand easier by remaining mindful to answer each question carefully, clearly, and truthfully. In this way, there is little cause for the defence to find fault or inconsistencies.

Reading the transcript

YOU WILL HAVE AN opportunity to read the transcript of your testimony before testifying at the trial. Reading the transcript may be emotionally difficult, but it is an important step in your preparation for trial. We suggest that you read it aloud with the Crown prosecutor. Reading aloud is a process that fosters greater awareness of the material, helps to keep the issues in perspective, and provides an opportunity to discuss issues as they arise. Share the transcript with nobody other than the Crown or your own lawyer. The defence may ask you in court if you have showed it to others, or if you have read the evidence others have given, and it is best for your credibility that you have not done so. If you were to read others' evidence, you could unwittingly incorporate this information into your memory by comparing your evidence to the versions given by others.

When reading the transcript prior to the trial, you may find places where you made mistakes, faltered, or gave incorrect evidence for one reason or another. As soon as you observe such discrepancies or omissions tell the Crown counsel, who will make note of corrections, the reasons for them, and then pass them on to the defence. The Crown can decide what, if anything, needs to be said or done about correcting any factual errors.

How the hearing ends

A PRELIMINARY HEARING CONCLUDES with an order by the judge for either discharge or committal to trial. If discharged, the accused is free to go, the charges are dropped, and no trial will take place on those particular charges, unless the Crown appeals the decision on a point of law. With a discharge, the law considers the accused to be innocent because there was not enough evidence for a finding of guilt.

If there is enough evidence, and a committal to trial is ordered, the judge states the offences that the accused will face in court. The court registry then provides a date for the superior court trial, normally within six months to a year. The accused has the option to appeal the results of a preliminary hearing, and the court will notify the complainant if the defence takes this route.

If authorities did not detain the accused before the preliminary hearing, the accused will likely remain at large until the trial. Any conditions of release imposed before the hearing remain in place until the trial. The court has the option to change release conditions before committal to trial, so if information has come to the attention of the Crown suggesting a change in release conditions is appropriate, this issue can be addressed while all parties are present in court.

PREPARING FOR A PRELIMINARY HEARING

IF YOUR COURT CASE includes a preliminary hearing, it can be as rigorous and challenging as a trial for everyone involved. It will be your first appearance in court to testify about the reported crime and for that reason it can be more stressful than a subsequent appearance. Furthermore, the challenges you face from the defence lawyer may be much rougher at this stage than at the trial. As always, the key is to be prepared. Make the same effort to prepare as you would for the trial. What you neglect to do at this stage could come back to haunt you down the road. Ideally, you and the Crown counsel can arrange sufficient opportunity to discuss your testimony in advance and prepare a course of action. In addition to what you read in this chapter, we encourage you to read carefully the material in Chapter 8, which describes in greater detail what you need to know when testifying in court. Thorough preparation for this arduous task is highly recommended.

Beyond preparation for the legal side of the proceedings, you will need to prepare for potentially strong emotional reactions. Talking about the explicit details of a sexual assault in such an emotionally charged situation takes courage. A complainant can feel vulnerable and exposed sitting in front of others recounting memories of events that may still be extremely painful to recall. Even thinking about testifying in court can trigger many negative thoughts, such as "I cannot stand this," "They want to hurt me," "I cannot relive this," "They will use this against me," "They just want this information to cause me more harm," or "I am going to lose." Conversely, you could view your court appearance as a rare opportunity to reveal the truth of your experiences in a meaningful, public way. It is sobering to consider that there are parts of the world where the systems of justice do not provide this opportunity to sexual assault victims. Countless victims have never had the chance to tell of their victimization or to hold the offender accountable. Considered from this perspective, you may appreciate having a legally sanctioned forum where you can tell your story.

Prepare for emotional turmoil

FOR SOME COMPLAINANTS, THE preliminary hearing can be a great shock, and they subsequently decide the legal process is just not for them. They want nothing more to do with the courts after going through a gruelling experience on the stand. Conversely, if you know what to expect, you can cushion the shock, take some control, and perhaps leave with a different perspective.

To begin, you will be physically close to the accused. In our provincial courtrooms, where all preliminary hearings take place, you may be seated within a few feet of the accused. This can be unsettling unless you mentally prepare yourself. In addition, the defence will likely launch an aggressive attack on your testimony. In one training session for defence lawyers, the instructor advised the attendees to metaphorically "whack" the complainant at the preliminary hearing. There is no doubt that many defence lawyers try to whack complainants by intimidation in the hope of discrediting them. They see it as their job. Their client says that you are not telling the whole truth, so they assume that you must be telling some lies. They may resort to intimidation while questioning you because the stakes are high and they believe such pressure will reveal any dishonesty. They want to rattle you so your testimony looks uncertain, strengthening their case for a discharge or eventual acquittal.

These intimidation attempts may be more aggressive at a preliminary hearing than at a trial. In superior court trials, defence lawyers are very careful about using aggression and intimidation because judges and juries typically take a dim view of such tactics and the strategy may backfire. In a preliminary hearing, however, there is no jury and no final resolution of the issues, so the defence really has nothing to lose in pushing you to your limit through relentless or aggressive actions.

Prepare for compound questions

BE MINDFUL THAT THERE are complexities and strategies involved in the questions lawyers will ask you. At the preliminary hearing, it is important to be prepared for these questions in their various forms. You need to listen carefully to the questions asked and then respond to every part of the question. One common form of question that creates problems is the compound question — two or three questions in one. When the witness responds to one part of the question only, the later transcript will not reveal which part that was.

The Crown will tend to ask you open questions, such as "Will you tell the court when you went to the police and why?" On the other hand, the defence will ask more pointed, leading, or compound questions. Consider the following compound question that defence counsel could pose to the mother of a child victim: "Did you go to the police because you were anticipating a custody dispute and your child had already made an allegation of abuse?"

The mother might be tempted simply to answer, "Yes," but which part of the question is she answering? Did she in fact go to the police? Was she anticipating a custody dispute at that time? Had the child made an allegation of abuse? Assume for a moment that the child did make an allegation, but the mother had not contemplated a custody dispute and this was not a motivating factor when she went to the police. What would be the truthful answer? Would a mere "yes" answer the question truthfully and give an accurate picture to the court?

With a simple "yes" to that compound question in a preliminary hearing, here is what the defence might ask her during the trial.

DEFENCE LAWYER: Isn't it true you went to the police because you were expecting a custody dispute and you wanted points in your favour so you would win the custody of the child?

MOTHER: No, that is not true.

DL: Do you recall testifying at the preliminary hearing?

M: Yes.

DL: And did you try to tell the truth?

M: Yes.

DL: And were you asked, "Did you go to the police because you were anticipating a custody dispute and your child had already made an allegation of abuse?"

M: If it says so here.

DL: And did you answer "Yes."?

M: Yes.

DL: And were you telling the truth?

M: Yes.

Instead of one simple "yes," it would be better for you to answer each component of the question. If, during the preliminary hearing, the mother had been careful to answer all parts of the question, she might have responded in the following way:

> I did go to the police and there had been an allegation from my child, but the last thing on my mind at that time was custody. Frankly, for what he had done, it never occurred to me there would be any question about that until we sorted out how to ensure my child was safe.

To be confident that you are responding to each part of the question individually, you can respectfully ask the defence lawyer to break a compound question into its parts so that you can answer each separately, for example, you may say, "That question seems to have many parts, could you simplify it for me?"

Say how you feel, out loud

SUPPOSE AT THE PRELIMINARY hearing you are highly anxious and feel faint, nauseous, or short of breath, causing you to pause, stutter, or hesitate. The court reporter cannot record your feelings so you need to articulate them clearly to the Crown or to the judge. If you suffer in silence, there will be no explanation for your stuttering or hesitating. Without any explanation, incorrect conjectures may be made about your behaviour. You may start to cry but want to push ahead without a break, responding to questions between sobs, perhaps making your responses disjointed and hard to follow. Unless someone explains your emotional state on the record, a person later reading the record could attribute the irregularities in your answers to uncertainty or inaccuracy. The Crown lawyer may intervene but if not, tell the judge and the lawyers that you need a break, and explain what is preventing you from giving a candid account of your story.

Some matters are not within the purview of the preliminary hearing

THE PRELIMINARY HEARING HAS a specific purpose, so certain matters are not relevant at this stage. Two such irrelevant matters are evidence of your previous sexual activity and access to your private records that are in the possession of third parties. If the defence wants to elicit evidence that the complainant in a sexual assault trial engaged in sexual activity at a time other than that which forms the subject matter of the trial, the defence lawyer must first seek permission to do so from the judge. The court does not permit such applications at the preliminary hearing, however. Similarly, if the defence wants access to private third-party records, the defence lawyer must apply for this and show grounds for the request, but this must wait until after the preliminary hearing stage. In either case, the defence lawyer may prepare for a later application by asking the complainant questions that indirectly relate to previous sexual history, mental health issues, and personal records. (For a checklist of things that you can do to prepare for the preliminary hearing, see Appendix 14.)

FOLLOWING THE PRELIMINARY HEARING

THE CROWN PROSECUTOR FOR your preliminary hearing is not likely to be the same one who will take your case when an accused is committed to trial. This is because Crown prosecutors generally serve in either provincial (lower) court or superior (higher) court. They seldom serve in both. The preliminary hearing takes place in provincial court, whereas the trial will generally take place in superior court. If you find this shift to a different lawyer disruptive and you want to work with the same prosecutor throughout the process, you can make your request either to the Crown counsel you know and prefer, or to the administrator at the Crown counsel office for superior court trials. This is not the same office as the court registry, which does not assign Crown lawyers to trials. If the preliminary trial lawyer is willing and available to take the trial forward, your request has a good chance of being granted.

If the judge discharges the accused at the end of the preliminary hearing, there will be no trial unless the Crown appeals the decision. If the Crown chooses not to register an appeal, and you want to pursue further legal avenues, you can sue in civil court. In Chapter 10, we discuss civil litigation and other avenues of redress or compensation for damages resulting from sexual abuse. Even when an accused is committed for trial, it is possible that no trial will take place. This happens when the accused pleads guilty.

THE GUILTY PLEA

MANY SEE A GUILTY plea as the ideal outcome of the criminal justice response to a sex crime. It is a formal acknowledgment to the court and the community that the accused takes responsibility for the crime. An accused charged with a sex offence can avoid a trial by pleading guilty to the charge at any time before the verdict. In so doing, the accused waives all rights under the *Charter of Rights* to a trial. There is always a chance that an accused will enter a guilty plea, and it is always worth the effort of trying to negotiate such a plea. A guilty plea saves a lot of time, expense, disruption to people's lives, and potential emotional suffering, so it is a very positive step in the resolution of a crime. It dispenses with the need for a trial with its adversarial roles of complainant against accused, provides an avenue for both to see what happened from the other's point of view, and potentially opens the door to healing.

When the accused says, in a court of law, "Yes, I am guilty of this offence against the complainant," the relationship between complainant and offender can undergo a fundamental change. For the first time since the crime took place, you are both on the same page. Up to this point, you, the police, and the Crown did not know what the accused had to say about the incident that led to the charges. There may be a police statement but concerned parties do not get to hear what the offender has to say until the latter testifies at the trial. With the guilty plea comes a first glimpse into the accused's perspective at the time of the crime, and state of mind about the offence. One may say that drinking or drugs caused impaired judgment, that one was under great strain and stress or was deeply depressed and not in a normal state, that one had misinterpreted your words or conduct, or that one could not have sex with a spouse or partner so sought it elsewhere. At first, these explanations may sound like excuses. Your reaction might be, for example, "Is that what the accused is saying?" "Is that what the accused thinks?" "Is that the accused's story?" or "Unbelievable!"

Upon further reflection, you may begin to understand the accused's internal dialogue, and the thoughts and feelings that compelled the latter to commit a sexual crime. The public verbalization of one's motivations can often be the first step on the journey to acknowledging and taking responsibility for one's actions. If nothing else, a guilty plea means the accused has publicly acknowledged responsibility and, from a legal perspective, the crime is resolved. From a complainant's perspective, a guilty plea may not indicate a clear admission of responsibility. For example, the complainant may think, "He says he did it but he's making all kinds of excuses ... says it was not really his fault, not totally," or "Why can't he just face up to it?" However, a guilty plea is a statement of responsibility, an important step for the offender, and a public gesture of admitting wrongdoing. With the adversarial process over, there is now an opportunity for further dialogue and resolution beyond the criminal process, particularly if the offender is an intimate or family member of the complainant.

The implications of a guilty plea

FOR SOME OFFENDERS, PLEADING guilty allows them to face their responsibilities voluntarily, rather than being convicted with a set of facts that they consider inaccurate. Some may see the possibility of a lighter sentence in exchange for this early plea. For others, it means they avoid facing the humiliation of the details of their crime being openly discussed in a trial, a prospect that often bothers them more than the sentence. For still others, the guilty plea is an opportunity to admit they were wrong, to turn things around, to get their life back on track, and to start making amends — that is, it seems the best way out of a bad situation. A guilty plea can be the catalyst that starts an offender on the path of self-discovery, and to learn what triggered the offence. Offenders are more likely to make significant changes in their behaviour when they admit their weaknesses and transgressions, so even a self-serving admission of wrongdoing is better than the prospect of going to jail while still maintaining innocence.

Offenders and complainants are frequently in intimate relationships of some sort. The offender may genuinely care for the complainant and may be motivated to enter a guilty plea with the hope of saving the complainant from further humiliation. A guilty plea can also be an opportunity to demonstrate remorse for the harm done by the offender's actions to the victim, as well as to others, such as family and friends who may also have been emotionally affected. This can be an opportunity for a fresh start in key relationships, a chance to wipe the slate clean and start over on a more honest, healthy footing.

Sexual assaults happen in all kinds of relationships. Apart from cases involving lovers, sexual assault cases can involve long-time platonic friends, where the man wants more intimacy than the woman is willing to give. In one case, a man sexually assaulted a woman who had considered him as her best friend. The assault occurred after a night of drinking, while they slept off the effects of the alcohol. The woman awoke to find her clothes in disarray and her friend lying beside her. When she asked if he had engaged in sexual intercourse with her, he admitted that he had, and offered no explanation. She asked him to leave, he did, and she went to the police. The man never denied the act. After the police charged him, he entered a guilty plea at the earliest possibility. He said that he had loved the complainant for a long time and felt sick about the fact that she did not seem to love him in the same way. When they got drunk, he acted on his love for her, but could tell immediately by her reaction that he had done a terrible thing, and now he felt horrified by his actions.

In this case, facing charges from a good friend and pleading guilty were the events that led this man to seek help, to begin looking inward for the first time, and to admit that his behaviour towards women in general needed changing. In the past, he had committed similar inappropriate acts and denied to himself and his friends that his behaviour was problematic. Following the charges, he was facing the facts and preparing to make personal changes.

Regardless of the consequences, a guilty plea is a major turning point in legal proceedings for the complainant. The complainant does not have to testify, and the legal outcome is certain; the accused will be held responsible. A guilty plea can put an end to further blame, embarrassment, confusion, or feelings of rejection and humiliation on the complainant's part. Is it more important that the complainant's version of events be put to the test in a trial, or that the offender accepts responsibility for having committed an illegal act and faces appropriate consequences as swiftly as possible? The answer to this will determine how satisfying the plea negotiation process is for the complainant.

HOW THE CROWN NEGOTIATES THE PLEA

AN OFFENDER DOES NOT simply say "I am guilty to all charges." The offender may offer to plead guilty to one charge and not to another, or agree to plead guilty if the charges are reduced to lesser offences. In some cases, the offender may be prepared to plead guilty to the *Criminal Code* charge, but will not admit to certain of the more serious facts of the case. The offender's decision will likely depend on the kind of evidence available to the prosecution, and the likelihood of a guilty verdict if the matter goes to trial. Some offenders would rather plead to physical assault charges than have a sexual offence on their record, and most offenders would prefer that adult, rather than child-related sex offences be brought against them. Some offenders will plead guilty to a sexual assault but will deny using a weapon.

The prosecutor will typically negotiate a guilty plea following a preliminary hearing and once a trial date has been set. By then, both the defence and the Crown counsel know the strengths and weaknesses of the case and can negotiate with those facts in mind. The offender may choose to plead guilty to one of the lesser charges and ask the Crown to drop the others. The Crown may deny this request and have the case proceed to trial on the remaining charges. If the offender pleads guilty to a lesser charge and then is acquitted by the court of the more serious charges at trial, the original guilty plea still stands; it is unaffected by the trial outcome.

On the other hand, if the accused enters a guilty plea to a lesser charge, for example, "I do not plead guilty to sexual assault with a weapon but I plead guilty to simple assault," and the Crown does not accept this plea, the trial will continue. The guilty plea to a lesser charge does not stand and the Crown has to prove the original charge. The accused will go to trial on the full charge of sexual assault with a weapon and if the Crown fails to prove the sexual assault, the accused is acquitted. If during the course of the trial, the accused formally admits the sexual assault and the defence raises reasonable doubt that a weapon was used, the court will find the accused guilty of the lesser offence of sexual assault.

Another plea option has the offender plead not guilty to one part of the offence and guilty to another part. The offender might agree that there was a sexual assault but take issue with the assertion that a knife was used. The Crown may consent to a plea to sexual assault, rather than sexual assault with a weapon. It is still open to the Crown to call evidence on the issue of the knife during the sentencing hearing, and the use of a knife would be an aggravating factor considered when determining a sentence.

Offenders must know details of all the allegations against them, and a plea must be voluntary and unequivocal. The prosecutor will not accept a plea if the offender, at the time of entering it, was intoxicated, using drugs, suffering from a mental disorder, or improperly pressured by another lawyer. The judge can also later withdraw the plea if any of the above conditions are found to pertain. If authorities charge more than one person in relation to a single incident (for example, sexual assault of a single female by several males), a guilty plea by one does not affect the plea of the others.

Certain issues are not negotiable in return for a guilty plea. For example, neither the Crown nor the defence can withhold information about the offender's previous convictions for sex offences from the sentencing judge. Similarly, the offender cannot negotiate with the Crown to have criminal charges brought against the complainant, and cannot negotiate to have conditions placed on the complainant's behaviour, or a peace bond being placed on the complainant.

What the defence and the Crown must agree on

IN CONSIDERING WHETHER TO negotiate a plea from the defendant, the Crown must first determine if it is in the best interest of the prosecution. Some of the factors to consider are as follows:

- Is the prosecution's evidence strong enough to get a conviction?
- What is the maximum penalty for each charge?
- Do the charges carry minimum penalties?
- Will the charge pled to accurately reflect the offender's behaviour on the criminal record, in case of future problems?

If the Crown determines that accepting a plea is a reasonable option, negotiations will utilize both *Criminal Code* case law and provincial policies as guidelines. Both parties should negotiate on principled positions and not merely on guesswork or whimsy. The defence and the Crown counsel will negotiate until they reach an agreement on enough factors to allow for the guilty plea; matters without consensus are argued in court where the judge can make a decision. Lawyers have to clarify and agree to which charges, outlined in the Information or Indictment, the defendant is willing to enter a plea of guilty. If they agree to a plea but do not agree about certain aggravating facts (such as the use of a weapon), the Crown still has the burden of proving these facts beyond a reasonable doubt. Most prosecutors do not want the defence to pressure them into an agreement any more than the judges want lawyers to pressure them into an agreed upon sentence. Of course, the law is clear that a judge is not bound by an agreement between the lawyers on what a sentence should be, and the accused should be warned about this when a guilty plea is entered. Judges may disregard what the lawyers have negotiated and make their own decisions about a sentence.

If the Crown and the defence counsel can agree on the resolution to some of the following questions, sentencing will run more smoothly:

- Where and when will the accused plead guilty?
- Will the accused undergo a psychiatric/psychological examination?
- Will there be a pre-sentence report ordered?
- Will the Crown ask for restitution for the victim?
- Will the Crown ask that the accused forfeit certain possessions (such as pornography or weapons)?
- Will the accused consent to give a blood sample for the DNA database?
- Will the accused agree to be added to the Sex Offender Registry (where it is not mandatory under the *Criminal Code*)?
- Will the accused be prohibited from possessing firearms (where it is not mandatory)?

Time and place for the guilty plea

WHEN THE OFFENDER DECIDES to enter a guilty plea to some or all of the charges, negotiations may be made with the Crown lawyer at that time. The Crown will want to hear details of the plea as soon as possible, and definitely before the trial date. The defence team may want to delay entering the plea, perhaps because it wants to first deal with other outstanding charges or, in some cases, because the accused is highly anxious about pleading guilty. A delay in pleading guilty also allows the offender to get life back in order before facing the judge. Anyone anticipating a jail sentence may need time to arrange one's affairs.

If the charge is an indictable offence, the offender must also make a decision about where the trial will take place. The defence may prefer to move the guilty plea from the superior court to the provincial court; the superior court justices in a given area may have a reputation for handing out tougher penalties, or the provincial court judge may know the offender and be sympathetic. A particular court may even be chosen simply based on scheduling and travel conveniences.

THE COMPLAINANT'S ROLE IN PLEA NEGOTIATION

THE PLEA NEGOTIATION OFTEN happens quickly and complainants may get little attention in the process. Unfortunately, in spite of legislated efforts to ensure authorities keep complainants informed, case dates and venues sometimes change without giving notification to the complainant. If you establish a rapport with Crown personnel early on and ask that they keep you informed, they are more likely to accommodate you.

The Crown may consult you about the guilty plea, or may simply tell you of the intention to do so. For you, consultation about the charges laid, sentencing, and similar issues may be vital. On the other hand, getting involved in the negotiations may cause more stress than you care to deal with. Interestingly, although victim impact statements were devised as a means for complainants to tell judges their experiences directly, a result not foreseen were protests by complainants that they had already given so much they did not want the added stress of giving another inventory of their suffering. If you want nothing to do with the plea negotiation, just tell the Crown. The Crown is keeping you involved and informed as a courtesy to you, not because you are a necessary part of the negotiation. There was a time when the process did not include complainants at all.

If the Crown consults you about the plea negotiation, you will likely review the charges and your version of what happened. The Crown will pay particular attention to any aggravating factors and may ask you about wording in the written statement of facts presented to the defence to ensure that it is accurate. If you express any doubts or uncertainty about any of these issues, or if other evidence casts doubt on these facts, the Crown may want to modify the original charges to ensure the defence will agree to a guilty plea.

You are more likely to be involved if the negotiations are lengthy. The Crown will ask if you have any concerns, and what you think of the charges chosen, the discussions about the facts and the range of sentence proposed. This offers you the courtesy of participation. You will not have the final say. It is the responsibility of the Crown to make the final decisions.

Discuss the plea only with the Crown

THERE ARE REASONS THAT you should keep any details of the plea negotiations in confidence. To begin, the matter is not resolved until the plea and relevant facts of the case are entered before a judge. A trial may still go ahead if negotiations break down and the parties cannot agree. Until the accused actually enters a plea, take particular care not to talk to any other victims. This can be difficult considering that support from other victims may be important to you, but to bring the offender to justice you must be vigilant to keep your story private during negotiations. If negotiations do fail and a trial ensues, the defence could use any discussions that you might have had with others during the plea negotiations as evidence to suggest there was collusion among the witnesses. In high profile cases, the media may obtain sensitive information and change the direction of negotiations. In general, it is best to be prudent and avoid giving rumours or innuendoes the chance to affect proceedings.

WHEN NEGOTIATIONS FAIL

IN SOME CASES, DESPITE compromises on both sides, an agreement cannot be reached and the trial goes ahead. Sometimes the accused may have a change of heart at the last moment, and not enter the agreed upon plea, or a judge may deny the plea. In some cases, you may still have to testify even if the offender has pled guilty to the charges. This can happen when there is a huge disparity in each side's version of the aggravating facts that could affect sentencing.

If the defence and the Crown counsel take up adversarial and hostile positions before the trial, a guilty plea is less likely. Acrimony can develop if opposing sides make numerous adversarial applications before trial. The defence lawyer might make disparaging comments about the complainant in front of the Crown or judge, or friends and family members may experience animosity and hatred. In the midst of such conflict, compromise is unlikely and the prosecution team buckles down to prepare for a full trial.

You can keep yourself up to date on the status of the offender's plea by checking in with the Crown in advance of the trial to ask if any negotiations have taken place. Tell the Crown what role you would like to play in any potential plea negotiations, and find out if any court dates or locations have changed.

CHILDREN TESTIFYING

NOT SO LONG AGO, children (defined as anyone less than fourteen years of age) were assumed to be unreliable witnesses in any criminal proceedings. Today, the court does not make this assumption. While children can make errors in both their perception of events and their recall, the courts, persuaded by courtroom experience and by research into children's cognitive capabilities, now recognize that children make no more errors than adults do, as long as authorities question them properly. In fact, when it comes to deception, adults can tell lies more adeptly than children can. A child's transparent nature can help to expose the truth in powerful ways that an adult's testimony might not. Children, however, do experience reality differently than adults. Children pay less attention to specifics of time and place than adults do. Adults, because of their adult responsibilities, are more attuned to when and where things happen.

Many cases in Canada have recently confronted the issue of child competency to testify in court. It is a complex matter and one that is in a state of change as courts continue to make new rulings. Recent amendments to the *Criminal Code* and the *Canada Evidence Act* presume a child under the age of fourteen is a competent witness unless a party convinces the court that its presumption is wrong. An inquiry into competency will only take place if someone challenges a child's capacity. The threshold test is simple; the court needs to know if the child can understand and respond to the questions asked.

Should a child testify?

THE COURT CAN SUBPOENA a child just as it does an adult. Although the law says the subpoena should be served personally, normally it is given to an adult guardian who can take the child to court. The Crown will not call upon a child to testify unless the evidence given by the child is essential to prove some or all the elements of an offence, and is crucial to the outcome of a trial.

Occasionally parents of a child victim will stipulate that they do not want their child to testify in a sex abuse trial for various reasons. For example, a non-offending spouse may try to protect the accused spouse by blocking the child's evidence, or a parent may feel shame that the child is a sexual assault victim, or that the child's testimony will irreversibly damage family relationships. Those who are motivated to protect a suspect may find themselves in a sticky situation if the local government protection agency determines that it must apprehend a child as protection from further abuse. Some people, out of desperation, decide to hide their child until after the trial, an action that can lead to criminal charges against the parent. As well, out of concern for their children, some parents try to prevent them from testifying because they may fear that the legal process will be emotionally harmful to them and not worth the effort.

If you have real concerns about your child testifying, you should seek legal advice to discuss what protections authorities can put in place. The courts now have an awareness of children's sensibilities that was not always apparent in the past. Some crimes simply will not be successfully prosecuted without a child's evidence, so the laws now go a long way to accommodate children.

If it is imperative that your child testify, make an appointment with the specialized prosecutor in your area who handles cases involving child witnesses. Ask about the various applications that the Crown can make to protect a child witness. For example, a child may testify from a different room or from behind a screening device, could make a pre-recorded statement, or could have a support person present. A judge will typically grant these accommodations but the Crown must use a special application process well before the trial. The defence can oppose the application, but the court will grant the requests of the child and the Crown unless there is good reason not to do so.

Apart from these special privileges granted in the courtroom, there may also be programs available in your community to orient children to the legal process, support them throughout, and advocate on their behalf. The many children who have testified with lesser supports in the past have not done so in vain. They have opened the eyes of the legal system to these important issues and have made testifying easier for today's children (see Appendix 15 for a more complete outline of courtroom accommodations that can be made for child witnesses).

The best way to help your child testify is to meet with the person responsible for witness preparation and work together to develop a plan based on the particulars of the case and your child's needs. The plan should include an age-appropriate orientation to the process and people involved in the case, emotional preparation for testimony, a means to debrief after court, and some means to honour the child afterwards for hard work and courage (see Appendix 16 for a checklist to aid the guardians of a child who is going to testify).

Preparing a child for court

THE CROWN PROSECUTOR, VICTIM services, or any other social agency with the mandate to prepare the child for a trial appearance, should address three important areas:

- *Discussion of evidence*: Explain the importance of telling the truth and getting the facts straight. This can be done by reviewing the child's statement and demonstrating how questions will be asked. Where appropriate, it is helpful to use appropriate props (for example, drawings) to assist the child in describing events. Preparation of the evidence is usually the responsibility of the Crown lawyer, but there are exceptions. In remote areas where the witness may live hundreds of kilometers from the courthouse, the Crown may have to rely on another professional to prepare the child.
- *Orientation to the court*: This includes a description of who will be in court, what the role of each person is, how the court looks, who sits where, and what is expected of the child. It may also include a visit to an actual courtroom.
- *Emotional support*: Addressing any fears or misconceptions to ensure that the child feels safe and is able to tell the story freely and fully.

Emotional support will come largely from family, friends, and others who are important in the child's life. This is critically important not only for the outcome of the trial, but also for the subsequent effect on the child. We urge you to do all that you can to provide the emotional support that your child needs. There are many places where the support offered helps your child grow and even have fun while learning new things. The main things that a child witness needs to know are the following:

- The child's support members will be there for all visits with the lawyer and the court appearances even if they cannot always be in the room.
- The child's participation in the trial is important — by testifying, other people, including other children are being helped. This is how adults work things out when they disagree.
- As much as possible, life will carry on with the usual routines.

Where to get help

EFFORTS ARE UNDERWAY TO standardize programs that prepare child witnesses. Currently, you can expect varying degrees of support and resources depending on where you live. Some jurisdictions (such as Toronto and London, Ontario, and Victoria, British Columbia) have established comprehensive programs to prepare child witnesses. In many locales, victim assistance programs may provide some pretrial orientation. A number of publications are available to help give you and the child witness the support needed (see the resource guide in Appendix 4).

As early as possible, find out who the Crown prosecutor is. The Crown will have to meet with the child well in advance of the trial or preliminary hearing. The earlier you can get in touch with the prosecutor and discuss orientation, the more time you will have to make appropriate arrangements.

VIGNETTE SEVEN: UNHELPFUL DISCLOSURE

WHEN THE CROWN LAWYER read Roy's journal she found it rich in detail about the abuse he had suffered; detail that was useful evidence against the accused. Roy indicated that the foster father had masturbated Roy, and had masturbated himself while Roy watched. He also noted where in the house the abuse had occurred, and described furnishings and articles in the room, and recorded the dates of some incidents. Roy also described one occasion, at the age of fifteen, when the foster father had anal sex with him. In light of this information, the Crown felt charges of indecent assault (masturbation of Roy and anal intercourse) and gross indecency (masturbating in front of Roy) were warranted. The Crown did not charge buggery because this section of the *Criminal Code* has been successfully challenged as unconstitutional in Canada.

In the journal, the Crown also found narrative about Roy's thoughts and feelings. She read that Roy's relationship with his foster father was complex. While the sexual abuse had been damaging, Roy had enjoyed the attention and favours he received from the foster father. Roy was in foster care because he was neglected in his biological home. In grooming Roy to be receptive to his sexual advances, the foster father had been attentive, playful, generous, and sympathetic. Roy had not previously experienced physical closeness, such as hugs and caresses, so he was grateful and felt special that the foster father was taking such interest in him. Roy felt valued as a person and talked about experiencing loving feelings toward the foster father at the time. As an adult, Roy worked out many of his feelings in therapy, and realized how this man had deceived and used him. He was angry at the way he had been manipulated.

During the trial, the defence lawyer, having also read the journal, called attention to the sections where Roy wrote about having had loving feelings towards the foster father, and he pointed out Roy's enjoyment of the hugs and caresses. The defence suggested that these statements indicated Roy was not a victim but was consenting to the man's sexual advances. Although the Crown did not believe Roy had consented to the sexual activity, she felt Roy's journal statements were creating doubt on the issue. If the court thought the doubt was reasonable, the foster father could be acquitted of those charges related to sexual activity that occurred after Roy was the age of fourteen. Since Roy's abuse happened during the period of 1976 to 1981, the 1983 legislation defining vitiation of consent (consent would be irrelevant where there was an abuse of authority) had not yet been passed and therefore did not apply to this case. Equally, the 1988 legislation prohibiting sex between those under eighteen years of age and an adult in a position of authority or power had not yet been passed. The issue of consent was important because authorities could charge the foster father with offences occurring before Roy turned fourteen years of age, but if there was reasonable doubt about consent, the foster father would likely be acquitted of those occurring after the age of fourteen. Under the circumstances, the Crown lawyer decided to negotiate a plea bargain whereby the actions that occurred after Roy had turned fourteen years of age were not included as part of the offences.

ENDNOTES

1   *Criminal Code*, R.S.C. 1985, c. C-46 [*Criminal Code*].
2   *R. v. Stinchcombe*, [1991] 3 S.C.R. 326, 68 C.C.C. (3d) 1.
3   *R. v. O'Connor*, [1995] 4 S.C.R. 411.
4   *R. v. Mills* (1999), 139 C.C.C. (3d) 321 at para. 118 (S.C.C.).
5   Jane Doe, *The Story of Jane Doe* (Toronto: Random House Canada, 2003) at 66–70.
6   *Ibid*. at 70.

8

The Trial

Vignette Eight

Morris, a fifty-year-old successful businessman, receives a phone call from his younger brother Charles, who says that he is finally going to report the sexual abuse perpetrated by their older brother Clem. Clem was very abusive and antisocial from a young age. He sexually abused his younger brothers in a sadistic, frightening way through their childhood and adolescent years, and he threatened worse if they ever told anyone. The abuse stopped only when Clem went to jail for the first time as a young adult on unrelated charges. Although apprehensive, Morris agrees to report his own abuse and strengthen the case against Clem. In his statement to police, Morris describes the abuse as "anal rape" and says Clem would sometimes choke him to near unconsciousness during sex. During the preliminary hearing, Morris is anxious but tells his story when questioned by the Crown counsel. The next day, under the pressure of cross-examination, Morris becomes increasingly agitated, blanks out, and cannot adequately answer many of defence counsel's questions. His demeanour is subdued and flat; from an observer's perspective, he seems disinterested and vague on details. Shortly afterwards, Morris asks for a meeting with Crown counsel and presents her with a letter from a psychiatrist saying he is suffering symptoms of Post-Traumatic Stress Disorder, including a dangerously high level of anxiety. Morris says that the pressure of testifying is making him too anxious and he cannot continue. The Crown says Morris' testimony is crucial to the case and she will have to drop some of the most serious charges if Morris does not testify.

CRIMINAL COURT IS AN adversarial process subject to the strengths and foibles of human nature. The outcome of a criminal case ultimately rests with the trier of fact, is never certain, and can hinge on a variety of factors including witness availability, memory, credibility, stamina, and motivation. In a sexual assault trial, the complainant is often the prosecution's most important witness and, as such, needs to be well-prepared to meet the courtroom challenges. This chapter explains the step-by-step process of a trial and prepares you for the demands of presenting your case to its best advantage.

Trials are the way society decides if a person accused of a sexual crime will be held accountable and subjected to legal consequences. Framed in this context, it is not surprising that sexual assault trials are a gruelling experience for everyone. The complainant, being the originator of, and typically the only witness to the complaint, bears the burden of clearly telling the story and consequently often suffers the greatest pressures. In a circumstance where the complainant may hope to find some empathy, compassion, or assistance, there may be anything but. For those who expect this to be a "truth-finding" process, it can feel like they are participating in an exercise of truth-limiting and victim-bashing.

The nature of our trial system means there is no certain way of knowing how any particular case will turn out. As outlined in the previous chapter, one reason for this unpredictability is that the accused does not have to reveal the details of the case in advance, even though the accused is aware what the Crown's case will be. The Crown prosecutor must reveal all details of the case against the accused in advance. This includes disclosing the identity of all witnesses, the order in which they will testify, and what they are expected to say. With minor exceptions, the defence is not required to do the same.[1] The defence does not have to indicate beforehand what the defence will be nor how the trial will be conducted. There is no requirement to inform the Crown if the defence will call evidence or if the accused will testify. Add to these procedural unknowns the human variables of fallible memory, performance anxiety in the courtroom, witness testimony of varying credibility, mistakes being made, or evidence being lost. With all these important variables it is not hard to understand why the outcome of a trial is never certain. As with any battle, stamina in the face of adversity can also play a significant role in the outcome.

Despite the adversity and unpredictability of a trial, you can count on some constant factors. As outlined in Chapter 4, you can count on meeting a typical coterie of courtroom personnel. To varying degrees, you will interact with these people during your case, so it is helpful to know what their roles are. Apart from the complainant, there will always be a Crown lawyer, an accused person or persons, and a judge in all trials. Usually a lawyer acts as defence counsel and represents the accused but not always; in some cases the accused will act as their own counsel. Sometimes a jury (if present) will determine the verdict, but more often it is a judge. Each of these participants has a critical role in the criminal trial. Each of them, at one time or another, is likely to expect something of you in the trial. The judge, the Crown counsel, and the defence lawyer will appear to have control over what you can and cannot do throughout the process. As the trial unfolds, the only person you will have any genuine control over is yourself.

If you need to refresh your understanding of court personnel roles, please refer to Appendix 5. Once you have read this chapter and are more conversant with the important issues of the trial process, there is a checklist in Appendix 17 that you can use when preparing for your day in court.

THE COMPLAINANT AS A WITNESS

YOUR ROLE, WHEN PURSUING a sex crime complaint, is to explain to the court as clearly, accurately, and honestly as you can, what happened to you. Based on what you say, the lawyers will make their arguments and the judge will decide if a crime has been committed. In this respect, you are the primary, and often the only witness to the crime. The details of how complainants testify, or whether they testify at all, will vary enormously from case to case. Testimony must comply with the procedural and evidentiary rules of the court, so it will be your task to understand and observe these rules to the best of your ability. Learn what limits are placed on your testimony; ask questions when you are not sure about procedures, and adhere to the restrictions placed on you when you tell your story. Articulate any needs that you have, but remain aware that the Crown counsel is not your lawyer and cannot always defend you or your actions. The Crown represents the state, but allies with you to prosecute the accused. As you will see later in this chapter, what you might expect the Crown to do for you out of common courtesy might be something that could actually damage your case. In fact, the judge will expect the Crown to guide you on the stand to ensure that you do not give inadmissible evidence or otherwise contravene legal procedure.

You should approach your witness role as if it were a job. Be punctual, and while you do not need to follow a dress code, you should be neat, clean, and dressed comfortably, as if this were a long work-day. In the ideal situation, you will come to court emotionally ready, motivated, factually well-organized, and prepared to tell your story in sufficient detail. You will have developed some rapport with the police during the reporting and investigation stages, and will have done your best to supply them with all of the details and the evidence that you can. You will have met with the Crown prosecutor, discussed your role in the trial, and gone over your statements in detail. Ideally, you will have sufficient support from family and friends, perhaps counselling support from a professional, and will have used victim services to your best advantage. Having done this, you will feel capable and well-prepared to talk about the crime in a public forum under oath or affirmation. This is a vision you can hold as your ideal while you strive to be the best witness you can be under challenging circumstances.

PRESUMPTION OF INNOCENCE IS PARAMOUNT

ALTHOUGH AUTHORITIES BRING CHARGES against the accused, the court will presume innocence and take whatever action is necessary to ensure a fair trial. The trial itself will determine whether there is sufficient evidence for the law to shift the accused person's status from innocent to guilty. It will help to keep this principle foremost in your mind as we examine the trial process. Although the legal system may not treat you as you expect, or may appear to be indifferent to your needs, the court must treat the accused fairly if justice is to be done.

Fairness to the accused does not mean the rights of the complainant must be abandoned. As we have noted throughout the book, the Canadian justice system has made particular progress over the past twenty years in developing ways to protect the safety and privacy of complainants and other witnesses, while being vigilant of the rights of the accused. The court's goal is to achieve a balance of these competing rights; where it cannot achieve a balance, it will make compromises. As an example, a complainant has privacy rights, and the accused has the right to provide a full answer in defence of the charges against him. When private information is relevant, and consequently important to a full defence, the right of privacy must yield in order to avoid the possibility of convicting an innocent person (see discussion of privacy issues in Chapter 7).

One of the duties and objectives of the court is to provide a forum for the complainant's story to be tested; it should not be a forum for public debate or recriminations. The complainant makes an accusation and the accused denies its validity in whole or part, and the judge's job is to resolve these differences and reach a verdict. This is done based on evidence presented according to well-established legal principles and evidentiary rules. In the end, it is not the job of the accused and the defence to prove the innocence of the accused; the burden always rests on the Crown to prove the accused's guilt. You will hear the court say this repeatedly throughout a trial, particularly when the facts are being determined by a judge and a jury (if present). Witnesses are an important part of this process, and Parliament has attempted to encourage participation by repeatedly amending the *Criminal Code* to make testifying easier.

Your courtroom role has limits

LEGAL PROCEDURE DICTATES THAT complainants cannot be in the courtroom until they testify. This can be frustrating because you do not hear the opening addresses, and do not hear where the facts support your story or where the defence refutes it. You will likely want to know exactly how the Crown intends to proceed, what witnesses will be called, what the police investigation showed, or what expert witnesses will say. The Crown will not consider it appropriate to give you any of this information until after the trial is over. If the trial is open to the public, then your family and friends may sit in the courtroom and you may be tempted to ask them what is going on. We recommend that you resist the temptation and do not ask. In fact, if they want to tell you, explain that they must not do so; it may compromise your own testimony. It can lead you, wittingly or unwittingly, to shape your testimony to fit the structure of the Crown's case or to match what others have said.

This is usually all too apparent to the observers, including the lawyers and the judge, and it can result in the perception that you have constructed your testimony to achieve a certain effect, rather than to report what you actually remember. If the judge discovers that you have integrated second-hand testimony into your story, it will seriously damage the way your evidence is weighed. The court will conclude that you are no longer an entirely reliable witness. If you are a key witness, the Crown's case may lose much of its strength. Do not forget that the police have documented your version of events in the original investigative statement; changing any part of your story now will not help your case. Some Crown lawyers prefer to call the complainant as one of the first witnesses; once you have given your testimony in the trial you can then stay in the courtroom for the rest of the proceedings and hear the remainder of the case.

Using legal channels to change the law

YOU MAY FEEL RESTRICTED in how the court allows you to bring evidence into the trial process. On the one hand, there is the pressure to obey the rules and show strict compliance with the law; on the other hand, you may have a desire to challenge what is patently wrong or unfair to you as a complainant. In our system of justice, each case can potentially create a shift in the path that subsequent cases follow. By appropriately asserting your right or legal position, and having a judge rule in your favour, new guidelines may be firmly established for those complainants whose cases will follow yours. As the court continues to address the tension between the rights of the accused and those of the complainant, there are landmark cases that dramatically change sexual assault law. You may be unaware that your case has contributed in this way because the effects are not likely to be felt until after your case is completed. Nevertheless, your struggle will not have been in vain if the system improves for those complainants, possibly even one of your relatives, coming after you.

Madam Justice Bertha Wilson, a former Supreme Court of Canada Justice, once reminded us in a speech that we must be mindful of the women before us who forged the path on which we walk, and the women who will come after us walking the path we forged. That you are a complainant in a sexual offence trial places you face-to-face with this possibility. Apart from preparing as best you can for your testimony, you may be able to note where you perceive integrity in the process, and where you do not; where you feel safe, and where you do not; where you feel there is a valid process of discovering the facts, and where there is not. Do not remain silent; talk to the Crown about your observations and concerns. Taking some action is the only way to foster change and build a justice system to protect all citizens — women, men, and children. You serve yourself and others effectively when you comply with the law while identifying how you can contribute to its betterment. The Crown will help you understand which procedures are acceptable and which are not, where there is room for change and where there is not.

There are examples of courageous complainants whose cases have moved the legal system in a direction that embraces the rights of sexual crime victims. The women in the *O'Connor* case (see Chapter 7 and Appendix 13), when ordered to release thirty years of personal records to the defence, told the Crown they wanted to challenge this order, a motion that eventually found its way to the Supreme Court of Canada. The Court established that there is a privacy interest in third-party records and devised a release procedure new to Canadian law. Now, as pointed out previously, the judge must review private, third-party records to determine which are essential to the case, rather than merely providing them unquestioningly to the defence. In response to the *O'Connor* case, Parliament amended the *Criminal Code* to make this release procedure codified law. The new legislation was quickly put to the test in the *Mills* case.[2] This case also made its way to the Supreme Court of Canada, which formally legitimized the new disclosure procedure by determining that the legislation was constitutionally sound. There are other examples of complainants who have made changes through their courage, tenacity, insight, and selflessness and Canadian law is better because of their efforts (see Chapter 11).

Another example of a system change is evident in the *Ewanchuk* case, which had a groundbreaking impact on the issue of consent to sexual activity in Canadian law.[3] A much older male who was a potential employer, sexually assaulted a young female during a job interview. He later defended his behaviour claiming he had her implied consent to engage in sex, despite her protestations against his advances. A lower court exonerated him on the grounds that his cultural beliefs led him to believe that a failure to openly consent (by the victim) can mean consent exists (see Chapter 1). In other words, the young woman was just being coy in her protests. The Supreme Court of Canada disagreed with this ruling and found that as long as the complainant does not clearly consent, an offence is committed, no matter how she may have behaved. This judgment is firm and unequivocal — there is no such thing as implied consent in Canadian law. It is not enough that the woman did not say "no," the law demands that she must say "yes" before her suitor can assume consent for sexual activity is present. If he is not clear on the consent issue because she has not said "yes," the accused cannot rely on an assumption of consent as a defence.

In other changes to the *Criminal Code,* there are now sections to protect a complainant from having the defence ask irrelevant questions about previous sexual activity. Tests of these changes have found them to be constitutionally sound as well. These are only some examples of the evolution of the law, and behind each of these changes are the personal stories of individual complainants whose cases altered the system to the benefit of everyone in this country.

Complying with the law is critical

THERE WILL BE TIMES when you are confused or frustrated by legal procedures and concepts, especially those that seem weighted in favour of the accused. You may balk at complying with some procedures that seem particularly onerous or unfair. However, in some situations, non-compliance can have little or no positive outcome and can harm your case. We suggest that you act prudently, accept that which you cannot change, and comply with the process and protocol as required. It is critically important that you and your supporters obey the law in the following ways:

- Attend court when ordered to do so by subpoena or other similar protocol.
- Do not destroy evidence.
- Do not threaten the accused or another witness.
- Do not simply refuse to answer questions in court.
- Do not lie to the police, the prosecutor, or in court to the judge.
- Do not act out violently, particularly against another person.

Any of the above actions could result in the authorities charging you and you subsequently having to attend your own trial. The Crown will give you further guidance about compliance issues, but if you find yourself in a legal corner, seeking legal advice independent of the Crown is the best approach. The best strategy is to remain solidly within the boundaries of law and legal procedure so you can devote all your energy to the task at hand: being the best advocate for the fair and honest prosecution of the accused in your case. You may find other avenues to advocate for legal change after the resolution of your case. We discuss ways of making your voice heard in the final chapter of this book.

PRETRIAL

LAWYERS FOR BOTH SIDES will have a number of matters to work out before you even get close to the courtroom. Before anyone gets a chance to address the sexual assault complaints, a case can be lost on a technical issue related to jurisdiction, the framing of the Indictment, or the *Charter of Rights.* The defence may argue that the case should not even proceed to trial because the charges are invalid, the court does not have jurisdiction, or the judge should enter a judicial stay because the accused's rights under the *Charter of Rights* have been violated. An example would be an application for a judicial stay of proceedings under the *Charter of Rights* because the accused has not been tried within a reasonable time, thus the accused's ability to fully defend himself has been infringed because crucial evidence is unavailable. Most *Charter of Rights* applications will take place before the trial begins and dates will be set to hear arguments on these points. It is also at this stage that the defence might seek to quash the Indictment due to a technical flaw. The defence may complain that the charge is not known to law or that the wording does not adequately inform the accused of the charges. The complainant will not likely be part of these applications, but the Crown will provide updates regarding the outcome and its affect on the case.

In some circumstances, *Charter of Rights* challenges are not heard until the end of the trial. For example, the accused may claim that a delay in the trial prejudiced his case. The court cannot determine whether the delay prejudiced the outcome until all the evidence has been presented. Regardless of whether the Crown proved its case based on the facts, the accused can still obtain a judicial stay at the end of the trial. If this happens during your case, the Crown will inform you.

Other pretrial matters may require participation by the complainant. If the defence requests access to private or third-party records, it must give the complainant formal notice of this application so the complainant's position on the release of these records can be articulated (see Chapter 7 for a discussion of disclosure rules). The defence could also request that evidence be included relating to the complainant's previous sexual activity. The lawyers would argue these issues and find some resolution before the trial begins. The complainant cannot be asked to testify at this application. Usually the same Crown lawyer who argues these pretrial applications will lead the case at trial.

Voir dire

IF THERE IS EVIDENCE in the Crown's case, the admissibility of which is in question, the Crown will ask the court to enter a process called *voir dire*. In this process, the judge will hear arguments from both sides and make a ruling on the admissibility of the evidence in question. Lawyers and the court prefer to determine these issues before the trial begins. Some of the evidence may not meet legal standards of acceptability and these issues are addressed in the *voir dire*. One such evidentiary issue would be a statement by the accused to a person of authority that the former committed the crime. The judge would have to be satisfied that the statement was voluntarily made before it would be admissible as evidence. Similarly, the defence lawyer may raise the issue that the client's rights under the *Charter of Rights* were infringed upon before the client provided the statement and, therefore, it cannot be admitted as evidence against the latter. An example of a *Charter of Rights* violation would be failing to provide a suspect access to counsel upon arrest before eliciting a statement from the suspect. As a trial judge, when one hears a confession in the *voir dire* and later rules it inadmissible, one must disabuse oneself of the evidence and not consider it in the deliberations.

The *voir dire* is a particularly important course of action in a jury trial because, once a jury is selected, the trial must continue without lengthy breaks to ensure that jury members are not seriously inconvenienced by being sent away while legal issues are sorted out. The following points summarize the most likely issues to be addressed in a *voir dire*:

- The admissibility of a statement the accused gave to the police. The court will likely examine whether the statement was voluntarily given and whether the police followed all the rules under the *Charter* of *Rights* to ensure that the accused's rights were not violated (see Chapter 6).
- The admissibility of similar fact evidence. Where the accused did the same act on more than one occasion with different victims (for example, robbery, sexual assault, or murder) these acts can be considered as evidence in one victim's case. This is very controversial evidence and the evidentiary value must outweigh the potential prejudice to the accused.
- An application to have evidence excluded because it was obtained by an illegal search and seizure. This is likely something found in the accused's home, place of work, or other place where privacy is expected.
- An application by the defence that the Crown not be allowed to ask the accused about a criminal record if the accused elects to testify. This is called a Corbett application.

THE TRIAL BEGINS

THE CROWN IS IN charge of presenting the evidence that supports the charges, and is required to identify to the defence, before the trial date, all evidence and all witnesses that will be called (see Chapter 7). There are no surprise Crown witnesses in a Canadian trial. If a significant new witness, unknown to the defence, were to surface in the course of a trial, the trial would be adjourned to allow the defence time to prepare as needed. As the trial continues, the defence will have an opportunity to call back certain witnesses for more questions on any new matters that arise.

The Crown prosecutor begins the trial with an opening statement to inform the judge (and the jury if there is one) of the Crown's case and the anticipated evidence to be called. If there are judge's rulings following the pretrial applications, the Crown will summarize that evidence in the opening. The opening statement should explain the relevant evidence and give some context so that when the witnesses testify, the judge or jury will already have an idea of how the case fits together. The Crown may have to prove multiple parts of the sexual crime to make its argument whole. These parts are the essential ingredients. The essential ingredients change depending on what crime the Crown seeks to prove. For example, the crime of level I sexual assault (see Chapter 1) requires that the Crown prove that the accused applied force to the victim named in the charge, the physical contact was sexual in nature, the victim did not consent, and the contact occurred on the stated date and in the stated location (city). As discussed previously, the complainant and other witnesses do not hear this opening statement, as they will not have given their testimony yet.

The defence is invited to make a statement

FOLLOWING THE CROWN'S OPENING statement, the accused is invited to make a statement, either personally or through the defence counsel. The defence team may not wish to reveal too much of its strategy at this point, and need not do so. On the other hand, it may want to make a strong statement to try to reduce the impact of the Crown's opening. In a jury trial, each side wants to provide the jury with a guide indicating what it should pay most attention to during the course of the trial. If possible, the lawyers want to begin to sway the jury's thinking early on. There are limits to what can be said during an opening statement, and if either side crosses these boundaries, the judge will warn the jury to ignore those statements.

THE CROWN'S CASE

THE CROWN PROSECUTOR HAS conduct of the case, although there are times when the defence attempts to influence or even pressure the Crown to conduct the case in a particular way. The defence may want the Crown to call certain witnesses who are not on the Crown's trial list in order to have them available for cross-examination, or to call the witnesses in a certain order. The defence may want the complainant to testify first, allowing the defence counsel to cross-examine the complainant and learn early in the process exactly how this important witness will present the evidence. Cross-examination may also produce information that will help the defence prepare any subsequent witnesses called. The Crown does not have to acquiesce to these demands and may have a different approach in mind.

Many Crown prosecutors feel that foundational evidence should be called first to create the context before the complainant testifies. Police witnesses who found evidence, such as furniture in disarray, blood splatter, soiled clothing, or other confirming evidence at the crime scene, can testify at the beginning of the Crown's case about their findings and show the photographs that they took. When the complainant later testifies, the exhibits already entered can be referred to as the court is already familiar with the crime scene when hearing descriptions of what happened there. The order of witnesses is up to the Crown but the defence may be allowed input if this promotes a fair and efficient trial.

To build a case, the Crown calls witnesses to testify about the facts relevant to the charges. This questioning of witnesses, called the examination-in-chief, usually consists of the lawyer making open-ended inquiries that help the witnesses tell their narrative. It can also include specific questions about certain exhibits, or about the defendant's identity. The defence lawyer plays a role in the examination-in-chief, listening carefully and objecting if something appears irrelevant or otherwise inadmissible to the case. Once the Crown has finished the examination-in-chief, the defence may question or cross-examine the witnesses. At the end of the Crown's case, the defence has the same opportunity to call witnesses and the Crown may then cross-examine them. Cross-examination provides an opportunity to challenge testimony, to ensure it holds up under scrutiny, or to ask questions in support of the opposing version of the story.

The witnesses who are likely to be called

THE CROWN PROSECUTOR HAS decided well in advance which witnesses will be called to make the prosecution's case during the trial. The first witness is usually the police officer assigned to be the investigation's exhibit person. The officer will bring all the relevant marked and ordered exhibits into the courtroom. Next, the Crown is likely to call the officer who is in charge of forensic evidence collected at the crime scene. This officer, who is responsible for any identifying evidence, will testify to the collection of any body fluids or fibres at the scene, and will likely be the main photographer. The officer will present the photographs one by one, describing what investigators found at the crime scene. In some cases, a blood splatter expert will show pictures of the crime scene bloodstains and will provide a theory regarding the nature and origin of these stains. If a person is hit hard enough to cause a spray of blood on a wall, the expert may be able to infer where and how the complainant was struck. Also among the first witnesses called may be a doctor or nurse who can give testimony regarding physical injuries.

Other potential witnesses in a sexual assault trial will be people who actually saw or heard events connected to the sexual assault. This could be a person who heard screams or cries for help, or someone who called the police. There may be witnesses who saw the complainant immediately after the assault and may have seen that the complainant's clothes were in a state of disarray, or that there were injuries to the complainant. In the case of delayed reporting or historical sexual assaults, persons who were involved in either the complainant's or the defendant's life at the time of the alleged assaults might be called upon. These people could substantiate parts of the complainant's story, or provide important details of dates, times, and places that might not otherwise be available.

Accommodations for witnesses

IN CHAPTER 7, WE outlined some accommodations the court would make for child witnesses. The option to testify from a place outside the courtroom or from behind a screen was once restricted to special circumstances where the witness was young or had a mental or physical disability. Now, any witness can apply for these measures if it will aid in giving a full and candid account of the witness' story. In addition, adult witnesses can request a support person if they feel it is necessary to help them through the process. The application process for these accommodations is more onerous for an adult than for a child; it will require the gathering of evidence to support an adult's request, and will take up court time. Making any such application well in advance will ensure that the lawyers, the judge, and the court service workers who will be providing any necessary equipment are properly prepared. Making an application early will also let you know in advance how your testimony will take place.

Bill C-2 is the legislation that amended the *Criminal Code* and the *Canada Evidence Act* to allow for the above accommodations and is new law at the time of writing this book.[4] Consequently, there are implementation strategies throughout the country to ensure that all justice personnel are aware of these changes, which are designed to encourage the participation of witnesses in the criminal justice system.[5] You can find a comprehensive and detailed list of these accommodations in Appendix 18. If you feel any of these would be beneficial to you, discuss the advisability of making an application with the Crown lawyer assigned to your case as early in the process as you can.

THE COMPLAINANT'S TESTIMONY

AS DISCUSSED IN CHAPTER 7, there are trials during which the Crown does not call the complainant to testify; it could be that this witness is either physically or psychologically unavailable to testify. The Crown will then have to prove the case by using other forms of evidence. These would include the complainant's police statement (assuming it meets hearsay exception evidentiary requirements), forensic evidence (for example, fibres, body fluids, or expert testimony), or the record of a confession (if the accused has made one). In one case, several years ago, a defence lawyer called two male child victims to deny the abuse that the accused had perpetrated against them. In the end, the court found that the boys were lying to protect the accused, and gave weight to the accused's admitted confession and convicted him.

If the complainant is able, available, and willing, the Crown will put the complainant on the stand at a time that best suits the strategy of the case. Taking the stand at the trial is a crucial experience for a complainant and important to the resolution of the crime. As noted, rules and restrictions influence how you can tell your story in court. Below we discuss these rules further and urge you to become familiar with them so you will perform to the best of your ability. It will be obvious to you by now that the best preparation is to meet with the Crown prosecutor beforehand and discuss how the testimony will proceed. If this is not possible, discuss your concerns and expectations with a lawyer, counsellor, or victim support worker who is familiar with sexual offence trials. Of all the responsibilities you have faced in the legal process, this is one of the greatest, and has no real precedent in one's daily life. While testifying in court is an enormous challenge for most who have suffered a sexual offence, diminishing the unknowns and allaying some fears will help you in your role. The best way to do this is through preparation and understanding, and the following sections should guide you in that direction.

Judging your credibility

THE COURT DOES NOT allow the Crown prosecutors to introduce evidence that bolsters your credibility. They cannot call character witnesses to say that you are someone who, in their opinion, tells the truth, nor can they call evidence describing the times you have told your story consistently as proof of its truth. Similarly, statements you make bolstering your own credibility are not permissible. The court would likely permit you to say, "I told my mother right away about the sexual assault," but you could not say, "I told her that he beat me and forced me to have sex." The court does not regard these statements as valid evidence of anything. Just because a witness previously made a statement does not make it more likely to be true in the eyes of the law. The court would look dimly upon any such statement, considering it an improper attempt to bolster your credibility. On the other hand, if the defence suggests that you made up the complaint against the accused in the recent past, the fact that you had earlier told someone about the assault could become relevant to refute the defence argument. A complainant must listen carefully to the instructions of the judge and the Crown counsel for guidance on when this type of evidence is admissible and when a full description of it is warranted.

The law guides judges on proper assessment of your credibility. The training and experience of judges ought to make them aware of their own biases so that gender, age, or race should not be factors in determining credibility. Rather than looking to the class of person, the court should assess each witness on the facts, on a case-by-case basis. The court will assess your credibility based on the internal consistency of your testimony, as well as on how it compares with other facts, evidence, and witness statements. Is the complainant's statement in the beginning essentially similar throughout the legal process or does it change in significant ways? Did the complainant say one thing to the police and something else on the stand? If there are contradictions in the complainant's testimony, the lawyers will ask for explanations and the court will consider the explanations when determining credibility. In some cases, a complainant may initially deny an assault took place or later retract the original accusation. This does not necessarily invalidate the complaint; the court will consider any reasonable explanations for the inconsistency, such as threats to the complainant, pressure from family members, or fear of reprisal.

When all the evidence is in, the court will make a judgment about the complainant's testimony. Either the jury (if present) or the judge will consider whether your version of events is consistent with the body of the other evidence provided. If the court rejects the defence's evidence and is satisfied with the validity of the complainant's version, it will convict.

When making a judgment about your integrity as a complainant, the court will listen to all your evidence and consider the following:

- Did you stick to the same story over time?
- Is your story internally consistent?
- When you told others what happened, did you exaggerate?
- Did you have a motive to lie?
- Did you respond intelligently to the questions?
- Did you demonstrate integrity?
- Of what quality was your power to observe?
- Did you show a capacity to remember what happened?
- Was the information you provided accurate?
- Were you honestly trying to tell the truth?
- Were you sincere and frank?
- Were you biased, reticent, or evasive?

Allowing for human nature

THE LEGAL SYSTEM RECOGNIZES that our recollection of events changes over time and that we may report things in different ways to different people, depending on our relationship with them. We may not tell our mother about a sexual assault in exactly the same way that we would tell our best friend or the police. The court understands this phenomenon and takes it into account; it will not expect faultless consistency and, at times, may be suspicious of picture-perfect, script-like recitations.

Keep in mind that judges will likely be aware if someone has coached you to respond in a certain way. If your trial version appears too studied, or if it includes specific phrases from the *Criminal Code,* or sounds like you have incorporated outside information, the court may call your credibility into account. Take care to stick with your memory of events, which most often is your first, authentic report. If there are subsequent experiences that have caused you to reconsider your initial version of events, explain this, rather than merely changing your story without explaining why. Your best strategy in this process is to talk about the event itself without second-guessing how the defence might challenge you. Do not try to figure out what the lawyers are attempting to do; instead, listen to the questions very carefully and answer them as respectfully and truthfully as you can.

TAKING THE STAND

ON THE DAY YOU testify, you will wait outside the courtroom and not enter until someone calls you in. The Crown will introduce you by saying something to the effect of "Your Honour, the next witness for the prosecution is (your name)." The Crown may ask permission to go and get you or you will be paged to the courtroom on a public address system. Ideally, you will be with a victim assistance worker who is familiar with this process and can guide you. You should look into the room where you are testifying before the proceedings start and familiarize yourself with it. Typically, someone will direct you to the witness stand when you enter the courtroom, but checking out the room ahead of time can relieve some anxiety.

When you have entered the witness box, the court clerk will ask you to remain standing and will give you the choice of either swearing an oath or affirming to tell the truth. Canadian courts allow people some flexibility in the way they pledge to tell the truth. You can do it without the use of a Bible or Koran, and without the use of the phrase, "so help me God." This accommodates those who do not believe in a God or follow a belief system other than Christianity, Judaism, or Islam. Children under the age of fourteen are simply asked if they promise to tell the truth. Once you have pledged to tell the truth, the court clerk will request that you identify yourself by stating your full name and then spelling your surname for the record. After stating your name, you can then sit down. Having announced you, the Crown prosecutor will already be standing, and will begin the questioning.

If, at any time during the course of your testimony, you become physically ill, overly fatigued, or extremely emotional, the court will allow you to ask for a break. Take the time you need before you come back and resume your testimony. If you feel you need medical assistance, ask the Crown or the sheriff for that. Some people have a tendency to vomit when they are very upset. If this is the case for you let the Crown know in advance. Having tissues, a towel, and a receptacle nearby can be reassuring and can diminish your anxiety during testimony.

Applying for an accommodation

AS DESCRIBED PREVIOUSLY, WITNESSES eighteen years of age or over may be entitled to testify with an accommodation if the court is satisfied this is what is required to receive a full and candid account from the witness. The accommodations available include the following:

- Testifying from a different room using closed-circuit television technology so that the accused cannot be seen
- Testifying behind a screen so that the accused cannot be seen
- Testifying with a support person (chosen by the complainant) nearby
- Being cross-examined by an appointed lawyer rather than by the accused

The Crown must introduce evidence to satisfy the court that the accommodation is required in order for a witness to give a full and candid account of the latter's experiences. This evidence may take the form of an affidavit or alternatively the witness may testify to this effect. It is not enough that the witness is uncomfortable testifying; there must be evidence that the witness' evidence would not be complete, or it would be deleteriously affected, if the accommodation was not granted.

There are situations where the accommodations are presumed to be required without the witness having to prove it. Witnesses with a physical or mental disability are presumed to be entitled to a support person. If the disability affects their communication, they are presumed to be entitled to out-of-court testimony. In a trial where the accused is charged with criminal harassment, the court presumes the complainant is entitled to be cross-examined by a lawyer, rather than the accused.

Describing your complaint

TESTIMONY TYPICALLY STARTS WITH the complainant giving some general background information. There is no requirement that a complainant provide private information, such as an address, on the stand. The Crown then asks questions to guide the complainant through the story of the latter's victimization. Your primary goal, discussed in detail below, is simply to answer the questions asked of you. Keep in mind that the judge and the jury (if present) have not read your statements in advance. They are hearing your account for the first time. Do not assume that they know anything about the case. Do not assume that they know who you are. They are making judgments about your reliability and credibility as court proceeds, so you can help them appreciate your account of events by being forthright, clear, and precise in your responses.

Simply answering the questions

IT SHOULD BE APPARENT by now that answering questions and responding to directives from the lawyers is all the court allows witnesses to do — you cannot volunteer any opinions or speak to your own agenda. The Crown may set the stage with non-controversial statements. The Crown prosecutor can ask you to confirm certain facts, such as "You are twenty-six years old"; "You live in a home with your husband and three children"; "You work at a convenience store close to your home"; "On the 1st day of January you called the police, the result of which they attended your store." In this way, the Crown can quickly establish some basic information and you are only required to answer "yes." You will then likely be asked to tell the story of the assault in your own words, for example, "Please tell the court what happened."

The court will insist on a straightforward account of the incident that has led to charges and to the trial: who, where, what, and when. Most prosecutors guide you with questions as you proceed, such as "Where were you when that part happened?" They will likely begin with open-ended questions then ask more specific questions when they want more details, for example, "You said he was carrying a gun. Describe the gun and tell us what he did with it." Questions by the Crown that lead you to give an opinion or make a statement about a controversial issue are not permitted. The Crown would not be permitted to ask you a leading question about whether or not you consented to the sexual activity. An example of such a question is

"Did you allow him to do this because you thought he locked the door and wanted to hold you in there against your wishes?"

When the Crown uses leading questions in an attempt to assist a troubled witness, and the questions are allowed, the court will give the answers less evidentiary weight than factual responses. Often, if you do not say something that the Crown expects you to say the first time asked, you might have your attention directed to the area. If you left out an important detail, such as the fact that the phone rang, the Crown might ask, "Was there a phone in the room?" or "Did anything occur related to the phone?" However, some defence lawyers, and judges as well, will be adamant that the Crown not suggest something to you that you have forgotten. In other words, the court will not allow the Crown to prod you, so you must be well-prepared to tell the story in a way that does not leave out any important facts. It is not enough to have the incident vivid and fresh in your mind; you will need to articulate it in a manner that other people can understand.

While on the stand, the court will allow you to refresh your memory by referring to your statement. Sometimes people get so nervous they forget the most obvious things. If this happens, just tell the judge that you forget and ask if you can read your statement. If you have read your statement in advance, you will be familiar with it and will know which parts are most useful to you. When you need to refer to it during testimony, re-read the relevant section then put the statement down and give your answer based on your refreshed memory. Police officers do this all the time using their police notes to check points, such as a licence number, the time of an event, or other similar details.

Avoiding hearsay evidence

YOUR DIRECT KNOWLEDGE AND experience is what the court wants from you as a witness. What someone else has told you and which is not your direct knowledge, is what the law terms hearsay and it is not admissible. Although there are some exceptions to this rule, the court generally forbids you to provide facts based on hearsay. For example, the statement, "My friend Susan told me later he (the accused) left his car at the house," is hearsay evidence and not admissible to prove where the car was left. The Crown will try to prevent you from giving hearsay evidence and you can expect the defence to object if you do. If a jury is present, the judge will explain the problem and tell them to disregard what you have said. If the hearsay is too damning, prejudicial, and cannot be remedied, it could result in the judge declaring a mistrial.

At times, things said to you are admissible if you are giving the evidence for a purpose other than determining the truth of what was said. For example, you could say that you heard someone yell "help," or say "ouch," or that you told someone to get out. These are all examples of direct knowledge that are not hearsay, and therefore admissible. There are some other exceptions to the hearsay rule. You can testify to anything the accused said to you; the actual words are considered admissible evidence. When giving this sort of evidence you should do your best to give the exact words as they were said to you. If you are unclear about what is or is not hearsay and what is admissible, clarify these issues with the Crown lawyer prior to your testimony.

Identifying the person who assaulted you

ONE OF YOUR TASKS as a complainant will be to positively identify the accused as the person who committed the offence against you. Normally, if you know the accused, and identification is not an issue, the Crown will just ask you in court to confirm the accused's identity by saying something, such as "Is the man you have called Bob in your evidence the man in the blue suit over there?" If you respond "yes" the Crown will then say something like "Let the record show that the witness has identified the accused." In other cases, the complainant need not even be asked to do this because the record already confirms that the accused is the person described so identity is not an issue.

If you did not know your assailant and identity is an issue in the trial, the procedure is different and must be done with greater care to ensure fairness to the accused. There is some skepticism about people's ability to identify strangers, especially when the stranger was seen only briefly. Research suggests that while identifications are often accurate, people sometimes make mistakes, and witnesses who say that they have great confidence in their identification skills are not guaranteeing their accuracy. To add to the complexity, when complainants or witnesses try to identify an unknown assailant, police or others can, wittingly or unwittingly, directly or indirectly, sway them to pick a particular person out of a lineup. For these reasons, there are procedures in place to ensure a witness is not influenced when identifying an assailant either during the investigation or at trial.

It is important both for the validity and the integrity of identification that witnesses comply with all procedures used. We cannot emphasize enough the importance of this point. One of the authors has seen a complainant actually pick out the wrong person in the courtroom. It was a man in the audience, rather than the accused, so the identification was clearly mistaken. The error made by the complainant was a startling reminder of the serious mistakes that can occur. In another case, a robbery victim asked if she was required to pick out the accused even though she was uncertain of his identity. These examples suggest a clear misunderstanding of what authorities expect of complainants. No police officer or Crown lawyer wants any complainant or witness to succumb to the pressure of having to point out someone as the offender if there is uncertainty.

For in-court identification, the Crown may ask you to describe the assailant from your memory of the assault. Once you have done this, the Crown will ask if that person is in the room. You must follow the instructions carefully. Describe the person as you remember from the time of the crime and then, when asked to do so, look very carefully around the courtroom to see if the assailant is there. If you see and identify a person in the courtroom as your perpetrator, you can either point to that person or describe what the person is wearing or both. If the perpetrator is not in the courtroom or if you are uncertain as to the identity of anyone there, tell the court your conclusions when you are given the opportunity. The Crown will ask that there be an indication on the record of whom you identified. In this situation, nobody should tell you if you have correctly identified the accused, so the Crown may say in your presence, "Your Lordship has the indication." After you have left the courtroom, the Crown will say on the record that you did or did not point out the accused.

If the police showed you a series of suspect photos during the investigation, the Crown could ask you to provide details about that exercise. You may be asked to identify any police form you signed and to confirm any comments you made on that sheet at the time you signed it. Either the defence or the Crown could ask you what instructions the police gave to you as part of this identification exercise or ask what you were told after you made a choice. Anything you said during the investigation related to identifying the assailant is an exception to the hearsay rule and either you or the police will be permitted to report this at trial.

Identifying exhibits and documents

IN THE COURSE OF telling your story, the Crown may ask you about the clothing or other personal articles relevant to the crime. The Crown may show you photographs or pieces of evidence (the exhibits) that the police entered earlier in the trial. Your testimony provides the necessary link between these exhibits and the crime scene. You may be shown articles of clothing, bedding, or other items that were seized by the police and that may have undergone laboratory analysis. Laboratory personnel look for the presence of body fluids (for example, blood, semen, or sputum) or try to identify physical evidence, such as hair and clothing fibres. The Crown may ask you to identify them by saying, "Do you recognize this shirt?" or "Where was this blanket the night of the incident?"

Forensic specialists may have identified samples of blood on these items as belonging to you. Testing may have confirmed that fluids or tissue from the accused were present on some items. The investigation may show fibres from an article belonging to you on the clothing of the accused. Of course, none of this will be explained to you at the time. At this point in the trial, it is simply a matter of your identifying the various articles and possibly explaining to the court how, for example, your shirt came to have blood on it.

You may not have seen some of the items in a very long time, perhaps a year or more, and it may be a shock to see them in court. Given the passage of time, it may also be difficult to recognize some of them. Normally, investigators place the items in special plastic bags to preserve the evidence, and do not clean them in any way, for the same reason. As a result, they can be very unpleasant to deal with. If it is necessary to remove them from their enclosures for identification, you may request gloves. Remember, if the courtroom pace is too fast for you, or if you are feeling overwhelmed, you may always request a moment to catch your breath, or sip a glass of water.

Questions about your memory

DURING YOUR TESTIMONY, THE lawyers are likely to ask questions concerning your memory. The Crown may ask you how certain events affected your memory. In contrast, the defence may refer to your previously recorded statements and suggest that your recall then, closer to the events, was better. Lines of questioning related to memory are important when the lawyer is trying to ascertain whether something has influenced your recall. You may be asked if either alcohol or drug use, at the time of the alleged crime or subsequently, affected your recall. If you suffered a head injury, you may be asked about its effect on your memory. In the case of historic sexual abuse, you could be asked about your ability to recall the details after a long delay in telling. In addition, you might be asked to assess your memory as a good or bad memory. These memory issues can be relevant when the court decides what weight to give to your testimony in the trial. If you face this kind of questioning, be mindful of the memory principles discussed in Chapter 4, and be honest about your own memory strengths and weaknesses.

A word of caution; the study of memory is a complex area conducted by experts with extensive knowledge of brain chemistry, physiology, and psychology. Terminology used to describe memory phenomena is specific and often poorly understood by non-professionals. A layperson might adopt a term to describe an experience without fully appreciating its meaning. Someone might refer to a "blackout" when describing a memory lapse, but the term has a much different meaning to a forensic psychologist using it to describe a client's symptoms. Similarly, the term "dissociation" may have a different meaning when used by professionals than when used by a complainant to describe what happens when the complainant is reminded of post-traumatic experiences. A psychologist talking about "repressed memory" likely has a different understanding of that term than a layperson who is describing the experience of forgetting something and later remembering it.

It is prudent to avoid jargon of this nature unless you are absolutely sure you understand its meaning and are using it with that meaning in mind. Otherwise, you may use a word to mean one thing whereas the lawyers and other professionals will attribute a significantly different meaning to that word. We suggest, as well, that you be very careful and precise in your language and avoid expressions like "out-of-body-experience," "body memories," or "psychotic" unless you are prepared to substantiate your description by demonstrating that you understand what those expressions mean.

Your memory is constantly being probed and tested while you are on the stand. An unexpected memory could be triggered by an unanticipated question or response, or your mind may go blank as you try to recall information. It is permissible to describe what you are going through. If you experience a temporary lapse of memory, ask the questioner to make a note and request that you come back to it later in your testimony.

THE CROSS-EXAMINATION

FOLLOWING YOUR EXAMINATION-IN-CHIEF, the defence will cross-examine you. Similarly, the Crown will subject any witness called by the defence to cross-examination. This opportunity to question the opposing side's witness is an integral part of the adversarial system. It is a strategic defence exercise prepared in advance, and it is inappropriate for the Crown to interfere or interrupt unless there are legally sound grounds to do so. Cross-examination by a defence lawyer in a public courtroom is one of life's unique experiences and calls for competencies not typically developed in the course of everyday life.

Although telling your story on the stand under the guidance of the Crown counsel may have been difficult, the cross-examination will likely be even rougher. The purpose, after all, is to question the validity of your accusations and your credibility as a witness. The complainant in a sexual crime case will always be cross-examined. When evidence given by the complainant is contrary to the interests of the accused, the cross-examination is never superficial, pleasant, or friendly. Recall that the onus is always on the Crown to raise a reasonable doubt on issues in dispute, such as consent or identity. Cross-examination is the defence's opportunity to raise reasonable doubt on issues, such as consent.

Cross-examination of the complainant offers an opportunity for the accused to deal directly with the evidence presented by the Crown. The defence does not have to prove the evidence is wrong; it just has to cast doubt on its validity. The most effective way to do this is to show that the witness should not be trusted. If the witness is not trustworthy, what the witness has said against the accused is of doubtful validity. Rather than attack each point of your allegation, the defence may focus its attack on your basic trustworthiness. "Should this person be believed?" is the ultimate question the defence will pose, and of course it will want to convince the court that the answer is "no."

Cross-examination is intended to raise doubts about your credibility and reliability. Our adversarial system allows an accused to put you under extreme pressure while under oath to see if your story will stand up, so a judge will allow an accused or defence counsel considerable leeway in this regard. Nonetheless, there are limits. The judge should take action to prevent any harassment, badgering, or intimidation from the defence. For example, if a defence counsel continues to cover ground that has already been responded to, counsel will be told to move on to something else. Similarly, if counsel argues with the witness or calls the witness names, the judge will intervene. Take your time before responding to questions. Again, breathe when you need to breathe. Some witnesses find it best to look at the judge while the defence asks the question. This can help you disengage from the personal aspects of the cross-examination and focus on the primary purpose of telling your story. If you do not understand a particular question or feel confused by a question, do not hesitate to ask for clarification. While you are doing all this, the judge has time to think and may decide that the defence has posed an inappropriate question.

There are some limitations placed on the cross-examination in the situation where an accused does not have a lawyer. As alluded to earlier, the court generally will not allow an accused to personally question any witness who is under eighteen years of age in a criminal trial. In addition, if the charges include criminal harassment, a complainant is presumed to be entitled to have counsel, rather than the accused, conduct the cross-examination . The Crown or the witness can make an application to have a lawyer appointed for that specific purpose and the application will normally be successful, unless the presiding judge is of the opinion that the proper administration of justice requires the accused personally to conduct the cross-examination. In a sex crime trial with any witness eighteen years of age or over, an application will only be granted if the court is satisfied that this procedure is needed in order to receive a full and candid account from the witness.

Having the person you are accusing of the crime cross-examine you is at best a challenge. If the court insists on this method, and you think you need assistance to give a full and candid account of your experiences, ask if you can at least be in a separate room and have the questions asked via closed-circuit television. Another allowable strategy would be to turn your body away from the questioner so that you are facing the judge during questioning. You could also diminish some of your stress in this situation by using the stress reduction techniques discussed in Chapter 5. Remember, you will need to practise these strategies prior to the trial so that they are well-learned when you need to use them. You might also want to examine and challenge some of your thoughts, feelings, or beliefs about the offender so that you will feel less intimidated. You might benefit from having a therapist help you devise and develop these strategies for counteracting the negative influence of the offender's presence in court.

Being tested on the stand

SINCE IT IS PART of the defence lawyer's task to test the accuracy of what you say, you are likely going to feel tested during cross-examination. The defence will frame questions in a manner that suggests that you are wrong, you have limited understanding of important issues, you are biased, or you have an ulterior motive, and so forth. Many of the questions asked will be the same questions asked by the Crown. The defence lawyer will have you go over it all again in order to see if you can repeat the same version as a test of your reliability. Alternatively, the defence lawyer may not have heard all that you said the first time, as a result of thinking about other things, or getting instructions from the accused while you were talking. Alternatively, the defence lawyer may be repeating a question merely to get a little more information about that topic.

There could be questions about your perceptual abilities. Individuals have different abilities when it comes to perceiving and giving an opinion about such things as height, weight, or speed of a car. Therefore, the defence might ask you questions about the lighting in the room, how far away you are from certain objects, or the relative position of the people in the room. The defence may want to know about your ability to see, and hear, and whether you were wearing glasses or hearing aids at the time of the assault, if that is relevant. You might be asked if you were paying attention at a critical time. The defence counsel might suggest that your recollections are inaccurate because you were attending to something other than the event you have described. You might be questioned about whether or not you had been taking intoxicants and whether or not you were impaired, drunk, or high at certain times. There might be questions about whether you were fatigued, and if that affected your ability to deal with the situation or your perceptions of it.

The defence counsel might specifically question your ability to recall details in a manner similar to the following: "I suggest to you that after this lengthy passage of time you cannot recall the order of events. Isn't that so?" "In fairness, witness, you do not really even know what happened here, isn't that so?" "Isn't it true that you are merely guessing about this point and you really don't know? Isn't that true?" "You could be mistaken and he wasn't even there that time; isn't that true?" or "You cannot remember now what you were wearing; you are just guessing, isn't that true?" This type of questioning hammers away at the details of your memory, because details are essential in a trial. Lawyers rely upon details in making their submissions and convincing the court of one position or another.

Language is important

AS WE HAVE POINTED out before, you need to consider the language that you use throughout the legal process, but most particularly during cross-examination. There will likely be things you are very sure of, while other things leave some room for doubt. If you are sure about your answer, say you are sure about your answer, not "I think that was the case." If you are certain about something, you should say so and not waver, even though the defence may be trying to convince you otherwise. Conversely, if you do not know the answer, do not make one up. It is not incumbent upon you to come up with an answer to every question. No matter how often counsel asks you or suggests that you should know an answer, if you do not have the answer, then do not give one. You can merely say, "I don't know," or "I don't remember." There may be instances when you have an answer but are somewhat uncertain about it. You may recall that something happened in the morning but are not sure of the exact time. Do not guess, say what you know, for example, "It was some time in the morning but I'm not sure exactly when." It is important to be precise. It is also important that the defence counsel does not sway you to give an inaccurate response when pressured by these questions. Clarity and authenticity are of primary importance.

It may be that during a sexual assault, the offender said things directly to you. As previously noted, this is important and permissible evidence. Whenever you are giving evidence regarding things that people said, always try to the best of your ability to give the exact words, rather than paraphrasing. In other words, saying "He said, 'I'm going to do want I want with you and you can't stop me,'" is better evidence than "He said that he was going to do what he wanted." In the first example, the witness provides the actual words, which are more powerful than the second example of a paraphrase. Try to put the words in the right order and, if you can, describe the tone of voice, the speed of the words spoken, the volume, or any other characteristics that convey the context and content of what was said.

Defence strategies and tactics

RECALL THAT THE DEFENCE has a right to full disclosure of the Crown's case before the trial begins. This means it has a list of all the exhibits, a description of the alleged perpetrator of the crime, the police reports, copies of all witness statements, and in some circumstances, if the court allows it, it may have copies of your diary, medical files, or other personal records. From all that information, the defence develops a strategy to challenge the Crown's testimonial evidence.

In raising this topic, we are not suggesting you attempt to second-guess the defence lawyer. As always, your best approach is to give honest, accurate responses, but it may help you to be aware of some lines of questioning you may encounter. Typically the defence attempts to raise reasonable doubt in two important areas, namely, did the accused commit the act and, if so, does the act constitute sexual assault? The defence will use various cross-examination lines of questioning to achieve this goal, most of which will have been prepared in advance after reviewing the material provided by the Crown.

Although there is no onus on the defence to show why a complainant might make a false complaint, the cross-examination will likely include questions about your bias and potential motives for lying. The defence may suggest reasons why you are motivated to cause trouble for the accused or to give a false complaint. If this happens, listen carefully to the questions and, if asked, honestly express your feelings. Be truthful and forthright about your motivations. You may well have very negative feelings toward the accused, which would be quite natural and understandable. Appropriately express the feelings necessary to answer these allegations against you; do not second-guess how your responses may be interpreted. Be prepared to use the psychological techniques outlined in preceding chapters to stay calm and to minimize being intimidated or threatened by the questioning. Your goal is to give a reasoned, balanced response as opposed to an emotion-based, reactionary one.

As noted previously, you particularly need to remain alert to compound questions during cross-examination. Defence counsel may ask you to agree with a number of facts that have been included in one question or one suggestion, such as "You got up in the morning, had breakfast, got on the bus, and arrived at work, and there you spoke to my client." All this may be true except that you actually drove to work, rather than taking the bus. Although the point of the statement may be to establish that you had a conversation with the accused, make sure you stop the lawyer and correct any errors made. Do not allow the defence to inaccurately assume certain things happened merely by the use of a compound question. It is allowable and prudent for you to say something such as "I did all those things, except I drove to work." If the issue or question is particularly complex, it is best to say, "Could you break that down for me please so I'm not confused?"

Defence lawyers may sometimes indicate that you said something when, in fact, you did not say it. They might misstate your evidence and suggest, for example, "You said yesterday that you didn't go to the park on Tuesday," when, in fact, you said that you did go to the park on Tuesday. This may happen because the lawyers misheard what you said or have so much to remember that they have forgotten some key pieces of information. Be aware of this possibility, and if it happens, bring it to the attention of the lawyer and clarify any misunderstanding.

It is common for the defence counsel to make forceful suggestions to the witness. The defence may repeat these suggestions in an aggressive, loud manner and may even make what feels like an intimidating approach to the witness stand. It is important that you respond to this according to the content, rather than the gestures and posturing of the lawyer. If you feel that you are being intimidated, do not hesitate to ask that the lawyer stop that particular behaviour. As an example, you can ask the judge to have the lawyer stand a comfortable distance away from you or request that the lawyer not stand beside the accused so that you have to look in that direction when addressing any questions. If you look away when answering, the lawyer may say, "Look at me when you answer my questions." There is no rule in law stipulating that you have to look at the lawyer when you answer the questions; you can look at the judge. Similarly, the defence counsel may demand a "yes" or "no" answer to a question, but there is no rule requiring this either. Answer "yes" or "no" if that is an adequate response to a question; otherwise use the words that you need to give a full and complete answer. Seek the help of the judge if the pressure becomes too intense for you to handle on your own.

Sometimes the defence lawyer may ask improper questions. The Crown lawyer should stand up and object when this happens, but there are limitations on the ability to do this. The court will be critical of a prosecutor who is felt to be inappropriately interrupting the cross-examination of the complainant. You may feel abandoned on the stand and, in many respects, you are on your own. When the questions are truly improper, the Crown will object, but in circumstances where propriety is in doubt for one reason or another, seek the assistance of the judge. In doing so you will get the necessary assistance and you will also alert the Crown to your concerns. For example, witnesses often tell the defence that they have been asked repetitive questions before and their answers are the same. A judge may agree with the witness on this point and tell the lawyer to move on, or may merely instruct the witness to not challenge the lawyer and answer the questions.

Not surprisingly, the intensity and rigour of a cross-examination often triggers memories you had not previously recalled. You may find that you remember something on the stand that you had not reported to the police or the Crown. Defence questions are often penetrating and may cover a lengthy period, raising topics you have not thought about in a long time, or touching on areas of your life that the investigators' or the Crown's questions did not. Again, the best approach is to tell the truth and answer the questions candidly. Explain why some information may be new and if you are not sure of the soundness of the memory make this known as well.

Listening carefully

YOU MAY HAVE NOTICED a theme in the previous section, namely, that you should always listen carefully to the questions asked. Be sure you understand the question being asked and try to give a specific answer without adding irrelevant information. For example, the defence counsel might ask: "Did you tell anyone about what happened before you went to the police?" The following answer is not responsive to that question: "I delayed telling my husband because the accused threatened me. I was scared he would carry out his threats. I was shocked and dismayed about what he did. I saw what he was capable of and was afraid his threats were real." The question actually being asked is "Did you tell or not?" and it should be answered accordingly.

On the other hand, the defence counsel might say: "I suggest your failure to tell your husband was because you felt guilty because you wanted this to happen. You have always been smitten by my client and this act was by your invitation, isn't that true?" Then the following response, "I delayed telling my husband because the accused threatened me. I was scared he would carry out his threats. I have told you this. I was shocked and dismayed by what he did. I saw what he was capable of and was afraid his threats were real. That is why I delayed telling my husband," would appropriately answer the suggestions made by defence counsel. Answering the defence's questions directly is very important, so you should listen carefully and respond appropriately. Giving a response that avoids the question may be seen as evasiveness.

Expressing your anger

WE HAVE MADE THE point frequently that a Canadian court of law is not a forum for victims of crime to rail against the accused, to berate the system, or to seek vengeance. On the contrary, a trial is expressly a forum that provides the accused an opportunity to refute your story, to challenge your allegations, question your credibility or motives, and examine your character. If you have made an effort to learn about the justice system, and prepare yourself beforehand, you will understand what you are facing. Your ability to meet the challenges and be an effective witness will be directly proportional to your resolve, strength, and preparation.

Nonetheless, as you proceed in your informed, conscientious approach to tell the facts of your ordeal, you may face surprising allegations and attacks. There may be times when it seems the only way to answer a question is by acknowledging your angry feelings toward the accused or about the impact of the crime. If this is the case, express your anger but direct it well and make sure it does not prevent you from addressing the question fully. Consider the following two examples that illustrate when angry expressions are or are not pertinent to the question being asked. If you are asked, "Why did you accuse my client?" you might answer, "I am angry with him because he raped me. And that was horribly wrong and he should go to jail for it." In this case, the expressions of anger are not pertinent to the question. On the other hand, if the defence lawyer challenges you with, "I suggest that you told this story because you are angry at the accused for dumping you for another woman," you might respond, "Yes, I am angry at him. But I am very angry because he raped me. And that was horribly wrong and I had to do something about it. And for me, that was reporting it." In this case, it is very appropriate to give voice to your anger and explain your feelings because they are directly relevant to the challenging statement.

RE-EXAMINATION

THE CROWN HAS A limited right to ask a witness questions after the cross-examination. Such a re-examination is only allowed if new matters arose in cross-examination that could not have been anticipated by the Crown or if it is obvious that you were not given an opportunity to explain certain answers in your cross-examination. Do not rely on the Crown to re-question you. If things do not go well during cross-examination, and you make some mistakes, try to correct them at the time, rather than thinking that re-examination can correct this. The difficulty is that the Crown does not get a chance to talk to the witness after cross-examination and before re-examination, so there is no opportunity to discuss potential misunderstandings or new information.

SPENDING DAYS ON THE STAND

IT IS TYPICAL FOR a complainant to be on the stand for two or three days, and in some cases longer. Sometimes, where there is more than one accused, the lawyer acting for each of the defendants will want to cross-examine the complainant, leading to days of testimony. This ordeal calls for considerable attention to your self-care. Think of this as an emotional marathon where encouragement, nurturance, nourishment, and intermittent rest are critical.

The emotional tension of testifying is heightened by the fact that you are on your own. Further, you are not allowed to speak with anyone about your evidence until all of your testimony, including cross-examination, is completed. The judge will warn you specifically, once cross-examination has started, not to discuss your evidence with anyone during beaks in your testimony, including Crown counsel. You cannot ask questions of the Crown counsel, family, friends, supports, or even your therapist. In the days and evenings between your periods on the stand, this can leave you feeling isolated. You might even be cross-examined to determine if you have had conversations about your evidence. Take this very seriously; you may be watched during breaks because other people involved in the case are suspicious that you might talk to someone and contaminate your evidence. Explain this situation to family and friends before you begin testifying so they understand your restrictions. You might prepare a pre-rehearsed spiel you can use if anyone tries to talk to you about the case, such as "This case is really important to me and I can't talk about it now. We'll talk about it after I'm finished." You can make plans to debrief with those close to you when the trial is over.

Being knowledgeable about the legal process, understanding the unique features of sexual crimes, and developing self-awareness will equip you not only to manage trial stress more effectively, but will also make you a more effective advocate for your case and for victim justice in general. Some stages of the trial can prove to be demoralizing, and your time on the stand could be one of them. There are times when the complainant and even the Crown may feel so discouraged they are ready to abandon the prosecution because the system does not seem to provide what victims need. Unless irrevocable harm to you or others is imminent, we encourage you to hang in there and employ some of the methods discussed in this book to see you through the difficult periods. Working through the crisis and adversity of a sexual assault and/or participating in the legal proceedings can lead to personal growth, empowerment, or transformation, and ultimately more control over your life.

Throughout the trial, make an effort to maintain a broad perspective on the criminal court process. Acknowledge your hopes and fears and separate these from the pragmatic task of participating in the legal proceedings. Take the opportunity to become familiar with the courthouse, the rules of court, and the legal personnel. Appreciate that this is not only the most acceptable but also the most preferable recourse to deal with significant conflict in our society. Compare the benefits of legal action to alternatives, such as avoidance, substance misuse, physical or verbal attacks, and criminal charges of your own. Examine with an open mind the advantages of human beings coming to a forum to provide their perspective in dialogue with a view to resolving a dispute. Recognize that, although you may not trust everyone along the way, the system is fundamentally sound, and you are contributing to it.

As the discussion in this chapter has illustrated, your time on the stand is likely to run a gamut from dull to exciting to stressful. Some of the evidence you give will be compelling; you will want to talk about it, and you will be enthusiastic. Other topics will be dull, uninteresting, and perhaps boring, making you feel tired and drowsy. This is particularly true when the lawyers are establishing the facts and you are required to go over minute details of your statements, identify exhibits, or look through many photographs. When you have an important story to tell, this kind of minutiae can be frustrating and tiresome.

As you give your testimony, you are not completely at the mercy of your questioners; you can exert some control over the situation. We have given examples illustrating situations in which you may ask the questioning lawyer for clarification, or you may turn to the judge for assistance or a break. Another useful tactic is to slow yourself down to diminish your anxiety and give yourself time to formulate a good answer. Slow your breathing and deliberately give your answers in slow, modulated speech. This will encourage the lawyers to keep their questioning slower so that you can process their words, understand the meaning, and then find the correct response, rather than being pressured into a response that is forced and perhaps not completely accurate. The other advantage of speaking slowly is that it provides more time for the judge and all the lawyers who are taking notes about what you have to say to do that properly.

Of course, some parts of your evidence may be difficult to talk about; you may want to avoid them altogether. This can happen when you are required to talk about intimate sexual details, or about things that frighten you. Some topics are extremely fear-provoking for witnesses; they are afraid there will be repercussions for talking. Equally, it can be difficult when the defence uses a style that suggests that you are not telling the truth, or you are fabricating or exaggerating. Questioning can be particularly difficult when your experiences have been devastatingly real for you and it is hard to understand how anyone could suggest the opposite. We encourage you to become well-versed and practised in using some of the stress-reducing strategies presented in Chapter 5. Learning effective ways to improve your concentration, remaining focused on the present time, and managing your emotional reactions will serve you well when you are in court.

In her book, *The Story of Jane Doe*, the author describes how she was so focused on giving truthful answers during her testimony that she was not aware of some of the things around her in the courtroom. Some professionals, such as police officers or expert witnesses who testify often, do not look at the examiner; instead, they just look at various objects in the courtroom so they detach themselves from the person asking the questions and avoid any potential interpersonal negativity. This strategy may be particularly helpful if the accused is in your line of sight when you are on the stand. You can sharpen your focus by concentrating on your breathing, keeping it regular and slow, and looking at a neutral spot in the courtroom while you think. Others maintain that the best strategy is to look at, and direct all responses to, the judge.

If you are able, and the Crown prosecutor does not object, you may want to take advantage of the opportunity to observe the trial after you have testified. It could help you come to terms with what transpires legally and may be helpful to the prosecution if you take notes of the evidence and alert the Crown to any concerns you have with the accuracy of the evidence introduced in the defence case. Neither you nor the other witnesses can have direct access to the Crown during the trial, but you may be able to meet during breaks.

LIKELY DEFENCE ARGUMENTS

IN CHAPTER 1, WE touched on the topic of essential ingredients of a charge, and which elements constitute a legitimate defence for the accused. To obtain a conviction, the Crown has an obligation to prove the essential ingredients of any offence, and for the crime of sexual assault these are as follows:

- There was activity of touching or threatening to touch the victim, or an invitation to touch;
- The offence was of a sexual nature;
- There was no consent; or
- Even if the victim cooperated with the sexual act, there were legal circumstances that invalidated the consent.

If the defence can demonstrate reasonable doubt that these essential elements were present, the court will acquit the accused. Below we discuss various avenues that are used by the defence in an attempt to demonstrate that at least one of these essential ingredients in the case against the accused is in doubt. These defences, in some cases, are relevant only to sexual assault, whereas others may apply to other sexual offences as well.

Denial

THE CROWN INTRODUCES THE prosecution's case first and has the onus to prove the charges beyond a reasonable doubt. The accused has no obligation whatsoever to either cross-examine or challenge the prosecution witnesses or to call any defence evidence. Practically speaking, however, the defence will always have questions to ask the complainant about the allegation. When the accused does not take the stand, the accused is saying that the Crown has not proved all the elements of the charge beyond a reasonable doubt and that there exists the right to remain silent on any involvement in the matter. Alternatively, the accused may take the stand and either deny having been with the complainant at the alleged time and place, or say that the events did not occur as the complainant says they did, or both. If the court believes the accused, or the defence raises a reasonable doubt about guilt, an acquittal is automatic. Normally in a trial, the accused will provide a version of events that explains each part of the implicating allegations, thus giving the trier of fact an alternative version to contemplate.

Alibi

DEFENDING WITH AN ALIBI means that the accused is saying that it is not possible to be the offender as charged because the accused was at a different place at the time of the offence. To use an alibi defence, the accused has an obligation to inform the Crown in advance because the law recognizes the impossibility of putting the onus on the Crown to disprove an alibi without notice. Once the accused has given notice to the Crown of an alibi, it is incumbent on the Crown, through the police, to investigate this evidence. If the police investigation reveals information that refutes the alibi, the prosecution then has the opportunity to call this evidence, which would introduce reasonable doubt that the alibi is valid. In the event that the accused introduces an alibi as part of the defence and the Crown does not refute it, then the court will presume that the alibi is true as the defence has described it, and this could raise reasonable doubt about the Crown's case.

Consent

THE DEFENCE MAY SAY that the Crown has not proven the case beyond a reasonable doubt on the issue of consent. If the complainant knew the accused at the time of the alleged assault and was old enough to consent legally, the case is likely to hinge on the issue of consent. It is an option for the defence to cross-examine the complainant on the subject of consent, and the accused can testify about all the indications given at the time that suggested that the complainant was consenting to sex. If the court believes the defence's evidence, it may determine that the complainant was not telling the truth or was exaggerating, and, in fact, did consent.

Faced with cross-examination on the matter of consent, you need to be clear in your own mind what did and did not take place. You need to be particularly clear about language and what was said or not said. Remember the common defence questioning tactics outlined above, and be alert to questions with multiple parts; avoid answering these complex questions with a simple "yes" or "no." The defence may wish to ask questions about your previous sexual activity. Under the old rape laws, it was common for the defence counsel to try to sully the reputation of a female complainant by providing evidence that she was sexually active with men other than the accused. Today, evidence regarding a complainant's previous sexual activity is subject to strict guidelines. It must be specifically relevant to the incident in question and cannot be introduced as a means to discredit the complainant or as an argument that, since sex was agreed to in the past, the complainant must have agreed on this occasion. As an example, the court will allow the defence to raise the issue of sexual history if it is legitimately needed to demonstrate that physical evidence consistent with unwanted sexual activity (such as injury) came from another source, or that a mistaken belief in consent was based on an understanding reached by the alleged offender and the complainant in previous encounters.

It is fair to say that courts in Canada now recognize that "no" means "no," regardless of whether one said "yes," on any number of past occasions, to the accused or anyone else. A sexually active person can have said "no" to the offender and expect the complaint to be taken as seriously as that of a person with little or no sexual history. Under the current law, prostitutes can bring charges of sexual assault against anyone to whom they have not given consent, and such cases, although rare, have been successfully prosecuted in Canada.

Mistake on the issue of consent

AS PREVIOUSLY STATED, THE Crown must prove both the guilty act and the guilty mind of an accused before the court will make a finding of guilt. The Crown needs to prove that the accused intended to engage sexually while knowing the complainant was not consenting. There are cases where the accused professes to believe that there was consent to sexual activity even though the complainant claims otherwise. The court will consider this defence if it has an air of reality. When the complainant does not signal a lack of consent, the accused may be successful in this defence. The *Criminal Code* specifies that an accused cannot rely on the defence of mistake on the issue of consent if the belief arose from the accused's voluntary drunkenness, recklessness, or wilful blindness, or if the accused did not take reasonable steps to ascertain that the complainant was consenting.

Mistake on the issue of age

THE CONSENT OF A sexual partner is invalid if certain circumstances exist whereby their agreement is not considered legal consent. For example, if the complainant is under the age of fourteen then, in law, the complainant does not have the capacity to consent to sexual activity and the court will hold an older sexual partner culpable of sexual assault.[6] There are instances where the accused thought that the complainant was both fourteen years of age and had agreed to sexual contact. The *Criminal Code* stipulates that, in these cases, there is an onus on the accused to conduct an inquiry to ascertain the age of the complainant before engaging in sex, even if that person agrees to the activity. The sort of inquiry expected is determined by the circumstances. The wider the age difference between the accused and the complainant, the more this is expected from the accused. A high standard of inquiry would go beyond just asking the complainant's age; it would include asking for identification or even questioning the parents of the youthful complainant.

Intoxication of the accused

EVEN IF THE ACCUSED was so intoxicated that judgment was impaired, or if intoxication blurs the issue of whether or not the complainant consented, the accused cannot rely on this as a successful defence. For public policy reasons related to protection of the public, this defence is not available to an accused as long as the intoxicant was voluntarily consumed.

Intoxication of the victim is an entirely different issue. If the victim is highly intoxicated and does not have the capacity to consent, in law no consent is present and the accused who knowingly engages in sexual activity in these circumstances is legally culpable for the crime of sexual assault.

Mistaken identity of the accused

IF THE ACCUSED IS a stranger, the defence may suggest the complainant is wrong about the identity of the offender. The defence may ask the following of the complainant: "Could it have been someone else, someone who looked similar?" "How good a look did you get?" "Was it dark?" "Do you wear glasses?" These sorts of questions could be asked during cross-examination in an attempt to raise doubt about the identity of an attacker. If the identity of the accused is in doubt, the case has to rely more heavily on other evidence, for example, physical, or forensic evidence connecting the accused to the incident, rather than eyewitness identification testimony.

In cases where the perpetrator wears a disguise or assaults the victim in the dark, and perhaps further confuses the situation by beating or blindfolding the victim, positive identification can be a significant issue. The victim may not have seen the assailant well enough to make a confident identification later. In some cases, the complainant may be able to identify a suspect in a police lineup at the time of the investigation, but is unable to make the identification in a courtroom a lengthy period later at the time of the trial. The court will be permitted to hear about the previous accurate identification in such a case.

Criminal law courts understand that there are serious weaknesses in eyewitness identification of strangers, particularly in situations where there may be confusion and panic. In his paper, Bruce MacFarlane notes that eyewitness misidentification is "the single most important factor leading to wrongful convictions."[7] The courts, therefore, treat this sort of evidence with great caution as serious mistakes have been made in the past.

The Federal Provincial Territorial Committee (FPT) Report on the Prevention of Wrongful Conviction released on 25 January 2005 summarizes some cases that illustrate these concerns. One case cited is that of Jennifer Thompson, a North Carolina woman raped at knifepoint as a twenty-two-year-old college student.[8] She explains the circumstances:

> During my ordeal, some of my determination took an urgent new direction. I studied every single detail on the rapist's face. I looked at his hairline; I looked for scars, for tattoos, for anything that would help me identify him. When and if I survived the attack, I was going to make sure that he was put in prison and he was going to rot.
>
> When I went to the police department later that day, I worked on a composite sketch to the very best of my ability. I looked through hundreds of noses and eyes and eyebrows and hairlines and nostrils and lips. Several days later, looking at a series of police photos, I identified my attacker. I knew this was the man. I was completely confident. I was sure.
>
> I picked the same man in a lineup. Again, I was sure. I knew it. I had picked the right guy, and he was going to go to jail. If there was the possibility of a death sentence, I wanted him to die. I wanted to flip the switch.
>
> When the case went to trial, I stood up on the stand, put my hand on the Bible and swore to tell the truth. Based on my testimony, Ronald Cotton was sentenced to prison for life. It was the happiest day of my life because I could begin to put it all behind me.

Eleven years later, DNA testing proved Cotton had not been the rapist; this evidence was further supported when another man later pled guilty to the crime. Recently developed methods of DNA analysis allowed the Innocence Project in New York City[9] to show that of 130 post-conviction exonerations, 101 or 78 percent involved mistaken identification. This was by far the biggest factor in wrongful conviction because in-court identification is deceptively credible; the complainant is typically honest, sincere, and convincing. However, the many factors described in Chapter 4 that influence our memory can quickly diminish the ability to identify a suspect correctly. So, if a defence lawyer questions you intensely about your identification of a client, realize that this is a particularly important legal issue and not necessarily a personal attack intended solely to discredit your character.

Mistaken identity of the complainant

IN SOME CASES, THE accused may say that a sexual act took place, that the complainant was consenting, but that the accused thought he was having sex with a person other than the complainant. The court has allowed this defence in circumstances where the sexual activity took place in a dark setting and the accused argues that, at the time of the sexual activity, the complainant was mistaken for the accused's girlfriend. In the event that the accused can raise a reasonable doubt on this point, the accused will be acquitted.

Behaviour was not sexual

WHETHER OR NOT BEHAVIOUR is sexual in nature is not always easy to distinguish. A football player may pat a teammate on the buttocks following a play without consequence, but a male patting a female colleague's buttocks after a successful business deal could find himself facing sexual charges. To raise doubt about this issue, the defence may argue that what an observer might have interpreted as a sexual act was not intended to be sexual by the accused, although the Crown need not prove sexual gratification for an assault to be considered a sexual assault.

The leading case of determining whether or not an assault is sexual is *R. v. Chase*.[10] Justice McIntyre suggested that the following test be applied to determine if specified conduct is sexual in nature and violates the sexual integrity of the victim: "is the sexual or carnal context of the assault visible to a reasonable observer?"[11] To make this determination, one must consider what part of the body was being touched, the nature of this contact, the situation in which it occurred, what words or gestures accompanied the touching, and if force or threats were used. The intention and purpose of the person committing the act is important, but may only be one factor in determining if the conduct is sexual. To continue with the example above, the woman might be successful in her complaint against her business colleague. The Crown will argue that football players patting each other is typical and accepted behaviour, whereas in a business office, handshaking is the typical way of congratulating a person. In that context, touching the woman's buttocks was a violation of her personal integrity.

This issue of sexual conduct is not always easy to address and has resulted in a diversity of court decisions. In one case, the court determined that grabbing a child's genitals to discipline him was a sexual assault, whereas a sergeant in the Canadian Forces who grabbed the buttocks of a private was not guilty of a sexual offence. In another case, the court found a stepfather who slapped his twelve-year-old stepdaughter on the buttocks, tried to touch her breasts, and then did succeed in touching them during horseplay was not guilty of sexual assault.

THE DEFENCE CALLS WITNESSES

FOLLOWING TESTIMONY BY THE Crown's last witness, the Crown will tell the judge that this is the case for the Crown. Then the defence team has the option to either call evidence or not. If it does not call evidence, it will likely argue that the Crowns' case was insufficient to prove the charges against the accused. In this situation, the Crown must then begin submissions to justify why the accused should be convicted. The defence will then make submissions as to why the evidence was insufficient. Conversely, if the defence feels that the Crown has a case it must meet, it will call evidence.

Unlike the complainant, who may be the prosecution's most important witness, the accused may have an essential but seemingly small part to play in the trial. If a defence lawyer has been retained, the accused's role may be limited to attending court, taking notes, and advising the defence counsel. The accused typically will only address the court through the defence lawyer. In Canadian law, an accused is not required to testify in a criminal trial; it is a choice, and the judge will not consider it unusual if the accused does not take the stand. When the accused does not testify, there is no direct contradictory story or challenge of the account given by the complainant, but there still could be weaknesses in the Crown's case. The court may acquit the accused of the charges whether guilt is denied on the stand or not.

The defence can face an ethical issue when deciding whether to call the accused to testify. In the event that the client has told the lawyer that the sexual assault took place as the complainant said, the defence cannot ethically put the accused on the stand to deny it, thereby committing perjury. If, on the other hand, the accused has a factual version that provides a legal defence, the accused will be free (but not required) to give this evidence on the stand. The story may be that sexual activity did indeed take place, but that the complainant consented or that the accused thought the complainant was consenting. The accused might argue that one of the defences outlined above mitigated the accused's actions. In one case, the accused admitted he touched the young complainant, but stated he did so to maintain his ruse that he was a professional and that there was no motive for sexual gratification in the touching. He was convicted because this is not an acceptable defence to the charges, but the judge heard the defence version of the facts and considered those facts in sentencing.

If the accused does not take the stand at trial, there will still be an opportunity to speak following conviction, but prior to sentencing, on matters related to sentencing. A judge will give those convicted an opportunity to make a statement by asking if they have anything to say at that time. Once again, the accused may or may not take the opportunity to speak.

Expert witnesses

EITHER THE CROWN OR the defence may call expert evidence in a sexual offence trial. Qualified experts have a different status than most witnesses, as the court permits them to give an opinion on a relevant issue when the judge or jury (if present) requires assistance. Expert witnesses must have a recognized expertise in a particular area of interest, and they must be able to support their opinion with sound, scientifically validated principles. The expert does not give an opinion on the ultimate question, that being guilt or innocence of the accused, or the veracity of testimony given, but instead, provides information to help the judge or jury reach its decision. The *Criminal Code* stipulates that either party must give thirty days' notice if it decides to call an expert witness. Notice must include the expert's name, qualifications, and areas of expertise. In addition, the Crown must provide a report, or at least the details of what the expert will say, within a reasonable amount of time before the trial starts. Although the defence must also give notice to the Crown when it intends to call an expert, the substance of what the expert will tell the court (known as "will say") need not be provided before the Crown's case is ended.

If the expert is asked to give an opinion about the complainant, such as an evaluation of physical injuries or the psychological impact of the crime, you may be required to attend for an assessment by the expert before the trial begins. The Crown will request that the complainant see the expert for an assessment but time to accomplish this may be limited. The defence cannot require, nor can a court order the complainant to undergo, an examination unless the complainant consents. Whenever a complainant sees an expert at the request of the Crown, the facts of the meeting and the opinion of the expert are matters that must be disclosed to the defence. The opposite is true if the defence lawyer asks the accused to see an expert. The defence has total control over what information is disclosed because what transpires between the expert and the accused is subject to the solicitor-client privilege. The defence has no obligation either to tell the Crown of the findings or to call the expert as a witness.

To subject the accused to an assessment of any nature in criminal proceedings is considered a serious intervention and is only permitted in law in the rarest of circumstances. The state cannot force the accused to undergo an assessment pre or mid-trial to determine whether the accused has a propensity to commit sex crimes. Even if the Crown had such psychological information about the accused, it is not admissible against the accused in a sexual assault trial. The only assessments of the accused permitted before the verdict are related to whether the accused is fit to stand trial, or was mentally disordered at the time of the alleged offence. These are matters that could give rise to a defence. If the accused undergoes an assessment pre or mid-trial in relation to sexual offending, it would likely be at the request of the defence lawyer and the solicitor-client privilege would attach to the findings.

In sexual offence trials, the courts have accepted expert opinions to provide the following:

* Assessment of the physical condition of the victim
* Evidence to counter the defence argument that the complainant did not act as expected of a victim (for example, had continued contact with an abuser)
* Psychological evidence of Post-Traumatic Stress Disorder
* An explanation of the testimonial characteristics of the class of persons to whom the witness belongs, which go beyond the ability of a layperson to understand (such as a child or witness with a disability)
* Psychiatric evidence lead by the defence to support the inference that the accused is not the sort of person likely to have committed the offence

Other witnesses

MANY COMPLAINANTS ARE SURPRISED to hear of witnesses who testify for the defence and contradict their evidence or paint a picture of them as being unreliable. As previously stated there is no requirement for the defence to provide a witness list in advance, so neither the Crown nor the complainant will know who is expected to testify for the defence until it happens. Little can be done to prepare for this, but the complainant can expect questions from Crown counsel mid-trial to assist with cross-examination of the witness where new issues or facts have arisen.

Reply or rebuttal evidence

THE CROWN HAS A limited opportunity to call witnesses in rebuttal after the defence has completed its case. The opportunity may arise when the defence has introduced evidence that could not have been contemplated by the Crown. It is not permissible for the Crown to split its case by presenting evidence in rebuttal after the defence has presented its case.

CLOSING STATEMENTS

AT THE END OF the trial, both counsel are invited to make submissions to the judge or jury (if present) to assist them in the determination of the verdict. When the accused calls evidence, the defence will start by emphasizing the Crown's onus to prove the charges beyond a reasonable doubt and stressing the weaknesses in the prosecutions case that raise such doubts. The Crown's final submissions will likely include the following topics:

- A general summary of relevant legal principles
- A recap of the offences that need to be proven
- A statement on what the issues are in this case
- An analysis of any legal issues that have arisen in the trial
- A summary of the evidence in the trial
- The elements of the victim's testimony that suggest the complaint is valid
- The corroborating evidence of the complaint
- Justification for any weaknesses in the Crown's case
- Highlighting weaknesses in the defence evidence
- An argument that the Crown has met the onus to prove the case beyond a reasonable doubt

When the accused calls evidence, the defence will follow the Crown with its closing statement, which takes a different approach, emphasizing the Crown's onus to prove the charges beyond a reasonable doubt and stressing the weaknesses in the prosecution's case that raise such doubts.

THE VERDICT

YOU HAVE GIVEN YOUR testimony, possibly sat through long hours of courtroom procedure, and probably endured a long wait, but all of that is behind you now. At this juncture, you may have an array of thoughts and feelings. You are likely to feel relief it is over; you have done well to come this far. Your relief may be tempered by self-doubt. You may be preoccupied with things you left out of your testimony, or questions you could have answered more clearly. You may feel somewhat powerless because you no longer have any influence on what the judge or jury (if present) will think, or how either will deliberate your case. Statistically, an acquittal is as likely as a conviction in a sex crimes trial, so you need to prepare yourself for either outcome.

The verdict is not only a judgment of the accused, but you have told intimate details of your life and you are also waiting to hear how you were perceived — did people believe you, and were you considered credible? If the court acquits and releases the accused, what does it mean that the accused will be free and at large in the community? Many of these questions cannot be answered until you hear the verdict.

Still, you have hopes or expectations that the justice system will come through and hold the offender accountable. At this point in the proceedings, legal precedent directs the judge or the jury (if present) on how either must make its decision when both the Crown and the defence have presented evidence to support their respective positions. Justice Cory has delineated these directions:[12]

> First, if you believe the evidence of the accused, obviously you must acquit.
>
> Second, if you do not believe the testimony of the accused but you are left in reasonable doubt by it, you must acquit.
>
> Third, even if you are not left in doubt by the evidence of the accused, you must ask yourself whether, on the basis of the evidence which you do accept, you are convinced beyond a reasonable doubt by that evidence of the guilt of the accused.

If you are feeling vulnerable, you may want to have a support person available to speak with immediately after the verdict. You could also book an appointment with your counsellor to debrief and work through your emotions following the court proceedings. First Nations groups sometimes have a drumming ceremony or a healing circle after hearing the verdict to help with the expression of emotion. Enlisting outside help is important because you cannot expect that the Crown will be available to provide the emotional support you need.

After the judge or jury (if present) convicts or acquits the accused, you may experience a wide range of emotions. You may feel relief, joy, and a sense of safety. You may feel disappointed, angry, or fearful. You may regret having taken your complaint to the authorities in the first place. You need a place to be able to express these emotions safely; it is not appropriate to do so in the courtroom. Be particularly mindful not to express your feelings to the judge; no good can come from it and you may affect your credibility in any future proceedings. You must turn to others and it is prudent to turn to others whom you trust to say the right thing in the circumstances and assist you in maintaining a level of privacy and decorum.

FOLLOWING THE VERDICT

THE VERDICT SIGNALS A trial's completion, but perhaps not the end of your case. In bringing a verdict, the court has judged the evidence and created a new legal reality that profoundly affects all parties. In some cases, where the court finds the accused guilty, this reality may be short-lived, because as occurred in some recent cases, the defence is successful in reopening the trial in order to call new evidence. This may happen when the accused has not testified at the trial but following the conviction feels that this was a mistake. The accused will typically argue that the defence lawyer at the trial made an error in not calling the accused to the stand.

If the accused does not successfully apply for a mistrial or a reopening of the trial in the lower court, there is an opportunity to appeal the conviction to a higher court. The appeal may be successful if the conviction is unreasonable, not supported by the evidence, involves a miscarriage of justice, or the judge in the lower court made an error in law. Usually a new trial will be ordered if the appeal is successful, and in some cases, the higher court will acquit the accused. This was the case some years ago when the Manitoba Court of Appeal determined that it was wrong in law for a psychologist to have said in her evidence that children do not normally lie about sexual abuse. The appeal court decision stated, "A witness, expert or otherwise, may not testify that ... any other witness, including the complainant ... is likely telling the truth."[13] Rather than order a new trial, the court entered an acquittal of the accused.

EMOTIONS AND PRINCIPLES

THE COURTS HAVE RECOGNIZED that the prosecution of sex crimes can be more difficult than many other crimes. Although the legal issues may be simple enough, such cases frequently bring with them an emotional factor not present in other trials. In spite of the often heinous facts brought before them, courts have to be vigilant not to deviate from the well-established rules of law. There are many historical examples of cases highjacked by passions and a desire to see someone held accountable for a horrific crime. Sexual crime cases in particular are vulnerable to the erosion of legal principles by emotion.

A sexual crime conviction carries serious consequences. Not only does the offender have a criminal record that can be a barrier to holding certain jobs or travelling outside Canada, but some may have to register as a sex offender and tell the authorities of their whereabouts long after the date of sentencing. There is also a social stigma associated with a sexual conviction that can affect people for the rest of their life. While some may argue that a sexual offender deserves all of these consequences and more, few would want to see an innocent person treated in this manner; but it happens.

Justice Galligan addressed this issue in the case of *R. v. J. (F.E.)*:

> While there is no scale upon which conflicting evils can be weighed, it should be remembered that, revolting as child sexual abuse is, it would be horrible for an innocent person to be convicted of it. For that reason, I think the courts must be vigilant to ensure that the zeal to punish child sexual abusers does not erode the rules which the courts have developed over the centuries to prevent the conviction of the innocent. [14]

Justice Wood warned about the potential of shifting the burden of proof to the accused:

> I noted the gender-related stereotypical thinking that led to improper assumptions about the credibility of complainants ... [will be] replaced by an equally pernicious set of assumptions about the believability of complainants which would have the effect of shifting the burden of proof to those accused of such crimes. [15]

Nevertheless, the justice system is a self-reflective process and ongoing procedural changes strive to make it an increasingly fair process for both the accused and the accuser. It is very important to society that we maintain faith in the system, participate in it when called upon to do so, and strive to improve our systems of justice. One only need to experience a society where there is no rule of law to appreciate that, even with its frailties, having the opportunity to make a complaint and testify in a process designed to examine culpability is far better than no process at all.

Maintain a healthy perspective

AS OUTLINED IN THE introduction to this book, we believe that the criminal justice system in Canada, although not perfect, is an evolving, viable method for responding to breaches of the criminal law. At the same time, this does not diminish the fact that the process of taking a case through the court system is very complex and beyond the control of one person. We have made the point that testifying can be a gruelling experience, and rather than being able to tell your story your way, you are required to tell it in a legally proscribed, arcane manner. Court officials often speak a different language that you do not understand, about matters that are not familiar to you. You may feel lost, excluded, and even exploited, as if you are there only for your piece of evidence without regard for your unique human qualities. These are all valid reactions but they do not reflect the total legal situation. We have discussed ways that you can broaden your perspective to encompass both the strengths and weaknesses of our criminal justice system. Increasingly, there are places in the legal system where your input to the process is invited and valued, and we explore some of these in the next chapter.

You now have a better understanding of what to expect in legal proceedings. We suggest you review this chapter prior to participating in a trial yourself; there is a lot of information to absorb. We feel strongly that you will fare better if you enter the process well-informed and prepared. The techniques and tools described in Chapter 5 can also be invaluable aids to you. Below is a summary of the steps you can take to build resiliency. You can refer to it when you are immersed in the trial process.

+ Make personal connections.
+ Take care of yourself.
+ Avoid seeing a crisis as an insurmountable problem.
+ Keep things in perspective.
+ Accept that change is a part of living.
+ Move towards your goals.

+ Take decisive actions.
+ Nurture a positive view of yourself.
+ Maintain a hopeful outlook.
+ Look for opportunities for self-discovery.

VIGNETTE EIGHT: MAKING ACCOMMODATIONS

THE CASE DESCRIBED IN Vignette Eight places the Crown counsel in a difficult position. The letter from Morris' psychiatrist explained that the sexual abuse at the hands of his brother was so traumatic that he suffered from Post-Traumatic Stress Disorder. At the age of fifty, Morris thought he had put the abuse behind him, but when he was required to recount the abuse in court with Clem present, many of his traumatic memories were triggered and he was overwhelmed with feelings of anxiety, shame, and fear. Morris' response to these feelings was to dissociate (see Chapters 2 and 4). Dissociation is a way some people protect themselves from overwhelming emotions. People who dissociate experience the world as a dreamlike, unreal place and they may blank out or have amnesia for the memories that are causing the distressing emotions. While Morris was re-experiencing his traumatic stress in the courtroom, other people could not understand why an otherwise highly functioning individual was doing so poorly in his testimony, and some were questioning his credibility.

The Crown counsel, after reading the psychiatrist's letter, understood Morris' problem, but she was also aware that people are expected to appear in court at the scheduled times and tell their story. The outcome of cases often depends on the performance of the witnesses on the appointed date and time. Without Morris' testimony, the case would lose much of its strength, so instead of letting his testimony drop the Crown decided to apply for some accommodations made allowable by Bill C-2. To begin with, the Crown had Morris undergo a full psychiatric assessment, which outlined specific triggers that had occurred during his testimony and the details of his emotional reactions. Morris himself then provided an affidavit that described his experiences and difficulty on the stand. Next, the Crown carefully analyzed the transcript of Morris' testimony so she was able to provide the court with examples of the questions and comments that had triggered Morris' emotional reactions and how these had caused observable shifts in his behaviour.

Based on this information, the Crown then sought to have Morris testify outside the courtroom during the criminal trial so that he would not see his brother nor have the added anxiety of the courtroom atmosphere while telling his story. These measures reduced Morris' anxiety to the point that he was able to testify. When he was questioned on parts of the preliminary hearing transcript where his recall had been poor, the reasons for this were explained. The court was also made aware that Morris had been able to recall these facts in his statement to the police, made at an earlier time without the pressures of testifying on the stand. Although it was difficult for him, and the defence challenged his credibility, Morris was ultimately able to tell his story at the trial and the trier of fact was able to judge his version with an informed awareness of his emotional challenges. Morris' testimony helped the Crown obtain a conviction on two counts of indecent assault on a male, and two counts of physical assault (choking). Considering that Clem showed no remorse, had made no effort to rehabilitate himself in the years since the offences, and had an extensive criminal record, the court sentenced him to a four-year term in federal prison.

ENDNOTES

1   The defence is required to give the Crown notice of an alibi before trial, in a timely fashion that will allow the police to conduct an investigation to determine if the alibi is legitimate. The defence is also required to give notice that it is calling an expert witness before that witness takes the stand.

2   *R. v. Mills*, [1999] 3 S.C.R. 668.

3   *R. v. Ewanchuk* (1999), 131 C.C.C. (3d) 481, 22 C.R. (5th) 1, 169 D.L.R. (4th) 193, 235 N.R. 323 (S.C.C.).

4   Bill C-2, *An Act to amend the Criminal Code (protection of children and other vulnerable persons and the Canada Evidence Act*, 1st Sess., 38th Parl., 2004 (assented to 20 July 2005, S.C. 2005, c. 32).

5   Both the *Criminal Code* and the amendments can be found online: http://laws. justice.gc.ca/en/C-46/index.html.

6   As noted in Chapter 1, at the time of writing, Parliament had introduced a Bill amending the age of consent to sixteen years.

7   Bruce A. MacFarlane, Q.C., "Convicting the Innocent — A Triple Failure of the Justice System," online: www.canadiancriminallaw.com/articles/articles%20pdf/ Convicting%20the%20Innocent%20Revised%202006.pdf.

8   FPT Heads of Prosecutions Committee Working Group, "Report on the Prevention of Miscarriages of Justice," online: www.justice.gc.ca/en/dept/pub/hop/PreventionOfMiscarriagesOfJustice.pdf at 42.

9   Online: www.innocenceproject.org.

10   *R. v. Chase*, [1987] 2 S.C.R. 293.

11   *Ibid.* at 300.

12   *R. v. W.(D.)*, [1991] 1 S.C.R. 742 at 758.

13   *R. v. Kostuck* (1986), 29 C.C.C. (3d) 190 at 192 (Man. C.A.).

14   *R. v. J.(F.E.)* (1989), 74 C.R. (3d) 269 at 271–72 (Ont. C.A.).

15   *R. v. K.(V.)* (1991), 68 C.C.C. (3d) 18 at 35 (B.C.C.A.).

Sentencing

Vignette Nine

The judge sentences a female high school teacher to a nine-month jail sentence for sexual abuse that happened five years previously. At the sentencing hearing are two of her former students, Elizabeth, aged nineteen and Mary, aged twenty-one, both of whom had been victimized by the teacher. Neither of them is happy with the sentence. At the trial, Mary testified that the teacher had touched her genitals on three occasions. Mary subsequently gave a victim Impact statement (VIS) during the sentencing hearing. In her VIS, Mary said the sexual assault made her feel "different" and alienated from her schoolmates, and said she had lost interest in sex. When contacted by police during the investigation, Elizabeth gave a statement in which she said the teacher had touched her genitals four times and had taken nude pictures of her. The police laid charges against the teacher for these offences but when the Crown counsel contacted Elizabeth to prepare for the trial, Elizabeth said she was too humiliated to testify, refused to come forward, and said that her police statement should be enough. When arrested, the teacher admitted that she had touched the two girls, but she denied taking nude photos of Elizabeth. Without Elizabeth's testimony, the Crown did not feel there was sufficient evidence to advance the aggravated factors of the case related to taking photos, so after Mary's testimony it negotiated a plea agreement in which the teacher agreed to plead guilty to two counts of sexual exploitation but without any reference to taking photos.

IN CANADIAN LAW, SENTENCING an offender found guilty of a crime is not an act of revenge. Above all, sentencing should promote respect for the law and contribute to the maintenance of a civil society. This chapter discusses the principles a judge uses to balance the needs of society, the victim, and the offender. We outline the various sentencing options and focus on the role a victim impact statement can play in sentencing hearings. The chapter ends with some practical advice on writing a statement and dealing with the emotional backdrop of the sentencing process.

When accused people are found guilty following a trial, their status changes in the eyes of the court; they then become offenders. The rights of an offender are different from those of an accused and, in fact, the offender may forfeit some rights, such as the right to freedom. Once convicted, the offender is accountable for the crime committed and will receive some consequence or punishment.

SENTENCING IS NOT REVENGE

THE CONCEPT OF PUNISHMENT for punishment's sake does not exist in Canadian law, and revenge is not the reason why judges impose sentences. The fundamental purpose of sentencing is specifically set out in the Canadian *Criminal Code*: it should contribute to respect for the law and maintenance of a just, peaceful, and safe society. The court does not sentence those convicted of a criminal offence solely to satisfy the understandable, human emotional need to see offenders suffer in some way for their actions; sentencing is done with the greater good of society in mind. There is a recognition that physically or emotionally traumatizing the offender does not contribute, in the end, to a healthy society.

When deciding on a sentence, the law makes a distinction between retribution and vengeance. Retribution is a repayment or recompense that reflects the moral responsibility of the offender, while vengeance is the inflicting of an extreme, hurtful punishment on the offender. In a 1996 ruling, the Supreme Court of Canada outlined the need to apply the principle of restraint in determining a just and appropriate sentence.

> Retribution in a criminal context, by contrast, represents an objective, reasoned and measured determination of an appropriate punishment that properly reflects the moral culpability of the offender, having regard to the intentional risk-taking of the offender, the consequential harm caused by the offender, and the normative character of the offender's conduct. Furthermore, unlike vengeance, retribution incorporates a principle of

restraint; retribution requires the imposition of a just and appropriate punishment, and nothing more.[1]

When the judge passes a sentence that revokes an offender's freedom or imposes conditions, it is done with certain objectives in mind, all meant to achieve a fundamental and positive purpose for society as a whole. The objectives include the following:

- Making a statement through the sentence that the actions of the offender in committing a specific crime will not be tolerated
- Showing both the offender and others that if crimes of this nature are committed, meaningful consequences will follow
- Separating the offender from society by court orders or imprisonment, if necessary
- Assisting the offender to rehabilitate in order to prevent further criminality
- Making reparation to the victim and the community for the crimes committed
- Promoting a sense of social responsibility and acknowledgment by the offender of the harm done to both the victims and the community

The court does not attempt to match the physical characteristics of the punishment with those of the crime. Those who steal may be imprisoned but the court does not steal the thief's rightful property (although stolen property and proceeds of crime will be seized and the offender may be ordered to compensate the victim). Those who assault others may be imprisoned, but the court will not order a physical punishment. In Canada, those who murder will be subject to imprisonment, but not to death by the state.

The justice system reflects the values of the community

THE PERSON WHO COMMITS a sexual offence against a member of our community has inflicted damage, not just to that individual, but also to the community as a whole. Such an act threatens the sense of security, safety, and well-being of all of us. Sexual crimes can change the perspective of an entire community, which may become less open, less trusting, less nurturing, and less secure. A conviction tells offenders they have committed an offence against society, and must therefore pay a debt, and be responsible to their community. These are our national values. We are an interdependent society and each of us has a responsibility to all other members of our community.

The concept of society's interconnectedness that calls for community participation in the criminal process (including the victim and the offender) has been entrenched in our criminal law both by legislation and case law. In *R. v. Gladue*, the Supreme Court of Canada had this to say about restorative justice:[2]

> In general terms, restorative justice may be described as an approach to remedying crime in which it is understood that all things are interrelated and that crime disrupts the harmony that existed prior to its occurrence, or at least that it is felt should exist. The appropriateness of a particular sanction is largely determined by the needs of the victims, and the community, as well as those of the offender. The focus is on the human beings closely affected by the crime.

If we accept that the justice system is not an institution separate from us all, but a manifestation of our community beliefs and ideals, we can appreciate how an offence against one person offends the greater public. The criminal justice system is one means to achieve social stability, civility, and justice. To function optimally, the justice system needs the responsible participation of community members, and sentencing is one juncture where community members can have direct input.

THE SENTENCING HEARING

SENTENCING CAN BE AN involved process, so in sex crime cases there is normally some delay between a guilty plea or verdict and the sentencing hearing. This time is required for both sides to prepare arguments for the sentencing judge. Having heard the facts, the experts, and the legal submissions at the hearing, most judges will reserve their decision on sentence. In other words, they will put the sentence over for a day or longer to consider all the information, and then hand down their decision.

The judge who sentences the offender following a trial is the same judge who presided at the trial. In contrast, if the defence enters a guilty plea, jurisdiction may be waived and the judge originally taking the plea may not be the one who eventually passes sentence. At a later date, the judge who hears the facts and submissions related to the case will sentence the offender. In either event, the sentencing judge may order that a report outlining the offender's risks and needs be prepared to assist with sentencing.

Parole officers, probation officers, or forensic mental health teams (such as psychologists, psychiatrists, social workers, and nurses) typically prepare these reports. It usually takes several weeks for the professionals to complete their assessment and report, so the sentencing hearing will be adjourned until this is done.

Not everyone agrees that offenders should have their motivations and risk assessed before sentencing, and there is no specific provision in the *Criminal Code* to order such a report when the offender objects. Although some judges have interpreted the *Criminal Code* as providing the jurisdiction to order the offender to undergo assessments when it is clear a psychological problem exists, others have objected to this interpretation and maintain that committing a sexual crime, even against a child, is not necessarily a sign of a psychological disorder. In practice, unless the offender agrees to a psychiatric assessment, the judge is not likely to order it.

Whether or not the sentencing judge orders an assessment, it is always an option for the defence to retain a psychologist or psychiatrist to provide an assessment of the offender. If the defence team has a report prepared for its own use, it can choose whether or not to submit it to the court. If the Crown thinks the assessment, prepared and tendered as evidence, is inaccurate, biased, or without foundation, a request can be made that the professional who wrote the report attend the sentencing hearing for cross-examination.

The judge could order that a report be prepared by a probation officer. This type of report will provide the offender's background and attitude towards the offence, the impact on the victim, and a summary of rehabilitative programs available. It may also address any other matters of interest to the court. The report will not make any specific recommendations about whether or not the offender should go to jail, but may recommend conditions that would be helpful in the event the court uses some form of community supervision (such as a curfew).

The complainant has an opportunity at this stage to provide input directly to the probation officer who can include it in the pre-sentence report, or to the Crown who will make submissions to the court. A third alternative is to prepare a document, read in court by the complainant or the Crown that directly communicates the impact of the crime. Although it can take a variety of forms, this is called a victim impact statement (VIS), and is discussed in more detail later in this chapter.

The facts

AFTER RECEIVING ALL THE necessary information, the judge will decide which sentence is appropriate to the facts of the case and the responsibility of the offender. If the matter has gone to trial without a jury, the judge has already heard all the facts and made a ruling based on them. In this case, the Crown will rely on the factual findings of the court to make submissions on an appropriate sentence. If there was a trial in front of a jury, lawyers may not always agree on what the jury meant by its verdict. For example, a complainant may have testified that her spouse sexually assaulted her fifteen times and on three of those occasions he caused bodily harm, but the accused denies both the sexual acts and the violence. If the jury returns a guilty verdict of sexual assault, but not sexual assault causing bodily harm, it suggests that the Crown did not prove beyond a reasonable doubt that bodily harm occurred. In such a case, the defence would likely argue that the verdict is ambiguous so the sentencing judge should consider only the non-violent acts in the sentence. The Crown will state its contrary position to the judge, who is entitled to decide which disputed facts are relevant to the sentence.

When the accused has waived the right to a trial and has entered a guilty plea, the court needs to hear the alleged facts of the crime initially from the Crown. If the defence disputes any fact that is an aggravating one that could lead to a harsher penalty, the Crown must prove it beyond a reasonable doubt by calling witnesses who will be subject to cross-examination. This means the complainant may have to appear as a witness even after a guilty plea has been entered if the accused is not prepared to admit the full extent of the charges. A complainant will likely discuss this eventuality with the Crown and decide if the disputed facts are important enough to warrant taking the stand at this late stage of the proceedings.

After hearing the facts on a guilty plea, the judge is seized of (a legal way of saying permanently assigned to) the sentencing, so the case will not be transferred to another judge.

The offender's criminal record

ONCE THE FACTS OF the current offence, including victim impact statements, are heard, the next important issue is the offender's criminal background. The Crown will therefore seek to file any criminal record, which is generally an easy task unless the offender claims there are errors. In that case, the Crown must demonstrate that the record is reliable. Once the record is filed and agreed upon, the court can use it in sentencing. The most relevant parts of the record will be convictions for other sexual offences that indicate the offender poses a risk of re-offending. Also important are previous breaches of court orders that suggest the accused may not be a good candidate for community supervision.

Neither the Crown nor the police will provide the offender's criminal record to a complainant. To do so would be inappropriate because that would be a breach of the offender's privacy and it could influence the complainant's testimony. Consequently, you may not even know the offender has a record unless you hear it from an outside source.

The Crown cannot include, in its sentencing submissions, details of other offences the accused committed that are not part of a formal criminal record. However, there are circumstances where the court can consider other sexual acts (which may or may not be criminal) that speak to the offender's character, conduct, attitude about the offence, or rehabilitation potential.

The Crown and the defence submissions

BOTH THE CROWN AND the defence lawyers will get an opportunity to tell the judge what they think the sentence should be and why, based on their interpretation of all the information (such as established facts of the crime, a criminal record, professional reports, the victim impact statement, and any letters supporting the offender). These interpretations come in the form of submissions that communicate the positions of each side. The Crown speaks first and focuses on complainant interests, community concerns, the serious factors of the offence, and the offender's real or potential danger to the complainant or the community. The defence focuses on the offender's redeeming qualities, and advocates for rehabilitation and a move back into the community as soon as possible. Both sides will give reasons for their recommendations. If a jail sentence is inevitable, the defence will focus on lessening the term by asking for maximum credit for time already served in custody (double or triple time) and in the case of multiple charges, the defence will ask for concurrent sentences. The Crown then has the option to reply to the defence's submission.

You may be frustrated to find that the court does not take into account things you know about the accused, for example, history of objectionable behaviour, poor character, or past unproven offences (such as thievery).

These sorts of wrong doings, unproven in court, cannot be used against the offender; it is information that does not meet a legal standard necessary to be considered in sentencing. There are circumstances where the defence calls character evidence to say what a fine upstanding person the accused is, but the Crown can then counter with cross-examination questions that suggest this is not true. Nevertheless, it may be irrelevant whether the Crown calls into question the offender's character, or the defence makes the offender out to be an upstanding citizen. The courts generally understand that even a person who is otherwise a fine, upstanding citizen may commit sex offences, yet a person who regularly steals from the community may not pose a similar risk.

The offender's chance to speak

OUR JUSTICE SYSTEM DEMANDS that the sentence be announced in a courtroom, by a judge, with the offender present; but before stating what the sentence will be, the judge must ask the offender if the latter has anything to say. Offenders are free to say anything that they want, and they will not be stopped as long as their comments do not show contempt for the court. This can be a difficult moment for a complainant especially if the offender shows no remorse, but can also be tough even when there is an expression of remorse. You may feel the offender's contrition is shallow, self-serving, or it is "too little, too late."

After the offender speaks, or indicates the choice not to speak, the moment arrives for which the complainant has perhaps waited years. The judge asks the offender to rise, addresses the offender by name, and then reads the sentence. The court will not lecture or shame the offender and will always be polite or even respectful while denouncing the crimes committed.

It may or may not be important for you to attend the sentencing hearing in order to resolve the effects of victimization, but you do have a right to be present. Other members of the public, including the offender's family and friends, can also be there. If the offender is given jail time, she will be taken away by the sheriff after being given a chance to talk to the defence lawyer. It is an emotional time for everyone. In Canada, it is a significant event when the court deprives a citizen of liberty, so it must be done with the utmost rigour, care, and respect for due process, even if the crimes committed are despicable.

SENTENCING PRINCIPLES

THE *CRIMINAL CODE* SETS out the principles, rules, and limitations of determining an appropriate sentence once a person is convicted.[3] While the *Charter of Rights* guarantees the convicted person the basic right to fair and humane treatment, it also affords the judge a good deal of discretion in determining an appropriate sentence. The sentence should reflect the nature of the crime and the unique character of the offender. The law allows the judge a wide purview to find the right sentence tailored for the particular offender. According to Justice MacKay,

> In measuring sentence, every circumstance should be taken into consideration, and in the exercise of judicial discretion regard should be had to: the age of the prisoner; his past and present condition of life; the nature of the crime; whether the prisoner previously had good character; whether it is a first offence; whether he has a family dependent on him; the temptation; whether the crime was deliberate or committed on a momentary impulse; the penalty provided by the *Criminal Code* or statute.[4]

Legal principles provide the bedrock supporting the judge's exercise of discretion, and some of these are set out in section 718.2 of the *Criminal Code*:

+ A sentence must be proportionate to the seriousness of the offence and the responsibility of the offender.
+ A sentence will be increased or reduced to account for any relevant aggravating and mitigating circumstances.
+ A sentence should be similar to the sentences imposed on similar offenders for similar offences committed in similar circumstances.
+ Where consecutive sentences are imposed, the combined sentence should not be unduly long or harsh.
+ An offender should not be deprived of liberty, if less restrictive sanctions may be appropriate.
+ All available sanctions, other than imprisonment, that are reasonable in the circumstances should be considered for all offenders, with particular attention to the circumstances of Aboriginal offenders.

Precedent and other sentencing issues

BEFORE DECIDING ON A sentence, the judge will hear information about the offender and about you. This process can take several months. There

may be a court hearing to decide the best sentence and the judge could order that a pre-sentence report be prepared to help in decision-making. Lawyers will present cases that show how the courts have previously sentenced
offenders in similar situations, having committed similar acts. Cases from
the Supreme Court of Canada or from the same province as the sentencing
court will be the most helpful references. However, precedent is not the
only factor a judge will consider. In current practice, even when precedent
indicates a particular sentence is appropriate, the judge may consider other
options. If a case presents unique characteristics suggesting that leniency is
called for, the court will err on the side of tailoring the sentence specifically
to the rehabilitative needs of the offender.

In exercising their discretion, judges consider many issues and try to
fit the sentence to the crime. One important consideration is what the law
refers to as "aggravating factors," namely, those circumstances that make
the crime more heinous than it might otherwise be. The *Criminal Code*
stipulates that some of these factors should result in a harsher sentence
than would normally be imposed for that crime. Canadian law considers
sexual abuse of a spouse, a common-law partner, or a child to be aggravating factors, as are sexual offences committed by such figures of authority as
teachers, parents, clergy, coaches, and peace officers. Use of violence, use of
a weapon, injury to the complainant, or the offender having a past criminal
history for the same offence are also aggravating factors. The court considers the offender deserving of a harsher sentence if any of these conditions
prevail.

There are also factors that can lead to less severe sentences. These are
called "mitigating factors" and can include demonstrated remorse for the
crime committed or no previous criminal record. If the offender is under
the age of eighteen, this is also a mitigating factor. Pleading guilty early in
the legal process is a mitigating factor. On the other hand, the court will
not consider defending the charge at trial (and thereby subjecting the victim to the rigours of the court process) as an aggravating factor unless the
prosecution can show that the accused actively ostracized the complainant
from family members and the community as part of the defence.

Maximum penalties are rarely imposed

EACH CRIMINAL OFFENCE HAS a maximum penalty that the court can
impose, and you can find these in the *Criminal Code*. Typically, maximum

penalties are lengthy jail sentences, so judges have significant latitude when deciding a sentence. In practice, they rarely impose a maximum sentence. Conversely, the *Criminal Code* directs that minimum sentences must be applied for only a few sexual offences; these relate to sexual crimes against children, including those involving prostitution. For any sexual offence in which the offender uses a firearm, a mandatory minimum four-year jail sentence is required. When the *Criminal Code* stipulates a minimum sentence for a crime, the offender can have time spent in custody while awaiting trial deducted from the sentence. This remand time is considered "dead time" and counts as double that of incarceration or sentenced time. For example, if an offender who committed a sexual assault using a firearm spends two years in custody waiting for the completion of the trial, the judge can deduct up to four years from the sentence. Thus, if the judge decided that a seven-year sentence is necessary, the offender would be sentenced to three years in the penitentiary even though the minimum penalty is four years.

For any prison sentence without a stipulated minimum length and of less than two years in duration, the judge may direct the offender to serve the time outside of the prison system with restrictive community conditions imposed (see conditional sentences below).

SENTENCING OPTIONS

LAWYERS WILL ALWAYS ASK the judge to consider the individual circumstances of the offender's case. They will argue for a customized sentence, not an "off-the-rack" penalty, as the judge has broad powers to impose conditions. Judges may sentence an adult offender to serve time in prison or may impose a conditional sentence order (CSO), which is a prison sentence served in the community under strict living conditions. With a prison sentence or conditional sentence of not more than two years, the judge may also include probation that applies once the offender leaves prison or completes the CSO. The maximum probation in Canada is three years. The judge may impose monetary fines alone or on top of jail and probation. For those offenders who present a particularly high risk to the public, a special sentencing hearing may take place to declare them either dangerous or long-term offenders. With a dangerous offender designation, the offender receives an indefinite jail term. The long-term offender receives at least two years of imprisonment followed by a maximum of ten years of community supervision.

Perhaps the most straightforward sentencing situation arises when many of the mitigating factors are present. If an offender convicted of a single incident has no previous record, appears remorseful, is motivated to change offending behaviours, and expresses a desire to engage in rehabilitative programs, the judge has some clear sentencing objectives. When a judge is presented with these conditions, it is a straightforward matter to impose a sentence properly reflecting the seriousness of the crime and society's needs. The judge can sentence the offender to time in jail where there is a suitable treatment program and can follow that up with restrictive conditions implemented when the offender returns to the community. Jail time should serve to demonstrate the seriousness of the offender's actions, and provide an opportunity to make positive life changes. Restrictive conditions and supervision in the community should lower the risk of re-offence and help to reintegrate the offender into society.

In the contrasting situation, where authorities consider the offender very dangerous and not immediately amenable to rehabilitation, choices are more difficult. The judge wants to impose a sentence that attempts to keep the offender off the streets while not giving up hope that rehabilitation can occur. Unless given an indeterminate sentence, the offender will return to the community one day. It is in society's best interest to have a prisoner return to the community as a changed, law-abiding citizen, rather than someone with deeply entrenched antisocial behaviour. In this respect, sentencing is a balancing act and a particularly tough one, because some offenders remain in denial and their problems are just not treatable. These individuals remain a high risk to others and may leave the courts no option but to impose long-term restrictive conditions on their lives.

No matter what sentence a judge imposes on a sex offender, there is often outrage by complainants, their friends and family, and members of the public. This is especially true in cases of brutal sexual assaults, but also in cases of less violent assaults committed by people in positions of responsibility or power involving vulnerable people or children. Given the repellant nature of sexual offences and our attempt to be a just, rather than vengeful society, probably none of the sentences legally allowable in Canada will satisfy all people. Sentences will seem either too lenient or too harsh, depending on where your sympathies lie. While acknowledging these legitimate human reactions, we also have to consider that the justice system reflects prevailing societal values. It is a progressive institution attempting to advance our cultural standards, which recognizes that the only real personal protection is each individual's sense of regard for others.

Circle sentencing

AN ALTERNATIVE TO THE justice system approach of dealing with criminals is called "circle sentencing" and comes from a First Nations practice called "talking circles." Indigenous people in North America have used talking circles for generations to resolve individual and community issues. The practice emphasizes living in balance with self, community, and the creator. In a talking circle, an assembled group sits in a circle and each person gets an opportunity to speak about the relevant issue, then the group discusses a solution.

The principles of the sentencing circle are predicated on the belief that when one person injures another it is essential that relationships be healed for future community harmony. Each member of the circle has a role and responsibility, and placement within the circle can be important. There is a keeper of the circle, a group facilitator of sorts, whose role is to promote effective communication. Often elders strategically place themselves throughout the circle to mitigate expressions and feelings of hatred, fear, and anger by bringing the conversation back to a compassionate and meaningful exchange.

When appropriate, the legal system can incorporate this alternative means of justice into the sentencing process. In current practice, the community gives its input regarding the case, but the judge imposes the final sentence. The *Criminal Code* contains a number of sections that apply specifically, and sometimes uniquely, to Aboriginal offenders. While the *Criminal Code* does not refer specifically to circle sentencing, it is an option judges can invoke at their discretion. The judge invites all community and family members to speak in court about the offender, the offence, the impact on the community, and ways to heal the damage. Once everyone has had an opportunity to give an opinion or testimony, the judge passes sentence. The process is quite informal but is a promising example of community participation in the justice system.

Sentencing circles are usually most appropriate when the offender's crime is not likely to result in a jail sentence. Because the *Criminal Code* specifies that jail must be a last resort for Aboriginal offenders, the sentencing circle fills an important need in many First Nations communities. Nevertheless, the court views sex crimes as a very serious matter, and the more forceful or violent an offence is, the more likely the offender will go to jail. This applies equally to both the Aboriginal and non-Aboriginal offender.

If the court does not invoke a sentencing circle, there may still be healing circles before or after the sentencing to assist with community healing. A court may order a healing circle as part of a sentence in cases where it may be a helpful step in rehabilitation of the offender.

PRISON

THE *CRIMINAL CODE* OF Canada is quite clear in stating that imprisonment should be the last resort in sentencing offenders generally; judges should impose a prison sentence only after careful consideration of all other reasonable measures. In making this decision, a judge will place a great deal of importance on whether the nature of the offence calls for a prison sentence and whether the offender appears to present a risk to the public. Even if an offender were likely to benefit from a treatment program available in prison, that condition alone would not be enough to warrant incarceration.

Here are some of the factors specific to sexual offences that a judge uses to determine if jail is necessary:

- The nature and gravity of the offence, including the use of threats, violence, psychological threats, or manipulation
- The frequency of the acts over the time they were committed
- The abuse of trust and the abuse of authority in the relationship of the offender to the victim
- Any mental or physical disorder underlying the offender's behaviour
- The offender's previous convictions including the proximity in time to the current offence
- The offender's behaviour after the offence, for example, confessions, treatment, potential for rehabilitation, and compassion and empathy for the victim
- The gravity of the crime, including physical or psychological injuries caused, age of the victim, nature and extent of the assault, frequency and duration of the abuse, vulnerability of the victim, abuse of authority or trust, and lingering effects

The law considers crimes against children to be particularly abhorrent. A lengthy period of jail is likely where the offender committed sexual assaults against young children over a prolonged period. One can expect a

sentence of four to nine years unless there is a significant intervening period with no subsequent offending. The court would consider this an indication that risk of re-offence is low.

Although there have been cases where conditional sentences have been
ordered in sex crimes against children, it is not the norm. With the passage
of Bill C-2, conditional sentences are not available for sexual crimes against
children because the court is obliged to impose minimum jail sentences
that generally range from either fourteen days (summary offence) or forty-
five days (indictable offence), but can de higher depending on the type of
offence. Crimes requiring a minimum sentence preclude the possibility of
a conditional sentence.

If the sexual assault is one that was committed many years in the past and
there was a delay in reporting, the intervening period between commission
of the offence and the trial may be a mitigating factor. If the offender has
made an effort to become rehabilitated, is no longer considered dangerous,
has dependants, and did not delay the report of the crime by threatening the
complainant, the sentence is likely to be in the lower end of the range and
may even be a conditional sentence. However, this is not always the case. For
example, when there are aggravating factors, or when deterrence and denunciation are important considerations in the case, the sentence may be longer.

Although the law suggests judges should not use a proscribed range of
sentences as a guide, when sexual intercourse takes place (the offence once
called rape), courts continue to suggest a sentence range of two to eight
years. When incest takes place over a period of years, the range is three to
five years, and when serious sexual misconduct takes place, the offender is
facing a sentence in the range of eight years. These sentence ranges can differ somewhat from province to province.

Sentence calculations and parole

HOW FEDERAL OR PROVINCIAL corrections authorities will deal with an offender is not usually a consideration when a judge is calculating a sentence. One
exception occurs when a judge invokes section 743.6 of the *Criminal Code*. This
section provides the court discretion to order that the offender not be released
before serving half the sentence or serving ten years, whichever is less. This section applies to sexual or violent offenders, prosecuted by indictment, who have
received at least two years' incarceration. Denunciation of the crime and deterrence are the governing principles in this section of the *Criminal Code*.

An inmate normally serves one-third of a sentence or seven years, whichever is less, before authorities will consider full parole. Release at this stage is never automatic, but once paroled the offender can serve the remainder of the sentence in the community. Parole may be suspended or revoked if the offender does not comply with release conditions, engages in criminal behaviour, or commits a new crime. After an offender has served two-thirds of a sentence, release on mandatory supervision is generally automatic. This is time earned for good behaviour while in prison. Whether released on parole or mandatory supervision, the offender will be required to comply with conditions set by the parole board. The National Parole Board (NPB) can hold an inmate until sentence expiry if Correctional Service Canada (CSC) recommends it. Authorities will deny release if a detention hearing determines that the offender is likely to commit an offence causing harm or death, a sexual offence involving a child, or a serious drug offence.

Participating in the parole process

IF A SEXUAL OFFENDER is sentenced to a federal penitentiary (a sentence of more than two years), the complainant has certain rights regarding information about the offender, including release dates. A complainant may contact any regional office of the CSC or the NPB to register for notification and information. The complainant may also observe parole hearings and has the right to provide input at certain stages of the proceedings. This right is outlined in the *Corrections and Conditional Release Act* and in the Mission Statements of the CSC and the NPB. The input of the victim will play a role in how and when the parole board chooses to release the inmate.

Visit the Corrections Canada website (www.csc-scc.gc.ca) for further information related to the calculation of sentences for inmates in the federal system (a sentence of more than two years). If the offender received less than two years in jail, and is serving time in the provincial system, contact your local provincial corrections office for details on your rights. For a list of the justice web pages for each Canadian province and territory for your convenience, see Appendix 19.

Prison sentences served in the community

IF THE JUDGE FEELS that a prison sentence is called for but the offender does not pose a danger to the public, the judge may impose what the law refers to as a conditional sentence. Conditional sentences only recently became part of the *Criminal Code* in Canada and are still a controversial sentencing option. Since sex offences are considered serious crimes, conditional sentences are generally not considered appropriate for these offenders. They reflect a philosophy that sometimes justice is best served when an offender is sentenced to a prison term of less than two years, but rather than serving that term in an actual prison, the offender serves it restrained and under supervision in the community. This sentence requires the offender to abide by a number of legally binding conditions set out by the judge. If the offender violates these conditions there will be a hearing in court, and if the violation is substantiated, the offender can be required to serve the balance of the conditional sentence in prison. A judge may use this type of sentence when the offence has no designated minimum prison term and the sentence is of less than two years' duration. Any *Criminal Code* sexual offence sentence can be made conditional, except in the cases of a class of offences against children and youth or sexual assault of any type in which a firearm was used. In these instances, the *Criminal Code* specifies a minimum sentence and the offender does not qualify for a conditional sentence.

Conditional sentences typically involve restrictions on the offender's behaviour. A judge may forbid a sex offender to be in the company of certain people or to be in places that might increase the chance of another offence. Offenders may be required to report in person to an authority on a regular basis and provide evidence that they are successfully self-monitoring their behaviour. Conditions frequently applied are abstinence from intoxicating substances, no contact with children, or a ban from public swimming pools. The restrictive conditions imposed would depend on the nature of the offence and those risk factors pertinent to the offender. The court would formalize these in a probation order or a conditional sentence order.

A good candidate for a conditional sentence is someone who is convicted of a first offence and the offence appears to be at odds with the offender's typical behaviour. On the other hand, those convicted of multiple offences over a period of years are the least likely candidates for this type of sentence. Sentences for offending behaviour between these two extremes are determined based on the offender's particular life circumstances, the nature of the crime, and characteristics of the community where the sentence is being served. Those who have abused positions of authority in committing sexual offences against children or vulnerable adults will have a tougher time convincing a court that they are candidates for a conditional sentence.

Conditions imposed on the offender

UNLESS THE COURT IMPOSES house arrest, offenders on a conditional sentence order are essentially at large and relatively free to move about and do as they wish within the bounds of court restrictions. Behaviour is self-monitored, rather than supervised, so the court must determine if the individual is capable of effectively abiding by conditions without external monitoring. The court must impose some conditions compulsory by law (section 742.3(1)) and has the option to impose others (section 742.3(2)), depending on circumstances of the case. A compulsory condition means the judge has no choice but to impose it; other conditions are at the judge's discretion and are therefore optional. The accused must abide by all conditions of an order, whether they are statutorily compulsory or judicially imposed.

Compulsory conditions require the offender to keep the peace, be of good behaviour, attend court when required, report to a supervisor, remain within the jurisdiction (unless the supervisor provides a written exemption), and notify authorities of any name, address, or employment changes. Optional conditions can require the offender to abstain from alcohol and non-prescription drugs, support any dependants, perform community service hours, or attend an approved treatment program. The court may also impose other conditions (such as a weapons ban) that it considers necessary to secure the good conduct of the offender and to prevent further criminal acts, particularly sex offences.

Under section 732.1 of the *Criminal Code,* an offender can also have conditions imposed through a probation order, which takes effect at the completion of the conditional sentence order. A probation order may be ordered alone as part of a suspended sentence or following a prison term (conditional or otherwise) of no more than two years. A probation order is not a conditional jail sentence, but the compulsory restrictions can be similar, for example, to keep the peace, be of good behaviour, attend court when required, and notify authorities of any change of name, address, or employment. Optional conditions imposed by a probation order can include: to report to a supervisor, not leave an area without permission, abstain from alcohol and non-prescription drugs, abstain from weapons, provide support to any dependants, or perform up to 240 hours of community service hours over eighteen months. The court may also impose other similar conditions it considers desirable for protecting society and for facilitating the offender's successful reintegration into the community. While probation and a conditional sentence are similar, the conditions imposed by a conditional sentence tend to be more stringent and allow authorities to keep closer supervision of the offender.

It is important for the complainant to provide any insights on what conditions would be of help in any community supervision order. Consider what conditions will assist you in feeling safe when the offender is in the community. Two conditions that you may particularly want to consider and talk to the Crown about are no contact with certain named persons or class of persons; and no going to certain named addresses or class of locations. Consider whom you do not want the offender to have contact with and what places (such as your school, work, or home) you do not want the offender going near to. If you do not want to name specific locations, then provide a grid or areas that should be avoided. Complainants often have insights about the unique nature of their community, the offender, or their personal situation that others may not have. If you know the offender, you may be familiar with certain habits, routines, and personal problems. Such insights can potentially help authorities protect you and other community members, so make any suggestions you have to the judge.

You might want to consider what conditions may be appropriate in your case and communicate these to the Crown lawyer, or to the probation officer writing the pre-sentence report. They can subsequently make your recommendations to the court. Below are examples of court-ordered conditions.

- *To monitor the offender*:
  - ▷ Report to corrections officers, police, and court as directed
  - ▷ Live in a designated place
  - ▷ Inform the probation officer of any address change
  - ▷ Surrender passport
  - ▷ Remain within a certain jurisdiction
  - ▷ Report any change of name, employment, or address

- *To protect others from the offender*:
  - ▷ No contact with designated persons or class of persons (for example, children under the age of fourteen)
  - ▷ Avoidance of certain places (for example, named addresses or classes of locations, such as public swimming pools)
  - ▷ No possession of weapons of any sort
  - ▷ No use of the Internet (if pornography or luring others are risk factors)

▷ No passengers in offender's car
▷ No possession of a camera

• *To rehabilitate the offender*:
  ▷ Take such counselling as required by the probation officer
  ▷ Attend an extensive treatment program
  ▷ Abide by any mental health recommendations that may serve to diminish the risk of re-offending
  ▷ Abstain from using alcohol or drugs
  ▷ Avoid places where alcohol is sold or served

Ordering the accused to undergo treatment

THE OFFENDER CAN BE ordered to attend treatment under a conditional sentence or but only under a probation order if the offender agrees to be subject to a treatment condition. The court will want to be satisfied that an offender is able to control the behaviours that increase the risk of re-offending.

Enforcing court orders

IF AN OFFENDER DOES not abide by the restrictions outlined in a conditional sentence order or a probation order, the offender faces the real possibility of being arrested and taken before the court either on new charges (breach of court order) or for a hearing to determine if the offender should remain at large under the original sentence.

The RCMP Behavioural Sciences Unit acknowledges that sex offending presents some unique law enforcement challenges. The nature of sex offending suggests that a productive approach is to have federal and provincial corrections agencies, in conjunction with the police, identify the crime cycles of known offenders. In this way, a proper assessment can identify when a breach of court-ordered conditions is likely to increase the risk of re-offending. Accumulating research indicates that a core group of men in the country is committing the majority of the sexual offences; assessing and monitoring these high-risk, intractable offenders can therefore go a long way to reducing the incidence of sex offending. A key part of this approach is a quick, effective response to breaches of court orders, thereby providing the Crown and the courts with background information to understand the significance of breaches and deal with them appropriately.

SENTENCES WITHOUT PRISON TERMS

MANY SENTENCING OPTIONS DO not include a jail sentence at all; these options include an absolute and conditional discharge, a suspended sentence plus probation, probation only, monetary fines, or a conditional sentence. There can be circumstances where the judge imposes a lenient sentence because, as described earlier, not all sexual assaults are as brutal and sadistic as attacks involving forced penetration; sexual assault can also be grabbing a woman's breast. The severity of an assault will influence the harshness of the sentence. If the offender appears to pose no risk to the public, and the offence does not warrant a prison term, the judge will not impose one.

Monetary fines

THE COURT MAY IMPOSE a fine in addition to, or as an alternative to, a prison term for a sexual offence. The fine limit for a summary conviction offence is $2,000. There are no limits to the amount that a judge may fine an offender found guilty of an indictable offence (which includes sexual crimes); however, there are many rules regarding fines. The key factor a judge must consider is the ability of the offender to pay a fine. When the court imposes a fine, the province then becomes responsible for collecting any money owed, and that money goes into the public coffers.

Restitution

FINANCIAL BENEFITS PAID SPECIFICALLY to the victim by an offender are known in law as "restitution." Restitution is different than a fine; the two are not equivalent under the law. Generally, restitution payments are for property damages and for financial losses when the accused has stolen or defrauded money from you. The nature of your loss in a sexual assault or sexual abuse case is not generally monetary. However, where the offender has inflicted bodily harm on you, the court can order the offender to pay for financial loss including loss of income if such loss can be demonstrated.

Restitution is a matter for the judge to decide and is an issue separate from other terms of the sentence. When the judge makes an order for restitution, it is filed in a civil court and enforced as a civil, rather than a criminal matter. Nevertheless, restitution does not prevent any other civil action that you may wish to pursue. Restitution can also be a condition of the offender's probation order. The advantage is that if the restitution is not paid, this is a violation of a court order and the offender can be charged with breach of probation. In cases of assault against a spouse, the law provides that restitution may include the costs associated with moving the spouse and the family out of the family home to a place of safety.

If the court orders an offender to pay restitution of a sizable amount, this could have an impact on any other punishment given in the sentence. For example, persons ordered to return sizable funds stolen or extorted are less likely to face a significant jail sentence as well.

Surcharges to support all victims of crime

THE *CRIMINAL CODE* OF Canada now requires that all those found guilty of an offence shall pay something for the general support of crime victims. This victim surcharge applies in addition to any other punishment contained in the sentence, and the amount should be 15 percent of any fine imposed. If there is no fine, the amount is $50 for a summary offence and $100 for an indictable offence, although the court may impose a larger amount if it believes more is appropriate and the offender is able to pay more. When the offender can prove hardship, then there is no surcharge, but this is the only exception. The money collected from these surcharges goes into a provincial fund for programs to enhance services for victims generally.

Firearms prohibition

UNDER *CRIMINAL CODE* SECTION 109, the court can prohibit an offender from possessing a firearm for a lengthy period up to a lifetime ban. The order is mandatory when the court convicts the offender of an indictable offence where violence was used, threatened, or attempted and the offence was one carrying a maximum penalty of ten years. The Crown makes an application for this condition at the time of sentencing. For the first offence, the court must prohibit the offender from possessing non-restricted firearms, crossbows, restricted weapons, ammunition, and explosive substances for at least ten years. The possession of prohibited and restricted firearms, and prohibited weapons, devices, and ammunition is banned for life. For a second or subsequent offence, the court must prohibit the possession of all firearms, crossbows, restricted weapons, ammunition, and explosive substances for life.

SENTENCING PROVISIONS TO PROTECT THE PUBLIC

MANY CONDITIONS IMPOSED THROUGH court orders are meant to help rehabilitate the offender and lower the risk of future offending, but some conditions serve a strictly protective function for society.

Providing a DNA sample

THE COURT HAS THE jurisdiction to order offenders, including young offenders, to provide a record of their DNA through samples of bodily substances; these can be hair samples, drops of blood, or swabs of saliva. For sexual offences (with some minor exceptions) the court will routinely make a DNA order when the Crown counsel requests it.

If, at some point in the future, the court-ordered sample matches some crime scene evidence, the police cannot use that sample for their investigation. For example, if ten years after the police have entered an offender's DNA in the data bank, this sample matches DNA recovered from a crime perpetrated by an unknown assailant, the investigators will not use the sample to bring charges. They are required to seek a warrant under a separate section of the *Criminal Code* compelling the suspect to provide another sample. The new sample will then be compared to the crime scene evidence and the results will be used in any subsequent prosecution.

The Crown will not likely tell the complainant about any request for a DNA sample, but you may want to ask about the merits of such an application before the sentencing hearing because afterwards it is too late. A sample in the data bank can be reassuring, as it might prove invaluable to investigators if the offender ever commits another sexual crime.

Safeguards for children

UNDER SECTION 161 OF the *Criminal Code,* the judge may order any offender convicted of sex crimes involving a child to abide by conditions that prohibit contact with children or being in places that children frequent. The courts can prevent offenders from the following:

- Attending a public park, public swimming area, daycare centre, school ground, playground, or community centre where persons under the age of fourteen years are present or can reasonably be expected to be present

- Seeking, obtaining, or continuing any employment (whether or not the employment is remunerated) or volunteering in a capacity that involves being in a position of trust or authority with persons under the age of fourteen years
- Using a computer system for the purpose of communicating with a person under the age of fourteen years

These can be lifetime restrictions, if the judge so orders. If the offender violates the order, authorities can then bring criminal charges that carry a maximum sentence of two years, even if that person did not commit another sexual crime at the time of the breach.

The Crown will likely tell you about any anticipated application for a child protection order, but as with many other issues, you can be proactive and broach the topic before the sentencing hearing. Again, you may have insights or information about your community that could aid the court in making meaningful orders.

The National Sex Offender Registry

LEGISLATION CALLED THE *SEX Offender Information Registration Act*, or *SOIRA*, became law on 15 December 2004 and created the National Sex Offender Registry. The stated purpose of the Act is to help police services investigate crimes of a sexual nature by requiring the registration of certain information.[5]

Section 490.012 of the *Criminal Code* establishes the procedure used by a sentencing judge who orders the offender to report to the sex offender registry. The Crown applies for the order and provides a form that the judge and the offender sign. Upon making the order, the court will inform the offender of this obligation. The following is a case example of a judge explaining to the offender what is required:

> Section 4(2) of the *Sex Offender Information Registration Act* requires you to report to a registration centre within 15 days after the order is made or, if a custodial sentence is imposed, within 15 days after being released from custody. When reporting to a registration centre you must provide, among other things, your name and every alias you use, your address, telephone number for your main residence, any secondary residence, your place of employment and where you may volunteer. Further, you must give your height and weight and a description of every physical distinguishing mark

on your body. If you will be away from your main or secondary residence for more than 15 consecutive days, but still within the country, you must provide every address at which you intend to stay and your departure and return dates.

I hereby direct that a copy of the order be given to JWR [initials of the offender].

If you fail, without reasonable excuse, to comply with this order, you are liable, in the case of a first offence, on summary conviction, to a fine of not more than $10,000 or to imprisonment for a term of not more than six months, or to both; and in the case of a second or subsequent offence, on conviction on indictment, to a fine of not more than $10,000 or to imprisonment for a term of not more than two years, or to both; or, on summary conviction, to a fine of not more than $10,000 or imprisonment up to six months, or both.[6]

The court shall make the registry order unless the offender satisfies the court that there should be an exemption under *Criminal Code* section 490.012(4). The court may permit an exemption if it can be demonstrated that the impact of the order on the offender's privacy and liberty would be grossly disproportionate to the public interest in protecting society through the effective investigation of crimes of a sexual nature, to be achieved by the registration of information under *SOIRA*. The court must give the reasons for requiring registration and the *Criminal Code* governs the duration of an order, which can be from ten years to life. Either the Crown or the offender can appeal any decision made by the judge.

Information about sex offenders goes into a database that is accessible to investigating police officers. The data can also be used for research and statistical purposes when authorized by the Commissioner of the RCMP. Only the offender, the police, the Crown, and the court can give permission to disclose information from the database. Authorities remove information from the database if the offender successfully appeals the order, is eventually acquitted of the offence, or receives a pardon.

Dangerous offenders

THE HARSHEST VERDICT IN the Canadian *Criminal Code* is the finding by a judge that an individual is a dangerous offender (DO). This designation is reserved for the offender who has repeatedly committed offences (including sexual crimes) that have inflicted serious bodily and psychological damage, who is a danger to the life, safety, or physical/mental well-being of others, and who gives little hope for rehabilitation.[7] When such an individual is identified, the Crown may apply to have that person declared a dangerous offender. This very serious designation brings with it a sentence intended, first and foremost, to protect the public.

A dangerous offender can be imprisoned indefinitely, meaning there is no maximum term after which parole must be granted. This is truly life imprisonment, although the law allows the offender periodic hearings after having served seven years, and every two years thereafter. Offenders can go before a parole board to argue that they no longer present a danger and therefore can be safely released. The occasions when this has succeeded are rare. Interestingly, although males get this designation, the court has only declared one female to be a dangerous offender in Canada, but her designation was later overturned on appeal.

Those who repeatedly commit serious sexual offences, including offences against children, are likely candidates for the dangerous offender designation. The process of having an identified offender declared a dangerous offender begins with a local Crown lawyer obtaining consent to proceed from the Attorney General of the province. The Crown then seeks to have the sentencing judge consider the dangerous offender option, rather than following the usual sentencing procedures. A number of preconditions must exist and a series of formal requirements that reflect the seriousness of the application are required. To be declared a dangerous offender, the court must find that there exists a pattern of unrestrained behaviour likely to cause danger; a pattern of aggressive behaviour with indifference as to the consequences of this behaviour; behaviour that is of such a brutal nature that ordinary standards of restraint will not control it; or a failure to control sexual impulses that are likely to result in harm to another. By deeming a person a dangerous offender, the court is formalizing the view that sentencing of the offender will not serve a rehabilitative function but is intended only to protect the public.

During a dangerous offender proceeding, the court must appoint a psychiatrist or psychologist to play a neutral role in assessing and helping to determine the risks and treatment needs of the offender. The accused will have substantial notice of the Crown's intention to apply for this status, and then a formal hearing is convened. The court will hear and weigh evidence from both the Crown and the accused, including evidence of the offender's behaviour associated with both the current offence and prior offences (see Appendix 20 for sentencing options).

Long-term offenders

THE *CRIMINAL CODE* PROVIDES a designation for repeat offenders who do not meet the criteria of a dangerous offender; the law classifies them as long-term offenders (LTO). When an offender has repeatedly committed sexual offences and appears likely to do so again, but is someone whom authorities feel they can control in the community, the Crown can make an application for a long-term offender designation. Alternatively, the court may apply this designation if it is not satisfied that the Crown has met its onus in an application for a dangerous offender designation and instead finds the offender to be a long-term offender. The court has recourse to this finding if there is substantial risk that the offender will re-offend, there is reasonable possibility of controlling that risk in the community, and it would be appropriate to impose a sentence of two years or more for the offence.

To represent a substantial risk, the offender has to be convicted of one or more of the offences that appears on a list of designated sex offences and must show a pattern of repetitive behaviours, of which the index conviction is a part, suggesting a likelihood to cause injury, psychological damage, or death to other people. The court has the discretion to apply the long-term offender designation if the offender's conduct in any single sexual matter, including the current offence, gives reason to believe the offender will cause injury or pain to another person, or commit other crimes in the future through similar conduct.

When designated a long-term offender, the individual receives a sentence that is a minimum two-year custodial sentence plus a period of community supervision that can be up to ten years. Therefore, the total potential sentence can be twelve years. Contrast this with the three-year maximum term of community supervision in a probation order for sentences less than two years. Although the court imposes the length of the community supervision, parole personnel determine the conditions of that supervision. There are cases in Canada where men who have been declared long-term offenders are on stricter living conditions in the community than they would be in prison. Community conditions can amount to house arrest with an escort at all times while in public.

Dangerous and long-term offender applications are extreme and rare procedures in Canadian courts. When they do occur, the defence will aggressively oppose them because the consequences are so grave for the offender. Of course, the Crown will be equally adamant in supporting the application because the risk to potential victims is serious if a dangerous person is freed. Arguments during these hearings are typically intense. Some see these measures as progressive and necessary while others feel they are harsh and a violation of human rights.[8] This intense polarization of opinion perhaps explains why the dangerous offender designation is infrequently made. Far more common are the cases where the court perceives a reasonable likelihood that the offender can go on to have a productive and crime-free future once a sentence is served.

The Crown may call victims of past sexual crimes to testify in a dangerous or long-term offender hearing, when the offender has acted out again and is being sentenced for new, unrelated offences. This could be many years after the victim thought that legal action was over and that neither a courtroom nor the offender would ever have to be seen again. The call to testify anew can be very troubling and can often stir up disturbing memories. Testifying at these hearings may be essential for the Crown's case and we encourage victims in this situation to speak with the Crown counsel about ways to present evidence using accommodations or by negotiated admissions that could avoid their having to appear in person at a hearing.

When the Crown applies for a dangerous offender designation, there are a number of sentencing options available to the court, and a full outline of these options is available in Appendix 20.

THE COMPLAINANT'S ROLE IN SENTENCING[9]

ALTHOUGH YOUR ROLE THUS far in the legal proceedings may have felt peripheral and restricted by courtroom procedures, the court views the victim of a crime as having a distinct and personal contribution to make in the sentencing and parole process. Incidental to this purpose is the potential to assist complainants to regain some lost control over their life. Taking an active role in the sentencing hearing can alleviate some of the frustration and detachment that often arises during criminal proceedings.

One way the courts have sought to achieve this goal is through the victim impact statement (VIS). Parliament amended the *Criminal Code* in 1988, which formalized the use of the VIS as part of the sentencing process. Section 722 of the *Criminal Code* allows victims to describe, in writing, the harm done to them or the losses suffered as a result of the crime. Initially, the court only considered a VIS when determining a sentence, but Bill C-41, proclaimed in September 1996, now requires the court to make use of the VIS. Initially, the VIS was not admissible in youth court, but in

December 1995, Parliament proclaimed Bill C-37, allowing the use of a VIS in youth court as well as ordinary court.

Through the VIS procedure, the complainant can help the offender, the lawyers, the judge, and the broader community fully understand the impact of the crime. The VIS is an opportunity to tell the court directly about the harm done by the crime, to ask for restitution, or to express concerns about community release of the offender. Statements by victims at this stage of the proceedings vary enormously. They can be in the form of letters, recordings, poems, or verbal expressions of pain, loss, and anger. Judges hear a range of sentiments including cries for harsh justice, appeals for leniency, and expressions of forgiveness. The law also allows statements from people, other than the victim, whom the crime has affected, typically family members, friends, relatives, or employers. To see a more formal account of the complainant's role in sentencing, as outlined by the Ontario Superior Court of Justice in *R. v. Gabriel*,[10] please refer to Appendix 21.

While it is mandatory for judges in criminal cases to make use of any VIS before sentencing, the option of preparing one is up to you. If you prepare a statement, you then have the opportunity to read it aloud in court for everyone to hear, but again this is not mandatory; it can be submitted by the Crown lawyer. This quote from Professor Wayne Renke helps us understand the importance of the VIS:

> The victim impact statement provisions of the *Criminal Code* presuppose victims' rights. These are not rights to vengeance, to the destruction of the offender, to negation of the offender's rights. The rights are to participate, to have a voice, to ensure that the real effects of the crime are not elided by professional talk. Fundamentally, the right claimed by victims is that they not be forgotten.[11]

In some circumstances where the judge seeks to ask you questions, or a dispute arises, the court may ask you to testify and the defence can cross-examine you based on your statement. For example, if the court considers it to be "in the interest of justice" and you are "reasonably available" the judge can require that you testify about the statement. We address some of these issues below.

Submitting a VIS

THE *CRIMINAL CODE* DESCRIBES a victim as a person to whom harm has been done, or who has suffered physical or emotional loss, due to a criminal offence. If you are such a person, you are permitted to submit a VIS. You can prepare the VIS on your own, or someone else can prepare it on your behalf. If you are having difficulty describing, in writing, how the crime has affected you, a friend, family member, or a victim services worker may assist you. If the victim is too ill to make the statement, relatives often take up the role. Where a victim has not survived an attack, the survivors — the parent or guardian, spouse, dependant, or other close relative — may prepare the victim impact statement. In this case, the court considers these relatives to be victims of the crime as well.

When you complete the VIS, the procedure for submitting it varies slightly from province to province and in the territories. Depending on local procedure, the police may give you a VIS form that you can fill out or they may refer you to a victim services agency where someone can guide you. When you have finished your statement, sign every page and attach the VIS pages to a dated cover page, and then mail, fax, or deliver it to the Crown counsel's office. The Crown may forward your completed VIS to the judge at the time of sentencing or may use the information you provide to tell the judge about the impact of the crime on you. You can add further information about the effects of the crime by giving a signed update to the Crown counsel or the Crown Victim/Witness Services after the conviction and prior to the sentencing or a review board hearing.

The Crown will either file the VIS with the court or ask you if you would like to present your statement orally. If you feel the need to make a personal statement in the courtroom, it might prove to be an important part of your healing. At the time of sentencing, the accused is now the offender and neither the offender nor the defence can intimidate you as long as you follow the guidelines given to you by the Crown. The court allows you to be emotional in your presentation; the VIS can and should include details about any pain and suffering resulting from the crime, including the long-term impact.

Will the offender have access to the VIS?

THE CROWN COUNSEL MUST provide a copy of your statement to the defence counsel or to the offender prior to the sentencing hearing. The offender will have access to it, since it is part of the information considered at the sentencing hearing. The offender (through the defence counsel) may question you about your statement.

New information

IN THE PROCESS OF preparing a VIS following conviction, a victim may recall new crime details or information that was not in the police statement. When criminal charges are laid, the Crown must provide all available evidence to the defence before the trial begins. If your VIS contains new information relevant to the case, information that is inconsistent with the evidence, or suggests an aggravating factor, the Crown must present this information to the defence. This is not the purpose of a victim impact statement; do not use a VIS to add more details about what happened to you. New evidence provided through the VIS will either be excluded or could take the case in a new direction. The defence might make an application to have the trial reopened following conviction on the grounds that the Crown did not disclose all the evidence. Once a victim adds new crime details, the Crown has no choice but to deal with them. Be mindful of this and realize that if you have more facts to give, provide them immediately through the proper investigative channels. The proper process for dealing with new information would be to go back to the investigating officer, or to tell the Crown (who may send you back to the police for another statement).

One way to avoid some of these evidentiary pitfalls is to have a copy of your police statement and/or transcript in front of you when you write your VIS. This will remind you to stay within the parameters of the case that successfully led to the finding of guilt. You can discuss your concerns about the content of your statement with the Crown. We reiterate that the Crown has a duty to provide all relevant information, so any discussions may have to be communicated to the defence and spoken about in court.

Editing, withholding, or sealing the VIS

VICTIM IMPACT STATEMENTS BECOME part of the official record of a crime, so they must meet certain legal requirements in order to be admissible. Your statement must only address the offence in question and must describe the effects that the offence had on you. Many statements stray off course and contain criticisms of the legal system, and while these concerns may be justified, this is not the place to air them. Judges really need to know how the crime, not the system, affected you. The Crown may edit the VIS so that it complies with the necessary rules to make it admissible. Ideally, the Crown will consult with you first so there are no surprises if changes are made. You should also be prepared to see your VIS withheld completely if the Crown believes it contravenes the legal requirements. Rather than file your document, the Crown may incorporate some of the content into its submissions. If the Crown does not edit the VIS, and the court finds it contains material that is irrelevant or prejudicial, the court may refuse to admit it or consider it in sentencing.

Predicting the judge's reaction

HOW THE JUDGE WILL react to your statement is not always easy to predict. The judge does not want to hear what sentence the offender should get; the judge makes that decision based on multiple sources of information, and your statement is just one of those. Your statement will be most effective if you focus on the task of informing those present about your personal experiences and suffering. The judge will then have valuable material to work with when articulating an appropriate sentence. The law encourages the use of victim impact statements and expects your participation in the process to be positive. As one Ontario Supreme Court stated in *R. v. Phillips* (1995),

> My experience has not been that victims wish to monopolize the sentencing process; they merely want to be able to participate in it in a meaningful way.[12]

Other uses of the VIS

THE INFORMATION IN YOUR VIS can be used in ways you might not anticipate, so it is important that your statement be thoughtful and accurate. The VIS could be used to assist the court at bail hearings (if the offender subsequently breaches court orders). This may be especially relevant if you have indicated that you do not wish the accused to have contact with you. National or provincial parole boards or individual parole and probation officers may also use your statement to help decide conditions of the offender's release.

The VIS and civil litigation

YOU SHOULD BE AWARE that your VIS could become evidence in civil litigation if you decide to go that route. When you prepare your statement, you may not be planning to proceed with a civil lawsuit, but you should write it with that possibility in mind. The guidelines for submission in civil court are the same as in criminal court. A good strategy to cover all these eventualities is to write the VIS as accurately as possible with a primary purpose of describing the impact the sexual crimes have had on you and your life.

PREPARING A VIS

ALL THE RULES AND guidelines discussed above can make you feel that your VIS will be limited and perhaps ultimately unimportant; be assured this is not the case. It is important for both you and for the criminal justice system to have these statements become part of the court record. Yes, there are constraints — you may feel you are not be able to tell the whole story, or the words do not express the depth of your emotional experiences, but there are those who will never be able to muster the strength to make any sort of statement. The expressions of pain, suffering, and life change must go on record if the justice system is to continue changing in a positive direction. Tell the story in your own words, in a manner that is comfortable for you, follow the guidelines, and do your best to educate society about the impact these offences have on individuals and their communities. Do not try to conform to some imagined legal format, but do be mindful of the guidelines.

Your statement is not the place to make complaints about the handling of the case or to offer opinions on the offender's character or on the justice system. The information in a VIS should accurately describe the harm done by the crime. You can refer only to the impact of the crimes for which the offender was found guilty. You should give details of the physical, emotional, medical, and financial effects of the crime on you. You can explain how it affected your relationships with others. You can talk about your losses. Your statement can be a factual account or may speak directly to the offender in the form of a letter. Some victims write a poem and the court will consider this with the same gravity as a prose statement as long as you follow the guidelines.

A case example

THE FOLLOWING ARE SOME excerpts from an authentic and recent victim impact statement. The VIS you will read below was written by a young mother who endured ongoing physical abuse and eventual stabbing by her spouse. This was not a sexual assault. We have deliberately avoided using the example of a VIS for a sexual assault case because we want to demonstrate some important writing principles without unduly influencing, by example, those who have yet to write their statements.

This wife and mother wrote her statement with passion and grace, eloquently describing the cycle of abuse and fear in her marital relationship. In her statement, you will see reflected courage, strength, and the responsibility taken for her own healing. We have omitted any names to protect the victim and her family. She has since recovered remarkably from her ordeal and we thank her for sharing it with us and for giving us permission to share it with you.

Emotional damages

In this excerpt, you will see how the statement gives us a vivid emotional picture of life with her abusive husband:

Example:

The impact of this crime on my life has been phenomenal. Before that date, I lived precariously between two lives. The one life was intense mutual love and adoration between the offender, myself, and our children. The other life was lived in trepidation of when the offender would next explode, and what the consequences would be.

My fears were well-founded. I became accustomed to physical assaults, uncontainable eruptions of violence, and threats on my life, person, and possessions. I became familiar with bone-chilling dread when suddenly, out of nowhere, the offender would plunge into wrathful tirades ....

Somehow, I managed to survive on a tightrope, and refined numerous techniques to do so. But I knew the tightrope could hold my weight for only so long ....

Emotional reactions to any significant event are very personal and unique. Do not assume that people will understand how you feel and similarly do not be afraid to report strong emotions that you think are unusual or "wrong." When it comes to emotional experience there is no wrong or right; take ownership of what you feel and do not hesitate to share it in an authentic way.

Example:

I face very real fears. Recurring nightmares confirm the past is still in my blood, and warn me the danger may never vanish .... The nightmares don't

happen a lot, but occasionally I wake up with a start in the same early morning hours, trembling and stiff with dread, bracing myself. It may take a
long time for these recollections to exhaust themselves.

Physical injuries

While a crime can cause physical, emotional, or financial harm, the degree
of physical harm done to the victim is an aggravating factor the judge will
consider. Assessing seriousness of the offence for sentencing purposes will
include physical damages inflicted.

Example:
I sustained five stab wounds, and scar tissue remains a problem. I sustained
several hospital wounds from the surgery, including a tracheotomy, lung
incision, and abdominal incision. I have continued weakness in my left
vocal chord, right lung, and diaphragm. I am on a program of therapy to
bring all of them back to their original strength. Part of the physical healing has been in the central organs — the stomach, spleen, and colon were
all affected by the injury to the lungs and diaphragm, though symptoms
did not occur for about ten months — a typical delayed reaction with
internal organs. Healing has progressed well through almost two years,
and has been successful due to alternative medicine, naturopathy, Shiatsu
therapy, and acupuncture. I am on a strict herbal regimen to bring balance
back to my body, and it is working.

Financial repercussions

Information about financial loss serves two purposes. For many offences, the
amount of financial loss speaks to the seriousness of the crime and can further assist the judge in deciding an appropriate sentence. As well, information about the financial loss, depending on the circumstances and the type
of case, may permit the judge to make an order that the offender repay the
victim for those losses. The judge in a criminal case is more limited in making such orders than the judge in a civil law suit is, but a criminal court can
order restitution or make probation orders that include payment of losses,
such as income, insurance deductibles, medical costs, counselling, moving
expenses, food costs, childcare, transportation, and property damages.

Example:
Though my work colleagues were understanding and supportive, and
lavished me with gifts and goodwill during my convalescence, I couldn't

work for two months. While I still had bandages on my neck and lost 60 percent of my voice, I had no choice but to resume work and meet demanding deadlines as quickly as possible. For the next six months it was difficult to carry on telephone conversations, but this did not affect my work so it had little impact on my income. I was very lucky.

Our old apartment had to be instantly vacated and I had to search for a new place to live. The vacancy rate in our city during this time was about 0.7 percent, and 2-bedroom apartments were going for between $1400 and $1800. Nothing was available in our neighbourhood. In the midst of intense emotional trauma, I had to find a way to mother two children on my own, support them financially, help them heal, and find a new home. We had no choice but to leave the city for more reasonable living quarters in a new town. This was a huge upheaval for us. Fortunately, my extended family provided immense support and help in looking after the kids and making the transition manageable.

The greatest challenge since the crime has been stick-handling in a sticky situation as the children's co-parent. All of the offender's possessions are still kept in our home, and the kids have photos of the offender on their bedroom walls. Through a separate cell phone, I finance the children's daily communications with the offender. I rent a mailbox so they can exchange letters. I drive them to the Detention Centre so they can visit regularly (this trip takes an average of four or five hours total depending on traffic), or pay a friend to do it for me. Though absolutely critical for the kids, it is emotionally draining for me. I also pay the children's allowance so they can finance the offender's canteen.

Safety and security

The court will want information that may be relevant to your safety and security. When it comes time to consider release from prison, community supervision, parole, or probation orders, the court will consider your need for protection and may be able to implement measures to reduce your risk of further harm.

Example:
The offender may never understand these feelings of terror, but they are based on [a history] of bruises, broken teeth, cuts, rashes, screams and tears. How can I be sure that he will not once again spiral into a mania or psychosis and find a way to hunt me down? If there is one constant theme

throughout all these episodes of rage, mania and psychosis — including the stabbing — it is unpredictability. I had no clue when anything would happen, and he always caught me completely off-guard. This is what my fear is based on: his rage and actions are unconnected with reason or reality.

In real terms, here's what this means to me.

I will have to hope he does not find out where I live. How can I do that when I am co-parenting the kids? I cannot expect the kids to be more loyal to my safety than they are to the offender.

I will have to find ways of protecting myself if and when I accompany the kids when they see the offender. I have no idea how to do this. As I said, unpredictability is the problem here.

History teaches me that the offender considers anyone else in my life a threat. Anyone could trigger rage. Anyone I speak with may be considered a potential lover and rival, and may well be at risk of this unpredictable wrath. Under what obligation am I to protect these innocent people, and under what risk am I that they might seek me for damages if something does happen?

You could say I am now living a different kind of tightrope, but I certainly hope it does not go back to that. I want to live in peace. With a very good counsellor, I am working through all the basic psychological wounds and struggles so I can live my life free of fear and based on love and faith.

I cannot take signs from a future I have not yet seen. I can only take signs from the past and protect myself as best I can ....

What not to include in a VIS

THE COURT WILL NOT lengthen the sentence based on the recommendation of the victim. While you may be justifiably angry about a system that did not protect you from the initial offence, or frustrated with the treatment that you received throughout the investigation and trial, we discourage you from including your comments about this injustice in your victim impact statement. Similarly, although you may be enraged, you must not suggest the amount of time that the offender should spend in jail nor call the offender names. Instead, you should write about the impact of this crime with as much passion as you can muster and focus that passion on producing an accurate, heartfelt account of how the crime has affected you. In the end, this strategy will provide a clearer insight regarding how the offender's behaviour impacted you, and your VIS will consequently be more effective as a court document than one filled with invective.

Victim impact statements should *not* contain the following:

- Any recommendation for a sentence (such as "he should go to jail for a long time") unless
  - ▷ The court specifically asks for one
  - ▷ An Aboriginal sentencing circle is considered
  - ▷ It is part of the prosecution's submissions where the victim seeks leniency
- Any psychiatric diagnostic terms to describe the offender (such as "he is a pedophile")
- Criticism of the offender (such as "he is a loser")
- Information about the offender's record
- Facts of the offence
- Suggestions that the offence is more serious than the charges indicate
- Writing for a child victim as if your words are the victim's

For a checklist to guide you in preparing your victim impact statement, please see Appendix 22.

PREPARING FOR SENTENCING

IF YOU WANT TO attend either the sentencing hearing or the actual delivery of the sentence (which may be on two different dates because sometimes the judge needs time to consider sentencing options), let the prosecutor know that you plan to be there and where you are in the courtroom before proceedings begin. Try to sit nearby in the public gallery so if the Crown wants to ask you a question, you are readily accessible. Ask the Crown what you should do if there is something important to add during the hearing as you sit and listen. Usually, the formality of most courtrooms does not allow you to interrupt and you must wait for a break to speak to the Crown about any issues that arise.

The emotional features

YOU MAY HAVE WAITED a long time for the court to pass a sentence; it may have been years of waiting for you. You have likely built up expectations about the sort of sentence you think will bring justice and perhaps closure. Although you may have expectations and desires for a particular sentence, you do not have any control over what the sentence will be. You perhaps contributed a VIS at the sentencing hearing, but your voice may not have the desired impact on the type or length of sentence the offender receives. While the sentencing may be extremely important to you, you do not know what the outcome is going to be, so you will be unable to predict if you will feel good about sentencing or just plain horrible.

After the judge sentences the offender, if you are in the courtroom you may feel a wide range of emotions. You may feel relief, or a sense of safety, but you may also feel disappointed, angry, or depressed, particularly if the offender is someone known to you. When the judge passes a sentence, the case has ended. It is not appropriate to try to talk to the judge after this. Do not count on the Crown counsel to provide the emotional supports you need; you must turn to others. You may want to hug family members, or tell someone how you feel. It is natural to have hopes and expectations for a particular outcome, but you will have to accept whatever result the process brings.

You should prepare yourself for the full range of outcomes. It is helpful to have a trustworthy support person with whom you can talk through your feelings as the time draws near. You might arrange in advance for a session with your counsellor to work through any emotional reactions following sentencing. Organize an activity with family or friends, or arrange a culturally significant gathering like a drumming ceremony to fill your day once you leave the sentencing hearing. You can refer to Appendix 23 for a more complete checklist of preparations for the sentencing hearing.

In most cases, the sentencing means the end of the case and the end of your role in it, but it can also mean the end of the personal support systems established to see you through the legal process. Sentencing can also mark the end of the attention focused on you. This is particularly true if you have been communicating with the media and your opinions have been sought after. You may feel some relief but also emptiness and the loss of an important motivating force; the challenges and stimulating forces are gone. Some complainants continue legal action through the civil courts (an option explored in the next chapter) while some may direct their energy toward advocacy work (see Chapter 11). Regardless of the path taken, for many, their legal experiences can start a psychological and self-development journey that will continue for years.

SENTENCING AND CLOSURE

REGARDLESS OF THE SENTENCE given to the offender, not everyone in the community will feel vindicated or relieved at the end of the trial. Some may want harsher jail sentences than the law provides, believing that this is the only way to punish the offender adequately. Sometimes even the offenders feel that they have gotten off easy. On the other hand, for some offenders, an order for counselling may be more onerous than time in jail because it means having to face the harsh reality of what they have done. With the exception of horrendous crimes that demand maximum penalties, the elements that constitute an appropriate sentence are complex and elusive. For some offenders a lengthy jail sentence exposes them to harsh treatment by other offenders in jail. Rather than bringing about insight regarding their victimization of others, it mostly brings anger and pain. Some will leave prison no better off and perhaps more dangerous than when they went in. For other offenders, it takes years in jail along with the guidance of others (sometimes another prisoner) before they fully appreciate the suffering they have caused.

Sentencing, no matter how creative or harsh, will not always bring closure for those affected by the crime. The pain and suffering caused by the offender's actions will not magically disappear with sentencing. Although some victims feel vindicated by the sentence, others feel demeaned. They see no parity between the offender's sentence and their own suffering. One thing a sentence does do is signal the end of this stage of the justice system proceedings, but perhaps not the end of the case.

Once the sentencing is completed, there may still be some challenges, such as appeals and perhaps parole considerations, but remind yourself of the good news: you have accomplished the goal of bringing an offender to justice. All the ways you have put your life on hold in order to deal with the legal proceedings have paid off and you can now give your attention to other important matters. This may not happen right away, and depending on the outcome of your case, you may need some time to adjust. Nevertheless, now is the time to shift your focus from the past and the harm you experienced, to the present and the future. Ideally, your healing journey is something you will continue, following a distinctly personal path to recovery and growth. You might already feel that the challenges you faced and the coping strategies you learned have helped you change for the better. If so, you may be particularly interested in those possibilities for continued growth and transformation that we explore more fully in the final chapter of this book.

VIGNETTE NINE: SENTENCING DISSATISFACTION

THE TEACHER DESCRIBED IN Vignette Nine received a nine-month jail sentence but her victims, Mary and Elizabeth, were both dissatisfied with the sentence for different reasons. Mary, who had participated in the trial and told her story, despite the emotional difficulty it caused her, felt that the judge gave the teacher a lenient sentence. She thought, since the teacher was female, she got off easier than a male teacher would have. She also felt the court minimized the impact that the teacher's behaviour had on her, despite hearing her victim impact statement. On the other hand, she felt good that she was able to face the courtroom challenges and that she had confronted her abuser. Even if the victim impact statement had not influenced the judge in the way Mary had hoped, it outlined for the teacher the impact that her behaviour had, and this was important to Mary. She carefully prepared her statement explaining in detail all the emotional and social consequences of the teacher's abuse. This statement allowed her to confront the teacher in a manner that would not have been possible on her own.

Elizabeth was also disappointed with the teacher's sentence but her feelings were different than those of Mary. Elizabeth was particularly angry that the teacher was not held accountable for taking nude photos of her; she was plagued by the idea that the nude pictures of her could be widely dispersed and could surface at some time in the future. Some of Elizabeth's anger was directed at herself for not testifying at the trial. After the sentencing hearing, she learned that the judge could have considered the taking of photos to be an aggravating factor in the case, particularly if the pictures were to be used for sexual purposes or for distribution. Elizabeth's testimony about the photos might have therefore resulted in a stiffer sentence. Elizabeth was also angry that the Crown did not explain early in the process that she was essential to this part of the case. She was also unaware that the Crown would have to tell the defence that a witness had refused to come forward. When Elizabeth refused to testify, the defence then knew the case for the aggravating factor of taking photos (a more serious circumstance) was weak and would consider this circumstance in plea negotiations.

ENDNOTES

1   *R. v. M.(C.A.)* (1996), 105 C.C.C. (3d) 327 at 368 (S.C.C.).

2   *R. v. Gladue*, [1999] 1 S.C.R. 688 at para. 71, on appeal from the B.C.C.A.

3   See *Criminal Code*, s. 718, which describes the fundamental purpose of sentencing and the objectives in imposing sanctions on an offender.

4   *R. v. Willaert*, [1953] O.R. 282, 105 C.C.C. 172, 16 C.R. 138 (C.A.), MacKay J.A.

5   *Sex Offender Information Registration Act*, S.C. 2004, c. 10, s. 2 [*SOIRA*].

6   *R. v. R.(J.W.)*, 2005 BCSC 75 at paras. 146–48.

7   Section 752 of the *Criminal Code* includes a list of sexual offences deemed to be serious personal injury offences.

8   See the John Howard Society web page for papers related to the issues of the rights of the offenders. Online: www.johnhoward.ca.

9   The authors acknowledge Lee Porteous for her input in this part.

10 *R. v. Gabriel* (1999), 137 C.C.C. (3d) 1 (Ont. S.C.J.).

11 Wayne N. Renke, "Flappers to Rappers: Criminal Law in 1921 and 1996" (1996) 35 Alta. L. Rev. 80.

12 *R. v. Phillips* (1995), 26 O.R. (3d) 522 (Gen. Div.).

Seeking Compensation

Vignette Ten

At the age of nine, Ralph was removed by child protection authorities from his family home and placed in the foster home of a respected businessman, his wife, and two other foster children. Within six months, the foster father began touching Ralph's genitals and performing fellatio on him, while wearing women's underwear. By the age of eleven, Ralph was frequently running away from the foster home. He tried to tell his social worker about the abuse, but at that time (1978), authorities dismissed Ralph's account as bizarre and unbelievable, and kept returning him to the home. After attempting suicide at the age of thirteen, Ralph was permanently removed from the home. He then lived in several other foster homes until he was able to live independently at the age of seventeen. Thirty years later, Ralph attended an alcohol treatment program to deal with his long history of addiction. During treatment, he was able to talk about his abuse and he learned how the sexual abuse might have contributed to his anger, relationship problems, and substance abuse. His therapist suggested the possibility of suing the offender to obtain compensation for the harm caused by the abuse. Ralph met with a lawyer who agreed to take his case. In researching the case, the lawyer discovered that the foster father had moved to another province where he had been criminally charged and convicted for sexual offences in that province. Ralph's civil lawsuit was commenced, naming the foster father and the provincial child protection agency as defendants. Three years later, Ralph's case was settled out of court.

IN PREVIOUS CHAPTERS, WE have focused on criminal proceedings as a means to seek justice for sexual crimes, but there are other legal options, or legal "remedies" or "redress," available. Legal redress may provide solace, validation, financial compensation, and a means of financing therapy; or it may provide none of these, depending upon the outcome of your particular case. Whatever redress you may receive from legal actions or crime victim programs, it is not likely to cure or fix your psychological wounds. Healing is something you accomplish on your own, albeit with help and support from others. Legal remedies can help you move along your own personal healing path, and perhaps open up new opportunities for you, but we caution you not to look for *the* solution or *the* resolution to your emotional problems in the courts. To do this could result in your being terribly disappointed or disillusioned, and your healing journey could become sidetracked. We do not want to discourage you from pursuing a legal remedy; we do, however, want you to approach it realistically. We encourage you to consider all your options — criminal prosecution of the offender, civil litigation, as well as other avenues of reparation.

In this chapter, we discuss a wide range of options available for seeking redress or compensation so you can make an informed decision about which path is best for you. We outline the step-by-step process of a civil lawsuit and reviews the differences between the civil and criminal legal systems. You will learn what you can realistically expect to gain or lose in civil litigation, and you will become familiar with some of the legal concepts and language that will be important should you choose to pursue a civil lawsuit. As well, we briefly review other compensation options, such as alternative dispute resolution and provincial crime victim compensation programs. If you have already made your decision to pursue a particular legal approach, the information in this chapter will acquaint you with the process so you will know what to expect and be better equipped to deal with issues as they emerge.

As you read the following section, keep in mind that the information presented here is neither all-inclusive nor meant to be a legal primer. We are not providing legal advice; this must be obtained on an individual basis from a competent legal professional. We provide you with a general overview of civil litigation and other legal procedures that we hope you will find useful. Once you have understood the material in this chapter, you will be in a better position to discuss the important issues with a lawyer and decide what course is best for you.

SEEKING COMPENSATION THROUGH CIVIL LITIGATION

IF YOU ARE TRYING to decide whether you want to bring a civil lawsuit against your offender or others who may be legally liable, the information here should help you make some decisions. If you have already decided to proceed, you will learn what to expect at the various stages of the civil litigation process. Having a better understanding of the process can help you to prepare for the inevitable stresses and avoid some of the potential pitfalls. Being an informed consumer gives you more control within the process itself and more control over your reactions to it.

This is a dense chapter, with a lot of information and terminology to absorb. It is understandable if you feel somewhat overwhelmed. Keep in mind that you do not have to remember the legal language or every point made. Just try to take away the general idea of what you read and become familiar with the overall process, as this will help you make informed decisions when necessary. If you pursue civil litigation, your lawyer should make sure that you understand the process and your role in it. You can revisit this chapter to re-acquaint yourself with the concepts and language and prepare for each stage of the process as it unfolds.

Similarities and differences between civil and criminal proceedings

PREVIOUSLY, WE DISCUSSED IN some detail the workings of our criminal justice system. Although there are similarities between criminal and civil proceedings, there are also some important differences. One straightforward, but potentially confusing difference is that victims of sexual crimes are generally referred to as "complainants" in criminal proceedings and as "plaintiffs" in civil proceedings. Below we highlight some of the more significant similarities and differences between civil litigation and criminal proceedings.[1]

Similarities
*   Both are adversarial processes, in which the goal is to be fair and just to both sides.
*   Both recognize the serious nature of sexual crimes.
*   Both may deter others from committing sexual crimes.
*   The outcome of both may be determined without proceeding to trial (for example, in a criminal case, the court can grant a stay of pro-

ceedings or the accused could plead guilty; in a civil case, the parties can negotiate a settlement).

* Both systems of justice are evolving; past legal precedents and current judicial rulings can affect future proceedings.
* Participation in both by the complainant (plaintiff) is inherently stressful.

Differences

* The purpose of civil litigation is financial compensation for the wronged party (victim of sexual assault) for the harm caused by the wrongdoer (offender). The purpose of the criminal law is to punish individuals who commit crimes (convicted perpetrator).
* A civil lawsuit can be brought against a deceased offender's estate, but a deceased offender cannot be charged criminally.
* Those found liable for the harm suffered by the plaintiff can include institutions and individuals other than the perpetrator of the sexual abuse.
* The burden of proof in criminal proceedings is beyond a reasonable doubt and rests on the Crown. The burden of proof in civil proceedings is less stringent than in criminal law (it is based on a balance of probabilities) and rests on the plaintiff.
* Commencing civil litigation lies at the discretion of the plaintiff (usually in consultation with a lawyer) and the plaintiff has relatively more control over this process than the criminal one. The plaintiff is responsible for retaining legal counsel.
* In some provinces, there are time limitations regarding the period in which the plaintiff can file a sexual assault civil lawsuit. In criminal law, there is only a limitation period for summary conviction offences. There is no limitation period for indictable offences.
* In civil proceedings, either party (the defendant or the plaintiff) can apply to have the case heard before a jury, rather than a judge alone. In criminal proceedings, only the accused charged with an indictable offence can choose a jury, rather than a judge alone.
* The types of hearings and examinations differ.
* A plaintiff's past history, including sexual history, is much more of an "open book" in civil proceedings.
* A wide range of documents, including personal information, will likely form part of a civil case.

- A plaintiff may be assessed by one or more mental health professionals (expert witnesses) to help in the determination of damages due to sexual assaults. In criminal proceedings, a complainant may be seen by medical or psychological experts as part of the criminal investigation to corroborate the complaint.

As you can see, both the criminal and the civil law systems provide some recourse for victims of sexual crimes to hold the perpetrators of these crimes responsible for their actions. Both attempt to balance the rights of the complainant (plaintiff) with the rights of the accused (defendant), both can serve as a deterrent for future sexual crimes, and in both, the offender's behaviour and actions are scrutinized in a public forum. While both systems can result in outcomes that benefit both society and the victim, this, of course, does not always occur. In contrast to criminal proceedings, civil litigation can result in financial compensation for the plaintiff, although this outcome is not guaranteed. On the other hand, civil litigation can have financial costs for the plaintiff that are not incurred in a criminal prosecution.

Both criminal and civil law are evolving, but the law pertaining to sexual assault claims has been changing especially rapidly in the last few years. For example, recent judicial decisions about determining liability have had major ramifications for victims sexually abused while in the care of government agencies or institutions. As we have discussed in earlier chapters, participating in either the criminal or civil justice system is inherently stressful for victims. With these general similarities and differences in mind, we turn to specific details about civil litigation as it pertains to sexual abuse crimes.

What is a sexual tort claim?

YOU WILL FIND THAT most people (including lawyers) talk about sexual assault claims using words, such as "civil sexual assault claims" or "sexual abuse litigation," but since these claims are based in tort law, the term "tort" is the technical legal term used. A tort is defined as "a civil wrong resulting in injury to the person or property of another, for which damages may be recovered."[2] Extending this definition, a sexual tort refers to sexual assaults perpetrated against victims that have resulted in recoverable damages. This means a sexual tort claim is what you pursue in the courts when you are seeking financial redress for damages suffered due to sexual abuse. In this section, we use the word tort to familiarize you with its usage, but elsewhere in the book we use the more familiar term of civil litigation.

Sexual tort claims generally name one plaintiff and one or more defendants. However, multiple plaintiffs assaulted by the same defendant(s) may be part of the same lawsuit, and all the plaintiffs will be named (perhaps with initials as discussed below). For example, many of the First Nations residential school sexual tort claims involve multiple plaintiffs who attended the same school and were victims of assault by sexual offenders affiliated with the school. The legal process, however, will be the same for an individual plaintiff whether a sexual tort claim is filed individually or as part of a multiple-plaintiff claim. This process is described below in some detail. These individual claims differ, however, from class action lawsuits, which also have multiple plaintiffs but use a different process to resolve the legal issues in the claim. We discuss class action lawsuits towards the end of the chapter.

The guiding principle in sexual tort claims is to attempt, as much as possible, to restore plaintiffs to the condition they were in prior to their sexual assault.[3] At the same time, people understand that no amount of money can provide complete restitution to a sexual assault victim. Not surprisingly then, there is considerable complexity, controversy, and disagreement about how to translate this principle into practice. For example, what does it mean to return a sixty-year-old man to the state he was in prior to his being sexually abused from the age of seven until the age of fourteen? Later in this chapter, we return to this central issue of how to determine damages in specific cases.

If you pursue a sexual tort claim, you will have to prove a number of things including the following: that you were, in fact, sexually assaulted; that an identifiable person or persons caused, or materially contributed to, the sexual assault; and that you have suffered injury, loss, or damages specifically due to the sexual assault. The standard of proof used in civil litigation is based on a balance of probabilities, which means that evidence is considered proven when it is judged as being "more likely than not." Literally, this means that the evidence must provide at least a 51-percent degree of certainty, in contrast to the "beyond a reasonable doubt" standard of proof in a criminal case.

Both society and the Canadian courts recognize sexual abuse as representing morally repugnant behaviour. Because sexual abuse allegations are serious accusations of "morally blameworthy conduct," and because victims sometimes file sexual tort claims many years after the abuse occurred, there have been court decisions requiring that the evidence presented by the plaintiff provide "clear and cogent" proof.[4] While this may require tightening the standard of proof in some cases, the evidentiary standard is still considerably lower than that required in criminal cases. This means, for example, that you can choose to pursue civil action even if the offender was acquitted of the crime against you in criminal court. Although an acquittal may weaken your case, a civil court may still award you damages. Most of you will be familiar with the *O.J. Simpson* case in the United States in which the criminal court acquitted Simpson of murder, but the civil lawsuit that followed held him liable for wrongful death and awarded the victim's family the consequent damages of several million dollars.

Why consider filing a sexual tort claim?

IF YOU HAVE SUFFERED damages due to a sexual assault, you have the right to bring a claim for compensation for your injuries and losses, and a civil lawsuit is a reasonable option to obtain financial redress. It is important to emphasize that civil litigation offers financial compensation only. Personal benefits (for example, feeling validated, holding the offender accountable, and experiencing emotional growth as outlined in Chapter 4) may flow from your participation in the process, but this is not the focus of the litigation. Understand that your claim may or may not be successful; the court may disallow your claim for a host of legal reasons that have nothing to do with you as a person. You should not bring a civil lawsuit expecting redress other than financial compensation (for example, an apology). Expecting non-financial redress in civil court can lead to significant distress, frustration, and disappointment. There are legal options besides civil court you can consider to address these other concerns. Those plaintiffs who fare best psychologically are those who take a broad and realistic perspective to litigation.

Although financial compensation is the central purpose of civil litigation, claimants undertake the process for a variety of non-monetary reasons. The following list illustrates some of the reasons, both realistic and not so realistic, that victims of sexual assaults have given for launching civil lawsuits:

- To have the defendant acknowledge that the abuse occurred and damaged the plaintiff. At the heart of this, the plaintiff often is seeking a sincere, meaningful apology.
- To have a judge or jury acknowledge that the assault occurred, and the defendant's actions significantly injured the plaintiff.

- To use the civil court as another opportunity to have the seriousness of the crimes acknowledged and the offender held accountable, because justice was not achieved in criminal court (for example, the case did not proceed to trial, or the offender received a light sentence or an acquittal)
- To hold government agencies or institutions liable, especially if the offender could not be held personally or financially accountable
- To address the unfairness of the offender seemingly doing well in life, while the plaintiff continues to suffer from the effects of the assault
- To be able to finance therapy needed to address the impact of the sexual assault
- To express solidarity and obtain support from others in multiple-plaintiff or class action suits that include others sexually assaulted in related circumstances
- To deter the offender and other potential sexual offenders from sexually assaulting anyone else
- To have a public forum in which to demonstrate how damaging sexual assaults can be
- To bring some closure in the plaintiff's life to the sexual assault experience(s) sometimes after considerable time has passed or after therapy

Clarify your expectations and motivations

YOU MAY HAVE REASONS similar to those above or you may have other motivations for pursuing civil litigation. If you have not thought much about your particular reasons for pursuing a civil lawsuit, take some time to do so. It is important for you to have some understanding of why you do or do not want to take this course of action. For your own well-being, you need to think about how realistic your expectations are. Ideally, you should engage an experienced lawyer who can help you determine the appropriateness of your expectations.

If your primary motivation is to have the offender sincerely apologize for the harm done to you, you should understand that, to date, such apologies have been highly unlikely. In the past, defendants have been loath to offer any sort of apology, as this was typically construed as an admission of guilt, but that may change. The *Apology Act* was enacted in British Columbia in 2006.[5] This Act is the first in Canada to essentially make an apology inadmissible in a court case for the purpose of proving liability. The Act has broad scope, covering apologies issued in private disputes along with statements by governments and legislatures. It is unclear at this time whether this legislation will provide a meaningful impact in sexual abuse cases.

Many civil defendants are unrelenting in their denial of wrongdoing. In some cases, defendants may acknowledge that sexual contact occurred, but not see their actions as being either wrong or harmful. These defendants, therefore, will never apologize in any meaningful way. In seeking an apology, you may be seeking something you are not likely to get. Part of your healing journey may be learning to let go of this hope or expectation and addressing your needs in another way.

If an apology is important to you, and you believe it might be possible to obtain one, you might want to look outside a civil courtroom to achieve this end. There are other means considerably less stressful and less costly than litigation. For example, in the *O'Connor* case, one of the complainants chose to have the former bishop apologize to her publicly in a First Nations healing circle near the community where she grew up. O'Connor himself agreed to this option once there was an agreement that the civil lawsuit would not be litigated further. The safest avenue for the offender may be to offer an apology in the presence of a lawyer because, in that circumstance, legal privilege may attach so that the apology could not be used against the offender in civil or criminal litigation proceedings.

Those who decide to sue the offender in order to promote healing or bring closure to the sexual abuse experience may also be setting themselves up for disappointment. Winning your case and having a judge or jury acknowledge that you have been assaulted and harmed by the defendant can empower you and give you a sense of vindication. On the other hand, if your case is not resolved as you hoped, you may feel that the offender has been vindicated and this may sidetrack your healing. Even if you achieve a positive outcome in court, it can come at such a high personal cost (in terms of time, energy, stress, and finances) that your well-being suffers and your healing is delayed. There are too many unknowns at the beginning of the litigation process to predict how your case will go or how it will be resolved.

As we have underscored throughout this book, it is a mistake to base your healing on the outcome of a legal action. To heal from harmful experiences or trauma, you must assume responsibility for the process. You need to draw on support and assistance, where you can, from family, friends, community, or spiritual sources, but it is important to keep in mind that the process and work of healing does not lay outside of you — it resides within you. If you think that your healing depends upon the offender's apology or a particular legal outcome, you are in danger of staying stuck where you are or regressing in your healing journey.

You will also need to talk about your reasons and motivations for pursuing civil litigation with your legal counsel and others who will examine or interview you during the process. The reasons you have for choosing to sue the defendant can be important to your case. The defendant's legal counsel could attempt to attack your credibility by demeaning your motives for suing. It will help enormously if you are clear about your motives and objectives. Thinking this through at the beginning of the process will enable you to convey your motives clearly, accurately, and sincerely across multiple interviews. As we have emphasized throughout this book, when you speak on the record (in court documents, at your examination for discovery, in court-ordered assessments, or at trial) people will pay attention not only to what you say, but also how you say it, and how consistent your responses are over multiple interviews.

THE FINANCIAL COSTS AND BENEFITS OF CIVIL LITIGATION

COMPENSATION AWARDED IN A civil lawsuit is very much dependent on, and specific to, the facts of a particular case. The court will carefully consider all the accepted facts in your case to determine the amount of compensation you should receive. Prior awards made in a particular province for similar types of damages will be a guide for the specific amount of money awarded in any one sexual assault claim. You can discuss with a lawyer the range of monetary compensation previously awarded in cases similar to yours in your province. This is information that you will need to make your own cost/benefit analysis of engaging in a civil lawsuit.

You will also need to take into account the financial costs of pursuing civil litigation. The cost of an average civil sexual assault trial has been estimated at between $20,000 and $50,000.[6] The primary monetary costs of litigation are your lawyer's fees and the costs of various "disbursements." Disbursements are the funds paid out by your lawyer for expenses incurred in your lawsuit, such as the costs of filing the lawsuit and obtaining typed transcripts or the fees charged by expert witnesses.

You can pay your lawyer's fees in one of two ways: by the hour or on a contingency basis. The latter arrangement is common in civil litigation. If your lawyer takes your case on a contingency basis, this means that you do not pay for your lawyer's time throughout the case. Instead, the lawyer receives an agreed-upon percentage of the money that the court awards you. With this arrangement, you may still be responsible for paying for disbursements. Your damage award may cover the majority of these expenses and provide a nominal amount of funds to offset your legal fees if it specifically includes an award of costs.

It is important to discuss payment of legal fees and disbursements in some detail with your lawyer so that you are very clear about your financial obligations. You have to know what happens if your claim is successful, if it is not successful, or if you decide to stop part way through the process. If you agree to proceed on a contingency basis, you will have to make a commitment to carry through with the case so that your lawyer can be compensated for the work done. If you want to pull out mid-stream, you will owe your lawyer money for work already done, even if you retained your lawyer initially on a contingency fee basis. You should discuss all these issues with your lawyer, and understand all your financial obligations before you embark on any course of action. As we suggest below, it would be to your benefit to ask for a printed copy of the lawyer's fee agreement in order to consider it for a few days before agreeing to its terms, signing forms, or retaining a particular lawyer.

WHEN CAN YOU SUE?

YOU MAY CHOOSE TO pursue civil action immediately after a sexual assault has been committed against you, but you can also bring a suit years after the offence. In some cases, the plaintiff did not commence civil action until forty or fifty years after the abuse ended. However, unlike indictable criminal proceedings, you may not always have an unlimited amount of time to sue the defendant. Some provinces, such as British Columbia, have excluded sexual assault from the actions that must be commenced within a specified period (no limitation period). Other provinces, such as Alberta, do have time limitations. Even where limitation periods exist, certain circumstances may extend this period to some degree. For example, if the sexual abuse took place when the plaintiff was a child, the limitation period will not start until the plaintiff reaches the age of majority or the age at which the plaintiff realized the extent of harm done by the abuse. It is important to check with a lawyer in your province to find out if there are any time limitations in your case. If you do not file your civil lawsuit within the legal time limit, you will forever miss your opportunity to bring your case forward in civil court.

WHOM CAN YOU SUE?

THE MOST OBVIOUS DEFENDANT in sexual assault cases is the person who committed the assault. However, the law can hold other parties legally responsible for the harm you incurred. Several different types of legal wrongs may apply in any one sexual abuse case. Below, we list the major legal wrongs giving rise to liability and to whom the liability might apply in a sexual tort claim.[7]

- *Battery*: Intentional harm caused through bodily contact (for example, sexual assault or childhood sexual abuse); liability attaches to the perpetrator of the physical acts.
- *Breach of fiduciary duty*: Harm caused in a relationship of trust and dependency; liability attaches to the offender in relationships, such as parent and child, doctor and patient, priest and parishioner. Liability may also attach to other individuals, such as non-offending caregivers who failed to protect their child, and institutions with a duty to provide care, such as churches, schools, and government agencies.
- *Negligence:* Unintentional harm caused as a result of a breach of a legally recognized duty of care to individuals; liability applies to individuals or institutions, for example, a childcare agency that failed to appropriately monitor staff that provided direct care to children.
- *Vicarious liability:* Harm caused by employees in the course of their employment when the employee's duties are connected to the sexual assaults in a meaningful way; liability attaches to the employers of the offending employees, for example, a residential childcare facility whose employees sexually assault children under their care or supervision.
- *Breach of rights under the Charter of Rights:* Harm caused when a person's rights or freedoms have been unjustifiably breached; liability

attaches only to people acting as agents of the state, for example, the police were found liable under the *Charter of Rights* when they used stereotypical views of women to justify their decision not to warn women about the potential for sexual assault in a high-risk situation.

We have briefly described the various types of legal wrongs that give rise to civil liability to give you some familiarity with the terminology and the ranges of accountability that can apply in sexual tort claims. It is beyond the scope of this book, and is not likely of interest to most readers, to discuss liability issues in any detail. This is a topic best discussed with your lawyer. In particular, you should ask for an update on liability claims, as this is a rapidly changing landscape in sexual tort cases. For example, there is considerable divergence among various courts across Canada regarding the scope of vicarious liability. Recent decisions from the Supreme Court of Canada have limited the scope of vicarious liability in some sexual assault claims.[8]

In one case, the Court determined that vicarious liability did not apply to a school district in which a janitor sexually abused a child.[9] The Court has also found that vicarious liability did not apply to the government for sexual assaults perpetrated by foster parents.[10] This latter ruling has obvious relevance to some current claims pertaining to sexual abuse while in foster care. If the government is not vicariously liable, the remaining liable defendant (the foster parent) may have no funds to pay a damages award. If you were sexually assaulted in foster care, discuss your case with a lawyer. Different types of liability, including vicarious liability, can apply depending on the circumstances of your case. Furthermore, case law in this area is especially fluid, so there may be further changes that affect your particular case.

WHAT DAMAGES HAVE YOU SUFFERED?

SEXUAL ABUSE CAN CAUSE a wide range of injuries, including immediate physical damage or subsequent medical conditions. If the plaintiff shows that these conditions are a result of the assault, the court can award financial damages. However, there is no requirement that the plaintiff must suffer physical injury in order to receive compensation for a sexual tort. Courts understand that much of the damage suffered by plaintiffs in these cases is usually emotional or psychological.

In sexual tort claims, the primary types of damage awards are non-pecuniary damages, awarded for the plaintiff's "pain and suffering," and pecuniary damages, awarded for past and future income and other economic losses. The courts may also award aggravated damages in cases where the defendant's conduct is particularly malicious, oppressive, or outrageous. Punitive damages, although rare, are damages awarded specifically to punish the defendant and deter others from similar behaviour. As these terms are important concepts, we will review them in more detail.

Non-pecuniary damages

NON-PECUNIARY DAMAGES INCLUDE THE harm that the law recognizes as being inherent to a sexual assault. As summarized in a 2001 report to the British Columbia Law Institute, these damages include "loss of dignity, personal integrity, autonomy, and personhood."[11] The following comments by Justice McLachlin in a civil sexual assault case illustrate the Supreme Court's opinion about the inherent harm in non-consensual touching:[12]

> The tort of battery is aimed at protecting the personal autonomy of the individual. Its purpose is to recognize the right of each person to control his or her body and who touches it, and to permit damages where this right is violated. The compensation stems from violation of the right to autonomy, not fault. When a person interferes with the body of another, a *prima facie* case of violation of the plaintiff's autonomy is made out ....
>
> The law of battery protects the inviolability of the person. It starts from the presumption that apart from the usual and inevitable contacts of ordinary life, each person is entitled not to be touched, and not to have her person violated. The sexual touching itself, absent the defendant showing lawful excuse, constitutes the violation and is "offensive."

Damages awarded for the inherent harm caused by sexual assault are consequently given in the non-pecuniary award in a successful sexual tort claim. Non-pecuniary damages typically also include other specific psychological injuries suffered by a plaintiff, such as depression, suicidal gestures, anxiety, substance abuse, interpersonal problems, or sexual difficulties — the types of difficulties described earlier in this book. Any psychological problems that the court finds causally connected to the sexual assaults (according to legal rules of causation) can be compensated. The court's goal is to provide "fair" compensation for damages that the victim has suffered. Non-pecuniary damages are difficult to quantify, as you will see in the discussion below.

Pecuniary damages

PECUNIARY DAMAGES COMPENSATE THE plaintiff for economic losses due to harm suffered due to the defendant's conduct. In contrast to non-pecuniary damages, "where the goal is to award 'fair' compensation, 'full' compensation is the goal in assessing pecuniary damages."[13] This means that the goal is to return a plaintiff, as much as possible, to the financial position the plaintiff would be in had the sexual assault not occurred. Pecuniary damages may include the following categories of damages:

- Loss of earning capacity, both pretrial and in the future. Since these damages are generally based on prior employment history, they are particularly difficult to determine in cases of childhood sexual abuse, where there is no previous employment history.
- Loss of homemaking capacity, which refers to the "impairment of the ... ability to perform normal household tasks."
- Cost of pretrial and future care, which refers to past or future expected expenses for treating injuries due to tort, including costs of therapy, medication, and educational or vocational upgrading.

Aggravated damages

ACCORDING TO THE SUPREME Court of Canada, aggravated damages should be considered in the following circumstances:[14]

> ... where the defendant's conduct has been particularly high-handed or oppressive, thereby increasing the plaintiff's humiliation and anxiety ....
> They represent the expression of natural indignation of right-thinking people arising from the malicious conduct of the defendant.

As the foregoing suggests, the court intends these awards as financial compensation for victims subjected to particularly malicious, intentional acts by the defendant. The court recognizes that these malicious acts can result in additional damages to the plaintiff's feelings, including "humiliation, indignity, degradation, shame, indignation, and fear of repetition."[15] Aggravated damages may be awarded either as part of the non-pecuniary damages or as a separate award.

Punitive damages

UNLIKE THE OTHER DAMAGES discussed above, the goal of punitive damages is not to compensate the plaintiff, but to punish the defendant for misconduct "so malicious, oppressive and high-handed that it offends the court's sense of decency."[16] Not often is the plaintiff awarded punitive damages in sexual tort cases. If the defendant has already been criminally convicted and sentenced, the court typically considers this to be sufficient punishment.

DETERMINING THE AMOUNT OR "QUANTUM" OF DAMAGES

THERE IS INHERENT DIFFICULTY in determining a reasonable and fair monetary value for the damages suffered in a sexual assault. Non-pecuniary damages are particularly hard to quantify because "pain and suffering" are nebulous, abstract legal concepts. The difficulty is magnified when damages are largely psychological in nature. A British Columbia Court of Appeal decision explains the issue well:[17]

> We are just beginning to understand the horrendous impact of sexual abuse. To assess damages for the psychological impact of sexual abuse on a particular person is like trying to estimate the depth of the ocean by looking at the surface of the water. The possible consequences of such abuse presently are not capable of critical measurement.

How does the court then determine the extent to which a person has suffered "pain and suffering" due to a sexual tort? The primary legal rule of causation is referred to as the "but for" principle. Damages are legally assumed to have been caused by the actions of the defendant if it is proven, on a balance of probabilities, that the plaintiff would not have suffered those injuries "but for" the actions of the defendant (for example, the sexual assault). Consider, as an example, the plaintiff who has Post-Traumatic Stress Disorder (PTSD) due to a sexual assault. If the plaintiff proves that the plaintiff would not have PTSD if it were not for the sexual assault, then the court considers the defendant's conduct to be the cause of the PTSD symptoms.

In many cases, there may be multiple factors that have contributed to the plaintiff's psychological injuries, and the court recognizes that there will be a number of other background events that contribute to the plaintiff's condition. In these cases, the question becomes to what extent did the defendant "materially contribute" to the harm that the plaintiff alleges. The court may award full damages in cases where the defendant's conduct caused part, but not all, of the plaintiff's injuries. In other cases, when the defendant's acts represent one among many other harmful acts, the court will determine to what extent the misconduct of the defendant contributed to the plaintiff's injuries, or made pre-existing conditions worse, and will then apportion damages accordingly.

GETTING STARTED: FINDING A LAWYER

HAVING CONSIDERED THE MAJOR issues above, you might want to further pursue the possibility of civil litigation. The first step is meeting with a lawyer to determine if the evidence available in your case is strong enough to legally support a sexual tort claim. Some small legal claims relating to non-personal injury actions may be simple enough for a layperson to take on without counsel, but civil sexual assault claims are a different matter. Whether the case is heard in a provincial court (for example, small claims court) or in a superior court (the most likely venue), the case will require the skill, knowledge, and resources of a lawyer who is familiar and comfortable with this area of the law. You can get a sense of the complexity of these cases from reading this chapter, but if you want a more in-depth analysis of how challenging this area is for plaintiffs, lawyers, and judges alike, we recommend that you have a look at *Civil Liability for Sexual Abuse and Violence in Canada* by Elizabeth Grace and Susan Vella.[18]

Most of us are acquainted with lawyers primarily through television and the movies. As is typical with such depictions, television lawyers have little resemblance to lawyers who are practising law in the real world. Lawyers tend to be typecast as "sharks" or "shysters," which does little to instill our trust in them. Although there are certainly unscrupulous people practising law (as there are in virtually all professions), it is inaccurate to paint the whole profession with that unflattering brush. Most lawyers will act with integrity, humanity, and competence and will look out for your best interests.

Just as we have advocated putting aside stereotypical views of sexual assault victims, we encourage you to put aside the stereotypes you may have about lawyers. This does not mean that you should automatically trust a particular lawyer to do the best job for you. Always use your discretion;

do not be indiscriminate in whom you place your trust. At the same time, try to be open to giving lawyers (and others) the opportunity to earn your trust. We have already discussed how trust issues can be paramount for some sexual assault victims, and the relationship with your lawyer is one in which trust is particularly important, as you will be relying on your lawyer for important legal advice and counsel. Having a trusting relationship with your lawyer can also go a long way toward reducing stress and helping the litigation process run more smoothly for you.

Although other factors are important, choosing the right lawyer can mean the difference between a successful claim and an unsuccessful claim. Unfortunately, finding a competent lawyer willing to take your case may not be easy. You may have trouble finding a lawyer with the knowledge and expertise specific to civil sexual assault cases, and if you do, the qualified lawyer may not have the time or the inclination to take your case. Sexual assault claims are complex and often difficult cases to prove with variable monetary rewards, for both the plaintiff and the lawyer. We advise caution if a lawyer actively seeks to recruit you as a client, perhaps as a member of a multiple-plaintiff or class action, or appears to have little understanding of the issues. Unscrupulous lawyers over-marketing their services have exploited victims of sexual assaults, including First Nations people abused in residential schools. A law firm in Saskatchewan was recently sanctioned because of these practices.

Where to look

YOU CAN BEGIN YOUR search for a lawyer with suitable experience in some of the standard places, such as your provincial law society (for example, the Law Society of British Columbia or the Law Society of Upper Canada). You can also get recommendations from victim support agencies, or you can inquire of friends who have previously worked with a lawyer. Most provinces have a legal referral service whereby you can call the local law society, which will refer you to a lawyer in your area with the specialty you require. These lawyers have agreed to be part of this service and the initial consultation is either free or only a nominal amount. Getting referrals from someone with first-hand experience in the litigation of a sexual tort claim (such as another plaintiff involved in a civil lawsuit) can be particularly helpful. Although you need to be cautiously selective, you also can refer to the yellow pages of the telephone directory or other advertising as an initial source. Alternatively, you can search the Internet; conducting a web search of a particular lawyer's name or the name of a successful case you have heard about can provide you with considerable information, including the particular lawyer's areas of specialty. Most provincial governments have websites that include information on the court system and court decisions. Combining this initial research with a face-to-face meeting can greatly assist you in choosing the appropriate lawyer for your specific needs.

The right experience

WHENEVER POSSIBLE YOU SHOULD look for a lawyer who has specific experience dealing with civil sexual assault claims. Litigation of these cases presents unique challenges to everyone involved and without specific experience in this area of law, a lawyer may not be able to provide you with the type of legal representation that you need. Furthermore, a lawyer who has some knowledge and understanding of the dynamics of sexual assault is more likely to be sensitive to your needs and less likely to misinterpret your reactions and your experiences. This can go a long way toward helping you develop a positive working relationship. Having a knowledgeable and understanding lawyer can also make it easier for you to openly disclose and discuss very personal information, including in-depth details about the sexual abuse.

The right qualities

IF YOU HAVE CONFIDENCE in your lawyer's competence and experience, the litigation process will be easier and less stressful for you. It will also go more smoothly if you feel that your lawyer treats you respectfully, listens to you, and advocates for your best interests. You will benefit from a lawyer who is up-front with you and can provide you with a realistic assessment of the strengths and limitations of your case. It is also important that your lawyer give you sufficient information so that you know what is happening and what to expect next.

It is particularly important to find a lawyer who will spend sufficient time with you to help you feel prepared to deal with the necessary examinations and the court proceedings. This is foreign territory for anyone without legal training, and this by itself is enough to induce stress. Although this book will acquaint you to some extent with the litigation process, it is not enough. You need an informed, patient, and instructive guide to walk you through the process, consult with you on decisions, and prepare you specifically for the questions you will have to answer and the testimony you will have to give. You need a lawyer who understands the importance of this instruction and who will take the time needed to help you feel prepared at each step in the process.

It is also important to know how available and accessible a particular lawyer will be. Balance your wants and needs for the lawyer's time with the understanding that most lawyers are busy professionals with other cases and demands on their time. If you are interested in retaining a specific person, you can ask how much time she will have to personally deal with your case. In some law firms, you may interact with office staff, legal assistants, or with lawyers other than the one that you retain. In other firms, you may have more direct access to the lawyer that you choose. Knowing how much time you will have with a particular lawyer is another valuable piece of information that can help you decide if a particular lawyer is the right one for you.

Evaluating these various qualities and the competency of a particular lawyer (or any professional) is not an easy task, especially given the short time that you are likely to spend together before you decide to retain either that specific lawyer or a certain law firm. Getting good referrals and checking with the law society is a good way to start your search; then, asking prospective lawyers the right questions will further help you to evaluate whether a certain person is the right choice for you. It is perfectly acceptable to have an initial consultation with several lawyers before you make a decision about which one to retain as your lawyer. We outline below the types of questions and issues you can raise with any lawyer that you might consider retaining.

Obtaining an opinion about the strength of your case

WHEN YOU MAKE A preliminary choice of lawyer and arrange an initial consult meeting, you should bring a list of questions and issues that you want to cover to the meeting (see Appendix 24). As well, you need to bring any documents that are relevant to your claim, and a pad of paper to jot down notes. Because this is a new experience for you and because what you will be discussing with the lawyer is very personal, it is understandable that you might feel nervous or even frightened, so it is advisable to write down any important information, instructions, or meeting dates that you have been given. Prior to going to your first meeting, it is important to ask if there is a cost for this initial consultation and, if so, what the cost will be. Whether or not you formally retain the lawyer, and even if your case does not proceed, the lawyer may bill you for this time spent.

In your initial meeting, the lawyer will review the circumstances of your particular case to determine if it is strong enough, and financially worthwhile, for you to proceed. This will likely include a review of the following types of information:[19]

- Your account of the sexual assault (for example, how much you re-member, or how clear your memories are)
- The source of your memories (for example, whether your recall has changed over time, or whether you have "recovered memories" and if so, how this occurred)
- Your history of therapy or psychological difficulties before and after the abuse
- Witnesses or evidence to corroborate or support your account of the sexual assault (such as a family member who witnessed the abuse, the person you told about the sexual abuse when it occurred, or other victims of the offender)
- The offender's position regarding your allegations and the evidence related to the allegations (for example, a confession, criminal convic-tion, or any institutional records)
- Any evidence that supports your claim of abuse and your damages (such as medical or hospital records, therapy records, or employment history)
- The offender's financial status

After discussing these issues, the lawyer will provide an opinion on whether or not it is worthwhile for you to proceed with a claim. If, in the lawyer's opinion, your case is not strong enough to proceed, or is not worth-while because the offender has no assets, you can then explore other forms of compensation discussed later in this chapter. It is always a good idea to seek another legal opinion, since different lawyers may view the same case in different ways. Each lawyer will have a unique perspective on the facts and may view the chances for success differently.

If you get feedback that your case is not considered strong enough to proceed, try not to over-personalize this. It is not a personal rejection; it does not mean that you are somehow inadequate, nor does it usually mean that the lawyer believes you are being untruthful. The lawyer is only giving you a legal opinion; an opinion about the strength of the evidence as the court is likely to view it and the provability of your case according to the legal requirements. In all areas of law, it is not uncommon to find a gap between what happened in a particular circumstance and what can be proved to have happened in a court of law.

Deciding to proceed

IF THE LAWYER BELIEVES that there is sufficient evidence to proceed with your claim, you then need to make some decisions. Lawyers experienced in dealing with sexual torts will likely ask you some specific questions to help them gauge your physical and psychological stamina and the support that you will need to deal with the rigorous litigation process. There should also be a discussion about the amount of money likely to be awarded in a case like yours and whether or not the defendant will have the resources to pay it. The questions asked and the information provided by the lawyer should help you both arrive at a decision about the feasibility and appropriateness of pursuing your case in the courts.

Here is a checklist with some of the important issues to consider when deciding if it is worthwhile for you to pursue a civil lawsuit.[20]

- Am I well within the limitation period that allows me to sue?
- Is there a reasonable likelihood that I will be granted damages and that I will be able to collect?
- Am I prepared for the financial cost and do I fully understand these costs?
- Am I prepared for the time commitment, knowing that this may take a substantial investment of my time and energy (this may include pursuing an appeal if you lose initially)?
- Am I prepared to deal with the emotional and psychological toll of litigation on my family, on myself, and on those close to me?
- Do I have adequate social support?
- Am I able to address my psychological concerns and find balance in my life outside of litigation?
- Do I have a reasonable understanding of the litigation process and realistic goals? Would I be able to accept and deal with a denial of my claim?
- Am I open to a negotiated settlement by legal counsel?

- Is there another type of compensation program where I could make a claim or am I better off going through civil court?

Retaining a lawyer

IF YOU AND THE lawyer agree that your case has legal merit, and that the benefits of proceeding appear to sufficiently outweigh the costs (in time, energy, stress, money, etc.), then you may be ready to take the next step and formally retain legal counsel. We recommend that you not sign forms or officially retain a lawyer during your initial meeting. This is a very big decision, with consequences that may affect you for years, so look at your initial meeting as part of the information gathering process. Even if you believe that a particular lawyer is a good fit for you, do not sign up while you are in the office for the first time. Whether you realize it or not, you may be feeling subtle (or not so subtle) pressure to go along with an authority figure. As a victim of sexual assault, you may be particularly vulnerable to these types of pressures. Before making any formal commitment or signing any forms, take some time to reflect and be sure that the particular lawyer is right for you. Unless you are facing a limitation period that is about to expire, if the lawyer has a problem with your taking some time to make your decision, you should consider that the lawyer may not be the best one for you.

When you are ready to proceed, a written agreement should be drawn up. The agreement is called an Hourly Fee Agreement or a Contingency Fee Agreement, depending on whether you have decided to retain the lawyer on an hourly fee basis or a contingency fee basis. Make sure the agreement contains clearly specified terms delineating the lawyer's services and fees, and the agreed-upon payment options. Take these forms away and think about them. It is always a good idea to talk to another lawyer and get a second opinion on terms and conditions of the proposed fee agreement.

These initial stages are also a good time to explore the broader aspects of your potential working relationship with your legal counsel. You should know how, when, and where you will be communicating with your lawyer. Any time you discuss confidential matters relevant to your claim with your lawyer and within the scope of the lawyer's legal practice (for example, in the office, rather than at the supermarket), this communication is "privileged." This means that there are legal protections in place to protect the confidentiality of what you discuss with your lawyer, unless you choose to waive that protection. Under the rule of privilege, no one can compel your lawyer to disclose what you discuss in the course of your professional contact, without your explicit permission. It is understandable that you might have concerns about privacy in these circumstances, so feel free to raise this issue.

Once retained by you, your lawyer may specifically ask that you not talk to anyone else about the details of your case, except when required in court proceedings. It is particularly important that you not discuss the specifics of your case with other witnesses because this can raise concerns about "collusion" between witnesses. Your lawyer may also request that you not engage in certain forms of therapy (for example, hypnotherapy) that might potentially contaminate your memories of the defendant and the sexual assault.

In summary, before you leave the lawyer's office after your initial consultation, and before you retain a particular lawyer, you should ensure that you have discussed or explored all of the important issues. Using the checklist in Appendix 24 is one way to make sure you address many of the relevant and important topics you need to consider. The lawyer will cover many of these issues, but you should raise the ones that are not covered at the initial meeting. The goal is for you to walk out of the lawyer's office with some information about that lawyer's experience, personality, and approach to sexual assault litigation. You also want to gain some understanding of the strengths and limitations of your case, how you would proceed, the role that each of you would play in the process, and a copy of any fee agreement you would be required to sign should you decide to retain the lawyer.

THE STEP-BY-STEP PROCESS OF A CIVIL SUIT

THIS SECTION OUTLINES IN some detail the usual steps in a civil lawsuit, which should help demystify the process and encourage a realistic outlook. Knowledge of the litigation process not only prepares you for the unfamiliar, but it will also help you develop realistic expectations about the process and outcome.

Data gathering and naming all the parties

ONCE YOU HAVE FORMALLY retained a lawyer, the first stage of launching a civil suit will include an initial collection of data to support your claim. To assist in this process, you will sign consent forms allowing your lawyer to speak with your therapist, physician, or others who can provide information about you, as well as obtain copies of relevant records and documents. Collecting data and speaking to others will give your lawyer an opportunity to evaluate both the strengths and limitations of your claim. This will also allow for an initial evaluation of the likely extent of damages.

In a civil lawsuit, the plaintiff and the defendant are called "parties" to the litigation. In discussion with you, your lawyer will determine which parties will be named in the suit. As discussed above, there may be defendants who are not obvious to you. Your legal counsel does not want to leave out parties whom the court might consider responsible. To do so could negatively affect your claim and potential compensation for damages. If, at the end of your litigation, the court decides that those named in your suit are not the responsible ones, but that others are jointly or solely responsible, you cannot add these defendants at this late stage in the process, and your efforts will be for naught.

Your lawyer will name all individuals, institutions, or organizations that may be liable in a Writ of Summons and Statement of Claim. These are the initial legal documents required to start your lawsuit to hold the named parties legally responsible for the damages that you have suffered, and they are filed at the court by your lawyer. To be complete and accurate, the writ may name a parent, family member, friend, or a professional whom you may not have thought to be responsible and whom you may prefer not to add. Be sure you ask your lawyer specifically which parties will be named as defendants in your case, so you can discuss and resolve any concerns you have early in the process and before the legal documents are filed.

Filing initial court documents

YOUR CIVIL ACTION BEGINS once your lawyer files the Writ of Summons and the Statement of Claim in the court registry. These documents set out the nature of the claim and the fundamental accusations against the defendant. The details must be sufficient to present your claim clearly to the defendant, and they must be accurate. This means you must be forthright and give a comprehensive, accurate account of the sexual assault to your lawyer.

Some plaintiffs do not fully disclose the details of their assault during their initial discussions with their lawyer because they feel uncomfortable talking about the abuse or because some of the details are particularly upsetting or humiliating. This can result in the lawyer not having sufficient information to conduct your case properly. We recommend that you think about these issues before you speak with a lawyer or proceed with litigation. What do you need in order to be able to talk openly with your lawyer about the details of the sexual assault? What support can you arrange, or what coping strategies can you use to reduce your anxiety or distress? Stack the deck in your favour — try to prepare yourself to tell your lawyer the whole story so the legal documentation is accurate from the beginning. If you find you are unable to discuss some details with your lawyer, explain that this is the case. Your lawyer can then appropriately deal with the situation.

If you have particular concerns about your privacy during the litigation, discuss this issue with your lawyer. There are things your lawyer can do at the outset to help protect your privacy. These protections include the following:

- Using your initials rather than your full name on the Writ of Summons, Statement of Claim, and other legal documents
- Banning publication of any reporting that identifies the parties other than by initials, or alternatively, banning any publication at all
- Sealing the court file
- Excluding the public from the courtroom

Your lawyer can request these various protections of your privacy; however, the court has the final say as to whether or not they will be put in place.

Legal response from the defendant

ONCE THE DEFENDANT HAS been served with the Writ of Summons and the Statement of Claim, the defendant will respond in a legal document called the Statement of Defence. You can expect the defendant to respond in one of the following ways:

- Deny many or all of the claims made in the plaintiff's Statement of Claim. This can be very upsetting and feel invalidating. The defendant may even deny knowing you. Try to avoid taking this document personally. Blanket denials are fairly common and to be expected in the early stages of litigation.
- Deny the plaintiff's claims and then countersue. In these cases, the defendant not only denies the misconduct, but also launches a lawsuit seeking damages from the plaintiff for harm allegedly caused by

the plaintiff's claims of sexual assault. This can be very upsetting, but it is not unusual. It does underscore the fact that untrue or false claims of sexual assault are serious and can result in sanctions.

- Admit some misconduct and name third parties. The defendant acknowledges wrongdoing (for example, that the assault occurred and caused harm) but denies being solely or even primarily at fault, and instead, suggests that the fault lies primarily with another person or institution (the named third parties).
- Admit wrongdoing and acknowledge harm. In this type of response the legal issue of liability is resolved and the question shifts to which damages are accepted or rejected as being legally caused by the wrongdoing and what the compensation should be for those damages.

Your lawyer will review the defendant's Statement of Defence with you, explain its significance, and discuss any concerns that you have. Your lawyer will then file a response if this is appropriate or necessary.

Disclosure and production of documents

THE RULES OF COURT require all parties to disclose relevant documents well in advance of trial. This enables each side in the litigation to elicit information from the other side concerning the facts in the case. The scope of disclosure of documents is very broad in civil litigation, much more so than in criminal proceedings, because the records required in civil matters cover a wider range of legal issues than in criminal cases. For example, besides any documents relevant to determining liability, those that assist in assessing causation of damages must also be disclosed. Both parties (defendant and plaintiff) are required to disclose and produce private records and personal documents considered relevant to the claim, such as diaries, calendars, and computer files, as well as the records of other sources of relevant information, including employers, physicians, and therapists. The range of documents available for disclosure is much wider than in criminal proceedings in which the *Criminal Code* provides limited access to such material by the defence.

The following list illustrates the type of documents that the plaintiff might be required to produce:

- Medical records
- Psychiatric or counselling records

- Drug or alcohol treatment records
- Medical Service Plan records
- Employment records
- Educational records
- Income tax records
- Police records
- Corrections Canada records
- Provincial government ministry records
- Photographs
- Letters and correspondence including e-mails
- Diaries
- Receipts for special damages (damages actually sustained rather than inferred by law), such as receipts for medication or therapy

Documents similar to those requested from the plaintiff can also be requested from the defendant, although there may be some differences. If, for example, there have been previous criminal charges against the defendant, records relevant to those proceedings could be requested.

The court places limits on the use of documents that are produced in the course of a civil lawsuit; their use is limited to the civil proceeding, and the parties must maintain confidentiality within that context. Although the scope of potentially pertinent documents is very broad, the court may rule that some documents are not relevant, or that the documents are privileged, and access to them is denied. A court ruling in British Columbia indicated that personal diaries, journals, or other writings may be considered privileged "if they are written in the expectation of confidentiality, are important to the writer's healing and if the disclosure of them would result in injury to the healing process which would outweigh the benefit of disclosure."[21]

In some cases, parties or their supporters have deliberately destroyed or intentionally not kept records in an effort to avoid disclosing that information. Destruction of evidence carries with it a rebuttable presumption that the evidence would have been adverse to the interests of the party who destroyed it. This means that during the trial, the destroyed records will be considered to have contained information unfavourable to the party who destroyed them. The court will view the evidence this way unless the party that destroyed the records can prove otherwise.

The legal term for the destruction, mutilation, or altering of evidence is "spoliation." Any party engaging in such practice can be held accountable in a separate tort of spoliation or may be liable civilly or criminally for contempt of court and an adverse cost award. Destruction of an expert's working notes may result in the exclusion of the expert's report. These legal consequences are designed to provide sanctions against the act of destroying potential evidence, making this strategy counter-productive in the end. Similarly, if your therapist keeps no notes on your work together, the therapist's expert testimony may carry little or no weight.

Examination for discovery

AFTER THE DEFENDANT AND the plaintiff have requested and exchanged the relevant documents, the Rules of Court require each party to attend a process known as an examination for discovery. This is a unique proceeding conducted in a neutral location, such as a boardroom or meeting room, rather than in a courtroom. It is much less formal than a trial, and has limited participants — only the person being examined (either the defendant or the plaintiff) and sometimes the other party (each party is allowed, but not required to attend the other's examination for discovery), the lawyers, and an official court reporter are permitted to attend unless the parties agree otherwise. The court reporter will administer the oath or affirmation to the person being examined and will record all the questions asked and all the answers given during the discovery.

The purpose of the examination for discovery is to provide an opportunity for each party to "discover" the evidence of the other party on relevant legal issues in the presence of legal counsel. In the plaintiff's discovery, you may be asked extensive questions about your claim, including your personal and family history, details of the sexual assaults, and details about your psychological difficulties or any other damages you are claiming. The court reporter transcribes the questions and answers, and then provides typed transcripts to both your lawyer and the defendant's lawyer upon request. The discovery transcript forms part of the evidence in the litigation and lawyers for either party may use it at the subsequent trial.

The examination for discovery is a stressful experience. You will likely be answering questions for several hours, and sometimes for several days. When there is more than one defendant, lawyers representing each of the defendants are likely to question you. Because the scope of the discovery is broad, all parties are required to answer a variety of relevant questions. Since no judge is present, the lawyers have much more latitude in the questions they can ask and the way they ask them than they would in a courtroom. Your lawyer will sit beside you throughout the discovery, but cannot answer questions for you. If inappropriate or irrelevant questions are asked of you, your lawyer will instruct you not to answer those questions without a court order, or to answer them after your lawyer's objection to the question is noted on the record. The style of questioning can be aggressive and may include leading questions that suggest what your answer should be. As you may be sensing, the discovery process can be particularly exhausting, confusing, upsetting, or insulting for any plaintiff.

As noted above, your lawyer will accompany you to the examination for discovery. In some cases, you can have a support person accompany you as well, but all parties have to agree on this. A support person cannot be someone who is going to be a witness at the trial since hearing your testimony at the discovery would severely weaken that person's testimony at trial. This means that some people, such as family members, a spouse, or a therapist, should not act as support persons during your discovery. If you want a support person with you at discovery, be sure you discuss the advisability of this with your lawyer and decide who the appropriate person would be to fulfill this role.

Consider also that a support person will be hearing everything you say about very personal life experiences, including the sexual assault. You need to think about how comfortable you will feel discussing these issues in the presence of that particular person. Think as well about the impact that this information will have on the support person and on your relationship with that person. This may be less of a concern for you if your support person is a victim support worker, rather than a close friend or family member. Because your choice of a support person can have significant ramifications for both of you, think carefully about whom you want with you. For example, in one case a husband, who was acting as his wife's support person, heard for the first time the graphic details of demeaning sexual acts an abuser had forced his wife to perform. The husband was subsequently unable to sleep with his wife or provide her with the comfort she needed. In this case, her choice of support person hindered instead of helped her. If you particularly want a family member or intimate partner with you, there are some options you could consider to help avoid a negative outcome. For example, you could have the support person available to you outside of the discovery room, where you can access them during breaks, at lunch, and at the end of the day. On the other hand, you might have your support person with you during the discovery, but arrange for the person to leave during discussions of difficult topics. It is prudent to discuss these options with your lawyer and your support person in advance. For some people, rather than attending the discovery with a support person, it is sufficient to meet with their therapist both before and shortly after the discovery process for support and an opportunity to debrief. Others will prefer that no one accompany them other than their lawyer.

The defendant has a right to be present at your discovery, just as you have the right to be present at the defendant's discovery. For some plaintiffs this is upsetting and intimidating, as it may be the first time in a long time (sometimes years) that they have been in the defendant's presence. While it is possible in some cases to have the defendant excluded from attending, there must be exceptional circumstances. The court can make an exclusion order when there is "demonstrated intimidation by one party towards the other or when the defendant ... has been criminally convicted for the same conduct."[22]

We recommend that you talk with your lawyer about your thoughts and feelings if you want to attend the defendant's discovery. This, too, can be a very upsetting experience. Given the choice, many plaintiffs choose not to attend, but some report positive outcomes from attending. Adults abused as children have reported seeing the defendant through a different lens. The defendant may no longer be physically larger than them, perhaps old or frail and in no position to control the discovery, and hence, may no longer be frightening. Your lawyer may request that you attend the defendant's examination because your knowledge of the defendant and the facts could be helpful. You will need to weigh the potentially negative effects of attending against the advantages this could have for your lawsuit and discuss this with your lawyer. If you do not attend, you still have the option of later reading the questions and the defendant's responses from the typed examination for discovery transcript and providing your comments to your lawyer.

In addition to your examination for discovery, you may be asked to provide written answers to a series of written questions prepared by the defendant's lawyer, called "interrogatories." The purpose of interrogatories is for one side to write out questions and present them to the other side as a means of determining facts, such as the times and dates of relevant events, names of relevant people, and details of your life. If the defendant wants you to answer interrogatories, the questions will be sent to your lawyer, who will then meet with you to obtain your answers and put them in the required format.

It is important that your lawyer prepare you for your examination for discovery. Being prepared does not mean that the lawyer gives you answers or tells you what to say. The purpose of this preparation is to familiarize you with the discovery process, the rules that govern it, and the methods you can use to handle difficult questions. Your lawyer should emphasize that the primary job is to tell the truth — plain and simple. Your personal integrity and your case will both suffer if you do not keep this in mind. You will not make a favourable impression if you fall into the trap of saying what you think others want to hear you say. Your role as a plaintiff, and as a witness to your own experiences, is to speak the truth, tell only what you know, and give that information as clearly and as accurately as possible.

Given the importance of the discovery, if your lawyer does not schedule preparation time with you, you should take the initiative to arrange a meeting yourself. Preparation can take time and effort, hours or even days in complex cases, but a lawyer who does not adequately prepare you for these important steps will not serve you well.

Being factually prepared for the discovery will also lower your level of anxiety and help you to be psychologically prepared. Nevertheless, no matter how informed you are, there will be inevitable stresses and strains. You may want to review Chapter 5 and refresh your understanding of stress-reducing and coping strategies. Practising these methods well in advance of attending the discovery will fortify you and emotionally prepare you for the process. Decide which of the techniques (for example, relaxation, deep breathing, grounding, or carrying a small comforting object) can best meet your needs. Will you most likely need to control your anger, lessen your anxiety, or perhaps deal with the distraction of intrusive memories? A good approach is to use a combination of coping techniques, choosing the one that is most appropriate for any particular situation.

Be especially gentle with the demands you make on yourself in the days prior to the discovery; practise appropriate self-care, eat well, exercise, and get sufficient rest. Be prepared to feel emotionally and physically drained afterwards. You may particularly need companionship and support the evening following the discovery. You may need a trusted, safe person with whom to debrief. Discussing painful and hurtful experiences during the discovery may trigger upsetting memories and may lead you to being preoccupied with these thoughts, images, or feelings. You may need to practise some of the grounding or distracting techniques you have learned. You may want to schedule activities afterwards that are particularly comforting or relaxing. You may just feel exhausted and want to go to bed. Be prepared to give yourself some latitude.

Nobody can predict how you as an individual will feel during and after the discovery. It is a stressful process for virtually everyone, but you may find the process either easier or more difficult than you anticipated. You are likely to experience a wide range of thoughts, emotions, and reactions, not all of which will be negative or upsetting. Some plaintiffs feel empowered by having the opportunity, often for the first time, to tell the defendant and the legal counsel how the defendant's conduct has hurt and damaged them. After it is all over, many plaintiffs feel considerable relief and are able to feel good about completing this challenging process. Give yourself credit for having completed a stressful but important ordeal. If you find yourself being self-critical or preoccupied with "I should have ...," have a look at our earlier discussion about how to let go of these feelings, or how to stop, confront, and effectively challenge unproductive negative thinking.

Independent psychological/psychiatric assessment

IN MOST CASES, YOUR lawyer will arrange for a mental health professional (generally a psychologist or psychiatrist) to assess you and provide an expert opinion about the psychological damages that you have suffered. As well, the mental health professional will typically give an opinion about your therapy or treatment needs and your prognosis. Since the defendant has the right under the Rules of Court to have you examined by an expert of his own choice, you could have more than one assessment. Although rare within our adversarial system, on occasion, lawyers for both sides agree to retain a joint expert for a psychological assessment.

Although one side or the other typically retains a mental health expert, this does not mean that the expert will always provide an opinion that supports the position of the side that did the hiring. Mental health experts who specialize in providing these types of assessments operate under professional and ethical guidelines that require them to give an independent, unbiased assessment. The role of these experts is to provide a fair and balanced opinion for the purposes of assisting the court in making its decisions, rather than assisting one party or the other. Experts with these ethical standards can make no guarantees to the party who retained them that the party will either agree with or benefit from their opinion.

Unfortunately, some mental health professionals consistently provide biased assessments favouring the party who retained them. With time, people recognize these professionals as "hired guns" and subsequently the court will give their opinion little weight; their value as expert witnesses then becomes short-lived. Similarly, damage assessments completed by the plaintiff's therapist may be given less weight because therapists are generally (and rightly so in the context of therapy) advocates for their client, and therefore biased.

Different mental health professionals conduct their assessments differently, depending on the type of assessment required. Some experts may meet with you for two or three hours; some may require several sessions with you over a number of days. No matter what the particular format, every mental health assessment should begin with an explanation of the purpose of the assessment and the limits to confidentiality. It is particularly important to understand that anything you talk about during the assessment can be recorded in handwritten notes (or electronically, if this is agreed to) and can then be used in the expert's report or testimony in court. Although information from the assessment may be disclosed to the lawyers of both parties and may appear in court, this information will not be shared with others, except in very specific circumstances. For instance, if you indicate that you are in danger of seriously hurting yourself or someone else, the mental health professional has a legal obligation to ensure your safety and the safety of others. The law also requires mental health professionals to disclose any reports of children being abused physically or sexually, or who are in imminent danger of abuse. The professional conducting your assessment should clearly spell out these limits to confidentiality.

During the assessment interview, expect to be asked questions about significant experiences in your life, including details of the sexual assault. The assessor will ask about your birth family, childhood experiences, education, work history, medical history, and relationships. You will also have an opportunity to provide your thoughts about the effects of the sexual assault on you. You will need to discuss in some detail any psychological problems that you have experienced and any treatment that you have received. If a psychologist is the assessor, it is likely you will be asked to complete some psychological questionnaires and perhaps some other types of tests. Many of these have no right or wrong answers; instead, they provide a standardized way of asking about your thoughts, feelings, and personality style. Some of the tests may also assess various abilities, such as your memory function, problem-solving ability, or language skills. Feel free to ask questions about any psychological questionnaires that are used.

Often plaintiffs feel anxious in anticipation of a psychological assessment because they do not know what to expect. The mental health professional who conducts the interview and testing generally has considerable experience in this area, and will treat you with respect and likely help you to feel at ease. Nevertheless, this will be one more occasion when you are required to talk about emotionally difficult issues. The assessment process can be long and physically draining, so take care of your needs as previously outlined for other trying experiences.

After the assessment interview and any required testing are completed, the mental health professional will communicate with the retaining lawyer. This generally takes the form of a written report but may be verbal communication. Depending on the circumstances, the lawyer may or may not enter the report as evidence at trial. If the lawyer submits the report, the lawyer for the other side is entitled to require the expert to appear for cross-examination on the expert's opinion.

Other expert evidence

YOUR LAWYER MAY RETAIN experts in areas other than mental health, such as medicine, vocational rehabilitation, actuarial, or any other field relevant to your case. A medical doctor could assess any physical damages that you may have suffered, while a vocation expert might be required to assess pecuniary damages resulting from lost or diminished employment opportunities. Expert opinions may be sought that do not require a face-to-face interview with you. Some experts provide an opinion, in either a written report or court testimony, based on a review of documents related to your claim or on relevant expert knowledge. An economist could provide an expert opinion about lost wages based on actuarial data, or an expert in memory might provide general information about the dynamics of remembering traumatic experiences.

In order to provide testimony in court, an expert must be properly qualified to give an opinion in a particular area of expertise. Lawyers must demonstrate to the court that their expert is qualified in the relevant area, and opposing lawyers can question the expert about those qualifications. The evidence presented by an expert must be relevant to your case; the opinion offered must be outside the scope of ordinary, everyday knowledge or common sense; it must be necessary to assist the court, but it cannot usurp the function of the judge or the jury.

Settlement and mediation

AT ANY TIME DURING the litigation process, either party may propose a settlement offer. The opposing side may accept, reject, or propose a counter offer. Although you can never count on a pretrial settlement of your claim, many civil cases are settled prior to the trial, sometimes within days of the scheduled court date.

Sometimes lawyers will suggest a mediation or settlement conference, in an attempt to reach a negotiated agreement between the parties without going to trial. In this instance, both parties must agree to mediation for the process to occur. The parties and their lawyers will then sit down to present their cases before a professional mediator. Mediators may be retired or supernumerary judges, or they may be professionally trained mediators (often a lawyer who has received special training in mediation). Though both parties and their legal counsel have the option to attend mediation, attendance by the defendant may be considered inappropriate. If both parties agree, the defendant would not attend.

The federal government has used settlement conferences in cases of First Nations people sexually assaulted in residential schools.[23] These are analogous to a "mini-trial," conducted before a judge. Before the settlement conference, lawyers on both sides provide the judge with relevant case information. The plaintiff has the opportunity to give an account of what happened and how this experience affected the plaintiff's life. The judge then gives an evaluation of the strengths and weaknesses of the case to the lawyers for both parties. The lawyers, in turn, discuss the issues of the case without the plaintiff or defendant being present. In this forum, the judge has the authority to impose a settlement on the parties, which can be a meaningful way to acknowledge the wrong suffered by the plaintiff without the stress of a public trial.

Unlike awards given at trial, pretrial settlements do not become part of the public record. The amount of money awarded in pretrial settlements remains confidential between the parties and their lawyers. Monetary awards given without a trial therefore do not affect case law or become benchmarks for financial compensation given in future court cases. In addition, unlike awards given at a trial that are always lump sum payments (see discussion below), settlement monies may be structured awards. This means that the defendant will pay the plaintiff the awarded money through an individualized payment plan or investment.

Your lawyer will advise you on whether or not to accept a settlement offer or engage in mediation. Some plaintiffs report satisfaction with the settlement process that allows them to avoid the stress of a public trial, whereas some plaintiffs express a desire to have their "day in court" and may feel less satisfied with a pretrial settlement of their case.

The trial

PRIOR TO THE COMMENCEMENT of the trial, your lawyer should explain the process and the procedures of court, the presentation of your evidence, and the kinds of questions that you likely will be asked. Your lawyer will not tell you what to say, but will prepare you to give your evidence in the best manner possible. This means speaking clearly, avoiding jargon, and asking to have questions repeated or rephrased if you do not understand them. Your lawyer should also prepare you to deal with the cross-examination by the defendant's lawyer. As discussed previously, the overarching principle is to tell the truth and to present your evidence as plainly and accurately as possible. Other relevant principles about testifying are discussed in Chapters 7 and 8.

A civil trial begins with the presentation of the plaintiff's case. After an opening statement by your lawyer, you will testify in court in front of a judge, possibly a jury, and the defendant. You will answer specific questions put to you by your lawyer. Most importantly, you have the opportunity to describe what the defendant did or failed to do that resulted in the damages you suffered. After your lawyer has finished questioning you, the defendant's lawyer will cross-examine you. Cross-examination is almost always a very stressful experience. Many of the tactics described in Chapter 8 may be used by the defendant's lawyer. Re-reading that section can help you prepare for the ordeal of being cross-examined.

Once your testimony and cross-examination is completed, your lawyer will call witnesses who can corroborate your claims about the sexual abuse or the impact that the alleged abuse has had on you. Your spouse or partner may be able to confirm specific problems and distress, such as nightmares or sexual difficulties. Your employer may describe changes in your work performance, if this is relevant to your case. This type of evidence is a combination of personal observations and lay opinions. It is very important that you not discuss your evidence with any of these witnesses throughout the litigation process or at the trial. None of these witnesses can hear your court testimony or the testimony of other witnesses until after their own testimony is given. In contrast, expert witnesses are not restricted in this manner. Expert witnesses can hear the testimony of other witnesses, and can give an opinion based on what was presented in evidence. Expert witnesses normally testify after the lay witnesses have completed their evidence because they may rely on it to formulate or substantiate their opinion. Sometimes an expert will give a rebuttal opinion. A rebuttal opinion is an opinion directed at the opinion or the basis of the opinion given by another expert. For example, the defence may call an expert to comment on, or give a rebuttal to, the opinion of an expert called by the plaintiff.

After the court has received all the evidence supporting the plaintiff's claim, the trial then shifts to the defendant's case. Since the burden is on the plaintiff to prove the case, the defendant may present no evidence of the defendant's own. Instead, the defendant may argue that the plaintiff's case should be dismissed because the plaintiff did not prove the case on a balance of probabilities. The defence does this by presenting a No Evidence or an Insufficient Evidence motion on which the judge rules. The judge dismisses the case if there is no or insufficient evidence to support the plaintiff's claim. If the evidence motions fail, the trial proceeds with the defendant's case. More likely than not, if still alive, the defendant will testify to give the other side of the story. Other witnesses, including expert witnesses, will also likely testify. At the close of the defendant's case, there will be closing arguments given by the lawyers for each side. The case then passes to either the judge or a jury for a decision. If there is a jury, the judge will give jury members specific instructions about the legal issues in the case and the applicable law and will remind the jury of its responsibilities before it starts deliberations.

Receiving the decision and compensation

IF A JURY HEARD your lawsuit, you will typically receive a decision quickly. Alternatively, if a judge alone heard your case, it could take a number of months to receive judgment. Once the court renders a decision, it can be appealed by either party, first to the provincial appellate court, and then, potentially, to the Supreme Court of Canada. The time it takes for appeals to be completed varies significantly from case to case.

If your claim is successful, and there are no appeals, the defendant must pay your monetary award in one lump sum (assuming the defendant has the capacity to pay the full amount awarded). The different types of damages awarded in your case (for example, pecuniary, non-pecuniary, aggravated, or punitive) will be combined together into one payment. This may include such things as costs for future care, so money for ongoing therapy may be included as part of the lump sum.

If your claim is successful and the defendant appeals the decision, the defendant must still pay out the judgment unless the defendant applies to the court to "stay the judgment." In making a decision whether or not to stay the judgment, the court will consider several factors, including the merits of the appeal, to determine whether your award should be withheld until the appeal is heard, or paid to you in whole or part pending the appeal. Your lawyer will discuss the appeal process with you so that you have a better understanding of its ramifications.

Completing a successful lawsuit and receiving fair financial compensation can help redress, at least to some extent, the damages that a plaintiff has suffered. The plaintiff may feel acknowledged, validated, believed, and vindicated by the court's recognition of the sexual abuse and the damages caused by that abuse. Monetary compensation can relieve some of the stresses in the plaintiff's life and may allow a plaintiff to seek treatment that would otherwise not have been financially feasible. However, for some plaintiffs the positive feelings associated with a successful lawsuit can be relatively short-lived. When difficulties in the plaintiff's life continue even after the award, the hopes that the lawsuit would "fix" everything are dashed. Some plaintiffs subsequently report feeling exploited or used by family and friends who seem more interested in their financial compensation than in their well-being. In too many cases, the plaintiff spends the money without careful thought or planning. In a short time, the funds can be gone, including money awarded for therapy to improve the plaintiff's mental health. Of course, the court will not replace misspent funds. If you are concerned about your ability to manage your award wisely, discuss this with your lawyer early in your case, as your lawyer can include, as part of your claim, a request for additional funds for financial management assistance.

In the event that the court denies a claim for damages, or the award falls far short of that expected, the plaintiff could feel devastated. Such an outcome can exacerbate pre-existing problems (for example, low self-esteem, depression, or mistrust) or can lead to emotional difficulties not previously experienced. In some cases, the plaintiff may feel re-victimized by the system and cynical about the world in general. Some plaintiffs become preoccupied, ruminating about the litigation or their victimization. Their thoughts may provoke self-blame, anger, anxiety, or depression and may increase the risk of unhealthy coping. These plaintiffs may have considerable difficulty moving on with their lives or managing these distressing thoughts and feelings.

DEALING WITH CIVIL TRIAL STRESS

AS DISCUSSED THROUGHOUT THIS book (especially in Chapter 4), participating in legal proceedings, whether civil or criminal, is stressful and presents another opportunity to employ the coping strategies discussed throughout this book. As in all experiences of adversity, we especially recommend that you turn to your support network for emotional support and assistance. You should also be aware that litigation might affect some of those from whom you seek support. Friends and family who have attended the trial may be dealing with their own stress related to hearing testimony or having to testify themselves. There may also be divisions among family and friends or within your community, as loyalties toward the plaintiff and the defendant become evident. Some who typically support you may be less emotionally available. You may want to protect others from further distress. Rather than seeking the support that you need, you may fall into a caretaker mode in an attempt to soothe the distress, hurt, frustration, or anger of those you care for. You may wonder if their thoughts or feelings toward you have changed due to the trial or because they have learned unpleasant details about your life or your experiences. On the positive side, friends and family can actually have more empathy and compassion for you following the trial.

Whatever your particular circumstances, we encourage you to have a wide range of supports available to you during and after the litigation process. Broaden your support network prior to the trial and try to have people available who are not themselves involved in the court process. Having professionals available to you who understand the litigation process and its stress, such as a therapist or victim support worker, can be invaluable. We once more encourage you to be alert to the possibility that the trial process itself may skew your perceptions of others. When you have gone through such an adversarial process, been repeatedly challenged, and have felt disbelieved or discounted, the way you see others can be significantly affected. It would not be surprising if you had negative feelings about people in general, trusted others less, and perceived negative reactions toward you, even if unintended. It might take a while to balance your view of others, so give yourself some time and space. Try not to let the experience influence the healing gains that you are making. Talk to a therapist, if need be, or seek guidance from someone that you trust. Find ways to get a "reality check" of your thoughts and perceptions. Discussions in previous chapters about challenging and changing your thoughts, letting go of negative feelings, or understanding relationships may assist you.

We have described several possible outcomes to help you look realistically at the costs and benefits of participating in civil litigation. If you are considering or are already pursuing civil litigation, you need to be ready to accept results other than the hoped-for outcome. To ensure your well-being, we encourage you to develop viable, healthy ways of coping with and accepting negative outcomes. Positive outcomes can carry stresses as well. If you receive any significant amount of financial compensation, you would be well-advised to obtain financial assistance to manage it.

CLASS ACTION SUITS

THUS FAR, WE HAVE been discussing the litigation process for plaintiffs who are advancing claims for damages caused by sexual abuse, either alone or with a group of other plaintiffs, using traditional procedural rules. In some provinces, class proceedings legislation has been passed allowing a group of individuals to bring a class action lawsuit where there is a common defendant and a sufficient number of legal issues that are common to the plaintiff group, such that a class action lawsuit is the preferred way to get those common issues resolved. A class action lawsuit might include a group of individuals who were abused by a church official, a sports coach, a teacher, or other type of authority figure. It also may include individuals who resided in an institutional or government-run facility where the institution or agency breached its duty by failing to protect the plaintiffs in its care from sexual assault.

This type of lawsuit differs from single or multiple-plaintiff lawsuits discussed previously. While a class action lawsuit includes multiple plaintiffs (referred to as "class members" or "the class"), the class action rules allow lawyers to select one or two of the plaintiffs to represent the class in the court proceedings on legal issues common to all members.

The primary advantage to class action suits is that only the representative plaintiff deals with the common legal issues in court. The other plaintiffs in the class action suit (which may number in the hundreds) do not have to be directly involved in the court processes regarding the common legal issues. Instead, the judge rules on the basis of evidence presented by the representative plaintiff and the judge's ruling applies to the entire class. Class members either benefit or lose, together. This can significantly decrease the cost (in time, effort, and expense) of litigation for the plaintiffs. It also can give the plaintiffs a psychological lift since they are pursuing their claims against a defendant (often an institution or government body) in large numbers, which tends to "level the playing field."

Another advantage of a class action is that the court must approve any settlement agreement reached by the parties, and the court can address issues in addition to financial compensation for the class members. For example, in the *Jericho Hill School* class action suit (see below), the settlement agreement included such things as a public acknowledgment by the province of British Columbia that the sexual abuse occurred, the government had failed in its responsibility to protect the class members, and steps would be taken to prevent this from happening again. The settlement also included educational and employment initiatives, counselling services, tuition money for families of class members to be used to learn American Sign Language, annual scholarships for visually impaired and deaf students, and commemorative plaques to honour the students who had been sexually abused.

It should be noted that only the legal issues common to all class members (such as liability for the breach of care by an institution) can be resolved through the representative plaintiff. Individual legal issues, such as the damages suffered by each particular class member (for example, non-pecuniary damages for psychological injuries, or pecuniary losses) have to be considered individually. Nevertheless, class proceedings legislation provides for the option of alternative means, other than a separate court process for each individual, to resolve any individual issues. For example, the court may approve an inclusive compensation plan, agreed to by all parties, which employs mental health professionals to assess the individual class members. These assessments are then used to help determine each individual's damage award based on the extent of that individual's injury. All class action legislation provides a mechanism for individuals who do not wish to be part of the class litigation to remove themselves from the proceedings and not be bound by the result.

The law has only recently allowed class actions for sexual assault to proceed in Canada. The first Canadian class action case to deal with the issue of institutional sexual abuse involved former students of the Jericho Hill School for the Deaf and Blind in British Columbia.[24] Sexual abuse had occurred there over a forty-two-year span, beginning in 1950. In 2004, the British Columbia Supreme Court approved a settlement of $15.6 million "new money" and various programs and services to approximately 350 former Jericho Hill School students (an excerpt from this Settlement Agreement that spells out the different components of this particular case appears in Appendix 25). Since that time, there have been several other successful class action suits in Canada, establishing this form of legal action as a viable alternative to launching large numbers of separate lawsuits in instances where there has been large-scale abuse of victims.

OTHER TYPES OF COMPENSATION

APART FROM THE CIVIL actions and criminal charges discussed at length in this book, sexual assault victims have other options that they can pursue for redress. These include the following:

- Criminal injuries compensation
- Human rights commissions and tribunals
- Compensation packages
- Community initiatives
- Ombudsman or other advocacy offices
- Public or private inquiries
- Alternative dispute resolution

Criminal injuries compensation is available in most Canadian jurisdictions to provide some financial compensation to victims of crime. The process of obtaining this compensation is relatively informal and fast, but the sums are not large. A person is still free to pursue civil action, but the criminal injuries award must be reimbursed out of any civil damages awarded.

Human rights tribunals are empowered to award modest compensation to individuals who have been discriminated against. This sort of compensation could apply to someone who was sexually assaulted in an employment setting. Again, this process is less formal or onerous than criminal and civil proceedings are, but can take some time to complete.

As an alternative to a civil action for damages, a compensation package may be negotiated by the victim or unilaterally offered by the potential defendant. These package awards tend to be less than those obtained through a civil lawsuit, and the terms are often confidential, precluding an outside review of the fairness. Nevertheless, a compensation package allows the victim to avoid the costs, both emotional and financial, of a trial process or lengthy civil proceedings.

Some forms of redress are centred in the community, and focus on its needs, and usually do not involve financial awards. These initiatives would typically address healing of the victim, offender, and the community. The Hollow Water First Nation, for example, began a Community Holistic Healing Program in 1987 after some individuals disclosed their abuse at a community workshop.

Another way to hold those responsible for sexual abuse accountable is through a provincial ombudsman's office. An ombudsman is an independent and impartial official who is empowered to investigate individual complaints. In the past, ombudsmen have investigated government culpability in sexual abuse matters and have recommended compensation, but there is no mechanism to enforce such recommendations.

A sexual assault case can be the subject of a public or private inquiry. While these inquiries do not offer financial compensation, they may lead to civil action or a negotiated compensation package.

Alternative dispute resolution (ADR) is a non-adversarial way of resolving disputes that is increasingly used in both the public and private sectors. ADR can help parties resolve their differences without resorting to more onerous court procedures. It looks at needs, interests, and solutions, and can promote healing. ADR is voluntary, and should be confidential, based on mutual agreement, and timely. It is designed to produce solutions that are adapted to the particular circumstances of individual cases, with a goal of solving problems, rather than imposing solutions through an adjudicative process. A recent example of ADR is the process set up by the federal government to settle claims by First Nations individuals who were victims of abuse in residential schools. A group or an individual can make a claim for sexual abuse, physical abuse, or wrongful confinement. To learn more about this process and access application forms, you can visit the Residential Schools Resolution Canada website.[25]

VIGNETTE TEN: NOT TOO LATE

WHAT IS WORTH NOTING about the vignette at the beginning of this chapter is that Ralph was able to bring his civil lawsuit some thirty years after the alleged sexual assaults occurred. Although there is a statute of limitations in his province, his lawsuit began within the allowable period under the statute. He sued within two years of the time he first realized, through therapy, that the sexual abuse had had a significant impact on his life. With the help of his counsellor, he began to examine the source of his personal problems, including anger, sexual confusion, impotence, frequent interpersonal conflicts, and violence. His therapist suggested that many of his difficulties were likely related to his sexual abuse history and, given the circumstances, Ralph might be able to sue. Ralph followed up on this advice and subsequently asked his therapist to write a report for his lawyer about the abuse. The therapist indicated that he preferred not to, because he wanted to maintain his role as Ralph's advocate in therapy, not as an evaluator in court. Instead, the therapist recommended that Ralph talk to his lawyer, who was experienced in dealing with civil sexual assault claims, to obtain the names of mental health professionals who specialize in providing independent assessments for court.

Ralph's lawyer arranged an appointment with a psychologist who met with him three times and prepared a report that became part of his case. Ralph was surprised at how in-depth the assessment was; it included a lengthy interview, tests of his cognitive abilities (for example, reading, math, and problem solving), and questionnaires with hundreds of questions on how he felt and thought about himself and his life. He had expected to talk mostly about the sexual abuse, but the psychologist asked in-depth questions about his family, schooling, relationships, other sexual experiences, and additional important events throughout his life. Although Ralph was emotionally drained by the assessment, he also felt the psychologist had carefully listened to his concerns. The overall review of his life also helped him to see himself from a different perspective — in some ways he felt "really screwed up," but he also could see how far he had come in the last few years since beginning his therapy.

When Ralph read the psychologist's report, he found it somewhat distressing to see his life laid out in writing, but he also found the psychologist's perspective on many issues informative. He was initially annoyed by the psychologist's opinion that some of his difficulties were related to other life experiences, rather than to the abuse, and he made this complaint to his lawyer. He reminded Ralph that the purpose of tort law is to award compensation that will return the plaintiff to the position the plaintiff would have been in had the sexual abuse not occurred. The court does not award compensation for all the past hurts Ralph had experienced in his life. Additionally, the lawyer pointed out that the court would likely give more weight to an objective, balanced report that acknowledged the impact of Ralph's broad life experiences, and included other damaging experiences besides the sexual abuse. The lawyer further suggested that Ralph share the report with his therapist to clarify any technical jargon or misconceptions.

When he discussed these issues in counselling, his therapist reminded him about the detrimental impact of the physical abuse by his father and the abandonment by his mother that occurred prior to going into foster care. Ralph and his therapist discussed some of the complexities of his personal development, and other important life events that had affected him.

Ralph also felt distressed by his examination for discovery. He was particularly upset about having to describe the sexual abuse in such detail. He became annoyed with being asked to tell about the first incident, then the second incident, and so on. How could they expect him to remember each separate incident after thirty years? The defence lawyer's suggestion that he "liked" the abuse because he had an erection particularly incensed Ralph. He lost his temper twice and had to take a break from the questioning. After the discovery concluded, Ralph desperately wanted to go out and get drunk but, instead, he telephoned his therapist as they had arranged, and debriefed with him. He was able to employ some healthy coping strategies that he had learned, rather than turn to alcohol.

Ralph was both dreading and looking forward to having his day in court. Having his life examined in such a public way was anxiety-provoking, but he was determined to explain how harmful the sexual abuse had been to him. He consequently had mixed feelings when his lawyer met with him to discuss a settlement offer made by the defence. After talking about the strengths and weaknesses of his case and the pros and cons of proceeding to trial, on Ralph's instructions, his lawyer submitted a counter offer for settlement that was accepted. On the one hand, Ralph was pleased with the settlement, which considerably improved his financial picture, gave him options for job retraining, and provided funding for further therapy. He felt vindicated after so many people disbelieved him as a child. However, he also felt let down. He believed that the offender got off too lightly; most of his property had been in his wife's name and was not subject to the lawsuit. Ralph also had expected his life to change more dramatically and more quickly than it did. He was still preoccupied with thoughts and feelings regarding the abuse and the proceedings. It took several months for these feelings to dissipate, and it took several more years to overcome some of his other personal problems, such as his unsatisfying sexual relationships.

ENDNOTES

1   These are general or typical differences that may not apply in all cases. Also, we are not specifically referring to class action civil litigation here; this is discussed later in this chapter.

2   From a glossary provided in Project Committee on Civil Remedies for Sexual Assault, *Civil Remedies for Sexual Assault*, British Columbia Law Institute Report #14 (Vancouver: British Columbia Law Institute, 2001) at 116 [*Civil Remedies*].

3   *Civil Remedies, ibid.* at 7.

4   *J.R.I.G. v. Tyhurst*, 2003 BCCA 224 at para. 6.

5   S.B.C. 2006, c. 19, received Royal Assent 18 May 2006.

6   *Civil Remedies*, above note 2 at 77.

7   Adapted from information provided in *Civil Remedies, ibid.* at v–vi and 19–30.

8   *M.B. v. British Columbia*, 2003 SCC 53; *K.L.B. v. British Columbia*, 2003 SCC 51; *E.D.G. v. Hammer*, 2003 SCC 52.

9   *E.D.G. v. Hammer, ibid.*

10 *K.L.B. v. British Columbia*, above note 8.

11 *Civil Remedies*, above note 2 at 16.

12 See *Non-Marine Underwriters, Lloyd's of London v. Scalera*, [2000] 1 S.C.R. 551 at paras. 15 and 22, as cited in *Civil Remedies, ibid.*

13 *Civil Remedies, ibid.* at 66, citing from *Andrews* at 462, as cited in Kenneth Cooper-Stephenson, *Personal Injury Damages in Canada* (Toronto: Carswell, 1996) at 108.

14 *Hill v. Church of Scientology*, [1995] 2 S.C.R. 1130 at 1205–6.

15 Cooper-Stephenson, *Personal Injury Damages in Canada*, above note 13 at 527, cited in *Civil Remedies*, above note 2 at 54.

16 *Hill v. Church of Scientology*, above note 14 at 1208, cited in *Civil Remedies, ibid.* at 57.

17 *Y.(S.) v. C.(F.G.)* (1996), 26 B.C.L.R. (3d) 155 at 172 (C.A.), cited in *Civil Remedies, ibid.* at 13.

18 Elizabeth Grace & Susan Vella, *Civil Liability for Sexual Abuse and Violence in Canada* (Toronto: Butterworths, 2000).

19 The following list is adapted from the presentation of Gail Dickson, Q.C., for Continuing Legal Education Society of British Columbia seminar, *Sexual Tort Claims*, 9 January 2004, Vancouver, British Columbia, 9 January 2004 [*Sexual Tort Claims*].

20 The following list is adapted from Sharyn A. Lynhart & Diane K.Shrier, "Potential Costs and Benefits of Sexual Harassment Litigation" (1996) 26:3 Psychiatric Annals 133.

21 As quoted in materials prepared by Barbara Yates, Q.C., for *Sexual Tort Claims*, above note 19; citation taken from *V.(K.L.) v. R.(D.G.)* (1994), 95 B.C.L.R. (2d) 322 (C.A.).

22 As quoted in materials prepared by Barbara Yates, *ibid.*; citation taken from *K.F. (Litigation guardian of) v. White*, [2000] O.J. No. 922 at para. 39 (S.C.J.).

23 The following description of this process is based on a presentation by Chief Justice Donald I. Brenner, Supreme Court of British Columbia, Vancouver, for *Sexual Tort Claims*, above note 19.

24 *Rumley v. British Columbia* (1999), 72 B.C.L.R. (3d) 1 (C.A.), aff'd (*sub nom. R. (L.) v. British Columbia*), [2001] 3 S.C.R. 184.

25 Online: www.irsr-rqpi.gc.ca/english/dispute_resolution_guide.html.

11

Personal Growth and Transformation

Vignette Eleven

A First Nations man who had sexually offended against many of the females in his extended family over a period of thirty years was eventually
convicted and brought to justice. His sentencing hearing was very dramatic
and moving as eight of his victims tearfully read victim impact statements.
A psychologist who specialized in the treatment of sex offenders also testified. He spoke about the psychological dynamics of sex offending, and
said, in the case at hand, the offender's impulses to have sex with female
children were so profound that even the offender himself could not accurately describe or assess his level of risk to re-offend. In the psychologist's
opinion, the risk of re-offending was so high that the offender should never
have unsupervised contact with children again, and nothing that the offender said about his sexual behaviour could confidently be believed. Observing the extensive human sadness that was the legacy of the offender's
crimes, the Crown counsel agreed with the victims that, with her help, they
would organize a healing circle to bring closure to the case. The women
asked the lawyer to provide the meeting place and to help get the circle
started. They wanted the meeting to be private. Although the Crown had
no particular expertise in leading healing circles, she was honoured by the
request and felt it would be disrespectful to refuse. The Crown said a few
words to begin the circle and the women in the group quickly took over as
the keepers of the circle, and one by one they spoke of their pain and guilt
at having been part of a family where so many children had been hurt.

SEXUAL VICTIMIZATION AND THE court process can challenge and shake
you, disrupting your accustomed ways of thinking and behaving. For some,

these experiences precipitate a crisis, signaling the clear need for personal change. Many people respond to this challenge and grow emotionally, sometimes inspiring change in those around them. In this chapter, we highlight the opportunities for growth presented by your experiences in the legal system and the ways that you may have grown during your personal struggle without realizing it. We also give examples of ordinary people who contributed to their communities in extraordinary ways. For those who find inspiration in these stories we provide some guidelines to a path of social action.

Sexual assault changes you. For some people, the change is immediate, profound, and goes to the core of their being. For others, the changes may be relatively minor or not immediately obvious. However, what appears to be a small change today can be the catalyst for broader changes in the future, both positive and negative. We have spent considerable time in preceding chapters reviewing the negative impact of sexual crimes. There is no doubt that a sexual crime can wreak havoc on a person's life, leaving pain and suffering in its wake. Sexual assault can take a terrible toll, not only on the victim, but its effect can radiate outwards from the victim, through family and friends, to the community as a whole. The effects are particularly complex when the offender is a well-respected authority figure, an intimate, or a family member. These offences can strain family relationships and potentially change the dynamics of community life.

Sexual assault and its repercussions, including participation in the legal process, can precipitate a crisis in a person's life. A crisis challenges and shakes our modes of feeling, thinking, and behaving, sometimes to the point of breakdown. In his insightful book, *Thriving through Crisis*,[1] Bill O'Hanlon defines a breakdown as something that "stops you and affects your life and your sense of yourself so completely that your life cannot go on as usual." O'Hanlon suggests that experiencing a breakdown can serve as a "wake-up call," alerting you to the need for personal change, and effecting changes that can lead you, ultimately, to a more fulfilling life.

According to O'Hanlon, when life events throw you "into the soup," you have the choice to "sink, swim, or find a crouton to float on."[2] A crisis can quickly sink us into this metaphorical soup of despair, depression, anxiety, and confusion. While some remain submerged in the soup, most of us manage to float on some sort of "crouton;" we survive our terrible ordeal. Examples of these psychological croutons include the basic coping strategies offered in Chapter 5 or, in other words, strategies that allow you to take a breather, calm down, soothe yourself, or distract yourself when needed.

Short-term coping strategies allow us to catch our breath, assess our situation, and get by day-to-day. To transcend or remove ourselves from the over-heated psychological soup, we have to develop some adequate swimming strokes. The resilience skills, also discussed in Chapter 5, can improve and strengthen your emotional swimming abilities. Even when a crisis in your life is unbidden, undesired, and not of your making, there is no going back. You cannot control what happened in the past, but you can exert control on the present; you can make the decision to swim, endure, develop new skills, and commit yourself to positive personal change. In the process, you will encounter new experiences, and grow as a person, and you may even transform yourself or those around you.

POST-TRAUMATIC GROWTH

PSYCHOLOGISTS KNOW A LOT about psychological damage and psychopathology, but we have spent less time looking at human resilience. Only recently have we begun seriously looking at the extent to which people can reclaim their lives and even transform themselves in the process of coming to terms with traumatic experiences, such as sexual crimes. In this final chapter, we shift from a focus on damage to one of the potential for growth and transformation inherent in a victim's struggle to find some new meaning in life. Psychologists interested in the phenomenon of positive change following a traumatic event refer to it as "post-traumatic growth" (PTG).[3]

When we talk about growth leading to transformation, we are referring to the ability not just to bounce back from trauma or to restore life to its pre-trauma functioning level, but also to grow beyond this, significantly changing the way that you view yourself, perceive the world, and live your life. Of course, growth or transformation does not occur simply because you experience a highly stressful or traumatic event — there is nothing positive about the direct effects of a sexual assault. Any growth that occurs comes through the victim's persistence and effort in dealing with the traumatic aftermath. Growth and transformation occur as a "by-product" of a victim's personal struggle. This is congruent with the wisdom contained in diverse religious and spiritual traditions that acknowledge the ways growth can come from suffering. When we are reasonably comfortable and satisfied with our life, we tend not to make the difficult or painful choices that could potentially be transformative. The possibility of growth or transformation becomes more likely when we are in a crisis, or when our complacency and sense of security have been shattered.

THINK ABOUT YOUR OWN GROWTH

AS YOU READ THIS chapter, think about the changes that you have undergone since being sexually assaulted. If you find motivation in your pain and suffering to move along a transformational path, there are several important points to keep in mind:

- Personal growth after a traumatic experience takes time, often a considerable amount of time. It may be months or years before significant positive change is apparent to you.
- Personal growth does not typically happen in leaps and bounds; it is cumulative, consisting of small incremental changes. Focus on small, daily changes — the big changes usually take care of themselves.
- We too often focus on our weaknesses, failures, and disorders — now is the time to reflect on positive change, find your strengths and nurture them.

Growth takes time

IN A SOCIETY SO used to instant gratification, we often have difficulty accepting those things that take some time to achieve. We occasionally need to remind ourselves that life is a process, not a destination, and time is the fabric of that process. It is through time that we heal and transform ourselves. The healing process is different for each of us, and it proceeds according to our unique needs, characteristics, and degree of conscious effort. It is through this conscious effort that we begin the healing process and shape its course over time. To begin, take notice of the changes that you have already made. With time, you will see that more changes have occurred and what initially may have appeared to be a small change has made a big difference in your life.

Incremental change

IT IS EASY TO read about the many ways that we could and should make changes; it is a much more difficult proposition to enact real change. Change is something that is inevitable for all of us. Life circumstances and the passage of time often demand changes of us, whether we are ready to make them or not. By your twenty-first birthday, most societies in the world will treat you as an adult; some societies will expect adulthood much sooner. Apart from certain extraordinary circumstances, when you reach the age of majority you will be held accountable for your actions. Our society will require you to pay taxes, punish you if you break the law, and ask you to vote. This passage from childhood to adolescence to adulthood happens gradually and mostly without conscious effort. As our genetic attributes meet environmental forces, we grow physically and emotionally in daily, largely imperceptible increments towards our inevitable maturity. However, when we encounter a crisis and its resulting emotional pain, we do not want to wait many years for a gradual unfolding of our destiny. We want change to come sooner, rather than later.

In seeking change, we are prone to making grand gestures, such as "Tomorrow I am going to jog, get in shape, and lose weight." If you are a middle-aged couch potato, and you actually remember your resolution the day after you make it, you will generally find that you just cannot easily "get there from here." Even if you manage to remember your resolution, you put on some jogging clothes and hit the road, you are not likely to get very far. You cannot simply leap up after years of inactivity and run any distance; something will likely give way, and you will end up limping back home sore and discouraged. Getting in shape and losing weight in a healthy manner takes time. You have to change long-held habits and build up endurance. If you expect to make yourself athletic and trim by next week, you will most certainly be disappointed. Proceeding with such unrealistic expectations can quickly make you feel like a failure. You may decide that getting healthy is just not possible for you and say, "Yes, I have a problem, but I tried and I just can't do anything about it." In this case, it is not the lack of ability, but the lack of a practical approach that is problematic.

The same principles apply to psychological change. It is easy for victims of sexual crimes to get stuck at an early stage of healing and believe that "Yes, I'm angry and depressed, but it's not my fault, and I can't do anything about it ." It is healthy to speak out about your anger, as it can be a necessary part of your healing journey, but it is easy to get stuck where you are and become preoccupied with these feelings. Concerning yourself with what others should be doing, rather than what you can do, or waiting for some momentous change to occur will stall your progress on the healing path. Do not wait for the court to punish the offender before moving on with your healing—what if the punishment never happens or seems inadequate? Do not wait until the justice system, the community, or your family and friends adequately acknowledge your suffering—suppose they never do?

What is most often successful in effecting personal growth is a progressive series of small steps instead of grand gestures or attempts to make major, sudden changes. Recovering from any crisis, whether it is from a stroke, car accident, or sexual assault, requires a first trembling step followed by increasingly confident and stronger steps, interrupted by side steps or stumbles. It is not a coincidence that some of the most successful recovery programs, such as Alcoholics Anonymous, Al-Anon, or Overeaters Anonymous, base themselves on a twelve-step process. These programs emphasize a "one day at a time approach," rather than a goal of instant and permanent sobriety or weight loss. As you begin your healing journey, plan on proceeding with small steps supported by patience, self-compassion, and regular doses of self-discipline.

Reflect on positive change

SMALL STEPS TOWARD PERSONAL growth and change can go unnoticed. Unfortunately, while looking for the grand changes, we often overlook or devalue small positive steps. Do not berate yourself if you cannot immediately identify any signs of growth; many important changes may lie ahead. If you are reading this book, you have taken an important step just by informing yourself. When you make the decision to report a sexual crime, whether you have actually done so or not, you have taken another step. Take satisfaction in each gesture or action that you make toward health and transformation. Below are some examples of steps that may appear outwardly small, but represent personal growth. You have taken a step

- By discussing your experiences with someone you trust, divulging the secret, and breaking the silence
- By talking to the police or making a report
- By realizing that you are powerless to change the past but can exert control over the present
- By no longer blaming yourself for an act that was not your responsibility
- By refusing to accept shame or guilt for an act that was not your responsibility

- By finding healthy ways to reclaim your personal power
- By defining yourself as a whole person, rather than as a victim

WAYS THAT PEOPLE GROW

PEOPLE GROW IN MANY ways: socially, emotionally, perceptually, and spiritually. You may grow more in some areas than in others. The concept of growth, when used in a psychological context, can mean different things to different people. It is perhaps best not to worry about somebody else's narrow definition of personal growth but decide what you want for yourself. We all have different goals, priorities, and values that are important to us; consequently, what makes one person feel good about herself is not necessarily meaningful to you. We can become exhausted and disillusioned if we attempt to achieve someone else's vision of success. So, what attitudes and activities do you, as an individual, pursue to feel good about yourself?

Perhaps the most important realization that you can make in your quest for personal growth is that no single formula defines the path to personal success. Dealing with the consequences of sexual assault can lead to personal growth and change in many different areas of your life. Research examining post-traumatic growth has found that victims of traumatic experiences exhibit positive life change in some of the following ways:

- Forming new relationships or improving existing ones
- Seeing new possibilities and new ways of life
- Developing spiritually
- Forming a heightened appreciation for the positive aspects of their lives
- Forming a greater sense of inner strength, even while feeling vulnerable

Meaningful relationships

HOW OFTEN DO YOU apply "social grease" in your relationships by saying things that are not particularly genuine, having trivial conversations, going through the motions, or playing a social role? Crisis often leads us to reach out to others for emotional support and, in the process, our relationships can become more authentic and forthright. We tend to drop our social façade when we reach out and those we turn to may surprise us with their compassion and support. Admitting to ourselves that we need the support of others and learning how to reach out is another example of personal growth. You may have to examine your friendships as you decide whom you are willing to trust. Your relationship skills will be honed as you learn to discriminate between those who truly respect and support you and those who are "fair-weather friends," or those who take advantage of you when the opportunity arises. It is easy to become cynical or judgmental of others and close yourself off and become isolated, particularly if you have been abused by someone close to you. Personal growth can involve developing empathy for others, including other victims of sexual assault, rather than becoming more cynical and judgmental of others. You might find that when seeking support, you can also give support and share the gift of compassion. Many individuals eventually work through their trauma and learn to cultivate loving relationships, rather than retreating from connections with others.

New Possibilities

A MAJOR EMOTIONAL UPHEAVAL will likely disrupt the ways that you normally think and behave. Old beliefs, attitudes, and habits may be shattered. Sometimes it takes a crisis to make us consider and try out new ways of living and behaving. During this time of upheaval, you might decide to change your job, move to a new residence, change your friendship circle, or find new interests. While we caution you against making major changes impulsively or carelessly, this could be a time for expanding your horizons, discovering what is most important to you, letting go of what is not working, and determining what will work for you.

Some victims rediscover neglected aspects of themselves. For example, during his recovery from childhood sexual abuse, one First Nations man returned to the artwork he had long ago abandoned. Creating art gave him considerable satisfaction and improved his self-esteem. It also reconnected him with his culture and he eventually developed his art into a livelihood. Even if you have never before considered yourself an artist, you can expand your horizons with the transformational power of art (for example, painting, sculpting, writing, making music, and dancing). We have worked with victims who have expressed their feelings and thoughts about their sexual assault experience in various art forms that have been transformative not only for the victims, but also for those who have seen their art.

Spiritual development

SOME PEOPLE FIND PERSONAL empowerment through their relationship with God, a Creator or a Higher Power. In North America, people are members of diverse religious communities, including those with Christian, Jewish, Muslim, Buddhist, or First Nations spiritual beliefs. Others take a more individualistic approach to spirituality, perhaps by practising yoga or meditation. Some may find spiritual connectedness in nature and the wilderness. The residential school system took First Nations children away from their communities and denied them their cultural and spiritual roots, but many later transformed their lives by re-connecting with Native spiritual traditions and ceremonies. Strong spiritual connections can give you meaning and direction in your life.

As we have emphasized often, the ultimate judge of your personal or spiritual growth is you. If your struggle with trauma leads you to a fuller understanding of spiritual matters and adds meaning to your life, you have grown. When you undergo an increased sense of purpose and you freely choose a new and better life, you are moving along a healing path. It is worth remembering that spiritual growth does not necessarily mean eliminating emotional pain; those who are most shaken by a crisis in their life are often those who experience the most spiritual growth. The struggle to reconcile your spiritual beliefs with the trauma that you have suffered may itself be a painful experience. As one shaken client asked, "How can I believe in a God who would let this happen to me?" Although being confronted with such a difficult question can be disturbing, the experience can also be the catalyst that promotes a deeper and more fulfilling spiritual understanding.

Appreciating the good things

IN TIMES OF DARKNESS and despair, it is hard to see the good things around us. Depression can cast a pall over even the most positive aspects of our life, but we should not lose sight of those things in our life that are good and sustaining. Rekindling an appreciation for the good things in your life is a sign of growth. This may include reordering your priorities in recognition of the preciousness of life so that you give more time to what really matters to you and less time to inconsequential trivialities. In this way, you can live each day more fully. We can get into weary habits, drift through the days, and unquestioningly do things in the same way week after week. There is comfort and security in routine, but it can become flat, stale, and unhealthy. A crisis can shake you out of these doldrums, and reveal what is most important to you. You may discover a new appreciation of family and friends, some of whom you may have come to neglect.

Inner strength

INNER STRENGTH IS A core human resource that we each rely on to deal with adversity and vulnerability. We often think this sort of strength is rare and reserved for successful, assertive people, but that is not true. We all have strengths and weaknesses that we discover during times of crisis. Sexual crimes often involve overpowering the victim both physically and psychologically. Being victimized this way can leave you feeling weak, defenceless, and vulnerable. In the process of dealing with this experience, getting through each day, learning how to cope, developing self-knowledge, making connections with others, and meeting the challenges of the legal system, many victims discover inner resources that they did not know they had.

The singular act of surviving a brutal attack can reveal previously unrecognized strength. Ironically, a heightened awareness of your vulnerability can create a more complex, balanced self-image that makes you feel stronger and more capable. Recognizing your strength is a step towards transformation and often requires a softening of self-criticism and the development of some compassion for yourself. We learn from mistakes, and when we can learn to be patient and tolerant of our human foibles instead of bemoaning our failures, we create an opportunity for growth. Each challenge we face can be an opportunity to exercise our resolve and resourcefulness. Inner strength is about living according to our own values and desires, not those imposed by circumstance or adversity. For many victims of sexual abuse, inner strength comes in the form of finally saying no to toxic, unhealthy relationships. For some, developing the ability to set healthy boundaries in their relationships may be the greatest reward of all.

SOCIAL ACTION

WE ARE ALL VULNERABLE as individuals. By living in communities, we gain strength and have the potential to develop into more complex and evolving civilizations. In most modern North American communities, we have developed adequate systems for accessing food, water, and shelter that ensure basic daily survival, but we require ongoing cooperation and the contributions of many to develop long-term security and protection from sexual assault. It is through the energy and social contributions of concerned individuals that we continue to develop our justice system, and evolve toward a more equitable and just society.

In his book *The Path of Least Resistance,* Robert Fritz argues that one of the fundamental principles for creating change is recognizing the relationship between inner healing and external actions:[4]

> There is a direct connection between what occurs in our consciousness and what occurs in our external life, and if we initiate change internally, a corresponding change will happen externally.

Mahatma Gandhi, the great Indian activist and social reformer, made this point in a slightly different way. He said, "You must be the change you wish to see in the world."[5] The internal changes you make during your healing journey are likely to be reflected in some external, observable way, and we have discussed some of those above. In the following section, we look at ways that you can move beyond personal change to perhaps making changes in the greater social fabric.

Bill O'Hanlon speaks eloquently about "following your wound," namely the hurt you feel inside that has not been resolved and that may never completely go away.[6] You may understand well his observation, "If you focus on your wound or your outrage and keep it inside, poisoning you, or if you use it to strike out at others out of bitterness it doesn't seem to heal. It makes you smaller and keeps you stuck ... [however] you can find both healing and meaning in what you are pissed or hurt by."

The wound of a sexual crime can move or energize you to heal yourself and to grow as a person. Over time, some of you may be moved to "follow your wound" into the realm of social action, to contribute to others, or to address injustices in our system and society toward victims of crime. You may find ways to transform your healing energy into constructive social change. Your efforts to make a positive social contribution may, in their turn, lead to further personal growth and transformation.

Social action is not for everyone

BEFORE WE CONTINUE FURTHER with this discussion, it is important to emphasize that direct social action is not for everyone; it is but one direction a person's healing path can take. As we have repeatedly indicated, the path that each person takes to resolve one's pain and trauma is unique. One path is no more valid than the next, and you are no less valuable as a person for the choices you make. If the path you choose is meaningful to you, causes no harm, and serves a healing purpose, your course of action is the right one.

Based on your own distinctive and valuable character, you can contribute to your social environment in your own unique way. Some choose to make a difference by getting angry at the system, writing letters, organizing protests, complaining to authorities, or giving press conferences. Others will make different choices, directing their energy to become a nurturing parent, a caring partner, or a school volunteer. Our hope for you is that you are able to make choices that are healthy and right for you.

No gesture is too small

SMALL ACTIONS CAN SOMETIMES have big, unforeseen consequences. This is an idea that has become known as the "Butterfly Effect." The Butterfly Effect is a popular phrase that captures a mathematic concept known as "sensitive dependence on initial conditions." Although this may sound abstract, the basic concept simply refers to circumstances in which small changes in initial conditions can make large differences in the outcome. For example, if you are standing at the pinnacle of a mountain and place a ball on the ground, it may roll in many different directions and come to rest in a variety of places, depending on where you initially place it. Placing the ball in spots only centimetres apart at the top of the mountain may result in it eventually rolling into different valleys kilometres apart below.

The Butterfly Effect is often used to illustrate the idea that there is meaning in everything we do. Every thought and every action, even as tiny as the flapping wings of a butterfly, can potentially have a large effect on the world. Everything you do matters, and even the smallest action today may make a difference with time. You never know when conditions are right for your actions to have a profound and lasting effect. The negative effects of sexual abuse, as discussed in earlier chapters, ripple outward from the victims, through their families, to the larger community. The same is true of constructive activities. A caring smile or a gesture of kindness toward someone can produce a shift in that person's day and perhaps have a ripple effect on others around them. We have all had the experience of someone's small attention making a disproportionate difference in our day. No gesture is too small or too insignificant to potentially be of value or to spur some sort of meaningful change. Even if your small gesture does not result in an observable, significant change of some sort, bear in mind the ancient aphorism attributed to Confucius: "A journey of a thousand miles begins with a single step." Although a small gesture can sometimes have a disproportionately large effect, the accumulation of small gestures or steps can also lead to meaningful change. Later, we will discuss some examples of ordinary people whose actions in response to their crisis had a significant impact on others and the community at large.

WAYS TO CONTRIBUTE

THERE ARE MANY WAYS that you might follow your wound to help others and your community. You might have an affinity for creative endeavours, such as painting, writing, making films, or playing music. Many people find an outlet for their rage in the creative process. Others prefer concrete, direct action, such as helping other victims to seek justice, volunteering at a rape crisis centre, organizing self-help groups, or educating others about sexual abuse issues. The list is virtually endless, and what you might choose to do will be based on your unique needs, talents, and desires. In the following sections, there are two paths toward social transformation that we want to discuss in more depth: supporting other victims and transforming our justice system.

Supporting other victims

SOME VICTIMS OF SEXUAL crimes take what they have learned from their own healing journey or justice system experiences and use this understanding to support others who are struggling with similar issues. This can be a very rewarding and fulfilling way to transform the pain of your own abuse into something good for others. For example, we know wonderfully compassionate and effective therapists whose own histories of sexual abuse have heightened their therapeutic work.

We caution, however, that providing effective emotional support directly to others can be a very demanding and difficult task. Good therapists have specialized training, a wide range of skills, and a strong support network. Getting the training and professional credentials you need to be a recognized therapist requires a considerable commitment of time, energy, and financial resources. If you choose this particular path as a way to make a difference, do your homework first. It is important that you understand the requirements and demands of being a therapist or counsellor — even on a casual basis. Perhaps more importantly, understand that being a therapist is not a means to do your own healing. A therapist's own emotional needs can easily diminish the value of his clinical judgments. As a counsellor, you will burden, rather than help, other victims by taking your own unresolved issues into therapy sessions. Even with the best intentions, a damaged counsellor can do more harm than good for another sexual assault victim who is seeking help.

We recommend that you take considerable time and care in making a decision about how to help other victims. In no way do we want to quash the impulse and desire you may feel to make this kind of contribution. Supporting those in need is a wonderful thing, but it is important that you find the helping avenue that is best for you and for those who need your help. Some people would make excellent, effective therapists; for others, the right choice may mean helping in other ways.

If you are contemplating some type of victim-support work, you might want to start by assessing which of your personal skills and attributes you can best utilize. Although a desire to help others may be your prime motivation, you do not have to work directly with victims of sexual crimes to make a difference. There are many ways to help. For example, you might assist victim support organizations with fund-raising, education, media presentations, financial donations, or other needed services. Depending on your particular skills and emotional needs, you might consider other activities, such as providing daycare services for at-risk children, conducting sports camps for youth, helping the homeless, teaching nutrition classes to young mothers, or supporting organizations that assist prostitutes to leave the streets. The list of social needs is virtually endless. While these activities may not, at first glance, appear to be relevant to sexual assault, your work could help prevent sexual assault in vulnerable populations, or could provide someone with the resources necessary to cope more effectively with the traumas of life.

Changing our justice system

YOUR OWN EXPERIENCES, INCLUDING your frustration, anger, or disappointment with the justice system, may motivate you to try to change the justice system. Studies of victims who attempt to translate their adversity into positive forms of social action suggest a common theme: a moral commitment inspired by a sense that personal and group trauma must be converted into a community asset.[7] Whatever your predominant emotions may be, you may feel committed to somehow converting your personal experiences of adversity into some sort of greater good, perhaps to smooth the way for those who will come after you. Although you may have some ideas about what you want to change, you may feel overwhelmed by the enormity of it all, and be unsure how to proceed. You may wonder if it is even possible for you to make a difference.

First, it is important to remind yourself that just by participating in the prosecution of an offender, by reporting an assault, and holding the offender accountable, you are making a valuable contribution. We have frequently made the point that the justice system is the sum of its parts; this includes the judge, lawyers, legislators, police, experts, witnesses, support staff, and the complainant. The participation of all these people makes the system work, and your participation may actually lead to changes in that system. You may feel like a small cog in a very large machine, but without your determined and often courageous effort as the complainant, justice is not served. It is not a small task to confront the offender in a courtroom. Any single case may set legal precedents and change the administration of justice in the future. Your case can make a difference that you never anticipated when you first made the decision to go to the police with your complaint.

For democracy to function well, all our great public institutions, and especially our justice system, must serve the needs and reflect the core values of all citizens. As a multicultural country, our core values are diverse, changing, and developing. There is frequently vociferous debate about our social values and an accompanying complaint that they are changing for the worse. Social change, as directed by government initiatives and legislation, should address the needs and desires of the communities affected. Only with the participation of people like you will the system truly reflect the needs within our local and national communities. In particular, to advance change that recognizes the needs and values of sexual assault victims, the justice system needs to hear the voices of the victims. If you want to influence any sort of change in the system, you can make your voice heard by participating in the prosecution of your offender or in civil litigation against those responsible for the harm you suffered. Whichever legal path you choose, your participation may provide you with an opportunity to contribute to the direction that our justice system ultimately takes.

GUIDELINES FOR SOCIAL ACTION

IF YOU ARE MOTIVATED to contribute to social change, but are not sure where to start, below are four principles, drawn from a variety of sources, that may help guide you as you endeavour to effect change within the justice system or within your community. You will notice that some of these steps draw on concepts, skills, and coping strategies that we have discussed in earlier chapters.

Create an inclusive circle

IN OUR LIVES, WE have friendship circles, circles of influence, cultural circles, and some have circles of power. We are aware, perhaps most acutely when we are young, of being excluded from some circles. People are excluded or left outside social circles for any number of reasons, including race, sexual orientation, poverty, religious belief, or disability. When you attempt to make changes or to shift other people's perspectives, you may be seen as a rebel or a threat to the normal way of doing business. As a result, you may find yourself outside the status quo circle.

In the following poem, Edwin Markham beautifully expresses the metaphor of social circles as a kind of personal boundary that can be either inclusive or exclusive:

> He drew a circle that shut me out
> Heretic, rebel, a thing to flout.
> But Love and I had the wit to win,
> We drew a circle that took him in.[8]

Many of us are accustomed to expending considerable time and effort attempting to enter someone else's circle of influence, power, knowledge, culture, or experience — but what happens when you create your own circle and invite others in? A sense of choice, control, and belonging then becomes yours. You are letting others in, rather than waiting for others to ask you in. Your energy may be much better spent allying yourself with like-minded people and creating your own circle, one that is an inclusive circle of influence or knowledge.

Many victims of sexual crimes and their advocates talk about feeling alienated and of being outside the circle of those in authority who just do not get it. This is what we earlier referred to as "secondary victimization." In large part, this is why so many advocacy groups exist. They are there to validate the experiences of victims, and to make sure that they get the support they need. Remember that, often, those who do not understand the needs and concerns of complainants are not necessarily spiteful people; they often lack awareness. Thoughtless or insensitive behaviour is frequently due to ignorance or limited personal resources, rather than due to any intention to hurt you. While there will always be people who intentionally hurt you, there are many others whose perspective can benefit from your knowledge and experience.

When the time is right, you might decide to let some of these people into your circle of knowledge and experience. They may not truly understand the impact of what you have experienced and perhaps they never will, but if a person is willing to listen and learn, that is an opportunity to invite that person into your circle. You can facilitate the inclusion of others in your circle if you are able to be as understanding of their weaknesses and vulnerabilities as you want them to be of yours. You can change their perspective by your example and through information that helps them understand the dynamics of sexual crimes. You will be gratified the first time someone who was initially indifferent, uncaring, or even hostile to you becomes one of your supporters. In this way, you can expand your circle and you may even build a close friendship or perhaps, in the case of a family member or intimate, a healthier, more loving, and supportive relationship.

Challenge the media messages

UNFORTUNATELY, WE DO NOT always get the whole story or the whole truth from what we read and hear in the media. Some media sources are thoughtful and well-intentioned, but others are less so. When the goal is to sell newspapers or advertising, the focus may be on sensationalizing an issue, rather than on providing an accurate or fair account of the story. We may encounter stories in the media that do not accurately reflect the experiences of victims or the functioning of the legal system. Both the news media and the entertainment media may present programming that glorifies or promotes violence or reinforces gender, racial, or ethnic stereotypes.

Because of the negative impact such distortions can have, there is value in providing another perspective by challenging myths, misperceptions, and stereotypes. To confront misrepresentations by the media effectively, it is best to begin by detaching yourself personally from the disagreement. This does not mean that your own experiences are not important to the points you wish to make, but people will better receive your comments if you do not deliver them with rancour, bitterness, rage, or defensiveness.

Your comments will also have more power and credence if they are carefully thought out and illustrated with facts and specific examples. Your interactions with others can effectively model how you would like to be treated and how you are advocating that others be treated. This means treating others (including media representatives) with respect, patience, and compassion. It can help to think of the person you are communicating with as being a "student of life" (as we all are) even when that person may view the world very differently than you do.

For those of you considering this type of advocacy, be aware that you likely will face resistance. The more you push, the more resistance you are likely to create. If you are hurt or enraged by resistance from powerful, established organizations, or from authority figures, advocacy of this type may not be for you. However, if you are fully aware that resistance is a natural step towards change, then you can challenge the status quo with conviction and assertion, rather than tentatively or aggressively.

Contribute to the tipping point of a value you believe in

IN HIS BOOK *THE Tipping Point: How Little Things Can Make a Big Difference*,[9] Malcolm Gladwell writes about that moment when an idea, a trend, or a social behaviour crosses over a threshold or "tipping point," causing it to spread quickly and widely. At its tipping point, an idea of previously little consequence can quickly become extremely influential. Just as one infected person can start an epidemic of the flu, so can one or a few people cause a fashion trend, a widespread popularity of a new product, or a change in social policy. To reach a tipping point, something has to jolt the social equilibrium, or the usual way that things happen. Gladwell postulates three principles that contribute to change by creating a tipping point: the law of the few, the stickiness factor, and the power of context.

The law of the few is something we all experience. Those in the working world know that in organizations, large or small, a small percentage of people generally do most of the work. Those who study crime know that a few highly dangerous criminals are responsible for most of the serious offences, and a relatively few drinkers receive the majority of impaired driving charges. So it is with trends and reforms; typically one person (or a few persons) contributes to the tipping point. It does not take an army to make a great change. A few well-motivated people with a genuine cause can create a tipping point of social change.

An idea or perspective is more likely to spread and take hold in the social consciousness if it has "sticky properties," something that makes it memorable to people. The stickiness factor suggests that people are more likely to remember a message if it is simple and poignant. Cluttered, complex, dry messages are not as likely to stick. People who use a public forum to berate the system, to vent their anger, or to achieve some personal gain are also unlikely to score high on the stickiness factor. An emotionally honest, heartfelt, balanced story is most likely to find resonance with the public and is therefore most likely to be sticky.

The context of the message can be as important as the message itself. As humans, we are very sensitive to social cues and the environment around us. Studies have shown that small changes in a neighbourhood, such as cleaning up garbage and fixing broken windows, can significantly lower its crime rate. An environment that others respect enough to keep clean is less inviting to criminal behaviour. At a more individual level, subtle changes in the delivery of a message can have a large impact on how people receive it. Personal characteristics of the messenger can be as important as the ideas they deliver. This is congruent with Gandhi's exhortation to be the change you want to see. Calls for balance and compassion in the justice system will be best received from a spokesperson demonstrating the same qualities.

One well-known example of a tipping point is the organization Mothers Against Drunk Driving (MADD), which was started by Candy Lightner after her young daughter was killed by a drunk driver. The lax laws and weak judicial response to her daughter's death so outraged Ms. Lightner that she decided to take action and found MADD in 1980. By 1982, the organization had reached national prominence and by 1984, it had hundreds of chapters around the world. Not only has MADD raised the national consciousness about the impact of impaired driving, its influence has led to the serious enforcement of impaired driving laws and mandatory penalties. MADD's efforts have significantly reduced the incidence of drunk driving and, consequently, countless lives have no doubt been saved.

The actions of a few people can be meaningful and, with time, small changes can lead to big results. As noted above, sometimes our actions and their impact are separated in time and space. The effect of your action today may not be realized for weeks, months, or even years. However, you may wake up one day to discover a noticeable difference has been made. You could be the one whose contribution added to all those who came before you, who takes a value or an issue to its tipping point, and who enables significant change to happen. Everything you do matters, whether it is seeking greater equality in court, nurturing victims of sexual assaults, or changing the way that litigation proceeds. You could be the one to start the ball rolling or tip the balance. On the other hand, you may be the one who inspires others to come on board who in their turn produce the tipping point for important change.

Seek out visionary leaders

SOME OF US HAVE leadership qualities while others are more suited to a support role, and thank goodness, the world provides for both. A society of nothing but leaders would be as doomed as a society composed only of followers. If you are strongly motivated toward social action, but do not relish taking a leadership role, you can seek out someone who does, someone who is a visionary leader. It is not hard to identify those people and institutions around us that influence social thought. They are the prominent people in places of power and education. Within this group of individuals, you can find visionary leaders who actively embrace change in our communities and welcome the support of others.

Although many of these visionary leaders work within large, mainstream organizations, some of them live and work in ways that are more peripheral. You can find them within the network of people working for causes that you want to support. You will find them working for rape crisis centres, women's organizations, homeless shelters, or with at-risk youth. Social visionaries concern themselves with issues that contribute to alienation and vulnerability in our communities, for example, homelessness, unemployment, poor health care, under-funded child services, and inequities in the criminal justice system. When seeking leadership, look for people who gain their authority not through appointment or organizational power, but through their beliefs, values, character, knowledge, and skills. Visionary leaders are people who want to achieve a vision or a goal, not people who simply manage or assign tasks to others.

Learn about these people, their beliefs, and the ways they facilitate change. You can read about or ask them about the specific measures they have undertaken to accomplish their goals. You could focus on societal values and government policies that contribute to the vulnerability of some and the subsequent physical or sexual violence that they are subjected to. Policies in need of change may relate to the lack of affordable housing, well-paying employment, or childcare. You may find an interest in policies that affect the funding of services to help victims of assaults, and to criminal justice system reform. You could then become involved in organizations that are attempting to address these issues, or take your own individual steps.[10] You can also contact your government representative to see what is being done to address these issues. When making this contact, do not be satisfied with a listing of past actions; remember that the initiatives that governments have already taken have not addressed the magnitude of the problem. Ask for specific commitments to implement particular recommendations made by the many commissions and studies conducted in the past two decades. Set a target date for action and follow-up to see if government representatives have kept their word.

The work of those who have gone before you is documented in a wealth of publications, many of these by governmental agencies. Health Canada sponsors the National Clearinghouse on Family Violence, a website where you can access information on violence within relationships, including sexual abuse.[11] This is a resource centre for all Canadians seeking information about violence and abuse or looking for new resources to address sexual abuse issues within the family. By sharing the latest research findings and information on all aspects of prevention, protection, and treatment, the Clearinghouse hopes to achieve its goal of helping Canadian communities work toward reducing the occurrence of family violence, including sexual abuse.

YOU ARE A WORK IN PROGRESS

AS WE HAVE POINTED out before, our healing journeys are unique and allow for some backtracking, side-trips, and even breaks from time to time. We also have latitude in how we decide to advocate for ourselves or for victims in general, and where we find some personal power. For those who choose advocacy, this kind of work becomes a part of the healing process. It involves self-exploration and discovery. It helps build self-confidence and

448 TRAUMA, TRIALS, AND TRANSFORMATION

self-discipline. As you continue along your own path, keep in mind that the circles you draw, your spheres of influence, and your choices are continually evolving and expanding. Self-doubt will likely wax and wane, but take regular notice of how far you have come and how much you have learned. To make it to this place, to the place where you have decided to make a difference, you have demonstrated inner strength, integrity, and courage. Once you have experienced these reserves in yourself, you can call upon them repeatedly. Recognizing and fostering these internal resources can propel you forward on a pathway that is distinctly yours.

EXAMPLES OF GROWTH AND TRANSFORMATION

THERE ARE COUNTLESS EXAMPLES of people who have dealt with extreme adversity or trauma in a way that is moving to all who hear their story. Witnessing other people's resilience, courage, perseverance, creativity, humour, and strength can spur us on and help us meet our own challenges. These life stories can be validating. Hearing about struggles that mirror our own makes us feel less alienated and alone. The stories can be ones of hope that show that it is possible to survive a terrible crisis and emerge on the other side to a fulfilling and new life. They can be stories of inspiration, showing us myriad ways to transform and change. Inspiration, from the Greek, literally means to breathe in, to draw life, and to enliven. Inspiration can motivate us to rise above what we believed were our limits, discover unacknowledged strength, change things in our own life, and, perhaps, transform those around us. Moreover, as you will see, the most inspirational stories are those of ordinary people who did extraordinary things. You do not have to be a superhero to make significant change; you only need the inspiration.

Below we present some validating, hopeful, and inspiring stories of other people's struggles. We begin with a listing of some memoirs written by people who have experienced terrible tragedy or trauma in their lives, and their subsequent journeys of personal growth or transformation. There are also examples of individuals who have dealt with their tragic circumstances by seeking social change, people who followed their wound to the benefit of us all. We end the chapter with some inspiring examples of Canadians whose actions have had a specific impact on our criminal justice system and those involved in that system.

Many of the stories we refer to here do not deal specifically with the trauma of sexual assault, because the themes of surviving and thriving through crisis are universal. We can be inspired by and learn from those struggling with a wide variety of personal crises or oppression.

Crisis memoirs

IN HIS BOOK *Thriving through Crisis: Turn Tragedy and Trauma into Growth and Change*, Bill O'Hanlon gives examples of what he refers to as "crisis memoirs" — stories of people who have survived extraordinary crisis and trauma.[12] For those interested in reading about how other people have faced tremendous challenges in their lives, *Survival Stories*, edited by Kathryn Rhett, is a good place to start. This book contains twenty-two excerpts from memoirs of people who have survived personal crisis.[13] Reynolds Price tells his story in *A Whole New Life: An Illness and a Healing.*[14] Mr. Price was paralyzed by cancer of the spinal column and eventually came to the conclusion that the person he used to be was gone. This book will challenge the reader who is undergoing a crisis to make some hard decisions and move on with life. At nine years of age, Lucy Grealy's face was disfigured by cancer. She recounts her story of reconstructive surgery, cruel taunts, and the morbid stares of others in *Autobiography of a Face.*[15] Ms. Grealy describes her struggle to find some self-esteem and the path that eventually led her to let go of her desire to be beautiful. Anatole Broyard was a *New York Times* critic and writer when he was diagnosed with cancer. He was therefore uniquely equipped to discuss issues of illness and death in a book entitled *Intoxicated by My Illness: And Other Writings on Life and Death.*[16] Mr. Broyard illuminates the life lessons that can be contained in overwhelming events.

A good general guide to self-help resources is the *Authoritative Guide to Self-Help Resources in Mental Health.*[17] This indispensable reference helps readers distinguish quality self-help resources from those that are potentially misleading or possibly harmful. The authors review a wide range of mental health references including Internet websites. Among referenced memoirs that focus on experiences of childhood physical or sexual abuse, Dave Pelzer's series of three books may be of interest. These books, which describe three periods in his life, are *A Child Called "It": One Child's Courage to Survive;*[18] *The Lost Boy: A Foster Child's Search for the Love of a Family;*[19] and *A Man Named Dave: A Story of Triumph and Forgiveness.*[20] The first of these books chronicles Mr. Pelzer's experiences as a young child who was emotionally and physically abused by his mother, almost to the point of death. He then spent nine years in foster care, which is the subject of the second book. The third book describes the author's life as an adult. Although these books graphically describe terrible experiences of abuse, the third book recounts how resilience, willpower, and the desire to survive can be instrumental in dealing with a horrific past and getting on with life. The message is simple — you can survive abuse and move on to a productive career and a satisfying life. Another valuable reference is *Daddy's Girl,* by Charlotte Vale Allen, which describes the author's struggles to deal with sexual abuse by her father between the ages of seven to seventeen.[21] Ms. Allen survived her experiences to go on to become a professional writer and an advocate for victims of child abuse and domestic violence.

Stories of social action

THERE ARE COUNTLESS INSPIRATIONAL stories of individuals not only surviving adversity and trauma, but also using their experience to transform society in some important way — people following their wound to social action. You are likely familiar with the following series of examples; they are famous people with well-known stories, but stories that bear retelling. If you want to know more about these people, their histories have been widely published and can be obtained though local libraries or bookstores.

IMAGINE LIVING IN A country where drinking out of the wrong water fountain was grounds for putting you in prison; where a man doing the same job as you would get paid more in a week than you did in a year because his skin was light and yours was dark; where you and your ancestors were not even considered to be fully human. South Africa was such a country. Nelson Mandela lived in South Africa and was imprisoned by authorities for approximately twenty-seven years due to his fight against racist governmental policies. However, even while in prison, Mandela continued to be a beacon of hope for his people and carried on the struggle against Apartheid. Finally freed from prison in 1990, Mr. Mandela was one of the driving forces in changing black South Africans' access to resources and giving them a role in government. His actions led to dramatic alterations in the racist policies that had previously imprisoned him. He became South Africa's first black president and received the Nobel Peace Prize. He also helped establish the Truth and Reconciliation Commission of South

Africa that has pioneered innovative ways to seek justice, accountability, amnesty, and forgiveness.

TERRY FOX IS A true Canadian hero. At the age of eighteen, Terry Fox was diagnosed with cancer, which required the amputation of his right leg. At the age of twenty-one, he set out on a cross-Canada run that he called the Marathon of Hope, in order to raise money for cancer research. Most of us have seen photographs or films of Terry Fox's enormously courageous run across the country with one healthy leg and one artificial leg. He ran for one hundred and forty-three days and covered 5,376 kilometres before having to stop due to a recurrence of cancer in his lungs. In a press conference Terry Fox said, "I just wish people would realize that anything is possible if you try. Dreams are made if people try."[22] When he died in 1981 at the age of twenty-two, Terry Fox had raised over $24 million for cancer research. Every year since his initial run twenty-five years ago, millions have participated in annual Terry Fox memorial runs to raise money for cancer research. These runs occur in over sixty countries, to date raising over $360 million, used in an effort to combat one of the most serious health problems of our time.

CANADIAN ACTOR MICHAEL J. FOX publicly disclosed his battle with Parkinson's disease and, hence, raised awareness of this disease and its effects. He has tirelessly campaigned to increase both the awareness of and the funds to fight this illness. He also created a foundation whose purpose is to find a cure and better treatments for this disease. He published an inspiring memoir of his struggles in 2002, entitled *Lucky Man*.[23]

The fight against sexual crime

THE FOLLOWING ARE STORIES of two Canadians who are not as famous as those noted above, but who expressed their rage about victimization and inequality in socially responsible ways. These are but two stories among many that inspire us.[24] For some individuals, their anger stemmed not only from their victimization, but also from the way in which the police, the media, and the justice system handled their cases. Their subsequent actions made a difference in how victims and their families are treated and changed the way police investigate sexual crimes while also improving the manner in which the justice system prosecutes offenders. Apart from their inspirational example, we are grateful for the contributions that each of these individuals has made to all victims of sexual crimes.

ART THOMPSON, A FIRST Nations' man and acclaimed Nuu-chac-nulth artist, attended a residential school for nine years as a child and adolescent in Port Alberni, British Columbia.[25] In 1995, Mr. Thompson, along with several other aboriginal men from the school, attended the trial of Arthur Plint, a dorm supervisor. Before entering a guilty plea to sixteen counts of indecent assault of boys aged six to thirteen years, Plint, then seventy-seven years old, demonstrated his defiance, disrespect, and lack of remorse, by striking out at people with his cane when he walked into the courtroom.

The court convicted Plint and at Plint's sentencing hearing, in the face of such ugliness, Art Thompson spoke with remarkable integrity and resoluteness. He attended the hearing proudly wearing the traditional clothing of his people — a headband and a ceremonial robe with a thunderbird on the back. He painted his face in the traditional black to ward off evil. Maintaining his dignity before the man who cruelly and sadistically had assaulted so many, Mr. Thompson addressed Plint by saying: "You're a constant reminder of cultural abuse. I want you to understand the anger and shame but, most of all, I want you to understand the dignity of these men."[26] A written account described this powerful courtroom moment, as Thompson stood before his tormentor, as "Snow-white particles of eagle down, representing truth and purity, floated from his cape to the bright-red courtroom carpet."[27]

Art Thompson demonstrated tremendous cultural pride, dignity, integrity, and courage in the way that he addressed the courtroom and the offender. He was able to speak powerfully and eloquently for all the men who had suffered so much at the hands of this offender, and the court and those present listened to him with respect. Mr. Thompson's comments, along with those of other courageous men who spoke at the hearing, standing "straight and proud," were likely taken into account as British Columbia Supreme Court Justice Douglas Hogarth sentenced Plint to eleven years in prison.

JANE DOE IS A young urban woman who became the fifth reported rape victim of a sexual predator in her Toronto neighbourhood while she was asleep in her bed. The offender entered her apartment through her balcony door, as he had done at other neighbourhood residences, and thus he became known as the "balcony rapist."

When the police refused to warn the neighbourhood that a sexual predator was on the loose, fearing that this would drive him underground and out of their grasp, Jane Doe challenged their procedures. Refusing to accept the status quo that she should be quiet and allow the investigation to unfold in a way that the police deemed appropriate, Jane Doe and her friends distributed posters on the streets and sent out media releases. She challenged a system that would not warn her and others in her neighbourhood that there was a dangerous predator among them. She also challenged the traditional belief that an official police warning would only cause unnecessary hysteria.

Jane Doe argued that, by not issuing a warning, the police were "using women as bait" to catch the rapist. This argument became the grounds for a civil lawsuit against the Toronto Police Services that was finally resolved twelve long, difficult years after her 1986 rape. Jane Doe collected over $200,000 in damages plus all her legal costs, an amount which surpassed a million dollars. During her ordeal, Jane Doe endured unmitigated verbal character attacks from the police, the mayor, the media, and the public.

Her lawsuit against the police was headline news in North America and abroad, and in the wake of her court victory, she received numerous awards and honours. A movie about her experiences, *The Many Trials of One Jane Doe*, aired to critical acclaim on television networks in Canada, the United States, and the United Kingdom. Tort law textbooks cite Jane Doe's case, which is studied in law schools internationally.

Jane Doe says that, even if she had known beforehand how long and difficult the journey was going to be, she would still have taken it. She is well aware of the difference she made not only in the Canadian legal system, but throughout the world as well. Jane Doe documented her story in a compelling book called *The Story of Jane Doe*.[28]

DIFFERENCES YOU CAN MAKE

IT IS OUR HOPE that you have found the foregoing examples to be inspirational. They illustrate not only human resilience, but also ways in which victims of terrible tragedy have been able to transform their lives or the lives of others. Sometimes we need reminders that these are not the stories of superhuman people. These are the stories of human beings, with flaws and limitations similar to our own. It is likely that none of these individuals could have accurately predicted beforehand how they would respond to the trauma and adversity that life brought their way. Sometimes our responses to adversity surprise not only those around us, but surprise us as well.

It is our human condition to have unexplored depths, accessed only in special circumstances including those of loss, adversity, trauma, or heartbreak. Sometimes just the task of surviving your current situation may feel overwhelming. The thought of transforming your life or the lives of others may not seem even remotely possible at this time, but remind yourself that surviving in and of itself can be an incredible feat and an enormous accomplishment. The tenacity and integrity of victims during the aftermath of their sexual assaults has deeply moved and inspired us. For some, it can be enough to celebrate having survived and being alive. Others may be on a different path. Perhaps you have experienced some personal growth or transformation through your struggles with adversity or trauma. Perhaps you have taken steps that have changed others or you are interested in pursuing a path that can lead to social transformation. These are all honourable paths and ways of being in the world that deserve celebration.

Wherever you may be on your own healing path, we invite you to appreciate and respect your unique achievements. Remember the "Butterfly Effect"; sometimes the smallest things you do can make the biggest difference. Whether or not the differences you make resemble those described in this chapter, realize that each of us has something to contribute, no matter how small it may seem. Just thinking in this positive way can be transformative. As professionals working with victims of sexual assault, we have been moved by the tenacity and courage of these individuals in coping with and overcoming their traumas, and we can attest to the power inherent in the simple decision to take a healing path. Change is inevitable; life unfolds without ever asking our permission, so the question we all have to answer is not will I change, but how will I change?

VIGNETTE ELEVEN: TURNING PAIN INTO ACTION

THE CROWN COUNSEL HELPED facilitate a healing circle for the women described in Vignette Eleven because the sentencing hearing and the emotional wounds described by the women in their victim impact statements illustrated to her the need for healing. She agreed with the women that there was an opportunity for them to bring some closure to their courtroom ordeal and begin the healing process. The Crown began the circle with a discussion of the offender and some of the women expressed a greater understanding of his behaviour after hearing the expert witness testify. Since the offender was directly related to most of the women, they wanted to think the best of him. For years they believed his expressions of regret and his promises never to offend again. It took their experiences in the courtroom to bring into full focus the danger he posed to children. Some expressed their guilt about not acting sooner to protect the younger generation of children from this man.

Several of the women in the circle, who were leaders in their own communities, took the initiative and began formulating a plan for a different, safer future for themselves and others. One woman apologized to some of the others for not supporting them when she had opportunities to do so in the past. Amidst more tears and comforting, the women vowed to support each other as a community in the future. They realized how a lack of support and communication within their group had contributed to the silence and fear that allowed the offender an opportunity to avoid consequences for his actions for so many years. The more they talked about a positive future, the more empowered they felt to make significant changes in their own lives and the lives of those around them. Some of the women pledged to begin an education program about sexual abuse on their reserve, and some committed themselves to accompany other victims to court and support them through the process. The faces of the women, which had been dark with suffering during the trial, took on a new light as they left their meeting. Their perspective was changed by new knowledge and understanding and they were empowered to make changes where they once felt incapable of preventing the abuse in their community.

ENDNOTES

1   Bill O'Hanlon, *Thriving through Crisis: Turn Tragedy and Trauma into Growth and Change* (New York: The Berkley Publishing Group, 2004) at xiv.

2   *Ibid.*

3   Richard G. Tedeschi, Crystal L. Park, & Lawrence G. Calhoun, eds., *Post-Traumatic Growth: Positive Change in the Aftermath of Crisis* (Mahwah, NJ: Lawrence Erlbaum Associates, 1998) [*Post-Traumatic Growth*].

4   Robert Fritz, *The Path of Least Resistance* (New York: Ballantine Books, 1984).

5   Online: www.mahatma.org.in/quotes/quotes.jsp?link=qt.

6   O'Hanlon, *Thriving through Crisis*, above note 1 at 66.

7   Sandra L. Bloom, "By the Crowd They Have Been Broken, By the Crowd They Shall be Healed: The Social Transformation of Trauma," in *Post-Traumatic Growth*, above note 3 at 181.

8   Edwin Markham, "Outwitted" in Hazel Felleman, ed., *The Best Loved Poems of the American People* (Garden City, NY: Doubleday, 1936).

9   Malcolm Gladwell, *The Tipping Point: How Little Things Can Make a Big Difference* (Boston: Little, Brown, 2000).

10 There are many victim support groups you can contact to offer assistance, such as the non-profit Canadian Crime Victim Foundation, online: www.ccfv.net, whose vision is "giving victims a voice." A Google search can access other groups.

11 Online: www.phac-aspc.gc.ca/ncfv-cnivf/familyviolence.

12 O'Hanlon, *Thriving through Crisis*, above note 1 at 80–82.

13 Kathryn Rhett, ed., *Survival Stories: Memoirs of Crisis* (New York: Doubleday, 1997).

14 Reynolds Price, *A Whole New Life: An Illness and a Healing* (New York: Plume, 1982).

15 Lucy Grealy, *Autobiography of a Face* (Boston: Houghton Mifflin, 1984).

16 Anatole Broyard, *Intoxicated by My Illness: And Other Writings on Life and Death* (New York: Fawcett Columbine, 1992).

17 J.C. Norcross *et al.*, *Authoritative Guide to Self-Help Resources in Mental Health*, rev. ed. (New York: Guilford Press, 2003) at 24–25.

18 Dave Pelzer, *A Child Called "It": One Child's Courage to Survive* (Deerfield Beach, FL: Health Communications, 1995).

19 Dave Pelzer, *The Lost Boy: A Foster Child's Search for the Love of a Family* (Deerfield Beach, FL: Health Communications, 1997).

20 Dave Pelzer, *A Man Named Dave: A Story of Triumph and Forgiveness* (New York: Dutton, 1999).

21 Charlotte Vale Allen, *Daddy's Girl* (New York, Berkley Books, 1980).

22 From CBC website, online: www.cbc.ca/greatest/top_ten/nominee/fox-terry.

23 Michael J. Fox, *Lucky Man* (New York: Hyperion, 2002).

24 See, for example, the story of the courageous contributions to the law made by Justice L'Heureux-Dubé, as recorded by Elizabeth Sheehy, ed., *Adding Feminism*

to Law: The Contributions of Justice Claire L'Heureux-Dubé (Toronto: Irwin Law, 2004). Also, you can read about the inspiring, determined recovery of Misty Cockerill, who survived an horrific sexual assault and recently received a scholarship to assist her in achieving her goal of becoming an advocate for crime victims, online: www.ccvf.net/events.cfm?pageID=events+eventID=8.

25 Suzanne Fournier & Ernie Crey, *Stolen from Our Embrace: The Abduction of First Nations Children and the Restoration of Aboriginal Communities* (Vancouver: Douglas & McIntyre, 1997) at 71–72.

26 *Ibid.* at 72.

27 *Ibid.*

28 Jane Doe, *The Story of Jane Doe: A Book about Rape* (Toronto: Random House Canada, 2003).

Appendices

APPENDIX 1: *CRIMINAL CODE* CHANGES

Historic sexual crimes

Rape and attempted rape:
- 1955–1970 ss. 135–137
- 1970–1982 ss. 143–145
- No longer an offence after 4 January 1983. Unwanted sexual penetration or attempted sexual penetration became sexual assault on or after 4 January 1983.

Sexual intercourse with a female under the age of fourteen, or with a female between the ages of fourteen and sixteen if of previous chaste character:
- 1955–1970 s. 138
- 1970–1982 s. 146
- No longer an offence after 1 January 1988.
- Sexual intercourse with a female under the age of fourteen became sexual assault if committed after 4 January 1983. Sexual intercourse with a female between the ages of fourteen and sixteen became an offence of sexual assault if there was no consent; sexual exploitation if there was a position of trust, dependency, or authority; and incest if there was a named blood relationship between the parties.

Indecent assault of a female and sexual assault of a male were separate offences:
- 1955–1970 ss. 141 and 148
- 1970–1982 ss. 149 and 156

- No longer an offence after 4 January 1983. Indecent assault of either gender, that is unwanted sexual touching, became sexual assault if committed on or after 4 January 1983.

Gross indecency was the offence of sexual activity that offended community standards. Usually oral sexual activity with a young person resulted in this charge before 1 January 1988. After this date, the charge is sexual assault if there is no consent or if the activity is with a child under the age of fourteen, and sexual exploitation if the young person is between the ages of fourteen and seventeen and there is a position of trust, authority, or dependency between the parties.

Other offences that were no longer chargeable after 1 January 1988:
- Sexual intercourse with an employee
- Seduction of a female passenger on a vessel
- Sexual intercourse with a stepdaughter, etc.
- Seduction under promise of marriage
- Seduction of a female between the ages of sixteen and eighteen

Sexual intercourse with a feeble-minded person was no longer chargeable after 4 January 1983. If a person engages in sexual activity with a person who does not have the capacity to consent, the person can be charged with sexual assault. Section 153.1 specifies where consent is present when a person who has a disability has sexual relations with a person who is in a position of trust, dependency, or authority.

APPENDIX 2: QUESTIONS ABOUT DRUG TREATMENT

- What is the name of this medication and is it known by other names?
- What is the medication meant to do?
- Are there any negative effects of the medication and what are they? Will the side effects get better or worse with time?
- How and when do I take the medication, and how long do you estimate I will have to take it?
- How will we know if the medication is working and how will my progress be checked?
- What are the risks if I do not want to take medication?
- If this medication does not work, are there others that I can try?
- Are there foods, drink, other drugs, or activities that I should avoid when taking this medication?
- Is this medication addictive, can it be abused, and can I overdose on it?
- Where can I get written information about this medication?
- What are the consequences if I forget to take the medication at the appropriate time? What do I do if I forget to take it?
- Are there laboratory tests that need to be done before, during, or after taking this medication?
- Have you treated other people with this medication and how helpful has it been?
- What is the procedure if I decide to discontinue the medication?

APPENDIX 3: QUESTIONS TO ASK A PROSPECTIVE THERAPIST

At the initial interview:

- Where did you get your training? What are your professional credentials and affiliations?
- What is your therapeutic philosophy? How do you view the healing process?
- How much do you charge and what are your billing procedures?
- Is it possible to reach you after hours in case of an emergency or crisis?
- What is your experience working with clients who are involved in court proceedings related to sexual assaults?
- Are you willing to write a report or testify, if requested, about my psychological difficulties or my therapy?
- How might your testimony affect my therapy?
- What is your policy about keeping notes and records of therapy sessions? Would you be willing to allow me to read those notes each week?

Following an initial evaluation:

- What do you feel are my treatment needs?
- What will the treatment goals be?
- What is the treatment plan?
- How often will I have to attend therapy and at what times?
- How will we evaluate if therapy is working?
- Do you see a need for medication to support therapy?
- Do you have experience with family therapy if I want to involve family members?
- Can you suggest any literature that would be helpful for me to read?

APPENDIX 4: RECOMMENDED SELF-HELP REFERENCES

Resource guide

Below we have listed many references on various subjects that we feel would be of interest to readers of this book. It is by no means an exhaustive list, nor is it meant to be a list of recommended reading. We intend it as a sample of the literature available and a starting point for those who are interested in learning more about these topics. There is an extensive annotated list of mental health resources (including books, films, and websites) in the following resource: John C. Norcross, John W. Santrock, Linda F. Campbell, Thomas P. Smith, Robert Sommer, and Edward L. Zuckerman, *Authoritative Guide to Self-Help Resources in Mental Health*, rev. ed. (New York: Guilford Press, 2003). We have drawn several of the references given below from this guidebook.

There are also countless resources available on the Internet addressing virtually all topics in this book. The difficulty lies in finding accurate, reliable sources of information. A good place to begin is with some of the available Internet guides, such as John M. Grohol, *The Insider's Guide to Mental Health Resources Online, 2002/2003 edition* (New York: Guilford Press, 2002).

Another resource to check is the Canadian National Clearing House on Family Violence, online: *www.hc-sc.gc.ca/hppb/familyviolence*, which provides a lot of information about sexual abuse within families.

An additional, broad-based resource is that of the National Institute of Mental Health, online: *www.nimh.nih.gov*, where there is information on a wide variety of mental health topics including those related to sexual abuse.

Below is an alphabetical list of topics that may be of interest.

Anger

Lerner, Harriet, *The Dance of Anger: A Woman's Guide to Changing the Patterns of Intimate Relationships* (New York: Harper & Row, 1989)

McKay, Matthew, Peter D. Rogers, & Judith McKay, *When Anger Hurts — Quieting the Storm Within* (Oakland, CA: New Harbinger, 1989)

Sonkins, Daniel Jay, & Michael Durphy, *Learning to Live Without Violence* (Volcano, CA: Volcano Press, 1997)

Anxiety disorders

Bourne, Edmund J., *Beyond Anxiety and Phobia* (Oakland, CA: New Harbinger, 2001)

——————, *The Anxiety and Phobia Workbook,* 3d ed. (Oakland, CA: New Harbinger, 2001)

Craske, Michelle G., & David H. Barlow, *Mastery of Your Anxiety and Panic III* (Albany, NY: Graywind, 2000)

Jeffers, Susan, *Feel the Fear and Do It Anyway*, reissued ed. (New York: Fawcett, 1992)

Internet resources

Anxiety Panic Internet Resource, The, online: www.algy.com/anxiety

Panic Anxiety Education Management Services, online: www.healthyplace.com/communities/anxiety/paems/index.html

Childhood sexual abuse

Allen, Charlotte Vale, *Daddy's Girl* (New York: Berkeley, 1995)

Copeland, Mary Ellen, & Maxine Harris, *Healing the Trauma of Abuse: A Woman's Workbook* (Oakland, CA: New Harbinger, 2000)

Courtois, Christine A., *Healing the Incest Wound: Adult Survivors in Therapy* (New York: Norton, 1996)

Davis, Laura, *Allies in Healing: When the Person You Love Was Sexually Abused as a Child* (New York: HarperCollins, 1991)

Engel, Beverly, *Partners in Recovery: How Mates, Lovers and Other Prosurvivors Can Learn to Support and Cope with Adult Survivors of Childhood Sexual Abuse* (New York: Fawcett, 1993)

Hagans, Kathryn B., & Joyce Case, *When Your Child Has Been Molested* (San Francisco: Jossey-Bass, 1998)

Lew, Michael, *Victims No Longer: Men Recovering from Incest and Other Sexual Child Abuse* (New York: Harper and Row, 1990)

Russell, Diana E.H., *The Secret Trauma* (New York: Basic Books, 1999)

Sonkin, Daniel J., *Wounded Boys, Heroic Men: A Man's Guide to Recovering from Child Abuse* (Stamford, CT: Longmeadow, 1992)

Warshaw, Robin, *I Never Called It Rape* (New York: Harper Perennial, 1994)

Internet resources

Information on child witnesses:

- www.courtprep.ca
- www.tcac.on.ca

◆ www.clarkprosecutor.org/html/victim/ctips.htm (American)

Chronic pain

Kabat-Zinn, Jon, *Full Catastrophe Living — Using the Wisdom of Your Body and Mind to Face Stress, Pain, and Illness* (New York: Dell, 1990)

Philips, H. Clare, *The Psychological Management of Chronic Pain — A Treatment Manual* (New York, Springer, 1988)

Radomsky, Nellie A., *Lost Voices: Women, Chronic Pain, and Abuse* (Binghamton, NY: Haworth Press, 1995)

Coping Strategies and Emotional Health

Borcherdt, Bill, *You Can Control Your Feelings — 24 Guides to Emotional Well-Being* (Sarasota, FL: Professional Resource Press, 1993)

Clarke, Jean Illsley, & Carol Gesme, *Affirmation Ovals: 139 Ways to Give and Get Affirmations* (Plymouth, MN: Daisy Press, 1988)

Goleman, Daniel, *Emotional Intelligence — Why It Can Matter More Than IQ* (New York: Bantam Books, 1997)

Kasl, Charlotte Sophia, *Finding Joy: 101 Ways to Free Your Spirit and Dance with Life* (New York: HarperCollins, 1994)

——— , *Home for the Heart: Creating Intimacy and Community with Loved Ones, Neighbors, and Friends* (New York: HarperCollins, 1991)

McKay, Matthew, & Patrick Fanning, *Prisoners of Belief — Exposing and Changing Beliefs That Control Your Life* (Oakland, CA: New Harbinger, 1991)

——— , *Self-Esteem — A Proven Program of Cognitive Techniques for Assessing, Improving and Maintaining Your Self-Esteem*, 2d ed. (Oakland, CA: New Harbinger, 1992)

Morin, Charles M., *Insomnia — Psychological Assessment and Management* (New York: Guilford Press, 1993)

Depression

Burns, David, *Feeling Good: The New Mood Therapy*, rev. ed. (New York: Avon, 1999)

——— , *The Feeling Good Handbook*, rev. ed. (New York: Plume, 1999)

Greenberger, Dennis, & Christine A. Padesky, *Mind Over Mood: Change How You Feel by Changing the Way You Think* (New York: Guildford Press, 1995)

Lewinsohn, Peter, Ricardo Munoz, Mary Ann Youngren, and Antonette Zeiss, *Control Your Depression* (Englewood Cliffs, NY: Prentice-Hall, 1996)

McGrath, Ellen, *When Feeling Bad Is Good* (New York: Bantam, 1994)

Real, Terrance, *I Don't Want to Talk About It: Overcoming the Secret Legacy of Male Depression* (New York: Scribner, 1997)

Yapko, Michael D., *When Living Hurts: Directives for Treating Depression* (New York: Brunner/Mazel, 1994)

Internet resources
Psychology Information Online: Depression, online: www.psychologyinfo.com/depression
Wing of Madness: A Depression Guide, online: www.wingofmadness.com

First Nations issues
Assembly of First Nations, *Breaking the Silence* (Ottawa: Assembly of First Nations, Ottawa, 1994).
Fournier, Suzanne, & Ernie Crey, *Stolen from Our Embrace* (Vancouver and Toronto: Douglas & McIntyre, 1997)
Johnston, Basil H., *Indian School Days* (Toronto: Key Porter Books, 1988)
Krawll, Marcia, *Understanding the Role of Healing in Aboriginal Communities* (Ottawa: Department of the Solicitor General, 1994)
Waldram, James B., *The Way of the Pipe: Aboriginal Spirituality and Symbolic Healing in Canadian Prisons* (Peterborough, ON: Broadview Press, 1997)

Internet resources
Aboriginal Healing Foundation, online: www.ahf.ca.
Alternative Dispute Resolution for Indian Residential School Abuse, online: www.irsr-rqpi.gc.ca.
Indian and Northern Affairs, Canada, *The Path to Healing*, online: www.ainc-inac.gc.ca/gs/pth_e.html

Inspirational stories
Broyard, Anatole, *My Illness: And Other Writings on Life and Death* (New York: Fawcett Columbine, 1992).
Doe, Jane, *The Story of Jane Doe: A Book about Rape* (Toronto: Random House Canada, 2003)
Fox, Michael J., *Lucky Man* (New York: Hyperion, 2002)
Grealy, Lucy, *Autobiography of a Face* (Boston: Houghton Mifflin, 1994).
Pelzer, Dave, *The Lost Boy: A Foster Child's Search for the Love of a Family* (Deerfield Beach, FL: Heath Communications, 1997)
————, *A Man Named Dave: A Story of Triumph and Forgiveness* (New York: Plume, 2000)
————, *A Child Called "It": One Child's Courage to Survive* (Deerfield Beach, FL: Health Communications, 1995)

Price, Reynolds, *A Whole New Life: An Illness and a Healing* (New York: Plume, 1982).

Sheehy, Elizabeth, ed., *Adding Feminism to Law: The Contributions of Justice Claire L'Heureux-Dubé* (Toronto, Irwin Law, 2004)

Rhett, Kathryn, ed., *Survival Stories* (New York: Doubleday, 1997)

Van Tighem, Patricia, *The Bear's Embrace: A True Story of Survival* (New York: Pantheon, 2001)

Internet resources

Terry Fox Foundation, online: www.terryfoxrun.org

Legal resources

Cameron, Angela, *Restorative Justice: A Literature Review* (Vancouver, The British Columbia Institute Against Family Violence, 2005), online: www.bcifv. org/pubs/Restorative_Justice_Lit_Review.pdf

Cooper-Stephenson, Kenneth, *Personal Injury Damages in Canada* (Toronto: Carswell, 1996)

Daylen, Judith & John Yuille, "Assessment of Adult Plaintiffs in Childhood Sexual Abuse Cases" in I.Z. Schultz & D. Brady, eds., *Psychological Injuries at Trial* (Chicago: American Bar Association, 2003) 1339–70

Fuerst, Michelle F., *Defending Sexual Offence Cases* (Toronto: Carswell, 2000)

Grace, Elizabeth K.P. & Susan M. Vella, *Civil Liability for Sexual Abuse and Violence in Canada* (Toronto: Butterworths, 2000)

Law Commission of Canada, *Restoring Dignity: Responding to Child Abuse in Canadian Institutions* (Ottawa: Law Commission of Canada, 2000)

Malesyk, Anna, *Crimes Against Children* (Aurora, ON: Canada Law Book, 2001)

Roberts, Julian V., & Renate M. Mohr, *Confronting Sexual Assault: A Decade of Legal and Social Change* (Toronto: University of Toronto Press, 1994)

Stewart, Hamish C., *Sexual Offences in Canadian Law* (Aurora, ON: Canada Law Book, 2005)

van Tongeren Harvey, Wendy & Paula Dauns, *Sexual Offences against Children and the Criminal Process* (Markham, ON: Butterworths, 2001)

Internet resources

Criminal Code of Canada available through the Canadian Legal Information Institute, online: www.canlii.org/ca/sta/c-46/

Links when preparing for court:

+ www.ag.gov.bc.ca/courts/general/beingawitness.htm.

- www.bccba.org/Guest_Lounge/dial-a-law.asp.
- www.clarkprosecutor.org/html/victim/wtips.htm (American)
- www.gvpvs.org/main.php?content=information

Information on justice in Canada: www.canada.justice.gc.ca

Meditation and Eastern spirituality

Chodron, Pema, *Start Where You Are — A Guide to Compassionate Living* (Boston: Shambhala Dragon Editions, 1994)

————, *When Things Fall Apart — Heart Advice for Difficult Times* (Boston: Shambhala Classics, 1997)

Epstein, Mark, *Going to Pieces without Falling Apart — A Buddhist Perspective on Wholeness* (New York: Broadway Books, 1998)

Kabat-Zinn, Jon, *Wherever You Go, There You Are* (New York: Hyperion, 1994)

Kasl, Charlotte, *If the Buddha Got Stuck — A Handbook for Change on a Spiritual Path* (New York: Penguin Compass, 2005)

Moore, Thomas, *The Care of the Soul — A Guide for Cultivating Depth and Sacredness in Everyday Life* (New York: HarperCollins, 1992)

Rabinowitz, Ilana, ed., *Mountains Are Mountains and Rivers Are Rivers — Applying Eastern Teachings to Everyday Life* (New York: Hyperion, 1999)

Memory issues

Brown, Daniel, Alan W. Scheflin, & D. Corydon Hammond, *Memory, Trauma, Treatment, and the Law* (New York: W.W. Norton & Co., 1998). [An essential reference on memory for clinicians, researchers, attorneys, and judges.]

Pope, Kenneth S., & Laura S. Brown, *Recovered Memories of Abuse: Assessment, Therapy, Forensics* (Washington: American Psychological Association, 1996)

Schacter, Daniel, *The Seven Sins of Memory — How the Mind Forgets and Remembers* (New York: Houghton Mifflin, 2001)

Post-traumatic stress disorder

Matsakis, Aphrodite, *I Can't Get Over It: A Handbook for Trauma Survivors* (Oakland, CA: New Harbinger, 1996)

Rosenbloom, Dena, & Mary Beth Williams with Barbara E. Watkins, *Life after Trauma: A Workbook for Healing* (New York: Guilford Press, 1999)

Rothbaum, Barbara Olasov, & Edna B. Foa, *Reclaiming Your Life after Rape* (Albany, NY: Graywind, 1999)

Williams, Mary Beth, & Soili Poijula, *The PTSD Workbook* (Oakland, CA: New Harbinger, 2002)

Internet resources

David Baldwin's Trauma Information Pages, online: www.trauma-pages.com

Sexual Abuse: Guide Picks, online: incestabuse.miningco.com

Articles on Trauma and PTSD, online: www.sidran.org/trauma.html

National Center for PTSD, online: www.ncptsd.va.gov

Resilience

Katz, Mark, *On Playing a Poor Hand Well* (New York: W.W. Norton & Co., 1997)

O'Hanlon, Bill, *Thriving through Crisis — Turn Tragedy and Trauma into Growth and Change* (New York: Perigee, 2004)

Reivich, Karen, & Andrew Shatte, *The Resilience Factor — 7 Keys to Finding Your Inner Strength and Overcoming Life's Hurdles* (New York: Broadway Books, 2002)

Sanford, Linda T., *Strong at the Broken Places — Overcoming the Trauma of Childhood Abuse* (New York: Random House, 1990)

Wolin, Steven J., & Sybil Wolin, *The Resilient Self — How Survivors of Troubled Families Rise above Adversity* (New York: Villard, 1993)

Sexuality

Berman, Jennifer, & Laura Berman, *For Women Only* (New York: Henry Holt, 2001)

Blank, Joani, *The Playbook for Women about Sex* (San Francisco: Down There Press, 1982)

Daniluk, Judith C., *Women's Sexuality — Challenging Myths, Creating Meanings* (New York: Guilford Press, 1998)

Dickson, Anne, *The Mirror Within — A New Look at Sexuality* (London: Quartet Books, 1985)

Engel, Beverly, *Raising Your Sexual Self-Esteem: How to Feel Better about Your Sexuality and Yourself* (New York: Fawcett, 1995)

Harris, Robie Harris with illustrations by Michael Emberley, *It's Perfectly Normal* (Cambridge, MA: Candlewick Press, 1995)

Heiman, Julia, & Joseph LoPiccolo, *Becoming Orgasmic: A Sexual Growth Program for Women*, rev. ed. (New York: Prentice-Hall, 1988)

Hutchinson, Marcia Germaine, *Transforming Body Image* (Freedom, CA: Crossing Press, 1998)

Kasl, Charlotte, *Women, Sex, and Additions: A Search for Love and Power* (New York: HarperCollins, 1990)

Maltz, Wendy, & Beverly Holman, *Incest and Sexuality — A Guide to Understanding and Healing* (Lexington, MA: Lexington Books, 1987)

McCarthy, Barry, & Emily McCarthy, *Sexual Awareness: Enhancing Sexual Pleasure*, rev. ed. (New York: Carroll & Graf, 1993)

Moore, Thomas, *The Soul of Sex* (New York: HarperCollins, 1998)

Northrup, Christiane, *Women's Bodies, Women's Wisdom: Creating Physical and Emotional Health and Healing* (New York: Doubleday, 1994)

Zilbergeld, Bernie, *The New Male Sexuality: A Guide to Sexual Fulfillment*, rev. ed. (New York: Bantam, 1999)

Sexual assault

Carosella, Cynthia, *Who's Afraid of the Dark: A Forum of Truth, Support and Assurance for Those Affected by Rape* (New York: HarperCollins, 1995)

Dobsey, D., & C. Varnhagen, *Sexual Abuse and Exploitation of People with Disabilities: A Study of Victims* (Ottawa: Health Canada, 1990)

Doe, Jane, *The Story of Jane Doe: A Book about Rape* (Toronto: Random House Canada, 2003)

Francisco, Patricia Weaver, *Telling: A Memoir of Rape and Recovery* (New York: HarperCollins, 1999)

Gabbard, Glen, *Sexual Exploitation with Professional Relationships* (Washington, DC: American Psychiatric Press, 1989)

Gonsiorek, John C., *Breach of Trust: Sexual Exploitation by Health Care Professionals and Clergy* (Thousand Oaks, CA: Sage, 1995)

Hoffman, Richard, *Half the House: A Memoir* (New York: Harcourt Brace & Co., 1995)

Ledray, Linda E., *Recovering from Rape — Practical Advice on Overcoming the Trauma and Coping with Police, Hospitals, and Court for Survivors of Sexual Assault and for Their Families, Lovers and Friends* (New York: Henry Holt and Co., 1986)

Maltz, Wendy, *The Sexual Healing Journey: A Guide for Survivors of Sexual Abuse* (New York: HarperCollins, 1991)

Internet resources

Coercion, Rape, and Surviving: http://ub-counseling.buffalo.edu/violence.shtml

Information for Victims of Sexual Assault and Their Families: www.connsacs.org

National Center on Elder Abuse: www.elderabusecenter.org

National Organization on Male Sexual Victimization, The: www.nomsv.org

Sexual Abuse: http://soulselfhelp.on.ca

Sexual assault issues:

- http://danenet.wicip.org/dcccrsa/saissues.html
- www.metrac.org/new/faq_sex.htm
- www.sace.ab.ca/non_flash/sao1b.html

WHOA (Women Hating Online Abuse): www.haltabuse.org

Stress management and relaxation

Benson, Herbert, *Beyond the Relaxation Response* (New York: Time Books, 1984)

———, *The Relaxation Response* (New York: Morrow, 1975)

Carlson, Richard J., *Don't Sweat the Small Stuff ... and It's All Small Stuff* (New York: Hyperion, 1995)

Davis, Martha, Elizabeth Robbins Eshelman, & Matthew McKay, *The Relaxation and Stress Reduction Workbook*, 5th ed. (Oakland, CA: New Harbinger, 2000)

Madders, James, *The Stress and Relaxation Handbook: A Practical Guide to Self-Help Techniques* (London: Vermilion, 1997)

Internet resources

Canadian Institute of Stress, online: www.stresscanada.org

Mason, L. John, *Basic Guided Relaxation: Advanced Technique*, online: www.dstress.com/guided.htm

Suicide

Thomas Ellis, & Cory F. Newman, *Choosing to Live* (Oakland, CA: New Harbinger, 1996)

APPENDIX 5: THE MAJOR COURTROOM PLAYERS

Crown prosecutor

A lawyer acting on behalf of the Crown is the Crown counsel or the Crown Attorney. This lawyer has a quasi-judicial role, which means acting fairly on behalf of the state, independent of inappropriate influence. Decisions are made based on sound legal principles, not on emotions. A Crown counsel is appointed, rather than elected, and represents all Canadians in a criminal proceeding. In doing so, the Crown counsel is seeking justice for all of Canada, which includes the victim, and has a duty of fairness to the accused. Although a defence lawyer acts for the accused, the Crown is not the lawyer for the victim but, rather, the strong advocate for the criminal justice system. The Crown pursues the finding of truth and ensures fairness. The Supreme Court of Canada has acknowledged that the Crown's role includes a vigorous pursuit of a legitimate result in a criminal trial.

All criminal cases in Canada are officially labelled *Regina* versus the *Name of the Accused*. *Regina* is Latin for the Queen, who stands for Canada and all Canadians in the system. Crown prosecutors are employed or contracted by the province's Attorney General's department. Those who do trial work may be assigned to a provincial court or a superior court, but may appear in either. Two or more Crown prosecutors may be assigned at different times to a particular case. If a case goes to a preliminary hearing before the trial, there will be a provincial court Crown counsel assigned. Then when the case goes to trial in a superior court, usually a different prosecutor is assigned to this type of work and may even be in a separate building for that assignment.

Every effort is made for a case to be handled by the same prosecutor throughout the process. You may ask to have the same Crown prosecutor for the hearings and the trial in your case. If the schedules allow for it, it just might happen.

The Crown counsel will do the following:

- Take responsibility for the conduct of the trial.
- Present arguments to the court relating to the strength of the case, your credibility, reasons why the public needs to be protected from the accused and the like.
- Listen to you and design how best to give your evidence based on how you best communicate.

- Make submissions based, in part at least, on the information that you provide.
- Explain the stages of the legal process to you as they arise.
- Assist you in preparing your evidence for court by reviewing your previous statements.
- Inform you of your rights in the *Criminal Code* related to privacy over any sexual activity not relevant to the trial and personal records that are in the hands of other people.
- Inform you of your rights in the *Criminal Code* related to accommodations for giving your testimony, such as closed-circuit television, testifying behind a screen, having a support person with you, and prohibiting the accused from cross-examining you.
- Provide to you, once the trial is over, non-confidential details of the investigation that are still not known by you; to have provided these details to you earlier would have taken away from your credibility and the integrity of the case.

The Crown lawyer is not your personal lawyer; rather, this lawyer represents the state. As such, the Crown prosecutor will *not*

- Advance your positions or views to the court where they detract from the lawyer's responsibilities or role as Crown counsel to provide an effective prosecution, including fairness to the accused.
- Provide confidentiality on matters discussed with you that are relevant to the case and not protected in law.
- Provide legal advice to you personally on matters that arise affecting your privacy rights.
- Engage in a personal relationship with you.
- Approve financial or other support outside of the mandate of the Ministry of the Attorney General.
- Provide details of the investigation and the case in the event that this would negatively reflect on your credibility or the integrity of the case.

Defence counsel

The role of the defence counsel is to represent the accused and make sure that the accused gets a fair trial.

In most sexual offence trials, the accused and the victim know each other before the alleged offence(s). Therefore the usual defence arguments are

- It did not happen at all.
- It happened but there was consent.
- It happened but the accused thought that there was consent.
- It happened but the accused thought that there was consent and that the victim was aged fourteen or over.
- It happened but there was consent and there was not a position of trust, dependency, or authority, nor was there a sexually exploitive relationship between the older accused and the teenaged victim.

The defence lawyer will ensure the accused's perspective is heard, will cast doubt on the evidence presented by the Crown that is inconsistent with the defence version, and will show why the accused should be treated fairly throughout the trial and with leniency, if shown to be accountable for the wrongdoing. This can be done in a number of ways. It may involve statements at the beginning and the end of the trial intended to refute the claims of the Crown and show that they have no merit. As well, it may involve the calling of witnesses and the presentation of exhibits in a manner every bit as believable and as complex as the Crown's case.

Accused persons in Canada may choose to appear at trial without legal representation, but they are entitled to that representation and will be encouraged to seek it. For sexual assault charges, prison time is a possible outcome, so a judge will strongly advise an accused to agree to be represented by counsel.

The defence counsel may be selected and paid for by the accused, or may be selected by a provincial legal services association and paid for by the people of the province through their taxes. In some cases, the defence lawyer is paid for by the Attorney General's department, for example, when the accused does not qualify for legal aid, but is entitled, according to a court ruling, to be represented. Clearly, an accused who feels the need for counsel should be entitled to assistance with the trial and this is particularly true in trials involving sexual offences where the potential outcome is very serious for all involved.

Cases that go through the preliminary hearing and on to a superior court, particularly jury trials, are the ones most likely to feature an active defence strategy, and centre on your credibility as a victim.

Trial lawyers may be called barristers in some provinces. Some specialize in defending people accused of sexual offences and have developed strategies over the years for refuting evidence and casting doubt on allegations.

These strategies can involve a combination of building up the character of the accused in the eyes of the court and tearing down the credibility of the Crown's witnesses, particularly the complainant. The process can be dramatic, and may be emotional and even nasty.

The defence counsel will be a part of all the applications that take place and, therefore, will be an essential part of the dialogue that contributes to the fairness of the trial. Equally, throughout the trial, this lawyer will be explaining to the accused the rules and procedures that ensure fairness. Indirectly, you benefit from the defence lawyer being on the case because this will assist the trial to move more smoothly than if the judge and the Crown had to explain everything to an unrepresented accused who does not know or agree with the process. Also, the Crown can ask the defence lawyer for an undertaking to do or not do certain things that are enforceable by the provincial law society. An undertaking from the accused would not have the same weight. Although you may not feel positively about the defence lawyer on the case, it is always better for the case than not having one at all. In summary, a defence lawyer will assist in providing the following:

- Assistance to ensure that your privacy rights are respected on issues relating to third-party records and previous sexual activity, identity, and place of residence and work
- Protection of the accused's rights, thereby ensuring that the trial is fair for the accused which, in turn, will have the peripheral result of assisting to keep the trial on track and avoiding grounds of appeal
- Cross-examination of the complainant, which provides an opportunity for the complainant to remember anything that was naturally forgotten and introspect and scrutinize the complaint, as well as to think of those aspects of it that have not been thought of before when in a more sympathetic environment
- Some encouragement to the accused to obey court orders relating to the safety of the complainant
- Encouragement to the accused to refrain from knowingly presenting a false story on the stand as a defence, when the defence lawyer knows the true version of facts from the accused; in other words, it is unethical, once the defence lawyer hears a confession from the accused that the latter committed the act, to put the accused on the stand to suggest otherwise

- A pathway for discussions between the Crown and the defence law-yer relating to the possibility of a guilty plea
- A contact person to go to if the complainant feels an obligation to support the accused and the accused's version, rather than the com-plainant's original complaint to the police

The defence counsel will not do any of the following:

- Keep matters learned about, either through the trial or through the disclosure of documents, confidential; the defence lawyer must dis-close these matters to the accused
- Advance information about what the defence will be if it would negatively impact the defence trial strategy
- Gorm a personal relationship with the complainant
- Hive financial or other support to the complainant
- Negotiate to drop charges in exchange for consideration

The accused

Although there are some procedures that allow proceedings to take place without the accused in the courtroom, generally, a trial under the *Criminal Code* cannot occur without the presence of the accused. There is no provi-sion in Canadian law for trials *in absentia* for serious cases, even for notori-ous individuals who have fled to another country. In Canada, we recognize that it is essential for a person to be present if that person is to be tried for a crime. It is one of the basic tenets of the system.

When charged with an indictable offence, an accused has the right to elect where the trial will take place — either in a provincial court or in a su-perior court. If the superior court is chosen, the accused then has the right to choose to be tried by a judge alone or by a judge and a jury.

While our system does not prescribe a role for the accused beyond being present, one expects that an accused person who has chosen to plead "not guilty" will take an active role in refuting the charges. This is sometimes called "mounting a defence." In many cases, the defence lawyer will present a case and will include witnesses and possibly exhibits with the intention to cast doubt on the allegations of the Crown.

Since the accused is presumed innocent, the accused person does not have to disprove the charges or prove anything else. Rather, the burden of proof is on the Crown.

Not every trial involves an elaborate defence. Once the Crown's case is seen by the defence to be weak, the strategy might well be to not call a defence — to let the inherent doubt in the Crown's case be the reasonable doubt that leads to an acquittal. The Crown must prove all of the essential ingredients of the offence and to not do so results in an acquittal.

If the accused refuses to be represented by a lawyer, the judge may take a fairly active role in protecting the rights of the accused during the trial, such as asking certain questions during cross-examination of the Crown witnesses. This can be unsettling to you and your allies, since it may seem that the judge is on the side of the accused and against you. But in such cases, the law permits and even encourages judges to assist an accused if it appears that the accused is not mounting an effective defence — that is, to err on the side of protecting the rights of the accused. There is a provision of the *Criminal Code* that allows for the judge to disallow the accused from personally cross-examining the witness and to appoint a lawyer to conduct the cross-examination instead.

The judge

Superior court judges are federally appointed. A superior court judge in a Canadian court is addressed orally as "My Lord" or "My Lady," and in writing as "Mr. Justice" or "Madam Justice" by everyone, whether a lawyer or a witness. The Attorney General of the province appoints provincial court judges. Provincial court judges are referred to as "Your Honour."

The judge's job is to ensure that the rules are followed and the rights of the accused are protected while, at the same time, the interests of the public and of justice are served. It is a difficult balancing act. When a dispute arises over the evidence or the procedure, the judge decides what evidence is admissible and what is not, what procedure is to be followed and what is not, and which questions are appropriate and which are not. There will be objections by either side and rulings on the objections. Counsel may test the limits of the court and the judge may rule on inappropriate behaviour, including that of witnesses or the public attending the trial.

Where a jury is present, the judge will instruct the jury about points of law. This can happen during the trial and will most certainly happen before the jury leaves the courtroom to discuss or deliberate on a verdict. Where there is no jury, the judge must decide on the facts of the case and render a verdict.

The judge is like a referee in a sports contest, enforcing the rules of the game to ensure that it is fair and that the truth is revealed. The goal is not to see that the best team wins, rather that those proven guilty in law are convicted and those who are not so proven are acquitted. It is a big job, crucial to our system, and one of tremendous responsibility. The judge is not to participate actively in the case. The Crown has conduct of the prosecution and the defence has conduct of the defence.

During the course of the proceedings the judge will

- Inform the complainant of any rights under the *Criminal Code* where it is articulated that there is an obligation to do so
- Provide guidance on the appropriate demeanour in court
- Direct the Crown and the defence to conduct the trial within the perimeters of the law
- Assist to ensure orderliness and protection of the victim within the trial scenario, including protection from outbursts by the accused and other persons
- Provide dispassionate decision-making based on a critical analysis of the facts and the law

The judge cannot provide:

- The appearance of empathy or sympathy beyond demonstrations of respect

The jury

The jury is present, if requested by the accused, in a superior court trial but not a provincial court trial. Once a court date is set, the panel of potential jurors is assembled and that is quite a ritual in itself.

Jurors are ordinary citizens chosen from voters' lists in the jurisdiction where the trial is to be held. The law intends that a jury should represent a cross-section of the people who live in the area where the trial takes place, such that they are considered peers of the accused. Their gender, age, education, income, and political and moral beliefs should mirror the larger population from where they come.

The method used to achieve this is simply to choose randomly or blindly, without any pre-determined criteria, from the population as a whole, as if we dipped our hand into a jar filled with different coloured balls. Dozens of citizens will be summoned for consideration as jurors. When jury selection takes place, the Crown only, without any of the witnesses from the

Crown's case, will be there. Those who have been summoned enter and are seated in a large superior court courtroom. The Crown tells the panel who the witnesses and lawyers are to ensure that no panelist knows the parties involved. Then the court clerk chooses cards from a box with the names on them and calls those persons to the front. About thirty panelists come forward and one-by-one the lawyers indicate if they challenge or are content with the panelist as a juror. It is up to the potential juror to let the judge know if there exist any circumstances that prevent the person from sitting. It is wrong for a juror to know the parties. And it is wrong for the police, the Crown, or the defence to investigate the jury panel in an effort to find the best picks. The jurors must take on their role unbiased and without prejudgments of the case.

In most jurisdictions, the lawyers continue to choose until fourteen jurors are selected. This ensures that alternate jurors are available in case one or two of the twelve people cannot serve, for example, due to illness or hardship.

The juror in a criminal trial must attend every court session. If a juror is late or absent, the day's proceedings may be delayed. In other words, each juror is critical to the case and is expected to participate fully in learning the facts of the case as they are presented, and in deliberations to reach a verdict.

The decision must be unanimous. If it is not, the jury reports its failure to the judge, who may call a mistrial, which means starting all over with a new judge and jury.

Laws regarding the behaviour of jurors during a trial are intended to preserve jurors' impartiality. Jurors are advised not to discuss the case before the evidence is complete and the judge has given directions to them. They are also not to discuss the case with others. Sometimes they will even be sequestered during the trial in a particular place in order to prevent such discussions, though this is rare. At the end of the trial, they must be sequestered during deliberations. In Canada, it is a criminal offence for a jury member to discuss the deliberations made by a jury.

The jury can provide:

- A commitment to sit and listen for the entire trial to bring the matter to a final resolution
- Serious deliberations of the facts after listening to them

The jury cannot provide:

- A decision based on sympathy or emotion
- Personal communication between the jurors and the complainant
- The complainant with reasons for its decision

The court clerk

Every trial has a court clerk assigned to it. The court clerk assists the court by ensuring that the courtroom is ready for the trial (with water, microphones, electronic equipment, exhibits and the like on hand) by preparing the lawyers and the public for the judge's entry, leading the witnesses through the oath or affirmation, keeping records of the process and judgments, handing articles out to the witnesses, counsel and the judge, and in some jurisdictions, recording the process where there is no court reporter.

The court clerk can provide:

- Advice and instructions to the complainant relating to where the complainant sits at the microphone, the recording of evidence, and the like
- Assistance with providing the plaintiff accommodations, such as water and Kleenex
- Assistance with equipment, such as tape recorders, closed-circuit television, and videoconferencing
- Information relating to the courthouse and the services that are provided there

The court clerk cannot provide:

- Counselling services
- Support of one party over another that gives an appearance of bias

The court reporter

All things said when court is in session must be recorded. It used to be that each court session had a court reporter who would manually take notes in shorthand, which would be prepared into a transcript, if needed. In the new technologically-equipped courtroom, one person acts as both the court clerk and the court reporter.

Although all evidence, submissions, and judgments are recorded, transcripts are not automatically prepared. One has to order a transcript of something that transpired in court. The cost of a transcript is about $4.50 a page, which becomes quite expensive considering a trial will fill hundreds of pages of transcript. The judge approves any transcript of an order he has given once it has been prepared. Most of the superior court, Court of Appeal, and Supreme Court of Canada judgments are in writing and can be found on the Internet at www.canlii.org. If you cannot find judgments on the Internet, it is not because someone is trying to hide them. Rather, it is because no one asked for a transcript, or if there is a transcript, it has not found its way to legal editors, or a ban on publication of the transcript is preventing people from dealing with the rulings openly. The judgments that will least likely be available are interlocutory rulings and provincial court judgments.

The court reporter can provide:

- The service of recording the complainant's evidence confidently to ensure that there will be a good and valid transcript
- Instructions to the complainant to speak in such a way as to ensure proper recording of the complainant's voice
- Information relating to the ordering of transcripts

The court reporter cannot provide:

- Other services

The sheriff

The sheriff is present for all criminal trials. Sheriffs often call the Crown in advance for a risk assessment of a case. Sometimes there is information that members of the public who are related to the accused or the victims may breach the peace or disrupt the trial. The Crown counsel will tell the sheriff's department if there is some risk of a disruption or even an attack at the trial. If an accused is in custody, the sheriff will search the accused to ensure there are no weapons and escort the accused into and out of the courtroom.

If there is an incident in the courtroom or courthouse, the sheriffs will act immediately to quash the problem and the police will follow up with an investigation if a criminal offence has been committed. Most Crown counsel have experienced incidents where their witnesses were intimidated by others during a trial in an effort to prevent witnesses from testifying.

The sheriff can provide:

- Assistance with paging the complainant to come into the courtroom
- Observation of the goings-on in the courtroom to ensure its safety and integrity

- Protection for the complainant from the accused and other members of the public in the courtroom
- The signals necessary to alert and bring others to the courtroom in the event that a crisis exists

The sheriff cannot provide:

- Legal or other advice relating to the safety of the complainant
- Support of one party over another that gives an appearance of bias

The victim services worker

A victim services worker becomes an important player in supporting you through the trial. There are victim service workers from different agencies including the police, the Crown, the court, and the community. Victims have, over time, expressed a particular trust in dealing with workers from community-based programs because their guidelines for confidentiality are more protective of the victim. These people provide a very helpful service to victims. The police and the Crown cannot refer you to the agencies unless you consent to this. Often victims do not consent because of the stigma of the name, concerns about privacy, or ignorance of the services that can be provided, and in rejecting the service, they lose meaningful support in the process.

A victim services worker may accompany you to pretrial interviews with the Crown counsel and to court, provide you with information, and sometimes liaise with the Crown counsel to ensure that you are properly supported. You may choose to have the victim services worker as the support person who sits near you in court. This is available upon request if you are under eighteen years of age or if you need this type of support in order to give your evidence even if you are over eighteen years of age. The advantage of doing this is that the victim services worker is not, on the face, considered to be a witness in the trial and knows what is required to fulfill that role. At times, the support person is called to the stand to allow the defence to ascertain the person's role and whether the person qualifies as a witness or not. After the court process is complete, the victim services worker may debrief with you and can be of assistance in referring you to other services should you need further counselling. After a conviction, the victim services worker will ensure that you know where the accused serves prison time and can participate in future parole hearings if you so choose. Victim service workers make it their responsibility to know of the resources that are available in your location and are a helpful source of information for the multitude of issues that arise where you may need help from others. In addition, the victim services worker knows that it is important to get back to normal routines as soon as possible and will encourage and help you to do so.

APPENDIX 6: SUPPORT TEAM CHECKLIST

	Your therapist
	Personal coaches and inspirational people
	A trusted friend or family member whom you can talk to
	Great cooks and comfort specialists
	Caregivers for your children
	Special people who can stay the night
	Connections through victim support services or local crisis centres
	A spiritual guide or religious leader
	A trusted neighbour
	An inspiring person who has handled adversity well
	A Native Elder or older wise person whom you respect
	A physiotherapist or massage therapist
	A family physician
	Friends with whom you can do fun, safe, and healthy activities
	A lawyer dealing with current legal proceedings

APPENDIX 7: STEPS OF THE COURT PROCESS

- Open a file — as soon as you contact police with a complaint, they open a dispatch or complaint sheet and assign an officer to your case.
- Ensure your safety — if the assault has just occurred, the first police officer to contact you will ensure you are safe and have the medical attention you need.
- Start an investigation — The next responsibility of the police is to determine if further inquiry is necessary. They will take a statement from you and begin an investigation. If they believe the perpetrator is at-large and dangerous, they will get a description and broadcast it to other officers and departments.
- Transfer the file — Your case will then be transferred to personnel who specialize in sexual charges. These officers will likely interview you in-depth.
- Charge assessment — Authorities will determine if there is sufficient evidence to lay criminal charges.
- Trial and hearings — If there is enough evidence, the case will proceed to court. The proceedings in court could include a variety of hearings to deal with issues, such as the remand, bail, arraignment, pretrial applications, and verdict.
- Sentencing — If convicted, the perpetrator receives the penalty at a sentencing hearing.
- Parole — If sentenced and sent to jail, the perpetrator may apply for parole. This request for release is heard at a parole hearing.

APPENDIX 8: LIFE STRESSORS SCALE

Rate each area of your life out of 10 with 5 being average functioning in that area. As a rule of thumb, subtract 3 from each category to estimate the effect of the prosecution stress on your life. Ask yourself which specific areas are currently, or will be, problematic for you, and what you can do to make improvements.

Work situation: satisfying, manageable, supportive *or* heavy work load, new job, out of work, conflicts, stressful work environment Add other:	
Social situation: stable, supportive relationships, secure *or* single parenthood, childcare difficulties, relationship problems (marital, intimate, family, friends), divorce, change in residence, unhealthy living conditions, school pressures, substance abuse Add other:	
Finances: adequate income, no or only minor financial worries *or* mortgage or other burdensome debt load, no or low income, credit problems Add other:	
Physical health: good health, no serious illness, physically capable *or* major medical treatments, chronic disease, recovering from surgery/injury/disease, pregnancy, out of shape, run down, children with health issues Add other:	
Emotional conditions: stable mood, eating and sleeping well, happy *or* anxiety (heart palpitations, exaggerated fears, avoidance), depression (poor appetite, poor sleep, chronic low mood), death of a loved one Add other:	
Spiritual well-being: life has meaning, belief system intact, experience connectedness *or* loss of life direction, alienation, no purpose, have let your religious practices slide Add other:	

APPENDIX 9: A CHECKLIST FOR REPORTING

Adapt these tips to your situation, depending on whether reporting a sexual assault is urgent or may be delayed.

	Consider talking to a lawyer first about the consequences of reporting.
	Consider taking a neutral friend with you when reporting.
	Ensure that you have sufficient time for the reporting process.
	Ensure matters of concern (such as childcare) are looked after.
	Tell the truth.
	Ask for a business card from the first responder.
	Start a file and notebook of your own that lists the date and the factual events from now on.
	Ask questions about things that concern you.
	Ask the police how best to fulfill your role as a witness.

APPENDIX 10: FACTUAL INCONSISTENCIES AND CREDIBILITY

In the reported case of *R. v. Francois*, [1994] 2 S.C.R. 827 at paras. 13–14, Madam Justice McLachlin addresses the challenge of the trier of fact when there are inconsistencies and falsehoods in a witness' evidence in the following excerpt:

> Review for credibility may involve consideration of the basis for conclusions which the witness has drawn. For example, a witness may say, "That is the man who hit me". If other evidence indicates that the witness was unable to see the person who hit him at the time of the assault, the witness's identification might be considered unreasonable and a verdict dependent solely upon it overturned under s. 686(1)(*a*)(i). This sort of challenge for credibility is not much different in practice than the challenge on other grounds in *Corbett* and *Yebes*. More problematic is a challenge to credibility based on the witness's alleged lack of truthfulness and sincerity, the problem posed in this appeal. The reasoning here is that the witness may not have been telling the truth for a variety of reasons, whether because of inconsistencies in the witness's stories at different times, because certain facts may have been suggested to her, or because she may have had reason to concoct her accusations. In the end, the jury must decide whether, despite such factors, it believes the witness's story, in whole or in part. That determination turns not only upon such factors as the assessment of the significance of any alleged inconsistencies or motives for concoction, which may be susceptible of reasoned review by a court of appeal, but on the demeanour of the witness and the common sense of the jury, which cannot be assessed by the court of appeal. The latter domain is the "advantage" possessed by the trier of fact, be it judge or jury, which the court of appeal does not possess and which the court of appeal must bear in mind in deciding whether the verdict is unreasonable: *R. v. W. (R.), supra*.
>
> In considering the reasonableness of the jury's verdict, the court of appeal must also keep in mind the fact that the jury may reasonably and lawfully deal with inconsistencies and motive to concoct, in a variety of ways. The jury may reject the witness's evidence in its entirety. Or the jury may accept the witness's explanations for the apparent inconsistencies and the witness's denial that her testimony was provoked by improper pressures or from improper motives. Finally, the jury may accept some of the witness's

evidence while rejecting other parts of it; juries are routinely charged that they may accept all of the evidence, some of the evidence, or none of the evidence of each witness. It follows that we cannot infer from the mere presence of contradictory details or motives to concoct that the jury's verdict is unreasonable. A verdict of guilty based on such evidence may very well be both reasonable and lawful.

APPENDIX 11: DEFINITIONS OF SEX ACCORDING TO UNIVERSITY STUDENTS*

What is sex?

Behaviours	Definition of having sex for:		Definition of unfaithfulness for:	
	females	males	females	males
Deep kissing/tongue kissing	1.9%	3.2%	92.2%	88.7%
Being touched on genitals to orgasm	11.0	9.7	99.0	98.4
Being touched on genitals; no orgasm	8.8	6.4	97.1	96.8
Oral stimulation of another's genitals to orgasm	22.0	24.0	99.0	98.4
Oral stimulation of another's genitals; no orgasm	21.0	18.0	98.0	96.8
Being orally stimulated on genitals to orgasm	24.0	23.0	99.0	98.4
Being orally stimulated on genitals; no orgasm	23.0	16.0	98.0	96.8
Touching their genitals to orgasm	15.0	13.0	98.0	98.4
Touching their genitals; no orgasm	7.8	9.6	97.1	96.8
Intercourse with orgasm	97.0	98.0	100.0	98.4
Intercourse with no orgasm	96.0	90.0	99.0	98.4
Anal intercourse with orgasm	83.0	84.0	99.0	98.4
Anal intercourse with no orgasm	80.0	77.0	99.0	98.4
Masturbating to orgasm in each other's presence	3.9	3.2	95.0	93.5
Masturbating to orgasm while in telephone contact with each other	2.9	1.6	83.3	88.7
Masturbating to orgasm while in computer contact with each other	2.9	1.6	78.4	79.0

* Reprinted with permission from Hilary E. Randall & Sandra E. Byers, "What Is Sex? Students' Definitions of Having Sex, Sexual Partner, and Unfaithful Sexual Behaviour"(2003) 12:2 Canadian Journal of Human Sexuality 91.

APPENDIX 12: CHECKLIST TO HELP YOU TO GET READY FOR COURT

	Read the section in this book titled, The Road to Resilience (Chapter 5) and search out additional information in books or on the Internet designed for lay people going to court.
	Find out the date of the trial and mark it in your calendar. Examine your calendar for changes that are needed to accommodate the trial.
	Identify and implement lifestyle changes that will strengthen you for the trial.
	Discuss with a friend positive objectives for your testifying experience that will enhance your personal development and growth.
	Identify family members, friends, and professionals who can provide appropriate support and who will contribute to your success as a witness.
	Create an organization strategy that you can rely on to keep track of all your appointments to recount later, if you need it, and to file your previous statements and court-related documents.
	Contact your local victim assistance program and discuss expectations for your court preparation.
	Visit the courthouse and watch a trial. Pick a trial that is not a sexual assault case.
	Meet with the Crown prosecutor and design the preparation required to meet mutually established objectives.

APPENDIX 13: THE STORY BEHIND PRIVACY PROTECTIONS — THE *O'CONNOR* CASE

The *Stinchcombe* (1991) case was a property crime case where the Supreme Court ruled that the Crown file was not to be seen as the property of the Crown and the contents were to be provided to the defence whether they supported the Crown's case or not. The Court did not address the unique nature of sexual crimes in its judgment. Until 1997, there was no process in place to protect the complainant's privacy in sex crimes prosecutions, and it was easy for the accused to gain access to personal records. In 1991 a Roman Catholic bishop from British Columbia, Hubert O'Connor, was ordered to stand trial for sexual offences against four Aboriginal women. Following the preliminary hearing in 1992, counsel for the bishop requested all employment, psychological, or medical records of all persons to whom any of the women had said anything at all to about the bishop and the assaults. Because there was no established process for this type of application, neither the women nor those who were in possession of the records were given advance notice of the application by the defence, and the trial judge granted the request without having heard from them and without placing any conditions on the release. The court order was worded to order that the women consent to the release of the records even though none of them were present for the hearing and one of the women and her therapist lived and worked out-of-province. The order embraced up to thirteen years of records and required, for example, that if one of the women had even briefly mentioned the bishop or the assault during a medical or other examination, all of her records had to be produced, regardless of their relevance. These records had not been previously gathered by the police and were therefore still in the possession of the therapists and other professionals who had provided service to the women over the years.

The women did not want to have their records gathered or released. The Crown supported the women's concerns and attempted to deal with the order. The process was clumsy because this was what is called an "interlocutory order" and it could not be appealed. After facing severe criticism from both the defence and the court for not collecting and handing over these records forthwith, the Crown mounted an extraordinary effort to obtain all the identified records and disclose them to the defence. But when the case came to trial, the judge agreed with the defence that the Crown had not shown sufficient compliance with the court order and subsequent demands for disclosure and stayed the charges.

The Crown appealed, however, and a new trial was ordered by the British Columbia Court of Appeal. The Supreme Court of Canada dismissed the defence's appeal and in doing so, acknowledged the need to create a process for the release of third-party records in sexual offence cases that respected the privacy rights of the complainant. The new trial in 1996 resulted in Bishop O'Connor being convicted of rape and indecent assault of three women who were former students at a residential school in British Columbia. The defence appealed the conviction to the British Columbia Court of Appeal, which in 1998 allowed the appeal and acquitted the bishop of the crimes involving two of the women and ordered that he be retried in relation to one of them. The second trial never took place and instead, with the agreement of the one complainant involved, the Crown decided not to pursue the case any further formally in criminal court. Instead, O'Connor admitted he broke his vow of chastity and publicly apologized to the woman in an Aboriginal healing circle in a community near Williams Lake in British Columbia. In 2004, the women complainants had a homecoming at the Sugar Cane reserve near Williams Lake to celebrate their fourteen-year journey of both criminal and civil litigation to hold the bishop and the government responsible for his actions while he was principal of the school forty years beforehand.

The life-altering journey of these courageous women did much more than bring attention to violations of trust at a residential school. It also changed the law in Canada to protect complainants from unfettered violations of their privacy in sex crimes trials. The process was legislated into the *Criminal Code* with some changes. Of significance is the fact that, even if the Crown has private third-party records in its possession, it is not to hand them over willy-nilly to the defence. The Crown is to tell the defence of their existence and the latter must embark upon a procedure of review before they will be ordered released. Any release comes with conditions. The *Criminal Code* amendments were unsuccessfully constitutionally challenged in the *Mills* case in 1999.

APPENDIX 14: CHECKLIST FOR THE PRELIMINARY HEARING

	Ask immediately whether you have been subpoenaed for a trial or for a preliminary hearing.
	Ask for an interview with the Crown in advance of the preliminary hearing date.
	Go to your appointments and be on time.
	Prepare as if this is the final trial.
	Read your statement transcript very carefully.
	Become familiar with how lawyers communicate in court.
	Be alert when answering questions, being aware that everything you say in court is being recorded and a transcript may be made to use later to test your credibility.
	Learn how to respond to compound questions.

APPENDIX 15: ACCOMMODATIONS TO HELP A CHILD WITNESS TO TESTIFY

To help ensure child witnesses get every opportunity to tell the whole truth, they may be given special protections, such as the following:

- Unlike most witnesses in a criminal trial, they may not have to face the accused in the courtroom. Upon request, they should be allowed to testify via closed-circuit television, behind a screen, or by facing the judge and not looking towards the accused.
- Their testimony can be videotaped and played in court while they are present or, in rare cases, in their absence.
- They should be given the right not to be directly questioned by the accused, who may be self representing without legal counsel.
- They are entitled to orders excluding the public from the court, and banning publication of information that could identify them.
- They should be allowed a support person to join them in court if they ask for this. Judges have recently allowed children to hold someone's hand during testimony, or even to sit on someone's lap while they testify.
- They may be given extraordinary supports in the courtroom, such as a special chair or a microphone.

APPENDIX 16: CHECKLIST FOR CAREGIVERS OF CHILD WITNESSES

	Contact your local victims assistance agency and discuss what services it provides and what resources are available for you or for child witnesses. Ask when it is necessary to start the child in an age-appropriate court orientation program.
	Start to talk to the child about what is coming up in a positive light. Listen to the child and the child's needs and work with the Crown and the victim services worker to design a preparation that integrates the needs of both the child and the caregiver.
	Recruit friends and family members to form a support team for the child through this process. Create an objective around positively supporting the child through this by making connections, taking care of the child's health needs (diet and sleep, etc.), keeping things in perspective (ensure that the child can enjoy the usual routines of school and sports), taking decisive actions, nurturing a positive view of the child and the team members, maintaining a hopeful outlook, and looking for opportunities for learning and self discovery by the child. Do not discuss the evidence.
	Arrange to talk to the Crown prosecutor well in advance of the trial about any concerns you have and ask for a description of what is expected from the child and how you might help.
	Well in advance of the trial, determine what kind of protections the child will need in court, and ask the Crown prosecutor to complete any necessary applications.
	Be reliable. Show up for the child. Sit outside the courtroom patiently and greet the child positively when the child is done.

APPENDIX 17: CHECKLIST FOR GOING TO TRIAL

	Ascertain the name of the Crown prosecutor assigned to the case right from the beginning, and ask for a copy of a business card with the spelling of the prosecutor's name, address, and phone number. Although this person is not your lawyer, the Crown prosecutor will be responsible for the prosecution and for preparing you for your role as a witness and answering questions that you may have.
	Ask where you need to go and what you should do when you first come into the courtroom. Ask if you will be escorted into the room by the Crown or by someone else.
	Ask how you will be paged or brought into court so you do not miss your cue. If you do not want to be paged, ask that this not be done with the understanding that you will stay very close to the courtroom so that when it is your time to come the Crown counsel or sheriff can easily find you.
	Each time you meet with the prosecutor or go to court, if it is of concern to you, ask how long you should expect to be that day so that you can make any necessary plans.
	If you have never testified before, make sure that you tell the prosecutor this and ask for preparation prior to the procedure if you need it.
	Ask what courtroom you will be in and at what time the proceedings start, the breaks are, and the session ends for the day.
	Ask where the restaurants are near the courthouse and whether you will be provided with lunch money before or after the lunch break.
	Ask where you should wait in order to avoid contact with the accused and the accused's family and friends.
	Ask if there are others that you should not talk to while the trial is pending, for example, friends or family who are witnesses in the trial.
	Ask that you be shown where the witness box is in advance. The usual procedure is that the witness comes into the courtroom, goes immediately to the witness box, and remains standing. The Crown usually will have told the court clerk in advance whether or not you wish to swear on the Bible or affirm. You remain standing for that purpose and then you have the choice of either remaining standing or sitting down during your testimony. If you would like to swear on another religious book, tell the Crown about this in advance so that it can ensure that the book is available, or in the alternative, bring your own copy of the religious book or other sacred object for you to swear on or use as part of your affirmation. Your testimony begins with questions from the Crown lawyer.
	Ask the Crown if you can bring a pad of paper to the stand with you. Some witnesses just like to take some notes as they testify because it helps them with their short-term memory.

If your story is long and complicated, create structure documents to help you organize it. For example, create an age chart that shows your age, grade, and where you lived at the time of the offence(s) if this type of information is important to the organization of your complaint.
Take your time to answer the questions. There is no requirement that you do this in a speedy fashion. If the lawyers are going too quickly for you, respectfully ask them to give you time to think and answer your question. If the question was asked in too quick a manner, ask that it be repeated. Do not start to answer a question until it is fully asked. Do not interrupt the lawyer. Answer the question that you are asked. It is quite common for witnesses not to answer questions that they are asked. For example, the question might be "What dress were you wearing?" and the answer may be "I always like to wear what is comfortable." This is not a response to the question. The answer that responds to the question would be, for example, "My blue dress."
Everything that you say is recorded. Keep your head up and your voice up to avoid people repeatedly having to remind you to ensure that your voice is picked up by the recording device. In addition, if you nod your head or gesture, this is not recorded so whatever you gesture must actually be described in words for the recording.
You may be asked to leave the courtroom during your testimony when lawyers are dealing with procedural matters. Do not go far away because you will be called right back in. If there are things that you take with you to the stand, you can be expected to be asked about them. Some witnesses like to take a comfort object. You may be asked about this and why you feel you need it. You may be asked the history of the object. Similarly, if you take any notes or any other documents and you are asked about them and it becomes apparent that you have used them in some way to prepare your testimony, you can expect that the defence will want to see them and maybe even ask for a copy of them.
Many complainants find the experience of testifying very difficult and may keep their voices at a low volume as a result. This brings little sympathy from those who seek to hear what is said. The judge, jury members, and lawyers will ask for your voice to be raised and your answers to be repeated, and there may be attempts to move you, bring you a microphone, or other such strategies. Sometimes, resignation takes over and those who need to hear just do not hear vital facts and the case rests on that which is heard.
If you forget to say something in your testimony in chief you can ask the Crown about it during a break. If you recall something during cross-examination, you cannot talk to the Crown at this time.

APPENDIX 18: BILL C-2 AMENDMENTS TO THE *CRIMINAL CODE* — MODIFICATIONS TO ACCOMMODATE WITNESSES

1. *Publication prohibited.* Section 276.3 prohibits the publication of any document or broadcast or transmission in any way of the contents of an application made related to the admissibility of previous sexual activity. Although the publication was prohibited in the past, now the law specifies that publication includes a broadcast or transmission.

2. *Publication prohibited.* Section 278.9 prohibits any person from publishing any document or broadcasting or transmitting in any way matters that are part of an application to gain access to third-party records. The concern here again is that the publication ban includes broadcast or transmission.

3. *Exclusion of public in certain cases.* Section 486 says that all proceedings shall be in open court unless the judge orders the exclusion of all or any members of the public for all or any part of the proceedings. The justice makes such an order in the interest of public morals, the maintenance of order, or the proper administration of justice.

    Section 486(2) says that the "proper administration of justice" includes ensuring that the interests of witnesses under the age of eighteen years are safeguarded in all proceedings. This means that a closed court will be more likely if the witness is under the age of eighteen. Also, in section 486(3), where the accused is charged with a sexual offence, whether it be against a child, youth, or adult, and the prosecutor or accused applies for an exclusion of the public, where no order is made, the judge must state the reasons for that on the record.

4. *Support person.* Section 486.1(1) allows for an application by either the prosecutor or witness who is under the age of eighteen or who has a mental or physical disability, to apply to have a support person of her choice who will be permitted to be present and to be close to the witness while the witness testifies. As long as the application is made, the court shall allow the support person to be present unless it would interfere with the proper administration of justice.

    In section 486.1(2) where the witness is aged eighteen or older, the prosecutor or witness can make the same application for a support person and it will be allowed if the judge is of the opinion that the order is necessary to obtain a full and candid account from the witness of the acts that are complained of. The application for the support person can be made either during the trial or before the trial begins.

This means that if you want a support person you can communicate this to the Crown prosecutor assigned to your case, and the application can be made in advance of the trial beginning. The advantage of an early application is that it will provide certainty for you in who will be with you when you testify.

During this application for a person who is aged eighteen or older, the Crown will look to the following factors:

- The age of the witness
- Whether the witness has a mental or physical disability
- The nature of the offence
- The nature of any relationship between the witness and the accused
- Any other circumstances that the judge considers relevant

This means that evidence relating to these variables will be introduced to the court and may require you to testify during the application if it is disputed and if the Crown feels that mere submissions from the Crown or hearsay evidence from others would not be adequate.

Where the judge allows a support person to sit with you, the judge may also order that you and the support person do not communicate with each other while you testify. This is provided for in the *Criminal Code*. Do not consider this an affront or an insult. It was added to the *Criminal Code* to appease the concerns of opponents of the procedure of allowing a support person. Discuss with the Crown the meaning of the order. It does not normally mean that you cannot talk with your support person during the breaks, for example, as long as you do not discuss your evidence.

5. *Testimony outside the courtroom or from behind a screen.* Section 486.2 allows for an application to be made to allow certain witnesses to testify outside of the courtroom where necessary. The application can be made either by the witness or by the prosecutor.

   Once the application is made, the judge will allow the witness, in some circumstances, to testify either from outside of the courtroom or behind a device that screens the accused, for example, where the witness is under the age of eighteen or is an adult who is able to communicate the evidence but may have difficulty doing so by reason of a mental or physical disability. The only time the judge will not allow the application is if the order would interfere with the proper administration of justice.

The court will also allow the testimony to be given from outside the courtroom or behind a screening device by a witness aged eighteen or older even without a disability affecting the testimony, when the court is of the opinion that to do so is necessary to obtain a full and candid account from the witness of the acts complained of.

If you need to testify during the application, the *Criminal Code* allows you to provide your testimony from a room separate from the courtroom in the same way. Where an adult makes the application, the court will look to the same considerations as when determining if an adult witness can sit with a support person. You may be required to provide evidence, either in the courtroom, or by affidavit, or by other means, in order to assist the prosecution in making an application on your behalf.

6. *Accused not to cross-examine.* Section 486.3 gives the court jurisdiction to disallow an accused from personally cross-examining a witness and allows the court to appoint a lawyer to conduct the cross-examination of a witness when the accused is not represented by a lawyer in the trial. If the witness is under eighteen years of age, the appointment of counsel to conduct the cross-examination shall be made unless the proper administration of justice requires that the accused personally conduct the cross-examination.

Where the witness is aged eighteen or older, the court will appoint new counsel, upon application, if the court is of the opinion that it is necessary to obtain a full and candid account from the witness of the acts complained of. In determining whether to appoint counsel to conduct this cross-examination, the court will look to the same factors that a court will look to in an order allowing a support person to sit with the adult witness, or allowing the witness to testify from outside the courtroom.

In circumstances where the accused is charged with criminal harassment as well as a sexual offence, section 486.3(4) allows for an order to appoint counsel to conduct the cross-examination instead of the accused. The *Criminal Code* allows for an application to appoint counsel to conduct the cross-examination to be heard at the earliest possible time before the commencement of the trial, and it is certainly to the advantage of all to do so. If this is a concern of yours, bring it to the attention of the Crown immediately. To appoint a lawyer to conduct a cross-examination is a complex process that may result in a delay of the proceedings if it is not done promptly.

APPENDIX 19: WEBSITES OF PROVINCIAL CORRECTIONAL SERVICES

Alberta: www.solgen.gov.ab.ca/corrections

British Columbia: www.gov.bc.ca/bvprd/bc/channel.do?action=ministry &channelID=-8391&navId=NAV_ID_province

Manitoba: www.gov.mb.ca/justice/

New Brunswick: http://app.infoaa.7700.gnb.ca/gnb/Pub/EServices/List-ServicesBySector.asp?SectorID1=70&AreaID1=5

Newfoundland and Labrador: www.justice.gov.nl.ca/just/PUBLICPR/community_corrections.htm

Northwest Territories: www.justice.gov.nt.ca/

Nova Scotia: http://gov.ns.ca/just/correcservices.htm

Nunavut: www.justice.gov.nu.ca/english/index.html

Ontario: www.mpss.jus.gov.on.ca/english/english_default.html

Prince Edward Island: www.gov.pe.ca/oag/cacs-info/index.php3

Quebec: www.justice.gouv.qc.ca/francais/accueil.asp

Saskatchewan: www.cps.gov.sk.ca/

Yukon Territory: www.justice.gov.yk.ca/

APPENDIX 20: SENTENCING OPTIONS FOR DANGEROUS OFFENDERS (DO) AND LONG-TERM OFFENDERS (LTO)

Type of Sentence Available	When Applicable	Sentence Calculation
Determinate sentence	The court does not designate the offender a DO or an LTO and sentences the offender to a jail term.	The offender is eligible for • day parole 6 months prior to full parole eligibility • full parole after 1/3 of term • statutory release at 2/3 of term • except if sexual or violent (s. 743.6) • lesser of half of sentence or 10 years • can be held until expiry by National Parole Board as recommended by Corrections (CSC)
Indeterminate sentence after the 1997 legislative amendments	Where the court makes a finding of DO, the offender automatically receives an indeterminate sentence if the commission of the offence is after 1997.	The offender is eligible for: • day parole 3 years prior to full parole eligibility • full parole after 7 years from the date of arrest • ongoing review for both day and full parole every 2 years
Long-Term Offender sentence combines a determinate sentence imposed by the court with an LTO status for a maximum of 10 years	Only available after the 1997 amendments. Court finding of LTO.	Determinate part of sentence: • minimum 2 years • (range in research 2–13 years) • day parole 6 months prior to full parole eligibility • full parole after 1/3 of term • statutory release at 2/3 of term • except if sexual or violent (s. 743.6) • lesser of half of sentence or 10 years • can be held until expiry by National Parole Board as recommended by Corrections (CSC) • followed by a maximum of 10 years community supervision from the date of warrant expiry • time determined by the court (range in research 5–10 years)

APPENDIX 21: THE VICTIM'S ROLE IN SENTENCING

Hill J. describes the purpose of the victim impact statement in the following paragraphs from an Ontario case called *R. v. Gabriel* (1999), 137 C.C.C. (3d) 1 (Ont. S.C.J.).

The victim impact statement serves a number of purposes, including:

(1) Nature of the Offence

The court receives relevant evidence as to the effect or impact of the crime from the person(s) able to give direct evidence on the point. The evidence is not filtered through a third party reporter. The evidence is relevant to the seriousness of the offence which, in turn, assists the court in imposing proportionate punishment (s. 718.1 of the *Criminal Code*).

(2) Victim Reparation

Sections 718(e) and (f) recognize that a just sanction by the court should have amongst its objectives reparation for harm done to victims and the promotion of acknowledgement by the offender of harm done to a victim. Resort to the best evidence on the subject of victim loss, the victim himself or herself, not only assures an accurate measure of any necessary compensation but also serves to bring home to the offender the consequences of the criminal behaviour.

(3) Repute of the Administration of Criminal Justice

Victim participation in the trial process serves to improve the victim's perception of the legitimacy of the process. The satisfaction of being heard, in the sense of a direct submission to the court, enhances respect for the justice system on the part of the harmed individual, and over time, the community itself. Incidental to the victim impact statement process is the ability of the victim to secure a sense of regaining control over his or her life and the alleviation of the frustration of detachment which can arise where the victim perceives that he or she is ignored and uninvolved in the process.

(4) Parity of Identity

A significant concern of the sentencing hearing is finding a disposition tailored to the individual offender in an effort to ensure long range protection of the public. As a consequence, much becomes known about the accused as a person. In this process, there is a danger of the victim being reduced to obscurity — an intolerable departure from respect for the personal integrity of the victim. The victim was a special and unique person as well — information revealing the individuality of the victim and the impact of the crime on the victim's survivors achieves a measure of balance in understanding the consequences of the crime in the context of the victim's personal circumstances, or those of survivors.

The victim impact statement is not, however, the exclusive answer to the civilized treatment of victims within the criminal process. Communication with victims of crime by prosecutorial authorities, victim/offender reconciliation projects, and community support initiatives for victims, are as, or more, essential.

Victim impact statements contribute significantly to a just sentencing process. Sentencing is a reasoned, not an arbitrary, exercise. Context remains important. It is to be remembered that there is a civil justice system to address actionable wrongs between individual citizens. The criminal court is "not a social agency" (*R. v. M.(E.)* (1992), 76 C.C.C. (3d) 159 at 164 (Ont. C.A.), Finlayson J.A., in dissent in the result).

Without, in any fashion, diminishing the significant contribution of victim impact statements to providing victims a voice in the criminal process, it must be remembered that a criminal trial, including the sentencing phase, is not a tripartite proceeding. A convicted offender has committed a crime — an act against society as a whole. It is the public interest, not a private interest, which is to be served in sentencing.

APPENDIX 22: CHECKLIST FOR PREPARING YOUR VICTIM IMPACT STATEMENT

	Write about your experience in your own words.
	Describe the physical pain, including the lasting effects.
	Write about the financial impact and speak in detail about the costs (may vary in some provinces).
	Describe the emotional pain, including the lasting effects and your efforts to heal.
	Write about your fear of the offender should the offender be released.
	Write about how your life has changed since this crime.

APPENDIX 23: CHECKLIST TO HELP PREPARE FOR THE SENTENCING HEARING

	Ask the Crown when the sentencing hearing will take place. Discuss the preparation of a victim impact statement.
	Prepare your victim impact statement with a victim assistance person and ensure that it gets to the Crown as soon as you are done. Check that the Crown has received it and has read it.
	If there is financial loss, ask the Crown about restitution and the chances of payment.
	Where a community sentence is expected, communicate to the Crown what conditions you would like to make you feel safe.
	Anticipate that both the hearing and the passing of sentence will be emotional for you and others around you. Attend the sentencing hearing with a supportive family member, friend, or support person.
	Arrange in advance where you will go when the court appearance is over.
	Schedule a session with your counsellor to work through any emotional reactions following sentencing.
	Prepare yourself emotionally for the full range of potential outcomes.

APPENDIX 24: TOPICS FOR DISCUSSION WHEN RETAINING A LAWYER

	The scope and limits of "privileged communication"
	The lawyer's experience in dealing with sexual assault claims
	The strengths and limitations of your claim
	Any relevant statutes of limitation
	The range of possible awards for similar claims
	General understanding of overall litigation process and time estimations for the litigation
	The terms for retainer agreement and payment of fees
	The next step in litigation process and your role
	The primary contacts in the lawyer's office (for example, the names and contact numbers of appropriate staff)
	The availability of your lawyer (for example, a contact number and the preferred method of contact and frequency)
	The lawyer's approach to and the time allowance for preparing you for court
	Instructions for communicating with others about your sexual assaults
	Discussion of your current circumstances and the support network available to you to assist you during the litigation process

APPENDIX 25: JHS CLASS ACTION — *RUMLEY v. HMTQ*

Settlement Agreement

1. This memorandum reflects the settlement agreement (Settlement Agreement) reached by the Negotiating Committee of the Jericho Hill Class Action, Counsel for the Jericho Hill Class Action (Class Counsel), and Her Majesty the Queen in Right of the Province of British Columbia (Government) to resolve the dispute between the Government and class members (Class Members) in *Rumley v. HMTQ*, SCBC Vancouver No. C980463 (Class Action), which will be presented to the Supreme Court of British Columbia (Court) for approval pursuant to section 35 of the *Class Proceedings Act* (Court Approval).

2. The goals of the negotiations leading up to this Settlement Agreement have been to achieve a fair, efficient and transparent settlement through a mediation process that addressed:

    a. Compensation to individual Class Members;

    b. Improved access to employment opportunities through existing Government programs to enhance these programs through measures responsive to special needs and concerns identified by Class Members;

    c. Healing of Class Members through measures responsive to special needs and concerns that have been identified by Class Members and enhancements to other existing Government programs and services; and

    d. Legal Fees.

3. The parties acknowledge that:

    a. The settlement negotiations have addressed important questions of Government policy and programs responsive to special needs and concerns identified by Class Members;

    b. They will continue to engage in discussions pending Court Approval; and

    c. There will be ongoing discussions involving Government and individual Class Members through committees like the Community Advisory Committee for the Well-Being Program, and the Jericho Hill Legacy Trust ("JHLT") subsequent to Court Approval.

Monetary Compensation — (Individual Compensation)

4. (a) Upon Court Approval, the Government will pay $10,500,000 for individual compensation into the Individual Compensation Fund (ICF).

   (b) The ICF will be distributed to Class Members through a distribution system, designed by Class Members (ICF Distribution System).

Jericho Hill Legacy Trust

5. Upon Court Approval, the Government will pay $2,000,000 to the JHLT.

Opt Outs

6. The parties acknowledge that the last date to opt out of the Class Action has passed and no Class Member can opt out of the Class Action or Settlement Agreement.

Undertakings of Class Counsel

7. Class Counsel will provide undertakings as described in Appendix C.

Court Orders

8. Appearances will be made before the Court jointly to request orders:
   a. For Court Approval;
   b. To extinguish all claims or causes of action, of persons who fall within the definition of the Class in relation to their attendance at Jericho Hill School; and
   c. To dismiss the Class Action without costs to either party.

General

9. Each Class Member or Legal Guardian for that Class Member will execute a written release releasing the Government from all causes of action whatsoever in relation to their attendance at Jericho Hill School (Release). For the purposes of this agreement, Legal Guardian is defined in the ICF Plan.

10. The Release form is defined in the ICF Plan.

11. Money, which a Class Member receives from the settlement, will not disqualify or otherwise affect that Class Member's entitlement to benefits under the *Employment and Assistance Act* and the *Employment and Assistance for Persons with Disabilities Act*, and will be treated by

the Government in the same manner as payments made under the previous Jericho Hill Individual Compensation Program (JICP).

12. Upon Court Approval, the parties will formulate a joint press release announcing the settlement.

13. The Settlement Agreement is subject to Government approval and approvals under the *Crown Proceeding Act*.

Programs

Well-Being Program

14. The parties acknowledge that the Well-Being Program was developed for persons who are Deaf, Hard of Hearing, and Deaf/Hard of Hearing and Blind, who had been sexually abused and has been expanded to include counselling and other services for all persons who are Deaf, Hard of Hearing, Deaf/Hard of Hearing and Blind, and their families. The parties further acknowledge that the funds allocated to the Well Being Program as a result of a recent policy review now come from the Ministry of Children and Family Development's budget.

15. The Government will maintain funding for the Well Being Program at the current budgetary allocation of $1,246,524 per year for a period of 5 years commencing April 1, 2004.

16. The payment of money by the Government to fund the Well Being Program is subject to:

    a. there being sufficient monies available in an appropriation, as defined in the *Financial Administration Act*, to enable the Government, in any fiscal year or part thereof when any payment of money by the Government to the Well Being Program falls due, to make that payment; and

    b. Treasury Board, as defined in the *Financial Administration Act*, not having controlled or limited, under the *Financial Administration Act*, expenditure under any appropriation referred to in subsection (a) of this section.

Literacy and Education

17. The Government requested its designated representative (Gary Mullins) to advocate to the appropriate officials for advancement of literacy and education programs with Universities and Colleges located in British Columbia in ways that are more responsive to the needs of the deaf. The Government has fulfilled its obligations, and has discharged

its duty, with respect to this clause. Gary Mullins, in his personal capacity, intends to continue these discussions.

American Sign Language

18. The Government confirms the acknowledgment it made on June 28, 1995, of the importance of American Sign Language (ASL) to the Deaf community and its culture.

19. The Government will establish a committee within the Ministry of Children and Family Development to enhance the quality of ASL interpretation in relation to the Ministry, which will include two Class Members, and for the work of which the Government will allocate $5,000.

20. Upon Court Approval, the Government will pay $6,000 to the Trustee of the ICF to be paid by the Trustee to recognized institutions for tuition for family of Class Members to enroll in advanced ASL training to a maximum of $600 per family.

Commemoration

21. The Government will create two plaques (Plaques) to commemorate the experiences of former students at Jericho Hill School. The Plaques will be inscribed with "This plaque is dedicated to the former students who were sexually abused while attending Jericho Hill School. The Government of British Columbia recognizes the impact on these individuals, the steps they have taken to heal themselves, and the action they took to prevent this from happening again"

22. The Government will seek approval to locate the Plaques at South Slope School in Burnaby, and the British Columbia head office of the Canadian National Institute of the Blind (CNIB).

23. The parties will establish scholarships of $2,000 to be awarded annually to a British Columbia student who is visually impaired, and a British Columbia student who is deaf or hard of hearing, who demonstrate leadership abilities and a commitment to community service and ongoing education. These scholarships will be administered by the board of the JHLT and paid from the JHLT.

24. The Government will, by a Minister, make a statement similar to what has already been said by Government in respect of the experience of class members at Jericho Hill School and will honor the importance of the proposed settlement having been achieved by class members and in furthering the public interest. This acknowledgment will be

conveyed in a public forum and use methods that can be made available to class members at different locations in the Province.

Full text of settlement agreement available online: www.jhsclassaction.com/settlement.html.

Legal Glossary

ABSOLUTE DISCHARGE: A situation in which an offender is deemed not to have been convicted of the offence. However, since the offender pleaded or was found guilty, the offender will still have a federal criminal record. A judge can only order an absolute discharge if this is in the offender's best interests and is not contrary to the public interest. An absolute discharge cannot be given if the offence carries a minimum punishment or is punishable by imprisonment for fourteen years or life.

ACQUITTAL: A finding of not guilty in a criminal case.

ACT: A law passed by Parliament or a provincial legislature (also called a statute).

ACTION: A judicial proceeding in either civil or criminal law.

ADJOURNMENT: A temporary postponement of court proceedings.

AFFIDAVIT: A sworn, written declaration that a certain set of facts is true.

AFFIRMATION: A non-religious oath given before testifying.

ALLEGE: Suggest that something is true without necessarily being able to prove it.

APPEAL: Examination by a higher court of a lower court or tribunal decision. The higher court may affirm, vary, or reverse the original decision.

APPEARANCE NOTICE: A notice issued by a police officer requiring the accused's appearance before a judge or justice of the peace to answer a charge. This is typically given instead of arresting the accused.

ARRAIGNMENT: The process in criminal law by which the accused's name is called, the charge is read, and the accused pleads either guilty or not guilty. If the offence is one that gives the accused a choice, the accused will elect at the arraignment to be tried by a judge alone or with a jury in a higher court, or by a judge in a lower court.

BAIL: Monetary or other security put up by the accused or on his behalf to ensure that the accused appears at trial.

BENCH WARRANT: A court order empowering the police to arrest a person. These warrants are most often issued in cases of contempt of court, failure to appear, or where an indictment is being laid.

BEYOND A REASONABLE DOUBT: The evidence here must be so complete and convincing that any reasonable doubts as to the guilt of the accused are erased from the minds of the judge or jury. This is the rigorous standard of proof that the Crown prosecutor is required to meet for each element of the offence in a criminal case.

CAUSE OF ACTION: The legal basis underlying the plaintiff's civil suit against the defendant.

CLASS ACTION: An action or lawsuit brought by a representative plaintiff(s) on behalf of a group of people who have been similarly affected.

CONDITIONAL DISCHARGE: Similar to an absolute discharge, except that the offender is subject to specified conditions contained in a probation order. If the offender violates these conditions, the discharge may be revoked. A conviction will then be entered, and an appropriate sentence imposed.

CONTEMPT OF COURT: A criminal offence that typically involves interfering with the administration of justice, ignoring the rules of court, or defying a judge.

CONTINGENCY PAYMENT: The payment made to the lawyer at the end of a case that is based on an agreed-upon percentage of the money awarded. This means that money is not paid to the lawyer for time spent during the case.

CORROBORATING EVIDENCE: Evidence that confirms or strengthens evidence already presented to the court.

COUNTERCLAIM: An action brought by a defendant against a plaintiff. The defendant's counterclaim is dealt with in the same trial as that of the plaintiff.

CROWN ATTORNEY: The lawyer representing the Crown in a criminal prosecution.

DAMAGES: Monetary compensation for financial or property losses, emotional or physical injuries, loss of earnings, and costs of care.

DANGEROUS OFFENDER: A designation reserved for the offender who has repeatedly committed offences (including sexual crimes) that have inflicted serious bodily and psychological damage, and who is a danger to the life, safety, or physical/mental well-being of others and gives little hope for rehabilitation.

DEFENDANT: The person who is sued in a civil action or charged with a criminal offence.

DISBURSEMENTS: The funds paid out by the lawyer for expenses incurred in the lawsuit, such as the costs of typed transcripts and the fees charged by expert witnesses.

DISCLOSURE: The compulsory, pretrial disclosure of documents relevant to a case (law); it enables one side in a litigation matter to elicit information from the other side concerning the facts in the case.

DUAL PROCEDURE OFFENCE: In a dual procedure, the Crown prosecutor has the choice to proceed by summary conviction or by indictment for a hybrid or Crown electable offence. (In Canada, all criminal offences are divided into one of three categories: summary conviction, indictable, and dual procedure offences.) The distinction between summary conviction and indictable offences is based on the formality of the procedures used to try them. Once the Crown has made its decision, the offence is subject to the normal rules of procedure for a summary conviction or indictable offence.

ELECTION BY THE ACCUSED: The choice given by the *Criminal Code* to the accused who is charged with certain offences to be tried by a judge with or without a jury in a higher court, or by a provincial judge in a lower court.

ELECTION BY THE CROWN: The choice given to the Crown to decide whether to prosecute cases involving dual procedure offences as a summary conviction or an indictable offence. The Crown is more likely to proceed by indictment if the circumstances of the offence are more serious than a typical case, or if the accused is a repeat offender.

EXAMINATION FOR DISCOVERY: An opportunity given in civil actions to the parties to question each other prior to trial to discover the details of the other side's case. The examination for discovery allows the parties to narrow the issues and focus the trial on contested matters.

HABEAS CORPUS: A writ issued by a judge ordering the release of a person who is being detained or imprisoned unlawfully.

HEARSAY: Indirect knowledge learned from what someone else said or told another person.

INDICTABLE OFFENCES: The category of criminal offences that are subject to formal and complex procedures. Generally, indictable offences are more serious than summary conviction offences are, and they carry lengthy maximum sentences. For example, impaired driving causing death is an indictable offence and is subject to a maximum sentence of fourteen years imprisonment. Most indictable offences give the accused the right to elect to be tried in a higher court by a judge alone or with a jury.

INFORMATION: May be laid, in writing and under oath, before a judge or a justice of the peace, by someone who reasonably believes that a person has committed an indictable offence. If the judge or justice of the peace concludes that there is sufficient evidence of an offence, either a summons or warrant for the accused's arrest may be issued.

INJUNCTION: A court order restraining a party from the performance of some act (prohibitory injunction), or requiring the performance of some act (mandatory injunction). Injunctions may be permanent or temporary.

INTERMITTENT SENTENCE: A sentence of imprisonment that is served in intervals (usually on weekends) over a period of time. Under the *Criminal Code*, a judge can only impose an intermittent sentence if the term of imprisonment is ninety days or less. The offender must comply with the conditions of a probation order when not in confinement.

JUDICIAL INTERIM RELEASE: A judicial order that releases the accused from custody prior to trial. The release is unconditional unless the prosecutor shows cause to impose certain conditions. A judicial interim release cannot be granted for certain serious criminal offences, for example, murder, mutiny, or treason.

LEGAL AID: A program that assists those who require a lawyer but cannot afford one. In some provinces, legal aid may only be available for more serious criminal offences.

LITIGATION: The process of trying a dispute in court.

MANDATORY PAROLE: The term used to describe a situation in which the inmate is released as a result of accumulated, earned remission. In most circumstances, an inmate will be credited with one day of earned remission for every two days served in prison. Inmates released under mandatory parole are subject to mandatory supervision by a parole officer.

OCCURRENCE NUMBER: The identification number assigned by the police to a particular crime under investigation.

PAROLE: The release of an offender from prison prior to the end of the sentence. The offender continues to serve the sentence outside of prison under the supervision of a parole officer and must obey specific conditions or risk returning to custody.

PLEA-BARGAIN: Negotiations between the defence counsel and Crown prosecutor concerning the charges and pleas of the accused. The Crown may accept a guilty plea on a lesser charge instead of incurring the expense and time of a trial on the original charge. The Crown may also agree to make a joint submission to the judge on the appropriate sentence, if the accused agrees to plead guilty.

PRE-SENTENCE REPORT: A report that summarizes the accused's family life, personal situation, and background, which may be ordered of a probation officer by the judge prior to sentencing. This report is used to help the judge decide on an appropriate sentence for the offender.

PROBATION: A sentence that requires the offender to obey certain stipulated conditions. Some conditions, for example, keeping the peace and being of good behaviour, are compulsory in every probation order. Other conditions are left to the judge's discretion. Probation is only available where the offence does not carry a mandatory jail term. The probation order can be no more than three years in duration. It is a federal criminal offence to violate any term of probation without a reasonable excuse.

PROTHONOTARY: The chief clerk of the civil court. The word is of Greek origin and means "First Clerk." All civil litigation is filed with the Prothonotary. The Prothonotary or one of the Prothonotary's deputies must be present in court during all civil cases in order to administer oaths to witnesses and juries and keep track of exhibits. All records maintained by the Prothonotary are available to the public unless they are sealed by the court.

RECOGNIZANCE: A formal promise made by the accused to appear and respond to criminal charges. Depending on the circumstances, the accused may enter the recognizance before a police officer or a magistrate.

REGULATION: A form of legislation enacted under the authority of a statute by the Governor-in-Council (the federal cabinet), the Lieutenant-Governor-in-Council (the provincial cabinet), a Minister or government official, or an administrative board. Typically, the regulations will set out those detailed provisions that are not essential to be included in a statute. The power to enact regulations permits the government to act expeditiously and introduce changes without having to enact a new statute.

SEXUAL TORT CLAIMS: Claims that describe civil litigation in sexual crime cases.

SUMMARY CONVICTION OFFENCES: The category of criminal offences that are subject to less formal and complex procedures. Summary conviction offences are tried by justices or provincial court judges. They are usually less serious crimes than indictable offences and carry lower penalties.

SUSPENDED SENTENCE: A judge may choose to suspend the imposition of the sentence and, instead, put an offender on probation. If the offender breaches probation, the judge may then order the offender returned to court and impose a jail term for the original offence. At this time, the offender may also be charged with the federal criminal offence of breaching probation. In issuing a suspended sentence, the court must consider the accused's age and character, the nature of the offence, and the circumstances surrounding its commission.

TESTIMONY: Statements made in court by a witness under oath or affirmation.

TORT: A civil action arising from a wrongful act or omission, in which a plaintiff may sue a defendant for damages.

TRIER OF FACT: The person or people in court who assess the facts of the case, namely, the jury, when it exists, or the judge.

WRIT: A written order of a court.

YOUTH CRIMINAL JUSTICE ACT: A federal statute that establishes how young people will be treated, tried, and sentenced for criminal offences. The Act applies to suspects who are over twelve but less than eighteen years of age. In certain limited circumstances involving very serious offences, those who are aged fourteen or older may be transferred to adult court. Among other things, the *Youth Criminal Justice Act* dramatically limits the maximum punishment that might otherwise apply for an offence, and it creates special record-keeping provisions to protect young offenders from the adverse publicity and consequences of having a criminal record.

About the Authors

DR. JUDITH DAYLEN received her M.A. in cognitive psychology in 1985, and her Ph.D. in clinical psychology in 1994 from the University of British Columbia. For the past twenty years, Dr. Daylen has worked primarily with victims of sexual and physical assault. She has worked as a volunteer in a rape crisis centre and has provided individual and group treatment to sexual assault victims as well as training to a wide range of mental health and legal professionals. Currently, Dr. Daylen works as a clinical and consulting psychologist, providing consultation to lawyers and assessments of sexual assault victims in civil litigation, class action lawsuits, and the Indian Residential School Alternative Dispute Resolution process. Dr. Daylen has published research on victims and witnesses of crime and has expertise in the dynamics of sexual assaults and childhood sexual abuse, assessment of the effects of trauma on psychological functioning and memory, and assessment of the credibility of allegations of abuse.

WENDY VAN TONGEREN HARVEY received her B.A. from the University of British Columbia in 1973 and her LL.B. from Queen's Law School in 1976. She is a member of both the Ontario and the British Columbia Bars. Since 1981, Ms. van Tongeren Harvey has specialized in the prosecution of sex crimes and crimes against vulnerable persons, such as children and persons with disabilities. She has lectured throughout Canada and internationally and has been an expert witness on Canadian legislative reform before parliamentary committees. In addition, she has played a significant role in training police, Crown, and social workers across the country. In 2005, she had two secondments: first, as a headquarters lawyer assigned to implement Bill C-2 and to assist with policy review of the British Columbia child abuse and sexual assault policies; and second, as a visiting instructor to the Pacific Region Training Centre to train RCMP police officers. In 2006, she joined the Office of the Prosecutor at the Special Court of Sierra Leone in Freetown, Sierra Leone. She has numerous publications to her name including *So, You Have to Go to Court* (1986), a book written for child witnesses, and *Sexual Offences Against Children and the Criminal Process* (2001).

DENNIS O'TOOLE received his Ph.D. in clinical psychology from the University of British Columbia in 1989. Since that time he has maintained a largely forensic clinical practice and has appeared as an expert witness in Family Court, Youth Court, and other courts. He has worked with both sexual offenders and victims of sexual assault. He has lectured on forensic issues at the University of British Columbia and the University of Northern British Columbia. Until recently he was the Clinical Director, Northern Region, of Youth Forensic Psychiatric Services.